AUSTRALIA
Law Book Co.
Sydney

CANADA and USA
Carswell
Toronto

HONG KONG
Sweet & Maxwell Asia

NEW ZEALAND
Brookers
Wellington

SINGAPORE and MALAYSIA
Sweet & Maxwell Asia
Singapore and Kuala Lumpur

Civil Evidence:

The Essential Guide

by

Martin Iller

LONDON
SWEET & MAXWELL
2006

Published in 2006 by
Sweet & Maxwell Limited
100 Avenue Road
Swiss Cottage
London NW3 3PF
www.sweetandmaxwell.co.uk

Typeset by Servis Filmsetting Limited, Manchester
Printed by Athenaeum Press, Gateshead

No natural forests were destroyed to make this product; only farmed timber was used
and replanted.

A CIP catalogue record for this book is available from the British Library.

ISBN-10 0-421-94710-1
ISBN-13-978-0-421-94710-8

© Martin Iller 2006

Dedicated to the memory of the late Professor Sir John Smith
C.B.E., Q.C., LL.D, F.B.A. and Professor Alan Pritchard

Preface

This is not so much a book about the "rules" of evidence, after all there would be very little to write about, as about "evidence": what it consists of, what you can or cannot do with it and why civil litigators need to "think trial from day one". In theoretical terms we have almost achieved Jeremy Bentham's ideal of abolishing the rules of exclusion in their entirety. The rule against hearsay went on January 1, 1997, and two of the remaining exclusionary rules, relevance and non-expert opinion are, to say the least, applied somewhat flexibly. The only rules that continue to operate more or less "absolutely" are privilege and public interest immunity. Has this had the effect, as Jeremy Bentham fondly hoped it would, of increasing the likelihood that "justice" will be achieved? I remain an optimistic sceptic. The major theme that runs through this book is that, in the vast majority of situations, all that now matters is "weight". The philosophy of the CPR points in the same direction. Legal advisers are expected to be able to sort out the "strong" cases from the "weak" ones, to pick out the few remaining determinative issues and either settle quickly or proceed to a speedy and economical disposal. But concepts such as "relevance", "weight" and that overworked newcomer "proportionality" possess no identifiable jurisprudence: they exist, at best, as an ill-defined set of value judgements.

The main purpose of this book is to provide a structure within which it will be possible to identify what facts need to be proved or refuted, the substantive rules that govern their admission or exclusion as evidence and the procedural requirements that have to be met before they can be placed before a court. Chapters 1 to 7 largely deal with the mechanics of how to prove facts, including the profound effect that the abolition of the rule against hearsay has had. Chapter 8, by far the longest chapter, deals with privilege and public interest immunity. Chapters 9 to 13 deal with the ways in which the Civil Procedure Rules regulate the disclosure, management and ultimate admission of evidence at trial. Finally, Chapter 14 deals with that statistical rarity, the trial itself. I very much hope that those who use this book will find that it provides them with not only a thorough text on the relevant law and procedure but also a valuable guide on how to "win" cases, whatever that may entail and however it is ultimately achieved. Although not intended to be a primary text on the art of advocacy, I also hope that it will be of assistance to those who are preparing for applications and trials. I also have attempted to offer some insight into the factors that are likely to influence and persuade judges in achieving justice.

The starting point is the need to recognise that there is no longer a single "law of evidence", but two entirely separate systems, one dealing with criminal cases and the other dealing with civil claims. This division of the law of evidence into two entirely separate streams with very few features in common has been accelerated by the introduction of the Civil Procedure Rules. As the 10th Edition of *Cross and Tapper on Evidence (2004)* acknowledges (at page 5), ". . . it is still impossible to be sure precisely how these rules will affect the law of evidence". However, even in the two years since that statement, things have moved on at a pace. The House of Lords in *Three Rivers* has reasserted the wide boundaries of legal advice privilege set by Taylor L.J. in *Balabel v Air India*. In *Polanski v Conde Nast* they have not only given valuable guidance on the circumstances in which the court should allow evidence by video link, but have also considered the extent to which the court should exercise its discretion to exclude evidence under CPR 32.1(2). In *O'Brien v Chief Constable for South Wales* the House has also confirmed that, unlike in criminal cases, the only "gateway" through which a litigant must pass to secure the admission of "similar fact" evidence" is that of relevance. The House also continues to be engaged in dealing with problems over proof of causation, especially in clinical negligence cases, *Chester v Ashfar* and *Gregg v Scott* being the most recent examples.

The Court of Appeal has also been kept busy, most notably on the evaluation of hearsay evidence in *Moat Housing v Harris and Hartless* and the problematic interrelationship between privilege, CPR 35 and expert evidence. However it is in the cases that do not deal with major points of principle that the workings of the system are best revealed: the broad inclusionary approach to justice exemplified in decisions such as *Bansal v Cheema, Hayes v Transco* and *Binks v Securicor* being prime examples. Perhaps the most valuable case of all though, and one covered in great detail in Chapter 5, is *Gow v Harker*, a clinical negligence appeal, in which Lord Justice Brooke provided invaluable guidance on how judges should go about deciding "difficult" cases.

Although the European Convention of Human Rights has not, as yet, had a major impact on the domestic law of evidence (such impact as it has had is examined in Chapter 2) there have been a number of important developments in the field of substantive law, the most significant of which has been the implementation of the Freedom of Information Act 2000 furnishing as it does opportunities for wide ranging evidence collection. There have also been a number of changes in the Civil Procedure Rules, most notably the introduction of the Expert Evidence Protocol from October 2005.

In this book I have tried to pull all these disparate strands together into a coherent whole to enable the conscientious litigator not only to prepare for trial and present his or her case, but to recognise those points which, properly presented will bring about a speedy negotiated settlement.

I would like to conclude by offering my thanks to the editorial team at Sweet & Maxwell, in particular James Douse, Emma Wilkin and Lisa Bruce for the assistance and encouragement they have given me in the preparation of what I hope will be the first of many editions of this book. I would also like to offer my heartfelt thanks to Dominic Regan who nobly volunteered to act as proof checker and "nit picker". I have taken all his stimulating suggestions on board, but take ultimate responsibility for any errors that the text may contain. On a personal note I would like to thank those of my friends who provided me with support during the long and lonely task in writing this book, in particular Denise Turton for her numerous encouraging text messages, Anne Giddings for her beguiling emails of rural life in France, my children Emma, Wendy, Olivia and Jude for tolerating my daily absences at the word processor and last but not least John Malpass and Tom Crosthwaite with whom I was able to share a number of mind-refreshing musical interludes. Finally, I would like to make brief mention of the two dedicatees of this work, the late Professor Sir John Smith and Professor Alan Prichard, who I am delighted to say is still very much alive. Those of us who, like me, had the privilege of learning at the feet of these two brilliant but remarkably humane and civilised men, during their lengthy tenures at Nottingham University, will no doubt understand the reason for this dedication. I only hope that readers will consider it worthy of them. The law, so far as I am able to do so, is stated as at May 1, 2006.

As always, the law never stands still. The commentary on *Fairchild v Glenhaven [Funeral Services Ltd]* [2003] AC 32 at 3–25 has now been overtaken by events. On May 3, 2006 the majority of the House of Lords (Lord Rodger dissenting) held in *Barker v Corus (UK) plc* [2006] UKHL 20, *The Times*, May 4, 2006 that where a claimant had contracted mesolthelioma after tortious exposure to asbestos by more than one employer, damages are to be apportioned according to each employer's degree of contribution to the likelihood of the worker contracting the disease.

Martin Iller, Ipswich, May 1, 2006

Contents

Table of Cases

Table of Statutes

Table of Statutory Instruments

Table of Civil Procedure Rules

Table of Practice Directions

Chapter 1

Civil Evidence in Context

This chapter summarises the principles which put all that follows into context. It outlines those aspects of evidence which will be addressed in the remaining chapters, namely: **1–01**

(1) What facts do we have to prove or refute in order to succeed and how do we go about achieving this objective?

(2) What categories of evidence are subject to legal rules as to whether and in what circumstances they may be admitted?

(3) To what extent do the Civil Procedure Rules ("CPR") govern the admission of evidence in civil proceedings?

(4) At what stage and to what extent is a litigant (and his legal adviser) obliged to disclose the evidence that they have collected to their opponent (and vice versa)?

However, when dealing with the law of evidence it is very easy to get sidetracked by the CPR. A good example of this is expert opinion evidence, in which the substantive law is a mixture of common law and statute. Nevertheless a litigator's first port of call when confronted with any problem on expert evidence will almost certainly be CPR 35. Although evidential aspects of the CPR will be covered in detail where necessary, those seeking a fuller commentary will be referred to the relevant sections in *O'Hare and Browne: Civil Litigation* (12th Edn, 2005) ("*O'Hare and Browne*") as is appropriate.

I OVERVIEW

1. Why Rules of Evidence are Important
"Evidence"—the very mention of the topic produces an adverse reaction from some lawyers ranging from, "As dry as dust" to, "Who **1–02**

cares—everything goes in anyway these days". Although there is more than a grain of truth in the last statement, you ignore the rules of evidence at your peril. In the past, the rules of evidence were largely seen as a body of law designed to regulate something *that hardly ever happened*. Civil trials have always been the exception rather than the rule, hence the lack of thought that was often given as to whether there was actually any *evidence* to support the assertions that had been so boldly pleaded at the start of the case. But things have changed. Under the CPR, with their emphasis on early disclosure of evidence and identification of issues (see most recently the remarks of Buxton L.J. in *Denton Hall Legal Services v Fifield* [2006] EWCA Civ 169 at [80]), how you prove your case and what you prove it with have become matters of the greatest importance. Changes to litigation funding have also placed a premium on early risk analysis and made early examination of evidential issues an essential component of modern file management (for greater detail on this minefield see Chapter 2 of *O'Hare and Browne* for a review of current funding options). Furthermore, evidential issues can arise at any stage of the proceedings and assume major strategic importance, for example:

(1) On a strike out-application under CPR 3.4. In *Unilever plc v The Proctor and Gamble Co* [2000] 1 W.L.R. 2436 the subject matter of the claim was held to have been made on an occasion covered by "without prejudice" privilege. Accordingly the strike-out application succeeded (see 08–93).

(2) On an application to discharge a "freezing order" under CPR 25. In *Somatra Ltd v Sinclair Roche and Temperley* [2000] 1 W.L.R. 2453, reliance by the defendants on "without prejudice" communications without the consent of the claimants led to the admission of what had taken place at all of the parties' negotiations (see 08–98).

(3) On an application for specific disclosure. In *Paragon Finance plc v Freshfields* [1999] 1 W.L.R. 1183, the Court of Appeal refused disclosure of the claimants' legal advice from their new solicitors in a professional negligence claim against their former solicitors on the ground that it was protected by legal professional privilege (see 08–70).

(4) On an application to strike out a witness statement on the ground that its contents were protected by Public Interest Immunity as in *Powell v Chief Constable for North Wales* [2000], *The Times*, February 11 (see 08–123).

(5) Where a party seeks leave to admit evidence that has been excluded for breach of a sanction imposed by the CPR as in *Woodward v Finch* [1999] C.P.L.R. 699 (see 1–50).

(6) Where an issue arises on the sufficiency of evidence to discharge the burden of proof on a summary judgment hearing under CPR 24 as in *Royal Brompton NHS Trust v Hammond* [2001], B.L.R. 297 or an application to set aside judgment, as in *Pugh v Cantor Fitzgerald* [2001] C.P.L.R. 271 (see 09–15).

(7) Where the admissibility of "similar fact" evidence arises as a case management issue as in *O'Brien v Chief Constable of South Wales* [2005] 2 A.C. 534 (see 04–31).

Practitioners must therefore be aware of evidential issues at every stage of the case and be alive to any tactical opportunities and challenges these may present.

2. *What are Rules of Evidence for?*

In practical terms they serve three purposes. First, they tell us how, as   **1–03** a matter of law, we may prove (or seek to refute) those facts which are material to the relevant claim. Since January 1, 1997, the law could not be simpler:

> "A party can seek to prove relevant facts (more or less) any way that he likes".

This is because evidence ceased to be liable to exclusion on the ground that it was *hearsay* as a result of s.1 of the Civil Evidence Act 1995. Hearsay as a concept will be addressed later in this chapter at 01–16 and is covered more fully in Chapter 3.

Secondly, the rules of evidence embrace those *procedural rules* that a party must comply with to ensure that evidence is received at trial. In practical terms evidence is more vulnerable to exclusion for failure to comply with a case management direction or a specific provision of the CPR than it is for breach of the substantive rules of evidence (these rules are covered in detail in Chapters 10 to 12).

Thirdly, although strictly speaking a matter of procedure, the rules on *disclosure* of evidence under the CPR are so closely related to the substantive law of evidence, especially on matters relating to privilege and public interest immunity, that, in effect, they now form part of its jurisprudence (see, in particular, Chapters 9 and 10).

II HOW DO WE PROVE FACTS?

A Basic Case Analysis

Before considering how we prove facts we need to identify what   **1–04** facts we need to prove or refute in order to succeed at trial. Many sophisticated forms of case analysis have been devised, for example by Jeremy Bentham, Dean Wigmore and Professor William Twining. For those seeking a fuller introduction to case analysis, Anderson, Schum and Twining *Analysis of Evidence* (2nd Edn, 2005, Cambridge) ("*Anderson, Schum and Twining*") is a helpful starting point. Chapter 5 is of particular interest for those who wish to take case analysis further since it is there that the authors explain the highly sophisticated "Chart Method" of analysis devised by John Henry Wigmore during his lengthy tenure at Northwestern Law School in the United States. However, in simple (and arguably simplistic) terms every potential claim can be broken down into three levels:

"LEVEL I"   WHAT ARE THE "ELEMENTS" OF THE CLAIM?
            (The "*Ultimate Probandum*", see *Anderson Schum and Twining* at page 60)

"LEVEL II" WHAT MATERIAL FACTS MUST I PROVE/
            REFUTE TO PROVE/REFUTE EACH ELEMENT?
            (The "*Penultimate Probanda*", see *Anderson, Schum and Twining* at page 61)

"LEVEL III" WHAT EVIDENCE DO I HAVE TO PROVE/
            REFUTE EACH MATERIAL FACT AND CAN
            I USE IT?

1. "Level I": Elements and Legal Analysis

1–05   Whenever a client takes his case to a lawyer, a complex interaction takes place in which, as the facts emerge, the lawyer should be able to identify whether or not, as a matter of law, the client has a claim or sustainable defence. Sometimes this task will be relatively easy because the facts fit into a well-recognised legal template.

The victim of a simple road traffic accident is an obvious example. Like any potential claimant in the tort of negligence he must prove four essential elements of his claim in order to succeed:

I	II	III	IV
(LAW/FACT)	(LAW/FACT)	(LAW/FACT)	(LAW/FACT)
EXISTENCE	**BREACH OF**	**CAUSAL LINK**	**DAMAGE**
OF A DUTY	**DUTY**	**BETWEEN**	

A similar template exists in contractual claims, namely:

I (LAW/FACT) EXISTENCE OF A CONTRACT	II (LAW/FACT) A TERM OF THE CONTRACT WHICH TRIGGERS ELEMENTS III-V	III (LAW/FACT) BREACH OF ELEMENT II	IV (LAW/FACT) CAUSAL LINK BETWEEN III AND V	V (LAW/FACT) DAMAGE

Whenever litigation looms, analysis of the relevant elements from the starting point, whether the claim is for possession of a secure tenancy under the Housing Act 1985, recovery of a debt, infringement of a patent, recovery of protected goods under s.90 of the Consumer Credit Act 1974, and so on.

2. "Level II": Material Facts and Factual Analysis

Having identified the relevant legal "template" and whether it is sustainable or capable of being defended, it is then necessary to identify those material facts the client will need to prove or resist in order to succeed at trial.   1–06

Example: Arnold Jones comes to see you having been involved in a road traffic accident whilst driving his Ford Mondeo LK51 ABC. He tells you he was struck in a rear end shunt by a 10 ton truck TI44 AMN driven by John Hart, an employee of Hanover Transport plc. He tells you his car is a write-off and he has suffered an unpleasant "whiplash" type injury.   1–07

To prove each of the four "elements" in the tort of negligence he will have to prove the following material facts: 1–08

ELEMENT I: EXISTENCE OF A DUTY

To prove that the relevant duty situation has arisen, namely, that owed by one road user to another, he must prove:

"MATERIAL FACT" (1)   Arnold Jones was lawfully using the highway in his car.

"MATERIAL FACT" (2)   John Hart was at the same time using the highway in the truck.

If, as he probably will, Arnold Jones also wishes to sue Hanover Transport plc he will also need to prove:

"MATERIAL FACT" (3)   At the time of the collision John Hart was driving in the course of his employment.

ELEMENT II: BREACH OF DUTY

"MATERIAL FACT(S)"   Arnold Jones will need to prove that John Hart's driving fell short of the standard of care it was reasonable to expect from a road user in the circumstances.

In practical terms, the claimant must adduce evidence which points to John Hart having driven in a particular way, for example, too fast, with insufficient attention and so on, that falls short of the required objective standard.

ELEMENT III: CAUSAL LINK BETWEEN ELEMENTS II AND IV

"MATERIAL FACT"   That the rear end shunt caused both Arnold Jones' Ford Mondeo to be written off, and his whiplash injuries.

Generally you should have little difficulty in persuading a court that the pristine vehicle that existed a split second before John Hart's 10–ton truck came into contact with its rear end, has been transformed into a wreck by the force of the impact from John Hart's vehicle. However, on occasions issues of factual causation both in tort and contract may be more complex (see 03–21). Indeed, Arnold Jones' whiplash injury may throw up problems if, for example, the medical evidence suggests that there is some pre-existing cause for his discomfort or the low speed of the collision does not tie in with the symptoms of which he now complains ("LVI cases" (low velocity impact) as they are now called (see further 12–17)).

ELEMENT IV: RESULTANT DAMAGE

"MATERIAL FACT"   (1) That the writing-off of Arnold Jones' car has caused relevant foreseeable losses, in particular:

- The cost of repair or replacement of the vehicle as a result of the collision;
- The value attributable to loss of use and/or the cost of replacement car hire;
- Storage charges.

"MATERIAL FACT"   (2) That Arnold has suffered losses as a result of his personal injuries that come within the recognised heads of recoverable damage, entitling him to compensation for his pecuniary and non-pecuniary losses.

Even the most basic case analysis of this kind will produce the essential material from which:

(1) The first detailed letter of claim or response will be drafted as required by the relevant Protocol or Protocol Practice Direction;

(2) The parties' lawyers will begin to analyse available evidence and consider what further evidence needs to be collected;

(3) The particulars of claim (CPR 16.4(1)) or defence (CPR 16.5(1)) will be drafted;

(4) The relevant facts "in issue" will be identified for the purpose of case management by the court under the CPR;

(5) The parties' lawyers will be able to carry out a preliminary risk analysis and monitor the claim as it progresses;

(6) The claim can be valued for the purpose of making or responding to offers of settlement.

3. Level 3: Evidence
As we shall see in Chapter 5, there are three basic methods of proving (or refuting) facts: **1–09**

(1) Calling witnesses ("oral evidence");

(2) Producing documents ("documentary evidence");

(3) Inviting the court to find facts through the production of an object or interpretation of material by means of its own unaided senses ("real evidence").

However, on occasions, facts can be proved without, in theory, calling any evidence at all.

Proof Without Evidence
The need to prove or refute facts by *evidence* will often not be necessary by the time a claim comes to trial, because many facts will no longer be in issue. For example, some will have been *admitted* in the parties' case statements (see for example CPR 14.1 and 06–02). Thus, for example, if the defendants in Arnold Jones' case were to admit liability in their defence this would stand as conclusive proof of their negligence (see further 06–03). Other facts may also be susceptible to proof without evidence, for example, by inviting the court to take "judicial notice" of certain facts (see 06–15) or relying on one of the "presumptions" that exist at common law or under statute (see 04–46).   **1–10**

B Proof by Evidence: Key Concepts

So far as proof by evidence is concerned, two important points need to be emphasised from the outset.   **1–11**

1. Methods of Proof are Cumulative

1–12   Because there are three methods of proof it is easy be misled into thinking that facts are proved *either* by oral, documentary or real evidence alone. This is not so, they exist as cumulative methods of proof, as the following examples show.

1–13   Example 1: C wishes to rely on a term in a written contract, the original of which is in his possession. D defends the action, alleging that his signature is forged. Although C wishes to rely upon this written contract (documentary evidence) to establish his claim he may need to call a whole succession of witnesses (oral evidence) including a handwriting expert to satisfy the court to the required standard that D did indeed sign the document and it is legally binding.

1–14   Example 2: The way a particular item of machinery was operating on a particular day may be crucial in establishing a claim for personal injuries brought by C. Although the judge may be invited to inspect the machine on site or view a video recording of it in operation (both forms of "real evidence"), this may of itself be an insufficient basis for making findings as to material facts without assistance from lay and expert witnesses ("oral evidence") as to its method of operation along with inspection of the relevant maintenance records ("documentary evidence").

A recent example of this process in operation can be seen in *Capital Bank plc v McDiarmid* [2006] EWCA Civ 226 in which the defendant's signature on a guarantee was proved by a combination of (1) the hearsay statement of the Company Secretary who witnessed the signature; (2) the tentative expert opinion evidence; and (3) the defendant's unconvincing performance under cross examination.

2. Most Relevant Evidence will be Admissible

1–15   Provided evidence is relevant to an issue in the case a party will have little difficulty in securing its admission provided:

> (1) It is not liable to exclusion under one of the few mandatory rules of exclusion that remain in civil proceedings, in particular, legal professional privilege (see 08–04); and

> (2) A party complies with the court's Case Management Directions, in particular as to documents (CPR 31) (see Chapter 10), oral evidence (CPR 32) (see Chapter 11) and expert evidence (CPR 35) (see Chapter 12).

One major reason why admissibility issues feature so rarely in civil trials in the United Kingdom is because so few cases are now tried with a jury. The only claims that may currently be tried by judge and jury are for defamation, fraud, malicious prosecution and false imprisonment (see CPR 26.11, s.69 of the Supreme Court Act 1981 and s.66 of the County Court Act 1984). As we shall see again and again throughout this work, the general approach is to allow all relevant evidence in and deal with it all according to its *weight*. The only potential problem with this approach that there are no clearly defined legal rules for determining weight, hence parties are very much at the mercy of unproven generalisation. The only legal control devices are the prohibitions against irrelevant evidence and non-expert opinion evidence, both of which, as we shall see, are somewhat loosely enforced.

3. *"Goodbye Hearsay": The "Blank Canvas"*
In the days before the Civil Evidence Act 1968, the rules on hearsay in civil and criminal proceedings were more or less the same. Broadly speaking, a party could not prove facts by means of hearsay evidence unless it came within one of the, then relatively few, available exceptions. So what is (or was) hearsay, why was it viewed with such suspicion, and why, since it has been abolished as a rule of exclusion by the Civil Evidence Act 1995 do we need to understand it as a concept at all?   **1–16**

Example: *Jones v Hart (1) and Hanover Transport plc (2)* A bystander   **1–17** ("EW") witnessed the rear-end shunt referred to earlier and his evidence is material proof of the fact that John Hart was driving carelessly.

Effectively the hearsay rule is best thought of as the "eyewitness   **1–18** rule" (or to be strictly accurate, the "proximate human perceiver rule"). In order to prove or refute a fact by means of human perception it will be hearsay evidence if you attempt to do so other than by calling the eyewitness (or "perceiver" if you wish to be pedantic) to give oral evidence on oath. Thus, if instead of calling "EW", the claimant were to try and prove what "EW" saw by, for example:

(1) Calling a person at trial (who did not witness the accident) to give oral evidence of "EW's" reported account of the collision (hearsay in the lay sense);

(2) Tendering "EW's" signed statement giving his account of the collision (at common law this would, technically, have been hearsay even if "EW" had also been called to give oral evidence as well);

(3) Producing a video recording in which "EW" gives his account of the collision;

(4) Producing a newspaper report of the collision in which "EW's" account is given to a reporter.

Now hearsay has been abolished as a rule of exclusion, *all* the above methods of proof would be permissible (although they might well be accorded less weight than "EW's" first-hand account given from the witness box). This is now the case *whatever the degree of hearsay* (s.1(2)(b) of the Civil Evidence Act 1995). The effect of this has been to largely remove any admissibility problems concerning the *medium* through which a relevant piece of factual material is adduced in evidence, provided it is not otherwise liable to exclusion. The only practical issues that remain in relation to most evidence are:

1) "Is it liable to exclusion on the grounds of privilege or public interest immunity?"

2) "If not, is this the best quality evidence available?"

3) "If not, what is the best way to maximise its quality?"

4) "Irrespective of the answer to the above questions, what aspects of the CPR do I need to comply with in order to introduce it in evidence?"

Hearsay evidence is fully discussed in Chapter 7.

1–19   *Conclusion*   Provided evidence is not liable to exclusion under one or more of the (relatively limited) mandatory or discretionary rules, the medium of presentation will not *of itself* affect its admissibility. However it is obvious that a vivid first-hand account of an event given by a totally reliable witness will help your case more than a garbled account contained in a letter written by a person who, for no good reason, is not prepared to reveal his identity.

However, evidence may still be vulnerable to exclusion on grounds other than the fact, that it is hearsay. The exclusionary rules fall into two broad categories:

(1) Evidence that the court *must* exclude; and

(2) Evidence that *may* be liable to exclusion as a matter of discretion.

III RULES OF EXCLUSION

1–20   The House of Lords in *A v Secretary of State for the Home Department (No.2)* [2006] 1 All E.R. 575 have, not surprisingly, confirmed that evidence extracted by torture within the United Kingdom would not be admissible in any circumstances. The same also goes for evidence extracted by torture in an overseas jurisdiction. However this is more a constitutional right than a rule of evidence (see Lord Bingham at

587). That being said, there are very few exclusionary rules in civil proceedings, and in practice, privilege excepted, they are rarely invoked directly. Nevertheless, one needs to be aware of them, if for no other reason, than that several of them are still relevant to weight.

A Evidence Which Must Be Excluded

There are four categories of evidence which a court is *obliged* to exclude, only two of which, privilege and public interest immunity, operate as genuine exclusionary rules.

1–21

1. *Mandatory Exclusion 1: Irrelevant Evidence*
The classic definition of relevance is contained in Stephen, *Digest of the Law of Evidence*, (12th Edn) Art.1; namely that:

1–22

> "any two facts to which it is applied are so related to each other that according to the common course of events one either taken by itself or in conjunction with other facts proves or renders probable the past, present or future existence or non-existence of the other."

The key words in this definition are:

> "according to the common course of events"

because these emphasise the fact that, to a significant extent, relevance is not a matter of law at all but is founded on a nebulous combination mixture of logic, common sense and experience, the presence or absence of which may depend to some degree upon the life-experience and professional background of the judge trying the case. The other question that needs answering is:

> "Relevant to what?"

The answer to this question will be found by studying the parties' case statements from which it will be possible to identify what material facts remain "in issue" in the proceedings. A party is only obliged to tender, and a court may only receive, evidence (in whatever form it is adduced) which tends to render more or less likely the existence of one of the remaining facts in issue. One of the objectives of the court-led case management introduced by the CPR was to encourage the parties to reduce the number of outstanding issues and hence the material facts in issue thereby reducing the amount of relevant evidence a court is required to receive (the fact that this is not always happening is borne out by the remarks of Buxton L.J. in *Denton Hall* referred to at 1–02). However, although relevance is usually a

1–23

question of fact there are certain categories of evidence which have developed their own legal rules, in particular:

(a) *Evidence of Character and Disposition*

1–24   The so-called "rule against similar fact evidence", of huge importance in criminal proceedings, also applies (albeit somewhat more flexibly) in civil claims. Put simply, it operates on the principle that a party's conduct (or misconduct) on an occasion *other than that which is the subject matter of the claim* is likely to decrease in relevance the further it is removed in place and/or time from the events that are in issue. The problems caused by similar fact evidence are fully discussed further at 4–24.

(b) *Credit and Credibility*

1–25   As a general rule, in contrast to the position on "similar fact" evidence, any party may cross-examine his opponent's witnesses (including a party) as to their previous bad character insofar as this is relevant to their *credibility as a witness* on any matter on which they testify. However, quite apart from the court's power to control cross-examination under the CPR (see CPR 32.1(3)), as a general rule, answers on questions as to credit are subject to certain exceptions. The most important of these relate to previous convictions and previous inconsistent statements and are discussed at 7–40 and 14–50.

(c) *Previous Judgments*

1–26   Another general principle is that the decision of an earlier court on an issue that also arises in the instant litigation is inadmissible both on the grounds of irrelevance and because the decision of the earlier court is regarded as being inadmissible opinion evidence. However, this general rule is subject to a number of important exceptions contained in ss.11–13 of the Civil Evidence Act 1968.

1–27   **Example:** *Jones v Hart (1)* and *Hanover International Transport plc (2)*
As a result of the collision, John Hart is prosecuted and convicted of careless driving. Arnold Jones wishes to adduce his conviction in the civil claim to prove Hart was driving negligently.

1–28   At common law, the conviction would have been inadmissible (*Hollington v Hewthorn & Co Ltd* [1943] K.B. 587), but as a result of s.11 of the Civil Evidence Act 1968 the conviction would now be admissible as presumptive proof of negligence. Section 11 is further discussed at 04–54 and earlier finding in general at 06–24 onwards.

2. *Mandatory Exclusion 2: Opinion Evidence*

1–29   As a general rule a party may only adduce evidence of *facts*, since to do otherwise would usurp the role of the court as arbiter on all disputed issues. Accordingly, if a witness were to be called by the claimant in *Jones v Hart (1)* and *Hanover International Transport plc (2)* to give evidence as to the circumstances of the collision, although he would be permitted to give his account of what he observed he could *not* be asked:

Q. "So who, in your opinion, was at fault for the collision?"

because that is the very issue that the court is being asked to decide. It operates, subject to exceptions, as an *absolute rule of exclusion*.

There are, however, exceptions, the most important of which, by far, is *expert* opinion evidence, a category of evidence which is rendered admissible by s.3(1) of the Civil Evidence Act 1972, subject (and it is a very big "subject") to compliance with CPR 35. In view of the persuasive influence of CPR 35, opinion evidence is left until Chapter 12.

3. Mandatory Exclusion 3: Privilege
There are certain well known situations in which a party or witness   1–30
may, however relevant the evidence may otherwise be:

(1) Refuse to answer a question; or

(2) Produce a document

on the ground that the information sought to be elicited is protected from disclosure because it comes within one of the four recognised categories of privilege, "Without prejudice" privilege excepted, they exist for all time and may be raised in any proceedings, not simply within the legal context in which they originally arose.

(a) *"Legal Advice Privilege"*
Confidential communications between a legal adviser and advisee   1–31
which are made for the purpose of giving or receiving *legal advice* (on *legal* matter, not simply litigation) are privileged. As will be discussed later (see 08–04), the term "legal advice" has been construed to embrace any confidential advice given by a legal adviser within a "relevant legal context".

(b) *"Litigation Privilege"*
Confidential communications between either: 1–32

(1) The person claiming privilege; and/or

(2) His duly authorised agent (for example the solicitor)

and a third party (and material generated as a result of such communication) where the predominant purpose of such communication (or generation of material) is preparation for actual or reasonably contemplated *litigation*. In one sense it is therefore wider than "Legal Advice Privilege" since it covers communications outside of the lawyer/client relationship. In another sense, however, it is narrower because the predominant purpose *must* be to prepare for litigation; if there is some collateral purpose of equal importance such as a health and safety enquiry, the privilege will not be available. The scope of the privilege is fully discussed at 08–39.

(c) *Self Incrimination*

1–33 If answering a question or producing a document will have a tendency to increase the exposure of a party or witness (or his or her spouse) to the risk of criminal prosecution, forfeiture or a penalty, he or she may refuse to answer or produce the document (see further 08–71). It is one part of the multi-faceted "right to silence" that exists at common law and is now underpinned by Art.6(1) of the European Convention of Human Rights.

(d) *Communications Made "Without Prejudice"*

1–34 Any oral or written communication made in good faith with a view to compromising a dispute will be privileged in the context of any ongoing or subsequent litigation between the parties concerning that dispute. It is, to a large extent, based on the premise that it is in the public interest to encourage warring parties to reach a negotiated settlement rather than litigate (see further 08–83).

4. *Mandatory Exclusion 4: Public Interest Immunity*

1–35 Production or admission in evidence of certain documents or information may be resisted on the ground that it is of such a confidential nature that to reveal its contents (or in some cases even its existence) would be contrary to the public interest. Traditionally, resistance used to be based on the assertion that either:

(1) The document or information, by its nature was protected (a "class claim"); or

(2) The content of the document or information was protected (a "contents claim").

The claim was usually, but not exclusively, raised by government departments, local authorities or other public officials such as Chief Officers of Police. As we shall see (08–122), its attractiveness as a basis for resisting production has diminished as a result of recent developments.

1–36 *Mandatory Exclusion in Practice* It is unlikely that any of the above exclusionary rules will give rise to major problems in straightforward cases: everyone understands how legal professional privilege and "without prejudice" works (well more or less!) and on expert opinion evidence, CPR 35 occupies centre stage. However as we shall see in later chapters, when the stakes are high, the taking of a point under one or other of these rules may turn out to be pivotal to the ultimate result. It is now time to turn to the discretionary rules of exclusion.

B Evidence Which May Be Excluded

The reality is that, apart from easily identifiable rules of exclusion **1–37** such as privilege, you are far more likely to have material evidence excluded because of a failure to comply with rules of *procedure* than because it is inadmissible under the substantive law. There are three (or possibly four) grounds on which evidence is vulnerable to exclusion as a matter of discretion. All but the last of these derive from powers conferred on the court by the CPR.

1. Discretionary Exclusion 1: "Automatic" CPR Sanctions

There are a number of situations in which failure to comply with a **1–38** relevant requirement of the CPR will prohibit the party in default from relying on the evidence without the permission of the court. The most notable categories of evidence which are vulnerable to exclusion on this basis are:

(1) Oral evidence of witnesses of fact; and

(2) Expert opinion evidence.

In both cases, parties will be required, as part of the "cards on the table" approach encouraged by the CPR, to give disclosure of such evidence in written form by a prescribed timetable date. Failure to comply will lead to automatic exclusion (see CPR 32.10 (witness statements) and CPR 35.13 (expert reports)) unless the court grants relief. As we shall see when examining this topic at 01–50, relief tends to be granted relatively generously. Nevertheless, failure to comply with case management timetables still carries a major costs risk.

2. Discretionary Exclusion 2: Breach of Specific Case Management Directions under the CPR

A court has power to make specific directions regarding evidence **1–39** quite apart from the "automatic" sanctions referred to above. In particular, the court has specific power to:

(1) Make an order for the purpose of managing the case or furthering the overriding objective (CPR 3.1(2)(m)); and

(2) Control the evidence generally under CPR 32.1.

The court also has a general power to specify the consequences of failing to comply with any order that it makes (CPR 3.1(3)(b)). There is therefore always the possibility that it will impose a specific sanction debarring a party from adducing a particular piece of evidence unless he complies with the court's order (often referred to as an "unless order"). Any party seeking relief from such a sanction will be able to invoke the exercise of the court's discretion in accordance with the principles contained in CPR 1.1 and 3.9. As with relief from automatic sanctions, such case law as there is suggests that the court should be relatively generous in granting relief (see in particular 11–24).

3. Discretionary Exclusion 3: General Discretion to Exclude Under CPR 32.1

1–40 As well as its specific power to control evidence under CPR 32.1(1), the court has now for the first time been given a specific discretion to exclude evidence that would *otherwise be admissible*. As yet there is little judicial guidance as to how this discretion should be exercised. However, once it has been established that an item of evidence is relevant to an issue in the case and is not inadmissible under any other exclusionary rule, it would require special circumstances before a court would exclude it. This is discussed further at 1–52.

4. Discretionary Exclusion 4: Breaches of ECHR: Does This Provide a Further Discretion (or Obligation) to Exclude?

1–41 Some commentators predicted that the introduction of the European Convention of Human Rights into our domestic law would create new grounds for exclusion both in civil and criminal claims. In particular it was thought that the admission of *hearsay* evidence might be liable to exclusion under Art.6(1) (right to a fair trial) and evidence obtained as a result of *intrusive surveillance* might be equally vulnerable if it involved breach of Art.8 (right to respect for private and family life). So far, as Chapter 2 will outline, this has not proved to be the case. Indeed it can be stated with a degree of confidence that, as yet, the ECHR has not extended the court's powers to exclude evidence. However what it undoubtedly *has* done is to place upon the court an obligation to consider all the evidence with care and to give clear reasons as how particular evidence has been treated. This is the minimum requirement imposed by Art.6 (See *English v Emery Reimbold and Strick Ltd* [2002] 1 W.L.R. 2409 discussed further at 02–28).

C Proof at Trial: Case Theory and Advocacy

In practical terms, most civil trials are relatively relaxed so far as   **1–42**
matters of evidence are concerned since, by the time a case comes to
trial:

(1) The documentary evidence will almost invariably be in an
    agreed trial bundle or bundles. This means that from the outset
    the parties will be able to use any document in the bundles as a
    means of proving or refuting a fact in issue or, where relevant,
    putting any of its contents to a witness in cross-examination.
    (The fact that 95 per cent of them are never actually looked at
    and play no part whatsoever in the trial is a matter that will be
    considered further in due course.)

(2) Witness statements, as well as being riddled with hearsay
    (which is now of course permissible) will also often contain
    blatantly inadmissible statements of opinion.

(3) It will be rare indeed for any admissibility points to be taken,
    let alone be available, at trial.

Of far greater significance is the *use* to which that evidence is put by
the advocate presenting it. The ability to create the most plausible
"story" out of the available material is central to forensic success. This
is where "Case Theory" comes in. Construction of a viable case theory
that is consistent with the applicable law, the realistically provable
facts and the client's own instructions, is one of the most important
and creative tasks the trial advocate (and the litigator who is preparing the case) has to perform. This is because the plausibility of the
"story" and the persuasiveness and conviction of the "storyteller"/
advocate who tells it, can win or lose a case. The subject is considered
in greater detail at 14–21 and 14–59.

IV EVIDENCE AND THE CPR: AN OVERVIEW

As has already been pointed out, evidence may be vulnerable to exclu-   **1–43**
sion because a party has failed to comply with one or more of the
requirements of the CPR. The role that these rules play in the management of evidence therefore needs to be addressed in greater detail,
since it runs as a theme through all the remaining chapters. Not only
that, the expectation of early disclosure of material evidence means
that the process of evidence collection and analysis has to start as
soon as you receive instructions.

A "Thinking CPR From Day 1"

1–44   Evidential issues can no longer be left to the last minute as was so often the case in the days before early disclosure became a normal requirement. This trend started in the mid 1970s with the introduction under the Civil Evidence Act 1972 of rules empowering the court to require disclosure of expert evidence as a pre-condition of its admission. Now, disclosure of *all* the evidence a party intends to rely on at trial will be required under the CPR once proceedings have begun. More importantly though, the Pre-Action Protocol Practice Direction and the individual Protocols create an expectation that any material evidence will be disclosed to the other side *before proceedings have even started.*

B "Case Analysis from Day 1"

1–45   There is now far greater need to analyse the available evidence so as to be able to carry out an accurate Risk Analysis (the basis on which this exercise is carried out for the purpose of calculating the appropriate "uplift" in a Conditional Fee Agreement ("CFA") with a "success fee" is helpfully summarised in *O'Hare and Browne* at 38.027). The cost-benefits of bringing or defending any claim must now be fully explored and have a particular relevance to, for example:

(1) The Client Care letter required by r.15 of the Solicitors' Practice Rules 1990;

(2) In the case of Conditional Fee Agreements, providing details to the client explaining why the percentage success fee has been set at that level. This is especially important since the letter will have to be disclosed to the paying party and the court on detailed assessment of costs if the CFA funded client is successful (CPR 44.15 and Costs PD Section 11).

Although the detailed provisions of the Conditional Fee Agreements Regulations (SI 2000/692) will not apply to CFAs entered into after November 1, 2005, it is unlikely that we have seen the last of attempts by a paying party to wriggle out of his liability to pay the successful party's costs by reference to some alleged defect in the agreement or the client care letter (see, in particular, *Garbutt v Edwards* [2006] 1 All E.R. 553).

Furthermore, the provisions of the "Overriding Objective" in CPR 1 must always be borne in mind. CPR 1.3 places an obligation on the parties, and hence their legal advisers, to deal with claims "justly".

This includes (CPR 1.1(2)):

"(b) saving expense;
(c) dealing with the case in ways which are proportionate:

    (i)   to the amount of money involved;
    (ii) to the importance of the case;
    (iii) to the complexity of the issues;
    (iv) to the financial position of each party;

(d) ensuring that it is dealt with expeditiously and fairly;".

Failure to follow these principles, particularly by raising and continuing to litigate inappropriate issues may, at any stage in the proceedings, have an impact on costs. This is because CPR 44.3, which sets out the principles upon which the court must exercise its discretion as to costs, requires the court to have particular regard to "litigation conduct" (CPR 44.3(3)(a)). CPR 44.3(4) then goes on to give specific examples of such conduct to which the court have regards:

"(4) The conduct of the parties includes:

(a) conduct before, as well as during, the proceedings, and in particular the extent to which the parties followed any relevant pre-action protocol;
(b) whether it was reasonable for a party to raise, pursue or contest a particular allegation or issue;
(c) the manner in which a party has pursued or defended his case or a particular allegation or issue;
(d) whether a claimant who has succeeded in his claim, in whole or in part, exaggerated his claim".

From this it is clear that a party who, for example:

(1) Does not adequately gauge the strengths and weaknesses of his claim by reference to the available evidence; or

(2) Fails to comply with Protocol and CPR requirements as to disclosure of evidence; or

(3) Fails to concentrate only on those issues which are clearly provable;

runs major costs risks. The message rings out loud and clear:

"if you try to flog a dead horse it will cost you".

A good illustration is the case of *Kastor Navigation v Axa Global Risks (UK) Ltd* [2004] EWCA Civ 277.

Facts. The claim concerned a vessel called the *"Kastor Too"* which had caught fire and sunk off the coast of Yemen. The owners were claiming against the insurers on the basis that the vessel was an "actual total loss" as a result of the fire. The insurer's case was that, because the fire had not caused the vessel to sink it was not covered under the policy which, as was normal, only covered "perils of the sea". It was common ground that the entry of seawater due to ordinary wear and tear was not covered under the policy. Although the insurers did not advance a positive case that the ship had been scuttled, they nevertheless wished to put the owners to proof that the loss was due to a risk covered under the policy. It was common ground among the experts that a steel ship of this kind would not normally sink as a result of an engine room fire, and for it to sink within 15 hours was highly unusual. The agreed value of the vessel was *US$3 million* and the estimated cost of repairs to the damage suffered by the time of its sinking was *US$7/8 million.*

Anyone who deals with simple road traffic cases must already be thinking, "well, surely it was a write-off anyway". Indeed it was, and some nine months into the claim, the owners amended their claim to add an alternative case based on "constructive total loss" (which rendered the cause of its sinking irrelevant if it were to succeed). However, the owners pursued both limbs of their claim to trial. The net result was that although they lost on the "actual total loss" limb of the claim they won on the "constructive total" loss part. Not only that, they were awarded a sum of *US$3.48 million* having made an earlier "Part 36 offer" to settle for *US$2.8 million.* A detailed consideration of CPR 36 is outside the scope of this work (see further, *O'Hare and Browne,* Chapter 29) but suffice it to say that, generally speaking, a claimant who beats his own Part 36 will have "hit the jackpot" so far as his costs are concerned. This is because, under CPR 36.21, he will usually be entitled to his costs on an indemnity basis from 21 days after the date of his offer.

However in the *Kastor* case, most of the costs had been incurred fighting the issue on which the owners had *lost.* On the trial judge's (Tomlinson J.) view, the length of the proceedings (a 17-day trial with nine days of expert evidence) was largely attributable to the owner's insistence on pursuing the "actual total loss" claim when the "constructive total loss" claim could have been determined summarily over a day or so without the need for any live evidence. Accordingly, he ordered the "successful" owners to pay 70 per cent of the insurer's costs. Bearing in mind that each side's costs were estimated at £850,000, one can see how this represented a somewhat Pyrrhic victory for the owners. Although the claimants were partially successful on their appeal before the Court of Appeal (the court substituted an order of "no order as to costs"), this still meant that, in effect, the owners only recovered 75 per cent of their loss.

Conclusion Of course, it is all too easy to be wise after the event, or **1-46** "rewrite history" as it was put to the Court of Appeal in *Kastor*. It takes an extraordinary amount of courage and conviction to advise a client to abandon a material part of his claim half way through an action. However, the above decision is but one of many instances (*Denton Hall* referred to at 01–02 being other) where a party who has pressed on all fronts has found it to be a very expensive experience.

C "Cards on the Table from Day 1"

One of the major features of the individual Protocols and the **1-47** Protocol Practice Direction is the requirement that each party sets out at an early stage the factual basis of his claim and the evidence which tends to support or undermine it. Under this philosophy parties are expected to provide their opponents with the essential information they need to enable them to make or respond to offers of settlement (see *Brawley v Marczynsici* [2002] 4 All E.R. 1060 discussed at 09–04). A party who fails to do so runs serious costs risks either under the general costs rules (CPR 44) or the special provisions on offers of settlement in CPR 36. It may not always be easy to convince clients that the duty extends to early disclosure of material that undermines their case or supports that of their opponent; however the philosophy of the Protocol Practice Direction and the individual Protocols requires precisely that.

D "Full Case Statements from Day 1"

It has always been a feature of civil litigation that both parties should **1-48** at an early stage, set out and serve on their opponent a written summary of the facts upon which their claim or defence is based. The purpose of this exercise is to identify the issues in the proceedings. However these documents which, prior to the introduction of the CPR used to be known as "pleadings", were often drafted in such vague and general terms that the true issues were obscured. Plaintiff's (claimant's) pleadings were often couched in the broadest and most optimistic of terms with little thought being given as to what evidence there was to support the claim until the door of the court loomed. Defences often consisted of little more than a blanket denial with virtually no contrary assertions of fact at all. Indeed, before the introduction of exchanged witness statements a party would often have very little idea indeed of the claim or defence he had to meet until the day of the trial. This unsatisfactory state of affairs lay behind many of the reforms introduced over the last three decades. The Practice

Direction to CPR 16 now contains detailed requirements as to the particulars and supporting documents a claimant must supply when he serves his Claim Form and Particulars of Claim. Even more crucial, so far is the defendant is concerned is CPR 16.5(2) which states that:

> "(2) Where the defendant denies an allegation:
>
> (a) he must state his *reasons* [emphasis added] for doing so; and
> (b) if he intends to put forward a *different* version of events from that given by the claimant, he must *state his own version* [emphasis added]."

Subject to certain exceptions (see CPR 16.5(3) and (4)), failure to do this will constitute a deemed admission of that allegation (discussed further at 06–05). Furthermore, all case statements (and certain other key documents must be supported by a "Statement of Truth" signed by the party, his legal representative or, alternatively, in the case of a company or corporation, by a person holding a "senior position" (the detailed requirements are set out in CPR 22 Practice Direction; see further, *O'Hare and Browne* 12–005 to 12–006 and 14–005). One of the effects of this requirement is to make case statements evidence in their own right for certain purposes, in particular for interim hearings and final hearings other than trials (CPR 32.6). The form of statement is prescribed by CPR 22 PD para.2.1:

> "[I believe [the (claimant or as may be) believes] that the facts stated in this [name the document being verified] are true."

Other documents that must be verified by a statement of truth include (see CPR 22 Practice Direction):

(1) Responses to requests for further information under CPR 18;

(2) Witness statements;

(3) An Application Notice where a party wishes to rely on matters contained in it as evidence at an interim hearing;

(4) Certificate of Service of a document required by CPR 6.10.

Elevating the status of case statements and other prescribed documents in this way means that they need to be drafted with far greater care than pleadings were. If, as will often be the case, the signatory will also be giving oral evidence at trial, any material discrepancies between the facts in the case statement and those in his subsequent witness statement may seriously damage the credibility of his case (albeit not always fatally (see *Binks v Securicor Omega Express Ltd* [2003] 1 W.L.R. 2557 discussed further at 11–71)). For those who seek general guidance on the role and drafting of case statements reference should be made to Chapter 12 of *O'Hare and Browne*.

E "Case Management from Day 1"

The court will expect the parties to have identified all the relevant   **1–49** issues, and any evidential problems that they are likely to create, at the earliest possible stage. A good example is the use of covert video surveillance evidence. In *Rall v Hume* [2001] 3 All E.R. 248 the Court of Appeal stated that, at the very latest, such a document should be disclosed as part of Standard Disclosure under CPR 31.6. However the court went further by stating that a party intending to rely on such material should make this fact known to the court at the earliest available opportunity; this will often be at Allocation Questionnaire stage. Furthermore, even before the claim has been allocated to its relevant track (for a full explanation of the track allocation system see *O'Hare and Browne* 09–040 to 09–068) broadly:

CPR 27 (Small Claims—claims not exceeding £5,000 (*subject to exceptions*))

CPR 28 (Fast Track—claims not exceeding £15,000 (*subject to exceptions*))

CPR 29 (Multi Track—claims exceeding £15,000)

The court will expect parties (other than in small claims) to have:

(1) Fully analysed what facts remain in issue;

(2) Decided what evidence they need and whether any of it involves special directions or is liable to exclusion;

(3) Be able to provide the court with an appropriate case summary should the court fix a Case Management Conference;

(4) Be able to give the court any information it needs to decide whether the claim needs to be transferred to a higher track than the one its financial value suggests.

Case management of fast-track and multi-track claims is discussed very fully in Chapters 21 and 22 of *O'Hare and Browne*. Once directions have been given, parties will also be expected to keep the court up to date as to the claim's progress and, in particular:

(1) At the Pre-Trial Checklist or Listing Hearing stage (the final stages of case management are set out fully in *O'Hare and Browne* at 21–015 (fast track) and 22–023 (multi-track) to have honed down the issues and necessary evidence required to an irreducible minimum; and

(2) In the final stages of preparation for trial to ensure that the court only has placed before it that evidence which it needs in order to resolve the issues that remain in dispute.

As already noted, failure to observe these requirements may in the short or long term have serious costs consequences.

F Think Timetables from Day 1

1–50 As already noted, evidence may be vulnerable to exclusion for breach of a specific case management direction or a breach of the CPR which carries an automatic sanction. A commonly encountered example is under CPR 32.10 (failure to serve a witness statement). The effect of this rule is that a party who files to file and serve his witness statements on the date required by the case management directions will be debarred from calling oral evidence at the trial without the court's permission. However, any litigator who fondly assumes that if his opponent is as much as one day late in serving his witness statements, the court will refuse him relief, is in for a shock. The court will generally grant relief and admit the evidence unless it genuinely feels that, having regard to the balancing exercise required by CPR 3.9, the imposition (or upholding) of the sanction is just and proportionate. In every case involving a sanction the court must, in deciding whether or not to uphold it, consider all the circumstances and, in particular, go through the checklist set out in the rule. And consider:

(a) the interests of the administration of justice;

(b) whether the application for relief was made promptly;

(c) whether the failure to comply was intentional;

(d) whether there is a good explanation for the failure;

(e) the extent to which the party in default has complied with other rules, practice directions, court orders and any relevant pre-action protocol;

(f) whether the failure to comply was caused by the party of his legal representative;

(g) whether the trial date or the likely trial date can still be met if relief is granted;

(h) the effect which the failure to comply had on each party; and

(i) the effect which granting relief would have on each party.

Although the granting or refusal of relief is a matter of discretion in each case, the following general principles have now emerged from Court of Appeal decisions:

(1) Breaches of the rules will be less tolerated than in the past, but with costs, sanctions and/or interest penalties being more likely (see *Biguzzi v Rank Leisure* [1999] 1 W.L.R. 1026).

(2) If the breach is serious the court may still refuse relief but the judge has a broad discretion which will only be interfered with in the case of serious error. For example, in *Woodward v Finch* [1999] C.P.L.R. 699 the Court of Appeal held that a circuit judge was not wrong to allow late service of the claimant's witness statement even though this was in flagrant breach of judge's own unless order made in the claimant's presence and explained to him.

(3) When exercising its discretion either to grant relief from sanctions, the court should go through each aspect of CPR 3.9(1) like a checklist. In *Bansal v Cheema [2001]* C.P. Rep. 6, another case involving late service of witness statements, the Court of Appeal granted relief because refusal without due consideration of CPR 3.9 produced a result that was "wholly disproportionate". In effect, it gave to the defendant what Brooke L.J. described as a "windfall judgement".

(4) The "punishment must fit the crime" (*Bansal v Cheema*) and the court should consider whether other forms of sanction such as costs, interest penalties and exclusion of issues from consideration will suffice to do justice between the parties.

(5) When the court makes an "unless" order with a sanction in default and the order must be drafted with sufficient clarity to enable the party against whom it is made to be clear what he must do to comply. Thus in *Morgan v Needhams* [1999], *The Times,* November 5 an order for specific disclosure was held to be of no effect on the grounds that it was "hopelessly vague". Likewise in *Keith v CPM Marketing* [2000], *The Times,* August

29 the Court of Appeal held that an "unless" order which stated:

"Unless the defendant do serve the outstanding equipment requested in the claimant's solicitor's letter of September 8, 1999 and September 24 within 21 days, the defence be struck out."

was of no effect because it gave no indication as to when the 21 days for compliance ran from.

1–51   *Conclusion*   In practical terms therefore, it is unlikely that any evidence which is served late will be at serious risk of exclusion for a breach of the CPR. However it is still advisable to ensure that directions are complied with, since failure to do so slows the claim down thus increasing costs. Furthermore, any application you have to make for relief will usually involve your client being ordered to pay the other side's costs. The court's approach to sanctions in relation to specific types of evidence is discussed further at 10–29 (disclosure of documents), 11–19 (witness statements) and 12–45 (expert evidence).

G   The Courts' Powers to Control the Evidence: General Discretion to Exclude

1–52   We have already noted how the "cards on the table" approach requires that certain types of evidence will have to be disclosed under case management directions with the sanction of automatic exclusion unless the court grants relief. Such sanction-based disclosure will invariably be ordered (at any rate in Part 7 claims) in respect of:

(1) Documents forming part of the order for Disclosure (CPR 31.21);

(2) Written statements of the oral evidence of factual witnesses (CPR 32.10);

(3) Expert evidence (CPR 35.13).

It is notable that there is no similar sanction for failing to indicate an intention to rely on *hearsay evidence*, even in those cases where notice has to be given under CPR 33.2. This is because s.2(4) of the Civil Evidence Act 1995 specifically provides that failure to serve a hearsay notice does not of itself constitute a reason for excluding the hearsay evidence although it will be relevant to the weight of the evidence and costs.

However there is in addition an important general power to control the evidence under CPR 32.1 which provides that:

"(1) The court may control the evidence by giving directions as to:

(a) the issues on which it requires evidence;
(b) the nature of the evidence which it requires to decide those issues; and
(c) the way in which the evidence is to be placed before the court.

(2) The court may use its power under this rule to exclude evidence that would otherwise be admissible
(3) The court may limit cross-examination."

These wide ranging powers may be exercised at any stage in the proceedings and will often fall for consideration during case management. As yet, there has been little judicial guidance on the scope of the discretion, but it is clear that it is very wide. It was used in *Rall v Hume* [2001] 3 All E.R. 248 to limit cross-examination on and use of a covert video which the defendants had taken of the claimant to "edited highlights" with no more than 30 minutes of cross-examination. Its use was also approved of by the Court of Appeal in *Tomlinson v CC of Hertfordshire* [2001] EWCA Civ 461 to exclude irrelevant evidence of allegations of police harassment after the alleged incidents of false arrest on which the claim was based, and in *Watson v CC of Cleveland* [2001] EWCA 1547 to limit cross-examination of the claimant on his previous convictions to those relating to dishonesty. Perhaps its most notable feature is the power in CPR 32.1(2) to exclude evidence *that would otherwise be admissible*. It clearly empowers the court to exclude evidence that is insufficiently relevant to justify the expense of adducing it, or evidence that goes over the same ground as other highly cogent evidence. But what of otherwise highly relevant evidence that has been obtained illegally, especially if this involves a breach of Art.8? For reasons discussed in Chapter 2 it is suggested that as a general rule CPR 32.1(2) would only be used for this purpose in the most extreme of cases. The power could also be exercised to exclude evidence where there had been a serious breach of the CPR. The existence of this power was acknowledged by the House of Lords in *Polanski v Conde Nast Ltd* [2005] 1 All E.R. 945. This decision is fully considered at 07–33 and 13–24.

V WHAT EVIDENCE MUST I DISCLOSE (AND HOW MUCH OF MY OPPONENT'S CAN I SEE)?

This topic, although not strictly speaking part of the rules of civil evidence, is closely related to it, not least because of the importance that the CPR attach to the "cards on the table" approach to litigation. Disclosure is also directly related to issues of privilege and public   **1–53** interest immunity. Four important aspects of disclosure will be addressed here before looking at the detailed rules in Chapter 10:

(1) Protocol disclosure;

(2) Pre-claim disclosure;

(3) Non-Party disclosure;

(4) Inter-Party disclosure.

A Disclosure Under the Protocols

1–54   The purpose of the pre-action protocols and the Pre-Action Protocol Practice Direction is to encourage all parties to exchange information concerning the nature of their claim or defence at the earliest stage so as to facilitate settlement without the need to commence proceedings. The topic is comprehensively covered in Chapter 2 of *Documentary Evidence* by Charles Hollander Q.C. (8th Ed, 2003 (*"Hollander"*)) (see also, "Pre-Action Protocols—Editorial" at C1A–001 of the *White Book* for a full background to the origins and development of the protocols). At present, as well as the Protocol Practice Direction (which applies to *all* claims not governed by an individual protocol; for the full text see the *White Book* C1–001), there are nine approved protocols dealing with:

- Personal injury (*White Book First Supplement (Summer 2005)* C2–001 and the commentary at C2A–001);
- Industrial disease and illness (*White Book* C9–001 and C9A–001);
- Clinical negligence (*White Book* C3–001 and C3A–001);
- Housing disrepair (*White Book* C10–001 and C10A–001);
- Construction and engineering disputes (*White Book* C5–001 and C5A–001);
- Defamation (*White Book* C6–001 and C6–001A);
- Judicial review (*White Book* C8–001 and C8A–001);
- Professional negligence (*White Book* C7–001 and C7A–001); and
- Expert evidence (available at the DCA website *www.dca.gov.uk*).

Other protocols are anticipated including one on possession proceedings for rent arrears. All of them (with the exception of the Expert Evidence Protocol) follow the same pattern, requiring:

(1) An early (and relatively detailed) letter of claim;

(2) A response within a prescribed time period;

(3) Early contact with a view to narrowing issues and reducing costs;

(4) A less adversarial climate with regard to expert evidence including, where possible, joint instructions;

(5) A climate in which voluntary disclosure of relevant documents is pursued;

(6) Encouragement to pursue ADR as a means of resolving the dispute or specific issues within it.

All the protocols are backed by the Pre-Action Protocol Practice Direction whose stated objectives (para.1.4) are to encourage:

- Early exchange of information;

- Early settlement;

- Effective pre-action preparation;

- In particular parties are (para.2.2) expected:

> "to have complied in substance with the terms of an approved protocol".

Furthermore, in cases not covered by a protocol (para.4) the parties will be expected to:

(1) Comply with CPR 1(a), (b) and (c) ("equality", "economy" and "proportionality");

(2) Act reasonably in exchanging information and documents relevant to the claim; and

(3) Act generally in trying to avoid litigation.

As already noted, trying to explain to your client that he not only has to disclose his strong cards but also his *weak* ones before proceedings have even begun is not easy. The idea that negotiation should be conducted on the basis of a full and frank exchange of *all* relevant evidence, good and bad, does not square with the way some clients approach negotiation in their day to day dealings (see further, Chapter 1 of *Hollander*).

1. So What is a Breach?
The CPR do not provide a specific machinery for enforcement of the 1–55 protocols. Nevertheless there can be no doubt that a party who holds

back relevant information in an attempt to secure tactical advantage will find himself penalised in costs if he is found out. Examples of what might constitute a breach can be found in para.3 of the Pre-Action Protocol Practice Direction. A claimant (3.1) will be in breach if he:

(1) Does not provide sufficient information about his case to a prospective defendant; or if he

(2) Fails to follow the procedure required by an individual protocol. By way of example, the paragraph specifically cites failure to follow the procedure for instruction of an expert set out in paras 3.14 to 3.17 of the Personal Injury Protocol (discussed further at 12–54).

A defendant (3.2) will be regarded as being in breach if he:

(1) Fails to make a preliminary response within the time stipulated in a relevant protocol;

(2) Fails to make a full response within the time stipulated in a relevant protocol;

(3) Fails to disclose documents required to be disclosed by the relevant protocol.

1–56   *Conclusion*   It now becomes clear why it is so important to analyse the available evidence at an early stage. If that is not done, a litigant runs a serious risk of being penalised in costs later in the claim if it emerges that he put forward or contested issues on the basis of inadequate evidence.

2. Sanctions
1–57   So what if evidence is not disclosed as soon as practicable? This topic is discussed fully in the *White Book* at C1A–01. In particular, CPR 3.1 provides that:

"(4) Where the court gives directions it may take into account whether or not a party has complied with any relevant pre-action protocol;

(5) The court may order a party to pay a sum of money into court if the party has, without good reason, failed to comply with the appropriate rule, practice direction or pre-action protocol".

Although protocol points are rarely taken at the case management stage, they may have a significant effect on costs at the conclusion of the case. This is because the court is obliged when deciding what order to make as to costs to consider "in particular" whether or not a party has complied with any relevant pre-action protocol (CPR 44.3(5)(a), and see further the *White Book* at para.4.3.13). There are also very explicit statements in the Protocol Practice Direction as to conduct that might constitute a breach. In particular, para.2.3 of the Practice Direction appears to assume that the "trigger" for court-imposed sanctions is where there has been:

(1) Commencement of proceedings; or

(2) Incurring of costs;

where this would not "otherwise" have happened. The power to impose sanctions is thus intended to be *compensatory* not punitive. This is confirmed by para.2.4 which specifically states that:

"The court will exercise its [power to impose sanctions] with the object of placing the innocent party in no worse a position than he would have been if the protocol had been complied with".

Paragraph 2.3 gives four examples of sanctions the court might impose as being:

(1) Costs; including

(2) Indemnity costs;

(3) Depriving a claimant of interest for a specified period or giving it a lower rate;

(4) Ordering a defendant to pay interest at a higher rate (up to *10 per cent* above base).

Any client who wants to know what risks he runs by "failing to play the game by the rules" should also be advised that a failure could lead to:

(1) An application under CPR 31.16 for pre-action disclosure with an order for costs against the party in default if it can be shown that he acted unreasonably (see CPR 48.3);

(2) Sanctions later in the proceedings (see CPR 3.8) or refusal or modification of relief from a sanction (see in particular CPR 3.9(1)(e));

(3) A stay under CPR 3.1(2)(f) where a party has commenced prematurely;

(4) Refusal of permission to call an expert who has been instructed in breach of a protocol (CPR 35.4(1)) and/or disallowance of the cost of instructing that expert;

(5) The award of costs (CPR 44.3(5)(a)) or their assessment (CPR 44.5(3)(a)(i)) being affected by inappropriate pre-action "conduct";

(6) Payment into court under CPR 3.1(5) for failure to comply without good reason with a:

"rule, practice direction or relevant pre-action protocol".

1-58 *Conclusion* All in all therefore non-disclosure of material evidence at the earliest practicable stage carries with it major costs risks, even though these will probably not emerge until much later, possibly at the trial itself. The tasks facing a legal adviser when initially instructed are admirably set out in Chapter 1 of *Hollander*, and will be considered in greater detail in Chapter 10 of this work. The facts of *Brawley v Marczynski (No.1)* [2002] 1 W.L.R. 813 (discussed further at 09–04) also serve as a warning to those clients who try to negotiate with their cards close to their chests.

B Pre-Claim Disclosure

1-59 Prior to the introduction of the CPR, pre-claim discovery was only available to prospective plaintiffs (and defendants) under s.33(2) of the Supreme Court Act 1981 in proceedings for personal injuries or death. This could cause major difficulties, in particular for a prospective plaintiff who had more than an inkling that he had a potential claim but lacked the ability to obtain access to the documents he needed in order to confirm his suspicions. His only pre-claim remedy was an action based on *Norwich Pharmacal v Commissioners of Customs and Excise* [1974] A.C. 133. However, as the decision in *AXA Equity and Law v National Westminster Bank* [1998] P.N.L.R. 433 showed (see further 10–33), this remedy was only available against an innocent third party who had unwittingly become involved in the actions of a tortfeasor where the tortfeasor's identity was unknown. It did *not* enable the aggrieved party to obtain access to documents in the third party's hands where the identity of the alleged tortfeasor was already known. To coincide with the introduction of the CPR, s.33(2) was extended to cover all potential defendants (and claimants) whatever the nature of the claim. Pre-claim disclosure will be considered in detail in Chapter 10.

C Non-Party Disclosure

1-60 Similar reforms were made to s.34(2) of the Supreme Court Act 1981 to give the court power in any proceedings, once they had been commenced, to order disclosure against a *non-party*. Although the effect of this is most likely to be felt in larger claims the Court of Appeal in *Clarke v Ardington Electrical Repair Services (Appeal Against Order for Disclosure)* [2001] EWCA Civ 585 (a case discussed further at 10–37) has shown a willingness to uphold the decision of a circuit judge to order non-party disclosure in a credit repair claim worth only £1,000. This remedy is discussed further at 10–37.

D Inter-Party Disclosure

Although strictly speaking a rule of procedure rather than evidence,   **1–61** disclosure is so bound up with the rules of evidence that its influence is felt at every stage. It is ironic in a sense that, before the Civil Evidence Act 1995 came along and abolished hearsay, many "discoverable" documents were potentially inadmissible because they contained hearsay. Now that hearsay no longer operates as a rule of exclusion this means, in effect, that *all* disclosable documents will be potentially admissible. One of the main objectives of the Woolf Reforms was to put a stop to time-consuming and expensive "paper chase" applications for discovery. However the abolition of hearsay, not to mention the increase in electronic communication, has vastly extended the scope of potentially relevant material. The basic principles under which the court controls the process are summarised below.

1. "Basic Principle 1": No Disclosure Without Order
"Full" discovery used to be automatic, either under RSC O.24 r.1   **1–62** (High Court) or under CCR O.17 r.11 (county court) following close of pleadings. This is no longer the case. Orders for disclosure, if any, are now made under the court's case management powers and can no longer be taken as a given entitlement. As already noted, however, parties will have been expected to provide voluntary pre-action disclosure where a protocol in the Pre-Action Protocol Practice Direction applies.

2. "Basic Principle 2": Standard Disclosure is the "Industry Standard"
Traditionally, the concept of discovery embraced far wider cate-   **1–63** gories of documents than those which were relevant and admissible at the trial and extended to documents which came within the so called *"Peruvian Guano" [1882] 11 Q.B. 55* text (see 10–03). Such was its potential scope that pre-CPR, it was not unheard of for cases to get bogged down for years, during which period the court would be bombarded with successive applications for further discovery.

One of the prime objectives of the CPR was to bring this process under control by limiting it to documents that were truly relevant to the issues in the case (see further 10–07). The CPR attempts to do this in three ways:

(1) By giving the court control over how much disclosure should be ordered. In exercise of its case management powers the court can, for example, identify key issues and limit disclosure to those, or even dispense with disclosure altogether.

(2) By prescribing "Standard Disclosure" as the norm, at any rate in the first instance. In effect, the definition of a Standard Disclosure in CPR 31.6 limits disclosure to those documents which are likely to be relevant to the issues in the claim.

(3) By requiring a party who seeks further disclosure to make an application for "Specific Disclosure" under CPR 31.12. Applications for Specific Disclosure must be supported by *evidence*, which must identify the documents or classes of documents of which disclosure is sought and show why such further disclosure is relevant and proportionate to the issues in the claim.

Interestingly (and encouragingly) there has been remarkably little case law on the scope and meaning of any of the new concepts in CPR 31.6. Anecdotal evidence suggests that parties are now being much more co-operative in relation to documents. For an interesting summary of how disclosure now operates in practice, see Chapter 9 of *Hollander*, especially 9–20.

VI SUMMARY

1–64   This chapter has highlighted a number of major themes that will recur through the remainder of the book, in particular:

(1) Subject to it being sufficiently relevant and proportionate, you can get evidence before a court irrespective of the medium in which it is presented.

(2) The circumstances in which a court is *obliged* to exclude evidence are relatively limited; legal professional privilege and "without prejudice" negotiations being by far the most commonly encountered examples.

(3) The risk of *discretionary* exclusion is most likely to arise as a result of non-compliance with the CPR, and, even then, such instances are rare. Application of the overriding objective in

CPR 1, and the balancing exercise required by CPR 3.9 on applications for relief, dictate an inclusionary approach.

(4) In some instances, especially in the case of expert evidence (CPR 35), the *procedural* rules governing the admission of evidence have become more important than the substantive law.

(5) There is now a much higher expectation that parties will *voluntarily* disclose their evidence but, failing this, procedures for securing compliance are available.

(6) Parties who litigate (or even offer to mediate) issues which lack credible evidence to sustain them run major *costs risks*. The expectation of the CPR is that weaknesses will be identified and conceded at an early stage in the proceedings.

Conclusion   Understanding how the rules of evidence operate in the   **1–65** four ways identified at the start of this chapter has assumed a far greater importance than was the case before the CPR came into force. In the past, a party could fire off a Writ or county court summons with very little, if any, thought being given as to what the case was really about, let alone whether there was any evidence capable of supporting it. Those days are, hopefully, long gone.

Chapter 2

The Impact of The European Convention of Human Rights and The Human Rights Act 1998

It is not possible in a work of this kind to do more than scratch the   **2–01**
surface of this enormous area of new, and to many English lawyers, unfamiliar area of jurisprudence. The cynical among you might be tempted to ask:

"Why bother at all?"

because so far as rules of *evidence* are concerned, it seems clear that, for the time being at any rate, the ECHR has little to add to our domestic law. This chapter summarises the key features of the ECHR and the Human Rights Act 1998 and considers the case law that has developed so far. The subject is more comprehensively covered in *Phipson on Evidence* (16th Edn, 2005) ("*Phipson*") at 1–45 and the paragraphs that follow. You will also find an informative commentary in Chapter 7 of *Hollander*).

I A BRIEF LEGAL HISTORY OF THE EUROPEAN CONVENTION AND THE HUMAN RIGHTS ACT 1998

A Background

The European Convention for the Protection of Human Rights and   **2–02**
Fundamental Freedoms (1950) (Cmnd 8969) ("the ECHR") was drafted and adopted by the Member States of the Council of Europe over 50 years ago. The United Kingdom has been a signatory from its

inception in March 1951, but it was not directly incorporated into our domestic law until October 1, 2000 when the Human Rights Act 1998 ("the 1998 Act") came into force. The ECHR has five major characteristics:

1. *Minimum Rights by the Signatory Nations:*

2–03   The ECHR secures:

> "to everyone within their jurisdiction the rights and freedoms defined in Section I of this Convention [Articles 2 to 18]".

"Everyone" extends to legal as well as natural persons irrespective of whether they are lawfully present within the jurisdiction concerned. The key articles for the purposes of civil proceedings are:

Article 2*:   The right to life

Article 3*:   Freedom from torture and inhuman or degrading treatment or punishment

Article 5:   The right to personal liberty

Article 6:   The right to a fair trial

Article 8:   The right to respect for private and family life, home and correspondence

Article 10:   Freedom of expression

Article 14:   The prohibition on discrimination in the delivery of rights

Note in particular that those rights which have an asterisk against them (*) are *absolute* in that they cannot be derogated from even in a national emergency. Others are *qualified* either by:

(1) Their individual wording (for example, Arts 2, 5 and 8, 10 and 14); or

(2) By implication (for example Art.6) provided such "derogations" are both in accord with legality, and are "proportionate".

The effect of this qualification is that the European Court of Human Rights accords a generous "margin of appreciation" to individual member states. Therefore a rigid "common law" style approach is inappropriate; it will not be possible to assert, for example:

> "This piece of evidence was obtained in breach of Art.8 therefore it *must* be excluded under Art.6".

2. Wide Imposition of Convention Obligations

Although primarily aimed at national governments and other public or *quasi*-public authorities, Art.17 of the ECHR is more widely drawn: **2–04**

> "Nothing in this convention may be interpreted by implying for any State, group or person any right to engage in any activity or perform any act aimed at the destruction of any of the rights and freedoms set forth herein or at their limitation to a greater extent than is provided for in the Convention."

In the context of civil proceedings, the practical effect of this is that the court, as a public authority, is obliged to uphold the rights conferred under the ECHR irrespective of the status of the litigants appearing before it (see the commentary on s.6 of the 1998 Act 02–13).

3. A Machinery for Enforcement

Any person whose Convention rights had been violated could apply to the European Commission and Court of Human Rights in Strasbourg; since November 1, 1998 application is made to the European Court of Human Rights in Strasbourg. Article 34 of the ECHR provides as follows: **2–05**

> "The Court may receive applications from any person, non-governmental organisation or group of individuals claiming to be the victim of a violation by one of the High Contracting Parties of the rights set forth in the Convention or the protocols thereto. The High Contracting Parties undertake not to hinder in any way the effective exercise of this right."

However, this has always been subject to the provisos in Art.35.1:

> "The court may only deal with the matter after all domestic remedies have been exhausted according to the generally recognised rules of international law, and within a period of six months from the date on which the final decision was taken."

It is fair to say that you are unlikely, if ever, to reach a stage at which you might consider taking a case to Europe on a pure point of evidence, not least because, as we shall see shortly, the ECHR, especially Art.6 (right to a fair trial) does not directly engage domestic rules of evidence. However, in the extremely unlikely event that you do, you will need to have "gone the distance", as far as you are allowed to, through the English courts first.

4. A System of Compensation

2–06 This is provided for in Art.41 as follows:

> "If the court finds that there has been a violation of the
> Convention or the protocols thereto, and if the internal law of the
> High Contracting Party concerned allows only partial reparation
> to be made, the Court shall, if necessary, afford just satisfaction to
> the injured party."

Although Art.41 is not one of the Articles specifically scheduled to the
1998 Act, it is nevertheless reflected in it by s.8. This incorporates the
effect of Art.41 into domestic law. It is important to bear in mind
however that the ECHR is intended to protect basic human rights, not
to provide a system of compensation. The approach of the European
Court to violations is therefore, in general, to treat the finding itself
as "just satisfaction". Even if it does award compensation, the
awards have tended to be modest in the extreme (see Lord Bingham in
*R. (On the Application of Greenfield) v Secretary of State or the Home
Office* [2005] 2 All E.R. 240 at para.17).

5. The Right to Rely Domestic Law if this is Superior

2–07 It is important to emphasise that the ECHR only lays down
minimum standards and that, accordingly, if domestic law provides
superior protection the individual (or body) concerned is in no way
restricted from taking advantage of this. Article 53 specifically
states:

> "Nothing in this Convention shall be construed as limiting or dero-
> gating from any of the human rights and fundamental freedoms
> which may be ensured under the laws of any High Contracting
> Party or under any other agreement to which it is a party."

One of the main reasons why the ECHR will never directly arise in
matters relating to the admissibility of *evidence* is because the specific
safeguards laid down in our domestic law and procedure generally go
beyond the minimum standards laid down by the ECHR. Some
obvious examples spring to mind:

(1) The safeguards in ss.2–5 of the Civil Evidence Act 1995 in the
     case of hearsay evidence;

(2) The general rule that non-expert opinion evidence is inadmis-
     sible;

(3) The law of privilege;

(4) The "cards on the table" approach to early disclosure of evidence required by the CPR.

Thus, it will rarely be necessary for a party to turn to the ECHR on the grounds that the domestic rules of evidence violate his human rights (for a possible example in the context of legal advice privilege, see Lord Hobhouse in *Medcalf v Mardell* [2003] A.C. 120 at para.60).

B Human Rights Act 1998

The 1998 Act, which came into force on October 1, 2000, made major changes to the applicability of the Convention in English Law. The full text of the 1998 Act along with valuable commentary can be found at para.3D-1 of the *White Book*. The most significant sections are set out below.   **2–08**

1. Section 2: "Europrudence"—The Court's Duty
The court must "take into account" European Human Rights case law when determining any questions regarding a "convention right". However as we shall see shortly the courts have made it clear that if, as a result of domestic jurisprudence, the issue does not engage a human right the court will pay scant regard to the lengthy list of European authorities you seek to rely on. Although we shall return to the decision on a number of occasions during the course of this book, the words of Latham L.J. in *Daniels v Walker* [2001] 1 W.L.R. at para.34, an appeal concerning the court's power to order a single joint expert under CPR 35.7 (see further 02–32), should provide a suitable antidote to those advocates who unthinkingly invoke the ECHR: **2–09**

"I read the authorities with interest but with growing incomprehension as to their relevance to the case in question".

2. Section 3: Duty of Compatible Interpretation
Section 3(1) of the 1998 Act imposes a duty on the courts to: **2–10**

"read and give effect to"

primary and subordinate legislation in a manner which is compatible with Convention Rights whenever it is "possible" to do so. However, there is an important distinction which needs to be drawn between *primary* and *subordinate* legislation so far as the court's powers are concerned. In the case of primary legislation, if a compatible interpretation is not possible, the court *has* to apply the law as it stands, incompatibility and all. The aggrieved party may seek a Declaration of Incompatibility under s.4 of the 1998 Act, but this will have *no effect on the actual result of the case itself*. However, in the case of subordinate legislation (of which the CPR are an important example), if a compatible interpretation is not possible the court (by which is meant a judge of any level, even a deputy district judge) may "read down" the provision, that is, read words into the provision in order to achieve compatibility. This power has been considered by the Court of Appeal on two occasions.

In the first case, *Goode v Martin* [2002] 1 All E.R. 620, the court used this technique to interpret a provision of the CPR (CPR 17.4(2)) in such a way as to secure compliance with Art.6. In it, a claimant sought to amend her Particulars of Claim outside the limitation period under s.35(5)(a) of the Limitation Act 1980 in circumstances where the amendment was based on facts put forward for the first time by the defendant in his *defence*. CPR 17.4(2) provides that such an amendment may only be entertained if:

". . . the new claim arises out of the same facts or substantially the same facts as are already in issue on any claim *previously made in the original action* [emphasis added] . . ."

On a strict reading this only appeared to allow a new claim if it was based on facts originally asserted by the *claimant*. However, Brooke L.J., giving the judgment of the Court of Appeal, followed the guidance given by Lord Steyn in *R. v A (No.2)* [2002] 1 A.C. 45 at [44] at which he stated:

"In accordance with the will of Parliament as reflected in s.3 it will sometimes be necessary to adopt an interpretation which linguistically may appear strained. The techniques to be used will not only involve the reading down of express language in a statute but also the *implications* [emphasis added] of provisions."

Employing this technique and allowing the amendment to secure compatibility with Art.6, Brooke L.J. construed CPR 17.4(2) as reading:

". . . if the new claim arises out of the same facts or substantially the same facts as are already in issue on *a claim in respect of which the party applying for permission has already claimed a remedy in the proceedings* [emphasis added]".

In the second case, *Anderton v Clwyd CC* [2002] 1 W.L.R. 3174, the Court of Appeal came to a rather more surprising conclusion. In an earlier decision, *Godwin v Swindon BC* [2002] 1 W.L.R. 997, the Court of Appeal had held that CPR 6.7(1), which states that a claim form served by first class post to the defendant's correct address:

"... shall be deemed to be served ..."

the second day after it was posted, created an irrebuttable presumption to that effect. This was so, even if that day fell on a Sunday, a Bank Holiday, Christmas Day or Good Friday. However, what *Godwin* did not address was whether this somewhat startling conclusion was compatible with Art.6. The Court of Appeal in *Anderton* held that it was, on policy grounds, sufficiently "proportionate" to be compatible. Their main justification for reaching this conclusion was that having to produce evidence of when the claim form was actually received would lead to unnecessary uncertainty and satellite litigation.

Conclusion   You may be wondering why the Court of Appeal needed   2–11
to invoke the ECHR and s.3 of the 1998 Act at ll in *Goode v Martin*. "Surely," you may be thinking, "can't the court just apply the overriding objective in CPR 1?" The answer is "No," the reason being that CPR 17.4(2) is one of those few provisions of the CPR in which the court may "only" exercise its discretion in the circumstances set out in the rule itself. That crucial word "only" has the effect of shutting out CPR 1 (see *Vinos v Marks & Spencer plc* [2001] 3 All E.R. 784). It is a word that does not appear very often in the CPR, but when it does, it may be (although is it pretty unlikely) that you would need to refer to the ECHR on an evidence matter.

3. Sections 4 and 5: Power to Declare Incompatibility
Section 4 gives (among others) the High Court, Court of Appeal   2–12
and House of Lords power to declare that primary legislation is incompatible with a Convention Right. A county court has no power to grant a Declaration of Incompatibility. You should note in particular that a declaration:

(1) Is not binding on the parties to the proceedings (s.4(6)(b));

(2) Does not, of itself, affect the continued validity of the relevant provision (s.4(6)(a));

(3) Confers power on the relevant Minister to amend the offending legislation by "remedial order" (s.10 and Sch.2);

(4) Such order may contain:

"Such incidental, supplemental, consequential, or transitional provision as the Minister considers "appropriate";

(5) Under s.5 of the 1998 Act the Crown is entitled to be given notice whenever the court is considering incompatibility.

It is unlikely that any rule of civil evidence is likely to receive scrutiny under these provisions. Applications under s.4 fall outside the scope of this book; however a useful summary of the relevant case law can be found in the commentary to s.4 at para.3D 6–1 of the *White Book*. There is also a very helpful summary of cases in which declarations have been sought in the speech of Lord Steyn at para.[52] of *Ghaidan v Godin-Mendoza* [2004] 2 A.C. 557. The relevant procedure is conveniently set out in *O'Hare and Browne* at 1–029.

4. Section 6: Duty of "Public Authorities"

2–13 Section 6(1) of the 1998 Act provides that it is unlawful for a "public authority" to:

"... act in a way which is incompatible with a convention right".

This applies not only to any person whose:

"... functions are functions of a public nature"

but also to courts (s.6(3)(a)). Since, therefore, the court is itself a public authority, it is particularly important to bear in mind that it has a duty to uphold the human rights of *all* the parties appearing before it, irrespective of their individual status. So far as matters of evidence are concerned there are a number of issues that could potentially arise, in particular:

(1) Has a court discharged its duties as a public authority, in particular with regard to Art.6 (right to a fair trial), in such a way as to secure compliance with the Convention and the Act?

(2) Has any individual appearing before the courts behaved in a manner, especially in the way it has presented its case or collected evidence that involves a breach of the other party's human rights?

2–14   **Example:** In a claim the defendant's lawyers or insurers obtain evidence such as documents or covert video footage in a manner that infringes Art.8 (right to privacy). Should the court as a "public authority" uphold the claimant victim's human rights by imposing a sanction such as exclusion?

In the above example the fact that the defendant or his insurers are   **2–15** not themselves a "public authority" is irrelevant because the court as a public authority must ensure that the claimant's Art.8 rights are not violated. In this respect, in the writer's view, the impact of the ECHR on the judiciary has been profound. Whenever a judge of any level is hearing a case either at trial or on an interim application there is that little voice whispering in his or her ear saying:

> "Remember, if you do not uphold each party rights under the ECHR you are breaking the law".

The Court of Appeal decision in *English v Emery Reimbold and Strick* [2002] 3 All E.R. 385 (considered further at 02–28) sets out how this principle should operate in practice.

5. *Sections 7 to 9: Right to Remedies*

Under s.7 of the 1998 Act, "victims" and, most importantly in civil   **2–16** proceedings, prospective victims, may either:

(1) Bring proceedings (s.7(1)(a)) (generally within one year of the act complained of (s.7(5)); or

(2) Rely on their Convention rights in existing proceedings (s.7(1)(b)).

Claims under s.7(1)(a) of the 1998 Act are outside the scope of this work. In any event, parties involved in ongoing litigation are far more likely to exercise their rights under s.7(1)(b).

Under s.8 of the 1998 Act, if the court finds there has been a breach of the ECHR by a public authority it may:

> ". . . grant such relief or remedy, or make such order, within its powers as it considers just and appropriate".

In the context of evidential issues, this relief could take the form of:

(1) Exclusion of evidence or dismissal of an application for disclosure on the grounds that it would involve infringement of a party's human rights;

(2) Striking out a claim or defence on the grounds of an abuse of process arising from a gross violation of a party's human rights;

(3) Granting relief from a sanction or dismissing a strike out application on the ground that it is disproportionate under Art.

(4) An adjournment to ensure a party's right to a fair trial was not compromised.

However, as must by now be obvious, the court will almost invariably have all the powers it needs to deal with these issues under the CPR and the general rules of evidence. However two final points need to be made:

(1) If ever the court needs to grant a party procedural relief by reference to the ECHR because it is not covered by domestic law, it is, in a sense, immaterial whether s.7 is engaged, because the court itself is a public authority charged with upholding all parties' rights under the ECHR; and

(2) If a litigant feels that the court has violated his or her human rights then the only remedy available is by way of appeal (s.9(1)(a)) although the appellate court does have a limited power to award damages (s.9(3)).

In the unlikely event that you are ever instructed to claim damages against a judge for violating a party's human rights on a matter of evidence, the best starting point will be to go to the relevant section and commentary to it at 3D–11 of the *White Book.*

II THE ARTICLES MOST RELEVANT TO EVIDENCE AND DISCLOSURE

2–17   There are only two Articles that require detailed consideration at this stage, namely Arts 6 and 8. The full texts of both have been set out along with some general commentary. Individual cases of specific relevance to matters of evidence are delay with in greater detail in Section C. The full text of those parts of the ECHR which have been scheduled to the 1998 Act can be found in the *White Book* at 3D–26 and the paragraphs that follow.

A Article 6: "The Right to a Fair Trial"

2–18   This states that:

"6.1   In the determination of his civil rights and obligations or of any criminal charge against him, everyone is entitled to a fair and public hearing within a reasonable time by an independent and impartial tribunal established by law. Judgment shall be pronounced publicly but the press and public may be excluded from all or part of the trial in the interest of morals, public order or national security in a democratic society, where the interests of juveniles or the protection of the private lives of the parties so require, or to the extent strictly necessary in the opinion of the court in special circumstances where publicity would prejudice the interests of justice.

2. *Everyone charged with a criminal offence shall be presumed innocent until proved guilty according to law.*
3. *Everyone charged with a criminal offence has the following minimum rights:*

   (a) *to be informed promptly, in a language which he understands and in detail, of the nature and cause of the accusation against him;*
   (b) *to have adequate time and facilities for the preparation of his defence;*
   (c) *to defend himself in person or through legal assistance of his own choosing, or, if he has not sufficient means to pay for legal assistance, to be given it free when the interests of justice so require;*
   (d) *to examine or have examined witnesses against him and to obtain the attendance and examination of witnesses on his behalf under the same conditions as witnesses against him;*
   (e) *to have the free assistance of an interpreter if he cannot understand or speak the language used in court."*

Nearly all of the ECHR and domestic decisions on evidence have been in criminal proceedings. Nevertheless, the following points are of general application and therefore need to be borne in mind whatever the nature of the litigation.

1. *Article 6 Engages the Whole Proceedings*

Traditionally, the ECHR has had regard to the proceedings as a whole rather than individual aspects of the litigation (including the admission or exclusion of a particular piece of evidence) in deciding whether or not a party has received a fair trial. Among other things this means that it will rarely be appropriate to raise ECHR points until, at the earliest, the start of the trial itself (see *Official Receiver v Stern* [2001] 1 All E.R. 633, discussed further at 2–41). However, it is important to bear in mind that ECHR law is a much more flexible and "growing" body of jurisprudence than our domestic law. Accordingly, since there

2–19

is no doctrine of precedent in the common law sense, nothing is written in tablets of stone.

2–20   *Conclusion*   If you start raising ECHR points at an interim hearing or case management conference, you had better have a very good reason for doing so.

2. *Evidence is a Domestic Issue*

2–21   The admissibility of an individual item of evidence is largely a matter for domestic law under the "margin of appreciation" principle. It is only if its admission has rendered the *whole trial* unfair that a potential breach of Art.6 arises. This principle was first clearly articulated in *Schenk v Switzerland* [1990] 13 E.H.R.R. 242, but has been restated by the ECHR on a number of occasions. By far the most portentous application of this principle was in *Khan v UK* (2001) 33 E.H.R.R. 1016 decided a few months before the ECHR was brought directly into force.

2–22   *Facts:* K had entered the country with his cousin who was found to be in possession of £100,000 worth of heroin. Although K was arrested and questioned, he was released without charge. He then went to stay at an address in Sheffield with B, a known drug dealer. Without the knowledge of either K or B, the Chief Constable of South Yorkshire authorised the attachment of a listening device to B's premises. As a result, the police were able to secure a tape recording of a conversation in which K admitted that he had been party to a conspiracy with N to import the seized heroin. As a result he was jointly charged with N and convicted.

2–23   Despite attempts by the defence to have the tape recording excluded under s.78 of the Police and Criminal Evidence Act 1984 (the Crown accepted that the attachment of the device constituted a civil trespass), the trial judge admitted the evidence. As a result of this ruling, Khan changed his plea to one of guilty and received a sentence of three years' imprisonment. Having exhausted his domestic routes of appeal (see *R. v Khan (Sultan)* [1997] A.C. 558) Khan took his case to Europe, in effect alleging two fundamental breaches of the ECHR, namely that:

(1) The attachment of the device was a breach of Art.8, not least because there was no accessible statutory framework governing the circumstances in which a surveillance operation of this kind could be set up other than Home Office Guidelines circulated to chief officers of police in 1984; and

(2) Section 78 of the 1984 Act (for a full explanation of the scope of s.78 see *Phipson* 38–10 *et seq.*) afforded inadequate

protection to an accused in that it did not provide an effective system for challenging the admission of evidence obtained in breach of Art.8.

The hopes of those who imagined that the ECHR was going to create new opportunities for excluding illegally obtained evidence were dashed. The European Court of Human Rights held that:

(1) Although there had been a clear breach of Art.8 in attaching a covert listening device to the outside of the house in which Khan was residing;

(2) The admission of the evidence obtained as a result of this trespass at the subsequent trial was not a breach of Art.6;

(3) Even though it was the only evidence against the accused.

Domestic decisions applying this decision are considered at 02–46, but its effect has been in essence to pre-empt any attempt to argue that the ECHR created new exclusionary rules of evidence. To quote Lord Hobhouse in *R. v P* [2002] 1 A.C. 146:

"[under Article 6 a party] is entitled to an opportunity to challenge its use and admission in evidence and a judicial assessment of the effect of its admission on the fairness of the trial . . ."

Although made in the context of criminal proceedings, this statement is equally applicable to civil claims. A civil judge does, of course have a general discretion to exclude evidence under CPR 32.1(2). The extent to which this engages Art.6 was considered by the Court of Appeal in *Jones v The University of Warwick* [2003] 1 W.L.R. 954 discussed further at 02–48.

Conclusion   Although the method by which evidence is obtained is   **2–24**
a legitimate issue for consideration by the court, your chances of having such evidence totally excluded are likely to be remote (see further 02–46).

3. The Concept of "Proportionality"
The "right" to a fair trial is not an absolute one: it is subject to the   **2–25**
doctrine of "proportionality". This concept, and its effect on the "right to silence" was examined in considerable detail by the Judicial Committee of the Privy Council in *Stott (Procurator Fiscal) v Brown* [2003] 1 A.C. 681 in which Lord Bingham of Cornhill stated:

"The jurisprudence of the European Court very clearly established that while the overall fairness of a criminal trial cannot be compromised, the constituent rights compromised whether expressly or implicitly, within Article 6 are not themselves absolute. Limited qualification of these rights is acceptable if reasonably directed by national authorities towards a clear and public objective and if representing no greater qualification than the situation calls for."

Again, although made in the context of criminal proceedings, this statement is equally applicable to civil claims. Indeed, the concept of proportionality is already written into the CPR in the form of the overriding objective in CPR 1.

4. Right to Examine Witnesses

2–26   Article 6(3)(d) on the face of it creates a "right" to cross-examine your opponent's witnesses. Although apparently confined to criminal proceedings, it was generally accepted that the "right" was equally available to civil claims on the basis that it simply highlighted an essential component of a fair trial. Accordingly, some enthusiasts anticipated that it would be possible to mount a root and branch challenge to the compatibility of s.1 of the Civil Evidence Act 1995. After all, what could be a more flagrant breach of Art.6.3(d) than the wholesale admission of hearsay evidence? However, hearsay does not exist as a rule of exclusion in other EC countries: accordingly the European Court has little to offer on the subject. However what ECHR jurisprudence does acknowledge is that the lack of an *opportunity to challenge* material evidence may compromise the fairness of the trial (see, for example, *Unterpertinger v Austria* (1986) 13 E.H.R.R. 175 and *Trivedi v UK* [1997] E.H.R.L.R. 521). Provided that this opportunity is afforded to the party wishing to challenge the hearsay evidence, ECHR jurisprudence does not require every material witness to be available for cross-examination at the trial itself (see, for example, *Kostovski v Netherlands (1989) 12 E.H.R.R. 434* and the detailed discussion of this topic in *Phipson* 30–59 *et seq*). This approach had already been adopted by the United Kingdom courts in criminal cases when considering the circumstances in which hearsay evidence could be admitted under ss.23–26 of the Criminal Justice Act 1988 (see, in particular, *R. v Radak* [1999] 1 Cr.App.R 187, *R. v Gavin*, unreported, May 3, 2000 CA and *R. v Sellick* [2005] 2 Cr.App.R 211). A similar approach has been adopted towards the hearsay provisions in ss.114–120 of the Criminal Justice Act 2003 (in force April 4, 2005) *R. v Xhabri* [2006] 1 All E.R. 776. Interestingly, much of the recent case law on hearsay evidence has been in *civil* proceedings, largely due to the increasing use by police and local authorities of the anti-social behaviour provisions introduced by the Government in the Crime and Disorder Act 1998 and the Anti-Social Behaviour Act 2003. Although these cases are considered in greater detail at 02–44 suffice it to say that for the time being the Civil Evidence Act 1995, has been given the ECHR seal of approval by the Administrative Court in *R. (On the Application of Clingham) v Marylebone Magistrates' Court* [2001], *The Times,* February 21 (affirmed by the House of Lords at *[2003] 1 A.C. 787).*

Conclusion Do not stand up and argue for the exclusion of hearsay   2–27
evidence on the ground that to admit it would be a breach of Art.6
solely on the grounds that it is hearsay. However, Art.6 is directly
engaged when the court decides what weight, if any, should be
attached to it.

5. Right to a Reasoned Judgment
This facet of Art.6 is, on a day to day basis, of major practical impor-   2–28
tance. Although the Court of Appeal in *English v Emery Reimbold
and Strick Ltd* [2002] 3 All E.R. 385 was of the view that Strasbourg
jurisprudence on the giving of reasons goes no further than that contained in domestic law (see Lord Phillips M.R. at [13]), Art.6 does add
a new dimension. Put simply, under s.6(1) of the 1998 Act, a judge is
acting unlawfully if his or her judgment does not comply with
the requirements laid down by the court in the *English v Emery* decision. This means that, as a general principle (see Lord Phillips M.R.
at [19]):

". . . the judgment must enable the appellate court to understand
why the judge reached his decision. This does not mean that every
factor which weighed with the judge in his appraisal of the evidence
has to be identified and explained. But the issues the resolution of
which were vital to the judge's conclusion should be identified and
the manner in which he resolved them explained. It is not possible
to provide a template for this process. It need not involve a lengthy
judgment. It does require the judge to identify and record those
matters which were critical to his decision. If the critical issue was
one of fact, it may be enough to say that one witness was preferred
to another because the one manifestly had a clearer recollection of
the material facts or the other gave answers which demonstrated
that his recollection could not be relied on."

This does not mean that every case management decision or trial
ruling on the weight or admissibility of evidence justifies a 10 page
written judgment, as the Strasbourg court itself said in *Torija v Spain*
(1994) 19 E.H.R.R. 553 at [29]:

"The Court reiterates that Article 6(1) obliges courts to give reasons
for their judgments, but cannot be understood as requiring a

detailed answer to every argument. The extent to which the duty to give reasons applies may vary according to the nature of the decision."

However what it *does* mean is that, at the very least a litigant is entitled to a reasoned ruling as to *why* a particular piece of evidence has been admitted or excluded, and, if admitted, the *weight* that the court has attached to it.

6. The "Right to Silence"

2–29 The Strasbourg Court has emphasised on numerous occasions that the so-called "right to silence" lies at the heart of Art.6 so far as criminal proceedings are concerned (see, for example, *Condron v UK* (2000) 31 E.H.R.R. 1 and *Heaney and McGuiness v Ireland* (2001) 33 E.H.R.R. 264). However, no similar principle applies in civil proceedings. As a general rule, adverse inferences can *always* be drawn from a party's failure to respond in circumstances where he might reasonably be expected to have done so. However it is important to bear in mind that an adverse inference may not be drawn against a party (or witness) who refuses to answer a question or produce a document on the ground of privilege (*Wentworth v Lloyd (1866); L.R. 2* Eq *607* more recent affirmation of the principle can be found in *Sinclair Roche and Temperley v Somatra Ltd* [2001] 1 W.L.R. 2453). The topic is discussed in greater detail at L.A. 08–83.

B Article 8: Right to Privacy

2–30 This provides that:

"(1) Everyone has the right to respect for his private and family life, his home and his correspondence.

(2) There shall be no interference by a public authority with the exercise of this right except such as is in accordance with the law and is necessary in a democratic society in the interest of national security, public safety or the economic well-being of the country, for the prevention of disorder or crime, for the protection of health or morals, or for the protection of the rights and freedoms of others."

"Family life" extends, not surprisingly, to single (*Ghaidan v Godin Mendoza* [2004] 2 A.C. 557) and dual-gender (*Kroon v Netherlands* (1995) 19 E.H.R.R. 263) cohabitees. "Private life" goes beyond the traditional nuclear family and, in particular, protects the confidential relationship between an individual and his or her legal advisers (see, in particular, *Niemietz v Germany* (1993) 16 E.H.R.R. 97 (search of lawyer's office a breach of Art.8)). As with Art.6, the right is "qualified" in the sense that violation is justified under Art.8(2) provided that first, it is in "accordance with the law" and secondly, it is "necessary" as specified in Art.8(2). This means that not only must the interference be compliant with domestic law, it must also be compatible with Art.8. However, notwithstanding its importance in a wider context its effect on the rules of evidence is peripheral because:

(1) As a result of *Khan v UK*, it is clear that evidence obtained in a manner that infringes Art.8 will not automatically be liable to exclusion. This point was considered by the Court of Appeal in *Jones v University of Warwick* [2003] 1 W.L.R. 954 and will be considered further at 02–46;

(2) Although the domestic law on legal professional privilege clearly engages Art.8, there will be few if any occasions upon which reference to Art.8 will be necessary. The absolute nature of the privilege under our domestic law makes it unlikely that recourse to Art.8 will provide wider protection (the relationship between Art.8 and privilege is considered further at 02–42 and 08–12).

C Case Law

Although cases on civil evidence are still thin on the ground (and are likely to remain so) some interesting pointers are beginning to emerge.   **2–31**

1. Prepare ECHR Points Carefully
Lord Woolf M.R. stated this in the strongest terms in *Daniels v*   **2–32**
Walker [2000] 1 W.L.R. 1382 at [26]. In this appeal the court had to deal with Art.6 based arguments concerning a case management decision on expert evidence. Interestingly, judgment was handed down on May 3, 2000, five months before the 1998 Act came into force. Lord Woolf M.R. had this to say on the Art.6 point:

"It would be unfortunate if case management decisions in this jurisdiction involved the need to refer to the learning of the European Court of Human Rights in order for them to be resolved. In my judgment, cases such as this do not require any consideration of human rights issues, certainly issues under Article 6. It would be highly undesirable if the consideration of those issues was made more complex by the injection into them of Article 6 style arguments. Certainly, on this occasion, this court gave [counsel] short shrift. Notwithstanding my high regard for [him], I consider that that was the only way in which that argument could be treated. When the 1998 Act becomes law, counsel will need to show self restraint if it is not to be discredited."

In *Daniels v Walker*, the defendant appellants had sought to argue by reference to a wealth of authority, in particular *Mantovanelli v France* [1997] 24 E.H.R.R. 370, that the court's power to impose a single joint expert on the parties under CPR 35.7 infringed their right to a fair trial under Art.6. The Court of Appeal in effect held that the duty to deal with a claim "justly" under the overriding objective in CPR 1 would almost invariably secure compliance with Art.6. As already noted when discussing *Goode v Martin* at 02–10, the effect of this approach is to render ECHR jurisprudence largely superfluous, at least so far as case management issues are concerned.

2. Determination Without Trial or in a Party's Absence may Comply with Article 6

2–33　Some commentators, and indeed some first instance judges, thought that early determination without trial would contravene Art.6. However the Court of Appeal has taken a more robust view.

(a) *Judgment Given in a Party's Absence*

2–34　It has always been a core principle of our domestic law that a party who has had a judgment pronounced against him in his absence has a right to apply to have the judgment set aside. This right currently exists both in respect of default judgments (see CPR 13.3 and *O'Hare and Browne* 15–014) interim orders (see CPR 23.11 and *O'Hare and Browne*, Chapter 43) and judgments (see CPR 39.3 and *O'Hare and Browne* 37–009) given at a hearing or trial in that party's absence. However the right to have the judgment or order set aside is not an absolute one and will, in particular, require the applicant to show that he has a sustainable claim or defence. Are these requirements compatible with the applicant's right to a fair trial under Art.6? *Barclays Bank plc v Ellis, The Times, October 24, 2000*, another appeal heard some months before the 1998 Act came into force (on August 9, 2000), concerned an application to set aside a judgment given at trial in the defendants' absence.

2–35　**Facts:** A claim on a guarantee and a loan account started as long ago as September 28, 1993 against the defendants Mr and Mrs Ellis was finally listed for trial at Central London County Court at 10.30 on July 21, 1999. Neither defendant was present and accordingly, having heard from counsel for the claimant, H.H. Judge Knight gave judgment for the claimants in the sum of £780,164.85 plus costs. The defendants applied to have the judgment set aside under CPR 39.3 on the basis that they thought the trial was due to start at midday. H.H. Judge Knight refused their application so the defendants appealed to the Court of Appeal.

The relevant rule, CPR 39.3(5), provides that a court may "only" **2–36** set aside a judgment given at trial in a party's absence if *all three* of the requirements in CPR 39.3(5)(a) to (c) are met. The Court of Appeal held that requiring a party who had had a judgment pronounced in his absence to comply with CPR 39.5(5)(c) by satisfying the court that his case has a reasonable prospect of success did not automatically involve a breach of Art.6(1). Since the claimant's claim was unanswerable it was not "unfair" to deny the defendant his retrial. The decision is also a good illustration of how *not* to raise an ECHR point. To quote Scheimann L.J. at [36]:

". . . At the last minute and without any warning, either to his opponent or to the court, [counsel] thought it appropriate to make reference to Article 6 of the European Convention on Human Rights. He was asked by the court whether he wished to develop his submission by reference to any case law. He declined. Neither he nor his opponent, who had been caught entirely by surprise by this particular line of argument, furnished any material to the court.

[37] The Human Rights Act of course has yet to come into force. But if counsel wish to rely on any provisions of the Human Rights Act then it is their duty to have available for the information of the court any material in terms of decisions of the European Court of Human Rights upon which they wish to rely or which will help the court in its adjudication. A mere reference in a case to an Article does not help the court in any way to do justice to a possible argument. To do an argument justice it needs to be formalised and advanced in a plausible way.

[38] For my part, I see absolutely no reason to suppose here that there has been any infringement of the right to a fair trial in the circumstances as they have been described by [Lord Woolf]."

The defendants' appeal was accordingly dismissed.

Conclusion This case has important implications so far as evidence **2–37** (especially evidence at interim hearings; see further Chapter 9) is concerned because it emphasises the fact that no party has an absolute right to put his opponent to proof at trial. In appropriate circumstances, a court may refuse to set aside a judgment in the absence of *evidence* that he has a reasonable prospect of success. Indeed, it may even be Art.6 compliant to require this of a party where, unlike Mr and Mrs Ellis, he maintains that he has not even had notice of the proceedings. You will recall that the Court of Appeal in *Anderton v Clwyd* [2002] 1 W.L.R. 3174 confirmed that the conclusive presumption of service by first-class post in CPR 6.7(1) was Art.6 compliant. In *Akram v Adam* [2005] 1 All E.R. 741 a defendant appealed against a refusal to set aside a possession order made in his absence where, as he asserted, he had never received the claim form. He argued that it was a breach of Art.6 to require a person who had received no notice of the proceedings to satisfy the court that he had a defence that stood a real chance of success before the judgment could be set aside. The Court of Appeal considered that it *was not*, even where it was accepted that the defendant had never received due notice of the proceedings. Brooke L.J. stated (at [43]):

> "The fair trial guarantees in Art.6 of the Convention must entitle a defendant to be heard, but if he cannot show the court that his defence would have a real prospect of success, or that there is some other compelling reason why a trial should be conducted, it does not require the parties and the court to indulge in an expensive and time-consuming charade. In *James v UK* (1986) 8 E.H.R.R. 123 [at 81] the European Court of Human Rights said that Art.6(1) extends only to 'contestations' over (civil) 'rights and obligations' which can be said, at least on arguable grounds to be recognised under domestic law. If a court, like Judge Yelton, is satisfied that the defendant would not have an arguable defence if the default judgment were set aside, Art.6 does not in my judgment entitle the defendant to a trial (or oblige the claimant on some other occasions to show that the defendant has no arguable defence)."

The importance of this decision cannot be overemphasised. The most likely occasion on which you will encounter an Art.6 argument is on an application to set aside a default judgment or a possession order granted in the defendant's absence. Unless the defendant adduces *evidence* (as to which see 09–15) which supports his application the court, as a general rule, has no choice in the matter; it *must* dismiss his application.

(b) *Dismissal (or Exclusion of Evidence) for Breach of the CPR*

2–38   As noted in Chapter 1, evidence that is *prima facie* admissible is in practical terms most at risk of exclusion if there had been a failure to comply with a case management direction, for example an order which states:

> "Unless the claimant serves and files written statements of each witness upon whose oral evidence he intends to rely at trial by

4.00pm on November 29, 2005 he shall be debarred from calling those witnesses to give oral evidence".

Could it be argued that such a Draconian order breached Art.6? The answer given by the Court of Appeal is "No". Indeed, the court has gone even further, holding that a serious failure to obey case management directions could lead to the striking out of all or part of a party's case statement under CPR 3.4. In *Arongundade v Brent LBC*, unreported, November 15, 2000 the claimant sought to argue that an order striking out her claim and giving the defendant's judgment on their counterclaim for a series of failures to file particulars of her defence to counterclaim was a breach of Art.6. The court dismissed this argument out of hand holding that such an order did not of itself constitute a violation of Art.6. Laws L.J. stated (at [21]):

". . . It would be wholly lamentable if the salutary provisions of the Human Rights Act—and here in particular, Article 6 of the Convention—were allowed to be deployed to run a coach and horses through properly considered and established procedural rules whose purpose is to ensure a fair trial to all parties and to the litigation to which they applied. This application, it seems to me is misconceived".

It must follow that to debar a party from relying on a particular item of evidence for serious and persistent breach of court orders will also not infringe Art.6.

(c) *Summary Judgment*
A party may apply under CPR 24 to have all or part of his opponent's   **2–39**
claim or defence determined summarily, in particular if he can show that it has no real prospect of success. The nature and incidence of the burden of proof on such applications is considered further at 03–14 and 05–16; for a fuller explanation of the uses and nature of this procedure see *O'Hare and Browne*, Chapter 19. On such applications May L.J. has stated in *S v Gloucestershire CC* [2000] 3 All E.R. 346 that the "fair trial" requirement imposed by Art.6 will have been complied with if:

(1) All the substantial facts that are reasonably capable of being before the court are before the court;

(2) These facts are undisputed or there is no real prospect of successfully disputing them;

(3) There is no real prospect of oral evidence affecting the court's assessment of the facts; and

(4) The grounds required by CPR 24 for granting summary judgment are met.

2–40   *Conclusion*   What all these cases make clear is that the "right to a fair trial" is a very flexible concept; in particular, no party has an absolute right to insist that every item of evidence is fully rehearsed and tested at trials

3. Article 6 and the "Right to Silence"

2–41   As will be explained more fully at 04–19, there is no "right to silence" at common law in civil proceedings (unlike in criminal cases; see *Phipson*, Chapter 34). Has Art.6.1 modified this? The Court of Appeal in *Official Receiver v Stern* (No.1) [2001] 1 W.L.R. 2230 upheld the decision of Sir Richard Scott V.C. to the effect that Art.6 did not as such automatically debar the Official Receiver from using statements taken from directors under s.235 of the Insolvency Act 1986 in subsequent proceedings against them under the Directors Disqualification Act 1986. The court stated that:

(1) Use of statements obtained under compulsion under s.235 of the Insolvency Act 1986 in subsequent civil proceedings did not necessarily breach Art.6.1;

(2) In each case it would be necessary to balance the degree of coercion employed against the prejudice generated by the replies;

(3) Issues of fairness of this nature were best left to be dealt with by the judge at trial or on pre-trial review.

As will be discussed more fully later (see 08–83), many investigating agencies are entitled to compel persons to answer questions on pain of prosecution or contempt of court proceedings. It means that statements taken in the course of such investigations will almost invariably be admissible in evidence against the maker in subsequent civil proceedings. The position is, of course, radically different in criminal proceedings where such evidence will rarely, if ever, be admissible against the maker (see in particular, Sch.3 to the Youth Justice and Criminal Evidence Act 1999 which would now, to a large extent, prevent the statements in the *Stern* case being inadmissible against the directors in a prosecution). Furthermore, it is now clear that the "right to silence" in any event only covers the answering of *questions*. It does not apply to material "independent" of the person concerned; in particular it does not cover documents produced under lawful compulsion. This was confirmed by the ECHR in *L v*

UK [2001] 2 F.L.R. 322, a decision applied domestically in *Attorney General's Reference No.7 of 2001* [2001] 1 W.L.R. 1879. The only basis upon which a party can resist production in such a case is if privilege or public interest immunity is available.

4. Privilege

The domestic law of privilege in all its forms will be considered more   **2–42** fully in Chapter 7. Although the ECHR is not directly engaged, the courts have been willing to uphold the absolute nature of legal professional privilege by invoking Art.8-based arguments. In *General Mediterranean Holdings v Patel* [2000] I W.L.R. 272 Toulson J. held that CPR 48.7(5) which, as it was then drafted, gave the court power to override the client's privilege in a wasted costs enquiry was *ultra vires* and a breach of Art.8. The rule was rapidly repealed. However, as is pointed out in *Phipson* at paras 23–11 to 14, there is still a potential conflict between the absolute nature of legal professional privilege as laid down in *R. v Derby Magistrates Court Ex p. B* [1996] A.C. 487 and the concept of proportionality which is at the core of both Art.8 and Art.6. Indeed Lord Hobhouse went so far as to say in *Medcalf v Mardell* [2003] 1 A.C. 120 at [60] that:

"It may be that, in the context of Articles 6 and 8 of the European Convention on Human Rights, the privilege may not always be absolute and a balancing exercise may sometimes be necessary."

Nevertheless, in *Medcalf v Mardell*, the House of Lords held that no breach of Art.6.1 was involved. The case concerned a wasted costs application against two members of the Bar who, it was alleged, had made various allegations of fraud against the claimant on the basis of inadequate instructions. Their client was not prepared to waive privilege to enable them to rebut this allegation. The barristers concerned were thus precluded from revealing their true instructions. This was held not to constitute a breach of their right to a fair trial under Art.6. However the House went on to state that when a wasted costs order was sought against a lawyer, who was prevented by legal professional privilege from revealing his instructions, the court should proceed with extreme caution before making such an order and only on the basis of incontrovertible evidence. Accordingly the appeal against the wasted cost order succeeded.

On the one other occasion when the House of Lords have had to consider legal professional privilege in the context of Art.8, in *R. v IRC Ex p. Morgan Grenfell & Co Ltd* [2003] 1 A.C. 563, they emphasised that the introduction of the Human Rights Act 1998 had changed the approach to statutory construction. As a result, the House held that a statutory provision can only be construed as having overridden privilege if that is a "necessary implication", based on clear unambiguous words in the statute.

2–43   *Conclusion*   The courts have sought to reinforce the absolute nature of legal professional privilege by invoking human rights principles on every occasion it had fallen to be considered. The absolute nature of the privilege was re-emphasised by the House of Lords in *Three Rivers District Council v Bank of England (No.6)* [2004] 3 W.L.R. 1274.

5. *Article 6(3)(d) and Hearsay*
2–44   Commentators anticipated on early attack on the type of evidence frequently given in "anti-social behaviour" cases by local authorities. This often consists of:

(1) Hearsay evidence given by local authority employees and/or police officers which repeats; or

(2) Complaints passed on to them, often by neighbours, whose identities are not revealed.

The use of this type of evidence in possession proceedings was endorsed by the Court of Appeal in *Leeds City Council v Harte* [1999] April Legal Action 23 but was regarded as vulnerable to Art.6 by many human rights lawyers. An attempt was made in *R. v Marylebone Magistrates Court Ex p. Clingham* [2001] The Times, February 20 to mount a full scale attack on the 1995 Act. The case concerned an application for an Anti-Social Behaviour Order ("ASBO") under s.1 of the Crime and Disorder Act 1998. Although, as we shall see at paragraph 3–58, many applications for ASBOs are civil proceedings, the criminal standard of proof applies. Is it contrary to Art.6 to admit hearsay evidence of the type indicated above, especially when breach of an ASBO constitutes a criminal offence? The High Court has held that:

(1) There was nothing either in the Human Rights Act 1998 or ECHR jurisprudence which required the automatic exclusion of hearsay evidence;

(2) It was for the trial court to consider what weight, if any, should be attached to the evidence by reference to the factors set out in s.4 of the Civil Evidence Act 1995. This decision has since been upheld, *albeit* obiter, in *Clingham v Kensington and Chelsea RLBC* [2003] 1 A.C. 787.

The *Clingham* decision and the Court of Appeal decisions on anti-social behaviour orders and injunctions ("ASBIs") which have followed are considered in greater detail at 07–36.

Conclusion   There is no mileage in trying to get hearsay evidence   2–45
excluded by direct reference to Art.6. However, as discussed at 7–36,
Art.6 provides a useful point of reference when it comes to considering how much weight, if any, should be attached to it.

6. Article 8 and Covert Videos

As with hearsay, some commentators argued that evidence obtained   2–46
by subterfuge, for example secretly video recording a claimant in a
personal injury case, would be liable to exclusion on the grounds that
it breached Art.8 and Art.6. It is interesting to note that in *Rall v
Hume* [2001] 3 All E.R. 248, a case concerning the use of a covert
video at trial, the Court of Appeal, and indeed every level of court
involved, appeared to accept that:

(1) Those parts of the video filmed whilst the claimant was in a
    public place were *prima facie* admissible; whereas

(2) Those taken of her inside her home and at her child's nursery
    were not.

However, no specific reference was made to Art.8. The argument that
intrusive covert evidence was prima facie inadmissible by reference to
Art.8 was questionable. The Criminal Division of the Court of
Appeal in *R. v Loveridge* [2001] 2 Cr.App.R 38, following *Khan v UK*
had already upheld the admission of covert video footage obtained
by the police in a gross breach of Art.8 (and indeed the criminal law).
They had secretly filmed the accused within the precincts of a magistrates' court. It was hardly likely therefore that they would adopt a
stricter approach to such evidence in civil proceedings. The fact that
breaches of Art.8 will not automatically result in exclusion has now
been confirmed by the Court of Appeal in *Jones v University of
Warwick* [2003] 1 W.L.R. 954.

Facts: The claimant had suffered a minor cut to the webbing between   2–47
the fourth and fifth fingers of her right hand as result of a full cash
box falling on her wrist. She claimed that this had led to the development of a condition known as *focal dystonia*, a spasmodic condition involving abnormal muscle contraction. She alleged severe
continuing disability and claimed damages in excess of £135,000. An
inquiry agent, posing as a market researcher gained access to her
property and filmed her with the aid of a hidden camera. The film was
shown to the defendants' expert who concluded that she had an
entirely satisfactory function in her right hand. The claimant's expert
took a different view. The claimant then sought to have the video
excluded on the ground that it had been obtained in breach of Art.8.

2–48   In a lengthy judgment Lord Woolf C.J. held that:

(1) Part of a judge's duty under CPR 1 is to consider the effect a case management ruling may have on the conduct of litigation generally;

(2) The fact that there has been a breach of Art.8, and in this case a trespassory entry, was a fact the court was entitled to take into account in exercise of its case management powers;

(3) An insurer is not a "public authority" but the court *is*, hence the need to ensure that the admission of such evidence is within Art.8(2);

(4) If the insurer's conduct is not so outrageous that their defence should be struck out, then it would be "artificial and undesirable" not to admit the evidence;

(5) It might well be appropriate for the court to show disapproval of the insurer's conduct by the imposition of costs sanctions (the report does not state what order for costs was actually made).

As Lord Woolf points out at para.[21] of his judgment:

"It is not possible to reconcile in a totally satisfactory manner the conflicting public policies . . ."

Nevertheless, as in *Khan v UK* discussed earlier, the decision places the seal of approval on the pragmatic (some might say cynical) approach that the English courts have always adopted towards illegally obtained evidence. Again, to quote Lord Woolf at para.[21]:

"The approach of Judge Harris was consistent with the approach which would have been adopted in both criminal and civil proceedings prior to the coming into force of the CPR and the 1998 Act. The achieving of justice in the particular case was then the paramount consideration of the judge trying the case. If evidence was available, the court did not concern itself how it was obtained."

At para.[27] he goes on to state that that type of evidence can be dealt with as a case management issue under CPRs 1 and 32 because, in so doing, the court is complying with the ECHR.

The most intriguing statement appears at para.[28]:

"This is not a case where the conduct of the defendants' insurers is so outrageous that the defence should be struck out."

Just how "outrageous" would a party's conduct have to be before it justified striking out? The obvious example that springs to mind is a party who persistently obtains evidence in this way, having been found out in the past. Surely there must come a time when a party who persistently flouts human rights law will be vulnerable to having his whole claim or defence struck out.

Two other points are worth noting. First, do bear in mind that where evidence has been obtained in a questionable manner for use in an injunction application different considerations may apply.

Example: A seeks a freezing order because he has reason to believe   **2–49** that D is removing his assets from the jurisdiction. This information is based upon evidence from an inquiry agent who has hacked into D's computer/broke into his office/obtained information in breach of data protection regulations/intercepted his telephone calls, etc.

Not only will the source of the evidence have to be revealed under   **2–50** the duty of full and frank disclosure (see *Memory Corporation plc v Sidhu* [2000] 1 W.L.R. 1443), but, since A is seeking an equitable remedy, the court may refuse him relief because it regards his conduct as unacceptable (for further discussion see generally *Hollander*, Chapter 3, especially 3–40).

Secondly, if you do have strong prima facie evidence that a party has obtained evidence illegally (including in breach of Art.8) do remember that litigation privilege will not apply (see further 08–30, and *Dubai Aluminium v Al Alawi* [1999] 1 All E.R. 703 and *Kuwait Airways Corp v Iraqi Airways Co* [2005] EWCA Civ 286).

Conclusion The ECHR adds little or nothing *directly* to the   **2–51** domestic law of evidence. Nevertheless it represents an important resource which, if used selectively, will assist in the presentation of arguments on matters of evidence. Section 6 of the Human Rights Act 1998 is of particular relevance because of the duty it imposes on the court, as a public authority, to uphold human rights. Individual applications of ECHR jurisprudence will be found at various places in the following chapters.

Chapter 3

Proof and Probability

This chapter will deal with the following topics: 3–01

(1) Who has to prove what in a civil claim? and

(2) To what standard is he required to prove it?

Before embarking on a study of each of these areas it is perhaps as well to remind ourselves of the three stage process of case analysis discussed at 01–04, namely:

LEVEL 1—"WHAT ARE THE ELEMENTS OF THE CASE THAT THE CLAIMANT IS BRINGING?"

LEVEL 2—"WHAT MATERIAL FACTS MUST THE CLAIMANT PROVE IN ORDER TO SATISFY THE COURT OF THE PROBABLE EXISTENCE OF EACH ELEMENT?"

LEVEL 3—"WHAT EVIDENCE DO WE HAVE/NEED IN ORDER TO PROVE EACH MATERIAL FACT?"

It is all too easy to assume that this structured approach is only necessary in large claims. The Court of Appeal decision in *Sunrule Ltd v Avinue Ltd* [2004] 1 W.L.R. 634 graphically illustrates the danger inherent in this assumption.

Facts: Sunrule ("S") were appealing against a judgment for £4,058.97   3–02
for the price of goods sold and delivered to them by Avinue Ltd ("A").
S was a clothing retailer, A sold leather jackets. They made numerous deliveries to S on a weekly basis. The claim related to a number of items which S maintained had never been delivered. The system which S maintained involved a member of staff recording a delivery in the stock book when it arrived. At the end of each month the stock book would be reconciled against copies of delivery notes. There was

no record in the stock book of the invoiced items. In addition, A Ltd. were unable to produce any delivery notes. Oral evidence was given at the hearing by C, A's deliveryman. His evidence was that he had delivered the items in question but he was unable to produce relevant delivery notes confirming this. The judge nevertheless held him to be a credible witness and gave judgment in favour of A.

3–03 In allowing the appeal and ordering a retrial Arden L.J. had this to say (at [38]):

"The mere fact that [C] was a credible witness and gave evidence about items he delivered, did not mean that he was saying that the items were delivered which were shown by invoices but not by delivery notes".

3–04 *Conclusion* A debt claim for the price of goods sold and delivered requires the claimant to prove four elements.

ELEMENT 1   **A contract of sale between the claimant and the defendant**

ELEMENT 2   **Performance of the contract by the claimant**

ELEMENT 3   **Liability to pay the price under the contract (on delivery, unless the contract provides otherwise; see s.28 of the Sale of Goods Act 1979)**

ELEMENT 4   **All or part of the price is still due and owing**

It could not be simpler could it? A debt claim is one of the first documents that many of us are given to draft on our first day in practice. However a moment's analysis of the essential elements reveals the evidential gaps in the claimants' case. How is he going to prove **ELEMENTS 1** and **2**? The existence of an invoice is *some* evidence of a contract between the parties. However, without clearer oral evidence from the delivery man, or evidence that the invoiced goods were loaded onto his vehicle at the warehouse before he started his delivery round and that they were no longer there on his return, the claimant is in difficulties. As stated above, all it needs is a moment's thought.

I BURDENS OF PROOF

A Introduction

3–05 The general principle can be stated simply. A claimant will fail unless he can prove *every* element of his claim (LEVEL 1), or, put another way, every material fact (LEVEL 2) needed to prove each element of his claim to the required civil standard. That standard is, almost without exception "on the balance of probabilities". However, it is not always as simple as that. It is far more commonplace than in criminal cases to find that *both* parties will be faced with burdens of proof. This process is sometimes referred to as the "shifting of the burden". Sometimes this does actually happen on a particular issue (presumptions being the major example, see 4–46). However, it is more likely that each party will have different burdens at particular stages in the trial.

1. Burden on Claimant Throughout

In *Sunrule v Avinue*, discussed earlier, Sunrule were maintaining that   **3–06** they had never received the invoiced goods. In that instance, Sunrule do not have to prove *anything*. Unless Avinue can prove all four elements of their claim they are bound to lose.

2. Burden Shifts to Defendant

There are a number of special defences that place a burden of proof   **3–07** on the defendant. One of the most commonplace is contributory negligence, a defence frequently raised in road traffic and employers' liability claims. If raised, the claimant will have the initial burden of establishing primary liability. If he fails, the defendant is left with nothing to prove. If however the court were to find in the claimant's favour on primary liability, the burden would then "shift" to the defendant, but only in the sense that it would now be his turn to prove contributory negligence; at no stage is the claimant required to prove that he was *not* contributorily negligent. In other words, both parties end up with the same burdens of proof that they started with but they were at different stages.

3. Both Parties Have Burdens Throughout

A common example of this is where a landlord seeks possession of   **3–08** rented premises under the 1985 or 1988 Housing Act on the ground of rent arrears and the defendant brings a Pt 20 counterclaim for damages for breach of the implied repairing covenants in s.11 of the Landlord and Tenant Act 1985. Both parties have to prove all the relevant elements of their respective claims. However, because the Pt 20 counterclaim may also provide a defence by way of set-off, it may be that the defendant's damages claim will wipe out the alleged rent arrears. This commonplace scenario requires a carefully structured approach.

Example: C local authority seeks possession against its tenant D   **3–09** based on rent arrears of £1,500. The defendant is counterclaiming for damages for disrepair which, re. assets, exceeds the amount of the rent arrears. Accordingly there is, in fact, no rent "lawfully due" under Ground 1 of Sch.2 to the 1985 Act. In terms of burdens of proof the judge would have to address the case in the following order:

Q1   Has C proved the relationship of landlord and tenant under a secure tenancy?

Q2   Has C commenced proceedings by service of a valid Notice Seeking Possession?

Q3   Has C proved that there is a £1,500 debit on D's rent account?

Q4   If the answers to Qs 1 to 3 are "yes", has D satisfied the court that C is in breach of the implied repairing covenant in s.11?

3–10   This where it starts to become more complicated. If the answer to Q4 is "No", the court will then have to go on and decide whether or not it is reasonable to make a possession order, in respect of which the burden will be on the *claimant*. If however the answer is "Yes", the court will next have to assess the amount of damages that the defendant should receive. On that issue the burden will be on the defendant. Having assessed quantum the burden of proof may shift yet again. If the damages (say, £3,000) were to *exceed* the rent that was due, the judge would dismiss the claim and give judgment for the *defendant* on the balance of the claim (£1,500), having first set off any rent "lawfully due". If however the damages were *less* than the rent arrears (say, £1,000), the court, having given judgment for the defendant on the counterclaim (such amount to be set off against the rent arrears) would now have to go on and consider whether it was reasonable to make a possession order based on the fact that there were only £500 of rent arrears. In the latter case, the burden would fall upon the *claimant*. Again however both sides have been stuck with their respective burdens throughout.

4. Burdens of Proof in Practice

3–11   In reality, since so few civil claims end up going to trial, the burden of proof tends to operate indirectly.

(a) Negotiating Burdens

3–12   As we have seen (see 1–48) the CPR create an expectation that parties will not "hide behind their pleadings", but will disclose their case and the evidence which supports it at the earliest stage practicable. The prime objective of the CPR is to manage *negotiated settlement*, not preparation for trial. It is therefore no longer so easy to use the threat of litigation as a negotiating tactic. The CPR and in particular the protocols create an expectation that a party will make out a sustainable case or defence from the outset and that, in the event of his being unable to do so, he will abandon it or face the consequences in costs. On a day to day basis therefore it is perhaps better to think of the burden of proof as being the:

"Burden of being taken seriously".

In practice, only occasions when the burden of proof is regularly put to the test at trial are in the Small Claims court or where one or both of the parties are litigants in person.

(b) *Evidential Burdens*
It is by no means easy to define precisely what is meant by the term   **3–13**
"evidential burden" let alone identify the party upon whom it falls. All it really boils down to though is the fact that:

"if you haven't got any evidence, you haven't got a case,"

a brutal truth that applies as much to a defendant as it does to a claimant.

(c) *Interim Burdens*
In *E D and F Mann Liquid Products v Patel* [2003] C.P.L.R. 384, a case   **3–14**
on setting aside a default judgment under CPR 13.3 (see further 9–15), Potter L.J. stated that:

". . . the burden of proof is of only marginal importance in the assessment of evidence".

Suffice it to say for the moment that there are occasions during the preliminary stages of case management when, although not having a burden of proof as such, an applicant, or a respondent, is going to lose unless he has at least *some* evidence in his favour.

Indeed, on occasions (see *Royal Brompton Hospital NHS Trust v Hammond* [2001] B.L.R. 297 discussed at 9–16) an applicant may have a higher burden of proof than at trial.

B Burdens of Proof: Legal Theory and Practice

There is a large amount of case law on burdens of proof in civil as   **3–15**
well as criminal cases, much of it dating from the nineteenth century at a time when trials by jury were still the norm in civil proceedings. The relevant detail is comprehensively surveyed in Chapter 6 of *Phipson*. However the burden of proof continues to throw up problems, especially in relation to causation in clinical negligence and industrial disease claims. They are discussed at 3–21.

1. The Legal Burden Defined

3–16 A number of attempts have been made by commentators to define what *Phipson* describes at 6–02 as:

> ". . . the obligation imposed on a party by a rule of law to prove (or disprove) a fact in issue to the requisite standard of proof. A party who fails to discharge [. . . this burden] placed on him to the requisite standard of proof will lose on the issue in question".

Phipson uses the term "persuasive burden" to describe this obligation, but it has also been variously described as the "legal burden" or "the ultimate burden". Whatever definition one employs, it comes down to the same thing; in order to succeed, the party upon whom the burden lies must be able to convince the trial judge that *every* material fact (LEVEL 2) needed to prove the elements of his case is more probable than not. It follows that a party who fails to establish every single one of those material facts to a probability level of 51 per cent will lose.

However, in practice, the evidence is usually clear cut one way or the other. But supposing the judge simply cannot choose between two competing versions of events; does he have no alternative but to fall back on the burden of proof as the only means of deciding the case? The answer to that question is, provisionally, "yes". As the House of Lords stated in *Rhesa Shipping Co SA v Edmunds* [1985] 1 W.L.R. 948 at 955:

> "No judge likes to decide cases on the burden of proof if he can legitimately avoid having to do so. There are cases, however on which owing to the unsatisfactory state of the evidence, or otherwise, deciding on the burden of proof is the only just cause for him to take".

However, as the Court of Appeal has recently made clear in *Stephens v Cannon* [2005] EWCA Civ 222 this technique should only be relied on as a last resort.

3–17 <u>Facts:</u> C and D entered into an agreement for the sale of a property belonging to C under which D was obliged to (1) obtain planning permission to erect additional buildings on the property, (2) erect the buildings, (3) sell the property and (4) account to C for 50 per cent of the sale proceeds insofar as they exceeded £1 million. D only ever carried out stage (1) of his obligations and accordingly C claimed damages from D based, ultimately, upon the value that the property would have sold for in the summer of 2002 if D had performed all his obligations under the contract. The jointly instructed valuer's figure was *£1.5 million*. A second valuer, whose evidence the court had permitted C to rely on valued it at *£1.9 million*.

The Master, faced with the conflicting valuation evidence "went" **3–18** with the jointly instructed valuer. He applied the burden of proof test because he was unable to choose between the two of them. The Court of Appeal allowed the claimant's appeal. The leading judgment was given by Wilson J. In it (at [46]) he set out the principles to which a judge should have regard when resolving conflicts of evidence (including expert evidence), namely:

(1) Situations in which the court has to fall back on the burden of proof are exceptional;

(2) A "legitimate state of agnosticism" can arise in respect of any issue, even after careful enquiry;

(3) A court should not fall back on the burden of proof unless, after due enquiry, it cannot legitimately make a finding of fact on a particular issue;

(4) If the court does fall back on the burden of proof it has to explain clearly why it has had no choice but to do so; unless

(5) The circumstances are such that such an explanation can be readily inferred.

The decision also serves as a reminder that, when faced with two conflicting assertions, namely:

"£1.5 million" vs "£1.9 million"

it is not necessarily a case of "either/or". As Wilson J. states (at [49]):

". . . Of course I do not wish to be misunderstood as commending any unprincipled splitting of differences, such is a practice which furious advocates sometimes suspect to be in hidden operation, which encourages submission of unreasonable figures and which brings the law into disrepute. But, had the master asked himself not "which of the two valuations should I accept?" but "what, in the light of the evidence of the two valuers, was the probable value of the property?" and had then not merely noted some of the specific differences between the valuers but sought to adjudicate in relation to them, he might well have been able to answer it".

Conclusion   Although the concept of the legal or persuasive burden   **3–19** of proof is analysed in great detail in *Phipson*, in practical terms, it will usually be possible for the judge to determine who has "won" or "lost". Accordingly, it will only be in the rarest of instances that the judge if left with no choice but to say:

"I cannot choose between the claimant and the defendant; claim dismissed".

Not only that, but as *Stephens v Cannon* shows, a judge is not necessarily left with having to choose between two polarised assertions. She may, on occasions opt for the "third way". However the judge can only opt for a "third way" if this is available to her on the parties' cases as presented in their case statements at the evidence led (see *Al Meddeni v Mars* [2005] EWCA Civ 1041 in which the Court of Appeal held that it was not open to the trial judge to adopt such a course on the *evidence*).

2. Who Has the Legal (Persuasive) Burden?

3–20   As we have already seen (3–05) burdens are nowhere near so much one way traffic as they are in criminal proceedings. The following is not an exhaustive list, but covers most of the examples that you are likely to meet in practice. The first two, causation and damage, will be examined in detail because they highlight the practical problems that discharging the burden of proof can sometimes cause.

(a) Causation

3–21   Whether the claim is in contract or tort, the burden is always on the claimant to prove on the balance of probabilities (51 per cent) that the alleged breach of contract or duty has caused him *some* loss in order to succeed. This may on occasions, especially in the field of tort law, produce what, at first sight, appear to be unfair results. However (see 3–34) the *quantification* of future loss is determined by reference to the "chance" that the claimant would have suffered that particular loss. This is so, even if that chance is *less* than 50 per cent. These two principles, as we shall see (3–31) are not always easy to reconcile (a notable exception is claims brought under s.7 of the Human Rights Act 1998, see *Colle v Chief Constable of Hertfordshire Police* [2006] EWHC 360 (QB)).

3–22   (1) *Causation Proved*   In the following instances, the courts have been prepared to modify the claimant's burden to avoid leaving him with an impossible task. In the first decision, the claimant was faced with the problem that his injury was caused by one or other of two concurrent activities but he could not prove which one.

3–23   In *Bonnington Castings Ltd v Wardlaw* [1956] A.C. 613: The claimant had contracted pneumoconiosis from inhaling air containing silica dust at the factory where he was employed. The dust was caused partly by the operation of steam hammers in respect of which the defendants were *not* in breach of any duty (the "innocent dust"), and partly by the operation of swing grinders that *did* involve a breach of duty (the "guilty dust"). The claimant was unable to prove on the balance of probabilities that the "guilty dust" had caused his disease. The House of Lords held that, faced with the above situation, all the claimant had to prove was that the "guilty" ingredient had *materially contributed* to the disease. The reasoning of the House was that since pneumoconiosis is a progressive disease, any activity that lengthens the period of exposure must increase the risk to which the employee is exposed. Proof of that material fact was sufficient to prove the necessary causal link. In *Bonnington* the two acts were both positive, the operation of the steam hammers and the swing grinders, but what if one of the acts complained of consists of an *omission*? The next House of Lords decision appears to take the *Bonnington* a stage further.

McGhee v National Coal Board [1973] 1 W.L.R. 1: The claimant, **3-24** who worked at the defendants' brick kilns contracted dermatitis after working in them for only four and a half days. The work inside the kiln was very hot and dusty and the kilns were not ventilated. Although the claimant was able to prove that the exposure to the dust was what had caused his dermatitis he could *not* prove any negligence or breach of duty in relation to the working conditions. He maintained however that the defendants ought to have provided showers that would have meant that the dust would not have remained in contact with his skin until he got home. However, the medical evidence did not establish on the balance of probabilities that "but for" the failure to provide showers he would not have contracted dermatitis. All he could establish was that the provision of showers would have *reduced* the risk.

Once again, the House of Lords was prepared to hold that as a matter of *law*, he had done enough to discharge the burden imposed on him. In a decision based to a large extent on policy, Lord Reid (at [5]) stated:

"... it has often been said that that the legal concept of causation is not based on logic or philosophy. It is based on the practical way in which the ordinary man's [or woman's] mind works in the everyday affairs of life. From a broad and practical viewpoint I can see no difference between saying that what [the NCB] did materially increased the risk of injury ... and saying that what [they] did made a material contribution towards his injury."

More recently, the House of Lords has had to consider the situation where the injury has been caused by one of two employers but it has not been possible to prove which one.

In *Fairchild v Glenhaven Funeral Services Ltd [2003] A.C. 32*: **3-25** The appeal concerned three employees (two deceased by the time of the hearing) who had contracted mesothelioma, an incurable cancer of the pleura or (rarely) the peritoneum. All three employees had suffered prolonged exposure to asbestos dust as a result of employment with

Employer A and *Employer B*. The causal link between lengthy exposure to asbestos and mesothelioma has long been established, but, unlike in the case of many other pulmonary industrial diseases, the precise point at which exposure to asbestos dust triggers the cell changes which lead to the development of mesothelioma is not known; the causal agent could even be one single fibre. Accordingly, the three employees could not prove whether inhaling asbestos dust while working for Employer A or B caused their illnesses.

The Court of Appeal ([2002] 1 W.L.R. 1052) had taken the view that, on those facts, the claims must fail against *both* sets of employers. However, once again, based on an extension of *Bonnington* and *McGhee*, the House held that the claim was established on proof of the following material facts:

ELEMENT 1: C WAS OWED A DUTY OF CARE BY EMPLOYERS A AND B

ELEMENT 2: BOTH A AND B WERE IN BREACH OF THEIR DUTY OF CARE/STATUTORY DUTY IN EXPOSING C TO ASBESTOS DUST

In order to establish **ELEMENT 3** (Causation) all the claimants had to prove was that:

(1) They were suffering from mesothelioma;

(2) Their mesotheliomas were caused by the inhalation of asbestos dust *while working for A and B*.

On proof of these facts they could recover *in full* against each of A *and* B even though they could not prove, having regard to the current limitations of medical science, whether they had contracted the mesothelioma while working for Employer A or B.

What distinguishes all of the above cases is the fact that, although a very hallow list of probable causes can be identified, it is impossible to go on and identify which of those causes is the more probable. However, if that calculation is practicable, there is nothing to prevent the court:

(1) *Apportioning liability* between two defendants on a percentage basis (see, for example *Holtby v Brigham & Cowan (Hull) Ltd* [2000] 3 All E.R. 421 (a claim concerning asbestosis which, unlike mesothelioma, is a progressive disease) and *Fitzgerald v Lane* [1989] A.C. 328 (a claim in which the claimant was cumulatively injured by two motorists in immediate succession but it was not possible to separate with any degree of precision the injuries caused by the respective vehicles)), the court fell back on 50:50 apportionment;

(2) Making a defendant liable only for that period of the claimant's damage that can be clearly identified as being attributable to the defendant's negligence (see, for example, *Thompson v Smith (Ships Repairers (North Shields) Ltd)* [1984] 1 All E.R. 881: an industrial deafness case, again, a progressive disease).

Another recent instance in which the House of Lords has adopted a broad-brush approach to causation is in relation to "informed consent" in clinical negligence claims.

Chester v Afshar [2005] 1 A.C. 134, the claimant suffered from **3–26** lower back pain. The defendant, her consultant neurosurgeon with considerable experience of disc surgery, recommended an operation but failed to warn her that it carried a one to two per cent risk of a seriously adverse result. The operation went ahead and she suffered significant nerve damage as a result. The trial judge found that, although the operation had been correctly performed, the defendant had been negligent in not informing the claimant of the risks involved. He also found that if the claimant had been informed of the attendant risks, she would not have had the operation but would have sought a second or third opinion. On that basis the judge found that causal link between the negligence and the injury had been established and therefore found for her.

The defendant appealed on the basis that it was not sufficient to prove simply that the claimant would have decided against having the operation that injured her; she was required to prove that she would not at any time have consented to run the relevant risk. The House of Lords (3:2) dismissed the appeal. As with so many of these cases, there are strong policy elements at play (see, in particular, Lord Steyn (at [25])):

"On a broader basis I am glad to have arrived at the conclusion that the claimant is entitled in law to succeed. The result is in accord with one of the most basic aspirations of the law, namely to right wrongs. Moreover, the decision announced by the house today reflects the reasonable expectations of the public in contemporary society".

The policy element inherent in all of the above cases starting with *Bonnington* can be seen when contrasting them with the recent decision in *Clough v First Choice Holidays and Flights Limited* [2006] EWCA Civ 15 in which the Court of Appeal held that the trial judge had been correct to dismiss the claimant's claim. The claimant had suffered catastrophic injuries when he had fallen into a shallow paddling pool whilst on holiday at a resort in Lanzarote. Although the owners of the resort were found to have been negligent in not applying non-slip paint to the edge of the pool, the claim failed because the claimant was unable to prove on the balance of probabilities that but for the defendant's negligence he would not have slipped and fallen. The President of the Queen's Bench (with whom Hallett and Richards L.JJ agreed (at [43])):

> "...the distinction sought to be drawn by [counsel for the appellant] between material contribution to damage and material contribution to the risk of damage has no application to cases where the claimant's injuries arose from a *single incident* [writer's emphasis]. In this court any modification of the principles relating to causation in the context of claims for damages for personal injury must be approached with the greatest caution."

Although this statement can be reconciled with *Bonnington* and *Fairchild*, it is harder to reconcile with *McGee* which was also in effect a "single incident" case. Perhaps, ultimately, *Clough* should be seen on its own facts, not least that:

(1) Nobody directly saw how the claimant fell;

(2) He had consumed at least six pints of lager; and

(3) There was no clear evidence that anyone else had slipped whilst walking along the poolside.

3–27   (2) *Causation not Proved*   The following cases show how narrow the dividing line between success and failure may be; literally:

51 per cent proof = 100 per cent recovery

50 per cent proof = zero per cent recovery

a result that can seem even harsher when one takes into account the fact that once there is 51 per cent proof of *some* loss, the claimant can recover for future loss even though the chance of it occurring is less than 50 per cent (see 3–34).

As was noted at 1–08 there will often be no dispute that the defendant's breach of duty caused the claimant's loss. However if the claimant would have suffered the same loss notwithstanding the defendant's breach of duty he will recover nothing. A particularly stark example of that principle in operation is the case of *Barnett v Chelsea and Kensington Hospital Management Committee* [1969] 1 Q.B. 428. The deceased was sent home from a casualty department by a doctor without treatment, even though he had presented with arsenical poisoning from which he subsequently died. The doctor had undoubtedly been negligent, but, based on the level of medical knowledge at the time, even if he had been treated properly it would have been too late to have saved him. The claim consequently failed. This type of argument is not exclusive to claims in clinical negligence. For example, in *McWilliams v Sir William Arrol & Co Ltd* [1962] 1 W.L.R. 295, the widow of a steel erector who had fallen to his death failed to recover in a claim based on the defendants' failure to provide the deceased with safety belts. On the evidence, she was unable to prove that he would have worn a safety belt on the occasion in question *even if they had been available.* The evidence showed that he had rarely worn a safety belt in the past and, accordingly his widow could not prove that he would probably have been wearing one on the occasion in question.

However there is no doubt that clinical negligence claims have given rise to the greatest problems in this area, as a summary of the following cases shows. The first case to be discussed shows that the *Bonnington* approach will not assist if there is *a multiplicity* of potential causes, one of which is a negligent act on the part of the defendants.

Wilsher v Essex Area Health Authority [1988] A.C. 1074: C was   **3–28**
born prematurely and subsequently become blind as a result of a condition known as retrolental fibroplasia (RLF). There was no doubt that the hospital and its staff had been negligent in administering too high doses of oxygen to C and that this was one of a number of possible causes of the onset of RLF.

The claim failed on the basis that there were at least five possible causes of RLF. The claimant was unable to prove that the negligent administration of oxygen was at least 51 per cent likely to have been the operative cause of the RLF and, hence, the blindness. The House of Lords specifically approved the dissenting judgment of Sir Nicolas Browne-Wilkinson V.C. in the Court of Appeal (where the claimant had succeeded) in which ([1987] Q.B. 730 at 779) he had stated:

"the position in my mind is wholly different from that in *McGhee*, where there was only one candidate (brick dust) which could have caused the dermatitis and the failure to take a precaution against brick dust was followed by dermatitis caused by brick dust . . . A failure to take preventative measures against one out of five possible causes is no evidence as to which of those five caused the injury".

So far, so good. The claimant has failed to prove that one *past* event (excessive administration of oxygen) has caused another *past* event (RLF leading to blindness). But what if one or more of the past events is an *omission* rather than a failure to act? This difficulty arose in the next case.

In *Bolitho v City and Hackney* H A [1998] A.C. 232 C, a two year   **3–29**
old boy, suffered irreparable (and ultimately fatal) brain damage as a result of cardiac arrest caused by a condition known as "croup", an obstruction of the bronchial air passages leading to asphyxia. The

defendants admitted negligence because a doctor who was treating the patient did not attend in response to calls. It was found as a fact that the cardiac arrest could have been prevented if a doctor had attended and intubated the patient thus clearing the obstruction. However, the trial judge found that (1) the treating doctor would not have intubated at that stage even if she *had* attended, and (2) a responsible body of medical opinion would have supported a decision not to intubate at this stage. The appeal to the House of Lords failed on the basis that, in order to prove causation the claimant had to prove that if the doctor had attended, either:

(1) She *would* have taken the requisite action (even though it would not have been negligent if she had decided not to do so); or

(2) The proper discharge of her duty would have required that she take that action (even though she would have decided not to).

The claimant's personal representatives failed under (1) above because the doctor's evidence that she would not have intubated at that stage was accepted (how can you succeed if the doctor says that she would not have taken that step, unless you can destroy her credibility as a witness?). They also failed under (2) above because they were unable to prove on the expert evidence that no responsible doctor would have taken the decision *not* to intubate.

Even greater problems arise when the claimant has to prove that there is causal link between a *past* act (or omission) and some *future* hypothetical event that has not yet taken place. This tends most commonly to arise in those cases where the claimant is complaining of failure on the part of the defendant to diagnose a past condition that has damaged his prospects of future recovery. In some cases, causation may not be that hard to establish.

Example: C presents at his GP on January 1, 2004 with a particular condition. His GP fails to recognise it as being a potentially malignant lesion which is highly curable if caught in time. A year later, on January 1, 2005, C presents again at which point it is clear that something is seriously amiss. On referral it now transpires that C has an advanced and inoperable cancer from which he will shortly die. Assuming negligence is provable, C can prove the causal link between the negligence and his loss if he can establish (to a level of at least 51 per cent):

(1) The stage his condition had reached at January 1, 2004;

(2) That, on the basis of the fact established at (1) there would have been a better outcome if the cancer had been correctly referred on January 1, 2004 and subsequently diagnosed and treated accordingly.

However, in real life the facts are not always that simple, as the following example shows.

Hotson v East Berkshire A H A [1987] A.C. 750: C fractured his hip **3–30** when he fell out of a tree. As a result of negligence on the part of D his injury was not properly treated for five days. He subsequently suffered severe and permanent disability due to the development of a condition in the femur known as avascular necrosis. However, on the basis of the available clinical evidence, there was a 75 per cent likelihood that the blood vessels to the femur had been so seriously damaged by the fall that it would not have been possible to have prevented the condition developing *even if he had been treated promptly*. The trial judge awarded his damages based on 25 per cent of the full value of his claim and this was upheld by the Court of Appeal.

However the House of Lords allowed the defendants' appeal holding that the claimant had failed to prove the crucial material fact essential to establishing causation, namely, that at the time the defendants assumed responsibility for the claimant's treatment, the condition of his hip was such that there remained a better than even prospect of it being successfully treated. Accordingly, the claimant had failed to prove that he had suffered any loss as a result of the defendants' negligence. This decision therefore serves as a stark reminder of the "all or nothing" approach to proof highlighted at 3–27.

At least in *Hotson* here was available evidence as to the claimant's condition at the time that the defendants assumed responsibility for his treatment, but what if, as a result of the defendant's breach of duty, there is simply *no available evidence* as to this? This issue taxed the House of Lords in yet another case on causation in clinical negligence, the most recent, but undoubtedly not the last to come before it.

In *Gregg v Scott* [2005] 4 All E.R. 812 C went to see D his GP on **3–31** November 22, 1994 with a lump under his left arm. D told him it was a benign lipoma. On August 22, 1995, having moved house, he went to see another GP who decided to refer him to Lincoln County Hospital where the lump was diagnosed as being a particularly severe form of cancer of the lymph system known as ALK negative subtype non-Hodgkin's lymphoma. There was no doubt that:

(1) D had been negligent in not referring C in November 1994; and

(2) The disease had spread during the nine month period it had remained undiagnosed.

However what C was unable to prove was that, on the balance of probabilities, it was the *spread of the disease during the nine month period* that had reduced his prospects of survival. All that he had available to him was expert statistical evidence to show that prompt treatment of this condition produced a 10 year survival rate of 45 per cent whereas C's prospects of survival at the time treatment actually began had reduced to 25 per cent.

The problem in this case was that the claimant's condition as at November 22, 1994 was *an unknown*. It was therefore not possible for the claimant to prove to a level of 51 per cent or better that it was the spread of the cancer during the nine month period of delay that had reduced his chances of survival. The claimant tried to get round this in two ways, the first based on a creative application of existing principles, the second based on an argument that the law needed to be changed. The arguments are summarised below.

(1) *The "Quantification Approach"*

3–32   There was no doubt that the defendant's negligence had caused *some* injury, in particular the reduced susceptibility to treatment. Accordingly the loss of expectation of life claim was part of ELEMENT 4 (damage) and fell to be determined on normal damages principles in which the court was no longer concerned with probability but only future possibility (see further 3–34). For reasons that are by no means easy to extract, the House (3:2) rejected this argument holding that, since the claimant had based his claim on loss of *expectation of favourable outcome* rather than any other damage that he had suffered (for example the pain and discomfort of the intensive treatment) he had no choice but to prove that it was the delay that caused the spread that had in turn caused that loss. In other words, proof of that factual chain was part of ELEMENT 3.

(2) *The "Policy Approach"*

3–33   The claimant further argued that having proved that he had suffered a "loss", namely the reduction of his chances of recovery from 45 to 25 per cent it would be a gross miscarriage of justice if he were not to be compensated for that loss. Suffice it to say that, in the teeth of strong dissenting speeches from Lord Nicholls and Lord Hope, the majority of the House rejected that approach. One is therefore left with the somewhat crude "zero option" situation in which, if the claimant could have proved that the delay in treatment was 51 per cent likely to have reduced his prospects of recovery, he would have recovered the full value of his "loss of chance", such as it was. However, since he was only able to adduce evidence that there was a statistical likelihood that his prospects of recovery would at best have only been 45 per cent if he had been referred to hospital on November 22, 1994, he recovered nothing. Ultimately the claim failed because there was a crucial gap in the *evidence*; his medical condition on November 22, 1994.

So is it ever possible to recover damages for a loss of chance where the prospects of success are less than 50 per cent? Tantalisingly, the answer is "Yes". The position when the claim is based on contract has been long established (see *Chaplin v Hicks* [1911] K.B. 286). However in recent years it has become commonplace to base claims in negligence against other professionals, for example, solicitors (*Allied Maples Group v Simmons and Simmons* [1995] 1 W.L.R. 1602 and *Stovold v Barlows* [1996] P.N.L.R. 1) and accountants (*First Interstate Bank of California v Cohen Arnold & Co* [1996] P.N.L.R. 17) on "loss of chance" of a successful outcome even though the value of that "chance" is less than 51 per cent. The reason for this distinction is inadequately explained by the majority in *Gregg v Scott* (surely it cannot be based simply on the fact that the claim is in contract rather than tort?). The only justification must be, that once the claimant has proved that he has suffered *some* loss as a result of the defendant's negligence (ELEMENT III) it becomes a matter of quantification of future loss (ELEMENT IV) which is governed by different principles. For the time being, so far as matters of evidence are concerned it is simply a distinction that you will need to be aware of when identifying the material facts you will need to prove at LEVEL 2 of your case analysis.

Conclusion   Although often seen as cases of the substantive law, all   3–34
of the above cases are, in reality, cases on *evidence*, all of which address the core issues of, "What do I have to prove?" and "How do I go about proving it?" Thus, case analysis is all important when it comes to ensuring that your client's claim or defence starts off down the right road at the earliest opportunity.

(b) *Damage*

A party seeking damages must prove each head of damage that he   3–35
claims to have suffered as a result of the other party's conduct. Furthermore, there are detailed rules, for example in tort, contract and landlord and tenant claims, setting out what heads of damage are maintainable and how they are to be quantified. However, the approach to quantification of *future* loss, especially in the field of personal injury law, is different to that in causation, as the following extract from Lord Nicholls' speech in *Gregg v Scott* [2005] 4 All E.R. 812 at [9] shows:

"In the normal way proof of facts constituting actionable damage calls for proof of the claimant's present position and proof of what would have been the claimant's position in the absence of the defendant's wrongful act or omission. As to what constitutes proof, traditionally the common law has drawn a distinction between proof of past facts and proof of future prospects. A happening in the past either occurred or it did not. Whether an event happened in the past

is a matter to be established in civil cases on the balance of probability. If an event probably happened, no discount is made for the
possibility it did not. Proof of future possibilities is approached
differently. Whether an event will happen in the future calls for an
assessment of the likelihood of that event happening, because no
one knows for certain what will happen in the future".

This means, as Lord Nicholls goes on to explain, and based on principles summarised by Lord Diplock in *Mallett v McMonagle* [1970]
A.C. 166 at 76, that in deciding whether, as a result of an injury proved
on the balance of probability to have been caused by the defendant's
tort, the claimant will suffer adverse consequences in the *future*, the
court will seek to evaluate the *chance* of that event occurring. As we
have seen, the claimant will be entitled to recover damages under that
head even though that chance is assessed at 50 per cent or less.

(c) *Other Common Examples of Burdens of Proof*

3–36   The other instances in which one or other of the parties has a recognised burden of proof can be dealt with relatively briefly. The most
well-recognised ones are set out below.

3–37   (1) *Contract*   The claimant, as well as having to prove causation and
damage must prove:

- The existence of the contract;

- Performance of any conditions precedent;

- The applicability of relevant consumer protection legislation, for
  example, the Unfair Terms in Consumer Contracts Regulations
  1999 ("the 1999 regs").

Conversely, the defendant will have the burden of proving:

- Any relevant exemption clause;

- Special defences such as infancy, release, rescission and fraud;

- Numerous specific statutory defences, for example, that a term
  of a contract to which the 1999 regs applies was individually
  negotiated (1999 regs, reg.5(4)).

It should also be noted that contracting parties may, subject to certain
statutory exceptions (see, for example, reg.5(6) of the 1999 regs)
include a term in the contract which specifies the incidence of the
burden of proof (see *Levy v Asscurazioni Generali* [1940] A.C. 791).

(2) *Negligence* The burden of proving negligence (claimant) and 3–38
contributory negligence (defendant) has already been covered. In
addition, the defendant will have the burden of proving special
defences such as:

- Volenti non fit Injuria;

- Illegality.

(3) *Consumer Protection Act 1987* Once the claimant proves that he 3–39
has suffered damage from the supply of a product to which s.2 of the
1987 Act applies, the burden is cast upon the defendant to establish
one of the special defences set out in s.4 of the Act.

(4) *Defamation* Having proved that the defendant has published a 3–40
statement that is defamatory of him the burden is then cast upon
the defendant to prove one or more of the special defences available
to him such as justification, fair comment or absolute or qualified
privilege. Crucially, it for the defendant to prove that the statement is
true rather than the other way round.

(5) *Malicious Prosecution* The claimant must prove not only the 3–41
prosecution was unsuccessful but also that the defendant initiated the
prosecution without "reasonable and probable cause".

(6) *False Imprisonment* The burden is upon the claimant to prove 3–42
that his liberty was restricted (characteristically by his arrest and subsequent detention). However the burden is upon the defendant to
prove that that restriction was lawful.

(7) *Bailment* Once the claimant has proved the circumstances of 3–43
the bailment and that the chattel has been lost or damaged while in
the defendant's possession, the burden is cast upon him to disprove
negligence. This is the case whether the bailment was gratuitous or for
reward.

Example: C (bailor) leaves, say, his overcoat in D's (bailee's) posses- 3–44
sion. When he returns it is gone, or is damaged. D will be liable for
this loss or damage unless he can prove that it was not due to his negligence. This will be the case irrespective of whether or not D took
possession of it on payment of a fee, for example at a hotel cloakroom. The latter type of case will also often give rise to further problems on burdens of proof if, as it often will, the cloakroom ticket has
an exemption clause on the back.

3–45 (8) *Mitigation* A claimant both in contract and tort is generally expected to take reasonable steps to mitigate his loss. However it is not for him to prove that he has, it is for the defendant to prove that he has not. However, the CPR recognise that it would be oppressive if the defendant, faced with this burden, were ignorant of the steps that the claimant had taken for this purpose. It is for this reason that CPR 16, Practice Direction, para.8.2(8) requires a claimant to set out in his particulars of claim:

"any facts relating to mitigation of loss or damage".

Even if he does not give any particulars, it now makes it much easier for the defendant to set out the steps that he ought to have taken.

3–46 (9) *Undue Influence* There have been numerous cases in which a party (usually a wife) has sought to have a mortgage or guarantee that she has entered into to provide security for her husband's business borrowings set aside as against the lender on the grounds of undue influence. The relevant law (see, in particular, *Barclays Bank v O'Brien* [1994] A.C. 180 and *Royal Bank of Scotland v Etridge* [2001] 4 All E.R. 449) is well beyond the scope of this book. However readers need to be aware of the House of Lords decision in *Barclays Bank v Boulter* [1999] 4 All E.R. 513 in which the House held that:

(1) It was for the party seeking to have the transaction set aside to plead and prove the facts which rendered the charge or guarantee invalid;

(2) In a husband and wife case this would involve no more than proving knowledge on the part of the lender that they were living together and that the transaction was not, on its face to her financial advantage (this aspect of the case is open to question following *Ettridge* referred to above);

(3) The burden then lies on the lender to plead and prove that it took appropriate steps to satisfy itself that her consent was properly obtained (again, reference should be made to *Ettridge*).

This is a very complicated area of the law, but it illustrates, once again, how one cannot address evidential issues without having first carried out a thorough research of the relevant substantive law.

3–47 (10) *Limitation* Although the defendant must plead any limitation defence that he wishes to rely on (see CPR 16, PD, para.31.1), once raised, it is generally accepted that it is for the claimant to prove the facts which bring him within the relevant limitation period. This complex topic is fully covered in Chapter 5 of *O'Hare and Browne*; the full annotated text of the Limitation Act 1980 can be found in s.8 of the *White Book* for 2006.

Conclusion It will be relatively straightforward to identify which   **3–48**
party has the burden of proof once proceedings have begun and case statements have been exchanged. However it is an issue that cannot wait until then. In the first instance you will always need to identify the elements in your client's case that must be proved or asserted. This may on occasions require you to make a detailed study of the substantive law, for example on causation in a clinical negligence case, before you can even begin to address the evidential issues.

3. Evidential Burdens
This concept has already been addressed briefly at 3–13 and there is   **3–49**
not much more than can usefully be said about it. The existence of the evidential burden is of far greater practical importance in criminal cases than it is in civil claims. The reason for this is easy to identify; if a defendant in a criminal trial denies the charge then, short of the prosecution deciding to offer no evidence, the only way of determining guilt is by way of trial. In civil claims, the likelihood of trial is statistically remote. Nevertheless the principle is, in theory, the same in both types of proceedings: unless the claimant adduces sufficient evidence to entitle, albeit not oblige the court to find in his favour, the claim must be dismissed. This is often referred to as establishing a prima facie case. Failure to hit this target leaves the claimant vulnerable to a successful submission of no case to answer by the defendant. However as we shall see (14–66) submissions of no case to answer are a rarity in civil proceedings (see, most recently, *Benham Ltd v Kythira investments Ltd* [2003] EWCA Civ 1794 discussed further at 14–66). One major reason for their scarcity compared to criminal proceedings is the fact that there are so few civil jury trials. Furthermore, the "cards on the table" approach to litigation has meant that the holes in a claimant's (or a defendant's) case are likely to become apparent at a much earlier stage than at trial. Accordingly a party will find his case is under attack as soon as the gaps in his evidence become apparent, especially after exchange of witness statements.

2. "Secondary" Burdens
A party who wishes to rely upon a particular piece of evidence may   **3–50**
on occasions be faced with an objection to its introduction. The general rule is that the party who seeks to uphold the admissibility of the evidence has the burden of satisfying the court to the civil standard that the evidence should be admitted. For example, the party

introducing the evidence will, if called upon to do so, be required to prove:

- A witness's competence to testify;
- The authenticity of a document;
- That an admission made by his opponent was not made on an occasion covered by privilege.

Although secondary issues of this kind are of great practical importance in criminal cases, largely because of the separate roles of judge and jury (see *Phipson* 6–04) it is most unusual to find them arising in civil claims. There are a number of practical reasons for this, the most notable being:

(1) Documentary evidence is almost invariably agreed;

(2) Even if it has not been directly agreed a party will usually have been deemed to admit all documents appearing in Pt 1 of his List of Documents under CPR 32.19 unless he serves Notice of Non-Admission within the prescribed period (see further 5–40);

(3) Most objections to the admission of evidence will arise because of a party has failed to comply with a rule or case management direction. Since, in deciding whether to grant relief from a sanction, the court will be exercising a discretion, burdens and standards of proof do not directly come into it.

C The standard of proof

3–51 Whoever has the burden of proof has to discharge it on the "balance of probabilities". As we saw when discussing causation, this "all or nothing" approach can operate harshly on occasions. It is for that reason that the court strives to find facts with a rather greater degree of certainty if at all possible. Three issues call for further discussion.

1. Is There a Higher Standard for Quasi-Criminal Issues?

3–52 There has always been a general consensus that:

"the more serious the allegation on the consequences the stronger the evidence needed to prove it".

In practical terms, judges bear this in mind when making findings of fact at trial or on "paper hearings"—the ruthlessly exacting standards imposed in "accelerated possession" cases involving assured shorthold tenancies (see CPR 55.12) being a prime example. If you can "get home" on a version of events that makes it easier for the judge to tell the other side that they have lost, you should, on the whole, go with it.

Example: C and D have been involved in a road traffic accident. They   **3–53**
are now before the court and present starkly different version of how the accident took place (ever was it thus!). However C calls W to give evidence on his behalf. W's evidence strongly supports C's version of how the collision took place. D, through her advocate, suggests that W has been induced by C to give false evidence.

Quite apart from the ethical constraints that exist before this line of   **3–54**
cross-examination can be pursued (see further, 14–45) the defendant is setting her advocate a pretty stiff task. The defendant is effectively obliging the judge to find that there has been such a conspiracy to pervert the course of justice if she dismisses the claim. Nevertheless, there have, in the past been suggestions in some judgments that there is somehow a "higher" standard of proof in the case of serious allegations, for example, of fraud. The impracticability of adopting a "mathematical" approach, say:

"51 per cent for breach of warranty, say, 76 per cent for fraud"

to a specific set of facts was highlighted by Denning L.J. in *Hornal v Neuberger Products* [1957] Q.B. 247. As he pointed out, in a claim based alternatively on breach of warranty and fraudulent misrepresentation, such an approach might result in the judge finding that there was sufficient evidence to prove the breach of warranty but not the fraudulent misrepresentation. The most recent statement of this principle can be found in the House of Lords' speeches in *re H and R (Minors) (Sexual Abuse: Standard of Proof)* [1996] A.C. 563 in particular in the speech of Lord Nicholls (at 586):

"The balance of probability standard means that a court is satisfied that an event occurred if the court considers that, on the evidence, the occurrence of the event was more likely than not. When assessing the probabilities the court will have in mind the factor, to whatever extent is appropriate in the particular case, that the more serious the allegation the less likely it is that the event occurred and hence, the stronger should be the evidence before the court concludes that the allegation is established on the balance of probabilities".

"Fair enough" you may be thinking: there is nothing particularly controversial in that statement. However, he then continues by stating:

"Fraud is usually less likely than negligence. Deliberate physical injury usually less likely than accidental physical injury. A stepfather is usually less likely to have repeatedly raped and had non-consensual oral sex with his underage stepdaughter than on some occasion to have lost his temper and slapped her. Built into the preponderance of probability standard is a generous degree of flexibility in respect of the seriousness of the allegation".

The immediate thought that springs to mind is "How does he know this?" (Lord Lloyd of Berwick dissented (see 577–8), stating that there was only one standard whatever the nature of the allegation). However, on reflection, most people would probably agree with Lord Nicholls and apply the same principles if called upon to make findings of fact at the end of a trial. Although the appeal arose in the specialised field of care proceedings, it is clear that Lord Nicholls was intending this to be a general statement of the law. It is interesting that Lord Nicholls concentrates on the *seriousness* of the allegation made as opposed to the *consequences* that may follow if the burden is discharged. The making of a care order is an extreme measure since it involves separating a child from its parent. There are however numerous other orders in civil proceedings that will have a profound effect on the life of the party against whom they are made: possession orders, anti-social behaviour injunctions ("ASBIs"), freezing orders and search orders (see generally, *O'Hare and Browne*, Chapter 27) being notable examples. Inevitably, the court will require a higher standard of proof when being asked to evict a tenant from her home on the grounds of anti-social behaviour than when called upon to adjudicate between two insurers as to which one should bear the cost of repairing the claimant's crash-damaged motor car. Consequence came to the fore in *R. (N) v Doctor M* [2003] 1 W.L.R. 562.

3–55   **Facts:** It was alleged that N suffered from a psychotic illness for which she was refusing to undergo recommended treatment including the injection of anti-psychotic drugs. Dr M, a consultant psychiatrist issued a certificate under s.58(3)(b) of the Mental Health Act 1983 stating that she required the recommended treatment. N challenged the decision.

3–56   In upholding the certificate and the decision of Goldring J., the Court of Appeal confirmed that a high standard of proof was required before a court could properly be satisfied that it was appropriate to give permission for treatment to which a patient did not consent. Dyson L.J. stated (at [17]):

". . . it is common ground that the standard of proof required is that the court should be satisfied that medical necessity has been 'convincingly' shown".

Dyson L.J. then went on to emphasise that the standard is not the same as the criminal standard but, that apart, it required no further elaboration.

Conclusion   As a general rule, the more serious the allegation or the   3–57
consequences that will flow from its proof, the stronger the evidence that you will need to prove it. Unfortunately, some clients are not prepared to accept this. To their way of thinking:

* All witnesses are liars and, moreover, will readily reveal themselves as such under cross-examination;

* All material documents are forgeries:

* The other party is deliberately refusing to disclose or is shredding material documents;

* Photographs and video recordings have been deliberately edited to present a false picture;

* The other side's expert witness has been bribed to express an opinion that favours his paymaster.

As Charles Hollander Q.C. suggests (see *Hollander* 11–10) perhaps post-Enron a greater degree of cynicism is appropriate. However, for the time being at least, one should assume that judges will follow Lord Nicholls' approach to standards of proof in civi cases.

2. "Weight"
One must also never overlook the fact that some facts within a case   3–58
are bound to be more probable than others. Although, as a matter of common logic, some items of evidence are more persuasive than others, there are no legal rules for determining weight. Evidence is evaluated by reference to common logic and generalisation. However, although the ultimate issue will be decided on the balance of probabilities, many of the findings of fact that a judge will be invited to make during a trial will, in effect, be virtual certainties. Once this "matrix of certainty" has been identified, it may be much easier to assess the probability of those that remain in issue (see, in particular, the analysis of Brooke L.J.'s judgment in *Gow v Harker* [2003] EWCA Civ 1160 at 5–11). This incremental approach to determining the ultimate issue was acknowledged by Wilson J. in *Stephens v Cannon* [2005] EWCA Civ 222 (for a summary of the facts see 3–17) at [48]:

"Giving rise to the global difference of £400,000 between the experts were about 16 specific issues between them . . . The Master made no finding in relation to any of them . . . I believe that, had he sought to work his way through the specific issues between the experts . . . he might well, in the light of all the other evidence, have found his way to a conclusion, one way or another, without resort to the burden of proof."

"Looking for certainties" is one of many ways in which the successful advocate will assemble his or her case theory, but it is a simple technique that can be employed at any stage to identify the strengths and weaknesses of your client's case. As *Stephens v Cannon* shows, it also mirrors the approach a judge will employ in resolving difficult issues on the burden of proof.

3. When the Criminal Standard *Does* Apply

3–59 There has always been a small number of cases in which the criminal standard ("beyond reasonable doubt") has been imposed upon a party. It is here that the influence of consequence becomes most apparent. Traditionally, the only situation in which the criminal standard applied was in proceedings for contempt of court (for a fuller explanation of the technical difference between "criminal" and "civil" contempt in the civil courts see *Murphy on Evidence*, page 106). However, the civil courts are being given ever-increasing powers to make orders in civil proceedings, the breach of which may lead not only to contempt proceedings but also to criminal prosecution. Examples include:

(1) Anti-Social Behaviour Orders ("ASBOs") under s.1 (magistrates' court) and s.1B (county court) of the Crime and Disorder Act 1998; see *R (On the Application of McCann) v Manchester Crown Court* [2003] 1 A.C. 787 at [37] (note however that the *civil* standard has been held to apply for applications for Closure Orders under ss.2(3)(a) and (b) of the Anti-Social Behaviour Act 2003 see *Chief Constable of Merseyside Police v Harrison* [2006] W.L.R. (D.) 100);

(2) Injunctions under s.3 of the Protection from Harassment Act 1997 (county court); see *Hipgrave v Hipgrave and Jones* [2005] 2 F.L.R 174;

(3) Applications for sex offender orders under s.2 of the Crime and Disorder Act 1998 (magistrates' court); see *B v CC Avon and Somerset* [2001] 1 W.L.R. 340 at 354;

(4) Football banning orders under s.14B of the Football Spectators Act 1989 (magistrates' court); see *Gough v CC Derbyshire* [2002] Q.B. 1213.

So far as ASBOs are concerned the position after *McCann* is clear. Lord Steyn, with whom all their Lordships agreed stated (at [37]):

". . . in my view pragmatism dictates that the task of magistrates [author's note: and by analogy, judges in the county court] should be made more straightforward by ruling that they must in all cases under s.1 apply the criminal standard".

One might have hoped that the courts would always adopt this approach when being asked to rule upon the standard of proof appropriate to this type of case. However, this has not happened. For example, in *Hipgrave v Hipgrave and Jones* [2005] 2 F.L.R. 174, which involved an application for an injunction under the Protection from Harassment Act 1997, Tugenhadt J. held that the *civil* standard of proof applied notwithstanding the fact that conviction for breach of an order is punishable in the same way as breach of an ASBO. He justified setting a lower standard, albeit still, presumably, the *re H* standard, by virtue of the fact that orders under the 1997 Act are private as opposed to public remedies. It is respectfully submitted that, for the pragmatic reasons identified by Lord Steyn in *McCann*, the criminal standard should apply to all civil proceedings of this kind.

Conclusion   In this chapter we have considered the burden of proof   **3–60** in detail because it is a concept that has assumed a far greater degree of practical importance since the CPR came into force. You need to be aware of what you must prove or refute in order to:

(1) Create a structure within which you can assess your chances of success;

(2) Within that structure analyse the evidence that you have available and/or that you need to collect in order to persuade the other side that your case is a strong one;

(3) Weed out at as early a stage as possible those aspects of your case that should not be pursued;

(4) Set out the case to your opponent in a format that convinces him that early negotiated settlement is advisable;

(5) Respond promptly and constructively to your opponent's proposals (or lack of them).

Remember; the trial begins on Day 1 (see Chapter 1).

Chapter 4

Relevance

In this chapter we shall consider the following topics: **4–01**

(1) How do we determine whether or not an item of evidence is relevant to an issue in the claim?

(2) What part does presumption, inference and circumstance play in the fact finding process?

As we shall see, relevance is not, on the whole, a matter of law at all but, as with weight, largely a matter of supposed common knowledge and generalisation. However there are some aspects of the subject, for example *Presumptions*, that do have their own legal rules.

I RELEVANCE IN PRACTICE

Before we look at the legal principles, such as they are, for determin-   **4–02**
ing relevance, it is as well to stand back from the theory and examine the practice.

1. Evidence at Trial
Although, in theory, the court is obliged, in theory, to *exclude* irrele-   **4–03**
vant evidence, the reality is somewhat different. Applications for the exclusion of evidence on the grounds of irrelevance are a rarity. The general approach of judges is to allow everything in at the outset, and to curtail unnecessary cross-examination. Usually a remark such as:

"really, where is this going?"

if delivered with a sufficient degree of froideur, will suffice. Not only that, but as we saw at 1–52, the judge has ample power to control the evidence, including the scope of cross-examination under CPR

32.1(2) and 1(3). However, parties still place an enormous amount of irrelevant evidence before courts, usually in the form of huge bundles of documents or over lengthy witness statements. They would be well advised to follow the guidance given by Rose L.J. in *Re Freudiana Holdings Ltd, The Times*, December 4, 1995.

4–04   **Facts:** At the end of a 165 day trial of a claim under s.459 of the Companies Act 1985 (for which counsel had given an estimate of 15–20 days) the trial judge had made a "show cause" order as to wasted costs against the respondents' solicitors. In response to this the petitioner's solicitors had assembled a large amount of evidence including a 40 page Points of Claim. On the basis of this profligacy the trial judge discharged the "show cause" order.

4–05   In upholding the decision of Parker J., Rose L.J. had this to say:

> "The real remedy lies with the legal profession itself. The proper conduct of litigation does not require every point to be taken; it requires all those involved to concentrate on the vital issues in the case. The legal profession must re-learn or reapply the skill which was the historic hallmark of the legal profession but which appears to be fast vanishing: to present to the court the few crucial determinative points and to discard as immaterial dross the minor points and excessive detail".

That is probably as a good working definition of relevance that you will find; sadly, the CPR notwithstanding, it is advice that often still goes unheeded.

2. Relevance Pre-Trial

4–06   Relevancy is at the core of disclosure applications both pre-claim (CPR 31.16) and post-commencement, whether made against a party (CPR 31.16) or a non-party (CPR 31.17). However the court may, on occasions, permit the net to be cast wider or confine it to narrower limits (see generally, *Hollander*, Chapters 8 and 9). What one can be sure of is that accusations of "fishing expeditions" and cries of "disproportionate" will not be overcome unless one has a strong case, based on relevance, for being granted the disclosure or further disclosure sought (see in particular 10–22).

II RELEVANCE DEFINED

1. Stephen and Beyond

4–07   The classic definition is that given by Stephen in *Digest of the Law of Evidence* (12th Edn), Art.1 namely:

"any two facts to which it is applied are so related to each other that according to the common course of events one either taken by itself or in connection with other facts proves or renders probable the past, present, or future existence or non-existence of the other."

This definition does not please all commentators, not least because it appears to suggest that evidence is only relevant if it renders facts more probable than not (see, for example *Murphy* 2.8). It also fails to deal with the fact that evidence will also be relevant if it has a tendency to render another fact *less* probable. What Murphy describes as the "appealing simplicity" of American Federal Rule of Evidence 401 best fits the bill:

"[Relevant evidence] means evidence having any tendency to make the existence of any fact more probable or less probable than it would be without the evidence".

One cannot emphasise too strongly that relevance is not a rule of law. It is therefore at the mercy of commonly held views of society and the individual susceptibilities of the judge (for further discussion see *Cross and Tapper*, 71 to 81). One useful working test (suggested by Stephen and explained more fully in *Cross and Tapper*) is to create a form of syllogism in which the item of evidence is the Minor Premise and the Major Premise is a proposition that the court would regard as true. It is not therefore a "true" syllogism in that the Major Premise, far from being a certainty is often not even identified, but just assumed. Those seeking a deeper discussion of these principles should read Chapter 3 of *Anderson, Schum and Twining*.

Example 1:

Major Premise	If a car is hit by a truck it will probably suffer damage;	**4–08**
Minor Premise	(Evidence) D's truck hit C's car; therefore	
Conclusion	It is more probable that D's truck probably damaged C's car.	

All pretty uncontroversial stuff, but as we can see in the following examples, the relevance of a particular piece of evidence may become somewhat more controversial and the formulation of the Major Premise may be shaped by assumptions that lack any evidential basis. **4–09**

Example 2:

Major Premise	Witnesses with convictions for dishonesty are less likely to be truthful;	**4–10**
Minor Premise	(Evidence) W has a conviction for dishonesty; therefore	

| Conclusion | It is more probable that W's evidence is less worthy of belief that a witness who has no convictions for dishonesty. |

Example 3:

4–11

Major Premise	People who change their account of an event are at best inaccurate and at worst untruthful witnesses;
Minor Premise	(Evidence) W's oral evidence differs in a material way from the contents of his witness statement; *therefore*
Conclusion	It is less probable that W's evidence can be relied on.

Example 4:

4–12

Major Premise	Debtors who fail to respond to several letters from a creditor demanding payment are doing so to try and delay payment of the debt;
Minor Premise	(Evidence) D has failed to reply to 4 letters from C demanding settlement of an outstanding debt; *therefore*
Conclusion	It is more probable that D is evading payment of the debt he owes to C.

4–13   One could go on playing this game ad infinitum, but, as you can see, it does serve a useful purpose. However much you may agree or disagree with the Major Premises and the Conclusions drawn from them, it gets you thinking about whether or not the above inferences, which judges are regularly invited to draw, are actually tenable.

2. Circumstantial vs Direct Evidence

4–14   Those looking for a comprehensive analysis of what is meant by the term "circumstantial" as opposed to "direct" evidence are advised to begin by reading 31 to 50 of *Cross and Tapper*. Most of the examples that are given of circumstantial evidence tend to be in criminal cases largely because, as a matter of common sense, criminals will try not to commit their offences in full public view.

4–15   <u>Example:</u> D is charged with burglary of a dwelling. The evidence against him consists of the following testimony:

(1) Of W1, that he was seen behaving suspiciously outside the burgled house 10 minutes before the occupants went out for the evening;

(2) Of W2, a fingerprint officer, that D's fingerprints have been found inside the house;

(3) Of W3, the occupant, who identifies an item of jewellery as her own; which

(4) W4, the arresting officer, says was found on D's person when he was arrested near the scene of the crime later that evening.

In the above example the tribunal of fact is being asked to *interpret* the evidence in a way which requires a greater degree of inference than if it were confronted with the evidence of an eyewitness who had observed the offence being committed at first hand. Wigmore (see *A Treatise on the Anglo-American System of Evidence* (Tillers revision, 1983), vol.1A, para.43) sought to place circumstantial evidence into three categories:

(1) "Prospectant"—Events that *precede* a fact in issue: the evidence of W1 in the above example would fit into this category;

(2) "Concomitant"—Events that are roughly *contemporaneous* to a fact in issue: the evidence of W2 in the above example would fit this description; and

(3) "Retrospectant"—Events that occur *after* a fact in issue, the evidence of W3 and W4 above being examples.

The exigencies of practice are such that it will not be feasible to spend too much time subjecting evidence to the detailed analysis that Dean Wigmore sets out in his treatise, nevertheless, the above classifications have served their purpose if they get you thinking about the uses to which a particular piece of evidence may be put.

It is much easier to find examples of circumstantial evidence in reports of criminal cases, but the following examples from civil claims should be enough to give the general idea as to how far one can go in trawling for such evidence. In *Joy v Phillips, Mills and Co Ltd* [1916] 1 K.B. 849, a claim was being made on behalf of a stable boy who had been killed as a result of a kick from a horse. The defendants were permitted to adduce evidence that he had teased that horse on previous occasions. The speed at which a vehicle was being driven either shortly before or after an accident is some evidence of the speed it was being driven at the time of the accident (see *Beresford v St Albans Justices* (1905) 22 T.L.R. 1).

3. Examples of Circumstantial Evidence

It is important to bear in mind that since relevance is not a matter of law, the examples given below should not be treated as precedents. **4–16**

Nevertheless, there are some types of circumstantial evidence that are so generally accepted that it can be stated with a degree of confidence that no objection will be taken to their relevance.

(a) *Business Practices*

4–17   Perhaps the most important example is proof of postage, not least because of the provisions in CPR 6 as to service of the claim form. Now is not the time to furnish a treatise on the perils lurking within that rule (see Chapter 8 of *O'Hare and Browne*, in particular 8–014 to 8–021), but suffice it to say that the date upon which a claim form was sent by first class post may on occasions be crucial. The reason for this is that under CPR 6.7 (see, in particular, *Cranfield v Bridgegrove* [2003] 1 W.L.R. 2441) a claim form is conclusively presumed to have been served the second day after it was sent by first class post. This will be the case even if that day is a Sunday, Christmas Day or a Bank Holiday. If a claimant is put to strict proof of service he will be able to rely upon *Trotter v McAllen* (1879) 13 Ch. 574 in which it was held that proof of posting may be furnished by evidence that:

(1) The letter was entered in the office letter book; and

(2) According to the practice of the office, all letters so entered were posted immediately.

Interestingly, this method of proof came to the rescue of the claimants in *Anderton v Clwyd County Council (No.2)* [2002] 1 W.L.R. 3174, one of the numerous recent appeals on CPR 6.7 (see [71]). That apart, there are few modern examples of this type of evidence appearing in reported cases. However, it is not uncommon for evidence of business practices to be confidently presented as if the court is bound to accept them. A common example is the area manager of a retailer giving evidence in a consumer claim based on breach of an express warranty in which he states:

"All our staff are specifically instructed not to give express warranties on products."

If that is the defendants' only evidence, a successful result is by no means assured. However, on occasions, evidence of system may be crucial, as the case of *Wisniewski v Central Manchester Health Authority* [1998] P.I.Q.R. 324 discussed further at 4–20 shows.

(b) *Mechanical Devices*

4–18   A party will not normally be put to strict proof that a device such as a speedometer (*Nicholas v Penny* [1950] 2 K.B. 466) and traffic lights (*Tingle Jacobs & Co v Kennedy* [1964] 1 W.L.R. 638) were in working order at the relevant time. However there has to be an underlying assumption that, as a matter of common knowledge, the device is of a kind that is generally accurate or in working order before this presumption can be applied. It is interesting to note the way in which computer evidence, initially treated with such scepticism that proof of proper functioning was required under s.5 of the Civil Evidence Act 1968, is now admitted as a matter of course.

(c) *Silence*
A court may always be invited to draw adverse inferences from a party's conduct out of court, for example, silence in the face of accusations or the destruction or forging of material documents (see, for example, *Arrow Nominees v Blackledge*, unreported June 22, 2000). This is because there is no general equivalent to the "right to silence" (see *Halford v Brooks* [1991] 1 W.L.R. 428) which exists in criminal proceedings. The most notable recent example is *Francisco v Diedrick* [1998], *The Times*, April 1. In that case the parents of the deceased bought a civil action against the defendant, the prime suspect in their daughter's murder who as at the date of trial some years later, had still not been charged. The claimants succeeded largely on the basis of inferences the judge drew from his failure to attend trial or to answer questions when interviewed under caution by the police. He was, in fact subsequently re-arrested and tried and convicted of murder on the basis of DNA evidence.

4–19

(d) *Failure to Call a Material Witness*
The House of Lords made it clear in *Herrington v British Railways Board* [1972] A.C. 877 that such inferences were permissible. In that case, the infant plaintiff had suffered injury while trespassing onto a railway line owned and managed by the defendants. His ability to gain access was greatly facilitated by the fact that a chain link fence bordering the line had been pressed down so that it was now only 10 inches from the ground. It was alleged that this state of affairs had existed for some weeks before the plaintiff had trespassed on the line. The defendants elected to call no evidence as to the maintenance procedures in relation to the fence. Lord Diplock (at 930F–931B) stated:

4–20

"This is a legitimate tactical move in our adversarial system of litigation. But a defendant who adopts it cannot complain if the court draws from the facts which have been disclosed all reasonable inferences as to what are the facts which the defendant has chosen to withhold.
    A court can take judicial notice that railway lines are regularly patrolled by linesmen and gagders. In the absence of evidence to the contrary, it is entitled to infer that one or more of them in the course

of several weeks noticed what was plain for all to see . . . A court is accordingly entitled to infer from the inaction of the appellants that one or more of their employees decided to allow the risk to continue of some child crossing the boundary and being injured or killed by the live rail rather than to incur the trivial trouble and expense of repairing the gap in the fence."

This principle can also be seen operating in *Wisniewski v Central Manchester HA* [1998] P.I.Q.R. P 324.

4–21   **Facts:** C suffered catastrophic brain damage as a result of partial asphyxiation by the umbilical cord during delivery. The judge found that D was negligent due to the fact that the midwife sister had failed to alert the Senior House Officer ("SHO") Dr R sufficiently promptly. Since this was a case of "negligence by omission" C's team had to prove that either:

(1) If Dr R had been called he would have proceeded to emergency caesarean delivery; or

(2) That *any* competent doctor would have taken those steps.

Dr R, who was in Australia at the time made a short statement in which he simply said that he had no independent recollection of the incident. He did not deal with what he would have done if he *had* been alerted.

The trial judge found for the claimant under both limbs. Most significantly from an evidential point of view, having grudgingly admitted Dr R's statement as hearsay evidence, the judge went on to infer that if Dr R had been called to give evidence he would have admitted under cross-examination that he *would* have proceeded to emergency caesarean. Although the Court of Appeal was prepared to allow the defendants' appeal under the second limb of the "*Bolitho* test" (see 3–29), it upheld the judge's finding on the first limb, holding that that:

(1) Provided a party could establish a prima facie case by other evidence;

(2) The court may be entitled to draw adverse inferences from the absence or silence of a witness who might be expected to have material evidence to give on an issue in an action;

(3) The full inference could only be drawn if there was no reasonable explanation for failure to call the witness;

(4) If the court is willing to draw such inferences they may go to strengthen the evidence of the opposing party or weaken the case of the person who might reasonably have been expected to call the absent witness.

Three important features of this of this case merit further discussion. Firstly, it is essential that the claimant establish a prima facie case by other evidence. As Brooke L.J. states (at 343):

"In my judgment the judge was entitled to adopt the course he chose to adopt. The plaintiff had established a prima facie, if weak, case that a doctor who attended Mrs Wisniewski at 3.40 am would probably have adopted the course that the plaintiff's expert witnesses had told him it was his duty to adopt."

An example of a case in which a claimant failed to establish a prima facie case and, hence, could not rely on any adverse inference from the defendants' failure to call evidence can be found in the Court of Appeal decision in *Hughes v Liverpool City Council* (Lexis Transcript, March 11, 1988) referred to by Brooke L.J. (at 339). Secondly, the litigation conduct of the defendants in this case did not help them. They had ignored warnings from the trial judge given at pre-trial review as to the inferences he might draw if Dr R were not called. They had been so late with service of their witness statements that the plaintiff had been forced to obtain an "unless" order, and they had prepared a statement for Dr R which totally failed to deal with what he would have done if he had been alerted. Finally, they had only served a hearsay notice in respect of Dr R's statement at the eleventh hour. All of this was strong circumstantial evidence in its own right. The case also provides a useful illustration of the potential impact that "system" evidence (see 4–17) can sometimes have. Brooke L.J. stated (at 343):

". . . there was [also] a deafening silence from the other members of the relevant medical team at the hospital . . . If such evidence had tended to show that the doctors at the hospital would be likely to adopt a "wait and see" approach, it would have been much more difficult for the judge to make a finding that Dr R would have adopted a different course if he had in fact attended".

Wisniewski has since been approved and applied in *Society of Lloyds v Jaffray* [2002] EWCA Civ 1101 and *Benham v Kythira Investments Ltd* [2003] EWCA 1794. Of course, if a party does not attend *at all* there is nothing to stop the court proceeding in his absence under CPR 39.3 (see further 14–02 and *O'Hare and Browne* 37–009).

(e) *"Padding"*

It is commonplace to find that the material facts that are essential **4–22** to proving or refuting a claim are set in a narrative, much of which may not be directly relevant to determination of the claim. This is generally accepted on the basis that if the recital of the facts were too prosaic it would not have sufficiently "come to life" to engage the interest of the tribunal of fact. Such evidence is sometimes referred to as part of the *res gestae*, and in criminal cases has generated a significant amount of case law. So far as civil claims are concerned, no useful purpose is to be served by the use of a term that is essentially meaningless. From a practical point of view however it is important, especially when drafting witness statements not to overdo the "padding". This issue is discussed further at 11–50.

4–23   *Conclusion*   It is not possible to draw any hard and fast conclusions as to whether the above examples are matters of law rather than fact. Nevertheless, it may be appropriate on occasions to refer the court to previous decisions, *Wisniewski's* case being an obvious example.

III "SIMILAR FACT" AND CHARACTER EVIDENCE

4–24   *1. Identifying the Problem*
In every case involving "similar fact" evidence the problem is always the same, namely:

"Is evidence of an event ("Event A") so far removed in time (and/or place) from the events that constitute the facts in issue ("Event B") that it is to be regarded as a wholly separate event in some way logically probative of one or more of the material facts necessary to prove Event B?"

The terms "Event A" and "Event B" will continue to be used throughout this section for the purpose of explaining this concept. Perhaps it can be expressed more simply as:

"Is what happened on Tuesday or Thursday logically probative of what happened on Wednesday?"

A simple diagram will suffice to illustrate the problem and also its relative ease of solution.

EVENT A   EVENT B

(PROOF)   (MORE PROBABLE)

D'S CAR DOING 60 IN A   D DRIVING NEGLIGENTLY AT
30 MPH AREA   TIME OF COLLISION

If Event A takes place a few seconds before (or after) Event B, as a matter of common sense everyone would agree that it is highly relevant as to the speed that the defendant was doing at the time of the collision. As Lord Bingham states in *O'Brien v Chief Constable of South Wales* [2005] 2 A.C. 534 9 at [4]):

> "that evidence of what happened on an earlier occasion may make the occurrence of what happened on the occasion in question more or less probable can scarcely be denied".

But what if "Event A" took place half an hour before "Event B", or took place 5, 10 or 20 miles away? Again, basic common sense dictates that the relevance of "Event A" diminishes as it becomes further removed in time and space from "Event B" unless perhaps, there is something so striking about it that it assumes a peculiar relevance.

Example: D, a 19 year old driver is sued in negligence for knocking 4–25 down a small child in a residential estate. His defence is that he was driving sedately along the road when the child ran out in front of him giving him no opportunity to stop.

Supposing that there was evidence available from a number of res- 4–26 idents that he was in the habit of "hot-wheeling" round the estate at high speeds and several people had had to jump for cover to avoid being hit by him. There is no doubt that the claimant would want to get that evidence before the court. Furthermore, there is, arguably, a sufficient degree of probative force to make it relevant to the standard of driving of the defendant on the occasion in question. However, the problem is complicated by the fact that proof of "Event A" reveals *bad behaviour* by the defendant on an earlier occasion, a complication that would increase if he had been convicted of driving at a high speed in the estate (the extent to which previous convictions are admissible in civil proceedings and the use to which they may be put, is considered further at 4–54). The court would then have to consider whether admitting the evidence (often loosely termed "character evidence") would unfairly prejudice the defendant. Not only that, but there is the additional issue of whether the previous bad behaviour conviction is relevant to the defendant's *credibility* as a witness (again, loosely referred to as "character evidence"). As the following summary will show, "similar fact" and "character" evidence are in reality separate concepts albeit that they frequently overlap.

"Similar Fact" Evidence It can now be confidently stated as a result 4–27 of the House of Lords' decision in *O'Brien v Chief Constable for South Wales* [2005] 2 A.C. 534 that there are no special rules as to the

admission of similar fact evidence even where it does have the effect of revealing earlier (or later) bad behaviour, including previous convictions. In every case the only issues are:

(1) Is the evidence of "Event A" relevant to any of the facts in issue in the claim before the court ("Event B")? and

(2) Is the evidence of "Event A" sufficiently relevant and proportionate to justify its admission under CPR 32.1?

4–28   *"Character Evidence"*   Not Relied on as "Similar Fact" Evidence
As noted earlier (4–28), witness credibility is an important form of circumstantial evidence. The relevance of a witness's "character", in the sense of previous convictions or other reprehensible behaviour, to his credibility as a witness will be considered further at 4–38.

4–29   *"Good Character"*   At common law (see 4–44), a party has never been able to directly rely either on his own good character or that of his witnesses as being potentially relevant either to the facts in issue or their credibility as witnesses. This runs contrary to the principle in criminal cases where, exceptionally, an accused's good character is relevant both to disposition and credibility (see *R. v Aziz* [1996] A.C. 41, and the full discussion of the history of this anomaly in Chapter 18 of *Phipson*). Even if it were technically admissible in a civil claim, it is more than likely that it would be ignored on the grounds of irrelevance.

2. *"Similar Fact" Cases Where "Character" is not Involved*
4–30   There may well be cases in which "Event A", although removed in time and place, does not involve any reprehensible or criminal behaviour at all. Nevertheless such previous events may be highly relevant to facts in issue in the claim ("Event B"). For example the evidence in *McWilliams v Sir William Arrol & Co Ltd* [1962] 1 W.L.R. 295 that the deceased steel erector was not in the habit of wearing a safety belt, and that the deceased stable lad in *Joy v Phillips, Mills & Co Ltd* [1916] 1 K.B. 849 was in the habit of teasing the horse that caused his death, are hardly instances of "reprehensible" behaviour. Foolhardy maybe, even reckless, but hardly evidence of (bad) character in the sense that the term is employed in criminal cases. Another example of this type of similar fact evidence being relied on would be where a party was seeking to prove the terms of a contract by reference to the course of dealing between the parties. "System" evidence of the type referred to by Brooke L.J. in *Wisniewski v Central Manchester Health Authority* [1998] P.I.Q.R. (P) 324 (see 4–21) is another obvious example. Delving back into the past could, hypothetically, have produced a different

result. Suppose, for example, that there had been a similar incident in the past, the medical team had adopted a "wait and see" policy, and the same catastrophic consequences had ensued. Even if their conduct in the earlier case were held to be *entirely beyond reproach*, the claimant would have been anxious to introduce this evidence because it would be relevant to a known risk which the defendants should have taken steps to avoid in the future.

3. *"Similar Fact" Cases Where Character is Involved*

Even before the decision in *O'Brien* civil courts were more willing to admit this type of evidence than in criminal cases, especially in non-jury trials. The existence of this more relaxed approach was acknowledged by Lord Denning M.R. in *Mood Music Publishing Co Ltd v De Wolfe Ltd* [1976] Ch. 119. The claim was one in which the claimants asserted that the defendants had infringed their copyright in a musical composition known as "Sogno Nostalgico". The defendants asserted in their defence that although the infringing work was similar, the similarity was coincidental. The claimants were permitted to adduce evidence that this defence had been raised on previous occasions, one of which involved an "entrapment" operation by the claimants. In upholding the decision of the trial judge to admit the evidence, Lord Denning M.R. stated (at 127):

> "The criminal courts have been very careful not to admit such evidence unless its probative value is so strong that it should be received in the interests of justice: and its admission will not operate unfairly to the accused. In civil cases the courts have followed a similar line, but will not be so chary of admitting it. In civil cases the courts will admit evidence of similar facts if it is logically relevant in determining the matter which is in issue provided that it is not oppressive or unfair to the other side: and also that the other side has fair notice of it and is able to deal with it."

The civil courts were also more comfortable with the use of similar fact evidence even when it involved trying a number of similar allegations together. In *Maes Finance v Leftleys* [1998] P.N.L.R. 193 Jacob J. ordered five professional negligence claims involving conveyancing transactions to be tried together. He expressed confidence in the view that any Chancery judge would have no difficulty in deciding what probative value, if any, the findings of fact in *Claim 1* had in respect of *Claims 2* to *5*. Neuberger J. adopted a similar approach in *Bradford and Bingley BS v Boyce Evans Shepherd* [1998] P.N.L.R. 250, holding that the claimants were entitled to amend their original claim, which was for breach of contract, negligence and breach of fiduciary duty, to one of equitable fraud. This was based on the

4–31

allegation that the claimants had discovered that an employee of the defendants had acted on a similar suspicious transaction for the same client albeit through a different building society. The judge also made an order for discovery of the solicitor's file on the other transaction.

4–32   *O'Brien's Case*   As already stated, the law in this area has now been authoritatively considered and clarified by the House of Lords in *O'Brien v Chief Constable of South Wales* [2005] 2 A.C. 534. In effect the decision establishes that this type of evidence is not subject to any special relevancy criteria over and above those required for any other type of evidence.

4–33   Facts: In 1998 C was convicted along with two others of the murder of Philip Saunders. Having served 11 years of his sentence his conviction was quashed by the Court of Appeal (see [2000] Crim. L.R. 676). Having received substantial compensation from the Government (£670,000) he now was suing the Chief Constable for malicious prosecution and misfeasance in public office. The core of his claim related to the conduct of certain police officers at Cardiff Police Station who, it was alleged, subjected him and his co-accused to improper pressure in order to obtain convictions. He wished to introduce evidence relating to two other high profile prosecutions in which the same investigating team had been involved and the same categories of improper conduct were alleged. H.H. Judge Graham Jones, at a case management conference, ruled that evidence relating to the other two investigations was admissible. D appealed to the Court of Appeal who upheld the judge's ruling ([2003] EWCA Civ 1085). D appealed further to the House of Lords.

The main speech was delivered by Lord Phillips (with whom the other four members of the House agreed). In it, he established three important principles regarding "similar fact" evidence in civil claims.

(1) *The Relevance Issue*
4–34   Counsel for the defendant had sought to argue that in order to be admissible in civil proceedings a test of "enhanced relevance" or "higher probative value" had to be met. This argument was roundly rejected by Lord Phillips (at [53]):

> "I can see no warrant for the automatic application of either of these tests as a rule of law in a civil suit. To do so would build into our civil procedure as inflexibility which is inappropriate and undesirable. I would simply apply the test of relevance as the test of admissibility of similar fact evidence in a civil suit. Such evidence is admissible if it is potentially probative of an issue in the action."

(2) *The Case Management Issue*

The second argument advanced by the defendant was that the intro-   **4–35**
duction of such evidence would so affect the trial that it would be
overwhelmed by collateral issues (a misgiving that Lord Rodger
clearly held (see [64])). While accepting that the court had a wide discretion to exclude evidence that was technically admissible in the
interests of case management, the House was unanimously of the
view that Judge Graham's exercise of discretion was not susceptible
to review. Lord Phillips stated (at [54]):

> "[There] are policy considerations which the judge who has
> the management of the litigation will wish to keep well in mind.
> CPR 1.2 requires the court to give effect to the overriding objec-
> tive of dealing with cases justly. This includes dealing with the
> case in a way which is proportionate to what is involved in the case
> and in a manner which is expeditious and fair. CPR 1.4 requires
> the court actively to manage the case in order to further the over-
> riding objective. CPR 32.1 gives the court the power to exclude
> evidence that would other wise be admissible and to limit cross-
> examination".

As already noted at 1–52, the effect of the CPR, especially CPR
32.1(2) has been to make the admissibility of evidence in civil trials
to a large extent a matter of judicial discretion.

(3) *Prejudice*

The final argument put by counsel for the defendant was that the   **4–36**
admission of evidence of the other two investigations would be
unduly prejudicial to the defendant. Although, ultimately, the house
did not overturn the decision of Judge Graham Jones to admit the
evidence it is clear that discretion to exclude unduly prejudicial evidence does exist. Lord Phillips stated (at [41]):

> "Similar fact evidence will not necessarily risk causing any unfair
> prejudice to the party against whom it is directed . . . It may
> however carry such a risk. Evidence of impropriety which reflects
> adversely on the character of a party may risk causing prejudice
> that is disproportionate to its relevance, particularly where the trial
> is taking place before a jury. In such a case the judge will be astute
> to see that the probative cogency of the evidence justifies the risk
> of prejudice in the interests of a fair trial".

Conclusion Introducing evidence that is removed in time and place   **4–37**
from the "core" events is subject to the same relevancy principles as any
other type of circumstantial evidence, even if it has a tendency to reveal

bad behaviour (including conviction for a criminal offence) by a party. However, you may need to explain to the court in detail both why the evidence is relevant and why its admission will tend to further the over-riding objective. The need to do this may well arise at an early stage in the litigation, possibly, even on an application for pre-claim disclosure (for a recent example in injunction proceedings, see *Abbey National plc v JSN Finance and Currency Exchange Co Ltd* [2006] EWCA Civ 328). The Claimant in *O'Brien's* case ultimately succeeded because:

(1) He was able to highlight a significant number of similarities between the conduct of the officers in his case and in the other two investigations;

(2) There were major public interest issues involved.

The decision can be usefully contrasted with the earlier decision in *Tomlinson v Chief Constable of Hertfordshire* [2001] EWCA Civ 461 in which the Court of Appeal held that the trial judge had rightly refused the Claimant's permission to call evidence of an alleged campaign of police harassment. It was a jury trial on liability only, in which the claimants were seeking damages for false imprisonment and malicious prosecution. The allegations of harassment were all alleged to have taken place after the date of arrest and charge; accordingly they threw no light on the state of mind of the relevant officers at the time of the events in issue in the case.

4. "Bad Character Evidence" Generally
(a) *Overview*

4–38 As we can now see, "character" in the sense of a chequered past can become an issue in one of three ways, namely when:

(1) It is revealed as a result of "similar fact" evidence being admitted, as explained in the previous section;

(2) Rarely, a party's "character" in the sense of his reputation, is a fact in issue in the case in question;

(3) It is a relevant factor in assessing the credibility of a witness's evidence (including the evidence given by a party).

Basically, how a person has behaved on an occasion other than the one which gives rise to the claim is either relevant or it is not. Whether it is "good" behaviour or "bad" behaviour is secondary to the core issue of relevance. Civil trials also differ from criminal ones in the sense that individual character is often far less important in relation to the facts in issue.

Examples:

(1) C sues D in defamation;   **4–39**

(2) C sues D in negligence for injuries sustained in a road traffic accident;

(3) C sues D in contract for breach of the implied condition as to reasonable quality in s.14(2) Sale of Goods Act.

In example (1) the claimant's "character", in the sense of his reputation, may be a crucial issue when it comes to assessing damages. However, in examples (2) and (3) the defendant's character is largely irrelevant. Negligence is a tort of inadvertence in which the personality of the tortfeasor is often neither here nor there. In example (3) the defendant may be a quite admirable fellow or an absolute rogue; it is largely irrelevant to the issue of whether or not the goods sold complied with the implied condition in s.14(2). However, if there were to be a factual dispute in any of the above cases the court's approach might be different. For example, if the defendant in example (2) were to swear blind that he was only doing 25 miles per hour, or the defendant in example (3) were to state with equal conviction that he had specifically drawn the complained of defect to the buyer's attention before purchase, the court might be less inclined to believe their stories if they had a number of previous convictions. The court's scepticism might well be increased further if it were to be informed that, not only were they, respectively convictions for dangerous driving and dishonesty, but that on each occasion the defendant had pleaded "not guilty".

(b) *"Character" as a Fact in Issue*
The most commonly cited example is in relation to libel and slander,   **4–40**
but as stated in *Murphy* (see 5.4) even here, relevance has a role to play. As *Murphy* states, the local government official who maintains that he has been wrongly accused of corruption will no doubt have his financial dealings put under the microscope, but the court is unlikely to allow in evidence of his sexual habits or the fact that he is cruel to animals (for a full discussion see *Phipson* 17–04). A more everyday example can be found in the field of housing law. In deciding whether or not it is "reasonable" to make a possession order against a secure or assured tenant who has been found to have behaved anti-socially the court will often be asked to examine much wider aspects of the defendant's character, including the whole history of his response to complaints both before and after the behaviour complained of (see, for example *Solon Housing Association v James* [2004] EWCA Civ 1857). Similar "character" issues may arise in the aftermath of a possession order when the tenant applies for

execution of a possession warrant to be suspended (see *Sheffield City Council v Hopkins* [2002] H.L.R. 12).

4-41 **Facts:** D had a suspended possession order made against her on the grounds of rent arrears. The terms of the suspension having been broken, C issued a warrant for eviction. On D's application to suspend the warrant C wanted to introduce evidence of acts of nuisance by D. The DJ refused to admit them.

4-42 The Court of Appeal held that evidence of other incidents of this kind were admissible, subject to adequate proof, proportionality and the defendant being given due notice. Incidents both after and before the date of the order were admissible although those arising after the date of the original order were likely to be more compelling.

(c) *"Character" and Credibility*

4-43 As a general rule, character evidence, including evidence of previous convictions, is admissible if it is relevant to a witness's credibility. Parties to the proceedings are treated no differently to any other witness in this regard. However it is subject to two constraints. Firstly, under the Rehabilitation of Offenders Act 1974, a conviction becomes "spent" after the prescribed period has expired. The effect of this is, by virtue of s.4(1), to treat the convictions as if it had never taken place although there is a residual discretion to admit spent convictions under s.7(3) of the 1974 Act (see further 14–50). Secondly, the court has always had a discretion to curtail reference to previous convictions, especially in cross-examination on the grounds of irrelevance or oppression or in exercise of its powers under CPR 32.1(3) An interesting example of these powers in action can be seen in *Watson v CC Cleveland Police* [2001] EWCA Civ 1547. The claimant was suing the police for damages for assault and malicious prosecution. He had no less that 58 previous convictions, 31 for dishonesty and 27 for a mixed bag including numerous convictions for driving whilst disqualified, one for affray and two for assault. The trial judge restricted the cross-examination to the assault offences and the defendant appealed. Although the decision of the trial judge, taken on grounds of relevance and proportionality, was upheld, Sir Murray Stuart-Smith (with whom Chadwick L.J. agreed) indicated that he would have permitted cross-examination on *all* the convictions.

5. *Relevance of Good Character*

4-44 Here is not the place to go into whether or not respectable appearance and demeanour influence the court to any great extent. However, the usual advice given to clients and their witnesses is that they should be on their best behaviour when giving evidence. No one would suggest that that is bad advice. At common law, which still governs the admission of good character in both civil and criminal proceedings, good character evidence is inadmissible in civil proceedings both on the issue of witness credibility (including that of the parties) and on the main issues in the case. Nevertheless, as *Phipson* states at para. 18–23, practice has been somewhat lax in this area. A classic example is the paragraph that almost invariably appears in witness statements in road traffic cases stating that:

"I have held a driving licence for 15 years and have no motoring convictions."

One wonders why practitioners persist in including it; perhaps it is out of fear that if it were omitted, the court would infer that the witness had a whole string of motoring convictions.

IV CONTROL OF RELEVANCE UNDER CPR 32.1

We have already seen (see 1–52) how CPR 32.1(1) gives the court wide powers to control the evidence, including power in CPR 32.1(2) to exclude evidence that would otherwise be admissible and to limit cross examination (CPR 32.1(3)). The breadth of discretion given to the court can be seen from the earlier discussion of the *O'Brien* decision (see 4–31). Since the discretion is so wide, whenever you seek to rely on evidence that is not obviously relevant or seek disclosure of documents over which there is a similar question mark, it is essential that you analyse precisely what issue the evidence relates to. If you do not, you run the risk of your application failing. **4–45**

V PRESUMPTIONS

The writer has always been unable to understand why presumptions should be regarded as rules of law at all, bearing in mind that relevance as a general rule is not. Nevertheless they occupy an important place in the traditional rules of evidence. **4–46**

A Introduction

The term "presumption" is used somewhat indiscriminately to embrace three different concepts: **4–47**

(1) *Rules of law* that define aspects of the burden of proof such as "the presumption of innocence" and the "presumption of

sanity". These are not in reality rules of evidence as such but simply examples of well established principles of substantive law. They will not be discussed further.

(2) *"Legal Presumptions"*. These are situations in which either at common law or by statute, on proof of a certain fact or facts (FACT A) the court is bound to infer (FACT B). Common examples include the presumptions of legitimacy and death. This category of presumptions is further subdivided into:

- "Irrebuttable Presumptions": these speak for themselves; not only is the court bound to infer FACT B from FACT A, but the party against whom it is tendered is debarred from calling any evidence to try and rebut it; and
- "Rebuttable Presumptions" in which the other party is entitled to call rebutting evidence. Whether or not he is also charged with the burden of disproving FACT B or simply adducing evidence that is capable of rebutting it depends on the presumption involved.

(3) *"Evidential Presumptions"*. These are really no more than examples of circumstantial evidence that, due to regular usage have acquired quasi-legal status.

"Legal" and "Evidential" presumptions will now be considered in turn.

B "Legal" Presumptions

1. "Proof Without Evidence"?

4–48   Legal presumptions are often placed with Judicial Notice, Estoppal and Admissions (see further Chapter 6) as a method of proof in which the party relying on it is able to prove a material fact (FACT B) without adducing any evidence. With respect, this analysis is incorrect, because the party relying on the presumption has still got to prove the foundation facts (FACT A) before the presumption is triggered. They only differ from mainstream circumstantial evidence in that:

(1) FACT B is found not as a result of deductive judicial reasoning, but by operation of a rule of law;

(2) The foundation facts (FACT A) required to prove FACT B are fixed (it is no good seeking to rely on the presumption of death based on six years and 364 days absence); and

(3) Once FACT A is proved, the court is bound to find FACT B (subject on occasions to the other party's right to call rebutting evidence); there is no room for judicial reasoning.

The more important presumptions will now be considered in turn.

2. Irrebuttable Presumptions of Law

4-49 In truth, you could go through your whole legal career without ever encountering one of these in practice. The most well known is s.13 of the Civil Evidence Act 1968 (as amended by s.12 of the Defamation Act 1996) which provides that:

> "(1) In an action for libel or slander in which the question of whether [the claimant] did or did not commit a criminal offence is relevant to an issue arising in the action, proof that, at the time when that issue falls to be determined, he stands convicted of that offence shall be conclusive evidence that he committed that offence; and his conviction thereof shall be admissible in evidence accordingly".

An amendment introduced by the 1996 Act (1968 Act, s.2A) deals with cases where there is more than one claimant. It should be noted that, although this presumption only apples to defamation proceedings, if a claimant were to bring subsequent civil proceedings based on the fact that a previous conviction of his was erroneous, it is more than likely that his claim would be struck out as an abuse of process (see further 6–51 and *Hunter v CC West Midlands Police* [1982] A.C. 529. A rather more mundane, but vitally important, presumption is that created by CPR 6.7(1) which provides that:

> "A document which is served in accordance with these rules, or any relevant practice direction shall be deemed to be served on the day shown in the following table . . ."

That table contains a number of presumed dates for service, the most important of which is that a document, including a Claim Form, sent by first class post to the address for service (see CPR 6.5 and *O'Hare and Browne* 8–001 to 8–012) shall be conclusively presumed to have arrived on:

> "The second day after it was posted".

A line of Court of Appeal decisions, concluding with *Cranfield v Bridgegrove* [2003] 1 W.L.R. 2441 has confirmed that this presumption applies even though:

(1) The second day after posting is a Sunday, Christmas Day or Bank Holiday; and

(2) The recipient or the person serving it can prove that the document arrived on a different day.

The conclusive nature of the presumption will apply to any of the other methods of service referred to in the table in CPR 6.7(1); practitioners ignore it at their peril.

3. Rebuttable Presumptions of Law

4–50 These are somewhat more numerous although, once again, they do not have a very large part to play in mainstream civil litigation. For a fuller discussion see *Phipson* 6–16 to 6–31. The only two that will be considered in any detail will be previous convictions admitted under s.11 of the Civil Evidence Act 1968 and res ipsa loquitur.

(a) *Legitimacy*

4–51 It is presumed that a child born in wedlock is legitimate unless the child is born more than nine months after the parties ceased to live together or were judicially separated. In the latter case the presumption is reversed. Section 26 of the Family Law Act now specifically provides that the presumption is rebuttable on the balance of probabilities (see further *Phipson* 6–22—23).

(b) *Death*

4–52 It is possible to prove a person's death by adducing evidence that he has not been heard of for seven years by those who, if he had been alive, would have been likely to have heard of him. There is nothing to prevent a person seeking to prove a person's death before that date based on circumstantial evidence, and, indeed, a party seeking to prove that a person died on a specific date will always retain the usual burden of proof to the civil standard. The other important presumption relating to death is s.184 of the Law of Property Act 1925 which deals with the situation where two persons die in circumstances where it unclear which survived the other. The section provides that:

". . . such deaths shall (subject to any order of the court), for all purposes affecting the title to property, be presumed to have occurred in order of seniority, and accordingly the younger shall be deemed to have survived the elder".

The relevant law is discussed further in *Phipson* at 6–28.

(c) *Marriage*

4–53 There are two, theoretically, very important presumptions (see further *Phipson*, 6–24) both rebuttable only with the most cogent evidence, namely that:

(1) Any marriage that is proved to have been celebrated de facto is formally valid; and

(2) Cohabitation gives rise to a presumption that the parties are married.

It is the latter presumption that, presumably, gives rise to the still commonly held misconception among members of the public that cohabitation for a period of six months creates the legal status of "common law" marriage.

(d) *Section 11 of the Civil Evidence Act, 1968*

The extent to which judgments and findings of fact in previous proceedings are admissible in evidence is discussed in detail at 6–24. However, the use to which criminal convictions may be put needs to be considered separately because of the rebuttable presumption created by s.11. The circumstances in which criminal convictions may be relevant in subsequent civil proceedings are many and varied as the following examples show.

4–54

Conviction of a party to the claim

(1) D is convicted of careless driving. C later sues D for damages arising out of the *same* event and C wishes to rely on D's conviction as evidence of negligence.

4–55

(2) D, a secure tenant of C local authority, is convicted of supplying a Class A drug at the demised premises. C later wishes to rely on this conviction to establish a ground for possession under Ground 2 in Sch.2 of the Housing Act 1985.

(3) C is claiming damages for breach of an oral contract that D asserts was never entered into. D wishes to put in C's previous conviction for obtaining by deception in order to undermine C's credibility as a witness.

In the first two examples the conviction goes to an *issue* in the case, in the third, simply to C's *credibility* as a witness.

Conviction of a non-Party

(4) Same facts in (1) above except that the conviction is of X, an employee of D's whilst driving in the course of his employment. C wishes to rely on X's conviction to make D vicariously liable for X's negligence.

4–56

(5) Same facts as (2) above except that the conviction is of X, a local drug dealer, the offence being committed on the tenanted

premises. C again wishes to rely on X's conviction (X being a "person visiting") as evidence of Ground 2.

(6) C proposes to call a material witness (W) who has previous convictions for offences of dishonesty. D wishes to put these convictions to W in an attempt to undermine his credibility.

Once again, the first two convictions go to an issue whereas the third simply goes to credibility. At common law, none of these convictions could have been used for the desired purpose as a result of the decision in *Hollington v F Hewthorn & Co Ltd* [1943] K.B. 587. The rationale behind the decision was that, firstly, the conviction was implicitly based on *hearsay* (where were the "eyewitnesses" whose evidence had secured the conviction?). Secondly, it was based on *opinion* evidence (it was simply the opinion of the court that had convicted based on evidence that the civil court had not received). For any readers who find the present rules of evidence unduly permissive, this decision serves as a timely reminder of the difficulties that can arise if the gateways to admissibility are set too narrow. The rule has now been abolished so far as previous convictions in the United Kingdom are concerned by s.11 of the Civil Evidence Act 1968. Note however that the section does not apply to overseas convictions where the rule in *Hollington* will still apply. Furthermore, as we shall see in due course (6–54) the rule still applies, at least in part, to previous findings in *civil* proceedings. Section 11 now provides that:

"(1)   In any civil proceedings the fact that a person has been convicted of an offence by or before any court in the United Kingdom or by a court martial there or elsewhere shall . . . be admissible in evidence for the purposes of proving, *where to do so is relevant to any issue in those proceedings* [author's emphasis], that he committed that offence, whether he was so convicted upon a plea of guilty or otherwise and whether or not he is a party to the civil proceedings; but no other conviction other than a subsisting one shall be admissible in evidence by virtue of this section."

Section 11(2) goes on to provide that:

(1) Proof of the conviction creates a presumption that the person concerned committed the offence until the contrary is proved; and

(2) Proof of the facts on which the conviction was based may be based on the contents of any information, complaint indictment or charge sheet.

Initially there appeared to be some uncertainty as to whether or not the effect of the section was to render admissible merely the *fact* of the conviction as opposed to the *findings of fact* inherent in it (see, in particular, the somewhat conflicting interpretations of the section by Lord Denning M.R. and Buckley L.J. in *Stupple v Royal Insurance Co Ltd* [1971] 1 Q.B. 50 at 72 and 76 respectively). However, it now seems clear that the latter approach is accepted (for a recent example see *Bland v Morris* [2006] EWCA Civ 56). However, bear in mind that convictions introduced under s.11 are subject to the same principles of relevance as any other type of evidence. For example, a conviction for dangerous or careless driving is clearly a highly cogent piece of evidence in any subsequent claim in negligence against the driver because both sets of proceedings are concerned with the *manner* of the defendant's driving. However, some convictions will not fit into this pattern. Supposing instead that the conviction was for failing to stop or was a blood alcohol offence. Both of these convictions would have *some* probative force, but clearly not as much. Once again syllogisms can help determine the level of relevance:

Major premise: People who are responsible for causing accidents tend not to stop.
Minor premise: (Evidence) D was convicted of failing to stop after the accident; therefore
Conclusion: D is liable in negligence.

Clearly, the inference is permissible, and may be that much stronger after the defendant has been cross-examined and given an unsatisfactory explanation as to why he did not stop, but it does not flow as directly from a previous conviction which reflects on the manner of his driving.

Procedural requirements   A party who wishes to rely on s.11 must   **4-57**
give notice of his intention to do so along with prescribed particulars in his Case Statement under CPR 16, PD, 8.1. In particular he is required to state the issue to which it is claimed the conviction relates. The defendant must respond in his defence if he wishes to dispute the conviction in any way; if he does not, he will be taken to have admitted it (see CPR 16.5(5) and 6–05). Although the CPR no longer set out the prescribed responses (as did the former RSC O.18, r.7A) it is suggested that, in practice they should be followed, namely to either:

(1) Deny the conviction ("It wasn't me"); or

(2) Admit the conviction but dispute its correctness ("It was me but I was wrongly convicted"); or

(3) Admit the conviction but dispute its relevance ("It was me, but so what?").

It is only if the defendant pleads (2) above, that the s.11 presumption shifts the burden to him. The claimant would still, for example under (1) above, have to prove that the John Smith named in the Certificate of Conviction is the same John Smith that is now being sued (not necessarily an easy task, as the criminal cases on driving while disqualified show: see *R. v Derwentside Magistrates' Court Ex p. Heaviside* [1996] R.T.R. 601, but see also *West Yorkshire Probation Board v Boulter* [2006] 1 W.L.R. 232). It is now submitted on the basis of *Boulter* that coincidence of name and address will usually be enough to create a prima facie case for coincidence of identity. Proof of the conviction itself will, of course, involve the simple matter of producing a Certified Copy of the Certificate of Conviction from the relevant court records.

4–58 *Section 11 and Case Management*   The extent to which the presumption created by s.11 could be used to strike a "knock out blow", for example by applying to have the defence struck out as an abuse of process or for summary judgment, was considered in a number of cases before the introduction of the CPR. In *Brinks Ltd v Abu-Saleh* [1995] 1 W.L.R. 1448, a tracing claim against 57 defendants who had allegedly facilitated the laundering the proceeds of the notorious Brinks-Mat robbery, the claimants applied for summary judgment against two of the defendants based on their conviction for handling the proceeds. In granting the application Jacob J. held that, in order to stave off summary judgment the defendant must adduce new evidence to justify leave to defend. In fact, he went so far as to say that, in the absence of such new evidence, it was an abuse of process to put the claimant to proof of facts that had already been determined by a criminal court. Subsequent decisions were not prepared to go that far. In *McCauley v Vine* [1999] 1 W.L.R. 1977 the claimant sought summary judgment in a road traffic claim in which the defendant had already been convicted of careless driving. Significantly:

(1) She had pleaded not guilty and therefore there had been a full trial; and

(2) She had been represented by solicitors and counsel.

Although the claimant had succeeded both before the Master and on appeal to the High Court, The Court of Appeal held that, at the summary judgment stage the defendant was only required to raise a "triable issue"; accordingly the judgment was set aside. Crucial to the decision was the fact that the defendant had now obtained a report from an accident reconstruction expert that suggested that she had not been responsible for the accident. Potter L.J. (at 1984F), although acknowledging that Jacob J. may well have been right on the facts of *Brinks* to award summary judgment, felt that he went too far in saying that absent new evidence, it was an abuse of process to challenge the conviction in the later civil claim. He went on to state (at 1984G):

"Of course the provisions of section 11(2) may well enable a plaintiff to proceed under Order 14 [author's note; now CPR 24], relying on an earlier conviction of the defendant as proof of an issue of negligence or dishonesty in civil proceedings. He will be entitled to succeed unless the defendant puts before the court evidence sufficient to satisfy [it] . . . when hearing the [application] that there is in truth and reality an issue to be tried."

A similar approach was adopted by Brian Smedley J. in a strike out application. In *J v Oyston* [1999] 1 W.L.R. 694, the claimant had brought a civil claim for damages for assault based on the defendant's earlier conviction for raping her. The defendant wished to advance the same defence in the civil proceedings (albeit relying on fresh evidence) that the incident had never taken place. In dismissing the claimant's application the judge was clearly unhappy at the idea of the court treating as an abuse of process the very thing that s.11(2) permitted him to do, namely challenge the correctness of the earlier conviction by proving on the balance of probabilities that it was erroneous. He stated:

"Whilst it may be unwise to say that there can never be an abuse where the subsequent civil proceedings are brought against and not by the subject of the criminal proceedings, nonetheless, on the present facts I have no doubt that to use the doctrine of abuse of process so as to prevent the defendant from having reheard, with such new evidence as he seeks to adduce, the issue of guilt would be to cause manifest unfairness."

All of these decisions precede the introduction of the CPR, and one is tempted to suggest that, having regard in particular to the court's enhanced powers to manage cases actively, a defendant who sought to challenge the correctness of an earlier conviction would now have, if anything, an even steeper hill to climb. This is borne out by the recent Court of Appeal decision in *Raja v Van Hoogstraten and others* [2005] EWCA Civ 1235.

4–59   <u>Facts:</u> The family of the late Mr R brought a civil claim against D alleging that he was responsible for the late Mr R's death. It was alleged that he had hired two "hit men" (K and C) to murder him back in July 1999. K and C had both been convicted of murder, D had been convicted of manslaughter but his conviction had been subsequently quashed on appeal. In the civil proceedings the family sought to rely on the convictions of K and C as part of the case against VH. VH sought to challenge the convictions of K and C in the proceedings and that part of his defence was struck out. VH applied for leave to appeal.

4–60   In refusing the application based largely on the fact that the evidence that the defendant sought to introduce late in the day was not capable as it stood of disproving the convictions of K and C for murder, both Brooke and Pill L.JJ emphasised the breadth of discretion given to the case management judge.

4–61   *Conclusion*   It is relatively unusual for a party to dispute the correctness of a conviction, but if he does wish to do so, in practical terms he will need to:

>   (1) Raise the point as soon as possible (unlike in *Van Hoogstraten*);

>   (2) Set out clearly in his defence the basis on which the conviction is being challenged (unlike in *Brinks* or *Van Hoogstraten*); and

>   (3) (Ideally) have some cogent fresh evidence which raises a valid question mark over the propriety of the conviction (as in *McCauley*).

(e) *Res Ipsa Loquitur*

4–62   The so-called "maxim" of *res ipsa loquitur*, or, now that Latin has been declared a proscribed language, "it speaks for itself", is often seen as part of the substantive law of negligence rather than an evidential principle. In fact, it is not a "maxim" at all, but simply a form of circumstantial evidence. The principle is simply stated. In a negligence claim, where the claimant adduces evidence tending to prove that:

>   (1) The activity which caused the claimant damage was under the control of the defendant or his employees; and

>   (2) The incident was such as would not in the ordinary course of things happen without negligence;

the court is entitled to infer negligence unless the defendant adduces evidence which is consistent with the exercise of care on his part. Again, a syllogism will assist.

Major Premise: Cars that are being carefully driven do not mount the pavement for no obvious reason.
Minor Premise: D's car mounted the pavement and injured C for no obvious reason; therefore
Conclusion: D was driving negligently

The practical importance of the so-called maxim has to a large extent disappeared due to the changes in the pleading rules. It used to be the case that a defendant could "hide" behind a bare denial however precise and detailed the claimant's allegations of negligence were. Defences in response to a 54 paragraph Statement of Claim that were only a few lines long and simply stated:

"Paragraphs 5 to 54 are hereby denied"

were by no means a rarity. The *res ipsa loquitur* concept was therefore useful in that it was one way of trying to "smoke out" a positive defence. The CPR have changed the process significantly. As was pointed out at 1–48, CPR 16.5(2) obliges a defendant to "put his head above the parapet" and expressly set out any alternative version of events that he is relying on. Accordingly, if the facts stated in the above example were to arise now, a defendant who simply denied liability without saying why, would be debarred at trial from putting forward an explanation which exonerated him unless the court gave him permission to amend. He might even find that his defence was put under pressure at an earlier stage by an application for further information under CPR 18 (see 10–44) or for summary judgment under CPR 24. An example of the maxim being used in this way can be found in *Bergin v David Wickes TV Ltd* [1994] P.I.Q.R. 167.

Facts: C, a well-known American film actor suffered injury on the film set of "Frankenstein" that was being filmed at Pinewood Studios. A sledge on which he was sitting overturned without explanation whilst being pulled along the studio floor by a motor. As a result of this C suffered a spiral fracture to one of his arms. D served a defence which consisted of a general denial and offered no explanation as to how the accident might have occurred. On C's application under O.14, D simply argued that it was an accident. C's application was refused and he appealed. **4–63**

The Court of Appeal allowed his appeal holding that, since the defendants had accepted that the sledge was under their control and had advanced no explanation as to how the accident might have occurred in a manner that was consistent with due care on their part, for example, the negligence of an independent contractor or an **4–64** unforeseen, unavoidable or fortuitous occurrence, the claimant was entitled to the judgment sought. Although this application was brought under RSC O.14, it is submitted that the same result would have probably ensued if it had been brought under CPR 24 (see further 9–16). Steyn L.J.'s *dictum* (at 168) indicates how, in his view, the "maxim" is simply a label for a form of circumstantial evidence when he states:

> "[it] is in truth not a doctrine, nor a principle, nor a rule. It is simply a convenient label for a group of situations in which an unexplained accident is, as a matter of common sense, the basis for an inference of negligence".

4–65   The principle can also be seen operating at trial in *Widdowson v Newgate Meats* [1998] P.I.Q.R.(P) 138. In it, the Court of Appeal held that the claimant had established a prima facie case where the maxim had been triggered by the introduction of the defendant driver's police interview record. In it he had admitted that he had been unaware of the presence of the claimant at the side of the road until after he had felt a bang and, having stopped and got out, realised that he had hit him. Based on that uncontroverted evidence the Court of Appeal held that the trial judge had wrongly acceded to the defendant's submission of no case to answer.

It is important to bear in mind that providing an explanation will not suffice unless it is consistent with the exercise of due care on the defendant's part. This explains the House of Lords decision in *Henderson v Henry E Jenkins & Sons* [1970] A.C. 282. In that case, the deceased had been killed when a lorry owned and operated by the defendants had careered downhill and struck him. The explanation proffered by the defendants was that this was due to a sudden brake failure caused by corrosion in the brake pipe at a point that was hidden from ordinary visual inspection. The House of Lords ultimately found 3:2 in favour of the claimant's widow. Whether or not the decision sets the standard of care imposed on the defendants at too high a level is perhaps open to argument but, in terms of its evidential significance it is clearly open to a court to reason as follows.

Major Premise:	Vehicles whose brakes fail due to corrosion in the brake pipe probably do so due to poor maintenance;
Minor Premise:	(Evidence) D's vehicle crashed due to a brake failure caused by corrosion of the brake pipe; therefore
Conclusion:	C's death was probably caused by D's negligence due to their failure to maintain the vehicle.

Just like any other form of circumstantial evidence, some inferences are weightier and easier to draw than others.

Burden Stays With Claimant However the burden of proving neg- **4–66**
ligence remains on the claimant throughout. In particular, he will fail
unless he is able to prove that the object or activity that has caused
his injury was under the control of the defendant at the time (see
Easson v London and North Eastern Railway Co [1944] K.B. 421).
Furthermore, absence of explanation on the defendant's part is not
of itself enough. There must be a clear inference of negligence on the
facts as presented by the claimant, otherwise he will fail; see *Ratcliffe
v Plymouth and Torbay HA* [1998] P.I.Q.R. P170. In that case the
claimant had suffered severe nerve damage to his leg as a result of an
operation performed under spinal anaesthetic. All the experts were
agreed that the nerve damage had resulted from an adverse reaction
to the anaesthetic. However there was nothing in the clinical records
to suggest that it had been administered negligently, and nothing in
the patient's medical history to suggest that he was susceptible to such
an adverse reaction. The Court of Appeal agreed with the trial judge
that the fact that spinal injection had caused neurological damage
was not of itself prima facie evidence of negligence because there was
no clear explanation, suggestive of negligence, as to why it had. They
confirmed that the claim had rightly been dismissed on a submission
of no case to answer.

(f) *Statutory presumptions*
A number of presumptions have also been created by statute. A dis- **4–67**
cussion of these is outside the scope of this work. They may be found
by consulting the relevant substantive law. Two important examples
are given below.

Employers' Liability (Defective Equipment) Act 1969 s.1(1): This **4–68**
Act was passed to reverse the effect of the House of Lords' decision
in *Davie v New Merton Board Mills Ltd* [1958] A.C. 604 under which
it was held that an employer could not be held responsible for the
negligence of a manufacturer in respect of defects in tools, in that
case a hammer, that could not be discovered on reasonable inspection. It effectively makes the employer presumptively liable for the
negligence of the manufacturer where it has involved exposing the
employee to risk in the course of his employment. The Act provides
that where:

"(a) An employee suffers personal injury in the course of his
employment in consequence of a defect in equipment provided by his employer for the purposes of the employer's
business; and

(b) the defect is attributable wholly or partly to the fault of a third
party (whether identified or not),

the injury shall be deemed to be also attributable to negligence on the part of the employer (whether or not he is liable in respect of the injury apart from this subsection) . . ."

It should be noted that "equipment" includes any plant and machinery, vehicle, aircraft and clothing. The term has been construed to include a defective merchant ship (*Coltman v Bibby Tankers* [1988] A.C. 276) and material with which an employee has been working (see *Knowles v Liverpool City Council* [1993] 4 All E.R. 321).

4–69   *Consumer Protection Act 1987 s.2(3)*: The 1987 Act creates a tort of strict liability for damage caused to any person as a result wholly of partly of a defect in a product. Liability is primarily imposed on the "producer" of the product. Nevertheless, in order to assist a claimant in identifying the producer, s.2(3) contains a presumption that the supplier of goods in effect becomes the producer if he fails within a reasonable period of receiving a request from the person who suffered the damage to identify the producer or person who supplied the product to him.

(g) *Omnia Praesumuntur Rite Esse Acta*

4–70   The effect of this rule is that on proof that a person acted in a judicial, official or public capacity there is a presumption that:

(1) The act complied with any necessary formalities; and

(2) The person in question was properly appointed.

Many of the cases referred to in *Phipson* (see 6–29) date from the nineteenth century; the only recent example given is *TC Coombs & Co v IRC* [1991] 3 All E.R. 623 a case in which the House of Lords held that the presumption covered a tax inspector who had given a notice to the claimants requiring them to produce information concerning a former employee.

B Evidential Presumptions

4–71   In certain situations the court may draw inferences from the facts proved by a party. As already stated, these are no more than commonly recurring examples of circumstantial evidence. It is therefore a misconception to treat them as presumptions in the strict sense since at no time do they transfer the burden of proof to the person against whom the evidence is tendered. They have already been covered at 4–16, nevertheless because they are often, wrongly it is submitted referred to as "presumptions" they merit further brief consideration.

(a) *"Presumption of Continuance"*

Proof of the existence of a state of affairs at a particular time may **4–72** entitle the court to infer that it existed at a reasonably proximate time either before or after that date or time. A relatively recent example can be found in the case of *Coles v Underwood* [1983], *The Times,* November 2 in which the court was entitled to infer that the defendant had been driving on the wrong side of the road at the time an accident occurred based on evidence that he was seen driving in this manner one third of a mile from the scene of the accident. Another interesting example can be seen in *Chard v Chard* [1956] P. 259 in which the court held that it was entitled to infer that a woman of 26 would still be alive 16 years later (on the facts it was not possible to rely on the presumption of death, see 4–52).

(b) *"Presumption of Regularity"*

As already noted, a court is entitled to infer that if a mechanical **4–73** instrument is proved to have been working correctly either before or after the occasion in question the court may infer that it was working correctly on that occasion (see *Tingle Jacobs & Co. v Kennedy* [1964] 1 W.L.R. 638 referred to earlier at 4–18).

It has also been applied to office practices, for example, on proof that all solicitors' post in the post book is dispatched by first class post the court may infer that a document was so dispatched. However it is important to bear in mind that office practices are changing all the time, especially in the age of computers and "online" communication. It may well be therefore that the court will need to investigate the process of transmission with great care in order to be satisfied that it has been duly transmitted. A recent example of this can be seen in *Smith v Tyne and Wear Autistic Society* [2005] 4 All E.R. 1336. In it, the Employment Appeal Tribunal had to determine whether the applicant's unfair dismissal claim had been "presented" within the three month time limit as required by s.111(2) of the Employment Rights Act 1996. The applicant had used the Employment Tribunal's online facility in which the complaint of unfair dismissal was dispatched to a commercial host of the tri-bunal's website. Although the Appeal Tribunal found in his favour, holding that the application had been "presented" when it was successfully submitted online, he was only able to prove that it had been so submitted by producing the files and cookies within his own computer since the commercial host, it would appear, had failed to transmit the application to the Tribunal's website and had a practice of erasing applications from its own server three days after receipt. Perhaps using the normal post still has its advantages!

Conclusion

4–74 Relevance is crucial: it lies at the heart of the principles introduced by the CPR. Do not think of it as a subject fit only for academic theorists. Whenever examining any piece of evidence or line of investigation, keep asking the question:

"Where does this take us?"

You will need to be constantly asking this question in order to deal with the many relevancy issues that will arise during the course of a claim, for example:

(1) On an application for pre-action (CPR 31.16) or specific (CPR 31.12) disclosure when your opponent is complaining of "fishing expeditions";

(2) When a decision has to be taken on a particular line of investigation: you may need to consider whether or not the cost will be recoverable or whether it will be regarded as "disproportionate";

(3) In advising a corporate client as to the likely scope of their disclosure obligations in a large commercial claim: you may need to give early advice as to the installation of retention systems for masses of electronic data;

(4) When creating and refining your client's "case theory" in which relevance and, in particular, inference have crucial roles to play.

Always bear in mind that the core tasks of the litigator are not only to apply the law, but to know how best to make use of the facts at her disposal.

Chapter 5

Proof by Evidence

I INTRODUCTION

1. What this Chapter Covers
This chapter must begin with a word of warning. The main message   **5–01**
that it sets out to deliver is that proof of facts is infnitely easier and
less stultified by technicality than it used to be (for an overview see
Diagram 1). Accordingly, it should be read with a sense of propor-
tion. Many of the difficulties it confronts constitute the exception
rather than the rule. Having identified in the preceding Chapters:

(1) Who has to prove what;

(2) The standard to which it has to be proved; and

(3) What evidence is regarded as relevant to those issues;

this chapter will examine the practical methods of proof that the litigator has at his or her disposal. As already noted (1–09) the court may
receive evidence in one or more of three formats:

(1) *Oral* (sometimes referred to as "witness evidence" or "testimony");

(2) *Documentary* (which can be anything from a rough scrawl on a
scrap of paper to millions of emails stored on backup tapes);
and

(3) *Real* (an extraordinarily wide category which can embrace anything from a judge "sizing up" a witness to her travelling to the
other side of the world to view material evidence);

all of which operate conjunctively (see 1–12).

2. The Shape of a Civil Trial

5–02   Although some of the features of the civil trial have already been outlined at 1–11, it will be much easier to understand how the various
methods of proof operate if you have a clear picture from the outset
of what a civil trial actually looks and sounds like in practice. Not
only that, it will get you into the habit of "Thinking trial from Day 1".
At first sight, the order of proceedings does not appear to differ
greatly from that in a criminal trial. It consists of the following six
stages (see also 14–13 onwards).

(a) Claimant Opens

5–03   This may consist of anything from a few sentences to the respective
80 day and 113 day marathons of Gordon Pollock Q.C. and Nicholas
Stadlen Q.C. for the claimants and defendant in the *"Three Rivers"*
trial. It may even be dispensed with. This is by no means uncommon
in road traffic cases in the Small Claims or Fast Track list in a busy
county court. In longer cases it will normally be accompanied by a
"Skeleton Argument" which, if the trial judge has had time to pre-
read it, will often take the place of an opening speech. However, whatever its format it serves as a valuable opportunity for the claimant's
advocate to highlight not only the key facts and evidence, but also to
set out her "theory" of the case (discussed further at 14–21 and 59).

(b) Claimant's Evidence

5–04   This is the stage at which the standard civil trial will often take a very
different course from a criminal case. Although the primary methods
of proof (oral, documentary and real evidence) will be the same, the
way in which the three types of evidence will be introduced will be
markedly different (see also Diagrams 2 and 3).

- *Oral Evidence*: In a criminal trial, each witness will be called,
  sworn, and then examined in-chief by the advocate calling him.
  This means that notwithstanding the fact that a detailed statement will have been taken from the witness, his testimony will
  have to be extracted by an (often lengthy and laborious) question and answer session. He will then be cross-examined by the
  opposing advocate and finally, if he so chooses, re-examined by
  the advocate calling him. In contrast, you will rarely see an
  "old-style" examination in-chief in a civil court. The reason is
  that, in civil trials, a witness's examination in-chief will almost
  invariably be replaced by the use of their signed witness statement in substitution (see CPR 32.5 and a full discussion of
  witness statements in Chapter 11). The only notable exception
  is in the Small Claims track where witness statements are not
  obligatory (although normally directed): where the parties are

unrepresented it will often be carried out by the judge hearing the claim. Furthermore, in the case of expert opinion evidence (see further 12–24) there is a strong presumption *against* oral evidence being given (see, in particular, CPR 35.5); the trial judge will generally be expected to make do with the experts' written reports.

- *Documentary Evidence*: Here, the difference between the civil and the criminal trial is even more stark (although the difference may become less apparent now that parties can agree hearsay evidence in criminal trials since April 4, 2005 under s.114(1)(c) of the Criminal Justice Act 2003). In a criminal trial it will often be necessary for each important document to be formally "proved" by calling a witness to produce it, confirm its authenticity and introduce it as an exhibit. Not only that, but, at any rate in trials pre-April 4, 2005 a party who wished to rely on the contents of a document in a criminal trial often faced difficult hearsay problems. Conversely, in the vast majority of civil trials not only will all the documents be in one or more "Agreed Trial Bundles", but this will also have the effect of enabling all the parties to rely on their contents from the outset. Not only that, but much evidence that used to be given orally, lay witnesses and experts being the prime examples, is now largely received in documentary form. It is no longer the witness's oral testimony that forms the bulk of his evidence, but his pre-trial oral account that has been recorded and transcribed in the form of a written statement. In that sense, nearly all received evidence is now documentary evidence. As we shall see shortly however (4–33), there are a number of detailed rules relating both to the proof of documents and of their contents which we shall need to consider in some depth for the sake of completeness.

- *Real Evidence*: Here, there is little difference between civil and criminal trials as to the way in which such evidence is received except that in criminal trials real evidence is much more likely to take the form of exhibits such as weapons or other incriminating articles found in the accused's possession which will require a whole procession of witnesses, both expert and lay, to be called before the exhibit is capable of proving anything.

(c) *Defendant's Evidence*

The defendant's advocate will now introduce her evidence in precisely the same way. This will sometimes be preceded by an Opening Speech although in very heavy cases this will take place immediately after the claimant's opening.

5–05

(d) *Defendant's Closing Speech*

(e) *Claimant's Closing Speech*

5–06 The only notable difference here is the fact that, unlike in a criminal trial, the party with the burden of proof gets the last word (in the magistrates' court the prosecutor does not get one at all).

(f) *The Judge Decides the Case*

5–07 One notable characteristic of the English civil trial is the emphasis it places on the *ex tempore* oral judgment delivered while the facts and arguments are still fresh in the judge's mind. Although a judge may have to reserve judgment and call the parties back to receive his or her written judgment in more complex cases, judges are encouraged to give oral judgment at the conclusion of the trial whenever practicable. Whatever the level of case being tried the parties are nevertheless entitled to a structured judgment that should be set out in the following form:

(1) The nature of the claim, the parties and the issues that are to be decided;

(2) The relevant facts, identifying those that are agreed and those that are in dispute;

(3) The relevant law: often this will be non-controversial, but in the event that it is disputed, the judge will review the advocates' submissions and the submitted authorities;

(4) The material issues that are in dispute, summarising each party's principal submissions;

(5) The "core". This will consist of:

  • Rulings on matters of law with reasons;
  • Specific findings of fact under each of the disputed issues identified at (4) above with reasons;
  • The final decision (again with supporting reasons) based upon the earlier findings of law and fact.

This may all sound rather like "painting by numbers" but it is an essential component of the trial process and one which all litigators need to be aware of from the outset when preparing their clients' cases. Not only that, it is the format suggested by the Judicial Studies Board in s.10 of the *Civil Bench Book*, the full text of which can be accessed at *www.jsb.co.uk*. It also represents the "industry standard" necessary to ensure compliance with Art.6 of the ECHR (see *English v Emery Reimbold and Strick Ltd* [2002] 1 W.L.R. 2409).

3. "Weight": What Wins Cases?

The common assumption, much of it based upon courtroom dramas **5-08** seen on television or at the cinema, is that cases are won and lost on witnesses' evidence, the truth and accuracy of which is tested by the dazzling cross-examination skills of "star" advocates. Throw in some appropriately theatrical rhetoric from these advocates in their opening and closing speeches, and the popular image of the standard trial and the skill necessary to achieve success in it are complete. Although some trials do still loosely conform to this format, the reality is usually somewhat more mundane, not least because documents tend to play such a large part in civil trials. The reason for this is simple enough to identify, especially in contractual claims. Firstly, human recollection is notoriously inaccurate. Hence the contents of letters, memoranda, e-mails and electronically produced transaction data are much more likely to provide a factual matrix from which it is possible to make either direct or inferential findings of fact. Secondly, however honest a witness may be, there is always a tendency to place a gloss upon past events that favours their side of the case, the often totally honest motorist who is convinced the accident was not his fault in the face of clear evidence to the contrary being an obvious and recurring example. Conversely, documents that turn out with hindsight to be crucial may have come into being at a time when no thought was given to the possibility of future litigation. Such documents derive their weight from the fact that any possibility of self-serving on the part of its creator can be discounted. However a strong dose of healthy scepticism never comes amiss; some arch business folk may well have had the possibility of future litigation in mind long before the storm clouds started to gather.

Gow v Harker [2003] EWCA 1160: How Judges are Supposed to Decide Cases
Never forget that although the standard of proof is on the balance **5-09** of probabilities, some findings of fact can be predicted with a greater degree of certainty than others (see 3–57). The case cited above provides a valuable illustration of the correct judicial approach to different categories of evidence, especially in cases where there is a direct conflict in the oral evidence.

Facts: This was a clinical negligence claim in which the claimant alleged **5-10** that the defendant Dr Harker had so negligently taken a blood sample for a routine thyroid function test from the "houseman's vein" situated on the top of the wrist that the needle had gone right through the vein and penetrated into the underlying radial nerve. At the trial the claimant gave a very graphic account of the incident stating that she had immediately screamed out in pain causing Dr Harker to let go of the syringe and jump back. Ms Gow went on to say that when she looked down at her right wrist the needle was sticking out at or near an angle of 90 degrees, "like a dart stuck in a dartboard".

5–11   When Dr Harker gave evidence her account was somewhat different. She stated that she had no recollection of the incident. However her own brief notes did not record anything untoward having happened and were entirely consistent with the inference that this was a routine venepuncture for a thyroid function test. She stated that although the "houseman's vein" site was an unusual one (necessitated by the fact that Ms Gow had had so many samples taken at the more usual site on the inside of the elbow) she had taken blood from there on a number of previous occasions. She also demonstrated the usual method for taking a sample at this site indicating that it involved a shallow angle of entry—no more than 15 degrees. Both experts gave evidence as to the accepted method for taking a sample at this site, which accorded with Dr Harker's demonstration. Significantly there appeared to be no dispute that a sufficient sample of blood had been taken to be able to carry out the thyroid function test (3–5ml on the expert evidence—the results were there to confirm it). This was a crucial piece of evidence because, unlike with injections, the person taking the sample has to pull the plunger *out* in order for the patient's blood to flow into the syringe. The trial judge found for Ms Gow, influenced largely, it seems, by the graphic "dartboard" image projected by her when giving evidence. However the Court of Appeal thought differently and ordered a retrial. In his judgment Brooke L.J. explained how the evidence of witnesses as to fact should be approached in cases of this kind:

(1)   Firstly, test the credibility of their evidence by reference to objective facts proved independently of their testimony, in particular by reference to documents (in this case there was nothing in the clinical notes to suggest anything untoward had taken place);

(2)   Secondly, look at the overall probabilities. The experts were both agreed that a needle would have had to go in a long way to stick out in the remarkable way described by the claimant. More important still, they were puzzled as to how any blood ever got into the syringe on Ms Gow's version;

(3)   Finally, based on these findings, go on to evaluate each side's testimony.

Because the trial judge had not followed this approach, the Court of Appeal ordered a retrial. There is nothing groundbreaking in this approach as the following extract from Brooke L.J.'s judgment shows (at [22 to 27]:

"22. Trial judges would always do well to model their fact finding technique, in a case as difficult as this, on the approach adopted by Robert Goff L.J. in 'The Ocean Frost' [1985] 1 Lloyd's Rep. 1, 57 which was adopted by the Privy Council in Grace Shipping v Sharp [1997] 1 Lloyd's Rep. 207, 215. In "The Ocean Frost" Robert Goff L.J. said:

> "Speaking from my own experience I have found it essential in cases of fraud when considering the credibility of witnesses, always to test their veracity by reference to the objective facts proved independently of their testimony, in particular by reference to the documents in the case and also to pay particular regard to their motives and to the overall probabilities".

23. While spoken in the context of a fraud case, these words are equally apposite in a case like the present where the claimant's case is inherently improbable, where there is little or no objective evidence supporting her account of a radial nerve injury, and there may be a risk that she may have persuaded herself over the months that followed the incident in the doctor's surgery of a history of that incident which had materially departed from what actually occurred.

24. A judge who adopted conventional *traditional techniques* [author's emphasis] in a case as difficult as this would begin by considering the contemporary written evidence. This consisted of Doctor Harker's note on the Friday and Doctor Senior's note on the following Monday. Two matters in particular would have been of note;

(i) Although it was Doctor Harker's last day at work, her note contains no information to the doctor who would have taken over Miss Gow's case of anything resembling the dramatic incident to which Miss Gow testified. It was a completely routine note about a thyroid function test and the need for a urine test.

(ii) Miss Gow's vivid description of how her fingers and the back of her hand all swelled up over the weekend was belied by Doctor Senior's note.

The judge considered the second of these matters but not the first.

25. Conventional traditional techniques would then have led the judge to consider the inherent probabilities (or improbabilities) of the case. Such an approach would have led the judge to ask himself the following questions:

(i) How could any blood have entered the syringe on Miss Gow's account of the matter? All three medical witnesses said that Doctor Harker would have had to pull back the plunger, and on Miss Gow's account Doctor Harker jumped back and let go the syringe as soon as she shrieked with pain.

(ii) Into what would the needle have penetrated if it was inserted at Miss Gow's site? It could not have entered the anatomical snuff box because the radial nerve was not in that area. If it entered 'near' the snuff box, where did it enter, and what did it probably stick into (so that it did not fall out)? Bone? Subcutaneous fat? How did such a finding square with Doctor Hick's evidence?

(iii) Why should Doctor Harker have chosen Miss Gow's site? If the reason was, as Doctor Grock [Author's note: the neurological expert] opined, that the vein was more prominent there, how does this square with the dart board scenario?

26.   The judge did not address any of these issues in his judgment. If he had considered the evidence with even greater care he would have noted that Doctor Hick's evidence that the amount of blood normally required for a thyroid function test would be 3–5 millilitres, was not challenged by Doctor Grock or in cross-examination at the trial, and was supported by Doctor Harker. This part of the evidence was not explored at the trial, but it would have been picked up by a judge who considered the whole of the evidence carefully before he gave judgment, and would have given him further cause for concern about Miss Gow's account.

27.   All these points would have bound to have worried a judge who was otherwise inclined to believe Miss Gow's evidence. He would then have gone on to conclude, as [the trial judge] did, that Miss Gow must be wrong when she:

(i) described the needle as going in at an angle of about 90 degrees;

(ii) said that blood wells up in the other puncture sites when the tourniquet was released;

(iii) said that Doctor Harker took out the needle before releasing the tourniquet;

(iv) said that all the fingers of her right hand and the back of her hand swelled up over the weekend.

28.   And when you turn to Doctor Harker's evidence any judge weighing the evidence thoroughly would have been bound to consider the inherent improbability of a doctor with as much experience of performing the venepunctures, both as a GP and as an anaesthetist attempting to take blood in the extraordinary way described by Miss Gow.

29.   Against all this is the fact that something happened which led Miss Gow to complain of pain to Doctor Senior [Author's

note: one of Dr Harker's GP colleagues] on the Monday, and the additional and very important fact that the judge saw Miss Gow and Doctor Harker and we have not. But I do not see how these two facts, important as they are, can properly lead this court to uphold this judgment when on the evidence there were so many improbabilities and at least one apparent impossibility (the presence of a millilitre of blood in the syringe) that the judge simply did not address in his judgment adequately or at all."

This passage, essential reading for all litigators, advocates and judges contains four important lessons:

(1) Witness evidence is not necessarily the "best" evidence. Documents may sometimes provide a more contemporaneous, accurate and less self-serving source of evidence;

(2) Always seek out "certainties" and "impossibilities" when evaluating evidence: it can sometimes save an awful lot of time;

(3) Once a "certainty" or "impossibility" has been established it becomes much easier to evaluate the other evidence in the case; and

(4) It is very easy to be "led astray" by vivid imagery (the "dart in a dartboard") without standing back to apply some cold hard logic to the evidence that is being presented.

As noted when discussing relevance in Chapter 4, the use of simple syllogisms can sometimes provide a quick and useful method for evaluating the weight of a particular piece of evidence.

Example: The fact that there was enough blood in the syringe for a successful thyroid function test to be carried out in *Gow v Harker* was a particularly telling piece of evidence.   **5–12**

Major Premise: For a successful thyroid function test to be possible a   **5–13**
                minimum sample of 3–5 mililitres needs to be taken;

Minor Premise: (Evidence) A successful thyroid function test was carried out on the blood sample taken from Ms Gow; therefore

Conclusion: Dr Harker must have pulled out the plonger in the syringe sufficiently far to extract 3–5 mililitres of blood from Ms Gow on the occasion in question.

It does not require a lengthy chain of reasoning to reach the conclusion that Ms Gow's account of what happened, namely that she screamed as soon as the needle was inserted and that Dr Harker immediately let go of the syringe, does not square up with the above proposition. The cited passage from Brooke L.J.'s judgment also illustrates the questionable assumptions that may sometimes lurk within a Major Premise. Paragraph 23 of his judgment provides a notable example.

Major Premise: Experienced and conscientious doctors will make a careful record of any untoward incident during a routine blood test;

Minor Premises: (Evidence)

(1) Dr Harker is experienced and conscientious;

(2) She did not record any untoward incident when she took a blood sample for Ms Gow.

Conclusion: The incident that Ms Gow describes is rendered less probable.

The Major Premise, which is inherent in Brooke L.J.'s reasoning, raises a number of interesting questions. Do we all agree with it? Is it the only tenable Major Premise? Could we for example argue that people who make mistakes tend to cover them up? Where is the evidence to support the Major Premise or is it simply an example of "hidden" judicial notice? The only conclusion to be drawn, perhaps, is that a considerable amount of what we think of as "scientific" proof is in fact nothing of the kind. This at once presents a challenge and an opportunity. It shows how, from the outset, the litigator must examine the available evidence at his disposal and test it against what, as a trained professional with a reasonable knowledge of how the world works, looks and sounds plausible. With that thought uppermost in our minds, it is now time to examine the various methods of proof in greater detail.

II ORAL EVIDENCE (WITNESSES)

5–14   This section examines the general rules as to the capacity of a witness to give evidence ("competence") and the circumstances in which he or she may be compelled to do so ("compellability"). It will then go on to outline the manner in which a witness's evidence is received (examination-chief, cross-examination etc.) leaving further consideration until Chapters 11 and 14. It may assist to begin with three important reminders.

5–15   Reminder *(1): You Will Know What is Coming*
A party will not only receive advance notice of the oral evidence that his opponent intends to rely on in the form of written witness statements (CPR 32.4), but the witness statements themselves will, in effect,

stand as the witnesses' primary oral evidence at the trial (CPR 32.5). Not only that, but, unlike it the past, there is no prohibition against a witness giving hearsay evidence, subject to relatively minimal procedural requirements being met (see 7–26).

Reminder (2): *Oral Evidence is a Rarity Outside of Trials*   **5–16**
There are many types of proceeding in which oral evidence is not only unnecessary, but is subject to strict control by the courts. The relevant governing provisions are set out in CPR 32 which provides that:

CPR 32.2

"(1) The general rule is that any fact which needs to proved by the evidence of witnesses is to be proved:

(a) at trial, by their oral evidence given in public; and
(b) at any other hearing by their evidence in writing.

(2) This is subject to:

(a) any provision to the contrary contained in these Rules or elsewhere; or
(b) any other order of the court."

CPR 32.6

"(1) Subject to paragraph (2), the general rule is that evidence at hearings other than the trial is to be by witness statement unless the court, a practice direction or any other enactment requires otherwise.
(2) At hearings other than the trial, a party may rely on the matters set out in:

(a) his statement of case; or
(b) his application notice, if the statement of case or application notice is verified by a statement of truth."

CPR 32.7

"(1) Where, at a hearing other than the trial, evidence is given in writing, any party may apply to the court for permission to cross-examine the person giving the evidence;
(2)   If the court gives permission under paragraph (1) but the person in question does not attend as required by the order, his evidence may not be used unless the court gives permission."

A detailed commentary as to the effect of these provisions can be found in the current *White Book*; the general tenor of which is that, outside of trials, oral evidence is a rarity. Examples include:

(1) *Interim hearings*, for example, case management conferences; general applications (CPR 23), summary judgment applications (CPR 24) and Interim Injunctions (CPR 25): evidence at such hearings is dealt with in Chapter 9;

(2) Claims brought under *Pt 8* of the CPR (including judicial review under CPR 54).

For a full explanation as to the scope and nature of Pt 8 claims see, *O'Hare and Browne*, Chapter 10. As a general rule, claims brought under this procedure will concern the construction of a document or the determination of a point of law. Although the court has power to direct the giving of oral evidence (see CPR 8.6(2)) including (CPR 8.6(3)) attendance for cross-examination it is more likely that the court will direct that the claim proceed to trial as if it had been brought as a Pt 7 claim, especially if extensive cross-examination required.

5–17   So far as orders for cross-examination are concerned, it is clear that they will only be ordered if the circumstances clearly justify such an order. In the past, they were generally only made in relation to a defendant's affidavit of assets in proceedings for a freezing injunction (see commentary to CPR 32.7 in the *White Book* and the general discussion of the Court of Appeal decision in *Phillips v Symes* [2003] EWCA 1769). However, Peter Smith J. has recently stated in *Watford Petroleum Ltd v Interoil Trading SA* [2005] EWHC 852 (Ch.) that, post-CPR, there is a wider discretion to order cross-examination if it will narrow the issues or save court time. It may therefore be of assistance in cases where there are, for example, allegations fraud or dishonesty or of destruction or non-disclosure of evidence.

5–18   *Reminder (3): You can (more or less) Prove Facts Any Way that you Like* Since the abolition of the hearsay rule, there is nothing to stop a party proving his case at trial relying solely on documentary evidence provided that he does not need to call oral evidence to prove any of the relevant documents. However, as a matter of commonsense, the tendering of oral evidence on matters that are hotly in dispute will normally be essential.

A Competence and Compellability

1. *The General Rule*

5–19   All witnesses, including the parties and their spouses, are generally competent and compellable to give evidence on oath (the historical background is set out in *Phipson* 9–03 to 9–07). Thus, in theory, it would even be open to a party to subpoena his opponent to give evidence on his behalf, although, in practical terms, this would create difficulties due to the general prohibition against cross-examining your own witnesses (see 14–30). The general test of competence is whether the witness is capable of understanding the nature of the oath (this does not require any theological appreciation of its significance) and of giving rational testimony. There are however additional requirements to be met before a witness is competent to give expert opinion evidence (see generally, 12–03). Furthermore, there are two categories of witness that constitute exceptions to the general rule, namely children and adults who, due to physical or mental disability, lack the requisite testimonial capacity.

2. *Children*
A child is competent to give sworn evidence if the court is satisfied **5–20**
that he or she appreciates:

(1) The solemnity of the occasion; and

(2) The special duty to tell the truth on oath over and above the ordinary duty to so do.

Unlike in criminal cases (see s.53(3) of the Youth Justice and Criminal Evidence Act 1999) the test is still governed by common law, the leading case being *R. v Hayes* [1977] 2 All E.R. 288. It is likely that, if required to do so in civil proceedings, the courts will follow the approach adopted in criminal trials and refrain from treating children as a class of witness who are presumed to be incompetent until the *Hayes* test has been satisfied (see *R. v Hampshire* [1996] Q.B. 1 at 7). The court will simply raise the issue of competence as and when it considers it necessary. Furthermore, unusual though it would be in mainstream civil proceedings, a child, meaning a person under the age of 18 (s.105(1) of the Children Act 1989) may, under s.96(2) of the 1989 Act, give *unsworn* evidence if he or she:

(1) Understands that it is his/her duty to tell the truth; and

(2) Has sufficient understanding to justify his/her evidence being heard.

It is not entirely clear what type of child witness this provision embraces; presumably the child who does not understand the nature of the oath, but does understand that telling the truth is an important social duty. The subsection has been criticised by some commentators on the grounds that it lacks clarity and is ambiguous; for a comprehensive discussion of these difficulties, see *Phipson* 9–11.

3. *Adult Witnesses who Lack Capacity*

5–21   In practical terms, the court is much more likely to be faced with an adult witness who due to some permanent or temporary cognitive disability, is unable to understand the nature of the oath and/or give coherent answers to questions. The problem is particularly acute in county court possession lists where defendants not infrequently present with difficulties of this kind as a result of mental illness or substance abuse problems. The test for competence is the same as that to be applied at common law in the case of children; however one wonders whether the time has not come for a broader test to be applied more in line with that used in criminal proceedings. Under ss.55(2) and (3) of the Youth Justice and Criminal Evidence Act 1999, an adult witness is treated as competent provided he is able to:

(1)   Understand questions put to him as a witness; and

(2)   Give answers to them that can be understood.

It is submitted that this is the test that the civil courts should, and in practice largely do, now apply.

4. *The Oath*

5–22   The starting point must, in reality, be to recognise that unsworn evidence is the norm for the vast majority of civil trials. The reason for this is very simple: the bulk of civil trials take place in the Small Claims Track in which, under CPR 27.8(4):

"The court need not take evidence on oath."

In practice, it is virtually unheard of for a district judge to take sworn evidence. The rules in other trials are summarised below.

(a) *Oaths and Affirmations: Form*

5–23   A detailed discussion of the history and procedures for taking the oath is outside the scope of this work (see *Phipson* 9–26 to 9–44). The procedure is governed by the Oaths Act 1978 (for the full text see the *White Book* 9B–439), although the wording of the oath is still governed by a resolution of the judges of the King's Bench Division made as long ago as January 11, 1927 (see *Phipson* 9–30). The "standard" procedure (1978 Act, s.1) is for the witness to take the New Testament (or in the case of a person of Jewish faith, the Old Testament) in his uplifted hand and say or repeat the following words:

"I swear by Almighty God that the evidence which I shall give shall be the truth, the whole truth and nothing but the truth."

However, due to the wider range of belief systems that courts now deal with, there are more comprehensive procedures for swearing a witness. A helpful summary of these can be found in Section 3.2 of the *"Equal Treatment Bench Book"* prepared by the Judicial Studies Board, the full text of which may be accessed at *www.jsb.co.uk*. However, it may not always be practicable for an oath to be administered in the form requested by the witness. In that case, the witness may instead affirm (1978 Act, s.5(2)). Furthermore, a witness may not ascribe to a particular belief system and may wish to affirm in any event; a witness has an absolute right to do this without giving any reason (1978 Act, s.5(1)). The wording of the affirmation is prescribed by s.6 of the 1978 Act as follows:

"I [name] solemnly, sincerely and truly declare and affirm that the evidence that I shall give shall be the truth, the whole truth and nothing but the truth."

(b) *Who may Administer the Oath?*
The situation so far as courts of trial is concerned is still governed by s.16 of the Evidence Act 1851 which provides that: **5–24**

"Every court, judge, justice officer, commissioner, arbitrator or other person now or hereafter having by law or by consent of the parties, authority to hear, receive, and examine evidence, is hereby empowered to administer an oath to all such witnesses as are legally called before them respectively."

However, oral testimony is not the only form of evidence that is generally required to be sworn, affidavits (although they are now a rarity post-CPR) being the major example. Paragraph 9.1 of CPR 32 Practice Direction provides for this by stating:

"Only the following may administer oaths and take affidavits: (1) Commissioners for Oaths, (2) practising solicitors, (3) other persons specified by statute, (4) certain officials of the Supreme Court, (5) a circuit judge or district judge, (6) any justice of the peace and (7) certain officials of any county court appointed by the Judge of that court for the purpose."

In practice, there should always be a member of the court staff available at the High Court or a local county court empowered to swear a document when the need arises.

5. *Compellability*
As already stated, all witnesses that are competent are also com-   **5–25**
pellable in civil proceedings. This means that not only may they be

compelled to come to court by means of a Witness Summons (see CPR 34 and 13–15) but also to be sworn or affirmed and to answer questions. Disobedience to any of these requirements is punishable as contempt of court. There are however a number of exceptions which will entitle a witness not only to apply to have a Witness Summons set aside, but also to refuse to be sworn or answer questions. The most important examples are (see further *Phipson* 9–16):

(1) Where the witness is able to assert that the evidence that he would be able to give is privileged or protected by public interest immunity (see further Chapter 8);

(2) The Sovereign;

(3) Diplomats of foreign states and, subject to exceptions, members of their family (Diplomatic Privileges Act 1964);

(4) Foreign sovereign or heads of state and members of their households (s.20 of the State Immunity Act 1978);

(5) (To a limited extent) members of consular posts (Consular Relations Act 1968).

The position of judges was recently considered by the Court of Appeal in *Warren v Warren* [1997] Q.B. 488.

5–26   **Facts:** The parties were a husband and wife who had become involved in extremely acrimonious proceedings concerning the contents of the former family home, some of which had, so the husband alleged, been removed by the wife. The wife gave various written undertakings as to their return before District Judge C. When a dispute later arose in committal proceedings as to the precise terms of the undertakings, the husband's solicitors issued a witness summons requiring District Judge C to attend to give evidence as to what had taken place. The committal proceedings were subsequently withdrawn, but a circuit judge made a wasted costs order against the husband's solicitors on the grounds, among others, that it was unreasonable to summon the DJ who, in any event, was not a compellable witness.

5–27   Having considered the relatively limited authorities on the subject Lord Woolf M.R. laid down the following principles:

(1) In the normal course of events, judges of all levels are fully competent and compellable to testify except in relation to functions they have performed as judges;

(2) In the latter case, although they are competent to testify, they cannot be compelled to do so, although Lord Woolf did go on

to say [at 497] that they should give evidence if their testimony was vital.

The effect of this is that a judge may be compellable to give evidence as to what takes place while she is sitting if it relates to matters outside of her judicial functions, for example if one of the parties were to attack his opponent's solicitor. The problem encountered in *Warren* is less likely to arise in future due to the fact that not only will the court have the benefit of the judge's notes, but there will also normally be a tape recording of the proceedings.

B Witness Examination (in outline)

Although this subject will be addressed further later chapters (see 11–63 and 14–38) it is useful to have a broad understanding of the process for receiving and testing witness evidence, not least because of the constant need to "Think Trial from Day 1". Witness examination falls into three stages, each governed, to a large extent, by practice. The three stages are: 5–28

(1) Examination in-chief;

(2) Cross-examination; and

(3) Re-examination.

1. *Examination-in-Chief*

Examination-in-chief used to be a "memory test" because the advocate examining the witness was, as a general rule, prohibited from asking leading questions (see further 14–27). However the difficulties that this occasioned had largely disappeared even before the advent of the CPR. This was largely as a result of two procedural changes. Firstly, from October 1, 1990, parties were required to exchange written statements of all witnesses as to fact (see s.5 of the Courts and Legal Services Act 1990 and RSC O.38, r.2A and CCR O.20, r.12A). Secondly, *Case Management Practice Direction* [1995] 1 W.L.R. 262 provided that a witness statement exchanged under either of the above rules would normally stand as his evidence-in-chief. This process has now become more or less universal as a result of the Civil Evidence Act 1995 (see s.6(1) and 7–43), and the CPR (see CPR 32.5 and 11–63). As a result, in practice: 5–29

(1) You will hardly ever see a full examination in-chief in a civil trial; and

(2) Statements have tended to become over long due to the fact that they may only be amplified by oral evidence (with leave of the court) in relation to new matters or to supply amplification (see CPR 32.5(3) and 11–63).

However there is a more fundamental reason for their ever-increasing length. In many litigators' minds the primary purpose of a witness statement is not to provide advance disclosure of the evidence that the witness' will give if the claim goes to trial. In all probability the claim will not go to trial. Accordingly their primary purpose is seen as being for use in negotiation. This has led to bad habits in some quarters that will be dealt with at 11–46.

Note needs to be taken in passing of the one common law concession that still remains although its practical usefulness has largely been overtaken by events, namely the "contemporaneous note". At common law the only circumstance in which a witness could refer to a "prompt" in the witness box was if the court gave him permission to "refresh his memory" from a document provided that:

(1) It was "made or verified" by the witness;

(2) Substantially contemporaneously with the events to which the witness is testifying.

This concession has been preserved by the Civil Evidence Act 1995 (see s.6(4) and 7–46) but, in practice, it has largely been rendered redundant by exchanged witness statements.

5–30   *Conclusion*   In theory the advocate calling a witness may simply do no more than get him to confirm, identify his statement, confirm its contents and then tender him for cross-examination. Brief introductions of this kind are not unheard of, especially if the judge has indicated that time is short and he has read all the papers, but, in the vast majority of cases there will be some further examination in-chief even if its only purpose is to "get the witness comfortable". Sometimes a much fuller examination may be allowed: this topic is discussed further at 11–65. However, in the main, it is the written statement, standing as it does as evidence in its own right, that is received in evidence rather than oral testimony. The only oral evidence of any significance will be contained in the witness's answers to questions put in cross-examination and re-examination or those asked by the court.

5–31   *"Hostile Witnesses"*   Fortunately, "problem witnesses" are a rarity in civil trials. However they can cause difficulty on occasions, most commonly when the witness being called is a person who has refused to sign a witness statement but has essential evidence to give. As a general rule you cannot cross-examine or otherwise seek to undermine your own witnesses. Therefore if they turn out to be merely "unfavourable", that is, they do not give the evidence that you were hoping that they would give, you are stuck with it, unless either:

(1) The court gives you permission to have them treated as a "hostile witness", that is, a witness who is deliberately refusing to tell the truth. In that case an advocate will be permitted to cross-examine the witness; or

(2) Your opponent has served a hearsay statement on you and you wish the maker to be called so that he can be cross-examined. It is now possible to apply to the court for a "cross-examination order" under s.3 of the Civil Evidence Act 1995 and CPR 33.4. This procedure is fully explained at 7–31.

2. Cross-Examination
The opposing party has the right to cross-examine a witness. Although the techniques and scope of cross-examination will be considered further in due course (see 14–43) it is important to have some idea of the basic ground rules from the outset, the most important technical difference between examination in-chief and cross-examination being that leading question are permitted in cross-examination. A witness may be cross-examined on any matters that are relevant and not otherwise inadmissible (for example material that is covered by privilege) in particular:

5–32

(1) On his entire witness statement whether or not it was referred to in-chief (CPR 32.11, and see further 11–70);

(2) Any previous inconsistent statement made by him may be put to him and, if necessary, proved under ss.4 and 5 of the Criminal Procedure Act, 1865 (see 14–55);

(3) On any document that is relevant to his testimony provided the document itself is admissible and has been duly admitted; it usually satisfies both of these criteria simply by being in the agreed Trial Bundle (see CPR 39 PD/3.9);

(4) As to credit, which may include previous convictions admitted under s.11 of the Civil Evidence Act 1968. However, as a general rule answers on credit are final in the sense that if a particular allegation put in cross-examination is denied, the cross-examiner is not entitled to go further or to call rebutting evidence. However this is subject to a number of important exceptions (one of which is previous convictions) considered in greater detail at 14–54.

Whatever the basis of the cross-examination, it is important to be aware of the "Rule in *Browne v Dunne* (1894) 6 R. 607" which, considering that it is a House of Lords decision of some importance, only appears in an obscure series of nineteenth century law reports. This was remarked upon recently by the Court of Appeal in *Markem Corporation Ltd v Zipher* [2005] EWCA 267, a decision in which the court went to some lengths to remind practitioners that the rule still applies. To quote from the current edition (2005) of *Phipson* at 12–12:

> "In general a party is required to challenge in cross-examination the evidence of any witness of the opposing party if he wishes to submit to the court that the evidence should not be accepted on that point. In general the CPR does not alter the position.
>
> The rules [sic] serves the important function of giving the witness the opportunity of explaining any contradiction or alleged problem with his evidence. If a party has decided not to cross-examine on a particular important point, he will be in difficulty in submitting that the evidence should be rejected."

The rule nevertheless grates somewhat with the CPR's emphasis on proportionality, and the power to control cross-examination given to the court by CPR 32.1(3).

III DOCUMENTARY EVIDENCE

5–33   The CPR have placed far greater emphasis on the early disclosure of important documents: the "cards on the table approach" begins before the claim even starts. The CPR also give a party the right to apply for Pre-Action (CPR 31.16) and Non-Party (CPR 31.17) disclosure, and issue a Witness Summons to produce documents at trial (CPR 34) thus ensuring that they have access to all material documents. To this must now be added the power to obtain information from public authorities under the Freedom of Information Act 2000 and the Data Protection Act 1998. These topics are discussed further at 10–45 onwards.

A Introduction

1. Documents Matter

5–34   Documents play an increasingly important part in civil trials. This is partly due to the abolition of the hearsay rule, but also the far greater ease with which authenticity may now be proved than in the past. In the average modest commercial claim the judge will, characteristically receive as documentary evidence:

(1) The parties' *witness statements*. They may not strictly speaking be evidence until the signatory is called and confirms his signature, but even this may not always be necessary. If the maker of the statement is not to be called to give oral evidence, then the party tendering the statement as hearsay evidence will not be called upon to prove the signature by other evidence unless his opponent requires him to do so;

(2) One or more *trial bundles* (which will usually have been agreed (see CPR 39 PD 3.9) containing all the relevant transaction documents including the contract itself (assuming that it was reduced to writing) along with the relevant inter party correspondence relating to the breach;

(3) Documents relating to *quantum* and mitigation including, where relevant, corporate accounts;

(4) The *written reports* of any expert upon whose expert the parties have been given permission to rely.

On occasions therefore, the witnesses may have little to add other than, for example, to fill in the background to the transaction documents and explain, where necessary, their significance. The only oral element will be their evidence given under cross-examination.

2. Documents are Relatively Easy to Put in Evidence
Many of the problems associated with documentary evidence **5–35** stemmed from the fact that there were numerous arcane rules concerning proof of the documents themselves, in particular the so-called "best (or primary) evidence" rule (see 5–44). Furthermore, whenever a party wished to rely on the contents of a document to prove the facts stated in it, this often involved the introduction of hearsay evidence. As a result of changes, in particular the Civil Evidence Act 1995, many of these problems have now disappeared. This section will deal with the following issues:

(1) What is a "document"? This will involve considering among other matters, the increasing use of electronic methods of document generation, and multi-media formats.

(2) How does a party prove the *contents* of a document if called upon to do so? In this section we shall consider the distinction between public and private documents, the extent to which it is still necessary to produce the original and proof of due execution.

(3) To what extent is a party entitled to call other evidence to *supplement* or *explain* the contents of a document (the so-called "parole evidence rule")? This area is almost exclusively

concerned with written contracts and is treated by some commentators as part of the substantive law of contract rather than a rule of evidence. Accordingly it will only be covered in outline.

(4) Having proved that a document is firstly, authentic (if called upon to do so) and, secondly, introduced its contents into evidence, to what use may those contents then be put? Many of the restrictions that used to exist have been swept away by the abolition of the hearsay rule and will be considered more fully in Chapter 7. Nevertheless, it would not be going too far to say that once a party has introduced a document into evidence, it can (subject to general exclusionary rules) be tendered as proof of any relevant fact that it states or infers.

B What is a Document?

1. Historical Background
5–36 At common law, the courts were refreshingly ready to move with the times: of particular note is the judgment of Darling J. in *R. v Daye* [1908] 2 K.B. 333 in which he, classically, defined a "document" as:

> "any writing or printing capable of being made evidence, no matter on what material it may be inscribed".

This definition was then extended to include matters recorded other than in writing such as tape recordings (*Grant v Southwestern and County Properties Ltd* [1975] Ch. 185) and television film (*Senior v Holdsworth Ex p. Independent Television New Ltd* [1976] Q.B. 23). From relatively early on, the courts were also prepared to accept that for discovery purposes the definition extended to the business records of a company contained in a computer database (*Derby v Weldon (No.9)* [1991] 1 W.L.R. 652).

2. The Modern Position
5–37 This is now set out in s.13 of the Civil Evidence Act 1995, a statute which ostensibly deals with documents containing hearsay, but, it is submitted, can be taken to extend it to all documents whether or not they are admitted as hearsay evidence under that Act (see further 5–42). Section 13 defines a document as:

> ". . . anything in which information of any description is recorded, and 'copy', in relation to a document, means anything onto which information recorded in the document has been copied, by whatever means and whether directly or indirectly".

CPR 31, which deals with disclosure under the CPR also adopts this definition (see CPR 31.4). Although this recognition of modern realities is to be welcomed, it is not without its problems, not least because of the enormous range of disclosable documents it creates. Cases in which literally millions of internal e-mails are potentially disclosable are by no means uncommon in heavy commercial cases. Disclosure of documents generally is considered further in Chapter 10.

C Proving Documents

The common law drew a broad distinction between: 5–38

(1) *Public Documents*, for example, private Acts of Parliament, court orders and birth certificates, which were provable on production of a duly certified copy; and

(2) *Private Documents*, which, subject to certain narrow exceptions, could only be proved by production of the original (often referred to as the "Best" or "Primary Evidence Rule"). Any other evidence of the existence or contents of the document whether by production of a copy or by means of oral evidence was classed as "Secondary Evidence", whatever form it was in, and was generally inadmissible.

The detail and the historical background is fully set out in Chapter 41 of *Phipson* (see in particular 41–05 to 41–12 (Primary Evidence Rule), 41–13 to 41–37 (Secondary Evidence) and 41–38 to 41–84 (Proof of Public Documents).

1. The Usual Position
Issues concerning admission of documentary evidence rarely arise at   5–39
a trial because, in general, the authenticity and the contents are agreed. There are also three important provisions, two in the CPR and one in the Civil Evidence Act 1995, which make the task of proving documents immeasurably easier than it used to be.

(a) CPR 32.19: Notice to Admit
The vast majority of documentary evidence placed before a court will   5–40
have been in the control of the parties themselves and, accordingly dealt with under an order for disclosure (see Chapter 10). CPR 32.19 provides that:

"(1) A party shall be deemed to admit the authenticity of a document disclosed to him under Part 31 (disclosure and inspection

of documents) unless he serves notice that he wishes the document to be proved at trial.

(2) A notice to prove a document must be served:

(a) by the latest date for serving witness statements; or

(b) within 7 days of disclosure of the document, whichever is the later."

A number of points require further discussion. Firstly the rule is probably not confined to documents disclosed in Sch.1, Part 1 (see further 10–14) of the party's List of Documents. "Disclosure" is defined in CPR 31.2 as:

". . . stating that the document exists or has existed".

In *Smithkline Beecham plc v Generics (UK) Ltd* [2003] 4 All E.R. 1302, a case dealing with the meaning of disclosure for the purposes of CPR 31.22 (implied undertaking as to confidentiality, see further 10–31) the Court of Appeal held that, once proceedings have begun, documents which are:

(1) Disclosed voluntarily; or

(2) Referred to in a case statement, witness statement or expert's report;

rather than under an *order* for disclosure are nevertheless "disclosed" as defined in CPR 31.2 and, hence, subject to the implied undertaking in CPR 31.22. It is hard to see how the court could construe the term differently if an issue arose under CPR 32.19 even though CPR 31.2 ostensibly only applies to CPR 31. Secondly, if the term disclosure is to be construed as widely as the *Smithkline* decision suggests, it creates a hidden danger for any party who subsequently realises late in the day that he wishes to dispute the authenticity of a document. The time limits for serving Notice of Non-Admission are very tight and, in particular, are hitched to the last date for serving witness statements (CPR 32.19(2)(b)). The only safe course therefore is to diarise ahead as soon as case management directions are given. The Court of Appeal acknowledged this danger in *Rall v Hume* [2001] 3 All E.R. 248, a personal injuries case involving the admission of a covert video recording. As Potter L.J. stated (at [16]):

"For the purposes of disclosure, a video film or recording is a document within the extended meaning contained in CPR 31.4. A defendant who proposes to use such a film to attack a claimant's case [author's note: or indeed even if he does *not*, for example because it supports the claimant's case: see further 13–36] is therefore subject to all the rules as to disclosure and inspection of documents contained in CPR 31. Equally, if disclosure is made in accordance with CPR 31, whether as part of standard disclosure under CPR 31.6 or the duty of continuing disclosure under CPR 31.11, the claimant will be deemed to admit the authenticity of the film unless notice is served that the claimant wishes the document to be proved at trial".

A party who has been taken unawares by CPR 32.19 might well get a reasonably sympathetic hearing from the court if he applies promptly for permission to withdraw the admission, but it is safer to include a reference to CPR 32.19 in the diary entry for witness statements as a matter of routine.

(b) *Agreed Bundles: CPR 32 and 39 Practice Direction Paragraph 27*   **5–41**
CPR 39.5 and Para.3.9 of the accompanying Practice Direction urges parties where possible to agree the contents of trial bundles (see further 13–32). Accordingly, in the vast majority of cases, all the documentary evidence will be agreed long before the trial commences and the parties and the court will all be working from agreed copies. Although the upshot of this is often that the court has *far too much* documentation placed before it, it does nevertheless mean that issues of proof scarcely ever arise. However, one anomaly needs to be noted. Paragraph 3.3 of the Practice Direction to CPR 39 (which deals with the preparation of trial bundles) states:

"The originals of the documents contained in the trial bundle . . . should be available at the trial".

Quite why this should be considered necessary, save in the case of questioned documents, is beyond the writer. One wonders whether it is a distant echo of the long discarded "best evidence" rule. There is even a direction to this effect in the standard directions for cases allocated to the Small Claims Track (see CPR 27, PD 9 to 14). Although it is generally true to say that it helps to have the originals of key documents available in Small Claims (an obvious example is a standard form contract) because produced copies are often well-nigh illegible, one must question whether this insistence on originals accords with the modern substantive law on documentary evidence. Special provision is made in para.27.2 of PD 32 for the use to which agreed bundles may be put at hearings other than trials. It provides that:

"All documents contained in bundles which have been agreed for use at a hearing shall be admissible at that hearing as evidence of their contents, unless:

(a) the court orders otherwise; or
(b) a party gives notice of objection to the admissibility of particular documents".

One must assume that this rule means what it says and that, accordingly it has no application to "trials" but only to "hearings" for example, of Pt 8 claims and interim applications.

(c) *Civil Evidence Act 1995 s.9*

5–42 This important section, the provisions of which still appear to be relatively unused, provides that:

"(1) A document which is shown to form part of the records of a business or public authority may be received in evidence in civil proceedings without further proof.

(2) A document shall be taken to form part of the records of a business or public authority if there is produced to the court a certificate to that effect signed by an officer of the business or authority to which the records belong. For this purpose:

   (a) a document purporting to be a certificate signed by an officer of a business or public authority shall be deemed to have been duly given by such an officer and signed by him; and
   (b) a certificate shall be treated as signed by him if it purports to bear a facsimile of his signature.

(3) The absence of an entry in the records of a business or public authority may be proved in civil proceedings by affidavit of an officer of the business or authority to which the records belong.

(4) In this section: "records" means records in whatever form; "business" includes any activity regularly carried on over a period of time, whether for profit or not, by any body (whether corporate or not) or by an individual; "officer" includes any person occupying a responsible position in relation to the relevant activities of the business or public authority or in relation to its records; and "public authority" includes any public or statutory undertaking, any government department and any person holding office under Her Majesty.

(5) The court may, having regard to the circumstances of the case, direct that all or any of the above provisions of this section do not apply in relation to a particular document or record, or description of documents or records."

Although, strictly speaking, the 1995 Act only deals with admission of documents that would otherwise involve hearsay (see further 5–48) it is clear that there will be very few categories of documentary records that it will not embrace. It is even arguable that the section embraces all such records whether or not they are tendered as hearsay: s.9(1) specifically refers to "a document" in contrast to s.8(1) (see 5–48) which refers to a "statement in a document".

Discussion The three provisions set out above provide a flexible and comprehensive code capable of dealing with the vast majority of document handing issues that are likely to arise in the average civil trial. The practical consequences are that: **5–43**

(1) Very little court time should need to be taken up in calling oral evidence to prove documents.

(2) The court and the parties will normally all be working from a common set of agreed copies in the form of trial bundles.

(3) It will rarely be necessary to call for the production of an original in the hands of a third party because many such documents will be covered by s.9 of the 1995 Act; the certification process set out in s.9(2) will normally suffice.

(4) It is sometimes useful for the court to be able to see and inspect an original document in order to better appreciate its significance, especially where there is some feature of it, for example the colour and quality of the paper on which it is printed, that is relevant. Indeed, on rare occasions, the absence of the original documents may be fatal to a party's case (see *Post Office Counters v. Mahida Ltd* [2003] EWCA Civ 1583).

(5) Any party who wishes to challenge the authenticity of a document (for example the signature on a witness statement) must be on guard lest he inadvertently is taken to have admitted this under CPR 32.19.

(6) Any party who wishes to put a party to strict proof of documentary evidence had better have a good reason for doing so; any unreasonable running up of costs is likely to lead to costs penalties being imposed.

On the rare occasion that disputes as to the authenticity of a document *do* arise, the party seeking to rely upon it will have to prove the document to the required civil standard. The following paragraphs deal with how this can be done.

2. *Proving Private Documents*

5–44   The basic common law rule used to be that, unless agreed, the party seeking to rely on a document had to call oral evidence to:

(1) Produce the original; and

(2) Prove its authenticity

and that, subject to limited exceptions, nothing less would do. Accordingly, it was thought that as a general rule, secondary evidence of contents was inadmissible. However it is now clear from *Masquerade Music Ltd v Springsteen* [2001] 5 C.P.L.R. 369: [2001] EWCA Civ 513 that the so-called "best evidence" rule no longer exists and that the admission of secondary evidence of the contents of a document goes purely to *weight*. Section 8 of the Civil Evidence Act 1995 has also made it much easier to prove many classes of document without the need to produce the original. Quite apart from anything else, the increasing use of word processors and computers to generate and store documents means that it is now much harder to identify whether there *is* an "original" document. It was much easier to identify the "original" when all documents were handwritten.

(a) *The End of the "Best Evidence Rule"*

5–45   The historical background to the "Best Evidence" Rule, or, to be strictly correct, the "Primary Evidence Rule" is set out in *Phipson* at paras 41–03 to 41–37. In that section, readers will also find considerable detail as to the different forms of "primary" and "secondary" evidence that the courts have over the centuries permitted for the purpose of proving a document. Basically, secondary evidence was only permissible if the original had been lost or destroyed or could not be found after exhaustive search. Secondary evidence of the document was also permissible via a procedural route. A party could rely on secondary evidence of the contents of a document, the original of which was in the hands of his opponent, if having served Notice to Produce the original at trial, his opponent failed to do so. However, the "Best Evidence Rule", or what was left of it, has finally been laid to rest by the Court of Appeal in *Masquerade Music Ltd and Others v Springsteen* [2001] 5 C.P.L.R. 369: [2001] EWCA Civ 513.

5–46   <u>Facts:</u> The claim was brought by the famous rock singer and composer Bruce Springsteen ("S") and concerned his entitlement to the copyright in 19 songs composed by him in the early 1970s. In 1972, S had assigned the copyright in these songs to his management partnership who had assigned them on to X Ltd. Masquerade Music put S to strict proof of the chain of title in the songs.

It was beyond dispute that, in order for the assignments of the   **5–47**
copyrights to X Ltd to be effective, s.36(3) of the Copyright Act 1956
required them to be in writing and signed by the assignors. Neither
the original nor a copy of the written assignment could be found after
what Ferris J. described as a "reasonably thorough" search. The trial
judge permitted Mr Springsteen to prove the written assignment by
calling the New York attorney who had incorporated X Co. He, in
effect gave evidence of "system", stating that, as an experienced attorney in the music business, he was well accustomed to creating for
companies whose sole raison d'être was to act as a corporate vehicle
for exploiting an artist's works. On that basis, the judge found that
there *had* been a written assignment sufficient to satisfy s.36(3) of the
1956 Act. The Court of Appeal dismissed the defendants' appeal. In
the process, Jonathan Parker L.J. (with whom Waller and Laws L.JJ
agreed) after a comprehensive review of the case law going back to
Omychand v Burke (1744) 1 Atk. 2, administered the final burial rites
to the Best (Primary) Evidence Rule (at [81]) when he stated:

"In my judgment, the time has now come when it can be said with
confidence that the best evidence rule, long on its deathbed, has
finally expired. In every case where a party seeks to adduce secondary evidence of the contents of a document, it is a matter for
the court to decide, in the light of all the circumstances in the case,
what (if any) weight to attach to that evidence. Where the party
seeking to adduce the secondary evidence could readily produce
the document it may be expected that (absent some special circumstances) the court will decline to admit the secondary evidence on
the ground that it is worthless. At the other extreme, where the
party seeking to adduce the secondary evidence genuinely cannot
produce the document, it may be expected that (absent some
special circumstances) the court will admit the secondary evidence
and attach such weight to it as it considers appropriate in all the
circumstances. In cases falling between those two extremes, it is for
the court to make a judgment as to whether in all the circumstances
any weight should be attached to the secondary evidence. Thus, the
"admissibility" of secondary evidence of the contents of documents is, in my judgment, entirely dependent upon whether or not
any weight is to be attached to that evidence. And whether or not
any weight is to be attached to such secondary evidence is a matter
for the court to decide, taking into account all the circumstances of
the particular case."

Although no mention is made of s.8 of the Civil Evidence Act 1995
in his judgment, perhaps for reasons that are explained at 5–48 below,
it is suggested that the current law concerning proof of documents by

secondary evidence both at common law and under the 1995 Act is in effect the same. The above extract from Jonathan Parker L.J.'s judgment also provides a valuable point of reference whenever a party is put to proof of a document.

(b) *Use of Copies: Civil Evidence Act 1995 s.8*

5–48   Section 8 of the 1995 Act provides that:

> (1) Where a statement contained in a document is admissible as evidence in civil proceedings, it may be proved:
>
> > (a) by the production of that document; or
> > (b) whether or not that document is still in existence, by the production of a copy of that document or of the material part of it,
>
> authenticated in such manner as the court may approve.
>
> (2) It is immaterial for this purpose how many removes there are between a copy and the original.

"Statement" is defined in s.13 of the Act as:

> "Any representation of fact or opinion however made".

It is important to point out here that, traditionally, a distinction was drawn between:

> (1) Those documents tendered as *original* as opposed to hearsay evidence, such as conveyances, leases, written contracts and assignments of the type referred to in the *Springsteen* case; and
>
> (2) Documents tendered as *hearsay*, for example the written statement of an absent witness (for further discussion of the hearsay principle see Chapter 7).

Some commentators suggest that s.8 is sufficiently wide to embrace both classes of document. If that were to be the case, the *Springsteen* decision would be redundant. However, even on the assumption that s.8 *does* only apply to documents falling into category (2) above, it is submitted that *Springsteen* is on all fours with s.8 in any event. That being said, s.8 represents a refreshingly realistic approach to the realities of modern document origination, not least in s.8(2).

5–49   <u>Example:</u> An important original document, not covered by s.9 and located in New Zealand, needs to be brought before the court as a matter of urgency in circumstances where its importance could not have been anticipated. Section 8(2) (subject to appropriate evidence of provenance and as to the chain of transmission) would enable the document to be admitted in evidence even if it had been scanned into a computer in New Zealand, emailed as an attachment to a computer in England, printed out and then faxed to the court.

Very different from the days when all copies consisted of laboriously hand-written transcriptions.

(c) *Methods of Proof*

Although there is a large body of case law dealing with specific **5–50** methods of proof, it is submitted that, following the developments in the law referred to above, each case will depend upon what is in issue in relation to the document itself. The dispute may be, for example, as to whether:

- The document is indeed the original;
- The handwriting or signature upon it can be correctly identified;
- (In the case of a will) whether it has been validly executed or attested;
- Whether it has been materially altered;
- Whether it is a forgery;
- Whether it bears the correct date;

and so on. In every case the party seeking to rely upon it will need to adduce the most cogent evidence that he or she can, assisted by secondary evidence where appropriate. For example, the most cogent evidence of the fact that a document has been written or signed by a particular individual is by calling her to give evidence to that effect by producing the original to her and asking her to identify it; an obvious, and regularly recurring example of this is where a witness identifies the signature on her witness statement before giving oral evidence. However, handwriting may also be proved by calling other persons to testify either that they were present when the individual signed the document or to identify the handwriting as that of the person in question. Finally, subject to the court giving its permission under CPR 35, *expert evidence* may be received to identify the writer. Those seeking a comprehensive list of the permitted methods of proof by primary and secondary evidence should consult paras 41–05 to 41–37 of *Phipson*. Nevertheless it is respectfully submitted that under the current law, there are *no* prescribed methods of proof; in each case it is simply a question of weight. Finally, it should be noted that there are a number of rebuttable presumptions that may assist in cases where some aspect of a document is in dispute, namely:

(1) Section 4 of the Evidence Act 1938 provides that any document which is proved or purports to be more than 20 years old (sometimes referred to as an "Ancient Document"), and which is produced from proper custody, is presumed to have been duly executed. The effect of this provision is that once the foundation conditions have been satisfied no evidence of the handwriting, signature, sealing or delivery of the document needs to be given. The 20 years runs from the date of *execution* of the document; this rule applies in the case of wills even if the testator does not die until many years later. Furthermore, the rule applies to *all* documents. "Proper custody" simply means that it is produced from a place where you would expect to find it kept if it were authentic. The relevant law is fully set out in paras 40–21 to 40–23 of *Phipson*.

(2) A document is presumed to be executed on the date that it bears (*Anderson v Weston* (1840) 6 Bing. N.C. 296);

(3) Any *alteration* to a *deed* is presumed to have been made *before* execution; conversely any alteration to a *will* is presumed to have been made *after* that date.

Before finally leaving the topic two further important provisions need to be noted. First, the Electronic Communications Act 2000 provides for the authentication of electronically generated and transmitted documents to be authenticated by means of an electronic "signature", signature being widely defined by s.7(2) as:

"... so much of anything in electronic form as:

(a) is incorporated into or otherwise logically associated with any electronic communication or electronic data; and

(b) purports to be so incorporates or associated for the purpose of being used in establishing the authenticity of the communication or data, the integrity of the communication or data or both."

Secondly, the Stamp Act 1891 provides that no instrument requiring a stamp:

"shall be given in evidence, or be available for any purpose whatever"

unless it is duly stamped or the required amount along with any penalty is paid to the officer of the court. The law is fully set out in paras 40–33 to 40–34 of *Phipson*. The 1891 Act has frequently caught landlords unawares in county court possession lists where it is by no means uncommon to find that tenancy agreements have not been appropriately stamped.

3. *Proof of Public Documents*

It is not possible to do more than scratch the surface of this topic in **5–51** view of its vast range (see further *Phipson*, 41–38 to 41–76). The common law approach to public documents was, firstly that their contents could be proved by production of a copy on the basis that it would be oppressive to require the keeper of the original to produce it every time that a court required sight of it (see *Mortimer v McCallan* (1840) 6 M. & W. 58). Secondly, from early on, the contents of public documents were admitted to prove their truth by way of exception to the hearsay rule (see further 7–53). The classic definition of a public document is still that given by Lord Blackburn in *Sterland v Freccia* (1880) 5 App. Cas. 623 at 643:

> ". . . a public document . . . [means] a document that is made for the purpose of the public making use of it, and being able to refer to it. It is meant to be where there is a judicial or quasi-judicial duty to inquire . . ."

Although the common law rules relating to public documents have been specifically preserved by s.7(2) of the Civil Evidence Act 1995, there are now numerous statutes in force which permit public documents to be proved by production of copies. A few examples are set out below.

Document	*Method of Proof*
Public Acts and EU Treaties	Judicially noted
Statutory Instruments	Queen's Printer's copy
Byelaws	Certified copy (s.238 of the Local Government Act 1972)
Public Records	Certified copy (s.9 of the Public Records Act 1958)

There are a whole host of other statutory provisions, many of which overlap with ss.8 and 9 of the 1995 Act. One cannot help but wonder whether all this complexity serves any useful purpose. Proof of matters such as birth, death and marriage, along with many others are set out in 32–55 to 32–106 of *Phipson*.

Conclusion Whatever the nature of the document in issue, a party **5–52** will not generally be at a major disadvantage if he cannot produce the original in circumstances where it would be unreasonable to expect him to do so. In the case of a questioned private document the *Springsteen* decision (see 5–46) and s.8 of the Civil Evidence Act 1995 have swept away the so called "Best (Primary) Evidence Rule". In the case of public documents, quite apart from s.9 of the Civil Evidence Act 1995, many statutes permit proof by means of a copy or certified copy. Nevertheless, in any case where there is likely to be an issue over the proof of a document, it may be advisable to seek a direction as to the method of proof required by the court (see CPR 32.1(1)(b)).

D The Parol Evidence Rule

1. The Principle

5–53   Chapters 42 and 43 of *Phipson* devote no less than 101 pages of text to this so called rule and the exceptions to it. It is therefore no easy task to sum up this weighty jurisprudence in a few short paragraphs. However, the principle is very easily stated. To cite paragraph 42–01 of *Phipson*:

> "Where a transaction has been reduced to, or recorded in writing either by requirement of law, or agreement of the parties, the writing becomes, in general, the exclusive record thereof, and no evidence may be given to prove the terms of the transaction except the document itself or secondary evidence of its contents . . ."

It should be pointed out that the rule excludes *all* evidence, not simply oral evidence and is therefore more accurately described as the "extrinsic evidence rule". Applications of the rule have tended to arise almost exclusively in relation to contract and wills. So far as *contracts* are concerned its practical effect is that once the parties have reduced their agreement to writing, extrinsic evidence is not admissible for the purpose of contradicting, varying, adding to or subtracting from its terms. So far as *wills* are concerned, the "parol evidence rule" was abolished by s.21 of the Administration of Justice Act 1982 for wills taking effect after January 1, 1983.

At its core, the rule is based on principles of *relevance*, as was recognised by the Court of Appeal in *Beazer Homes Ltd v Stroud* [2005] EWCA Civ 265. One of its most important practical effects is that evidence of pre-contractual negotiations are generally inadmissible. The rationale behind this was stated by Lord Wilberforce in *Prenn v Simmonds* [1971] 1 W.L.R. 1381 at 1384E:

> "The reason for not admitting evidence of these exchanges is not a technical one or even mainly one of convenience. (Though the attempt to admit it did greatly prolong the case and add to its expense.) It is simply that such evidence is unhelpful."

Two further passages from Lord Wilberforce's speech reveal the true purpose behind the rule. Firstly at 1385A when he states:

"By the nature of things where negotiations are difficult, the parties' positions, with each passing letter, are changing and until the final agreement, though converging, still divergent. It is only the final document which records a consensus."

He then goes on to state at 1385C:

"... in a world of give and take, men have to be satisfied with less than they want."

All that matters is what the parties were intending at the *time that they reached agreement*, and the fact that they then expressed that intention in writing; nothing else matters.

2. Exceptions
Nevertheless, the rule is subject to so many exceptions that some **5–54** commentators have suggested that it is a mirage. This is clearly not so, as the recent *Beazer* decision referred to above shows. If nothing else, *pre-contractual negotiations* will not be admitted unless they can be brought within one of the exceptions listed below (see, in particular Lord Hoffman in *ICS Ltd v West Bromwich Building Society* [1998] 1 W.L.R. 896 at 251E). The following summary is, of necessity, cursory; for a more comprehensive review see *Cross* 715 to 729. On matters of detail you will need to go to *Phipson* or the standard works on the law of contract. Common arguments for the admission of extrinsic evidence include:

"It's not the whole contract".

Although the law requires that some contracts be wholly reduced to writing (contracts for the sale of land being the prime example: s.2 of the Law of Property (Miscellaneous Provisions Act) 1989) states that extrinsic evidence will be admissible as to the other terms if it can be proved that they exist.

"It's void/voidable".

Obviously, extrinsic evidence as to illegality or, more commonly, evidence of misrepresentation will be admissible.

"It's governed by statute".

There are common situations in which the receipt of extrinsic evidence necessarily follows from the operation of statute. Obvious examples are, evidence as to reliance on the seller's care and skill in a written contract to which s.14(3) of the Sale of Goods Act 1979 applies, or whether what a tenancy agreement describes as a "licence" is in fact an assured tenancy.

"There's a collateral contract".

Extrinsic evidence will be admissible in the situation where a party is alleging that he only entered into the written agreement on the basis of an oral "side contract".

"It's not a contract".

Parties will often draw up a document that, although lacking any contractual force, records that a level of understanding has been reached. It may be called a "comfort letter" or a "memorandum". Alternatively the parties may, having concluded an oral agreement record only certain "heads" of the agreement in a written memorandum. You are now probably beginning to realise why some commentators have dismissed the parol evidence rule as myth.

"It needs interpretation".

This is perhaps the most difficult area of all which engages the still not entirely resolved conflict between the literal and contextual schools of thought on matters of linguistic interpretation. Much of the current controversy stems from the speech of Lord Hoffman in *ICS Ltd v West Bromwich Building Society* [1998] 1 W.L.R. 896 in which he set out five "principles" of interpretation, only the first of which need be cited for the purposes of this brief summary:

> "(1)   Interpretation is the ascertainment of the meaning which the document would convey to the reasonable person having all the background knowledge which would reasonably have been available to the parties in the situation in which they were at the time of the contract".

This could have the effect of allowing in a large amount of extrinsic evidence that in the past would have been regarded as inadmissible even though he makes it quite clear in the third of his "principles" that evidence of *previous negotiations* will not generally be admissible. This difficult area has been revisited by the Higher Courts on a number of occasions, indeed, Lord Hoffman has himself sought to make the admission of such evidence subject to principles of relevance (see *BCCI v Ali (No.1)* [2002] 2 A.C. 251 at 269). Suffice it to say for the time being that extrinsic evidence *may* be admissible to resolve an ambiguity or to give the document practical effect (see, in particular, in the cases of notices, *Mannai Investment Co Ltd v Eagle Star Life Assurance Co Ltd* [1997] A.C. 749) but a strong case will have to made as to relevance. As with relevance generally, each contract will depend on its own particular facts (see *Phipson* 43–09): for a recent example in which the Court of Appeal was of the view that a claimant should at least have the *opportunity* of arguing for the admission of extrinsic evidence at trial, see *Proforce Recruit Ltd v The Rugby Group Ltd* [2006] EWCA Civ 69.

3. Wills

As already indicated, in the case of wills the law was changed by s.21   **5–55**
of the Administration of Justice Act 1982 which provides that:

"(1) This section apples to a will:

    (a) In so far as any part of it is meaningless;

    (b) In so far as the language used in any part of it is ambiguous on the face of it;

    (c) In so far as the evidence, other than evidence of the testator's intention, shows that the language used in any part of it is ambiguous in the light of surrounding circumstances.

(2) In so far as this section applies to a will extrinsic evidence of the testator's intention may be admitted to assist in its interpretation."

This welcome change in the law has removed many of the difficulties associated with the parol evidence rule in this area. However, it must not be forgotten that, if the testator's intention is in issue, any evidence adduced under this section will still have to satisfy the normal burden and standard of proof. Accordingly, if the testator's expressions of intent are vague and on the face of them not fully settled, the evidence so adduced will be of no effect (see *Re Williams, Wiles v Madgin* [1985] 1 All E.R. 964).

E Proving Admissibility of the Contents

The contents of many documents used to be inadmissible on the   **5–56**
grounds that they were hearsay. Although documents such as contracts, conveyances and leases were always treated as "proving their own contents", many other commonly encountered documents such as records, correspondence and witness statements were treated as hearsay because they were being tendered to prove the truth of their

contents. As already noted, this restriction has been removed by the Civil Evidence Act 1995 and will be discussed more fully in Chapter 7. Documents are, of course, subject to the other rules as to admissibility. For example, the contents of a document will not be admissible insofar as they:

(1) Are irrelevant;

(2) Consist of inadmissible opinion evidence;

(3) Are privileged; or

(4) Protected by public interest immunity.

The fact that evidence is contained in a document, however impressive that document may look, makes its contents no more (or less) admissible than evidence tendered in any other form.

IV REAL EVIDENCE

5–57   The final category of evidence consists of evidence which the court views and interprets with its own unaided senses, for example:

(1) The operation of machinery,

(2) The scene of an accident; or

(3) The way a witness gives his or her evidence.

Such evidence will however often need oral testimony (often that of an expert witness) to "bring it to life". It should also be noted that evidence may on occasions be received as both "documentary" and "real evidence". A good example of this is the covert video which is a "document" for the purpose of CPR 31 but is received as "real evidence" when it is played in court insofar as the judge is asked to make findings of fact based on what she has seen. *Phipson* (see 1–14) criticises the use of the term as being "indefinite and ambiguous" and questions whether the term is a very helpful one. It clearly extends beyond "material objects" if you include within the definition the way in which a live witness gives their evidence. On the other hand, to confine it to material objects other than documents also leads to inaccuracy because many material objects, for example a computer, will have no forensic significance whatsoever until expert evidence has explained whatever facet of its operation is relevant to a fact in issue.

Non-documentary evidence is specifically dealt with under the CPR. The court may make orders for the inspection and preservation of such evidence (see further, CPR 25.1(1)(c)(I) and (ii), 10–41 and *O'Hare and Browne* 27–052 and Chapter 3 of *Hollander*).

Conclusions

At the start of this chapter it was stated that, in the vast majority of **5–58**
cases facts are now much easier to prove than used to be the case
whatever medium they present in. The diagram on page 166 serves to
illustrate this fact. On successive pages you will find two further diagrams setting out the way in which the various methods of proof
interact. It is particularly important to keep three things in mind.
Firstly, once an item of evidence is admitted, it may be used for whatever forensic purpose an advocate wishes to use it for. For example,
documents that were originally in the control of the claimants' witnesses may be used to cross-examine the defendants' witnesses and
vice versa. Secondly, once an item of evidence is admitted, it is like
dropping a stone into a pond: its major significance may not emerge
until a long way into the trial, for example in cross-examination of
one of the last witnesses to be called by the defendants. A brief
perusal of these diagrams will enable you to readily identify the stage
at which its full impact is likely to emerge. Finally, these diagrams
enable you to take in at a glance the method by which certain crucial
facts may best be proven. One of the most interesting recent cases to
work through with these two diagrams is *Odyssey Re (London) Ltd v
OIC Run Off Ltd* [2000] EWCA Civ 71. A very brief, and extremely
simplified, summary of the facts is set out below.

C were involved in a huge re-insurance claim in which they were
seeking a declaration that a "Memorandum of Understanding"
reached between themselves and D in 1974 as to various run-off liabilities was not intended to be contractually binding. Their chief
negotiator at that meeting was a Mr Leslie Sage whose position had
always been that the results of the meeting were never intended to be
contractually binding. Six months before the date fixed for trial (late
1989) C realised that a document disclosed by the D consisted of a
written memo drawn up by Mr Michael Flint ("the Flint Note") a
member of the D's team. It began, "Leslie Sage. Goodwill agreement.
Not a legal contract".

When initially seen by the claimants' solicitors, Mr Sage had been
very vague about what had happened at the meeting; not surprising,
since the events had taken place some 14 years before. However,
having read the "Flint Note", in his final witness statement he exhibited a somewhat greater degree of certitude. Indeed, he expressed
himself in words that bore a remarkable similarity to the words in the
"Flint Note". Under cross-examination he was asked whether he had

always been that certain of what had been said or whether his certitude derived from having read the "Flint Note". He replied to the effect that he had *always* been that certain. After three lengthy trials before Hirst, Moore-Bick and Langley JJ. the Court of Appeal finally concluded that, in saying this, Mr Sage had committed perjury. What makes the case so interesting, albeit a very long read, is the fact that it begs the question as to whether Mr Sage should *ever have been shown* the "Flint Note" in the first place. He did not need to give oral evidence as to its contents because, having been disclosed by the defendants as part of their discovery, it had been deemed admitted (see now CPR 32.19). The note therefore derives its forensic impact from the fact that it is entirely independent *of Mr Sage*. Just a moment's glance at diagram 2 brings this home. The diagrams also provide a valuable cross-check when either sending instructions to counsel to advise on evidence or when preparing your own trial plan (see further 13–37).

Diagram 1

PROVING FACTS

	TYPE OF EVIDENCE	ACTION
1.	ORAL EVIDENCE FACT WITNESSES (TRIAL)	**PREPARE AND SERVE WS IN ACCORDANCE WITH RULES OR CM DIRCTIONS (CPR 32)**
	FACT WITNESSES (OTHER)	**SERVE WS IN ACCORDANCE WITH CPR 8 OR 23**
	EXPERT WITNESSES	**GET COURT'S PERMISSION (CPR 35) AND COMPLY WITH CM DIRECTIONS**
2.	DOCUMENTS OUR DOCUMENTS	**SERVE LIST: LIST IS NOTICE TO PRODUCE AND ADMIT: STRICTLY PROVE ONLY IF NOTICE OF NON-ADMISSION SERVED (CPR 31.19)**

THEIR DOCUMENTS	**ALL GO IN UNLESS YOU SERVE NOTICE OF NON ADMISSION**
OTHER DOCUMENTS	**CONSIDER: ss.8 AND 9 CEA 1995 NOTICE TO ADMIT (CPR 31.19) HEARSAY NOTICE (CPR 33.3)**

3. REAL EVIDENCE

OBJECTS EG. MACHINERY	**SEEK EARLY CM DIRECTION PLUS CONSIDER CPR 35 (EXPERTS)**

4. PROOF WITHOUT EVIDENCE

PRE CLAIM ADMISSIONS	**REFER TO IN CASE STATEMENT SEEK**
POST-CLAIM	**JUDGMENT UNDER CPR 14: CONSIDER NOTICE TO ADMIT FACTS (CPR 32.18)**

Diagram 2

THE COURSE OF A CIVIL TRIAL

PRE TRIAL

JUDGE READS TRIAL BUNDLES

<u>CLAIMANT'S CASE</u>

C OPENS (REFERS COURT TO ADMITTED AND AGREED FACTS)

C PRESENTS EVIDENCE

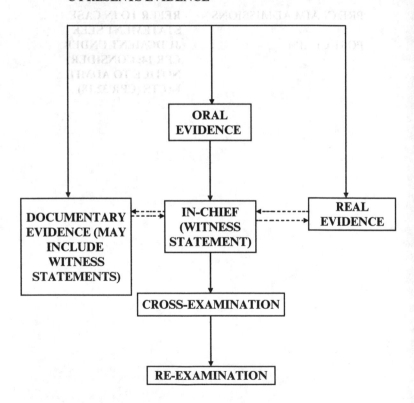

(RARE) SUBMISSION OF NO CASE

Diagram 3

DEFENDANT'S CASE
D OPENS (OPTIONAL)
CALLS EVIDENCE

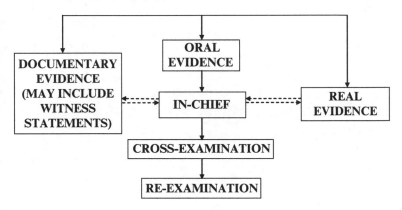

D CLOSES
C CLOSES
JUDGE DECIDES

Chapter 6

"Proof Without Evidence"

This chapter will look at a miscellaneous group of legal rules under   **6–01**
which facts may be proved or taken to have been proved. This category is sometimes classified, misleadingly in the writer's view, as
"Methods of Proof without Evidence". Facts are treated by most
commentators as being capable of proof without the need to adduce
evidence if they are:

(1) Formally admitted;

(2) Judicially noted;

(3) Created by an estoppal; or

(4) Presumed.

Presumptions have already been dealt with at 4–46 since they are best
regarded as a formalised category of circumstantial evidence.

I FORMAL ADMISSIONS

The common law drew a distinction between "formal" and "infor-   **6–02**
mal" admissions, the former usually, although not exclusively, being
made in pleadings and the latter generally being made orally by a
party or some other person acting as his agent or having an identity
of interest. Informal admissions used to constitute an important
exception to the rule against hearsay and could consist of anything
from a motorist saying "I'm sorry, it was all my fault" at the scene of
an accident to a party's solicitor or counsel conceding material facts
in the course of open negotiations. They are dealt with along with
hearsay in the next chapter at 7–48.

1. The General Principle

6–03   Formal admissions (whether made at common law or under CPR) are *conclusive* proof of the facts or issues admitted and accordingly relieve a party from having to call *any evidence at all* in support of that fact. A remarkable example of this can be found in the Court of Appeal decision in *Sollitt v D J Broady Ltd* [2000] 3 C.P.L.R. 259. The defendants sought permission to withdraw an admission of liability on the basis that the claimant had not sued the correct company. The Court of Appeal refused permission, albeit on most unusual facts, even though there was *no dispute* that the claimant had sued the wrong company. However, since the admission had been knowingly made on their behalf by their solicitors and with the benefit of legal advice, the defendants were bound by it. Their use is specifically addressed by the CPR at a number of points.

(a) Pre-Claim

6–04   Although the only specific reference to admissions is that contained in para.3.9 of the *Pre-Action Protocol for Personal Injury Claims* which provides that:

> "Where liability is admitted, the presumption is that the defendant will be bound by the admission for all claims with a total value of up to £15,000",

that is to say all claims within Fast Track trial limits, the clear tenor of the Protocol Practice Direction and many passages within individual protocols is that parties should, wherever possible, be prepared to narrow the issues by making appropriate admissions. There are numerous passages, for example in the *Protocols Practice Direction* (para.4.5), the *Pre-Action Protocol for the Resolution of Clinical Disputes* (para.3.25) and the *Professional Negligence Pre-Action Protocol* (para.B5.2) that implicitly encourage early admissions by requiring a reasoned response to any parts of the claim that are disputed. However, it now seems that, on the basis of strong *dicta* in *Sowerby v Charlton* [2005] EWCA Civ 1610, that pre-trial admissions are not covered by CPR 14 (see below). Accordingly since this means that they must be treated as *informal* admissions, a party who is met with a defence denying liability would simply have to rely on the pre-trial admission as *evidence* of liability which he would, no doubt, consider relying on in support of an application for summary judgment.

(b) Procedure During the Claim

6–05   A detailed discussion of the procedure relating to admissions under the CPR is outside the scope of this book; reference should be made to Chapter 16 of *O'Hare and Browne*, which covers the topic in detail. CPR 14.1 provides that:

"(1) A party may admit the truth of the whole or any part of another party's case.

(2) He may do so by giving notice in writing (such as in a statement of case or by letter)."

The rule then goes on to set out in some detail the circumstance in which a party may make an admission in respect of a money claim in his Acknowledgement of Service (CPR 14.3 to 7, see *O'Hare and Browne* 16–004 to 16–010). CPR 16.5, which deals with the drafting of the defence also addresses admissions. Not only is a defendant required to specify in his defence which allegations he admits (CPR 16.5(1)(c)) he also runs the risk of being *deemed* to have admitted any allegation in the Particulars of Claim that he does not deal with by way of denial, admission or putting the claimant to proof. However CPR 16.5 also provides that:

"(3)   A defendant who:

(a) fails to deal with an allegation; but
(b) has set out in his defence the nature of his case in relation to the issue in which that allegation is relevant;

shall be taken to require that allegation to be proved.

(4)   Where the claim includes a money claim, a defendant shall be taken to require that any allegation relating to the amount of money claimed be proved unless he expressly admits it."

In other words, provided that the "gist" of the defence is set out on a particular issue, a defendant is not taken to have admitted any pleaded facts within that issue that he does not expressly deal with. A claimant will always have to prove *quantum* unless it is expressly admitted. As well as being able to admit any facts in writing at any time under CPR 14.1, a party may also admit facts or whole issues in response to Notice to Admit served under CPR 32.18. This important and underused tactical device is considered further at 13–04.

(c) *Effect of Admissions*
A party will frequently be released from the need to prove large parts   **6–06**
of his claim as a result of admissions made by the defendant in his pleadings or otherwise under the CPR.

6–07   **Example:** In a road traffic claim the defendant in his defence admits
ELEMENTS 1 (existence of a duty—he can hardly do otherwise),
2 (breach of that duty) and 3 (causation) and simply puts the claimant
to proof of the damage he has suffered.

6–08   Although this is to a large extent a matter of procedure rather than
evidence, it is important to emphasise that the above admissions will
entitle the claimant to seek judgment on admissions under CPR 14.3:

"An amount to be decided by the court".

It is sometimes argued on the basis of *Parrott v Jackson* [1996]
P.I.Q.R. P394 that such a judgment is not possible unless the defendant has expressly admitted causation. Even though this may be
technically correct, it will usually be obvious on the Particulars of
Claim that the claimant has suffered *some* loss as a result of the defendant's admitted negligence so that, even if judgment under CPR 14 is
not available there will be an unanswerable case for summary judgment under CPR 24 (see further *Sowerby v Charlton* at [32]).
Defendants are often unwilling to admit causation on the basis that
this shuts them out from raising causation points on individual heads
of damage. It does not because, in conceding ELEMENT 3 (causation), the defendant is doing no more than admitting that he is
responsible for causing *some* loss to the claimant. He is not admitting
responsibility for *all* of the claimant's loss. He will still be entitled to
put the claimant to proof as to each head of damage. Furthermore,
he will not be precluded from adducing evidence that the claimant's
losses are also attributable to other factors sufficient to reduce his
overall liability. The Court of Appeal decision in *Lunnun v Singh*
[1999] 4 C.P.L.R. 587 illustrates the latter point. Although the judgment was entered in default of Acknowledgement of Service, the
decision would be equally applicable to a judgment entered on admissions or a summary judgment on liability.

6–09   **Facts:** C sought damages in nuisance against his adjoining occupiers
D for flood damage caused as a result of a cracked sewer on D's
premises. At the assessment of damages hearing D sought to put C
to proof of each of his heads of damage arguing in particular that
since the amount of water being pumped out of C's cellar each week
(70–100 gallons) exceeded D's total yearly water consumption, C had
the burden of proving that the alleged water damage was attributable
to D's nuisance. The judge hearing the case debarred D from raising
the causation issue. D appealed.

6–10   In allowing the defendants' appeal and following an earlier decision of Sir Richard Scott V.C. in *Maes Finance Ltd v Phillips & Co,*
unreported, March 12, 1997, Jonathan Parker J. (at 599) stated:

"... in the instant case all questions going to quantification, including the question of causation in relation to the particular heads of loss claimed by the claimant, remain open to the defendants at the damages hearing".

(d) *Withdrawal of Admissions*

Informal admissions, whether made by the defendant at the scene of the accident or by his insurers in a letter, cannot be withdrawn as such, they can be explained away or qualified, but they remain available as *evidence* that can be deployed against him. However, in the case of formal admissions the position is different. Under the CPR, a party may amend or withdraw an admission with leave of the court under CPR 14.1(5). However the Court of Appeal decision in *Gale v Superdrug Stores Plc* [1996] 3 All E.R. 468 continues to cause controversy.   6–11

Facts: C, an employee of D Ltd suffered an injury at work in October 1990 when she was unloading a delivery van. In November 1991 D's insurers wrote to C's solicitors stating: 6–12

"We can confirm that in the circumstances, we do not propose making any further dispute as to liability".

The claim failed to settle (although C did receive a voluntary interim payment) and, with the three year limitation cut off looming C's solicitors commenced proceedings in September 1993. D then served a defence denying liability. C's solicitor applied to have that paragraph struck out as an abuse of process. In evidence, he relied solely on the letter of admission.

The Court of Appeal (Thorpe L.J. dissenting) upheld the decision of H.H. Judge Wroath to dismiss the claimant's application, largely on the basis that there was no *evidence* that the claimant would suffer any prejudice if the defence were allowed to stand. In the subsequent Court of Appeal decision of *Sollitt v Broady* (see above) Lord Bingham C.J., while accepting that it was generally necessary to look at the respective prejudice each party would suffer if permission to withdraw an admission was granted or refused, acknowledged that the dissenting judgment of Thorpe L.J. had "very considerable persuasive force". It is submitted that the decision in *Gale*:

(1) Was never more than a fact specific decision that turned largely on the fact that the claimant had failed to adduce sufficient evidence in support of *his* application to strike out; and

(2) Has, in any event, been overtaken by the CPR because a "bare denial" defence of the kind served by the defendants would no longer be permitted under CPR 16.5(2): the defendants would have to assert facts sufficient to show that they had a defence on the merits or not strike out in any event;

(3) Predates the CPR and is therefore of little assistance not least because it is now clear on the wording of CPR 14.1(5) that it is for the *defendant* to make the application to withdraw the admission and therefore, at the very least, he will have the primary burden of adducing some evidence in support of his application (a point now confirmed in *Sowerby v Charlton* [2005] EWCA Civ 1610).

6–13   Subsequently, there have been at least four High Court decisions and two Court of Appeal decisions under the CPR. The first two High Court decisions were *Flaviis v Pauley* [2002] EWHC 2886 (Nelson J.) and *Hamilton v Hertfordshire County Council* [2003] EWHC 3018 (Keith J. on appeal). In *Flaviis*, the defendants had admitted liability for the very severe injuries that the claimant had suffered when the front wheel of the motorcycle he had hired from the defendants had become detached. However it later emerged that the claimant was an illegal overstayer who had been relying on a stolen Italian passport. The defendant now wished to defend on three grounds, firstly that the contract of hire was void for illegality and, secondly, that the accident was caused solely by the claimant's own negligence and, thirdly, that the claimant was guilty of contributory negligence. Nelson J.'s decision was based largely on the prospects of success of each of these proposed defences. He accordingly gave the defendant leave to withdraw the admission but only so as to allow him to run the illegality defence. In *Hamilton*, a similar approach was adopted by Keith J. on hearing an appeal against a refusal by the trial judge to allow the defendants to withdraw an admission of liability arising out of an accident a work. Once again the judge concentrated on the merits of the defence that was now being asserted and its prospects of success. Conversely, in *Lenton v Abrahams* [2003] EWHC 1104 and *Cluley v RL Dix Heating* [2003] EWCA Civ 1595 defendants were refused permission to make late withdrawals of admissions in circumstances where the claimants would have suffered severe prejudice as a result. The Court of Appeal in *Cluley* dealt with the appeal as a case on amendment under CPR 17, so it casts no further light on CPR 14.1. The final decision in this lengthy saga is the Court of Appeal decision in *Sowerby v Charlton* [2005] EWCA Civ 1610 which:

(1) Suggests but does not definitively state (see [33]) that CPR 14 only regulates admissions made *after* proceedings have begun; the practical effect of this being that the correct procedural route for judgment on a pre-claim admission would be an application for summary judgment (CPR 24) rather than judgment on admissions (CPR 14.4) (see [32]); and

(2) States that the decision in *Gale* should now be approached with caution ([34]).

The court concludes [35] by commending to practitioners the guidance given by Sumner J. in para.45 of his judgment in *Braybrook v Basildon & Thurrock University NHS Trust* [2004] EWHC 3352 Q.B.D. in cases where, by whatever procedural route, a party wishes to withdraw a formal admission:

"1. In exercising its discretion the court will consider all the circumstances of the case and seek to give effect to the overriding objective.

2. Amongst the matters to be considered will be:

   (a) the reasons and justification for the application which must be made in good faith;
   (b) the balance of prejudice to the parties;
   (c) whether any party has been the author of any prejudice that they may suffer;
   (d) the prospects of success of any issue arising from the withdrawal of any admission;
   (e) the public interest in avoiding where possible satellite litigation, disproportionate use of court resources and the impact of any strategic manoeuvring.

3. The nearer any application is to the final hearing the less chance of success it will have even if the party making the application can establish clear prejudice. This may be decisive if the application is shortly before the hearing."

It is respectfully suggested that this guidance should be followed irrespective of when the admission was made and whatever the procedural context in which the issue of withdrawal arises.

Conclusion The practical effects of the formal admissions rule are not only to reduce considerably the number of issues in a case that fall to be decided, but also to reduce the scope of the evidence that the parties are required to present to the court. Three points in particular need to be borne in mind at all times.

6–14

(1) The expectation under the CPR and Protocols is that parties will do all they can to narrow the issues by making early admissions whenever appropriate: those who fail to do so may find themselves paying the price in costs as the claim unfolds; and

(2) An admission of liability still leaves the field open to the defendant to raise individual causation issues on *quantum* as well as those relating to failure to mitigate loss and contributory negligence;

(3) A party who refuses to admit "certainties" can be placed under pressure by the Notice to Admit procedure in CPR 32.18 (see further 13–04).

II JUDICIAL NOTICE

1. The Principle

6–15 The effect of judicial notice is that the court accepts the truth of a fact without formal proof, on the ground that the fact is within the court's knowledge. The doctrine is divided into two broad categories within which, as we shall see, there are a number of sub-divisions:

(1) Facts that are notorious or can be shown to exist by reference to an authoritative source so that formal proof by evidence is not required; and

(2) Where provision is made by statute for judicial notice to be taken of a fact.

The basis for the doctrine is largely one of pragmatism; it saves a great deal of court time. However it can, on occasions cause a problem when the judge relies on her own knowledge rather than the evidence received. It is at this point that judicial notice and circumstantial inference blend almost imperceptibly into each other. As *Cross and Tapper* acknowledges at page 94:

"the tacit applications of the doctrine of judicial notice are more numerous and more important than the express ones. A great deal is taken for granted when any question of relevance is considered or assumed".

However what ultimately differentiates the two concepts is the fact that judicial notice, unlike relevance, is a matter of law and is therefore subject to the doctrine of precedent (although quite how far this goes in unclear, see *Phipson* 3–03).

2. *Notorious Facts*

As we shall see, this category can include facts that are not "notori- **6–16**
ous" at all, especially in cases where the judge consults learned texts
or on occasions, even receives oral evidence by way of assistance. This
section briefly examines four of the most commonly encountered
sub-categories; those seeking a more comprehensive review are
invited to consult Chapter 3 of *Phipson*.

(a) *Notice Without Inquiry*

There are numerous examples of the court accepting facts that are **6–17**
assumed to be a matter of common knowledge; cases which are often
cited by law lecturers seeking to inject some human interest. Some of
the most popular examples are:

(1) That a criminal's life is an unhappy one (*Burns v Edman* [1970]
2 Q.B. 541);

(2) If a man and a woman share a bed they are likely to have sex
(*Woolf v Woolf* [1931] P. 134);

(3) Television is a commonly enjoyed domestic pleasure
(*Bridlington Relay Ltd v Yorkshire Electricity Board* [1965] Ch.
436);

(4) Money has declined in value since 1189 (*Bryant v Foot* (1868)
LR 3 Q.B. 497).

A comprehensive list appears at 3–17 to 3–21 of *Phipson*. There is no
doubt that this method of proof can be very useful on occasions and
can provide assistance to the advocate is who is suddenly confronted
by a judge who says, "Where is your evidence for this?"

Example: C Ltd wishes to prove that a telephone call was made from **6–18**
their office to D Ltd's office on a particular day. There is no dispute
as to the parties' telephone numbers but the only evidence that C Ltd
has to support their contention is the computerised record of C Ltd's
telephone calls on that day which they have received from British
Telecom with their bill for that period. A judge could be invited to
take judicial notice of the fact that calls have been made to the
numbers indicated in the print out without having to strictly prove
those facts.

The crucial test is whether you can stand up in court and to say to
the judge with all due deference:

"Your Honour might I suggest that it is a matter of common
knowledge".

(b) *Notice After Inquiry*

6–19 The most commonplace example under this head is when the judge takes judicial notice of matters of law and procedure after consulting law reports or authoritative legal texts. A judge may also on occasions be invited to consult learned books of reference in order to be in a position to take judicial notice of matters such as the sovereign status of a state (*Duff Development Co Ltd v Government of Kelantan* [1924] A.C. 797), what constitutes acceptable religious practice (*Read v Bishop of Lincoln* [1892] A.C. 694), and whether a custom by usage exists within a particular trade (*Crawcour v Salter* (1881) 18 Ch. D. 30). A comprehensive review appears at 3–07 to 3–12 of *Phipson*. An interesting recent example of this process at work can be seen in *Co-Operative Bank plc v Tipper* [1996] 4 All E.R. 366. In that case the judge took judicial notice of the fact that a pencil alteration to a typewritten deed of guarantee was not intended to be a permanent alteration: if it had have been, it would have destroyed the bank's claim for rectification. Judicial notice was gleaned from consulting ancient textbooks and case law and from the judge's own acceptance of "life in the modern world". Now that the rule against hearsay has been abolished one wonders whether it would not make more sense to simply see this process as one of fact finding based on hearsay evidence, the weight of such evidence depending upon the ostensible accuracy and authority of the sources consulted.

(c) *Personal Knowledge*

6–20 There is large body of case law in criminal proceedings dealing with the extent to which jurors or lay magistrates are permitted to make use both of their local and specialist knowledge (see, in particular *Wetherall v Harrison [1976] Q.B. 773*). This decision suggests that lay magistrates and jurors are to be afforded rather more indulgence in making use of their personal knowledge than judges and arbitrators. As a general rule, judges should be extremely cautious in making use of their local knowledge or personal expertise (see, in particular *Reynolds v Llanelly Associated Tinplate Co* [1948] 1 All E.R. 140) and, especially in view of Art.6, should only ever do so after drawing this to the parties' attention and inviting representations. On the other hand, if you were involved in a very complex shipping case you would probably prefer it to be tried by a judge with Admiralty expertise rather than a childcare specialist. This issue arose recently in *Checkpoint Ltd v Strathclyde Pension Fund* [2003] EWCA Civ 84, a case in which an RICS arbitrator on a rent review clause had used his own personal knowledge, gleaned from acting as a land agent, when fixing the open market rent. The court held that there was a crucial distinction (see, also Lord Denning M.R. in *Fox v Wellfair Ltd* [1981]

Lloyd's Rep. 514 at 522) between an arbitrator (and by implication a judge):

(1) Using his specialist knowledge so as to *understand* and adjudicate upon the evidence that the parties place before him (which is generally permissible); and

(2) Using his specialist knowledge to *provide evidence* that the parties have not chosen to provide for themselves (which is not permissible).

The most intriguing recent case on use of local knowledge is undoubtedly *Mullen v Hackney LBC [1997] 2 All E.R. 906*. A circuit judge had fined the defendant local authority £5,000 for contempt of court because they were in breach of an undertaking to carry out repairs on the claimant's property. In setting the level of the fine the judge was influenced by the fact that the defendants had failed to take undertakings seriously in other cases. In the Court of Appeal Otton L.J. stated that the judge had been perfectly entitled to take judicial notice of the defendants' record in similar cases. He stated that in situations of this kind the judge had two points to determine, namely:

(1) Was the party's conduct notorious and clearly established? If it was, the judge could act on that fact without further enquiry; however, even if it was not,

(2) The conduct of a party in other cases before the court was clearly susceptible of demonstration by consulting court records.

We all know from experience that certain parties (and sometimes, unfortunately, their solicitors) have a certain "reputation" for the way in which they conduct litigation. *Mullen's* case indicates how this may on occasions be prayed in aid where, for example, yet again, a party has failed to comply with case management directions.

(d) *Reception of Evidence*

Finally, we come to the extraordinary decision of *McQuaker v 6–21 Goddard* [1940] 1 K.B. 687, the facts of which alone make it stand out from the crowd. The case concerned a claim against a zoo bought by one of their patrons who had been bitten by a camel. The judge was required to determine for the purposes of liability whether or not the camel is a naturally domesticated animal. In order to do this he received a large amount of sworn oral evidence including evidence from a former captain in the Camel Corps who amongst other matters imparted the intriguing fact that such was the level of the camel's domesticity that it was incapable of sexual congress without human assistance. The Court of Appeal decided that, in holding that the camel was naturally domesticated, the judge had taken judicial notice of that fact. The oral evidence received simply assisted him in (at 700):

> "forming the view as to what the ordinary course of nature in this regard in fact is, a matter of which he is supposed to have complete knowledge".

As *Cross and Tapper* points out a page 90, the only material difference between this process and fact finding, at any rate in non-jury trials, is that judicial notice is a matter of law and, accordingly, *McQuaker* is binding so far as camels are concerned. The case is probably best seen as a one-off decision in the context of the highly technical rules on strict liability for animals that existed at the time.

3. *Statutory Judicial Notice*

6–22   Many statutory provisions are explicitly made the subject of judicial notice (see further *Phipson* 3–07). For example under s.3 of the Interpretation Act 1889, judicial notice is to be taken of every Act passed after 1850. The importance of this can be more fully appreciated when contrasted with the position in the case of Scots, colonial or foreign law, all of which must be proved as a fact by expert evidence (see further 12–09). The only notable exceptions are EEC law (European Communities Act 1972, s.3, Sch.I, Part I), the various EEC Treaties and Judgment Conventions (s.2(1), Civil Jurisdiction and Judgments Act 1982) and decisions of the European Court of Justice (*ibid* s.3). The most commonplace example of judicial notice being taken under this heading is where the judge takes judicial notice of primary legislation after consulting law reports or legal texts, all of which are matters of which the English courts must take judicial notice. Interestingly, there is no similar provision in relation to statutory instruments, but, as already pointed out (see 5–51) now that the "best evidence rule" has been buried, absence of a Queen's Printer's copy surely only goes to weight.

III ESTOPPAL

6–23   The concept of estoppal derives from the Old French for a bung or cork ("*estoupail*"). It can arise in a variety of situations all of which have one key feature in common, namely the happening of some prior event as a result of which a party is precluded (or "stopped" if you want to keep it simple) from asserting in subsequent litigation that a different state of affairs existed on the occasion in question. When expressed thus, it is relatively easy to see why it has been traditionally regarded as a rule of evidence rather than of substantive law. However, its boundaries now extend so far and wide and are so ill-defined, that many aspects of it are treated as rules of substantive law. In terms of classification, estoppals have been traditionally divided into the following categories, namely:

(1) *Estoppal by Record*: this usually arises in circumstances where one party seeks to argue that the subject matter of current litigation has already been the subject of prior adjudication (to use the Latin archaism, "estoppal *per rem judicatem*");

(2) *Estoppal by Deed*: a rarely invoked form of estoppal whereby a signatory of a deed and those claiming through him are precluded from denying any of the facts stated in the deed or the recitals. However an estoppal cannot be set up in the face of an allegation of fraud, or illegality, and is no defence to a claim for recission or rectification (see, for example *Wilson v Wilson* [1969] 1 W.L.R. 1470). The current statutory requirements for a deed are contained in s.1 of the Law of Property (Miscellaneous Provisions) Act 1989.

(3) *Estoppal by Conduct*: a category of estoppal that has its core an objectively intentional representation by A (by words or conduct) as to a particular state of affairs that causes another (B) to act upon it to his detriment. In subsequent proceedings A will be precluded from denying the truth of the representation. It is subdivided into estoppals:

- By representation;
- By agreement;
- Proprietary estoppal;
- Promissory estoppal; and
- Negligent estoppal.

These forms of estoppal are not normally covered in textbooks on evidence (see, for example, *Murphy* and *Cross*). However the latest edition of *Phipson* covers estoppals in all their forms in great detail in Chapter 5.

This section will confine itself to consideration of Estoppal by Record.

1. General Concepts
The major problem with this area of the law of evidence is the virtually infinite range of circumstances in which the decision of an earlier court can affect subsequent litigation. Accordingly, there is a real

6-24

danger of becoming bogged down in detail and losing sight of the core principles. There are based on two policy consideration that are, somewhat unhelpfully, still expressed as Latin maxims, namely:

"*Interest rei publicae ut sit finis litium*"—("Finality in litigation ('closure') is in the public interest"); and

"*Nemo debet bis vexari pro eadem causa*"—("Nobody should be sued for the same thing twice").

However, as we have already seen (04–54), courts have also been reluctant to set too much store by judgments in earlier proceedings, especially where one or more of the parties to the later proceedings are different. The basis of this reluctance stems from the fact that the previous judgment is seen as no more than an expression of opinion based upon evidence that the later court has not had the advantage of hearing, at any rate in an identical form.

Another problem that has bedevilled this area has been, at least up until recently, a notable lack of consistency in the definition of terms, a difficulty that could, it is submitted, be ameliorated if the use of Latin were avoided. Throughout this section therefore the expression "estoppal *per rem judicatem*" will be replaced by "estoppal by previous adjudication". Before delving into the detail, it may be helpful to take in some broad generalisations by way of simple examples. Hopefully, that will make what follows easier to understand.

(a) *Where the Parties are the Same*

6–25   Adjudications in earlier proceedings are far more likely to bending in subsequent proceedings if the parties locking horns in the later proceedings are identical. Conversely, s.11 of the Civil Evidence Act 1968 excepted, if one or more of the parties differ, previous adjudications will generally be ignored in the later proceedings.

6–26   **Example 1:** C's car is involved in a collision with a truck driven by D. He sues D for damages for personal injuries and vehicle damage. If either:

(1) He wins; or

(2) He loses,

both parties are bound by the decision in the sense that C cannot bring a second action based on precisely the same claim.

There can really be no quarrel with that. It is hard to imagine that any non-lawyer would be surprised at this outcome. In a sense, it is not an estoppal at all, it is simply that the cause of action has "merged" with the judgment. Accordingly, this type of situation (a sub-category of Estoppal by Previous Adjudication) will be referred to hereafter as "Estoppal by Merger". As we shall see however it will only apply in cases where there has been a *final* judgment, so that if, for example the claimant had made an application for summary judgment that had been dismissed, this would not preclude him from taking the claim to full trial, or, indeed making a second application under CPR 24 based on different evidence. However, a subsequent application based on the same evidence would, in all probability, be struck out as an abuse of process (see Dyson L.J. in *Collier v Williams* [2006] EWCA Civ 20 (at [37])).

Example 2: Same situation as in Example 1 except that C, unaware   **6–27** that he has suffered any personal injuries attributable to the collision, only sues for the damage to his *vehicle*. Having obtained judgment based on a finding that D drove negligently, he later discovers that the excruciating backache he has been suffering from is attributable to the whiplash injury he received in the collision. He now brings a second action based on the *same facts* for damages for his personal injuries. The following issues now call for consideration.

(1) Does the earlier judgment create an Estoppal by Merger?

(2) Is D bound by the finding of negligence in the first action, given that the *facts* giving rise to the claim are identical?

(3) Is it nevertheless an *abuse of process* for C to bring a second claim based on the same set of facts if he could have included the claim for personal injuries in the first claim?

As can be seen, complexity can start to creep in even on relatively simple facts. Put broadly, the answer to each of the above questions in turn is:

(1) "No", because technically the claim for personal injuries is a separate cause of action and therefore there has been no merger;

(2) (Arguably) "Yes", because the parties are the same and the liability issue is the same. This type of estoppal (another sub-category of Estoppal by Previous Adjudication) is known as "Issue Estoppal" and will be so referred to hereafter. It goes without saying that if that essential congruence of subject matter is not present, no estoppal will arise via this route;

(3) "Possibly". It is a misnomer to regard this as a form of Estoppal by Previous Adjudication because the whole point is that there *was* no adjudication in the first claim because the claimant did not bring a claim for damages for his personal injuries. What renders the second claim potentially vulnerable

the fact that he *ought* to have done so (sometimes referred to as "the rule in *Henderson v Henderson* (1843) 3 Hare 100").

(b) *Where the Parties are Different*

6–28   As a general rule, estoppals are less likely to be encountered where the subsequent litigation involves different parties. The only partial exception to this (partial because it does not create an estoppal, only a rebuttable presumption) is a previous conviction admitted under s. 11 of the Civil Evidence Act 1968 (already considered at 4–54). It is important to recognise that s. 11 is an *exception* to the general rule that a previous adjudication is regarded as wholly irrelevant if the parties are not identical to those in the earlier proceedings (the "rule in *Hollington v Hewthorn [1943] K.B. 587*" discussed at 4–54).

6–29   **Example 3:** The same facts as Example 1. However, say that C had sued D and lost. What if a passenger in C's car, P, were to now bring a fresh claim for her injuries against both C and D? A number of possible issues arise here, in particular:

(1) What, if any, use may D, as against P, make of the fact that the claim brought against him by C in the earlier proceedings was dismissed?

(2) If P were to succeed against both C and D, would D be able to argue as between himself and C, that C should bear full responsibility for P's damages?

(3) Can D argue that P should have brought her claim at the same time as C and, accordingly her claim is an abuse of process under *Henderson?*

Dealing again with each of the above issues in turn, the answers would be as follows:

(1) "None", because the parties are different, hence there is no question of an Estoppal by Merger or Issue Estoppal arising;

(2) "Possibly", depending on whether the court took a broad or narrow view of whether the issue, namely C's responsibility for the collision, was sufficiently similar in both cases to create an Issue Estoppal;

(3) "No", because the rule in *Henderson* (Abuse of Process) can only be raised against those who were parties to the first proceedings (see *C v Hackney London Borough Council* [1995] 2 F.L.R. 681).

6–30   However, as already noted, there are three occasions on which a previous adjudication may either create an estoppal, give rise to an abuse of process argument or be admissible in evidence, notwithstanding the fact that the parties to the earlier decision were not identical to those in the current proceedings. These are, in summary, where:

(1) The *fact* of the previous adjudication and the *state of affairs* it creates is in issue rather than the *facts on which it was based*. Thus if, for example an employer were sued to judgment for £100,000 but his insurers sought to avoid liability under the policy he had taken out with them, in a subsequent claim under the policy, the insurers would be precluded from disputing the amount of the earlier judgment but would not be bound by any of the facts on which it was based. This type of estoppal is sometimes referred to as "Cause of Action Estoppal" to distinguish it from Issue Estoppal. A further distinction is also sometimes drawn between judgments *in personam* which only affect the parties' rights as between themselves and judgments *in rem* which affect status and are, hence, binding against the whole world. These definitions are explored in greater detail at 6–34.

(2) A special variant of abuse of process has arisen in recent years. This limits the ability of a party to mount a *collateral attack* an earlier decision of a court of competent jurisdiction. The classic example of this is the convicted criminal who subsequently wishes to sue the police for fabricating the evidence which secured his conviction in circumstances where the original conviction has not since been overturned on an appeal or referral by the Criminal Cases Review Commission. This is discussed further at 6–51.

(3) Sections 11 to 13 of the Civil Evidence Act 1968. Section 11 has already been considered in the previous chapter at 4–54. However, as we shall see (at 6–54), ss.12 and 13 create additional exceptions to the rule in *Hollington v Hewthorn*.

Conclusion There are therefore five categories of case in which a previous adjudication can have an evidential impact on later proceedings either between the same, or different parties, namely: **6–31**

(1) Estoppal by Merger (binding only on the original parties);

(2) Cause of Action Estoppal (binding on the rest of the world);

(3) Issue Estoppal (the writer would prefer to call it "Finding of Fact Estoppal" since it is beyond dispute that it extends to individual findings of fact, see Ward L.J. in *Pugh v Cantor Fitzgerald International Ltd* [2001] C.P.L.R. 271 at 288) (binding only on the original parties);

The above three are all subcategories of "Estoppal by Previous Adjudication".

(4) Abuse of Process applications under the *Henderson* rule (generally only available to one of the original parties (see 6–49)), or via the "collateral attack" route (parties can be different to those in the original action);

(5) Admissibility of previous decisions under the Civil Evidence Act 1968 (available to any party in relation to any person's conviction provided it is relevant to an issue in the proceedings).

The principles underlying these concepts will now be reviewed in somewhat greater detail than above. However, in view of the fact that the principle premise of this work is that proving facts is now easy, it is not proposed to deal with them in great depth. Those seeking a fuller analysis are invited to consult Chapter 44 of *Phipson*.

2. Estoppal by Merger

6–32   Lord Denning, as always, summed up the principle most neatly in *Fidelitas Shipping Co Ltd v V/O Exportchleb* [1966] I Q.B. 630 at 640 when he stated:

> "If one party brings an action against another for a particular cause and judgment is given on it, there is strict rule of law that he cannot bring another action against the same party for the same cause".

Nothing could be simpler, it is the reason why, for example, the claimant in a personal injury claim will be anxious not to settle until the prognosis is clear or, alternatively, seek a provisional award. If the loss turns out to be greater than expected, you cannot go back for more (the same rule applies in all claims, for example breach of contract, see *Conquer v Boot* [1928] 2 Q.B. 336). Provided that the judgment is:

(1) Final;

(2) On the merits;

(3) Relates to the same cause of action;

(4) Involves the same parties suing in the same capacity; and

(5) Was not obtained by fraud;

the cause of action dies with the judgment: there is simply nothing left to sue on. As stated, the principle only operates in respect of final judgments. Accordingly, for example, the dismissal of a summary judgment application will not preclude a further application based on fresh evidence (*Wagstaffe v Jacobowitz* (1884) W.N. 17) because it was not a final judgment. However, provided that the judgment is final, it matters not that it is by *default* (*Kok Hoong v Leong Cheong Kweng Mines Ltd* [1964] A.C. 993 or is a foreign judgment (see *Carl Zeiss Stiftung v Rayner & Keeler (No.2)* [1967] A.C. 853 and s.34 of the Civil Jurisdiction and Judgments Act 1982). However, for example, the discontinuance, strike out, or withdrawal of a claim will not have this effect (although it might constitute a procedural impediment to bringing fresh proceedings, see *O'Hare and Browne* 33–010 and 35–011). A party who wishes to challenge a judgment must either, in the case of a default judgment, apply to have it set aside (as to the effect of dismissal on issue estoppel see 6–40), or, in the case of judgment at trial, appeal or (in rare cases) bring a fresh action to have it set aside on the grounds that it was obtained by fraud or perjured evidence (a recent example of the latter is *Odyssey Re (London) Ltd v OIC Run Off Ltd* [2000] EWCA Civ 71 discussed at 5–58). The admissibility of fresh *evidence* on appeal is considered further at 14–73. In order to ascertain whether the later proceedings are in respect of a different cause of action you will need to refer to the relevant substantive law (and see *Phipson* 44–18) but, by way of example:

(1) A claim in negligence for personal injuries is a different cause of action from a claim for vehicle damage even though it arises out of the same event (*Brunsden v Humphrey* (1884) 14 Q.B.D 141); and

(2) A claim in debt is a different cause of action from a claim for damages even though both arise out of the same contract (see *Lawlor v Gray* [1984] 3 All E.R. 345).

It goes without saying that any party who "cherry picks" his causes of action in this way is extremely vulnerable to having subsequent proceedings struck out as an abuse under the *Henderson* principle, but the crucial difference is that merger applies automatically whereas strike out under *Henderson* is a matter of discretion. The position with fraudulent judgments is complicated, but basically requires the person attacking the judgment to adduce fresh evidence that was not reasonably available to him at the time (see *Phipson* 44–08). For a fuller discussion of merger generally, see *Phipson* 44–05 and 44–17 to 44–22.

Conclusion The basic principle is a simple and obvious one: it is **6–33** nevertheless still advisable to ensure that all relevant causes of action are included in the same set of proceedings to avoid vulnerability to a *Henderson* application.

3. Cause of Action Estoppal

6–34   Estoppal by Merger is often included under this heading but it is best seen as an entirely separate principle, not least because Cause of Action Estoppal may, at least to a limited degree, be raised even though the parties to the later proceedings are *different*; it goes without saying that the person against whom it is pronounced is bound by its effect. However, as already noted, a distinction needs to be drawn between the *state of affairs* ("Cause of Action Estoppal") created by the judgment (which is generally binding on the whole world) and the *findings of fact* ("Issue Estoppal)" upon which it was based (which generally only bind the parties to the earlier proceedings).

6–35   **Example:** C sues D to judgment in a breach of contract claim and is awarded damages of £250,000 at the conclusion of the trial on June 9, 2005. The sealed copy of the judgment will probably state tersely:

> "Judgment for the claimant in the sum of £250,000 plus costs to be determined by detailed assessment if not agreed".

Although the *facts* upon which that judgment has been reached will only bind the parties themselves, the *judgment* is conclusive evidence against the whole world that the defendant was ordered to pay £250,000 plus costs to the claimant on June 9, 2005. Accordingly, to cite the examples given in *Cross and Tapper* at 97:

(1) The fact of the claimant's acquittal on a criminal charge will be conclusive evidence of that fact and therefore proof of an essential element in a subsequent claim against the defendant police officer for malicious prosecution (*Purcell v Macnamara* (1807) 9 East 157):

(2) A judgment against a surety will be conclusive evidence as to the sum that he has been held liable for in a subsequent claim for an indemnity against the principal debtor (*Re Kitchin, Ex p. Young* (1881) 17 Ch. 668 at 673).

6–36   An interesting recent example of its application is the House of Lords decision in *Mulkerrins v Pricewaterhouse Coopers (a firm)* [2003] 4 All E.R. 1.

6–37   **Facts:** C brought a claim in negligence against D, who she had consulted as insolvency practitioners, alleging that as a result of their negligence she had been adjudicated bankrupt, thus suffering considerable financial loss. An issue arose in the bankruptcy proceedings as to whether this right of claim against D was vested in the trustee in bankruptcy on behalf of the creditors. A judge ruled that it vested in C. D later applied to strike out C's claim on the basis that it should be brought by the trustee.

The House unanimously held that since the effect of the order was to vest the right of action in the claimant to the exclusion of the trustee in bankruptcy, it was not open to the defendants to challenge it. As this decision shows, the effect of the judgment will naturally depend to an extent upon the subject matter of the litigation. Some judgments simply consist of a bald recital as to recoverable damages, others will go somewhat further than and declare a state of affairs (*Mulkerrins* is an example of this) or even change the status of a party affected by it. As already noted, the latter type of judgment is sometimes referred to as a judgment *in rem*, for example a decree of divorce, as opposed to a judgment *in personam* such as that given in a claim in tort or contract (which only deals with rights as between the parties). Whether this distinction serves any useful purpose is open to debate (see further *Phipson* 44–14). The following list sets out the most important examples of judgments that are treated as being *in rem*:

- Decrees of divorce, nullity and judicial separation (including analogous orders made under Civil Partnerships Act 2004);

- Adjudications in bankruptcy;

- Grants of Probate and Administration.

Some rather more exotic examples can be found in *Phipson* at 44–14 (p.1340).

Conclusion   One rarely encounters problems with Cause of Action   **6–38**
Estoppal in practice; the important point to remember is that strangers to the original proceedings will only be bound by the judgement itself, not any of the findings of fact made in it.

4. Issue (Finding of Fact) Estoppal
This is where matters can start to get rather more complicated, not   **6–39**
least because, firstly the factual matrix upon which the earlier adjudication is based may be extremely complex, and secondly, it may not always be easy to identify precisely what findings of fact the earlier tribunal actually made ("I find the case proved" being the most vivid example). Let us return to Lord Denning M.R. in *Fidelitas Shipping*, again at 640 where he states:

". . . within one cause of action, there may be several issues raised which are necessary for the determination of the whole case. The rule then is that, once an issue has been raised and distinctly determined between the parties, then, as a general rule, neither party can be allowed to fight that issue all over again".

Lord Brandon proceeded to develop the principles of Issue Estoppal in *DSV Silo und Vervaltungsgesellschaft mbH v Owners of the Sennar* [1985] 1 W.L.R. 490 at 499 when he set out the three criteria that must be satisfied before it can operate:

"The first requirement is that the judgment in the earlier action . . . must be (a) of a court of competent jurisdiction, (b) final and conclusive and (c) on the merits. The second requirement is that the parties (or privies) in the earlier action . . . and those in the later action . . . must be the same. The third requirement is that the issue in the later action . . . must be the same issue as that decided by the judgment in the earlier action".

The key questions in relation to the previous adjudication are usually likely to be firstly, "Was it the same issue?" and, secondly "Was it distinctly determined?" Nevertheless, it is also necessary to examine the components of the principle in greater detail.

(a) *The Earlier Judgment*

6–40   Firstly, the decision must be made by a court of competent jurisdiction: this will therefore exclude as a general rule findings made by inquisitorial tribunals such as inquests and public inquiries (see, in particular Steyn J. in *Speedlink Vanguard v European Gateway* [1987] Q.B. 206). The same principle applies to purely administrative decisions, for example, a refusal of planning permission (*Thrasyvoulou v Secretary of State for the Environment* [1990] 2 A.C. 273: see further *Phipson* 44–24). However adjudications by Employment Tribunals are capable of giving rise to Cause of Action and Issue Estoppals in subsequent proceedings before the civil courts (see *Barber v Staffordshire County Council* [1996] 2 All E.R. 748). The other three features identified by Lord Brandon in "*The Sennar*" are subject to the same principles as those discussed in relation to Estoppal by Merger at 6–32. Thus the findings of fact inherent in a default judgment, or a claim that has been formally dismissed on withdrawal (see, for example, *Lennon v Birmingham City Council* [2001] EWCA Civ 435) will bind the parties every bit as much as those made at trial. This means that, on occasions, Issue Estoppal will arise within a single set of proceedings; the classic example being a judgment entered on liability with damages to be assessed. As we have already seen in the discussion of *Lunnun v Singh* [1999] C.P.L.R. 587 at 6–09 this still has the effect of leaving *quantum* issues at large including, to a significant extent, those of causation, remoteness and contributory negligence (see *Maes Finance Ltd v A L Phillips & Co, The Times*, March 25, 1997). The circumstances in which a default judgment can create Issue Estoppals was considered in detail by the Court of Appeal in *Pugh v Cantor Fitzgerald International Ltd* [2001] C.P.L.R. 271. In that case the defendants had sought to have a judgment in default of defence to a claim for wrongful dismissal set aside on the ground that the dismissal was justified due to gross misconduct by the claimant. That application having failed, an issue subsequently arose at the assessment of damages stage as to whether the defendants could raise the same allegations of gross misconduct in relation to the claimant's alleged failure to mitigate. The Court of Appeal stated that:

(1) A point could not be taken on assessment of damages which was inconsistent with any issue that had been settled on the judgment on liability;

(2) When the court has refused to set aside a default judgment, the central question is whether the same issue is being raised in relation to mitigation as was raised in the set aside application;

(3) It does not always follow that a refusal to set aside a default judgment has resulted in a determination on the merits sufficiently clear and certain to found an estoppal; the language of CPR 13.3 (see *O'Hare and Browne* 15–017 to 15–019) has not altered this;

(4) The principle expressed by Viscount Radcliffe in *Kok Hoong v Leong Cheong Kweng Mines Ltd* [1964] A.C. 993 namely:

". . . default judgments, though capable of giving rise to estoppals, must always be scrutinised with extreme particularity for the purpose of ascertaining the bare essence of what must necessarily have been decided . . ."

still applied.

If, on the other hand, the relevant issue has never actually been decided, it naturally follows that no Issue Estoppal can arise; an example of this can be seen in *Blackburn Chemicals Ltd v BIM Kemi AB* [2004] EWCA Civ 1490 in which the relevant issue (breach of Article 81 of the EEC Treaty) had been stayed pending determination of whether or not the contract which was the subject matter of the claim had been determined by repudiation.

(b) *Same Parties*
This aspect does not create any obvious problems. More importantly it highlights the circumstances in which Issue Estoppal *cannot* arise.

6–41

The classic case illustrating the point is *Townsend v Bishop* [1939] 1 All E.R. 805.

6–42   Facts: A collision occurred between a car owned by F (father) and driven by S (son) acting as his agent, and a truck driven by D. In Claim 1 F sued D for the damage to the car but failed due to the fact that the court found that S was contributorily negligent (at that time still a complete defence).

In Claim 2 S claimed compensation against D for the personal injuries that he had suffered in the same collision.

D sought to argue that S was estopped from denying contributory negligence. On the trial of a preliminary issue as to whether D was entitled to rely on the finding in Claim 1, the court held that he was *not*. The basis for that ruling was that the son had not been a party to the earlier proceedings.

6–43   *"Privies"* Earlier findings of fact may bind not only the parties but also their "privies", namely those enjoying priority by blood, title or identity of interest (see *Phipson* 44–27). Thus, for example earlier findings of fact will be binding:

- If made against a testator, in subsequent proceedings on the same subject matter concerning his executor, devisee or legatee;

- If made against mortgagee, assignee or grantee, in proceedings involving subsequent successors in title.

However judgments against executors or administrators do not necessarily bind next-of-kin, devisees or residuary legatees because the personal representative does not represent the estate for all purposes (*Re Waring* [1948] Ch. 221). Likewise, the directors, managers or employees of a company are not bound by any findings of fact made against it in litigation.

6–44   *"Same Capacity"* It is not only the *identity* of the party against whom the estoppal is raised that is crucial but also the *capacity* in which he sues or is sued. A graphic illustration is provided by the decision in *Marginson v Blackburn Borough Council* [1939] 1 All E.R. 273.

6–45   Facts: Mr Marginson ("M") was a passenger in a car driven by his wife ("W") acting as his agent, which was in collision with a bus driven by an employee of Blackburn Bus Company ("B"). W was killed in the collision, M received injuries and certain adjoining houses were damaged.

Claim 1: In a claim for property damage brought by the house owners ("O") against both M and B, based on their vicarious liability for the negligence of their respective drivers, and by B against M for the damage to their bus the court found that:

(1) O's claim succeeded against M *and* B on the basis that their drivers were equally responsible for the accident; and

(2) It followed that B's claim against M failed (contributory negligence still being a complete defence at the time).

Claim 2: M brought claims against B for:

(1) His own personal injuries; and

(2) On behalf of the late W's estate as her PR.

B sought to raise the findings in **Claim 1** by way of estoppel.

Their argument was successful with regard to Mr Marginson's own claim (obviously now the position would be different, they would simply be entitled to argue 50 per cent contributory negligence). However, so far as the claim on behalf of his late wife's estate was concerned, there was no estoppal because he was not claiming in his personal capacity but as her personal representative.

(c) *Same Issues*

It is here that the greatest difficulty often arises. Although the **6–46** problem has proved particularly acute in road traffic claims involving more than one driver and one composite claim (see *Randolph v Tuck* [1962] 1 Q.B. 175 and *Wall v Radford* [1991] 2 All E.R. 814), it is by no means confined to that area (the recent Court of Appeal decisions in *Blackburn Chemical Ltd v BIM Kemi AB* [2004] EWCA Civ 1490 and *Kennecott Utah Copper Corporation v Minet Ltd* [2004] 1 All E.R. (Comm) 60 being cases in point). What is clear, especially from Chadwick L.J.'s decision in *Kennecott Utah*, is that in order to determine whether an Issue Estoppal arises, the court will have to examine:

(1) The material facts that the claimant in the current proceedings will have to prove in order to succeed; and then

(2) Examine the judgment in the earlier proceedings to ascertain whether any one or more of those material facts has been the subject of previous adjudication.

Clearly, this may well require a detailed textual examination of not only the earlier judgment, but also the case statements in both sets of proceedings. It is likely to be an extremely time consuming and expensive process in any claim of substance. So far as road traffic claims are concerned, the characteristic type of problem that can sometimes arise can be seen in *Wall v Radford* [1991] 2 All E.R. 741.

6–47   **Facts:** In Claim 1 C, a passenger in D1's car received personal injuries as a result of a collision with a car driven by D2. She sued D1 and D2, the driver of the other vehicle involved in the collision. Having succeeded against *both* of them, the court then apportioned liability between them 50:50.

In Claim 2 D1 now sought damages against D2 for the personal injuries that she had received in the same collision.

D2 sought to argue that D1 was estopped from disputing the fact that she was 50 per cent contributorily negligent. Theoretically, the issues are different (see a full discussion of "Running-down cases" in *Phipson* at 44–36) but Popplewell J. concluded that the *factual issue* was identical and therefore held that the claimant in Claim 2 was bound by the apportionment of 50:50 made in Claim 1. It should however be pointed out that if the same situation were to arise in the future, D1 would be at grave risk of having Claim 2 struck out as an abuse of process under the *Henderson* principle (see further 6–49) on the basis that she ought to have brought her damages claim within Claim 1.

6–48   *Conclusion*   Issue Estoppal is hardly part of the mainstream, and will involve a great deal of careful case analysis, however, on occasions it may enable a party to play a "trump card" that will obviate the need to go to trial.

5. *Abuse of Process*

6–49   This topic will only be covered in outline. It is in essence a procedural remedy, namely a strike out application under CPR 3.4(2)(a) (see *O'Hare and Browne* 33–010), rather than a rule of evidence. Nevertheless since it touches and concerns evidential issues, it cannot be ignored. Before doing so however it is important that we remind ourselves of two key principles relating to Issue Estoppal, namely:

(1) They only apply if there has been a previous adjudication on that issue; and

(2) They only bind the parties to those earlier proceedings and their privies.

Bearing those two principles in mind, this section will consider, firstly, strike out under the rule in *Henderson's* case and, secondly, abuse by way of collateral attack on an earlier decision.

(a) *Henderson's Case*
The source of this principle is the statement of Wigram V.C. in   **6–50**
Henderson v Henderson (1843) 3 Hare 100 at 14 that a party is entitled to raise estoppal:

> ". . . except in special cases, not only to points upon which the court was actually required by the parties to form an opinion and pronounce a judgment, but to every point which properly belonged to the subject of the litigation. And which the parties, exercising reasonable diligence, might have brought forward at the time."

Naturally, it cannot give rise to an estoppal in the strict sense because there has not been a previous adjudication, the mischief lies in the fact that there *ought* to have been. The historical background, scope and implications of *Henderson* abuse of process are fully rehearsed in *Phipson* 44–45 to 44–56 however some features of the principle require further explanation. One of the more significant decisions in this area was *Talbot v Berkshire County Council* [1994] Q.B. 290 which not only held for the first time that the principle applied in personal injury cases, but also struck out a second claim brought by a party to an earlier running down claim based on very similar facts to those in *Wall v Radford* discussed earlier. Following that decision, an approach seemed to develop under which the burden was placed on the party *resisting* the strike out application to satisfy the court that there was an exceptional reason that justified allowing the second action to continue. This approach on occasions produced harsh, if not downright unjust results (see for example *Wain v F Sherwood and Sons Transport Ltd* [1998] EWCA Civ 905). The rule has however now been authoritatively reviewed by the House of Lords in *Johnson v Gore Wood & Co* [2002] 2 A.C. 1 from which the following principles can be derived:

(1) Although bringing a claim or raising a defence in later proceedings might, without more, amount to an abuse of process, if the court was satisfied that it ought to have been raised in the earlier proceedings;

(2) It was wrong to hold that a matter should have been raised merely because it *could* have been;

(3) A broad approach should be adopted in which the key issue was whether, in all the circumstances a party was misusing or abusing the process of the court by seeking to put before it an issue that could have been raised before.

In *Johnson*, the claimant's professional negligence claim against his solicitors was allowed to proceed notwithstanding the fact that an earlier claim brought by a company of which he was the *alter ego* and based on closely related causes of action had been determined in that company's favour. Although it is too early to predict what practical effect the decision will have on applications to strike out under the rule, there is little doubt that it heralds a change of climate which, especially when considered in conjunction with CPR 1 and Art.6 issues, means that such applications will not be carefully scrutinised.

(b) *Collateral Attack*
It is also a potential abuse of process to mount a collateral attack upon an earlier decision of a court of competent jurisdiction even though the parties to the proceedings were *different* and, hence, Issue Estoppal cannot be raised. This form of abuse is of relatively recent origin and was first identified by the House of Lords in *Hunter v Chief Constable of West Midlands Police* [1982] A.C. 429.

6–51   Facts: The defendants in the notorious "Birmingham Six" case had sought to have their confessions excluded at their trial for murder on the basis that they had been extracted by violence. This argument was rejected by the trial judge at a *voir dire*. They then brought civil claims for assault based on the same alleged incidents.

6–52   Although Issue Estoppal could not arise because the parties were different (Lord Denning M.R. in the Court of Appeal tried to extend Issue Estoppal to cover the instant case), the House of Lords struck the claim out as an abuse of process. In so doing they identified a new category of abuse, analogous in many ways to Issue Estoppal, namely (Lord Diplock at 541B):

". . . the initiation of proceedings in a court of justice for the purpose of mounting a collateral attack upon a final decision against the intending . . . [claimant] which has been made by another court of competent jurisdiction in previous proceedings in which the intending . . . [claimant] had a full opportunity of contesting the decision in the court by which it was made".

The principle has regularly been invoked in cases where disgruntled clients wish to sue their former legal representatives for negligence (see, for example *Smith v Linskells* [1996] 1 W.L.R. 763) and it was a major factor in the House of Lords' decision in *Arthur J. S Hall v Simons* [2002] 1 A.C. 615 to remove advocates' immunity from being sued for professional negligence. In the Court of Appeal the court had indicated that there was a sliding scale of weight to be applied to previous judgments, with the greatest weight being attached to criminal convictions. Second on the list were civil judgments following fully contested hearings with interim judgments and consent orders in civil and ancillary relief proceedings being accorded the least weight. However following the House of Lords decision it is by no means clear whether and if so to what extent, the *Hunter* doctrine applies to civil cases (see further *Phipson* 44–58).

Conclusion   It will be rare indeed for a litigator to encounter either   **6–53**
of these forms of abuse of process in practice. If you do, it will be fairly easy to identify. Any application to strike out will however need to be considered with greatest care after the most thorough research.

6. Civil Evidence Act 1968
We have already seen how the rule in *Hollington v Hewthorn* [1943]   **6–54**
K.B. 587 rendered previous convictions inadmissible in subsequent civil proceedings as proof of the facts on which they were based (see 4–56). In fact it is arguable that the decision is authority for the general proposition that Issue Estoppal can only ever arise in later proceedings between the same parties and their privies. We have also seen how (4–54) s.11 of the Civil Evidence Act 1968 creates a partial exception so far as criminal convictions are concerned, namely a rebuttable presumption that the person convicted committed the offence in question. Sections 12 and 13 of the 1968 Act created two further statutory exceptions. Section 12(1) provides that previous findings of adultery or fatherhood shall be admissible in subsequent civil proceedings for the purpose of proving, where it is relevant to do so, that the person named committed the adultery or fathered the child as the case may be. The section closely follows the wording of s.11 and creates (s.12(2)) the same rebuttable presumption as to those facts. Section 13 provides that the fact that a claimant in an action for libel or slander has been convicted of a criminal offence shall be conclusive evidence that he committed that offence for the purpose of those proceedings.

Conclusion

As stated at the start of this chapter, it is somewhat of a misnomer to   **6–55**
regard admissions, judicial notice and estoppals as forms of "proof without evidence". In the case of *Formal Admissions*, the judge may need to receive real evidence in the form of, for example, perusal of the case statements, in order to determine whether, and if so to what extent, a party is absolved from adducing any evidence on the admitted issue. In the case of Judicial Notice, although its foundation ʃ
on occasion be laid by advocacy, there will be other occasions w
the judge will have to consult documentary evidence before notiɖ

be taken. In the case of Estoppals, especially Issue Estoppals, the judge may have to examine not only the case statements in the instant proceedings but also trawl through the evidence in earlier proceedings with a magnifying glass. Nevertheless, it is a term hallowed by usage and therefore no harm is done by employing it however technically inaccurate it may in fact be.

Chapter 7

Hearsay

I INTRODUCTION

The rule against hearsay, briefly explained at 1–16, has not enjoyed a good press in recent years. In *Myers v DPP* [1965] A.C. 1001 at 1019, Lord Reid stated that it   **7–01**

"is difficult to make any general statement about the law of hearsay which is entirely accurate",

and Sir Robin Auld in *Review of the Criminal Courts of England and Wales: Report* (2001) at para.11.96 described the rule as being "complicated, unprincipled and arbitrary". The writer has never entirely agreed with these damning verdicts, its rationale and objectives being entirely laudable. What better way of testing the truthfulness and accuracy of a witness's perception and recall than having him give live evidence on oath tested by cross-examination? Its deficiency lay primarily in its absolute nature: under it evidence was either in or out regardless of its potential weight. Its abolition as a rule of exclusion by s.1(1) of the Civil Evidence Act 1995 now means that the court can concentrate on evaluating that weight. This chapter will examine in detail both the 1995 Act and the relatively simple procedures that need to be followed in order to bring hearsay evidence before the court. However, before proceeding further, it may be helpful to lay down some ground rules:

> (1) *All* hearsay evidence is now admissible, whether oral or documentary, irrespective of how remote it is from the original perceiver unless it is liable to exclusion under any other rule of evidence or procedure;

(2) The notice procedure (1995 Act, s.2 and CPR 33) is relatively uncomplicated and only applies to trials and final hearings in the fast track and multi-track: it has no application to applications for interim orders or small claims;

(3) Failure to comply with the notice procedure will not debar a party from relying on hearsay evidence unlike with orders for exchange of witness statements, expert evidence and disclosure of documents when leave would be required;

(4) The reality is that in most cases very little thought is given to whether or not the evidence being led contains hearsay: on occasions one cannot help wonder whether this relaxed attitude by litigants has started to go too far;

(5) Sections 8 and 9 of the 1995 Act have made it much easier to admit documentary hearsay (and, arguably, any documentary evidence); this aspect of the 1995 Act has already been covered at 5–42 and 5–48.

Before embarking on this commentary however it is important to consider precisely what is meant by the term "hearsay evidence". Those seeking a fuller history of the rule and the reasons for its development should consult *Phipson* at 28–01 to 28–07.

1. Why Understanding Hearsay is Still Important

7–02 Although the rule against hearsay has gone, hearsay still remains important as a concept. You will still need to identify hearsay evidence in order to:

(1) Comply with the notice procedures under CPR 33 (see, in particular *Moat Housing Group South Ltd v Harris and Hartless* [2005] 4 All E.R. 1051 discussed further at 7–36);

(2) Direct arguments as to the effect this has on the weight to be accorded to it;

(3) Make or resist applications for exclusion under the general exclusionary discretion in CPR 32.1(2) (see, in particular *Polanski v Conde Nast Publications Ltd* [2005] 1 W.L.R. 637, discussed further at 7–33).

It should also be borne in mind that hearsay evidence can, on occasions, win or lose cases as the following simple example shows.

7–03 **Example:** Two drivers, C and D are involved in a collision in which each blames the other. They both set out a diametrically opposed version of how the collision took place in their witness statements, and both give their evidence with equal conviction and remain unshaken after vigorous cross-examination (by no means an unusual occurrence). There is nothing in the surrounding circumstances, for example the vehicle repair reports and road layout, to assist the court one way or the other. However there is a witness statement from X which, if accepted, clearly suggests that C rather than D was responsible. No reason is given for the maker's absence.

If the court admits X's statement as hearsay it will, in effect, decide the case unless it attaches *no weight to it at all*. Its admission may also give rise to other issues, for example:

(1) Can the defendant prove that the document is in fact X's statement, if so how?

(2) Did the defendant include X's statement in his list of documents and is the claimant therefore deemed to have admitted its authenticity under CPR 32.19 (see 5–40)?

(3) Have the defendants failed to serve a hearsay notice? If so, what effect does this have on the weight to be attached to it (see further 7–26)?

(4) Can an adverse inference be drawn against the defendant (see *Wiszniewski v Central Manchester HA* [1998] P.I.Q.R. P 324 and 4–20) from failure to call X?

This simple example illustrates why it is still important to identify hearsay evidence and know how to deal with it. It is also as well to bear in mind why direct evidence from X would be preferable: **7–04**

(1) The best source of human perception is X, the perceiver;

(2) Getting X to come to court, take the oath or affirm, and have his evidence tested by cross-examination gives the court the best opportunity of evaluating its accuracy and truthfulness;

(3) The longer the chain of communication, the greater the risk of distortion (the "Chinese Whispers Effect");

(4) It is inherently unfair to deny a party the opportunity of challenging witnesses against him face to face (the "Confrontation Principle", to some extent acknowledged in Art.6(3)(d) of the ECHR).

These are all arguments that can quite properly be addressed to the court on the issue of weight. For a fuller discussion see *Phipson* 28–08 to 28–12.

2. Definition

7–05   Although there have been numerous attempts in the past to provide a comprehensive definition of hearsay (see *Phipson* 28–02) the only definition that need concern us is that contained in s.1(2) of the 1995 Act which defines hearsay as follows:

> "(a) 'hearsay' means a statement made otherwise than by a person while giving oral evidence in the proceedings which is tendered as evidence of the matters stated; and
>
> (b) references to hearsay include hearsay of whatever degree".

Section 13 defines "statement" as meaning:

> "any representation of fact or opinion however made."

There is a minor complication as to what the term "statement" actually means. This is discussed further at 7–19, but is likely to be of largely academic interest.

(a) *"The Eyewitness Rule"*

7–06   As already stated (1–18), the concept is most readily grasped if it is thought of as "the eyewitness rule". Although this is not strictly accurate, it identifies the core objective of the hearsay rule, namely to ensure so far as possible that proof by means of human perception and recollection was tested by requiring the perceiver to attend trial in person, recount his perception on oath and have his recollection tested by cross-examination. In other words, if you had an "eyewitness" you had to bring him to court to testify. Interestingly, CPR 32.2(1) (see 5–16) still states that, as a general rule, witness evidence at trial should be given by the witness in person and on oath. However, as already pointed out, the reality is that that the vast majority of live witness evidence is adduced in documentary form via written statements. Furthermore, as we shall shortly see, there is nothing a party can do to prevent his opponent from adducing the written statement of an absent witness (assuming that he can prove that it is that witness's statement). One cannot help but wonder therefore what purpose CPR 32.2(1) serves other than as a "mission statement".

3. Some Examples

7–07   By now it is hoped that you will have a pretty good idea of whether or not an item of evidence consists of hearsay. However, some further practical examples may assist.

(a) *Hearsay*

7–08   Hearsay can exist in many forms, but the following two examples cover the most commonplace situations.

(1) *Calling another Witness to Testify as to what the "Eye-Witness" Perceived*
This is the most straightforward example because it accords with the   **7–09**
non lawyer's understanding of the term. Any lay person would regard
it as hearsay if a witness was called to say:

> "X told me he had seen an accident and this is what he said happened . . ."

It should be noted in passing that, now that the rule has been abolished, there is nothing to stop a party adducing evidence in this form.
How much weight will be given to it is another matter.

(2) *Adducing the "Eye-Witness's" Written Statement to Prove what he Perceived.*

Out of Court Statement when the Witness is not Called   This is a   **7–10**
form of hearsay that the non-lawyer might not so readily recognise:
most documentary evidence involves the admission of hearsay evidence. Supposing X in the example at 7–03 had signed a very full
written statement supported by a Statement of Truth. It had been
served in accordance with case management directions, but he was
not available to give evidence at trial. Even though you might have no
difficulty in proving the statement as a document, tendering his
written statement in substitution for his live evidence would constitute reliance on hearsay evidence. This was where the inflexibility of
the rule in its original form started to cause problems (see, in particular *Myers v DPP* [1965] A.C. 1001; for an example of a civil case that
produced similar potential difficulties see *Arab Monetary Fund v
Hashim (No.7)* [1993] 1 W.L.R. 1014).

Example: C wishes to prove that EW carried out a particular transac-   **7–11**
tion on D's instructions on a particular day, but the only evidence of
it is the record of the transaction that EW created once he had put it
into effect. Strictly speaking, the record is hearsay because, however
accurate it might be and however truthful EW might be, strictly
speaking EW is the "eyewitness" as to both the instruction, the transaction, and its implementation. If by now, many years later, EW had
no recollection of the transaction, or could not be traced, C would
have been in grave difficulty at common law.
   Viewed in a modern context, it would create hearsay problems with
virtually every single recorded transaction that formed part of everyday business or institutional practice: the countless millions of electronic communications being the most obvious case in point. It was
these inflexibilities, paying scant regard as they did to the realities of

modern business practices, that led to reforms, starting with the Bankers' Books Evidence Act 1879, via the Evidence Act 1938 and the Civil Evidence Act 1968, culminating in the wholesale abolition of the rule by the 1995 Act.

7–12   *Out of Court Statement when the Witness is Called*   However, even more perplexing to the lay person, adducing a witness's written statement in evidence constitutes reliance on hearsay *even if he is called to give live evidence.* Not only does reliance on the statement in support of X's testimony constitute hearsay, but the use of the statement in this way also offends against the so-called "rule against self-corroboration". Under this rule, even now, a witness cannot, in theory, refer to his out of court statement for the purpose of showing consistency or to fill in any gaps in his recall without the court's permission (see further 7–44). Before the 1995 Act swept many of these technicalities away, the giving of live evidence largely consisted of a memory test. The use of witness statements as a substitute for oral examination in-chief (it is hard to think of it as hearsay evidence but it is) has largely removed this problem. However, the use of other out of court statements is still controlled by s.6 of the 1995 Act (see further 7–43). To that extent, even though the rule against hearsay has gone, the "rule against self-corroboration" still, theoretically, lives on.

(b) *Not Hearsay*
7–13   The following examples address two of the most popular misconceptions concerning the meaning of the term. The following situations do *not* involve the admission of hearsay.

7–14   (1) *Calling a person to testify as to what someone else said, if what was said is the material fact.*
Calling a witness to testify as to what another person *said* will not necessarily constitute hearsay. This is because it may well be that what was said on a previous occasion itself constitutes direct evidence of a relevant fact. The following examples illustrate the point.

(a) D makes an oral statement to C which either:

(1) is false and induces C into entering into a contract with D; or
(2) constitutes an express warranty in a contract between D and C.

(b) In the course of treating C Dr X gives negligent oral instructions to nurse Y which cause C injury. At trial C gives oral evidence of what Dr X said to nurse Y.

In each of the above examples C can give evidence as to what was said without having to comply with the notice requirements in s.2 of the 1995 Act. A full list of examples appears at 28–17 to 28–19 of *Phipson*. The other most commonplace example is where evidence is given of an individual's statement as to his mental or physical condition or state of knowledge. For example:

(a) W testifies that "C told me that he was getting very worried about the situation".

(b) Dr W testifies that "On examination C complained of extreme sensitivity in the scar and tingling in the middle and index fingers".

(c) W states in evidence "D told me that he knew that he was taking a risk".

Of course, none of this really matters any more in a practical sense because it will all be admissible in any event but, on occasions, sifting out the hearsay from the non-hearsay may be important on the issue of weight, for example:

HO, a local authority employee in an anti-social behaviour order ("ASBO") case states in her witness statement "[Tenant X said she was too afraid to come to court to give evidence] because of the threats that had been made by D's children to her". HO now wishes to give this evidence at the subsequent trial of the possession action.

The passage in square brackets is not hearsay but the remainder is. The above example is by no means atypical of the kind of evidence that is given in ASBO cases and therefore should have been preceded by service of a hearsay notice (see further 7–26) before it was adduced in evidence at the trial of the possession claim.

(2) *Producing mechanically or electronically recorded evidence where the contents are direct perceptions by the machine of a material fact.*

The hearsay ("eyewitness") rule only applies to evidence that consists of *human* perception. If the ultimate "perceiver" is a *machine*, such as a computer, tape recorder, camera, CCTV surveillance system or other such device, and the information has been recorded without any human input, the evidence will not be hearsay.

7–15

Examples

(1) The print out from a cardiotochograph monitoring a baby's heart rate and her mother's contractions during delivery;

7–16

(2) A covert video of C taken by D to attack C's credibility at trial;

(3) A telephone bill which monitors C's telephone calls showing C telephoned D's number on a particular day.

In all of the above examples, the cardiotochograph, the video and the telephone bill, although requiring proof as documents, do not involve the admission of hearsay evidence because they record the perceptions of a device not a person. Most of the case law derives form criminal proceedings, the one notable civil case being *"The Statue of Liberty"* [1968] 1 W.L.R. 729 in which the court admitted the radar recorded trace movements of a ship; further illustrations can be found in *Phipson* at 28–23 to 28–24. Three additional points are of note. Firstly, not only may it be necessary to prove the recording as a document, for example by producing a duly authenticated copy of a CCTV recording, but also, to prove the ordinary method by which it operates if it is a new and unfamiliar form of device. This may even be the case with computer generated material (see, for example *Smith v Tyne and Wear Autistic Society* [2005] 4 All E.R. 1336 discussed at 4–73) although the special rules as to computer output formerly in s.5 of the Civil Evidence Act have been repealed. Secondly, secondary evidence of the contents of, for example a lost or "wiped" CCTV film, may not involve adducing hearsay evidence. It may be possible to prove the contents by calling a person who viewed the film and can give evidence as to its contents. He is the proximate human perceiver, and, hence, the "eyewitness" (see *Taylor v CC Cheshire* [1987] 1 W.L.R. 1479). Finally, there may well be many cases where video or computer evidence *will* contain hearsay and hence require the service of a hearsay notice. The most obvious example is where an audio-visual recording has been made of a potential witness's evidence. It is every bit as much hearsay as the contents of a written statement would have been. This type of evidence is discussed further at 13–23.

7–17   ## II THE DEATH OF HEARSAY: CIVIL EVIDENCE ACT 1995

The Civil Evidence Act 1995 embodies the recommendation of the Law Commission paper *The Hearsay Rule in Civil Proceedings* (Law Com. No.216, Cm. 2321 (1993)). It abolishes the hearsay rule as a rule of exclusion but very much keeps it alive as a concept relevant to weight. It needs to be read in conjunction with CPR 33 which deals with the minimal procedural requirements that need to be met in relation to such evidence.

1. Abolition: s.1

Section 1(1) of the Act states: **7–18**

> "In civil proceedings evidence shall not be excluded on the ground
> that it is hearsay".

Nothing could be clearer, hearsay as a rule of exclusion of gone. As
noted at 1–16, the effect of this is that, subject to the evidence being
relevant and not liable to exclusion under any other rule, the medium
in which it exists is immaterial. It has already been employed exten-
sively in possession proceedings against anti-social tenants and in
applications for Anti-Social Behaviour Orders ("ASBOs") and
injunctions ("ASBIs") and the Court of Appeal has acknowledged in
Chase v News Group Newspapers Ltd [2003] E.M.L.R. 11 that it could
form the basis of a plea of justification in a defamation claim. As
Phipson states at 29–07:

> "For many years there has been a contrast between the strict rules
> of evidence set out in textbooks and the rules applied in the
> civil courts on a daily basis, where evidence is regularly admitted
> without consideration of the rules of hearsay. The bundles of
> documents put before the court are often treated as thought their
> contents are evidence without any point being taken and without
> any problems arising. The Act seeks to narrow the gap between
> theory and practice."

(a) *Meaning of Hearsay*

The definition in s.1(2) has already been given at 7–05. You will recall   **7–19**
that it covers any out-of-court "statement" made by an individual
which is tendered as evidence as to its contents. This means that
although it is not essential to identify the maker of the statement by
name, it will nevertheless be necessary to show that it is the statement
of *somebody*. This point was emphasised by the Court of Appeal in
Moat Housing Group v Harris and Hartless [2005] 4 All E.R. 1051,
discussed further at 7–36. Some commentators have also suggested
that the definition of "statement", which replicates that in s.10 of the
1968 Act, is not without its complications (see *Phipson* 29–03 and
Cross and Tapper at page 616). Their argument is that, possibly, it
does not cover *implied* representations. This is based on the speeches
in *R. v Kearley* [1992] 2 A.C. 228, some of which suggest that not all
spoken words are "statements". It is hard to think of a concrete
example of how facts analogous to *Kearley* might arise in a civil
context:

> C Ltd suspects that D Ltd is producing and selling DVDs which
> infringe their copyright. They instruct an Enquiry Agent, Ms X, to
> obtain employment with D Ltd. Whist working there she overhears

requests from various individuals (Ws) asking if D Ltd can supply DVDs which consist of infringing works. C Ltd wish to call Ms X at trial to give evidence of what she has heard as proof that D Ltd were selling infringing copies.

The argument (no longer available in criminal cases, see s.115(3) of the Criminal Justice Act 2003 and *R. v Singh, The Times*, March 8, 2006) would be, that the inference to be drawn from Ws' requests for purchase namely:

> "I'm coming to you for these DVDs because I know you are selling infringing copies under the counter",

although hearsay, are not W's "statements" and hence are still inadmissible hearsay because they do not come within the definition of hearsay in s.1(2) of the 1995 Act or any preserved common law exception. As *Cross and Tapper* points out, if raised the point is unlikely to be greeted with a great deal of enthusiasm by the court. Although the Court of Appeal did express the view in *Ventouris v Mountain (No.2)* [1992] 1 W.L.R. 887, a case concerning interpretation of s.2 of the 1968 Act, that a secret tape recording of an individual's voice was not that person's "statement" because he did not realise it was being recorded, it is to be hoped that the term "statement" will be construed to include all human utterances. To do otherwise would be to introduce an unwelcome element of technicality.

There is also potential for confusion in the way that the term "statement" is often used to mean a written witness statement to which CPR 32 applies. So far as possible an attempt will be made to keep the two meanings distinct. Confusion is to some extent avoided by the use of the term "original statement" which appears at various places in the Act (for example s.4(2)(a)). Section 13 defines this as:

> "... the underlying statement (if any) by:
>
> (a) in the case of evidence of fact, a person having personal knowledge of that fact; and
> (b) in the case of evidence of opinion, the person whose opinion it is".

This definition makes it clear that for certain purposes, for example several of the "weight criteria" in s.4 of the Act, the court must focus on the *original source* of the evidence, the "eyewitness" not the signatory of the "witness statement" in which the "original statement" is contained.

7–20   **Example:** X (the "maker of the original statement"), a local authority tenant complains to HO, a housing officer, that D, a neighbouring tenant, has threatened her. In subsequent possession proceedings,

HO signs a witness statement which records X's complaints. On the day of the trial HO is unable to attend due to illness, so the local authority's advocate, as she is entitled to do, puts in her witness statement as hearsay evidence.

In deciding what weight should be attached to HO's statement the court is required among other matters to have regard under s.4(2)(a) to whether it would have been reasonable and practicable to have called "the maker of the original statement" as a witness. In the above example, that is X not HO.

(b) *Scheme of the Act*   **7–21**
Much of the Act is straightforward and easy to follow, in particular:

(1) Hearsay includes hearsay "of whatever degree" (s.1(2)(b)). It matters not therefore how many removes there are between the original perceiver and the statement that is tendered in evidence. There could, in theory, be a limitless number of intermediaries (this type of hearsay is commonly termed "multiple hearsay"). However, as Brooke L.J. emphasised in the *Moat House Housing Association* case (at [140]):

> "If the statement involves multiple hearsay, the route by which the original statement came to the attention of the person attesting to it should be identified as far as practicable".

In this type of case being aware of what is meant by the term "original statement" becomes particularly important.

(2) Although hearsay is admissible it is subject to four "statutory safeguards" in ss.2 to 5 set out below; the relevant procedural rule is set out in brackets.

- s.2: The giving of *notice* by the party proposing to rely on hearsay evidence (CPR 33.2)
- s.3: An entitlement on the party against whom the hearsay evidence is tendered to apply for an order that "the maker of the original statement" attend for *cross-examination orders* (CPR 33.4)
- s.4: A duty on the part of the court to have regard to the *weight* of the evidence having particular regard to the six factors listed in s.4(2), many of which focus on "the maker of the original statement"
- s.5: A right on the part of the party against whom the evidence is tendered to give notice that he intends to *impeach credit* of *any* person (not just the maker of the original statement) in the same way as if he had been called to give oral evidence (CPR 33.5)

(3) Section 7(2) of the Act retains a number of common law exceptions none of which are unlikely to be of great importance in practice. More relevant however is the fact that s.1(3) states that:

> "Nothing in this Act affects the admissibility of evidence admissible apart from this section".

The effect of this is to preserve a number of important statutory exceptions permitting the admission of hearsay evidence, for example, under the Bankers' Books Evidence Act 1879 and Children Act 1989, ss.96(3) to (7). The only practical difference in respect of hearsay admitted under any of the above provisions is that there is no need to serve a hearsay notice under CPR 33.2.

(c) *"Civil Proceedings": s.11*

7–22 These are defined as proceedings before any tribunal

> "to which the strict rules of evidence apply".

The most notable exception is claims allocated to the Small Claims Track where the strict rules of evidence are specifically disapplied (CPR 27.8(3)).

(d) *Power to Exclude on other Grounds: s.14*

7–23 The admission of hearsay is without prejudice to the right of the court to exclude evidence:

> "in pursuance of any [other] enactment or rule of law or for failure to comply with rules of the court or an order of the court, or otherwise."

Quite apart from the general power vested in the court by CPR 32.1(2) to exclude evidence that would otherwise be admissible (see 1–52), hearsay evidence is no more immune from exclusion than other evidence; a late witness statement is caught by CPR 32.10 whether or not it contains hearsay.

(e) *Proof of Statements in Documents: ss. 8 and 9*

7–24 These important sections have already been covered at 5–48 and 5–42. However CPR 33.6(1)(c) does require notice to be given in the case of records admissible under s.9 and is dealt with at 7–27.

III THE STATUTORY SAFEGUARDS

7–25 It is likely that these safeguards will prevent any breach of Art.6, in particular Art.6(3)(d). The House of Lords were clearly of the opinion in *Clingham v Kensington and Chelsea RLBC* [2003] 1 A.C. 787 that there was nothing in Art.6 that of itself prohibited reliance on hearsay evidence, provided the statutory scheme was followed. However there is also no doubt that any court faced with the task of evaluating hearsay evidence and making findings of fact based upon it will have to articulate carefully the reasons for doing so (see *Moat Housing Group Ltd v Harris and Hartless* [2005] 4 All E.R. 1051 at 1085).

A Safeguard 1: The Notice Procedure

1. 1995 Act Section 2
Section 2(1) provides that:

"A party proposing to adduce hearsay evidence in civil proceedings   7–26
shall, subject to the following provisions of this section, give the
other party or parties to the proceedings:

   (a) such notice (if any) of that fact, and
   (b) on request, such particulars of or relating to the evidence,

as is reasonable and practicable in the circumstances for the purpose
of enabling them to deal with any matters arising from its being
hearsay".

Under s.2(2) rules may be made:

"(a) specifying classes of proceedings or evidence in relation to
    which subsection (1) does not apply, and

(b) as to the manner in which (including the time within which) the
    duties imposed by that subsection are to be complied with in
    the cases where it does apply."

The original rules (RSC O.38 r.21; CCR O.20 r.15) provided for a Notice Procedure similar to that under ss.2 and 4 of the Civil Evidence Act 1968. These rules were superseded by CPR 33 for those actions commenced after April 26, 1999. Subsection (3) goes on to provide that the notice procedure may be excluded by agreement. The reality is that it is often excluded by default because neither party addresses the hearsay implications of the vast quantities of business documents containing hearsay that regularly turn up in trial bundles. However it worth observing that, unlike in criminal proceedings, parties have always been free to agree evidence, a rule of law that appears to have survived the advent of the CPR (see *Sunley v Gowland White (Estate Agents and Surveyors) Ltd* [2004] P.N.L.R. 15).

Although the notice requirement in s.2(1) appears to be mandatory, s.2(4) goes on to make it clear that failure to give notice cannot, of itself, provide a ground for exclusion. It states:

"A failure to comply with [s.2(1)] or with rules under [s.2(2)] does not affect the admissibility of the evidence but may be taken into account by the court:

(a) in considering the exercise of its powers with respect to the course of the proceedings and costs; and

(b) as a matter adversely affecting the weight to be given to the evidence in accordance with section 4."

As yet there are no reported cases to show how the court is dealing with failure to give notice. In the writer's own experience it is by no means uncommon for hearsay notices not to have been served, with very little notice then being taken of that fact. However it may be that after the *Moat Housing* decision a rather stronger line will need to be taken (see further 7–36).

2. Contents of Hearsay Notice: CPR 33.2

7–27 Unlike under RSC O.38 r.21(1) or CCR O.20 r.15(1) there is no longer any requirement to serve a detailed hearsay notice containing a prescribed reason for not calling the maker of the original statement. The regime is now much simpler. CPR 33.2 provides that:

"(1)   Where a party intends to rely on hearsay evidence at trial and either:

(a) that evidence is to be given by a witness giving oral evidence; or

(b) that evidence is contained in a witness statement of a person who is not being called to give oral evidence;

that party complies with s.2(1)(a) of the Civil Evidence Act 1995 by serving a witness statement on the other parties in accordance with the court's order.

(2)   Where paragraph (b) applies the party intending to rely on the hearsay evidence must, when he serves the witness statement,

(a) inform the other parties that the witness is not being asked to give oral evidence.

(b) give the reason why the witness will not be called."

The crucial distinction is *not* whether or not it is proposed to call the "maker of the original statement", but whether or not it is proposed to adduce the hearsay by means of *oral* evidence. The best way to explain this is by means of a simple example.

Example: A local authority housing officer (HO) has made a witness 7–28
statement for the purposes of defended possession proceedings
brought by the authority against one of their tenants, D. In it she
sets out several allegations of anti-social behaviour that have been
reported to her by tenants A, B and C, none of whom are willing to
come to court to give evidence due to fear of reprisals.

If the local authority intends to call HO to give oral evidence, she
will clearly be giving hearsay evidence so far as the statements of A, B,
and C are concerned. However the notice requirements will have been
complied with (see CPR 33.2(1)(a) and 32.2(4) below) simply by
serving HO's witness statement in accordance with the relevant case
management direction. It is up to those advising the defendant firstly,
to identify the hearsay evidence and secondly to decide how, if at all,
to respond to it. The only way in which the hearsay will be "flagged
up" is if HO's witness statement complies with CPR PD 32 para.18.2
and indicates those parts that are true to the best of her information
and belief, indicating the source and grounds thereof (see further
11–37). Conversely, if for any reason HO was *not* available to give oral
evidence at trial and, hence, the local authority intended to adduce
her witness statement as hearsay evidence, they would then have to
give *notice* to this effect under CPR 33.2(1)(b). Although there are no
longer any prescribed reasons that have to be given for her non-
attendance, clearly, the more plausible the reason, the greater the
weight that is likely to be attached to the evidence. One anomaly is
that the reason in the notice has to be given in respect of the witness
who was going to adduce the hearsay, in the above example HO,
rather than the *maker* of the original statement (the "eyewitness") in
this case A, B and C. One can only assume that this is an oversight,
in particular when, as we shall see, CPR 33.4 (cross-examination
orders) is worded differently. CPR 33.2(2) then goes on to deal with
cases where it is not intended to introduce the hearsay evidence by
means of a live witness *or* their witness statement.

> "(3)   In all other cases where a party intends to rely on hearsay evi-
> dence at trial, that party complies with section 2(1)(a) of the Civil
> Evidence Act 1995 by serving a notice on the other parties which:
>
> (a) identifies the hearsay evidence; and
> (b) states that the party serving the notice proposes to rely on
>   the hearsay evidence at trial;
> (c) gives the reason why the witness will not be called."

In theory this rule would require you to go through every single document that had been disclosed, examine it to see whether or not the
purpose for which it was going to be adduced involved hearsay
evidence and serve the appropriate notice to that effect. In reality,

as already suggested, this process usually goes by default and nobody raises the point. However, one possible situation in which you might wish to serve such a notice could be as follows.

C is claiming for serious injuries that he received in an accident at work. The accident was so serious that the Health and Safety Executive investigated and took statements from a number of fellow employees. None of them are now prepared to make statements or even be interviewed. You have now obtained copies of their statements from the HSE and wish to rely on them in evidence without calling the makers.

This is one of a number of situations in which you might need to serve a hearsay notice in view of the fact that the "eyewitness's" statement is not contained in a witness statement, by which one assumes is meant a witness statement as defined in CPR 32.4 (see 11–14).

CPR 33.2(4) sets out additional procedural requirements in respect of all hearsay notices:

"(4)   The party proposing to rely on the hearsay evidence must:

(a) serve the notice no later than the latest date for serving witness statements; and

(b) if the hearsay evidence is to be in a document, supply a copy to any party who requests him to do so."

Although the rule uses the word "must", the consequences for non compliance are not automatic exclusion (see s.2(4) referred to earlier). Note that there is no requirement that the notice should be served at the same time as any associated witness statement or document. However it will normally be good practice to serve the notice as part of the witness statement bundle or along with the relevant accompanying document.

3. Cases in Which No Notice Required: CPR 33.3

7–29   The following proceedings are exempt from the requirement to serve a hearsay notice under s.2(1) of the 1995 Act.

"(a) [hearsay] evidence at hearings other than trials;

(aa) . . . an affidavit or witness statement which is to be used at trial but which does not contain hearsay evidence;

(b) a [hearsay] statement which a party to a probate action wishes to put in evidence and which is alleged to have been made by the person whose estate is the subject of the proceedings; or

(c) where the requirement is excluded by a practice direction."

This accordingly exempts all interim applications and Pt 8 proceedings from the notice procedure. However, CPR 33.3(aa), to echo the words of the *White Book* at 33.3.1, is indeed a "curious provision" because it seems to exempt from the notice procedure the one situation that, perhaps more than any other would seem to cry out for notice to be given.

Example: W, an American citizen and key witness in a major commercial fraud has gone back to the United States. Although C has W's signed witness statement, none of the contents of which would be hearsay if he were to give oral evidence, W is adamant that he will not come to England to give oral evidence and is being extremely unco-operative about giving evidence by live video link. C simply serves his statement in the witness statement bundle but gives no indication that he is not calling W.

7–30

On the face of it, the claimant is perfectly entitled to do this according to CPR 33.3(aa); no doubt at some point this will require judicial interpretation if the stakes are high enough.

B Safeguard 2: Cross-Examination Orders: Section 3

1. 1995 Act s.3

This section provides:

7–31

"Rules of court may provide that where a party to civil proceedings adduces hearsay evidence of a statement made by a person and does not call that person as a witness, any other party to the proceedings my, with leave of the court, call that person as a witness and cross-examine him on the statement as if he had been called by the first-mentioned party and as if the hearsay statement was his evidence in chief."

It seems that this section is replete with problems and may, ultimately not be capable of fulfilling the purpose for which it was ostensibly intended. The first point that needs to be made is that it will only be activated if the hearsay statement is actually put in evidence (see *Tsaviliris Russ (Worldwide Salvage & Towage ltd v RL Baron Shipping Co SA (The "Green Opal")* [2003] 1 Lloyds Rep. 523). It is hard to see how this fits in with the time limits for applying for such an order in CPR 33.4. Secondly, CPR 33.4 is drafted more narrowly than s.3 in that it only provides for cross-examination orders against the "maker of the original statement" whereas s.3 provides for rules to made in respect of the maker of *any* hearsay statement. Finally, it is not clear either whose witness the person so summoned will be or, more significantly just how far cross-examination may go. Is it restricted to the contents of the hearsay statement or is he to be treated just like any other witness (for further discussion see *Phipson* 29–05)?

2. *Cross-Examination Summons: CPR 33.4*

7–32   This rule provides that:

"(1)   Where a party:

(a) proposes to rely on hearsay evidence, and
(b) does not propose to call the person who made the original statement to give oral evidence,

the court may, on the application of any other party, permit that party to call the maker of the statement to be cross examined on the contents of the statement.

(2)   An application for permission to cross-examine under this rule must be made not more than 14 days after the day on which a notice of intention to rely on the hearsay evidence was served on the applicant."

There are two practical problems which the courts have not yet been called upon to address. Firstly, what if the particulars given of the hearsay statement are inadequate? Presumably, one can simply seek further information under CPR 18 and apply to the court if the information is not forthcoming (see 10–44). Secondly, what factors will the court take into account when deciding whether or not to grant leave? There is no case law which provides any guidance on this but, presumably, leave will be considered in accordance with the overriding objective in CPR 1.

Note also that the application can only be made under CPR 33.4(1)(b) in respect of "the person who made the original statement". In the following example this is B not A.

7–33   **Example:** Midtown Council wish to tender the witness statement of Housing Officer A in which he sets out complaints received from B as to be anti-social behaviour of his neighbouring tenant D. Somewhat bizarrely:

(1)   The Hearsay Notice must be given in respect of A; but

(2)   The cross-examination application will be in respect of B.

CPR 33.4 has now been addressed by the Court of Appeal in two recent cases. Firstly, in *Douglas v Hello!* [2003] EWCA Civ 332, a case dealing with the use of an exchanged witness statement as hearsay evidence. This is discussed at 11–69. The second case, *Polanski v Condé*

Nast Publications Ltd [2004] 1 All E.R. 1220 involves a point of somewhat greater general interest, namely, what sanction, if any should the court apply if a person served with a cross-examination order fails to attend to give oral evidence? The well known film director Roman Polanski was suing the defendants, the publishers of *Vanity Fair* magazine, in respect of the publication of an article that was highly defamatory of him. He applied for permission to give evidence from Paris by live video link (see further 13–24). In refusing him permission (later reversed by the House of Lords), the Court of Appeal stated that:

(1) The fact that a witness who ought to be before the court is overseas would not of itself be a good reason for refusing an order under CPR 33.4;

(2) If a cross-examination order were made and the witness did not attend this would almost certainly lead to the trial judge refusing to even admit his witness statement;

(3) Non-admission of such hearsay evidence would not infringe s.1 of the Civil Evidence Act 1995 because under CPR 32.1(2) the court may exclude any otherwise admissible evidence (see s.11 of the 1995 Act).

However, the House of Lords in *Polanski v Condé Nast Publications Ltd* [2005] 1 All E.R. 945, although acknowledging that the power existed, were not prepared to be so dogmatic. In particular, Lord Nicholls stated ([36]):

"I agree with the Court of Appeal that the court's case management powers under CPR 32.1 are wide enough to enable the court to make the orders indicated by the Court of Appeal in this passage. But I do question whether, in the present case, had a VCR order been refused, the court would have been "bound" to make an order excluding Mr Polanski's statements from evidence if he did not present himself in court for cross-examination. Such an order should be made only if, exceptionally, justice so requires."

The simplest way to deal with it, surely, would be to admit the statement but invite adverse inferences from the witness's absence (see 4–20).

C Safeguard 3: The Weight Checklist: Section 4

As we have already seen (7–25) the House of Lords has stated that the admission of hearsay evidence does not of itself involve an infringement of Art.6 because of the emphasis that s.4 attaches to the weight **7–34** of the hearsay adduced. As a result, courts are frequently invited to take major decisions based upon such evidence, even to the extent in *Leeds City Council v Harte* [1999] 4 C.L.D. 423 *CA* of making a possession order against anti-social tenants based wholly upon such evidence. Nevertheless it is now clear from *Moat Housing Group South Ltd v Harris and Hartless* [2005] 4 All E.R. 1051 that the court is required to set out with some care the basis upon which s.4 has been applied.

1. Section 4(1): The General Rule

7–35   Under s.4(1) the court shall have regard to any circumstances:

"from which any inference can be drawn as to the reliability or otherwise of the evidence".

An obvious example of where an inference might be drawn is where the maker of the original statement has failed to attend in answer to a cross-examination order made under CPR 33.4. The subsection appears to have no obvious limits subject to relevance and is discussed further in the context of witness statements tendered as hearsay evidence at 11–67.

2. Section 4(2): "The Six Factors"

7–36   Under this subsection the court shall have particular regard to any of the following:

"(a) whether it would have been reasonable and practicable for the party by whom the evidence was adduced to have produced the maker of the original statement as a witness;

(b) whether the original statement was made contemporaneously with the occurrence or existence of the matters stated;

(c) whether the evidence involves multiple hearsay;

(d) whether any person involved had any motive to conceal or misrepresent matters;

(e) whether the additional statement was an edited account, or was it made in collaboration with another or for a particular purpose;

(f) whether the circumstances in which the evidence is adduced as hearsay are such as to suggest an attempt to prevent proper evaluation of its weight."

Although it is clear that the admission of hearsay evidence is not, of itself, a breach of Art.6 of the ECHR, see *Clingham v Marylebone*

Magistrates [2003] 1 A.C. 787. This decision has been applied by the Court of Appeal in *Solon SW Housing Association v James* [2004] EWCA Civ 1847, a claim for possession against anti-social tenants in which a large amount of evidence consisted of complaints by neighbouring residents given as hearsay by housing officers and members of the police. In it, Mance L.J. (at [29]) emphasised that, although the decision to admit hearsay evidence might not, of itself, furnish grounds for appeal, the *way* in which the judge then treated that evidence might do so. In this instance the court was satisfied that the judge had addressed the hearsay evidence appropriately, in particular because he had:

(1) First analysed the "live" evidence; and then

(2) Gone on to consider the extent to which the hearsay evidence (which consisted of both hearsay evidence from "live" witnesses and the witness statements of "absent witnesses") either supported or contradicted the "live" non-hearsay evidence.

The Court of Appeal has also had to consider a number of important points on hearsay in *Moat Housing Group South Ltd v Harris and Hartless* [2005] 4 All E.R. 1051. Although they arose in the specialised area of Anti-Social Behaviour Orders (ASBOs) and Injunctions (ASBIs) under ss.153A to E of the Housing Act 1996, many of the comments of Brooke L.J. are of general application. He made it clear that although hearsay evidence was admissible in civil proceedings, nevertheless:

(1) In future much greater care needed to be taken in drafting witness statements in support of "without notice " relief;

(2) Greater care should be taken by claimants in future to demonstrate with convincing and direct evidence why it was not reasonable or practicable to call the makers of witness statements which were being relied on as hearsay evidence;

(3) Judges should in future take greater care to begin by evaluating the available direct evidence before dealing with the hearsay statements; and, finally;

(4) Judges should, when dealing with hearsay evidence of the type relied on in this case, analyse its weight in their judgments by reference to the specific criteria set out in s.4(2) of the 1995 Act.

As a result of the above decision it seems clear that in future the court will be required to scrutinise the reason for not calling a witness with some care. The court will also need to consider whether adverse inferences should be drawn form the witness's absence (see 4–20).

D Safeguard 4: Competence and Credibility: Section 5

7–37 The final safeguard seems to have been largely ignored, at any rate so far as reported cases are concerned. Outside of fiendish examination questions, it is unlikely to be encountered very often in practice.

1. *1995 Act Section 5*

7–38 The purpose of this section is to enable a party against whom hearsay evidence is tendered to raise any points on competence and credibility that he would have been able to have raised if the witness had attended to give live evidence. The rules as to competence have already been covered at 5–19 and cross-examination on credit is dealt with at 14–47.

(a) *Section 5(1): Competence*

7–39 This subsection in summary provides that If it can be shown that the maker of a hearsay statement would not have been competent to testify at the time he *made* the hearsay statement by reason of:

(1) Mental or physical infirmity or lack of understanding; or

(2) (If a child) he would have not been competent to give unsworn evidence under s.96(2) of the Children Act 1989;

the statement *shall not* be admitted.

(b) *Section 5(2): Credibility*

7–40 The subsection provides that:

"Where in civil proceedings hearsay evidence is adduced and the maker of the original statement or of any statement relied upon to prove another statement, is not called as witness:

(a) evidence which if he had been so called would be admissible for the purpose of attacking or supporting his credibility as a witness is admissible for that purpose in those proceedings;

(b) evidence tending to prove that, whether before or after he made the statement, he made any other statement inconsistent with it is admissible for the purpose of showing that he had contradicted himself.

Provided that evidence may not be given of any matter of which, if he had been called as a witness and had denied that matter in cross-examination, evidence could not have been adduced by the cross-examining party."

The rules on cross-examination are set out at 14–43. In practical terms, it means that if an opponent seeks to rely on the hearsay statement of an individual and you have at your disposal evidence that he or she, (1) has previous convictions; (2) is biased; or (3) has made a previous oral or written inconsistent statement; you may adduce evidence to this effect. That evidence itself may be tendered as direct or hearsay evidence in the same way as any other. As yet, there has been no reported case on these provisions.

2. Notice Attacking Credibility: CPR 33.5

A party wishing to attack the credibility of the maker of a hearsay statement who is not called as a witness under s.5(2) of the 1995 Act must give notice of his intention to do so not later than 14 days after service of the relevant witness statement or hearsay notice under CPR 32.2. Although there is no reported case on this rule, it is likely to cause significant practical difficulties should the need to rely on it arise.

7–41

Example: You are acting for a tenant in a possession case. In the witness statement bundle you find a statement from a housing officer which includes serious allegations against your client being made by a neighbour X, who C does not intend to call. Enquiries reveal that X has made statements to other neighbours, A and B, to the effect that she has a grudge against your client. You take statements from A and B who you wish to call to attack X's credit.

7–42

Firstly, you will almost certainly be out of time with your notice under CPR 33.5; 14 days is an extraordinarily tight time limit. Secondly, you will be out of time with A and B's witness statements and therefore will need the permission of the court before they can be called to give oral evidence (CPR 32.10). No doubt the court would be highly sympathetic on both these points and be less than impressed by an opponent who raised technical objections but, it is submitted, the problem should never have to arise in the first place; CPR 33.5 is plainly inadequate for dealing with this type of evidence.

IV PREVIOUS OUT OF COURT STATEMENTS: SECTION 6

1. Purpose of Section 6

This section is concerned primarily with the interrelationship between the "Rule Against Self Corroboration", referred to briefly at 7–12. This common law rule provides that when a witness is called to give evidence, as general rule, it is not generally permissible to adduce in evidence any out of court statement made by him, whether oral of written, to support his oral testimony or fill in any of the gaps in it. The rule has significantly diminished in importance since written witness statements replaced oral examination in-chief. The section provides:

7–43

"(1) Subject as follows, the provisions of this Act as to hearsay evidence in civil proceedings apply equally (but with any necessary modification) in relation to a previous statement made by a person called as a witness in the proceedings.

(2) A party who has called or intends to call a person as a witness in civil proceedings may not in those proceedings adduce evidence of a previous statement made by that person, except:

    (a) with leave of the court, or
    (b) for the purpose of rebutting a suggestion that his evidence has been fabricated.

This shall not be construed as preventing a witness statement (that is a written statement of oral evidence which a party to the proceedings intends to lead) from being adopted by a witness in giving evidence or treated as his evidence.

(3) Where in the case of civil proceedings, section 3,4 or 5 of the Criminal Procedure Act 1865 applies, which makes provision as to:

    (a) how far a witness may be discredited by the party producing him;
    (b) the proof of contradictory statements made by a witness; and
    (c) cross-examination as to previous statements in writing.

This Act does not authorise the adducing of evidence of a previous inconsistent or contradictory statement otherwise than in accordance with those sections.

This is without prejudice to any provision made by rules of court under section 3 above (power to call witness for cross-examination on hearsay statement).

(4) Nothing in this Act affects any of the rules of law as to the circumstances in which, where a person called as a witness in civil proceedings is cross-examined on a document used by him to refresh his memory, that document may be used in evidence in the proceedings.

(5) Nothing in this section shall be construed as preventing a statement of any description referred to above form being admissible by virtue of section 1 of the matters stated."

As with s.5, the section largely deals with matters arising at trial (see 14–24 outwards). However it may be helpful to summarise its effect in relation to out of court statements introduced to show: (1) consistency (s.6(2)); (2) inconsistency (s.6(3)); and (3) memory refreshing documents (s.6(4)). It is important to note that any statement admitted under this section, whether oral or written will, by virtue of s.6(5) be admissible as *evidence of its contents*, unlike under the old common law rules when, extremely confusingly, it only went to the issue of the witness's *credibility*. It is also somewhat ironic that the rules in criminal cases (see the Criminal Justice Act 2003, ss.119 and 120) are now in many ways less restrictive than those in s.6. one cannot help but wonder whether the section continues to serve any useful purpose.

2. Consistent Statements: s.6(2)

So far as any witness statement served under CPR 32.4 and relied on as evidence in-chief there is no problem. Although it is, in a highly technical sense, hearsay (see 7–12) it will admissible in evidence without leave, provided the relevant case management direction has been complied with (see further 11–13 onwards). However, it is by no means unusual for witness statements to be prepared for signature many months or even years after the events in question. Supposing, for example, a crew member in a shipping claim had made a signed statement to an investigator shortly after the loss of the vessel when the events were much clearer in his memory. Strictly speaking, if you now wanted to rely on the earlier statement in support of the crew member's oral testimony, you would need to:

7–44

(1) Prepare a signed witness statement exhibiting the earlier statement and confirming the truth of its contents;

(2) (Strictly speaking) seek leave of the court under s.6(2) to adduce the earlier statement in evidence.

The reality is likely to be that neither party would ever take the point; it is submitted that these technicalities are, in any event wholly unnecessary. Previous statements should be fully admissible, the only issues being relevance and weight: after all, when would the court ever be likely to refuse leave? Subsection 6(2)(b) deals with the situation in which it is put to a witness in cross-examination that the contents of her witness statement is a "recent fabrication", in other words that she has indulged in a bit of creative fiction after the event. In this situation it has always been permissible at common law (see *R. v Oyesiku* (1971) 56 Cr.App.R. 240 now governed in criminal cases by s.120(2) of the Criminal Justice Act 2003) to adduce rebutting evidence either by calling a witness or producing a document to show that the witness under attack had made a statement to similar effect on an earlier occasion.

3. Inconsistent Statements: s.6(3)

7–45 The rules on use of previous inconsistent statements at trial are still, somewhat confusingly, governed by the Criminal Procedure Act 1865. These sections are designed to deal with two situations, namely when:

(1) Your own witness is treated as "hostile" (1865 Act s.3). Not only will you be able, with leave, to cross-examine him, but any inconsistent out of court statement will be fully admissible:

(2) You wish to cross-examine one of your opponent's witnesses and put a previous inconsistent statement to him (1865 Act, ss.4 and 5). This is discussed further at 11–67 and 14–30. Once again the statement so used will be admissible as hearsay evidence to prove the truth of any fact that it contains.

It must however be emphasised that both of the above situations, especially (1), are rarities: furthermore, witnesses are regularly cross-examined on documents in trial bundles which contradict the contents of their witness statements without any thought being given either to the 1865 Act or s.6(3).

4. Contemporaneous Note: s.6(4)

7–46 As already noted (see 5–29), in the days before exchanged witness statements, a witness was largely "on his own" in the witness box with very few, if any, "prompts" to assist him. In those far off days a written note or statement that had been made or verified at the first opportunity after the events in question, would often, subject to leave, supply the witness with a very valuable *aide memoire*. Now that witness statements have replaced oral examination-in chief, these rules are of rather less practical importance. However there may still be occasions on which the witness statement has been taken and signed long after the events have ceased to be a vivid memory. In those circumstances the ability to refer to contemporaneously recorded information, for example, in the form of clinical notes, observation logs, health and safety entries and so forth may be vital. However, great care needs to be taken when drafting the statement to make sure that the witness's current recall is not influenced by what he has read in contemporaneous documents as *Odyssey Re (London) Ltd v OIC Run Off Ltd* [2000] EWCA Civ 71 discussed at 5–58 so vividly shows. Strictly, speaking, even if exhibited to a witness statement, the leave of the court is required at common law. Again, it is suggested that the point is never taken and the records go in without objection.

V PRESERVED COMMON LAW AND STATUTORY EXCEPTIONS

Section 7 of the 1995 Act deals with a number of miscellaneous **7–47** matters of which the abolition of the informal admission rule is the most important. It also preserves a number of common law exceptions to the hearsay rule which merit no more than a brief consideration. The main difference with hearsay admitted under this section, other than informal admissions, is that it will not be subject to any of the four statutory safeguards in ss.2 to 5 of the Act.

A Informal Admissions (s.7(1))

Informal admissions differ from formal admissions (see 6–02) in that **7–48** a formal admission is conclusive proof of the facts admitted whereas an informal admission is merely evidence, albeit often highly persuasive evidence, that goes towards proof.

1. Abolition of the Informal Admission Rule
The subsection provides that: **7–49**

"The common law rule, effectively preserved by section 9(1) and (2)(a) of the Civil Evidence Act 1968 (admissibility of admissions adverse to a party) is superseded by the provisions of this Act."

The effect of this provision is to render such admissions subject to the same rules as any other type of hearsay evidence admitted under s.1 of the Act.

2. What is an "Informal Admission"?
Any admission made by a person against his own interest was gener- **7–50** ally admissible by way of exception to the hearsay rule by calling the person to whom it was made or producing the relevant document. The rationale for the rule was that any statement that a party made that was adverse to his interest was likely to be true. At first sight it may not be apparent why such an admission would infringe the hearsay rule.

Example: C is suing D, an aged aunt who has cared for many years, **7–51** claiming an interest in her house based on the doctrine of proprietary estoppal. C wishes to rely on the evidence of X in support of his case. X will say that D stated to him that she had promised C that if he looked after her house would be his. C wishes to call X to give evidence.
    Bearing in mind that the hearsay rule is, in effect the "eyewitness rule", in the above example it is D not X who is the "eyewitness" as to

her promise made to C. Accordingly in calling X, C would be adducing hearsay evidence. The rule was subsequently extended to those having an identity of interest with the party, including agents such as solicitors and counsel and predecessors in title (a fuller history of the rule's development can be found in *Phipson* at 4–19 to 4–23 and in *Cross and Tapper* at 608 to 613). Crucially, it was never extended to adverse statements made by employees, including directors of a company.

7–52   **Example:** After a car accident X gets out of his vehicle and admits to P that he was driving too fast. P could give evidence to this effect even though X was the "perceiver". The same rule would equally apply if after getting out of the car R, a bystander were to have said "you lunatic, you were driving too fast!", and X had made no reply.

However if X were, say, acting in the course of his employment, problems used to arise in an action against X's *employer* based on vicarious liability. X had to be made a nominal party in order for C to be able to give hearsay evidence of X's admission (although there was a somewhat convoluted way of getting it in under s.2 of the Civil Evidence Act 1968). The admissions rule has now been abolished so that a witness may now repeat an adverse hearsay statement made by:

(1) a party (or person having an identity of interest); or

(2) any other person (irrespective of their relationship to that party).

Informal admissions will however be subject to the "Four Statutory Safeguards" in ss.2 to 5 of the Act and notice will need to be given under CPR 33.2.

B Public Documents

7–53   As well as the common law rules preserved by s.7(2) of the Act, any other statute providing for the admission of hearsay evidence is expressly preserved and exempted from the provisions of ss.2 to 5 by s.1(4) of the Act. As well as briefly examining the preserved common law rules, this section will also summarise the principal features of the Bankers' Books Evidence Act 1879.

1. Common Law

7–54   The rules as to the admissibility of such documents are expressly preserved by s.7(2) of the Act. Under these exceptions a certified copy of a public document is admissible as proof of its contents, for example, certificates of birth, death and marriage (s.7(2)(b)). However since nearly all such documents are covered by specific statutory provisions, this exception is not as practically important as it might appear at first sight. Furthermore, many such documents will now be admissible as "records" under the simplified procedure in s.9 of the Act (see 5–42). An extremely comprehensive survey of public documents admissible at common law is to be found in *Phipson* 32–55 to 32–106. Section 7(2) also preserves the common law rules as to published works (s.7(2)(a)) of a public nature, for example dictionaries and maps, and various public records (s.7(2)(c)). The common law rules as to the admissibility of a person's reputation for the purpose of proving his good or bad character (s.7(3)(a)) and evidence of family reputation for the purpose of proving or disproving pedigree and other specific matters (s.7(3)(b)) are also preserved. The practical significance of this is minimal; those seeking a fuller explanation should consult *Cross and Tapper* at 621 to 631.

2. Bankers' Books Evidence Act 1879

Banker's books have their special scheme for admission under the   7–55
1879 Act. This provides, broadly, that a copy of an entry in a banker's book, defined in s.1(2) as including:

> "ledgers, day books, cash books, account books and other records used in the ordinary business of the bank, whether those records are in written form or are kept on microfilm, magnetic tape or any other form of mechanical or electronic data retrieval mechanism".

The 1879 Act provides that copy entries:

(1) Shall be receivable as prima facie evidence of such entry (s.3); provided that

(2) (Inter alia) the entry was in the ordinary course of business (s.4); and

(3) The copy has been examined with the original (s.5).

The Act extends to all mechanical and electronic data retrieval systems (Bankers' Act 1979, Sch.6). Not all documents recording client transactions held by a bank will necessarily come within the definition in the 1879 Act. For example, in *Re Howglen* [2001] 1 All E.R. 376 Pumfrey J. held that the minutes of a meeting between bank employees and customer were not within the definition of "other record" for the purposes of the Act since that term had to be construed *eiusdem generis* with the specific categories set out in s.1(2). Nevertheless, he went on to hold that the applicants were entitled to disclosure as against the bank of some of the documents sought under CPR 31.17 (non-party disclosure).

VI PROOF OF COPY DOCUMENTS AND BUSINESS RECORDS

7–56   It will be recalled that ss.8 and 9 of the Act had a far wider reaching impact in that they are regarded by many commentators as being applicable to all documentary evidence irrespective of whether its contents are being adduced as hearsay evidence. Both sections have already fully covered at 5–42, 5–48 and are dealt with further at 13–35.

7–57   *Conclusion*   This chapter has examined the 1995 Act and the accompanying procedure in CPR 33 in some detail. It has become apparent that some parts are not without their complications. Nevertheless, the reality is that hearsay evidence is regularly being receive in evidence and evaluated by courts without any of the accompanying technicalities that so used to bedevil this area of the law (anyone who laments the passing of the exclusionary rule should read *Ventouris v Mountain (No.2)* [1992] 1 W.L.R. 887). However, as stated at the start of this chapter, this does not mean that it is no longer important to identify hearsay evidence and to recognise the inherent weaknesses that it my sometimes exhibit. Furthermore, it may present significant challenges to the courts, as Brooke L.J. stated in *Moat Housing Group South Ltd v Harris and Hartless* [2005] 4 All E.R. 1051 (at [140]):

> "While nobody would wish to return to the days before the 1995 Act came into force, when efforts to admit hearsay evidence were beset by complicated statutory rules, the experience of this case should provide a salutary warning for the future that more attention should be paid . . . to the need to state by convincing direct evidence why it was not reasonable and practicable to produce the original maker of the statement as a witness. If the statement involves multiple hearsay, the route by which the original statement came to the attention of the person attesting to it should be identified as far as practicable. It would also be desirable for judges to remind themselves in their judgments that they are taking into account the s.4(2) criteria . . . so far as they are relevant."

Although this guidance was directed at claimants in anti-social behaviour cases, it is submitted that it is applicable to all parties in all types of claim.

Chapter 8

Privilege and Public Interest Immunity

As noted at 1–21, there are only four mandatory rules of exclusion in **8–01** civil proceedings: (1) irrelevance (see 4–03); (2) opinion (considered along with expert opinion evidence at 12–02); (3) privilege; and (4) public interest immunity ("PII"). Courts regularly receive irrelevant evidence and technically inadmissible opinion evidence, but rather than excluding it they tend to accord it little or no weight. However with privilege and PII the position is very different, not least because the evidence in respect of which they are asserted may be *highly* relevant. Although issues relating to privilege and PII tend to rise at the disclosure stage (see Chapter 10) they can crop up elsewhere, for example on an application for disclosure against a non-party under CPR 31.17, a freezing order, or to set aside a witness order.

SECTION I: OVERVIEW: THE CONCEPT OF PRIVILEGE

1. Privilege and Public Interest Immunity: the Reality
The law relating to privilege occupies a central place in the modern **8–02** law of evidence: it takes no less than 155 pages (Chapters 23 to 26) of *Phipson* and 128 pages (Chapters 11 to 18) of *Hollander* to cover the area comprehensively. Nevertheless, in practical terms, outside of the costly sabre rattling that sometimes takes place in high value claims, it does not give rise to many difficulties in practice. From an early stage in our legal careers we learn that the client's file is more or less a closed book to the outside world in every case; if we inadvertently disclose privileged material it may be too late to undo the damage; and our clients are not usually bound by anything said in negotiations to settle a dispute unless and until there is a concluded agreement. So

far as public interest immunity is concerned, one could easily enjoy a lengthy and distinguished legal career without ever encountering it in practice. However, the principles covered in this chapter are now recognised as being more than mere rules of evidence. They constitute a significant group of important constitutional rights. We have the "big hitters" of litigation to thank for marking out and cementing the boundaries of rights and protections for the individual that are perhaps taken too much for granted.

2. *The Basic Principles*

8–03 A person who is in the possession of information consisting of material (in whatever form), may legitimately refuse to make that information available by, for example, refusing to:

(1) Give oral evidence or produce a document at a trial or hearing (or answer individual questions);

(2) Disclose information under a Pre Action Protocol;

(3) Answer to a Witness Summons issued under CPR 34 to give oral evidence or produce documents at a trial or hearing;

(4) Permit inspection of documents or real evidence in his possession power or control during the course of pre-trial/action disclosure;

(5) Give access to documents or material to those executing a search warrant in criminal proceedings or a search order in civil proceedings;

(6) Answer questions or produce documents to a police officer or other investigator;

on the ground that the information is protected under one or more of the heads of privilege, or that it is immune for disclosure in the public interest. Before considering the privilege in detail, it is instructive to set out a very brief overview of how the major privileges inter-relate. It should be borne in mind at all times that whichever privilege is asserted: (1) no adverse inference can be drawn from reliance upon it; (2) it is immaterial how relevant and otherwise admissible the material would be.

I LEGAL PROFESSIONAL PRIVILEGE

8–04 Legal professional privilege ("LPP") comprises two categories which are not always clearly differentiated. Both are personal to the individual or institution asserting them, and must be upheld on their behalf by anyone who holds privileged information in confidence. Both classes of legal professional privilege can only be lost by the express or implied waiver of the person entitled to assert them or an agent with ostensible authority. They endure for all time, and are not confined in scope to the legal context in which they originally arose. It is also now clear (see 8–10) that LPP is more than a rule of evidence but amounts to a substantive legal right underwritten by Arts 6 and 8 ECHR, albeit that it is only accorded qualified exemption under s.41 of the Freedom of Information Act 2000.

1. "Legal Advice" Privilege
This consists of confidential oral or written communications between   **8–05**
a client/advisee and his legal adviser made with a view to enabling the advisee to obtain legal advice on any matter, provided the advice is not sought for a future criminal or dishonest purpose. It is "absolute" in the sense that once it is found to exist in respect of any communication, it is not subject to any exceptions; the only way in which it can be lost is by express or implied waiver. The privilege does not apply (subject to limited statutory exceptions) to other confidential communications, for example, with a doctor, accountant or priest, even if those communications touch and concern legal matters. However, that is not to say that the court will always compel such persons to divulge confidential information: the court will carefully scrutinise the relevance of such material before it compels a non-lawyer to betray a confidence.

2. "Litigation Privilege"
This consists of oral and written communications (and material   **8–06**
brought into being and enclosed with such communications) between:

(1) The litigant or his agent and third parties;

(2) Legal advisers and third parties;

provided that the communication (and any enclosure) was made in contemplation of existing or anticipated litigation and that its "dominant purpose" was to prepare for that litigation. In one sense it is *wider* than legal advice privilege in that it covers communications with third parties and can (probably) be invoked by a litigant in person. In another sense it is *narrower*. It is confined to communications whose predominant purpose is preparing for actual or anticipated litigation. It is also, unlike legal advice privilege, subject to exceptions, in particular, it cannot be raised in proceedings relating to children (see 8–14).

B Privilege Against Self Incrimination

8–07   As a general rule, any person called as a witness or summoned to produce a document is guilty of contempt of court if he refuses to answer questions or produce the document. However, a person is entitled to refuse if the information disclosed would have a tendency to increase the likelihood of his being prosecuted for a criminal offence or subjected to a penalty. The privilege can be asserted at any stage, for example on disclosure of documents (see 10–16) or in response to a search warrant or search order (see 8–83). It is an important facet both of the "right to silence" and the right to a fair trial under Art.6 of the ECHR. It can be waived by the individual entitled to assert it, but is subject to a much wider range of statutory exceptions than LPP (see 8–74).

C "Without Prejudice" Negotiations

8–08   It is regarded as being in the public interest that parties to a civil dispute should be encouraged to settle as quickly as possible. Thus evidence cannot be given by *any* party to those negotiations of any communication (including an offer or other points conceded) made in an attempt to settle a dispute if it was made expressly or impliedly "without prejudice". It differs in a number of important respects from the other varieties of privilege, in particular:

(1) It cannot be waived unilaterally, all parties to the negotiation must consent;

(2) It cannot be asserted against any individual who is not a party to the negotiations or the proceedings in which they arise;

(3) It is open to negotiating parties to agree that any communications made during negotiation should retain confidentiality thus rendering them contractually inadmissible should a dispute subsequently arise between them;

(4) It is subject to a far wider range of exceptions, at least eight, than the other privileges.

In civil proceedings, it also plays an important role in relation to protective offers on costs made under CPR 36 ("Part 36 Payments and

Offers"). A detailed commentary on Pt 36 is outside the scope of this work (see further Chapter 29 of *O'Hare and Browne*).

D Public Interest Immunity

Relevant evidence must be excluded on the grounds of public policy where it is found that the public interest in the administration of justice and the interests of the individual litigants are outweighed by some greater public interest. It is not possible to provide a rigid classification of types of evidence subject to public policy exclusion, but case law (see 8–123) has established that the categories of public interest immunity ("PII") are never closed and will change in line with the prevailing social and political climate. There used to be a time when the courts would not enquire into the justification for asserting PII, certainly when it was raised by a Government Minister. However (see 8–127), the courts now adopt a much more active role in ensuring that the assertion of PII is kept within its proper confines. In this sense, PII differs fundamentally from privilege. Once the court determines that privilege applies, it has no choice in the matter; disclosure must be refused unless the privilege has been waived. Conversely, whenever PII is asserted the court must carry out a "balancing exercise" to determine whether the public interest identified by the party resisting disclosure outweighs the potential forensic value it may have for the party seeking access. In theory, PII also differs from privilege in that it cannot be waived. If sensitive material *is* disclosed voluntarily this is rationalised by saying that PII never arose in the first place.

The relevant heads of privilege and PII will now be analysed in greater detail. Those seeking an even more substantial commentary should consult Charles Hollander Q.C.'s comprehensive review of the current law in Chapters 23 to 26 of *Phipson*.

SECTION 2: LEGAL PROFESSIONAL PRIVILEGE

As already pointed out, LPP is more than a rule of evidence, it is a substantive legal right. This was first explicitly acknowledged in *R. v Derby Magistrates Court Ex p. B* [1996] 1 A.C. 487, in particular by Lord Taylor CJ when he stated:

"Legal professional privilege is thus much more than an ordinary rule of evidence, limited in its application to the facts of a particular case. It is a fundamental condition on which the administration of justice as a whole rests."

This has since been reaffirmed by speeches in the House of Lords in *Morgan Grenfell* [2003] 1 A.C. 563, *Medcalf v Mardell* [2003] 1 A.C.

8–09

8–10

520, *Three Rivers (No.6)* [2004] 3 W.L.R. 1274, and in the Privy Council in *B v Auckland District Law Society* [2003] 2 A.C. 736. For a full commentary see *Phipson* 23–05 to 23–14.

I GENERAL CHARACTERISTICS

8–11   As noted earlier, litigation privilege has only been recognised as a separate head of LPP relatively recently and differs from legal advice privilege in a number of fundamental respects. Nevertheless, both heads still retain a number of common features.

1. Absolute Nature of Legal Professional Privilege

8–12   In both of types of LPP, the privilege belongs to the client/advisee but attaches to the communication provided it was made in confidence. Accordingly, it must be asserted on behalf of the client/advisee by the legal adviser (or any other person to whom it is communicated in confidence). Furthermore, once established it cannot be overridden by the court. This was confirmed by the House of Lords in *R. v Derby Magistrates* Ex p. B [1996] A.C. 487 in which Lord Taylor CJ stated:

> "The principle that runs through all [the authorities] is that a man must be able to consult his lawyer in confidence, since otherwise he might hold back the truth. The client must be sure that what he tells his lawyers will *never* [writer's emphasis] be revealed without his consent".

The potential importance of the evidence to the party seeking to rely upon it is immaterial and, unlike in the case of PII the court has no discretion to override the claim to LPP. The facts of *Ex p. B* provide a stark illustration of this:

B was charged with the murder of a teenaged girl following a highly publicised civil claim brought by her parents in which he had been held liable for killing her. He denied the murder and sought to cast blame on his stepson, X. Some years previously, X had been charged with the same murder. Initially he had confessed. However he later retracted the confession and was acquitted. At committal proceedings B's advocate wished to cross-examine X about the instructions X had given to his solicitor after the confession but prior to the retraction.

The potential relevance of X's answers in relation to B's defence is manifest. Furthermore, X himself was no longer at risk of prosecution because he had already been acquitted. Nevertheless, X's claim to privilege was upheld even though, in practical terms X no longer needed to rely on it.

Parliament, subject to the ECHR, has the power to override privilege, but as was confirmed in *Morgan Grenfell* (see in particular Lord Hobhouse at [45] and the commentary in *Phipson* at 23–37) any purported abrogation by Parliament of LPP will be scrutinised with the greatest care and only upheld if privilege has been expressly overridden or it is a "necessary implication" of the provision. The court would then have to go on and consider whether the abrogation was ECHR compliant. The only other glimmer of an exception is in relation to disciplinary enquiries by professional legal bodies such as the Law Society. It appears, based on the Court of Appeal decision in *Parry-Jones v Law Society* [1969] 1 Ch. 1 that the Law Society has such a power (see *Simms v Law Society* [2005] EWHC Admin 408) but the legal foundation for this is uncertain. The current position is by no means satisfactory (see further *Phipson* at 23–22 to 23–26). It will be interesting to see how public authorities and the courts will deal with the fact that information subject to LPP held by a public authority is not absolutely exempt from disclosure under the Freedom of Information Act 2000 (see 10–52).

2. Scope and Duration

Because LPP is a substantive legal right it can be asserted in any situation (see *Calcraft v Guest* [1898] 1 Q.B. 759 in which documents that were 100 years old were still privileged). Therefore the phrases "once privileged always privileged" and "a lawyer's mouth is shut for ever" are an accurate summary of the legal position. Accordingly, if a document is privileged in one action it will be privileged in any subsequent action even if there is no substantial identity of subject matter (see *Aegis Blaze* [1986] 1 Lloyds Rep. 203). It will survive for the benefit of a successor in title and survives the death of the person entitled to claim it, see *Bullivant v AG for Victoria* [1901] A.C. 196. The privilege also runs with the action when the right to this is assigned, see *Crescent Farm (Sidcup) Sports Ltd v Sterling Offices Ltd* [1972] Ch. 553. The same principles apply to pending litigation privilege (see *S County Council v B* [2000] Fam. 76).   **8–13**

3. Family Proceedings

There are special rules in cases involving children and, possibly, applications for ancillary relief in relation to *litigation privilege only*. The House of Lords has held in *Re L (a Minor) (Police Investigation: Privilege)* [1996] 2 All E.R. 78 that although legal advice privilege is absolute, litigation privilege does not attach to expert reports obtained by a party to proceedings under Pts IV or V Children Act 1989. It is in the non-adversarial nature of the proceedings that prevents litigation privilege from arising. This principle has since been extended to private Childrens Act proceedings in *Vernon v Bosley*   **8–14**

(No.2) [1999] Q.B. 18. In that case, damages had been assessed based upon a psychiatric report ("Report 1") which had given the claimant a very pessimistic prognosis. The Court of Appeal held that the claimant should have voluntarily disclosed a report ("Report 2") prepared in respect of residence and contact proceedings which had painted a much more optimistic picture. Since Report 2 was not privileged in the children proceedings it was not privileged for *any* purpose. Note however that the converse does not apply, the claimant in *Vernon v Bosley* could have asserted litigation privilege in respect of Report 1 if disclosure had been sought in the children proceedings (see *S County Council v B* (above)).

4. Loss of Privilege

8–15 As already noted both legal advice and litigation privilege can only be lost by the waiver of the person entitled to assert it or his authorised agent. Waiver is dealt with as a separate topic at 8–58. Most of the reported cases involve instances where the client's legal adviser has inadvertently waived privilege by permitting inspection of a privileged document. This topic is considered at 10–30.

5. Disclosure under the CPR: What Goes in Part II of the N265?

8–16 If the court makes an order for disclosure (see 10–14) a party must disclose the existence of privileged documents in Pt II of his List of Documents (Form N265) and then claim privilege or immunity from inspection. Under the RSC and CCR privileged documents could be described in such general terms that their true identity was never revealed (see *Derby v Weldon (No.7)* [1990] 1 W.L.R. 1156). However the N265 and PD 31 para. 4.5 appear to suggest that the documents which a party claims he is entitled to withhold from inspection must be *individually described*. If this were so, it would drive a coach and horse through LPP. To take an obvious example, what if an expert report was individually described in Pt 2 of the list but that party was not seeking the court's permission to rely on it in evidence? The obvious inference would be that he had reported unfavourably. Since there is no property in a witness (see 8–44, 11–60 and 12–44) the other party might be tempted to call that expert himself: failing that, it would still provide the opponent with useful ammunition in negotiations. If the point were ever to arise, it is likely that the court, applying *Morgan Grenfell* (see 8–12) would read the rule down. The topic is discussed in detail in *Phipson* at 23–97 to 23–98. Should the issue ever arise, CPR 31.19 enables a party to apply to the court as follows:

"(3) A person who wishes to claim that he has a right or a duty to withhold inspection of a document, or part of a document, must state in writing:

(a) that he has such a right or duty; and

(b) the grounds on which he claims that right or duty.

(4) The statement referred to in paragraph (3) must be made—

(a) in the list in which the document is disclosed; or

(b) if there is no list, to the person wishing to inspect the document.

(5) A party may apply to the court to decide whether a claim made under paragraph (3) should be upheld.

(6) For the purposes of deciding an application under paragraph . . . (3) (claim to withhold inspection) the court may:

(a) require the person seeking to withhold disclosure or inspection of a document to produce that document to the court; and

(b) invite any person, whether or not a party, to make representations.

(7) An application under paragraph . . . (5) must be supported by evidence."

In the meantime solicitors follow the time-honoured practice of describing the documents generically, for example:

"Those documents which were created for the purpose of giving or receiving legal advice and/or actual or contemplated litigation and are by their nature privileged . . ."

and nobody raises any objection.

II "LEGAL ADVICE" PRIVILEGE

The modern rationale of this branch of LPP was spelled out by **8-17** Bingham L.J. in *Ventouris v Mountain* [1991] 1 W.L.R. 607:

". . . actual and potential litigants, be they claimants or respondents, should be free to unburden themselves without reserve to their legal advisers, and their legal advisers give honest and candid advice on a sound factual basis, without fear that these communications may be relied upon by an opposing party if the dispute comes before the court for decision."

This statement is revealing because it goes to the core of why a party might want access to privileged information. It is not the *advice* they would like to be able to use in evidence: that would be inadmissible on the grounds of irrelevance in any event (although it would be useful in negotiations to know how the other side's lawyer rated his client's prospects of success). On the other hand the *instructions* given by the client to his legal adviser could contain significant admissions or inconsistencies which, in the absence of privilege, could be made use of in cross-examination: after all, that was what *Ex p. B* was all about. It would also raise the horrifying prospect of days of cross-examination on the minutiae of solicitor/client correspondence and attendance notes.

A Scope

8–18 The privilege covers confidential communications between an advisee/client and his legal adviser with a view to enabling the advisee/client to obtain legal advice. Thus it is not essential for there to be a solicitor/client retainer. This was the case in *Somatra v Sinclair Roche and Temperley* [2000] 1 W.L.R. 2493 in which advice given by the managing partner of the defendant firm to his co-partners regarding a dispute with the claimants was held to be privileged. Whatever the relationship, it is essential that the communication is made *in confidence*. There is a presumption that all lawyer/client communications are confidential unless there is evidence to the contrary (*Minter v Priest* [1930] A.C. 558 at 581 and see *Phipson* 23–18).

1. Who Qualifies as a "Legal Adviser"?
8–19 The privilege does not arise unless the communication is with a "legal adviser". This extends to:

(1) All *solicitors* and *barristers* in private practice, including fee earners acting under a solicitor's supervision. It also extends to overseas lawyers (*Re Duncan* [1968] P. 306).

(2) *In-house lawyers* provided they are acting as such. For example, in *Alfred Crompton Amusement Machines v Customs and Excise Commissioners (No.2)* [1974] 2 A.C. 405 it was held to extend to the Commissioner's salaried legal advisers in relation to the claimants' tax liability. However, if the in-house lawyer is acting in a purely executive capacity, the privilege will not arise see, for example, *Blackpool Corporation v Locker* [1948] 1 All E.R. 85 where it was held not to apply to communications between the town clerk (who happened to be a solicitor) and a Government Minister in circumstances where the communication was made in the town clerk's executive capacity. The privilege is even

capable of arising in the case of communications between a Chief Officer of Police and the Crown Prosecution Service or the Director of Public Prosecutions, but only if there is a genuine relationship of legal adviser and advisee (see *Goodridge v Chief Constable of Hampshire* [1999] 1 W.L.R. 1558). In that case, the claim to privilege failed in respect of a report prepared for the DPP pursuant to a statutory duty.

(3) *Other professionals* by way of statutory exemption. Examples include: patent agents (s.280 of the Copyright Designs and Patents Act 1988); trademark agents (1988 Act, s.284); licensed conveyancers (s.33 of the Administration of Justice Act 1985); and representatives of employees at industrial tribunals. There is also power in s.63 of the Courts and Legal Services Act 1990 to extend privilege to "authorised practitioners". As yet this power has not been invoked.

(4) *Journalists* enjoy a statutory immunity from disclosing their sources analogous to LPP under s.10 of the Contempt of Court Act 1981 unless the court is satisfied that disclosure is, "necessary in the interests of justice of national security or for the prevention of disorder or crime". The section is fully discussed in *Hollander* at 5–47 to 5–61.

However, it does not extend to other confidential relationships even if made in a legal context. For example, the privilege has been held not to arise in the case of: personnel consultants (see *New Victoria Hospital v Ryan* [1993] I.C.R. 201), industrial relations consultants (see *M and W Grazebrook Ltd v Wallens* [1973] 2 All E.R. 868) or; other professional relationships such as doctor and patient (see *Dunn v British Coal* [1993] I.C.R. 591), priest and penitent or personal financial advisers (see *D v D (Production Appointment)* [1995] 2 F.L.R. 694). This narrow definition also, in theory, denies the protection of privilege to the vast amount of legal advice given by lay advisers at advice centres. However, a court will hesitate before it compels a witness to reveal confidences.

Protecting Confidentiality Although the scope of LPP is limited to   **8–20** communications with legal advisers, this does not mean to say that the courts will unhesitatingly and unthinkingly force a person to divulge confidential information on pain of punishment for contempt of court. As Lord Denning M.R. stated in *AG v Mulholland* [1963] 2 Q.B. 477, a case on journalistic confidentiality at 489):

"Take the clergyman, the banker or the medical man. None of these is entitled to refuse to answer when directed by a judge. Let me not be mistaken. The judge will respect the confidences which such member of these honourable professions receives in the course of it, and will not direct him to answer unless not only is it relevant but also it is a proper and, indeed, necessary question in the course of justice to be put and answered. A judge is the person entrusted, on behalf of the community to weigh these conflicting interests . . ."

This passage was approved by the House of Lords in *British Steel Corp v Granada Television* [1981] A.C. 1096.

2. What Constitutes "Legal Advice"?

8–21 The modern position was first set out by Taylor L.J. in *Balabel v Air India* [1988] Ch. 317, a claim for specific performance of an alleged agreement to grant a lease. From this case it is possible to identify the following principles:

(1) The term "purposes of legal advice" should be construed broadly;

(2) It may extend to general commercial or property advice within the relevant legal context;

(3) The advice need not be specifically sought in the sense that every client letter must end with the words "please advise me as to my legal position";

(4) During a transaction the "continuum of communication" will normally be covered. Accordingly it will not be possible for a party to "cherrypick" individual communication within that continuum simply because no identifiable legal advice is sought or given within them. However, if a specific client communication were to constitute a *"fait accompli"* for example, by setting out the terms of a contract that had been entered into the position might be different.

The decision was considered at length by Colman J. in *NRG v Bacon and Woodrow* [1995] 1 All E.R. 976 in the context of a claim for professional negligence arising out of the acquisition of a group of reinsurance companies. During the course of discovery it became apparent that the claimants' solicitors, who were part of the claimants' acquisition team but not themselves defendants in the proceedings, had given general commercial advice as well as legal advice. The defendants sought discovery of the documents containing that advice. The key test applied by the judge was whether the advice was:

"directly related to the performance by the solicitor of his professional duties as legal adviser."

Following *Balabel*, Colman J. held that the solicitors' commercial advice was protected. This broad definition of communications attracting privilege was generally accepted until subjected to a degree of qualification by the Court of Appeal in *Three Rivers (No.6)* discussed at 8–38. However, the House of Lords has now restored the status quo in overruling the Court of Appeal in *Three Rivers (No.6)*. Accordingly both of the above decisions can be taken to have been correctly decided on their facts (if that was ever in doubt).

3. *Limits to the Privilege*
A client cannot confer privilege on a document simply by handing   **8–22**
it to his legal adviser for the purpose of receiving advice upon it. This was established by the Court of Appeal in *Ventouris v Mountain* [1991] 1 W.L.R. 607 in which the defendants sought to withhold from inspection a tape recording which had been handed to them by a third party. Since it was not privileged on any other basis (for example under litigation privilege) the claimants were entitled to inspect it. It also important to remember that it is only communications in relation to *legal advice* that are covered. There is therefore no guarantee that all documents created in the course of the solicitor/client relationship will be privileged. For example, in *R. v Inner London Crown Court Ex p. Baines and Baines* [1988] Q.B. 579, a case involving an application for a Production Order in criminal proceedings, documents recording conveyancing transactions, such as the conveyance, completion statements and entries in the Office and Client account relating to them, were held not to be covered. Furthermore, the communication must be by way of giving or receiving legal advice accordingly, it will not cover a request for a "quote" on a conveyancing transaction (see *C v C* [2002] Fam. 42) or information relating to the amount of costs that have been incurred to date on behalf of a client (the court has specific power to order a party to file a costs estimate at any stage in the proceedings see, Section 6 Costs PD 43). Nor can it be asserted in respect of *extraneous facts* learnt by the legal adviser otherwise than in the course of giving or receiving legal advice. All the recent case law has been in the criminal proceedings, but the decisions would be equally relevant in a civil context. In *R. v Manchester Crown Court Ex p. R* [1999] 1 W.L.R. 832 the record of a client appointment in a solicitor's diary was held not to be privileged and in *R. (App Howe) v South Durham Magistrates' Court* [2004] EWHC Admin 3077 a solicitor was held to be a compellable witness as to the identity of a client that he had represented at an earlier hearing. Finally, perhaps more importantly in a civil context, it will it cover a communication from a client which (*Balabel*) constitutes a *fait accompli*. The example Lord Taylor CJ gives is the client who writes a letter saying, "I have agreed with X to sell Blackacre for

£1,000,000, please draw up the appropriate documents". Further extensive examples are given in *Phipson* at 23–65 to 23–80.

Implied Breach of Privilege: "Betraying the Trend" It was thought that the privilege protected not only the communication itself but also any non-privileged communication(s) which might implicitly:

"betray the trend of legal advice"

such as a selection of documents collated by a party's solicitor from non-privileged material. This concept was recognised in *Dubai Bank v Galadari (No.7)* [1992] 1 W.L.R. 106. However, as will be discussed later (8–52), it has now been held by the Court of Appeal in *Sumitomo Corp v Credit Lyonnais Rouse Ltd* [2002] 4 All E.R. 68 to have been incorrectly decided.

B. Problem Areas

1. "Blanking Out"

8–23 It used to be thought that a document could not be sub-divided into privileged and non-privileged parts unless the two parts dealt with separate subjects. This is probably still the case if the document is deployed in evidence at trial as in *Great Atlantic Insurance v Home Insurance* [1981] 1 W.L.R. 529 (see further 8–68). However, the Court of Appeal decided in *GE Capital Corporate Finance v Bankers Trust Co.* [1995] 1 W.L.R. 172 that similar principles do not apply on discovery/disclosure of documents and that accordingly a party may legitimately seek to "blank out" (redact) privileged and/or irrelevant parts of an otherwise disclosable document (see further *Phipson* 23–42 to 23–43).

2. Problems with Business Clients

8–24 A number of difficulties may arise due to the fact that the "client" will frequently not be a single individual, but a corporate or institutional entity with numerous directors and departments individually or collectively seeking advice for the purpose of wider distribution. Fortunately, many of the potential difficulties can be resolved by ensuring that confidentiality is retained at all times however widely the advice is circulated within the organisation. If the information is sensitive it is probably wiser not to circulate it via internal email: one wrong click of a mouse could send it spinning round the world.

(a) Legal Advice Given at a Board Meeting

8–25 All kinds of potential problems can arise. What if the advice it is discussed, minuted and circulated afterwards? Provided confidentiality is maintained, the privilege will carry over into any confidential document created within the client organisation, which all employees will be under a duty to uphold (see *Phipson* 23–40). One recent authority in support of this is the decision of Mann J. in *USP Strategies v London General Holdings Ltd* [2004] EWHC 373 Ch. It would however always be a sensible precaution to set out in the heading of the document that it contained privileged material and was to be held subject to a duty of confidentiality. What if third parties such as auditors or other interested parties are present? Although it will constitute a waiver so far as those third parties are concerned, provided confidentiality is maintained, it does not operate as a waiver to the whole world (see *Gotha City v Sothebys* [1998] 1 W.L.R. 114 and *USP Strategies* (above)). Although it would be prudent to make it clear to any third parties that they were to respect confidentiality, the *Gotha City* decision (discussed further at 8–27) makes it clear that confidentiality will be readily implied. This is even more important if it is being shown to someone from a public authority because of the Freedom of Information Act 2000 implications (see 10–52).

(b) *Dissemination within the Organisation*

What if the advice (or the gist of it) is incorporated into a document   **8–26** which is then circulated within the organisation? As noted above, provided confidentiality is maintained, privilege will not be lost. The decision of Saville J. in *The Good Luck* [1991] 3 All E.R. 1, which has never seriously been questioned supports this view. The case concerned an internal memorandum within a bank containing legal advice. Saville J. held that, provided confidentiality was maintained either expressly or by implication, there was no loss of privilege. This must surely be right. However some doubt has been cast upon the precise nature of "the client" by the Court of Appeal in *Three Rivers District Council v Bank of England (No. 5)* [2003] Q.B. 1556. The court appeared to be of the view that "the client" within a corporate organisation would be those individuals charged with the task of *obtaining legal advice* on its behalf. Although the House of Lords were invited to rule upon the issue, they declined to do so. As *Phipson* states at 23–57 to 23–61, the position is less than satisfactory. However even if "client" is restricted to the "core team" within the organisation, legal advice disseminated within the organisation by the "core" will still be privileged in the hands of the recipients under the *Gotha City* principle.

(c) *Dissemination to Third Parties*

What if solicitors communicate legal advice to third parties such as   **8–27** auditors or insurers or some other interested party such as the CEO of a company within the same industry? It is now clear that. The privilege will be preserved against all persons other than the one to whom it had been disclosed, provided that the disclosure is made expressly or impliedly in confidence. This vitally important principle was established by the Court of Appeal in *Gotha City v Sothebys* [1998] 1 W.L.R. 114.

8–28   Facts: Sothebys (B) were shown legal advice given to the purported owner (A) of a valuable painting at the offices of A's solicitors. The Court readily inferred that the circumstances under which the advice was revealed indicated that it was being shown in confidence and hence was privileged from inspection by the claimant in subsequent proceedings brought by them against A.

The decision is significant because:

(1) The purported owner (A) never informed the third party (B) that they were being shown the advice in confidence: the fact that it was shown to B at the offices of A's solicitors was sufficient;

(2) At the time litigation was not contemplated against either A or B, hence litigation privilege was unavailable.

8–29   It appears that privilege may even be asserted against another party where legal advice has been disclosed to that other party's legal adviser in confidence "for his eyes only" (see *Oxford Gene Technology v Affymetrix* [2001] R.P.C. 18).

3. Advice Tainted with Criminality or Fraud

8–30   The decision of the Court for Crown Cases Reserved in *R. v Cox and Railton* (1884) 14 Q.B.D 153 covers two types of legal advice, namely communications which are:

(1) Criminal (or fraudulent) transactions in themselves; or

(2) Intended to further some future criminal (or fraudulent) purpose.

Privilege never arises because there is no legal retainer in the first place. The fact that the legal adviser is unaware of the client's dishonest purpose is irrelevant. Indeed the privilege may even be lost where the client is unaware that his "strings are being pulled" by a third party who does have such a purpose (see *R. v Central Criminal court Ex p. Francis and Francis* [1989] 1 A.C. 346). These principles have now been extended to also apply to litigation privilege, in *Dubai Aluminium v Al Alawi* [1999] 1 All E.R. 703 and *Kuwait Airways Corp v Iraqi Airways Corp* [2005] EWCA Civ 286.

(a) *The Scope of the Proviso*
Privilege is only lost if the advice relates to *future* conduct. The client **8–31**
who has *already* behaved dishonestly is protected if he makes a clean
breast of it to his lawyers (*O'Rourke v Darbishire* [1920] A.C. 581 at
613). However, it extends to conduct to which, although not technically criminal, is nevertheless prima facie fraudulent. In *Barclays
Bank Plc v Eustice* [1995] 1 W.L.R. 1238 the claimants were seeking
to set aside a transaction at an undervalue under s.423 of the
Insolvency Act 1986. The defendant had instructed solicitors for the
purpose of putting this transaction into effect. The claimants were
held to be entitled to discovery of the solicitor's file including the legal
advice given (for commentary questioning the breadth of this decision see *Phipson* at 26–73). As already noted, the crucial issue is the
purpose of the client or whoever stands behind him. The complicity
or knowledge of the solicitor is immaterial (see *Nationwide BS v
Various Solicitors* [1998] *The Times*, February 5, in which Neuberger
J. held that the giving of false information by a prospective borrower
in order to obtain a loan could result in privilege being lost).
Overriding privilege is a serious matter and accordingly, all privileged
communications are assumed to be untainted until the contrary is
proved (*O'Rourke v Darbishire* [1920] A.C. 581). In *R. v Governor of
Pentonville Prison Ex p. Osman* [1990] 1 W.L.R. 277 the following
guidelines were laid down:

(1) The applicant for disclosure must establish a prima facie case
of criminality;

(2) The court decides whether the communication is tainted;

(3) The court then conducts a "balancing exercise".

Further valuable guidance can be found in the criminal case of
R. v Gibbins [2004] EWCA Crim 311.

(b) *The Solicitor Whose Client is Under Investigation*
Although not strictly within the scope of civil evidence, it is appro- **8–32**
priate to include a short section on the relevance of privilege when a
legal adviser is required to produce documents by an outside agency.
Quite apart from the contractual and professional duties of confidence (*Law Society Guide to the Professional Conduct of Solicitors*,
8th Edn, 1999: 16.01) issues of LPP and the privilege against self
incrimination may well arise.

(1) *The Police* Unless the client expressly authorises disclosure, all **8–33**
material is held subject to the lawyer's professional duty of confidentiality and is therefore "Special Procedure Material" within s.14 of the

Police and Criminal Evidence Act 1984. Thus in order to obtain access even to non-privileged material, the police must apply for a Production Order (see *R. v Guildhall Magistrates' Court Ex p. Primlaks Holdings Co (Panama) Inc* [1990] 1 Q.B. 261 and *R. v Inner London Crown Court Ex p. Baines and Baines* [1988] Q.B. 579). However, "Items subject to legal privilege" are exempt from search, seizure or production under s.10(1) of PACE 1984 unless "held for a criminal purpose". This may include the purpose of a person other than the client. In *R. v Central Criminal Court Ex p. Francis and Francis* [1991] A.C. 346, a case involving a conveyancing transaction in which funds were supplied by an alleged criminal in order to finance a house purchase for an "innocent" relative, the house held that the criminal purpose of the "funder" removed any right of the "client" to assert LPP.

8–34   (2) *Other Agencies* The power of regulatory authorities to investigate individual and corporate financial misfeasance has been significantly modified since December 1, 2001 by the Financial Services and Markets Act 2000; its impact is covered in *Hollander* at 25–14 to 25–33.

8–35   *Liquidators* Under ss.235–7 of the Insolvency Act 1986 they have wide powers of investigation including, under s.236(5) powers to apply to court for warrants of arrest and seizure for failure to comply "without reasonable excuse" to requests made under that section. It is not entirely clear whether legal professional privilege constitutes "reasonable excuse" but it almost certainly does (see further *Hollander* 25–34 to 25–45).

8–36   *Inspectors* Investigations under ss.431, 432 and 442 of the Companies Act 1985 are expressly covered by legal professional privilege (1985 Act s.452(1)(a)).

8–37   *Other Agencies* Agencies such as the Inland Revenue and the Bank of England have power to override legal professional privilege unless the documents are in the hands of the client's barrister, advocate or lawyer (see the Taxes Management Act 1970, ss.20B and C and the Banking Act 1987, ss.39, 41, and 42). However:

   (1) The power must be expressly given; and

   (2) The court may still have to consider whether it is a justifiable inroad into the party's rights under Art.8 of the ECHR (*R. (on the application of Morgan Grenfell and Co Ltd) v Special Commissioner for Inland Revenue* [2003] 1 A.C. 563).

We are most unlikely to see any further inroads into LPP without the clearset possible expression of that intention by Parliament.

4. Documents Submitted for Legal Advice and the Scope of Legal Advice Privilege: The "Three Rivers Saga"

Very often problems arise where evidence is collected before litigation is contemplated in the course of, for example: **8–38**

(1) A compliance investigation;

(2) For submission to a public enquiry.

Frequently the material will be submitted to the corporate client's lawyers for legal advice, indeed the investigation may be directed or supervised by them. To what extent are such documents, for example interview records, and selections of (otherwise) non-privileged documents, subject to legal advice privilege? This difficult question has been considered by the Court of Appeal in *Three Rivers District Council v Bank of England (No.5)* [2003] Q.B. 1556. The relevant facts were, very briefly, as follows.

As a result of the highly publicised collapse of BCCI in 1991, Lord Justice Bingham was appointed to conduct a public inquiry ("the Bingham inquiry"). Knowing that they would be required to give evidence to that inquiry, the Bank set up an internal unit known as the Bingham Investigation Unit ("BIU") to collect evidence from Bank employees for submission to the Bingham inquiry. In subsequent proceedings for misfeasance in public office, the claimants sought disclosure of all the material collected by the BIU. The Bank resisted, arguing that all the collected material was subject to legal advice privilege because it been submitted to their solicitors, Freshfields, for them to advise on.

Clearly, if litigation had been in contemplation, the material would have attracted litigation privilege, but it was accepted by the Bank that preparation of material for submission to a public inquiry did not attract litigation privilege because the proceedings were non-adversarial. Tomlinson J. at first instance ruled that all documents prepared, collected and collated by the BIU acting on the advice of Freshfields, were protected by legal advice privilege. The Court of Appeal allowed the claimant's appeal, and laid down the following principles:

(1) Legal advice privilege should be kept within reasonable bounds; thus

(2) Where litigation was not yet in contemplation;

(3) Material collected from the Bank's employees by the BIU for submission to the Bingham enquiry;

(4) Were not privileged even though;

(5) They were initially prepared for submission to or at the direction of the Bank's solicitors.

Leave to appeal to the House of Lords having been refused, the claimants now sought disclosure of parts of the advice actually given by Freshfields to the BIU. The basis for this new argument was that that some of the advice was, in all probability, mere "presentational advice" and, hence, not legal advice at all. Effectively the claimants argued that, at least in some contexts, Freshfields were being retained as little more than "spin doctors". In *Three Rivers District Council v Bank of England (No.6)* EWHC Civ 2565 (Comm) the claimants succeeded in obtaining an order from Tomlinson J. requiring the Bank to review the disclosure given on the basis that:

". . . presentational assistance in relation to the Bingham Inquiry is not regarded by the Court of Appeal as advice as to what should prudently and sensibly be done by the Bank in the light of its legal rights and obligations. It is advice as to how the Bank's material might be presented in the way least likely to attract criticism, not advice sought by reference to any particular aspect other Bank's substantive rights and obligations which might in due course be the subject matter of adversarial litigation".

This decision was confirmed by the Court of Appeal in *Three Rivers District Council v Bank of England (No.6)* [2004], *The Times*, March 3. However, the Court of Appeal was reversed by the House of Lords in *Three Rivers District Council v Bank of England (No.6)* [2004] 3 W.L.R. 1274. Having heard not only from counsel for the parties but also from the Attorney General, the Law Society and the Bar Council, the House confirmed that:

(1) Legal advice privilege covers advice as to public rights, liabilities and obligations; and hence

(2) Includes presentational advice given by lawyers to a party whose conduct might be the subject of public criticism; and

(3) Would extend to advice and assistance given with reference to a range of inquiries including coroners' inquests, statutory and *ad hoc* inquiries; however

(4) If the lawyer became the clients' "man of business" advising across a wide range of non legal topics such as investment and other business matters the advice might lack the relevant legal context necessary to uphold the privilege;

(5) There does not appear to be a "dominant purpose test" as there is in litigation privilege, in other words it matters not if the lawyer's advice concentrates on commercial issues rather than purely legal ones, provided the advice is given within a relevant legal context.

However, they refused to reconsider the Court of Appeal decision in *Three Rivers (No.5)* although invited to do so. The net result of all this activity and expense is that the broad definition of "legal Advice" established in *Balabel* has been reaffirmed. However, so far as evidence *collection* is concerned, unless it is covered by litigation privilege (and there was never any assertion in *Three Rivers* that the BIU's endeavours were) the material will not be protected. The other notable recent decision is *United States of America v Phillip Morris and BATCO* [2004] 1 CLC 811, a case decided between the Court of Appeal and House of Lords decisions in *Three Rivers (No.6)*. In it, the Court of Appeal upheld a decision of Moore-Bick J. ordering a solicitor who had advised BATCO on their document retention policy to answer questions pursuant to Letters of Request issued by the District Court of Columbia. The court held that the solicitor was not entitled to make a blanket claim to privilege, but was required to raise privilege on a question by question basis. The Court of Appeal (based on its reading of the Court of Appeal decision in *Three Rivers (No.6)*) expressed the view that advice on a document's policy could be outside the scope of legal advice. The decision was not disapproved of by the House of Lords and therefore stands on its own special facts, for further commentary see *Phipson* at 23–68.

III LITIGATION PRIVILEGE

The separate existence of this form of LPP was not generally recog-   **8–39**
nised until relatively recently indeed; according to *Phipson* at 23–53 the term "litigation privilege" was first used as recently as 1984 by counsel in *Re Highgrade Traders Ltd* [1984] B.CL.C. 151 at 161. The historical development of the rule is traced at 23–54 of *Phipson*. As already noted it is both wider and narrower in various respects than legal advice privilege. It also seems to have caused fewer problems in practice, with the possible exception of experts' reports: a topic that is considered in greater detail at 12–53.

THE "THREE RIVERS" SAGA (Nos 5 and 6)

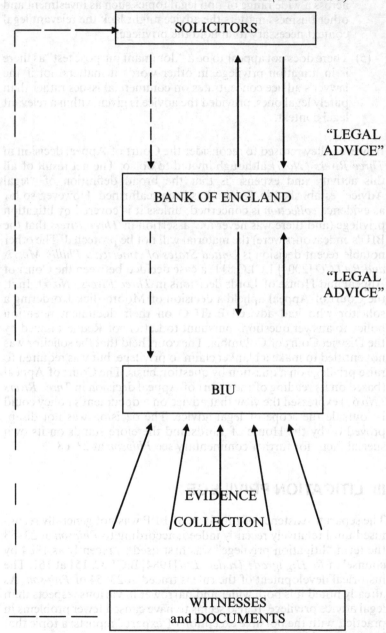

SOLICITORS

"LEGAL ADVICE"

BANK OF ENGLAND

"LEGAL ADVICE"

BIU

EVIDENCE

COLLECTION

WITNESSES and DOCUMENTS

A. General

1. The rule

Provided the communication is made with the sole or dominant   **8–40**
purpose of:

(1) Giving advice; or

(2) Obtaining advice; or

(3) Collecting evidence

for the purpose of actual or contemplated litigation, the privilege can
be claimed in respect of both:

(1) The communication itself, for example, a letter of instruction
to an expert, and

(2) Documents or materials (such as a sample for analysis) enclosed
with or referred to in the communication provided that they
have been brought into being for the privileged purpose (or are
otherwise privileged); and

(3) Documents generated as a result of the communication such
as expert reports or witness statements.

The extension of this principle to documents in categories (2) and (3)
was acknowledged, albeit with some reluctance, by Sir Richard Scott
V.C. in *Re Barings* [1998] 1 All E.R. 675. He appeared to take the view
that the Court of Appeal had taken a wrong turning in earlier cases.
His rationale was that the protection conferred by litigation privilege
had originally been confined to material collected for the purposes of
litigation, but only insofar as it had a tendency to reveal legal advice.
However, as *Phipson* rightly points out at 23–92, there are numerous
authorities to the contrary which cast grave doubt over this view (see
in particular, *Guinness Peat Properties Ltd v Fitzroy Robinson
Partnership* [1987] 1 W.L.R. 1027 and *Re Highgrade Traders* (above)).

2. Scope

It embraces a much wider range of communications than "legal   **8–41**
advice" privilege including those between:

(1) *The litigant's lawyer and third parties*—for example experts and
witnesses as to fact;

(2) *The litigant and third parties*—(possibly) whether or not he is
acting through a lawyer;

(3) *The litigant's agent and third parties*—for example statements taken by an enquiry agent,

but across a narrower spectrum than "legal advice" privilege in that the predominant purpose *must* be in preparation for actual or contemplated litigation. There is no authoritative decision on whether a litigant in person is entitled to claim litigation privilege: on Sir Richard Scott's analysis in *Re Barings* (above) he would not be able to do so. The writer's view is that once it is accepted that litigation privilege is separate head of privilege, the presence of a legal adviser is not essential. Apart from anything else, it would surely be contrary to the "equality of arms" principle under Art.6. What could be more unfair than requiring a litigant in person to disclose all his case file when the party having the benefit of legal representation could assert litigation privilege? The only alternative would be to confine the privilege within the narrow boundaries suggested by Sir Richard Scott V.C. in *Re Barings*.

3. "Litigation"

8–42   The privilege extends to proceedings before courts, arbitrators and tribunals exercising judicial functions. It is less certain whether the privilege extends to communications made in the course of preparing for proceedings before other fact finding tribunals see *Parry Jones v The Law Society* [1969] 1 Ch. 1). In that case, the Court of Appeal held that it did not apply to a request for production under the Solicitors' Accounts Rules. Each case will depend on its own special facts, but what seems to be clear following the *Three Rivers* saga is that the privilege will not be available for communications in the course of preparing for non-adversarial proceedings such as inquests or public inquiries even though litigation is more than likely once the inquiry has completed its work. It is not always easy to decide which side of the line a proceeding falls, for example, disciplinary proceedings are generally treated as attracting litigation privilege. The cases are fully reviewed in *Phipson* at 23–87 to 23–91.

4. "Reasonable Prospect"

8–43   There is such a thing as being too quick off the mark in collecting evidence. If the court were to decide that litigation was not yet in reasonable prospect, only the *legal advice* would be protected. The sending of a premature letter before action can have the converse effect; all your opponent's' preparation thereafter will be protected. Bear in mind in particular that any *expert report* obtained before litigation is in reasonable prospect will not be subject to legal advice privilege either and, hence, will be potentially disclosable in subsequent proceedings (see *Price Waterhouse v BCCI Holdings*

(Luxembourg) SA [1992] B.C.L.C. 583). As to the point at which litigation becomes "anticipated", each case will depend on its own facts, but, on the whole, the courts have leaned towards upholding the privilege wherever feasible. For example, in *Guinness Peat Properties v Fitzroy Robinson Partnership* [1987] 1 W.L.R. 1027 CA, an architect's report made to professional indemnity insurers on his first being notified of a prospective negligence claim was held to be covered. However, the mere fact that storm clouds are gathering over a particular industry, in the case of *USA v BATCO* [2004] 1 C.L.C. 811 tobacco companies in the United States, is not sufficient. The litigation must be in reasonable prospect as against the party asserting privilege.

5. *"Communications"*
As with legal advice privilege, the privilege only extends to "commu-   **8–44**
nications". Accordingly, as with legal advice privilege, it will not
extend to *facts* observed by the lawyer outside of the retainer. This
means that notes taken of court proceedings or conversations with an
opponent's legal representative (unless "without prejudice") are not
privileged, see *Parry v Newsgroup Newspapers Ltd* (1990) 140 NLJ
1719). It is therefore advisable to make separate notes of:

(1) The proceedings; and

(2) Attendances on the client or advice to be given to him (see
    further *Phipson* 23–65 to 23–66).

The privilege also does not apply to *extraneous facts* observed by
a third party. This can create difficulties with expert witnesses.
Although the instructions and report, if created for a privileged
purpose, will be "communications" and therefore protected, the
same does not necessarily go for facts observed by the expert and
his opinion thereon. The crucial issue will be whether the expert's
observations and opinions are based on the examination of privileged
material. If they were not, then, in theory, the expert could be
required to give evidence by an opponent (see further 12–44) since
there is no property in a witness. Obviously, your opponent would
need to be aware of the expert's identity, but mistakes do sometimes
happen. This occurred in *Harmony Shipping SA v Saudi Europe
Line Ltd* [1979] 1 W.L.R. 1380. The identity of a handwriting expert
instructed by the defendants was inadvertently revealed to the
claimants. It was held that he could be compelled to give opinion
evidence on behalf of the claimants as to whether or not a non-
privileged document sent to him for analysis by the defendant was a
forgery.

However, if the observations are based on examination of material which is itself privileged, the position is different. The two most recent instances arose in criminal appeals, but the result would have been the same if the issues had arisen in a civil claim. In *R. v R* [1994] 1 W.L.R. 758 a blood sample was sent to a haematologist for DNA analysis. The Court of Appeal held that since the sample had been created for a litigious purpose and had been sent to the expert along with privileged instructions, the sample itself was privileged. Accordingly, the expert should not have been required to produce the sample on behalf of the Crown and give evidence as to the results of his analysis. A similar situation arose in *R. v Davies (Keith)* [2002] EWCA Crim 85, *The Times,* March 4, 2002. In that case, a psychiatrist was instructed on behalf of the accused to examine him with a view to running a defence of diminished responsibility to a murder charge. As a result of interviewing him she formed the opinion the he was not suffering from any "disability of mind" and was called on behalf of the Crown to give evidence to that effect. Again, the Court of Appeal held that she should not have been called to give evidence because her opinion was based upon facts she had gleaned during the interview, an interview that consisted of a privileged communication with the defendant.

B The "Predominant Purpose" Test

8–45 Considering the potential this creates for argument, there have been remarkably few problems in practice since the current legal position was settled by the House of Lords in 1979.

1. The Basic Rule

8–46 This "predominant purpose" test is still the major limiting factor in raising litigation privilege. It is by no means uncommon for investigations to be conducted in the aftermath of a major incident that has caused serious personal injury or financial loss. For example it is normal for companies to carry out a health and safety investigation in the aftermath of a serious industrial accidents, sometimes with the objective of avoiding possible prosecution by the Health and Safety Executive. The leading decision is still *Waugh v BRB* [1980] A.C. 521 which involved statements prepared after a fatal rail accident. In this decision the House of Lords decided that in order to attract litigation privilege the communication had to satisfy the "sole- or dominant purpose" test. If there were two or more purposes of equal weight (in the instant case there *were,* namely rail safety and preparing for anticipated litigation) the claim to privilege would fail. This decision has had significant repercussions for all compliance investigations, because much of the collected material will not be subject to litigation privilege (or legal advice privilege following *Three Rivers (No.5)*).

2. *Examples*

Although each case must be evaluated on its own facts, the following cases are are provided by way of illustration.   8–47

(a) *Not Privileged*

Statements taken for a police complaint (see *Neilson v Laugharne*   8–48
[1981] 1 Q.B. 736), an NHS Circular report (see *Lask v Gloucester Health Authority* [1985], *The Times,* 13 December), an accountant's report into the financial position of BCCI (see *Price Waterhouse v BCCI Holdings (Luxembourg) Ltd SA* [1992] BCLC 583).

(b) *Privileged*

A report prepared for insurers on a fire at the insured's premises   8–49
(see *Re Highgrade Traders* [1994] B.C.L.C. 151); a letter written by architects to their professional indemnity insurers (see *Guinness Peat Properties v Fitzroy Robinson Partnership* [1987] 1 W.L.R. 1027); an accountant's report on the purchase of a business commissioned by the vendor (see *Plummers Ltd v Debenhams Plc* [1986] B.C.L.C. 447).

Where a party is already receiving legal advice the predominant purpose test can assume major significance so far as expert reports are concerned, because the report will only be privileged if it comes under the umbrella of litigation privilege (see *The Sagheera* [1997] 1 Lloyds Rep. 160).

C Litigation Privilege and Evidence Collection

Problems tend to arise in relation to documents not privileged in   8–50
themselves collected from the client or third parties or copied during the course of preparing for litigation. The starting point is simple. Original or copy documents that have at any time been in the client's control will be disclosable (see 10–09) unless privilege is available under some other head (for example, because they contain legal advice): the mere fact that the client seeks legal advice upon them or that they have been assembled for the purpose of the litigation will not cloak them with LPP. But what if the document or a copy thereof is obtained from a *third party* for the purposes of the litigation? There the position is different albeit not entirely free from uncertainty.

1. *Originals*

These are disclosable if they are or have been at any time in the   8–51
"control" (within CPR 31.8) of the party or his lawyer provided they

come within standard disclosure and are not otherwise privileged or subject to PII. However, they are not disclosable if they have remained in the "control" of a third party. This means that a party can avoid disclosing the information contained in such a document by arranging for his legal adviser to read it (and possibly take a copy, see below) without taking possession of the original. However, one cannot help but wonder whether such "games" really accord with the spirit of the CPR.

2. Copies

8–52   If a copy (not otherwise privileged) of an original document in the possession of a third party is taken for a privileged purpose, then, on the authority of *"The Palermo"* (1883) 9 PD 6, the *copy* is privileged in the hands of that party. In that case the Court of Appeal held that the copy of a transcript of evidence given to the Receiver of Wrecks which the plaintiffs had been permitted to take by the Board of Trade was protected by litigation privilege in the hands of the plaintiff as against the defendant. This was followed in *Lyell v Kennedy* [1884] 27 Ch. D. 1. However, these decisions have been doubted in *Buttes Gas and Oil Co v Hammer (No.3)* [1981] Q.B. 223 and discussed at length in *Ventouris v Mountain* [1990] 1 W.L.R. 1370. Nevertheless, the *"Palermo* principle" must still be regarded as good law (see further *Phipson* at 23–44 to 23–51). However, what is also now clear is that a litigant cannot claim litigation privilege for a copy if at any time the (non-privileged) *original* has been in his possession (see *Dubai Bank v Galadari* [1990] Ch. 98) or in the possession of his opponent (see *Lubrizol v Esso Petroleum* [1992] 1 W.L.R. 957). As already noted (8–22), this is now the case even where the copies consist of a selection by the lawyer from originals, following *Sumitomo Corp v Credit Lyonnais Rouse* [2002] 1 W.L.R. 479.

8–53   <u>Facts:</u> C was claiming against D, their clearing broker, for losses US$247m, allegedly sustained as result of D dishonestly assisting one of C's employees in carrying out a large number of unauthorised trades on the copper futures market. In the course of worldwide regulatory investigations and civil claims, C assembled some 6.9m documents, most of them in Japanese. C's lawyers had selected a very small number of those documents (about 0.4 per cent) for translation into English. D now sought disclosure of those translations. C resisted.

The claimants presented two arguments in support of their opposition to disclosure, both of which failed before the Court of Appeal. Firstly, they maintained that, since the translations were prepared for a litigious purpose, by analogy with the taking of copies from a third party, they were subject to litigation privilege. The Court of Appeal would have none of this stating that translations of documents that were in the control of the party claiming privilege were no more privileged than the originals. The second argument was that they were subject to legal advice privilege under the *Lyell v Kennedy* principle referred to earlier (8–22) on the basis that because the selection was so small, it of documents for translation would inevitably betray the trend of the legal advice that was being given to the claimants. This argument was also rejected by the court, who stated that the *Lyell v Kennedy* principle only applied to a selection from copy documents that had been taken from a *third party*. In the light of this, one wonders what is left of *Lyell v Kennedy* bearing in mind that the documents from which the selection is made will themselves be subject to litigation privilege under the "*Palermo* principle" (see above).

IV OTHER VARIETIES OF LPP

Although the two categories discussed below are not separate varieties of LPP as such, they are nevertheless sufficiently detached from the mainstream to merit separate consideration.   **8–54**

1. Joint Privilege
Obviously enough, if A and B both instruct the same legal advisers, there is no confidentiality between them and, hence, no claim to LPP of either category attaches to communications made during the joint retainer should they subsequently fall out. Two other significant consequences are that: **8–55**

(1) They may claim it against the rest of the world; and

(2) It can only be waived jointly.

Absence of privilege as between A and B might prove particularly significant if disclosure was sought by a successor-in-title, since this would include A's trustee in bankruptcy (see *Re Konigsberg* [1989] 1 W.L.R. 1257). However, privilege will arise as soon as a conflict of interest emerges between A and B. A recent example arose in *TSB Bank v Robert Irving and Burns (A Firm) (Colonia Baltica Insurance Ltd, third party)* [2002] 2 All E.R. 826 CA.

Facts: Counsel and solicitors were instructed to act for both the insured firm ("RIB") and the insurers ("CBI Ltd") on a professional negligence claim against RIB. Initially CBI Ltd accepted liability under the policy, but on exchange of expert evidence concluded that they were entitled to repudiate. Without informing RIB of this, they arranged a conference with counsel in which counsel was instructed to see if he could elicit damaging admissions from a partner in RIB who   **8–56**

was unaware of this subterfuge. Armed with the damaging admissions secured thereby, CBI Ltd then repudiated liability under the policy. In third party proceedings brought by RIB under the policy, CBI Ltd pleaded the admissions made by the partner in conference.

The Court of Appeal ordered that those admissions be struck out holding that:

(1) As a result of the joint instruction there was an implied waiver of privilege between the parties; but this was

(2) Limited so as to exclude communications made *after* an actual conflict of interest had emerged, but *before* the other party had been informed of that conflict.

Although, technically speaking the result was reached by a questionable route (how can you waive a privilege that never existed in the first place?) the result was undeniably correct (see further, *Phipson* at 24–02).

2. Common Interest Privilege

8–57   The precise boundaries of this relatively new variant of legal advice and litigation privilege are not easy to identify. The privilege was first recognised by the Court of Appeal in *Buttes Gas and Oil Co v Hammer (No.3)* [1981] Q.B. 223. The passage from the judgment of Lord Denning M.R. (at 243) cited below indicates its rationale if not its precise compass:

"It often happens in litigation that a plaintiff or defendant has other persons standing alongside him—who have the self same interest as he—and who have consulted lawyers on the self-same points as he—these others have not been made parties to the action . . . All collect information for the purposes of litigation. All make copies . . . in all such cases I think the Court for the purposes of discovery treat all the persons interested as if they were the partners in a single firm or department in single company. Each can avail himself of the privilege in litigation."

The first point that needs to be made is that, although Lord Denning M.R. was only addressing litigation privilege, the principle would equally apply to shared legal advice. Secondly, if privileged material is shown by A to B in confidence, which it must have been in order to retain privilege in the first place, privilege will still be retained as against the rest of the world under *City of Gotha* (see 8–27). One wonders therefore whether common interest privilege retains any significant practical role.

Insofar as the concept does retain any raison d'être, a brief summary of the relevant cases is given below. In *The "Good Luck"*

[1992] 2 Lloyd's Rep. 540 Saville J. held that the parties had to have sufficient community of interest to have been able to have instructed the same solicitor if they had wanted to, but a broader test was promulgated in *The "World Era" (No. 2)* [1993] 1 Lloyd's Rep. 363 and *Formica v Export Credits Guarantee Department* [1995] 1 Lloyd's Rep. 692. However one questions the need to even identify a community of interest following *City of Gotha*.

The one area in which common interest privilege may still have a life of its own is when it is employed as a "sword" rather than as a "shield", that is, where B is seeking access to documents in respect of which A is asserting privilege. An example of this can be seen in *Re Nottingham Forest Plc* [2001] 1 All E.R. 954 in which it was held that legal advice obtained by the directors of a company was not privileged as between them and the shareholders in subsequent s.459 proceedings. Evans-Lombe J. held that:

(1) It was immaterial that the company was a plc rather than a small private company;

(2) The fact that the company was only a nominal defendant in the s.459 proceedings was significant; and

(3) The relationship between shareholders and directors was analogous to that between trustees and beneficiaries.

The position would, of course, be different if there were a conflict of interest between the directors and the shareholders. Common interest privilege is discussed in greater detail in *Phipson* at 24–03 to 24–18.

V LOSS OF LPP BY WAIVER

The absolute nature of privilege is such that it can only ever be waived **8–58** by the party entitled to rely upon it or any agent with ostensible authority to do so on his behalf. It is particularly important to be aware of the fact that waiver is judged objectively (see *Great Atlantic Insurance Co v Home Insurance Co* [1981] 1 W.L.R. 529). The consequence of this is that if, for example, you enclose the "wrong" expert's report with a covering letter (something you surely did not intend to do) the court will only be concerned with an objective evaluation of what you *appear* to have done, namely waived privilege on your client's behalf.

A Waiver: General Principles

The principles set out below are common to both types of LPP. Even **8–59** if privilege is waived, there is no guarantee that the contents will be of any great assistance to the other party. As already pointed out, legal advice will often be inadmissible on the grounds of irrelevance and inconsistencies and admissions can often be explained away.

1. Nature of Waiver

8–60   Waiver may be either (1) express or implied; and (2) limited in scope. Each case will depend on its own facts. The latter point is particularly important because, if a party's waiver in respect of, say, a single document, were to constitute waiver of all privileged communications, no party would ever entertain volunteering limited disclosure of such material.

2. Some Basic Reminders

8–61   It is as well to remember that:

(1) Waiver to one does not constitute waiver to the whole world if confidentiality is intended to otherwise be maintained (see *City of Gotha v Sothebys* [1998] 1 W.L.R. 114);

(2) Waiver of privilege in an individual item or class of material does not necessarily entitle a party to disclosure of any *other* privileged material on the same subject matter. It will be for the court to decide in each case how far, in fairness, the waiver should be deemed to extend. A party cannot "cherrypick" and only waive privilege insofar as it helps his case (see *R. v Secretary of State Ex party Factortame* [1997] Admin L.R. 591 and *Dunlop Slazenger International Ltd v Joe Bloggs Sports Ltd* [2003] EWCA Civ 901). In effect, in an individual item or class of material what the court will do is consider how much additional material should be treated as waived to enable the disclosed item to be evaluated in its proper context (this approach was followed by Mann J. in *Fulham Leisure Holdings v. Nicholson Graham & Jones* [2006] EWHC 158 (Ch.));

(3) The privilege belongs to the client but may be waived by the client's lawyer on usual agency principles.

B Waiver and Disclosure During Civil Litigation

8–62   This is the stage at which waiver is most likely to arise in practice. Some of the more common situations are discussed below. In each case, the crucial issue will be whether the privileged document has simply been referred to, for example as a source of belief or its *contents* have been relied on in evidence. This distinction is not always easy to make (see, in particular, *Dunlop Slazenger* (above)).

1. Case Statements

Any reliance on a document referred to in a case statement will nor-   **8–63**
mally be taken to have waived privilege in the whole document,
although there are suggestions in *Buttes Oil and Gas v Hammer (No. 3)*
[1981] Q.B. 223 that a party could assert privilege and have the reference struck out. CPR 31.14 gives any other party the immediate right
to inspect such a document but there is nothing in the rule to suggest
the course suggested in *Buttes Oil* would not still be permissible.

2. Affidavits

The cases are unclear, but the position appears to depend upon   **8–64**
whether or not the contents have been "deployed in evidence". If they
have, privilege will be waived (see *Derby v Weldon (No.10)* [1991]
1 W.L.R. 1660). If not, privilege will have been retained, (see *Def
American v Phonogram* [1994], *The Times,* 16 August). So far as the
actual affidavit itself is concerned, clearly, service will constitute
waiver of privilege, furthermore, there is no collateral undertaking as
in the case of witness statements. Accordingly it will be admissible,
subject to relevance, in any subsequent proceedings (see 11–28).

3. Disclosure and Inspection

Inclusion of a document in Part I of a party's list of documents (see   **8–65**
further 10–16) will normally render it liable to inspection although
"blanking out" the privileged parts is permissible (see further 8–23).
However, if a party has inadvertently waived privilege by permitting
inspection of a privileged document, the party who has inspected it will
not be able to rely on its contents without the permission of the court
(CPR 31.20). Furthermore, it may be possible for the disclosing party
to seek redress by means of an injunction if the mistake should have
been obvious to the reasonably competent solicitor (see further 10–30).

4. Exchanged Witness Statements

It is now generally accepted that, once served, the contents of the   **8–66**
statement and documents referred to in it are no longer privileged (see
Youell v Bland Welch (No.3) [1991] 1 W.L.R. 122 and *Black and
Decker v Flymo* [1991] 1 W.L.R. 753). This is underlined by the fact
that under CPR 32.5 any party may put it in as evidence in certain circumstances (see further 11–68). Furthermore, CPR 31.14 gives other
parties the same right to inspect any document referred to in it, as
with case statements. However, it may not be used for a collateral
purpose unless one of the three exceptions in CPR 32.22 apply, in
particular, once it has been put in evidence in a public hearing (see
further 11–28). Up until that point however, although service waives
privilege in the instant proceedings, privilege could probably be
asserted in respect of subsequent proceedings (see *Phipson* at 26–41).

5. Expert's Reports

8–67   Expert witnesses' reports remain privileged until disclosed but, once disclosed, will no longer be privileged and any party may make use of their contents in evidence (CPR 35.11). So far the lawyer's instructions and documents submitted with those instructions are concerned, CPR 35.10(3) specifically provides that the expert's report must state the substance of all material instructions and the court may, subject to any Art.8 points, override privilege if it considers the report to be inaccurate or incomplete in this regard. This topic is considered further at 12–53.

6. Use at Trial

8–68   Reliance on part of a privileged document at the trial will normally constitute waiver of the whole document unless its contents can be divided into discrete topics, see *Great Atlantic Insurance Co v Home Insurance Co* [1981] 1 W.L.R. 529. This was a case in which the claimants, having disclosed the first two paragraphs of a memorandum claimed privilege in the remainder. Counsel read out the first two paragraphs in court at the trial. The Court of Appeal held that this had constituted waiver of privilege in the whole document because the part in respect of which privilege was claimed covered the same subject matter as the part that had been read out. This decision is probably now best classified as a "cherry-picking" case (see 8–61) and, as such, causes no difficulty. For a fuller discussion see *Phipson* at 23–42 to 23–43.

C Waiver Of Privilege In Professional Negligence Claims

1. Background

8–69   Until recently it was thought that legal advice privilege could be impliedly waived whenever a client sued his solicitor for professional negligence. This implied waiver was extended in *Lillicrap v Nalder* [1993] 1 W.L.R. 94 to cover legal advice given to the client concerning *other* transactions provided that they were relevant to the issues in the instant case. In *Kershaw v Whelan* [1996] 1 W.L.R. 358 this was further extended to cover advice given by a *different* solicitor in relation to the same subject matter as that in issue in the instant litigation. The concept of implied waiver was then taken even further by Parker J. in *Hayes v Dowding* [1996] P.N.L.R. 578. In that case, the claimant was suing his solicitor for so negligently conducting a claim that he was forced to settle on less advantageous terms. However, he had withdrawn instructions from the defendant and gone to new solicitors to advise him on the terms of settlement. Parker J. held that since the advice given by the new solicitors was relevant to issues of causation and mitigation of loss, there was an implied waiver of the privilege in the advice given to the claimant by the new solicitors.

2. The "Paragon" Case

However these assumptions were subjected to a major reappraisal by the Court of Appeal in *Paragon Finance Plc and others v Freshfields* [1999] 1 W.L.R. 1183 in which the nature of the claim was similar to that in *Hayes v Dowding*. In it the Court of Appeal held that:

8–70

(1) Although a client who sues his former solicitor, in bringing that relationship into the public domain, impliedly waives privilege in respect of all relevant privileged communications with that solicitor (*Lillecrap v Nalder* [1993] 1 W.L.R. 94);

(2) He does not bring into the public domain communications with any *other* solicitor he consults on the same transaction unless, perhaps, there are exceptional circumstances which make that material relevant (*Kershaw v Whelan* [1996] 1 W.L.R. 358 considered but doubted);

(3) The decision of Parker J. in *Hayes v Dowding* [1996] P.N.L.R. 578 to the effect that legal advice given prior to entering into an agreement was relevant if that agreement was later sued on was wrong and should be overruled.

It is important to note that if the defendants in *Paragon* had sought disclosure of the *negotiations themselves* on the grounds that they were relevant both to causation and mitigation of loss, the claimants would probably not have been able to assert "without prejudice" privilege for reasons given at 8–100.

SECTION 3: PRIVILEGE AGAINAST SELF INCRIMINATION

As already noted, this privilege forms an important component of the so-called "Right to Silence". Not only has its practical scope been significantly narrowed in the context of criminal proceedings, but the very need for its existence in civil proceedings has been challenged by some senior judges. In particular, Lord Templeman stated in *A T & T Istel v Tully* [1993] A.C. 45 at 53:

8–71

"I regard the privilege against self-incrimination in civil proceedings as an archaic and unjustifiable survival from the past when the court directs the production of relevant documents and requires the defendant to specify his dealings with the plaintiff's property or money".

Lord Griffiths (at 57) stated to similar effect. Many of the judges in the cases cited below have made similar statements. It has undoubtedly been subjected to far more statutory inroads than LPP, and goes beyond the ambit of the right to silence under Art.6 in that it extends to the disclosure of *documents*, whereas the Art.6 "right to silence" only engages to the answering of incriminating *questions* (see *L v United Kingdom* [2000] 2 F.L.R. 322).

A Principles

8–72   As with PII, it is fair to say that one could enjoy a lengthy career as a civil litigator without ever being involved in a case in which the privilege assumed significant practical importance. For example, although prosecutions frequently take place as result of road traffic accidents or accidents at work, the civil claim will usually not get off the ground until after the criminal proceedings have been disposed of. The use of any relevant convictions in such circumstances has already been covered at 4–54. The privilege is almost invariably invoked by defendants in claims based on fraud or corruption in response to orders to provide information as to their assets under freezing or search orders.

1. The Privilege in Civil Proceedings

8–73   Although the privilege has its origins in the sixteenth and seventeenth centuries as an antidote to the excesses of the Star Chamber, its existence in civil proceedings is based on s.14(1) of the Civil Evidence Act 1968 which provides that:

> "The right of any person in any legal proceedings other than criminal proceedings to refuse to answer any question or produce any document or thing if to do so would tend to expose that person to proceedings for an offence or for the recovery of a penalty:
>
> (a) shall apply only as regards criminal offences under the law of any part of the United Kingdom and penalties provided for by such law, and
> (b) shall include a like right to refuse to answer any question or produce any document or thing if to do so would tend to expose the husband or wife of that person to proceedings for any such criminal offence or for the recovery of any such penalty."

The reference to "penalty" will include certain kinds of non-criminal liability, for example, a fine for civil contempt of court. The section only extends to offences and penalties under United Kingdom law. It thus extends to European Union offences and penalties (see *Rio Tinto Zinc v Westinghouse Electric* [1978] A.C. 547). So far as a risk of *overseas* prosecution is concerned, the court nevertheless retains a discretion to prohibit disclosure. In *Arab Monetary Fund v Hashim (No.3)* [1989] 3 All E.R. 466 the first and second defendants as well as being husband and wife were Iraqi citizens. They sought to be excused from providing details as to their assets in response to worldwide freezing orders on the basis that this could expose them to prosecution in Iraq with dire consequences. Morrit J. decided the case under s.37 of the Supreme Court Act 1981 on the basis that the court always retains a discretion when granting an interim injunction to impose terms, which included in this case, restricting the persons to whom the information given by the defendants was to be disclosed.

2. *Exceptions*

There are numerous statutory exceptions to the privilege including, in **8–74** particular, the provisions listed below.

(a) *Theft Act 1968 s.31;*
This abolishes the privilege in respect of the witness and his/her **8–75** spouse in the case of questions put or orders made in proceedings for:

> "the recovery or administration of any property, the execution of any trust or for an account of any property or dealings with any property".

Defendants will often try to argue that they face the risk of being prosecuted for offences falling outside the relatively narrow ambit of the section. By no means every offence of dishonesty is covered, in particular, statutory or common law conspiracy to defraud (see, for example, *Sociedade Nacional v Lundquist* [1991] 2 Q.B. 310). However, if the defendant is clearly at risk of prosecution for an offence coming within s.31, it will not avail him to argue that he could also, technically, be at risk of prosecution for offences to which the section does not apply, for example, forgery (see *Khan v Khan* [1982] 1 W.L.R. 513).

(b) *Supreme Court Act 1981 s.72;*
This abolishes the privilege in relation to proceedings: **8–76**

(1) For infringement of rights pertaining to any intellectual property or for passing off;

(2) To obtain disclosure of information relating to any infringement of such rights or passing off;

(3) To prevent any apprehended infringement of such rights or any apprehended passing off.

This section was rushed through Parliament to reverse the effect of the House of Lords decision in *Rank Film Distributors Ltd v Video Information Centre* [1982] A.C. 380 which, if it had stood, would have made search orders almost impossible to obtain. However, it does not extend to "commercial information" relating to intellectual property rights unless the proceedings are concerned with the infringement of those rights (see *A T & T Istel v Tully* (above)).

(c) *Other Statutory Provisions*

8–77   There are numerous other statutes that override the privilege nearly all of which are subject to a proviso that the evidence thereby cannot be used in subsequent criminal proceedings against that person. For example, s.291 of the Insolvency Act 1986 requires that a bankrupt deliver up to the Official Receiver all documents which he has possession or control relating to his estate and affairs. Other statutes in which the privilege is overridden include s.434 of the Companies Act 1985 (production of documents and evidence to inspectors investigating companies). This stands in stark contrast to assertions of legal professional privilege which, as a general rule, cannot be overridden (see 8–32).

3. *Family Proceedings*

8–78   Although the rule applies in general matrimonial litigation, for example, applications for ancillary relief, and private Children Act 1989 applications, in public Children Act 1989 proceedings under Pts IV and V, s.98 of the 1989 Act provides that:

"(1) . . . no person shall be excused from:

(a) giving evidence on any matter; or
(b) answering any questions put to him in the course of his giving evidence,

on the ground that doing so might incriminate him or his spouse of an offence.

(2) A statement or admission made in such proceedings shall not be admissible in evidence against the person making it or his spouse in proceedings for an offence other than perjury."

B "Risk of Prosecution"

1. *What Danger?*

8–79   The danger must be "real and appreciable" *per* Cockburn J. in *R. v Boyes* (1861) 1 B & S 311. However the burden is on the person seeking to rely on the privilege and he must do more than simply state that he is at risk in order to discharge the burden, see *Triplex Safety Glass Co v Lancegaye Safety Glass* (1934) [1939] 2 K.B. 395 and *Sonangol v Lundquist* [1991] 2 Q.B. 310. However, it is clear that all he will be required to show is that, if he were to answer the question or produce the document, this *might*, to use the words of Staughton L.J. in *Sociedade Nacional* at 325, lead to him revealing:

". . . any fact which a prosecutor would wish to prove in order to establish the guilt of the witness on a criminal charge."

Nevertheless, the risk of prosecution must be real as opposed to fanciful (Staughton L.J. in *Sociedade Nacional* at 324).

2. "Deals"

Thus, the privilege will not be available if the Crown Prosecution **8–80** Service has undertaken not to make use of any evidence disclosed on discovery in subsequent criminal proceedings (see *AT & T Istel v Tully* [1993] 1 A.C. 45). However, the court has no power to make an order to that effect and *Istel* could equally be rationalised on the basis that the Crown already were in possession of all the evidence they needed. In *Norwest Co-Op v Johnstone* [1994], *The Times*, February 24, a fraudulent trading case, an order by the judge for disclosure which purported to override the claim to privilege was set aside by the Court of Appeal because the prosecuting authorities had never been involved.

3. Problems with Search and Freezing Orders

The effect of the privilege on the granting of freezing and search **8–81** orders that are not covered by s.31 or s.72 was acknowledged, albeit with some regret, by the Court of Appeal in *Den Norske Bank ASA v Antonatos* [1998] 3 All E.R. 74. Although, at any rate in the case of search orders, PD 25 makes it clear that the defendant must be informed in the order of his right to claim the privilege, the court took the view that:

(1) If the risk was palpable (absent an abrogation such as s.72 SCA) it might be appropriate to make no order at all without notice; and

(2) There was a similar risk with freezing orders.

Failure to draw the court's attention to this on a "without notice" application may lead to the injunction being discharged, see *Memory Corporation v Sidhu* [2000] 1 W.L.R. 1443.

4. Risk Arising in Litigation

8–82 What if a party exposes himself to the risk of prosecution or committal for contempt by something he does in court during ongoing litigation? This was considered fully by Neuberger J. in *Great Future International and Others v Sealand Housing Corp* [2001] 3 C.P.L.R. 293. In that case, which involved a freezing injunction he held that:

(1) Exposure to contempt proceedings does generally come within the privilege; and

(2) They should not normally be brought as a result of answers given under cross-examination on his affidavit of means.

5. Incidental Discovery if Incriminating Material

Practitioners need to be aware of the judgment of Lindsay J. in *O Ltd v Z* [2005] EWHC 238 (Ch). During the execution of a search order the objective of which was to protect the claimant's commercial interests, the claimant's computer expert discovered pornographic paedophilia in the defendant's computer. In ordering the expert to disclose this material to the prosecuting authorities, Lindsay J. held that:

(1) Granting access to the claimant's computer constituted a waiver of privilege of *all* material held in the computer;

(2) It was too late to assert privilege after access had been given (the defendant attempted to do this);

(3) Although the incriminating material was still subject to the implied undertaking in CPR 31.22 (see 10–31 onwards) the circumstances of this case were such that the claimant (and his expert) should be released from their undertaking, applying the factors set out by Swinton-Thomas L.J. in *Re C (A Minor) (Case Proceedings: Disclosure)* [1997] Fam 76 CA at 85–86.

(4) Bearing in mind that this was a s.72 case, consideration needed to be given as to whether defendants should, even in s.72 cases, be given notice of this right to assert the privilege against self incrimination.

In view of the implications of this decision, which is an essential point of reference for those advising persons served with a search order, it is essential for there to be a blanket assertion of privilege before any material is made available either to the claimant, the supervising solicitor or an expert. This will not affect s.72 material because it is not covered by the privilege in any event.

C The Privilege and the "Right to Silence"

As Lord Hoffman observed in *R. v Herts CC Ex p. Green Environ-* **8–83**
mental Industries [2000] 2 W.L.R. 373, the privilege against self
incrimination is part of a loosely linked group of rules and principles
of immunity. The following points need to be emphasised.

1. Adverse Inferences

In civil proceedings, unlike a criminal prosecution, the general rule is **8–84**
that adverse inferences *can* be drawn from failure to:

(1) Respond to an accusation or assertion when a response might
reasonably have been expected; or

(2) Disclose relevant documents; or

(3) Co-operate with a jointly instructed expert

unless one or more of the available privileges can be invoked, in which
case no inference can be drawn. This has recently been confirmed in
Somatra v Sinclair Roche and Temperley [2000] 1 W.L.R. 2493
(Without Prejudice) and *Oxford Gene Technology v Affymetrix*, unreported, November 23, 2000 (Legal Professional Privilege).

2. Use of Material Obtained under Compulsion

As already noted, many investigating agencies have wide powers to **8–85**
compel individuals to come before them to answer questions, produce
documents or make other materials available for inspection on pain
of prosecution or contempt proceedings. To what extent can material
obtained under such compulsion be used in subsequent civil proceedings bearing in mind, as already noted, that there are major
restrictions on its use in a criminal case?

(a) Statement of Witnesses

Although almost always inadmissible against the maker in a subse- **8–86**
quent criminal prosecution (usually under the statute granting the
power particularly as a result of Sch.3 to the Youth Justice and
Criminal Evidence Act 1999) there is no general restriction on the use
of such material in civil proceedings (s.33 of the Health and Safety
Act 1974 being a notable exception). The use of such material in
quasi-criminal proceedings such as Directors' Disqualification proceedings will not as a general rule infringe Art.6(1) ECHR either (see
Official Receiver v Stern [2001] 1 All E.R. 633).

(b) Documents and other Materials

These do not come within the "right to silence" as interpreted by the **8–87**
ECHR (see *L v UK* [2000] 2 F.L.R. 322). Accordingly, if they are

produced in response to a request from an individual, such as a liquidator or officer of the Health and Safety Executive or Environment Agency, who has statutory power to demand such information on pain of prosecution or contempt proceedings, the material will be admissible in subsequent civil proceedings notwithstanding its potential to incriminate. If however the person seeking access is not so empowered, for example, a solicitor executing a search order, the privilege can be invoked.

SECTION 4: "WITHOUT PREJUDICE" NEGOTIATIONS

8–88   As already noted, this privilege differs in a number of fundamental respects from the other privileges considered in this chapter. Although it causes remarkably few problems in practice, there has suddenly been a rush of cases on important points of detail. The relevant section in *Phipson* can be found at 24–14 to 24–29.

A The Principle

8–89   It has long been regarded as being in the public interest that parties to a civil dispute should be encouraged to settle as quickly as possible. This process has assumed even greater significance since the introduction of the CPR with their emphasis on encouraging out-of-court settlements. The protection conferred by the privilege means that:

(1) As a general rule no party to such negotiation may put in as evidence;

(2) Any statement (oral or written) made by any of the parties touching on the strengths or weaknesses of that party's case (including an offer or other points conceded in negotiations); provided it was

(3) Made in a bona fide attempt to settle the case; and

(4) Was made either expressly or impliedly "without prejudice",

(5) Unless:

- All parties consent to its admission;
- A concluded settlement is reached; or
- It is made in conditional form as to costs (whether or not it is a valid Pt 36 offer); or
- Disclosure is sought by an individual who is not a party to the proceedings in which the negotiations took place.

B The Detail

After laying relatively dormant for many years, there has been a posi-   **8–90**
tive deluge of cases on various aspects of without prejudice privilege,
much of which has not only extended its scope but also marked out
its boundaries with greater clarity.

1. *"Express or Implied"*
Provided that there is an identifiable "dispute", the privilege will be   **8–91**
readily implied. Thus, although it is customary to make communications expressly "without prejudice" it is not absolutely essential that
these words are used at every stage of negotiations. Indeed, once
negotiations have begun, a party faces a heavy burden in proving that
they have gone into "open mode". For example, in *Cheddar Valley
Engineering Ltd v Chaddlewood Homes Ltd* [1992] 1 W.L.R. 820 a pur-
portedly "open" letter was still held to be protected because, first, the
fact that it was intended to be open was not spelled out with sufficient
clarity and, secondly, negotiations were still ongoing. In contrast, in
Dixon's Stores Ltd. v Thames Television Plc [1993] 1 All E.R. 349, not
only had negotiations broken down, but the letter was explicitly
stated to be an "open offer".

2. *"An Attempt to Settle the Case"*
There must be a genuine dispute. However, this does not stop an   **8–92**
"opening shot" from being covered even if it is unsolicited (see, for
example *South Shropshire DC v Amos* [1986] 1 W.L.R. 1271): each
case will depend upon the content of the statement the context
in which it was made. Thus ostensibly cordial negotiations between
CEOs over a lengthy period concerning "spheres of influence" were
held (in the absence of a contractual agreement) not to be privileged; see *The Prudential Assurance Co Ltd v The Prudential
Assurance Company of America* [2003] EWCA Civ 1154: [2003]
ETMR 29. The case is of interest because Chadwick L.J. appears to
differentiate between "contractual" without prejudice which he
characterises as a substantive legal right and "public policy"
without prejudice which is a rule of evidence. The major practical
difference between the two according to Chadwick L.J. is that the
former variety may, in appropriate circumstances be made the
subject of a worldwide injunction.

3. *"Any Statement"*
Often the statement for which protection is sought amounts to con-   **8–93**
cessions or "admissions" (see Hoffman L.J. in *Muller v Linsley and
Mortimer* [1996] P.N.L.R. 39) but what of the party who states in the
course of such negotiations:

"I'll pay you £20,000 to get rid of it";
"If you go on infringing our patent we'll sue"?

Laddie J. had to consider statements of intent as opposed to concession in *Unilever plc v The Proctor & Gamble Co* [1999] 2 All E.R. 691.
The issue was of fundamental importance because the defendants had applied to strike out a "threats" claim on the basis that
the pleaded threat, to bring infringement proceedings against the
claimant, had been made in the course of without prejudice negotiations. Laddie J. stated (at 699g):

> "It seems to me that the rule against the subsequent use of without
> prejudice discussions is wide enough to cover all statements made
> by each party touching upon the strength or weakness of its own
> and its opponent's case, and any valuation, for whatever reason, it
> places on its or it opponent's rights. These are issues which go to
> the heart of any attempt to compromise litigation."

Accordingly, he struck out the claim as an abuse of process.

4. Exceptions

8–94   Laddie J.'s decision in *Unilever* was subsequently upheld by the Court
of Appeal at [2001] 1 All E.R. 783. Robert Walker L.J.'s judgment
contains a useful summary of the major exceptions, (see 791j to 793c).
He listed eight in all namely:

(1) Where the issue is whether or not there was a concluded agreement (see, *Tomlin v Standard Telephones and Cables Ltd* [1969]
1 W.L.R. 1378);

(2) Where misrepresentation, fraud or undue influence is alleged
(see *Underwood v Cox* (1912) 4 D.L.R. 66);

(3) Where, even though no concluded agreement is needed, a clear
statement is made on which the other party is intended to act
and does so act, giving to an estoppal (see *Hodgkinson and
Corby Ltd v Wards Mobility Services Ltd* [1998] F.S.R. 520);

(4) Where the statement was intended to cloak injury, blackmail or
other "unambiguous impropriety", provided the abuse is of
the clearest kind (see *Forster v Freedland* [1993], *The Times*,
March, 19);

(5) Where evidence of negotiations is admissible to explain delay
in a strike-out application;

(6) Where the access is sought by a third party provided the material is relevant (see *Muller* and *Murrell*);

(7) Conditional offers made "without prejudice as to costs", or, it would seem, conditional as to other matters;

(8) Confidential communications with a view to matrimonial conciliation (see *Re D (minors)* [1993] 2 All E.R. 693).

Three of these exceptions merit further examination.

(a) *Concluded Agreements*

Once a settlement has been reached a binding contract of compromise comes into existence and prior communications are admissible to prove the contract. A notable example is *Tomlin v Standard Telephones & Cables Ltd* [1969] 1 W.L.R. 1378 in which the Court of Appeal stated that an agreement as to 50:50 liability in a personal injury claim, could be pleaded in subsequent proceedings. However if, say, C settles with D1 but intends to continue the claim against D2, privilege can still be maintained as against D2. This was confirmed by the House of Lords in *Rush and Tompkins v GLC* [1989] A.C. 1280. Contrast this with the position where a non-party seeks disclosure. In *Muller v Linsley and Mortimer* [1996] P.N.L.R. 39 (discussed further at 8–100) the defendants were held to be entitled to disclosure of negotiations between the claimant and a third party even though the negotiations related to associated subject matter. **8–95**

(b) *Conditional Offers*

A party may make a "without prejudice" offer to a party whilst reserving the right to draw the attention of the court to the offer on the question of costs based on the decisions in *Calderbank v Calderbank* [1976] Fam. 93 and *Cutts v Head* [1984] 2 W.L.R. 349. This principle continues to apply to offers that do not strictly constitute "Pt 36 Offers" as set out in CPR 36, for example offers made on a summary judgment application (see *Petrotrade v Texaco* [2002] 1 W.L.R. 947). That decision confirms that CPR 36.1(2) means what it says: the court may take *any* admissible offer into account on costs (see further *O'Hare and Browne* at 29–006). **8–96**

(c) *"Unambiguous Impropriety"*

The precise scope of this exception has recently been subjected to intense scrutiny by the Court of Appeal. In *UYB Ltd v British Railways Board*, unreported, October 20, 2000 the Court had to consider whether a party who is supplied information on a without prejudice basis is entitled to lead it in rebuttal if his opponent gives different information at a trial or hearing. Apparently the Court could find no authority on the point. However Waller L.J. stated: **8–97**

"That at first sight may seem a powerful argument, but the difficulty is that it may often be possible to dress up an argument that something said in without prejudice negotiations could demonstrate that what is being said at a trial is untrue, and thus caution must be exercised."

The court was prepared to recognise that it could be open to a party to adduce such evidence, but ultimately got round the problem by holding that disclosure would have made no difference anyway. The problem has since been addressed further in two other recent decisions in which one of the parties wished to make use of statements made during negotiation in order to reveal the inconsistencies between what their opponents were saying in negotiation and their open positions. Both involved alleged admissions made by defendants during negotiations, and in both cases the claimants failed before the Court of Appeal. In the first, *Berry Trade Ltd v Moussavi* [2003] EWCA 715 the claimant sought to admit without prejudice statements made by a defendant to contradict assertions made in his witness statement in contested summary judgment proceedings. In the second case, *Savings and Investment Bank v Fincken* [2003] EWCA 1630 a claimant who was seeking to rescind a voluntary arrangement entered into with the defendant debtor on the grounds of misrepresentation applied to amend his Particulars of Claim to include alleged admissions made by the defendant in compromise negotiations. It was alleged that he had admitted a failure to disclose all his assets. The Court of Appeal over-ruled Pumfrey J. and refused leave. The combined effect of Rix L.J.'s judgment in *Fincken* and Peter Gibson L.J.'s in *Berry Trade* (which was cited at length in *Fincken*) is that:

(1) The "mere" fact that a party makes an admission during without prejudice negotiations which conflicts with his "open" case is not of itself a sufficient "unambiguous impropriety" to remove protection;

(2) The fact that the admission is unequivocal and/or undisputed is not, of itself, determinative;

(3) There must be some abuse of the negotiation process such as threats, blackmail or the commission of perjury to remove the protection afforded by the privilege.

It seems therefore that a party will have to have resorted to extreme conduct such as threatening to give perjured evidence and bribe witnesses, before the privilege will be lost (see, for example *Hawick Jersey International v Caplan, The Times,* March 11, 1988 and *Phipson* at 24–34 to 24–38).

5. *Loss of Privilege by Waiver*

Without prejudice privilege is unique in that it cannot be unilaterally **8–98** waived. What then is the position if one party purports to waive privilege without the other's consent? In *Somatra Ltd v Sinclair Roche and Temperley* [2000] C.P.L.R. 601, the defendants, who were being sued in professional negligence, obtained a freezing order against the claimants in aid of a counterclaim for their legal fees. The affidavit in support of the application made reference to two small extracts from the lengthy meetings that had taken place between the parties in an attempt to reach a negotiated settlement. Unbeknown to the defendants, these meetings had been secretly audiovisually recorded. The claimants now applied to set aside the freezing order. They argued that the partial waiver entitled them to put in evidence the entirety of the without prejudice negotiations including the recordings. The Court of Appeal held that they could do so on the basis that a partial unauthorised waiver could be accepted by the other party thus bringing all the negotiations out into the open. The court drew an analogy with contractual repudiation. The claimants could have insisted on holding the defendants to the privilege by having all references to the privileged material excluded. Alternatively, as here, they were entitled to accept the waver in its entirety. The decision also serves as an important reminder that:

(1) The duty of full and frank disclosure does not override privilege; and

(2) No adverse inference can be drawn against a party who relies on privilege.

In other words, the claimants need never have referred to the material in the first place.

C Problem Areas

The increased encouragement to settle cases heralded by the CPR has **8–99** inevitably meant that this area of the law has become one of the more fertile sources of reported cases, as the following paragraphs show.

1. *"Without Prejudice" and Third Parties*

As already noted, the privilege can only be invoked by the negotiat- **8–100** ing parties. This principle was identified in *Muller v Linsley and Mortimer* [1996] P.N.L.R. 39.

Facts: M was a former client of L & M, a firm of solicitors. M **8–101** claimed that he had been forced to settle severance terms with a company, S Ltd, of which he had been a director and shareholder on less advantageous terms due to L & M's negligence. L & M sought discovery of the antecedent negotiations between M and S Ltd on the basis that they were relevant to causation and M's duty to mitigate his loss.

The Court of Appeal held that they were entitled to the discovery sought. The reasons given by Hoffman L.J. with which the other two members of the court agreed are not easy to follow, not least because the hearsay rule has now gone (see *Phipson* 24–21 to 24–23). However, *Muller* has been followed and applied in *Murrell v Healey* [2001] 4 All E.R. 345, the facts of which are suggestive of questionable tactics on the part of the claimant. The chronology is significant.

(1) May 1995: C injured in Road Traffic Accident (RTA) 1.

(2) Nov 1995: C Injured in Road Traffic Accident 2.

(3) Feb 1996: C's solicitors informed D1's insurers that C might never work again as a result of RTA 1. Later RTA 1 settled.

(4) 1998: C brought proceedings against D2 for RTA 2 and claimed that the majority of his future losses were attributable to RTA 2.

(5) July 2000: on assessment of damages for loss caused by RTA 2 the trial judge ordered C to disclose the antecedent without prejudice negotiations in respect of RTA 1.

The Court of Appeal upheld the decision of the trial judge. Waller L.J. stated:

"I have no doubt the documents produced from the insurers' file [in respect of the first accident] were admissible. It seems to me that the circumstances of this case are a long way from *Rush & Tompkins Ltd v GLC* [1989] A.C. 1280. The evidence was relevant to an inquiry as to what injury the plaintiff had suffered in the first accident. *Muller v Linsley and Mortimer* [1996] P.N.L.R. 74 is the more relevant authority, and the reasoning of Hoffman L.J. would lead to the conclusion that this file was admissible."

The decisions are based, it would appear, on the principle that, since there is no public interest or contractual justification in withholding negotiations between A and B from disclosure to C when C is not a party to those negotiations, C's entitlement to access can be resolved by reference to general principles of relevance. It is also important to note that, first, even though, in both *Muller* and *Murrell*, the negotiations had led to a concluded settlement, that was not a material factor. Thus, for example, in *Murrell* D2 could have sought disclosure of the without prejudice negotiations between C and D1 prior to settlement. Indeed, it would appear that there would have been nothing to have stopped D1's and D2's insurers "swapping notes". Secondly, the decisions stand in notable contrast to *Paragon v Freshfields* (above) in which the defendants sought access to the *legal advice* prior to concluded settlement (see 8–70).

2. Without Prejudice and ADR

The privilege will not only attach to negotiations between solicitors **8–102** or the parties themselves but also to negotiations between the parties and other intermediaries, for example, mediators. Most mediation agreements, in fact, expressly state that the negotiations are without prejudice. Many courts now encourage ADR as a matter of course but cannot force parties to negotiate if they do not wish to (although an unreasonable refusal to do so may ultimately have adverse costs consequences: see *Halsey v Milton Keynes NHS Trust* [2004] 1 W.L.R. 3002). However, if the offer to mediate and the refusal were made without prejudice that fact would only become admissible if the offeree agreed to waive the privilege, which he would be unlikely to do (see *Reed Executive plc v Reed Business Information Ltd* [2004] 1 W.L.R. 3026). The Commercial Court offers an "Early Neutral Evaluation" service ("ENE") from a judge who is then disqualified from hearing the claim should it go to trial (see *Commercial Court Guide* G2 and *White Book* 2A 101). This is expressly stated to be on a without prejudice basis.

3. Open Offers

What about an offer that simply consists of, "As a gesture of goodwill **8–103** [to get rid of it/you] we'll pay/accept £x." Does that tie your hands in anyway? The Court of Appeal decision in *Amber v Stacey* [2001] 2 All E.R. 88 serves as a timely reminder that an open offer is, of itself, of no evidential significance at trial unless it contains admissions, for example, on liability. In *Amber* the defendants had made an open offer to settle early on in the proceedings. Much later on they made a payment into court which was lower than their open offer, but which the claimant failed to beat at trial. In giving the defendants their costs on a standard basis:

(1) 100 per cent post-payment in on the usual principles; and

(2) As to 50 per cent thereof from the date of the open offer

the Court of Appeal stated that the judge had been quite right to treat the open offer as irrelevant both as to liability and *quantum*. This raises two intriguing issues. First, when would a party ever wish to make an open rather than a Pt 36-type offer, and, secondly, if such an offer were made, at what stage would it be appropriate to place it before the trial judge? A possible answer to both of these questions appears in the judgment of Arden L.J. in *Johnson v Gore Wood (No.3)* [2004] EWCA Civ 14 (see also *White Book* 36.19.1). *Gore Wood (No.3)* decides that if a defendant makes a Pt 36 offer or payment that the claimant fails to beat, it cannot be prayed in aid on issues relating to interest or causation of damage because (1) the judge will not get to hear of it until after he has quantified damages and interest because of the "secrecy rule" in CPR 36.19; and (2) the whole tenor of Pt 36 is that offers and payments made under it only confer protection on *costs*. Arden L.J. suggested (entirely correctly in the writer's view) that there was nothing to stop a party wishing to protect his wider position from making an open offer in the same terms as that under Pt 36. Although she did not elaborate further, it is clear, following *Amber v Stacey*, that such an offer would not be admissible until the point at which it became relevant which would not be, at the earliest, until after liability had been determined.

4. Use in Interim Applications

8–104 Prior to the CPR the privilege did not apply to applications to strike out for want of prosecution (see *Family Housing Association v Hyde* [1993] 1 W.L.R. 354), where the negotiations were admissible to explain delay. Presumably this will apply by analogy where the application is based on CPR 3.4. However it has not traditionally applied to most other applications, for example on security for costs, see *Simaan Construction Co v Pilkington Glass* [1987] 1 W.L.R. 516.

5. Does it Protect from Prosecution under the Proceeds of Crime Act 2002?

8–105 There was some doubt as to the position if a party were to reveal evidence suggestive of "money laundering" during the course of negotiations, since the 2002 Act gave no specific immunity from prosecution for non-disclosure offence. The answer, at least for the time being appears to be that, provided the disclosure takes place during negotiations in a "litigious context" it will come within *Bowman v Fels* [2005] 4 All E.R. 609 discussed further at 8–110.

SECTION 5: SECONDARY EVIDENCE OF PRIVILEGED MATERIAL

8–106 As already noted at 2–23 the English courts have not been overly concerned about how a party has come by evidence provided that it is relevant and otherwise admissible. Therefore, at least in theory, there would be nothing to stop a party adducing secondary evidence, say, of privileged solicitor/client communications, by means of illegally taken copies or secret tape recordings. However, notwithstanding the fact that one does hear tales of dustbin bags being searched and builder's skips being scoured for such material, the aggrieved party will almost inevitably be entitled to reclaim his right to privilege if he takes appropriate action.

1. The Basic Position

Privilege (unlike public interest immunity) only attaches to the original document or communication. Accordingly an opponent could, in theory, give evidence of a privileged communication by adducing a copy of the privileged document or by calling a witness who had read its contents. This was established in *Calcraft v Guest* [1889] 1 Q.B. 759. Furthermore, there is no doubt that a party who through carelessness (see, for example *R. v Tompkins* [1997] 67 Cr.App.R. 181) or voluntary disclosure through his solicitor: (see *R. v Cottrill* [1997] Crim. L.R. 56): discloses a privileged communication may subsequently be confronted with it. However, the above two cases are not examples of secondary evidence at all, but instances in which a legal adviser with ostensible authority has, albeit unintentionally, waived the client's privilege.

8–107

2. Restraining Use

It was established in *Lord Ashburton v Pape* [1913] 2 Ch. 49, that if a party had obtained a copy of a privileged communication by means of a trick, the party entitled to the privilege could seek delivery up and an injunction restraining the use of the information contained in it, provided the application was made prior to its deployment in evidence (see further 10–00). The availability of these remedies has since been extended to situations in which a party has inspected a privileged communication as or as a result of an "obvious mistake" (see *Guinness Peat Properties Ltd v Fitzroy Robinson Partnership* [1987] 2 All E.R. 716). Furthermore, if a third party has received privileged information in circumstances of confidentiality, as already seen, waiver will only be in respect of that person. Hence an opponent may not compel the third party to give evidence or produce copies of documents disclosed to him (see *Gotha City v Sothebys* [1998] 1 W.L.R. 114 discussed at 8–27).

8–108

3. Article 8 and Privilege

It would now appear that it is no longer necessary for a party wishing to uphold privilege to rely upon injunctive relief prior to its deployment in evidence. Quite apart from the fact that CPR 31.20 places a general embargo against the use of privileged material that has been:

8–109

"disclosed inadvertently"

without permission of the court, whatever that may mean, it is now clear that a court may exclude evidence obtained in breach of Art.8 by exercising its general jurisdiction to exclude evidence that is otherwise admissible under CPR 32.1(2). This has been confirmed by the Court of Appeal in *Jones v University of Warwick* [2003] I W.L.R. 954 discussed at 2–47.

SECTION 6: PRIVILEGE AND MONEY LAUNDERING

8–110   The coming into force of the Proceeds of Crime Act 2002 ("POCA") on February 24, 2003 created new tensions between a solicitor's professional duty of confidentiality and his duty to uphold client privilege whatever its form. Some of the problems raised by the Act have been addressed in the recent judgment of Brooke L.J. in *Bowman v Fels* [2005] 4 All E.R. 609.

1. The Property

8–111   The Act created a whole range of offences in relation to "Criminal Property" defined in (s.340(2)) as:

> "(a) Property that constitutes a person's benefit from criminal conduct or represents such a benefit (in whole or in part and whether directly or indirectly): and
>
> (b) The alleged offender knows or suspects that it constitutes or represents such a benefit".

It matters not, in effect, what form the property takes s.340(9). "Criminal Conduct" is defined by s.340(3) of the Act as conduct which:

> "(a) constitutes an offence in any part of the United Kingdom
>
> (b) would constitute an offence in any part of the United Kingdom if it occurred there".

As a result, litigators were concerned that, whenever any suspicion emerged during proceedings that any of the assets were "tainted" by criminality, they would be liable to prosecution if they continued acting. These concerns were subsequently confirmed by the President of the Family Division in *P v P* [2003] 4 All E.R. 843. However, to a significant extent, *Bowman* has removed this risk of prosecution. The reasoning of the Court of Appeal is as follows.

(a) *"Arrangement"*
Neither (1) the pursuit of litigation to judgment, nor (2) the compromise or settlement of issues within a "litigious context" constitutes an "arrangement" for the purposes of s.328 (see 8–117). **8–112**

(b) *Privilege*
Nothing in the Act is sufficient to indicate a clear and unequivocal intention on the part of Parliament to make any inroads into the principles of legal professional privilege. **8–113**

(c) *Documents Revealed on Disclosure*
Because of the coercive nature of the disclosure process, documents disclosed by an opponent continue to be held subject to the implied undertaking as to confidentiality which overrides POCA (see CPR 31.22 discussed further at 10–31). **8–114**

2. *The Key Offences*
The most significant ones from so far as civil litigation is concerned are: **8–115**

(a) *"Concealing": s.327*
The offence consists of (1) concealing; (2) disguising; (3) converting; (4) transferring; or (5) removing criminal property from England and Wales, Scotland or Northern Ireland. The terms "concealing or disguising" include (s.327(3)): **8–116**

"concealing or disguising its nature, source, location, disposition, movement or ownership, or any rights in respect to it".

The Court in *Bowman* specifically stated (95) that the issue or pursuit of legal proceedings was not within this section.

(b) *"Entering into an Arrangement": s.328*
This offence, which caused the greatest concern to civil litigators, consists of ether "entering into"; or "becoming concerned" in an "arrangement" which the accused "knows or suspects" facilitates (by whatever means) the: **8–117**

"acquisition, retention, use or control of criminal property, by or on behalf of another person".

This was thought to embrace negotiations during the course of litigation (at least in an inchoate form of the offence) but begged the question as to when it became an "arrangement" for the purposes of the completed offence. *Bowman* is clear on this. A judgment or "settlement in a litigious context" is not an "arrangement", hence it is not possible to commit an inchoate form of the offence by settling in a "litigious context".

(c) *"Failure to Disclose": s.330*

8–118   If a person carrying on business in the "regulated sector" (which will include most solicitors) receives information in the course of such business which leads him to "know", "suspect" or "have reasonable grounds for suspecting" that "another person" is engaged in "money laundering" (which includes offences under ss.328 and 329) he commits an offence if he fails to make the "required disclosure" (usually to NCIS) as soon as practicable. However a legal adviser has a defence under s.330(6) if the information came to him on an occasion protected by: legal advice; or pending litigation privilege. The wording of the exemption is strange: it suggests that it is the occasion on which the information is received that is crucial rather than whether the information itself is privileged. The legal adviser therefore seems to be protected even more than under *Bowman* if he receives information covered by s.330 in the course of, for example, giving or receiving legal advice. *Bowman* makes it clear that in addition to the s.335(6) defence, a solicitor is protected by legal professional privilege and the implied confidentiality undertaking.

(d) *"Tipping off": ss.333 and 342*

8–119   Essentially these two offences deal with different phases of any investigation which might affect a legal advisor. Both consist of making a "disclosure" which is:

"likely to prejudice any investigation"

where the accused knows or suspects that either:

(1) An "authorised disclosure" has been made (s.333); or

(2) Any "money laundering" investigation is being or about to be conducted (s.342).

However a legal adviser has a defence under ss.333(2)(c) and 342(3)(c) if the disclosure is made on an occasion protected by legal advice; or pending litigation privilege. Again *Bowman* makes it clear that a litigator is not generally liable for the reasons already stated. However the s.342 offence can also be committed by a person, who:

"falsifies, conceals destroys or otherwise disposes of, or causes or permits the falsification, concealment destruction or disposal of documents which are relevant to the investigation".

Clearly the s.342(3)(c) defence is not available for this offence.

3. Defences
Crucially, a legal adviser (and every other potential party to the   **8–120**
offence) has a defence to an offence under s.327 ("concealing") or
328 ("being concerned in an arrangement") if, before doing the prohibited act he makes an "authorised disclosure" (s.338); and obtains
"appropriate consent" (s.335). For reasons already given, *Bowman*
makes it clear that a legal adviser engaged in actual or contemplated
litigation will not normally need to rely on this defence.

4. So How Does the Act Affect Privilege?
The inter-relationship between the Act, privilege and the duty of dis-   **8–121**
closure is a complex one which, one suspects, will involve further consideration by the courts in particular with reference to Art.8 issues.
However the following points appear to have been established following *Bowman*.

(1) There is no need to make an "authorised disclosure" in the
    course of pursuing or compromising litigation because this
    creates no offence under s.328.

(2) No offence is committed under s.330 simply from receiving
    instructions and giving advice to the client. However *Bowman*
    is not entirely clear where this leaves the legal adviser with non-
    privileged information. The writer's view is that he has a duty
    to disclose if the advice sought is caught by *R v Cox and Railton*
    (see 8–30) but not otherwise.

(3) Once a legal adviser receives information relating to "money
    laundering" on an occasion covered by "legal advice" or
    "pending litigation" privilege he or she commits no offence
    under s.330 by simply remaining silent (s.330(6)). The situation
    is no different when he or she comes by the information during:

    • Disclosure of documents or assets and/or
    • "without prejudice" negotiations

    because of the "implied undertaking" point (see CPR 31.22) in
    Bowman.

(4) Entering into or continuing litigation and negotiations once
    a legal adviser "knows or suspects" that it involves "criminal
    property" will not be an offence under s.328 and accordingly
    no "authorised disclosure" needs to be made before any further
    steps are taken (indeed, because of privilege it usually cannot
    be made).

(5) A legal adviser does not commit a "tipping off" offence under
    ss.333 or 342 by disclosing to the client or any other party that

she has reason to believe that her opponent has committed a money laundering offence provided it arises during the course of ongoing or contemplated litigation.

SECTION 7: PUBLIC INTEREST IMMUNITY

8–122 Public Interest Immunity ("PII") differs in a number of material respects from the privileges discussed earlier in that:

(1) It is a duty rather than a right and hence;

(2) Cannot ever be waived. However there is an ill-defined ambit of discretion on the part of the person or body with a duty to uphold it.

(3) Unlike privilege it is not in the first instance absolute: in disputed cases the court must carry out a "balancing exercise" between the competing public interests of:

- Giving access to litigants of relevant material they legitimately need to assist their case; and
- Protecting confidentiality of sensitive information;

it thus only becomes absolute once the court decides that there is a higher public interest in maintaining confidentiality.

(4) There are no clearly defined relationships such as lawyer and client or ongoing negotiations. In each case protecting confidentiality is at the core of the duty and accordingly the situations in which it may arise are potentially limitless.

(5) Secondary evidence in not admissible.

However it must be borne in mind that it is an entirely discrete ground for withholding evidence, and may be invoked in addition to any of the privileges discussed earlier. Indeed, it is by no means uncommon for a party who resists disclosure to argue that (1) it is subject to legal professional privilege; but (2) even if it is not, it is subject to PII; but (3) failing either of those, the material is irrelevant in any event.

1. The General Rule

8–123 As appears from the Court of Appeal decision in *Powell v CC for N Wales* [2000], *The Times,* February 11, relevant evidence must be excluded on the ground of public policy once the court finds that the public interest in the administration of justice and the interests of the individual litigants is outweighed by some greater public interest. In the above case, this led to the exclusion of a witness statement because its contents revealed the identity of a police informant. It is not possible to provide a rigid classification of types of evidence subject to public policy exclusion since:

"the categories of public interest are not closed and must alter from time to time . . . as social conditions and social legislation develop"

as stated by Lord Hailsham in *D v NSPCC* [1977] 1 All E.R. 589 at 605. *D v NSPCC* was a landmark decision because in it, the House held that the NSPCC was entitled to withhold the identity of an informant as to alleged child abuse. Prior to that, it had been widely assumed that PII was only available to the Crown, government departments and other quasi-governmental bodies such as police forces and local authorities, indeed, until relatively recently PII was often referred to as "Crown Privilege".

2. Pre-Wiley Case Law

Prior to *Ex p. Wiley* (see later) the courts appeared to have established **8–124** a presumptive approach to PII, often based on the *nature* of the document (a "Class Claim") as opposed to its individual *contents* (a "Contents Claim"), for example. Thus documents relating to confidential matters of central government or national security were treated as immune from disclosure irrespective of their contents. If the relevant Minister of the Crown issued a certificate to that effect the court would not seek to go behind it (*Duncan v Cammell Laird & Co. Ltd.* [1942] A.C. 624). However, the climate began to change as the result of the subsequent decision of the House in *Conway v Rimmer* [1968] A.C. 910 in which, contrary to what it had appeared to be saying in *Duncan v Cammell Laird*, the House stated that the courts had a duty to hold the balance between two public interests: the administration of justice and upholding the confidentiality of sensitive information. Since that decision the courts have become progressively more active in scrutinising claims to PII. This development is traced in detail in *Phipson* at 25–01 to 25–14.

3. The Effect of Wiley

An even greater change in the courts' approach took place as a result **8–125** of two developments in the mid-1990s, the first of which was the House of Lords decision in *R. v Chief Constable of West Midlands Ex p. Wiley* [1995] 1 A.C. 274. In a sense, the decision did no more than re-affirm, albeit in strong terms, the earlier decision in *Conway v Rimmer*. The decision is undoubtedly important on the narrow point that it established, namely that no class claim to PII exists for documents generated in the course of an investigation into a claim against the police, but its reverberations have extended much further. Although not quite abolishing the concept of a class claim to PII, the House nevertheless stated unequivocally that whenever PII is raised the court must conduct a "balancing exercise" between the two public interests namely:

> (1) that of the litigant in having access to material that is likely to assist him in his case; and

> (2) that of the other party to maintain confidentiality in the public interest.

Generally, where the applicant satisfies the requirements of the former the presumption will be in favour of disclosure. However, in cases of doubt it is for the court, having examined the documents to decide. Partly as a result of *Ex p. Wiley*, but also due to other factors outlined below, the Government no longer makes class claims to PII.

4. *"Matrix Churchill"*

8–126 The full effects of *Ex p. Wiley* have still not been fully realised although it is clear that the old distinction between "class" and "contents" claims has largely gone and that any party seeking to raise a class claim will have heavy burden to discharge. The terminal decline, if not as yet the demise of the class claim has been accelerated by the report of Sir Richard Scott V.C. into "Matrix Churchill" affair (*"Report of the Enquiry into the Export of Defence Equipment and Dual Use Goods to Iraq and Related Prosecutions"*) which criticised the use of class claims by the Government in criminal proceedings. As a result of the Scott Report, the Attorney General, in a statement made to both Houses on December 18, 1996, indicated that in future Government departments would only raise PII on a 'contents' basis. It is submitted that this approach should be followed by all other bodies or persons seeking to rely on PII; however this has not turned out to be the case.

5. *The Court's Role*

8–127 Following *Wiley* and the Scott Report, the court will have to scrutinise all claims to PII with the greatest care. This does not mean however that the court should ride roughshod over attempts to protect sensitive material so far as is practically possible. In sensitive cases it should always actively consider whether the information to which access is sought could be made available without breaching confidentiality. It is important to recognise that disclosure and inspection were originally equitable remedies and are also subject to the court's control under CPR 31 (see further Chapter 10).

Frequently PII issues arise on applications against non-parties under CPR 31.17 (see 10–57). A recent example of the modern approach can be found in *Frankson v Home Office* [2003] 1 W.L.R. 1952 in which the Court of Appeal held that statements taken by the police under caution from prison officers in the course of investigation into alleged assaults were not subject to PII. However because of their confidential nature:

(1) The makers should be informed of the intention to use them and be given the opportunity to make representations at HMP Wormwood Scrubbs; and;

(2) Their use, and the persons to whom they were shown should be strictly controlled.

The prospects of success on any application for disclosure will, therefore, be greatly enhanced if appropriate undertakings are offered.

6. The "Fallout"

Decisions subsequent to *Wiley* suggest that both "class" and "contents" claims to PII are now harder to uphold. This has especially been the case with financially sensitive material. For example, in *Kaufmann v Banque Lyonnais* (1995) 7 Admin L.R. 669) in which reports by the defendants' solicitors and accountants to the Securities and Futures Authority regarding the defendants' banking operations were held not to be covered by PII notwithstanding the fact that the defendants argued disclosure would discourage frankness when reporting to regulatory bodies. In *Soden v Burns* [1996] 3 All E.R. 967 statements given to a Department of Trade inquiry were sought by a liquidator under s.236 of the Insolvency Act 1986. The Court of Appeal held that PII was not available, but that the makers of the statements had to be notified and given an opportunity to object. PII was also considered by the Court of Appeal in *Wallace Smith v Deloittes* [1996] 4 All E.R. 403. The case concerned the issue of whether statements given by employees of the defendants to the Serious Fraud Office under s.2 of the Criminal Justice Act 1987 enjoyed immunity from disclosure and inspection in the hands of the employees that was separate from any claim to PII raised by the Serious Fraud Office (who were not themselves raising any objection). The Court of Appeal held that they did not.

8–128

As a result it is becoming more common for public bodies to resist inspection on the grounds of irrelevance or under a separate head of privilege. This is because, irrespective of whether immunity exists, disclosure will only be ordered if the party seeking it can prove that the document is within the scope of standard disclosure under CPR

31.6 and that inspection is "proportionate" (see further 10–15). The only area in which the courts still seem willing to uphold class claims to PII is an claims against the police, see *O'Sullivan v Metropolitan Police Commissioner* [1995], *The Times*, July 3 and *Kelly v MPC* [1997], *The Times*, August 20, in which information passing between police officers and the Crown Prosecution Service concerning decisions to press charges were held to be subject to PII as a class. Having regard to the potential importance of such evidence in these cases, both of which were claims for damages for malicious prosecution, it is somewhat surprising, post-*Wiley*, that class claims were upheld.

7. Without Notice Applications: CPR 31.19

8–129 These enable the party raising PII to make a "pre-emptive strike". They are governed by CPR 31.19 which states:

"(1) A person may apply, without notice, for an order permitting him to withhold disclosure of a document on the ground that disclosure would damage the public interest.

(3) Unless the court orders otherwise, an order of the court under paragraph (1):

(a) must not be served on any other person; and
(b) must not be made accessible to any other person."

As yet, there has been no reported case on the use of this exceptional power. It is also open to a party to make an on notice application under CPR 31.19 in the same way as with a claim to privilege.

Conclusion

8–130 As stated at the start of this chapter, it is quite possible to go through a lengthy and distinguished career without ever encountering a case involving a major issue on PII. Indeed, following the developments during the 1990's referred to above, that likelihood has increased. Nevertheless, in constitutional terms it is a subject of major importance. Only time will tell how far the courts will go in permitting a litigant to have access to confidential information in the hands of public bodies. A full list of material in respect of which a successful PII claim might still be raised appears in *Phipson* at 25–25 to 25–39.

Chapter 9

Case Management and Interim Applications

The rules of civil evidence are shaped by the process within which **9–01** they operate. At the centre lies the CPR philosophy of "cards on the table". Case management is, to a large extent, concerned with that process, as the standard package of directions on disclosure of documents (see Chapter 10), exchange of witness statements (Chapter 11) and service of expert evidence (examined in Chapter 12) shows. The first section of this chapter examines wider disclosure issues and the second section deals with a topic largely ignored by writers on evidence, namely, evidence in interim proceedings.

I DISCLOSURE UNDER THE CPR

The procedures under which a party secures disclosure of his oppo- **9–02** nents' evidence also forms an important part of any text on civil evidence because:

(1) The use of the CPR to secure disclosure is an important component of evidence collection;

(2) Failure to comply with directions on disclosure of evidence triggers a number of important exclusionary rules under the CPR, notwithstanding that they are rarely imposed in practice; and

(3) Disputes over disclosure tend to engage the substantive rules of evidence, especially relevance, privilege, and public interest immunity.

However, once again, one must not lose sight of the fact that, in the vast majority of cases, all parties comply, more or less, with case management directions and, as a result, settlement is achieved at some point during that stage. The next four chapters are largely concerned with the ones that go wrong or go to trial because settlement cannot be achieved.

A "Information, Information, Information"

9–03 There is now far more to "disclosure" than there was to "discovery" of documents as the following summary shows; in effect, every scrap of evidence that a party intends to rely on has to be revealed in advance of trial: in the case of pre-existing documents, it will normally go even further.

1. "Cards on the Table" and the CPR
9–04 We now operate within a climate in which prospective as well as actual parties to litigation are expected to operate a policy of voluntary disclosure of documents and other information even if it harms their own case or assists that of their opponent. Sanctions for non-compliance may include an application for pre-claim disclosure under CPR 31.16 combined with an adverse costs order if it can be shown that disclosure was unreasonably refused (see CPR 48.2 and the commentary in the *White Book*). Indeed, adverse costs consequences may follow at any stage if the court decides that there has been inappropriate "conduct" in relation to disclosure (CPR 44.3(4) and 5). For example in *Brawley v Marczynski* [2002] 4 All E.R. 1060 the Court of Appeal upheld a decision of Laddie J. to award indemnity costs against a defendant in a patent claim. The claim had settled at the door of the court, but the parties were unable to agree costs. The indemnity award was due in part to the defendant's conduct on disclosure of documents, many of which had been held back for tactical reasons. The Court approved the following passage from Laddie J.'s judgment:

> ". . . it was wholly contrary to the proper way of conducting litigation for the defendants to refuse to hand over the necessary documents to enable [the claimant] to assess his claim, or, more importantly, to allow him to assess the offers which were made from time to time by the defendants".

A failure to disclose evidence may also, in extreme cases, lead to its exclusion at trial. A rare example of this can be seen in *Martin v Steelforce Plc,* unreported, June 13, 2000 CA (considered further at 11–22). Non disclosure of material evidence may also constitute grounds for appeal (see, for example, *Orford v Rasmi Electronics Ltd* [2002] EWCA Civ 1672) a case in which failure to disclose a factory plan in accordance with CPR 33.6 (see 13–35) led to a retrial being ordered. As a last resort, wholesale non-disclosure, especially if it is combined with the falsification or destruction of documents, may cause such severe prejudice as to justify strike-out (see *Arrow Nominees v Blackledge* [2000] 2 B.C.L.C. 167 (at [193–4]) and the commentary in *Hollander* at 11–10 to 11–34).

2. *"All the Cards All the Suits"*
Although the term "disclosure" is specific to disclosure of documents,   **9–06**
CPR 31 is part of a far wider disclosure regime that, in essence, gives the court power (and sometimes an obligation) to ensure that *all* relevant information and evidence is disclosed in accordance with the "overriding objective" in CPR 1. However, each part of the disclosure regime operates somewhat differently.

(a) *Documents: CPR 31*
The court's powers to order disclosure of documents, defined in CPR   **9–07**
31.4 as "anything in which information of any description is recorded" are almost entirely *discretionary* in that:

(1) Pre-Claim (CPR 31.16) and non-party (CPR 31.17) disclosure "may" be ordered provided that the applicant can first establish the detailed criteria laid down in the relevant rules. This was made abundantly clear by the Court of Appeal in *Black v Sumitomo Corp* [2002] 1 W.L.R. 1562 and *Three Rivers DC v Bank of England (No.4)* [2002] 4 All E.R. 881 discussed at 10–37.

(2) The court is not obliged to order disclosure between the parties either under CPR 28.3 (Fast Track) or CPR 29.2 (Multi Track). Furthermore CPR 31.5(2) states that the court may ". . . dispense with or limit standard disclosure".

(3) Under CPR 31.12(3) (orders for specific disclosure and inspection) and 31.3(2) (right to resist inspection on the grounds of disproportionality) the court may control *inspection* of disclosed documents.

Under CPR 31.21, by way of sanction, "A party may not rely on any document which he fails to disclose or in respect of which he fails to permit inspection unless the court gives permission." Persistent breaches of orders for disclosure may even lead to a party's claim or defence being struck out under CPR 3.4(2)(c).

(b) *Expert evidence: CPR 35*
As discussed further at 12–21, CPR 35 makes expert opinion evidence   **9–08**
inadmissible unless the court gives permission to the parties to rely on

it. Advance disclosure of the experts' written reports will always be imposed as a precondition for their admission. The sanction for non-disclosure is in CPR 35.13 which provides that:

> "A party who fails to disclose an expert's report may not use the report at the trial or call the expert to give evidence orally unless the court gives permission".

Although the court, in theory, retains a discretion to permit a party to rely on undisclosed expert evidence, the circumstances in which this would be permitted are hard to envisage. Disclosure of expert evidence is considered further at 10–27 and 12–45.

(c) *Witness Evidence: CPR 32*

9–09   CPR 32.4(2) appears to give the court *no* discretion, at least at the case management stage. It states that, "The court will [writer's emphasis] order a party to serve on the other parties any witness statement . . .". Service of witness summaries under CPR 32.9 is also, in effect, mandatory. Non-disclosure of any statement (or summary) will debar the party concerned from calling the maker without the court's permission (CPR 32.10). Although relief will normally be given if the application is made in good time (see further 11–19) the court will be less willing to do so if the issue is raised for the first time at trial.

(d) *Other Evidence*

9–10   In effect, no evidence which a party wishes to rely on at trial or an interim hearing may be kept back. Notable examples include:

(1) Notice of intention to rely on hearsay evidence should be given in accordance with the procedure laid down in CPR 33.2, although as noted at 7–26, s.2(4) of the Civil Evidence Act 1995 specifically provides that non-compliance will *not* result in automatic exclusion.

(2) Any plan, photograph or model; or document receivable under s.9 of the Civil Evidence Act 1995 *must* be served at the same time as witness statements (CPR 33.6(4)), or (where it is referred to in an expert's report) at the same time as the report is served (CPR 33.6(6)). As to be expected, non-compliance debars a party from relying on it without the court's permission (CPR 33.6(3)).

(3) Any evidence in support of an Interim Application must be served with the Application Notice (CPR 23.7(1)) or as prescribed by the relevant rule (CPR 23.7(2)). These requirements are discussed further at 9–26.

3. *"All Cards are Playable"*

As already noted, one major consequence of hearsay being abolished   **9–11**
as a rule of exclusion, has been to make *any* factual information that
is relevant to an issue admissible in evidence irrespective of its format.
Hence it is now much easier to use information, whatever its nature
or provenance, to prove or refute facts. Ironically, this has had the
effect of increasing rather than decreasing the scope of a party's documentary disclosure obligations under CPR 31: not quite what Lord
Woolf was aiming for.

4. *"Cards Cannot Usually be Withheld"*

Information that is otherwise relevant and liable to disclosure cannot   **9–12**
be withheld from inspection unless a party can rely upon one of the
available heads of privilege or claim public interest immunity. These
topics have already been covered in Chapter 8.

II EVIDENCE ON INTERIM APPLICATIONS

Throughout the text there are references to occasions on which the   **9–13**
court requires an application to be supported by *evidence*. Indeed,
claims are frequently won or lost on an interim application and therefore evidential issues need to be taken every bit as seriously as they
would be at trial. However what passes for evidence in so many interim
hearings is witness statements that are crammed with argument but
remarkably light on fact (see further 9–32). It is also by no means
uncommon for advocates to make all manner of assertions which are
wholly unsupported by any of the evidential material that has been
placed before the court,

"My lady, my information is/instructions are . . ."

being the characteristic preamble to the advocate assuming the role of
witness in his client's cause. Although a certain amount of discussion
and information exchange has its place on occasions and can oil the
wheels at a case management conference, there are limits. However
persuasive an advocate's rhetoric may be, it is still not *evidence.*

A Burdens of "Persuasion"

Remarkably little attention has been paid to burdens of proof at interim   **9–14**
hearings. This is unfortunate because many of the issues that a judge
has to determine will affect the overall result of the claim. Furthermore,
they can be every bit as complex as those arising at trial. Even though

findings of fact at an interim hearing will not generally create any estoppal (see 6–26 and 6–32) there will often be, at the very least, a "burden of persuasion" upon the applicant. It is also quite clear that if an applicant fails to hit all the targets required by an individual rule see, for example CPR 31.16 at 10–36) his application is *bound* to fail. Some of the more commonly recurring instances are discussed below.

1. Setting Aside Judgment: CPR 13, 39 and 3.6

9–15 The defendant's burden in an application to set aside a regular *default* judgment under CPR 13 is onerous. First, the rule requires the applicant to support his application with *evidence* (see CPR 13.4(3) and *Pugh v Cantor Fitzgerald* [2001] 3 C.P.L.R. 271 discussed further at 9–32). Secondly, that evidence must show that the defendant has a real prospect of successfully defending the claim or that there is some other compelling reason why he should be allowed to defend (CPR 13.3). Unless the defendant can meet these stringent requirements his application must be dismissed: the overriding objective gives no further leeway. However, in some cases, the claimant may have the initial burden of persuading the court that the judgment is a regular one. For example, he may be required to prove that postal service has been validly effected in accordance with CPR 6 (see, for example *Mersey Dock Property Holdings v Kilgour* [2004] EWHC 1638 approved in *Collier v Williams* [2006] EWCA Civ 20). A party who applies to set aside a judgment entered against him at a *trial* or hearing from which he was absent also has a heavy burden of persuasion (see, CPR 39.3(5)). He will have to satisfy the court that (1) he has applied promptly; (2) there was a good reason for his absence; and (3) that, if reinstated, he has a reasonable prospect of success. He must succeed on all three limbs, otherwise his application is doomed to failure. Finally, the Court of Appeal decision in *CPL Industrial Services Holdings Ltd v R & L Freeman and Sons* [2005] EWCA Civ 539 has highlighted an important difference between applications to set aside default judgments under CPR 13 and 39.3(5), and those entered in default of compliance with an "unless order" under CPR 3.6. In the latter case, the court is not concerned with the merits of the applicant's claim or defence, only with whether relief is appropriate as a matter of discretion under CPR 3.9 (see further 1–50).

2. Summary Judgment: CPR 24

9–16 Applications for summary judgment under CPR 24 also impose significant burdens on the applicant, arguably greater than those that existed under RSC O.14 and CCR O.14. Whereas the burden used to lie with the defendant to show that there was a "triable issue" entitling him to defend; the burden (notwithstanding PD 24/4) now seems to rest solely on the applicant to show that the respondent has no realistic prospect of success, and that there is no other compelling reason why the case or issue should be disposed of at a trial. The relatively limited availability of the remedy became apparent in *Swain v Hillman* [2001] 1 All E.R. 91. In that case, Lord Woolf M.R. stated that the term "real prospect of succeeding/successfully defending" was not susceptible to any specialised definition since the procedure was designed to dispose of cases that had a "fanciful" as opposed to a "realistic" prospect of success. He stated:

> "Useful though the power is under Part 24, it is important that it is kept in its proper role. It is not meant to dispense with the need for a trial where there are issues which should be investigated at the trial . . . the proper disposal of an issue under Part 24 does not involve the judge conducting a mini trial, that is not the object of the provisions; it is to enable cases, where there is no real prospect of success either way, to he disposed of summarily."

What this decision, a defendant's application in an employer's liability claim, made clear was that if credibility of witnesses is in issue and that can only be tested by cross-examination, summary judgment will not be available. Furthermore, the burden of proof is a heavy one and is to a higher standard than the normal civil standard of proof. This was made clear in *Royal Brompton NHS Trust v Hammond* [2001] B.L.R. 297. In that case the Court of Appeal stated that it was not open to a judge to dispose summarily of a claim or issue on the basis that the party was unlikely to succeed on that issue at trial "on the balance of probabilities". The test laid down in *Swain v Hillman* had to be applied in every case: effectively the judge has to be satisfied that the party's case is a "no hoper". If you are ever in doubt as to whether your case is sufficiently strong to justify an application for summary judgment, the test laid down by May L.J. in *S v Gloucestershire CC* [2000] 3 All E.R. 346 provides a useful yardstick against which to measure your chances of success. Although the application arose in the highly specialised field of a negligence claim against a local authority social services department the guidance given can be applied to any type of case by deleting the words in square brackets.

> "For a summary judgment application to succeed [where a strike-out application would not succeed], the court will need to be satisfied that all substantial facts relevant to the allegations [of negligence], which are reasonably capable of being before the court, are before the court, that these facts are undisputed or there is no real prospect of successfully disputing them; and that there is no real prospect of oral evidence affecting the court's assessment of the facts."

So far as compliance with the ECHR was concerned, May L.J. concluded by saying that if this process was followed:

> "there will, in my view, have been proper judicial determination of the detailed facts of the particular case such as to constitute a fair hearing in accordance with Article 6 of the Convention."

The Court of Appeal has also recently considered the interrelationship between applications for Summary Judgment and those for Setting Aside Judgment in *ED and F Mann Liquid Products v Patel* [2003], *The Times*, April 4. The court concluded that the phrase "real prospect of success", which is common to both rules, meant the same. Accordingly they approved the "realistic as opposed to fanciful" test laid down in *Swain v Hillman*. They also concluded that although the burden of proof (interestingly the court *used* the term "burden of proof") theoretically lay on a different party depending upon whether CPR 13.3 or 24 was being applied, all this really amounted to was that a court might look rather more kindly on a respondent who asserted facts in timely opposition to a Summary Judgment application, than one who only raised those same facts after a regular judgment had been entered against him. Finally, one needs to bear in mind that if an applicant is seeking a conditional order as a "fallback", especially if that condition requires the respondent to pay money into court as a condition of being allowed to proceed with his claim or defence, the court will need to be persuaded that the condition is a reasonable one (see *M V Yorke Motors v Edwards* [1982] 1 W.L.R. 444). Rather than run the risk of an adjournment so that the court can receive evidence as to the respondent's means, it may be prudent for the applicant to put the respondent on notice in advance of the first hearing by letter written "without prejudice save as to costs" (see *Anglo-Eastern Trust Ltd v Kermanshahchi* [2002] EWCA Civ 198). For a full discussion of the relevant procedure on summary judgment see Chapter 19 of *O'Hare and Browne*.

3. Interim Relief: CPR 25

9–17   At the risk of digressing too far into the realms of substantive law and procedure, it will by now be clear that significant burdens of persuasion are imposed on applicants for various forms of order, for example:

(a) *Interim injunctions*

9–18   The applicant will have to satisfy the court with *evidence* that the "balance of convenience" favours the grant of injunctive relief in order to satisfy the requirements laid down in *American Cyanamid v Ethicon* [1975] A.C. 396. However, there may be somewhat more stringent requirements laid down where the relief is sought under a specific statute, for example under s.153A of the Housing Act 1996 (see, for example *Moat Housing Group South Ltd v Harris and Hartless* [2005] 4 All E.R. 1051). Where a mandatory injunction is being sought, the applicant will also in general have to show that he has a high prospect of success at trial (see *Zockoll Group v Mercury Communication* [1998] F.S.R. 354). Interim injunction procedure is covered in Chapter 27 of *O'Hare and Browne*.

(b) *Freezing orders*
A freezing order, formerly known as a "*Mareva* injunction" restrains   **9–19**
a party from removing assets from the United Kingdom and from dealing with his assets wherever located save insofar as the court permits him. It is normally granted without notice in the first instance and, as well as restraining the respondent as set out above, will require him to file a detailed affidavit as to his assets. It is one of the most common situations in which a party will assert that he is entitled to rely on the privilege against self-incrimination (see 8–71). Because of its swingeing nature, the applicant is required to hit three very clearly defined targets if he is to succeed, namely evidence, supported by affidavit, of:

(1) A good arguable case;

(2) The existence and location of assets that are capable of being frozen; and

(3) A real risk that the respondent will dispose of those assets in an endeavour to frustrate the execution of any judgment the applicant may obtain.

The relevant procedure is discussed in *O'Hare and Browne* at 27–025 to 27–039.

(c) *Search orders*
Formerly known as "*Anton Piller* orders", search orders are the   **9–20**
nearest that the civil courts can get to a search warrant (see further 10–40). In view of the uniquely intrusive nature of such orders, the applicant will have to show not only that he has a strong case on the merits, but also adduce compelling evidence, supported by affidavit, that serious harm or injustice will result if an order is not made. He will also have to identify with some precision both the premises and the documents or property to which access is sought. The procedure is set out in *O'Hare and Browne* at 27–040 to 27–043. As with freezing orders, a respondent may seek to fall back on the privilege against self-incrimination, although his ability to do so has been severely curtailed by s.72 of the Supreme Court Act 1981 (see 8–76).

(d) *Interim payments*

9–21 There are no less than five grounds on which such an order may be made under CPR 25.7; all of them contain clearly defined burdens of persuasion which must be supported by evidence (CPR 25.6(3)). The most significant in terms of the burden imposed on the applicant are CPR 25.7(c) in which the claimant has to satisfy the court that he "would", that is, *will* recover substantial damages if the case goes to trial, and CPR 25.7(e) under which he must satisfy the court that if the case went to trial he:

> ". . . would obtain judgment for a substantial sum of money . . . against at least one of the defendants (but the court cannot determine which)".

The latter provision reverses the decision in *Ricci Burns Ltd v Toole* [1989] 1 W.L.R. 993 under which the claimant had to prove his entitlement against *each* individual defendant. Nevertheless, in either case the burden is still a heavy one unless judgment has already been entered on liability (see generally, *British and Commonwealth Holdings plc v Quadrex Holdings plc* [1989] Q.B. 842 and Chapter 25 of *O'Hare and Browne*).

(e) *Other applications*

9–22 There will be numerous occasions on which issues are the subject of dispute, all of which will involve the exercise of a discretion. These are in some ways the hardest type of application to present, especially where the decision involves relief from a sanction. As such, there are no burdens of persuasion in the CPR 3.9 checklist. However it is suggested that, on the whole, if the consequences of the sanction appear to be more severe than those of lifting it, the party seeking to uphold it has the task of persuading the judge that it is a just and proportionate course to adopt. On other occasions, the Court of Appeal have laid down specific guidance as to the factors to be taken into account. A recent example can be found in the case of applications made *within* the four month period (CPR 7.6(2)) to extend the time for service of the claim form (see *Hastroodi v Hancock* [2004] 1 W.L.R. 3206 and *Collier v Williams* [2006] EWCA Civ 20). On other occasions, the CPR themselves prescribe the factors that the judge may take into account; this may on occasions have the effect of shutting out the overriding objective, especially where the factors are prefaced by the word "only" (see for example, *Vinos v Marks and Spencer plc* [2001] 3 All E.R. 784, a case concerning an application to extend the time for service made *outside* the four month period under CPR 7.6(3)). Whatever the nature of the application, it is essential that you make a list of the targets that you will need to hit to obtain the order that you seek, either by reference to the relevant rule or a guideline Court of Appeal judgment such as *Hastroodi*, before assembling your evidence in support.

(f) *Case management*
All manner of issues may arise during the course of a substantial case   **9–23**
in which the court will be involved in major decisions on disclosure and expert evidence. An ability to analyse the issues and point to the relevance of individual items of evidence to those issues by reference to the principles set out in Chapters 1, 3 and 4 will greatly assist both you and the court in making sure that all essential evidence is made available at trial.

(g) *Enforcement*
Most textbooks on evidence seem to take no interest in what happens   **9–24**
after judgment has been given or entered. Nevertheless, the rules of evidence continue to apply, and within the CPR (and RSC and CCR) there are a number of situations in which an individual party is placed under a clearly defined burden. For example:

(1) A party who seeks leave to enforce a judgment that is more than six years old will need the leave of the court (RSC O.46 r.2 and CCR O.26 r.5). The burden on the judgment creditor is a very high one (see *Patel v Singh* [2002] EWCA Civ 1938).

(2) Although the judgment creditor has the primary burden of establishing by evidence that there are grounds for making an *interim* Third Party Debt Order (CPR 72.3(2)) or interim Charging Order (CPR 73.3(4)) the rules make it clear that any party who objects to a *final* order being made must file written evidence in support (see CPR 72.8 and 73.8).

(3) An application to commit to prison for breach of an injunction (RSC O.52 and CCR O.29) must be supported by evidence on affidavit: the criminal standard of proof applies (see further, the *White Book* at S.52.4.6).

Conclusion   In order to make and resist interim applications   **9–25**
effectively it is essential to identify the issues that the court is being required to rule on. This process will also provide you with a valuable tool for analysing the tactical benefits, if any, to be gained from interim skirmishes.

B Use of Witness Statements at Interim Hearings

An application for an interim order can vary from a five minute   **9–26**
appointment in which no evidence as such is adduced, to a heavy

application for an interim injunction involving many hundreds of pages of evidence. Evidence at such hearings is governed primarily by CPR 23 along with CPR 32 and the supporting Practice Direction (see further *O'Hare and Browne* Chapters 19 (Summary Judgment); 25 (Interim Payments); and 27 (Interim Injunctions). Further guidance on the drafting of witness statements in general is given at 11–31.

1. Is there a General Rule?

9–27   The answer, quite simply, is "No". Some rules specifically require evidence in support, for example, an application for Summary Judgment under CPR 24. However para.9 of PD 23 states:

(1) As a practical matter the court will often need to be satisfied by evidence on a contested issue (9.1).

(2) The court may always give directions for the filing of evidence (9.2).

(3) Respondents should serve evidence in reply as soon as possible or in accordance with any directions given (9.4). The same goes for any evidence in reply (9.5).

(4) All evidence must be filed as well as served (9.6).

However, if written evidence is to be given, it is subject to the provisions of CPR 32.2(1) and 32.6 set out at 5–16 and further discussed at 11–29.

2. Use of Affidavits: CPR 32.15

9–28   From being the norm pre-CPR, affidavits, defined in the CPR glossary as "a written, sworn statement of evidence", have become a rarity. CPR 32.15 provides:

"(1) Evidence must be given by affidavit instead of or in addition to a witness statement if this is required by the court, a provision contained in any other rule, a practice direction or any other enactment.

(2) Nothing in these Rules prevents a witness giving evidence by affidavit at a hearing other than the trial if he chooses to do so in a case where paragraph (1) does not apply, but the party putting forward the affidavit may not recover the additional cost of making it from any other party unless the court orders otherwise."

The following points should be noted:

(1) The court may order evidence to be given by affidavit: either on application or of its own initiative (PD 32/1.6)

(2) Affidavit evidence may be required by statute for example, in proceedings under the Protection from Harassment Act 1997, s.3(5)(a)) or a rule, for example, RSC O.115 rr 2B and 14 (confiscation and forfeiture orders in connection with criminal proceedings) and RSC O.110 r.1(3) (environmental control proceedings).

(3) A party may always choose to give evidence by affidavit (PD 32(1.2)), but see CPR 32.15(2) above.

(4) Practice Direction 32/1.4 requires affidavit evidence for:

- Search orders (formerly known as *Mareva* injunctions: see *Hollander* 3–54 to 3–78)
- Freezing orders (formerly known as *Anton Piller* orders: see *Hollander* 3–10 to 3–53).
- Applications to commit for contempt of court.

In practical terms, the format of an affidavit will not differ from that of a witness statement except that the written confirmation that it has been sworn (known as the *jurat*) will appear at its foot.

3. *Practical Issues*
Although it is often overlooked, witness statements (and affidavits) at interim hearings should only contain *evidence* not advocacy. Drafting is discussed in greater detail at 11–31, nevertheless, there are some important ground rules that need to be observed in interim hearings.

9–29

(a) *"Grounds" and "evidence"*
CPR 23.6 provides that an application notice must state:

9–30

(1) What order the applicant is seeking;

(2) Briefly, why the applicant is seeking the order.

It is important that the grounds are set out where they belong, in the N244 in Part A or in a separate document. What one often sees in the application notice is:

"The grounds are set out in Part C [the witness statement of X]".

It is suggested that this tends to encourage bad habits. It creates a tendency for the statement to become, in effect, a Skeleton Argument with a few crumbs of fact scattered within it.

(b) *"Findings of fact"*
Most interim applications involve the exercise of a discretion. Discretion cannot be exercised in a vacuum. Therefore consider:

9–31

(1) What requirements are prescribed by the CPR before an order can be made?

(2) Are there any specific matters to which the court must have regard under the CPR when exercising its discretion?

(3) What preliminary or presumptive findings of fact must the court make prior to exercising discretion?

4. Should Statements for Use in Interim Hearings Contain More Argument?

9–32   There is a common tendency for witness statements in interim hearings to contain a great deal more "advocacy" than "fact". This has on occasions led to adverse comment from the Court of Appeal, for example, in *Pugh v Cantor Fitzgerald* [2001] C.P.L.R. 27I the defendants were seeking to set aside a regular default judgment. This requires the applicant to adduce evidence that he has a defence with a "real prospect of success" (CPR 13.3). Ward L.J. had this to say about his solicitor's statement in support:

> "7. Mr A . . . put in a second witness statement, and, unlike the first, this is with our papers. It deals at length with the failure to return the acknowledgement of serve in time but when he dealt with the sustainable defence he said little more than this:
>
>> '9. I believe the defendant has discovered matters which constitute . . . a valid defence.
>>
>> 11. With respect, Mr . . .'s assertion that this defence is a sham is wholly incorrect. The matters set out in the draft defence demonstrate a valid and sustainable defence to the claimant's cause.'
>
> 8. I will not quote more from this statement. It was practically useless for the purpose it was designed to serve. It may have been long in argument and comment but it was woefully short on facts, especially any which went to the basis of the defence sought to be advanced."

An even clearer example can be found in *Alex Lawrie Factors v Morgan* [2001] CPR2: [1999] *The Times*, August 19. In Summary Judgment proceedings the defendant filed an affidavit which stated:

> "As I have already stated in this affidavit, had I seen the letter dated February 5, 1996, I would have taken independent legal advice as to the contents. However, given the ruling of the House of Lords in *Barclays Bank Plc v O'Brien*, in particular the judgement of Lord Browne-Wilkinson, my view is that Alex Lawrie did not go far

enough with just writing the letter of February 5, 1996. It is clear that Alex Lawrie should have insisted that I attend a private meeting in the absence of Mr Morgan with a representative of Alex Lawrie with them explaining the extent of my liability as a surety. This did not happen. There was no communication whatsoever between Alex Lawrie and myself and as far as I am concerned, communication is a vital part of any agreement. The only time I received any communication from Alex Lawrie was in their letter dated October 13, 1997, advising me that I owed them £130,996.96."

Not surprisingly, Douglas Brown L.J. approached her affidavit on the following basis:

"Her affidavit includes other sophisticated points about the evidence. It is hardly surprising that in those circumstances, without seeing her, the judge formed the view that she was a woman of intelligence and decided in these circumstances that her evidence was simply incredible."

Although her appeal was ultimately allowed, it was not surprising Brooke L.J. stated:

"The case is a very good warning of the grave dangers which may occur when lawyers put into witnesses' mouths, in the affidavits which they settle for them, a sophisticated legal argument which in effect represents the lawyer's arguments in the case to which the witnesses themselves would not be readily able to speak if cross-examined on their affidavits. Affidavits are there for the witness to say in his or her own words what the relevant evidence is and are not to be used as a vehicle for complex legal argument. Those considerations apply just as much to statements of truth under the Civil Procedure Rules as they do to affidavits."

H.H. Judge Dean Q.C. in *E, D and F Man Liquid Products Ltd v Patel* [2002] EWHC Civ 1706 was somewhat more forthright. He was considering a submission on costs based on the fact that a solicitor's witness statement was unduly lengthy. According to the costs schedule, it had taken a week to prepare. In defence of the statement it was argued that, in the Commercial Court, there was "a long and honourable history" of very full witness statements because they facilitated settlement. The judge stated:

"Matter of that sort should not be in any witness statement, and I do not think that there is any encouragement to make submissions in witness statements in the Commercial Court or in any other court."

The issue then arose as to whether the legal arguments should have been put in the witness statement. The judge stated:

"I have to read it twice and it wastes time, and it is inappropriate in a witness statement. He should not make submissions and neither should he make extensive reference to documents. A witness statement is a written statement signed by a person who gives evidence and only evidence . . ."

Was there a distinction between witness statements for interim proceedings at trials? The judge had this to say:

"Witness statements are not the place for argument. It means you have to read everything twice . . . A lot of it is tendentious comment which is bound up with fact. I think this witness statement is an example of what a witness statement should not be whether in the Commercial Court or anything else. It is a tendentious advocate's document. I am minded to disallow the cost of it actually".

The judge had still not finished:

"Look how long it goes on for . . . 41 paragraphs. That is just a solicitor giving information on what his client has said. He expresses a reference to his client's belief which is not only irrelevant but inadmissible. I think that this is a statement of an enthusiastic solicitor who wishes he was an advocate. I am going to cut quite a lot off this. I do not think that this is a proper statement at all . . . It adds to the time of the hearing and it adds to the time of preparation. Here we have the Commercial Court practice which says that witness statements must comply with the rules. They should be as concise as the circumstances allow. They should not engage in argument. They must indicate which statements are made from the witness's own knowledge and which are from other sources and state what is the source of the information and belief".

These are, perhaps, extreme examples, but it shows how important it is to observe the guidance given at 9–29 above.

C Evidence on Interim Applications: Practical Guidance

9–33   The main characteristic of interim proceedings is that although oral evidence is possible, it is rare. Evidence is characteristically given by witness statement (see, CPR 32.6(1)) with documents to be relied on exhibited to the statement. However, a greater degree of flexibility is now afforded under CPR 32.6(2) which permits reliance on the contents of case statements and application notices (Form N244) provided they are supported by a statement of truth. In many ways, preparation of witness statements for interim hearings is harder than for trial because the issues are so many and varied and, as has been shown, often more complex. Some general advice follows.

1. "What am I Asking for?"

In the writer's view, applications are not preceded by the type of analysis recommended at 9–29. Until you have examined the relevant rule under which you are applying or opposing, and analysed what decisions the court is being asked to make under it, you will not be ready to deal with it. Carrying out this preliminary exercise, which will only take a minute or two will enable you decide firstly, whether you should be making or opposing the application at all, and secondly having taken the decision to go ahead, what evidence you will need to assemble for that purpose.

9–34

2. Attractive Paperwork Helps

It goes without saying that well organised paperwork tends to have a persuasive effect. Remember also, that unless you have a lengthy appointment, your application will often appear as one of many in a busy list. It will therefore help if you set out your evidence in a format that can be quickly assimilated. For example, if there has been a series of delays extending back to the pre-action protocol stage, set them out in tabular form as an exhibit. Set out the dates on which each step should have been taken. Next to it then put the dates, if any, upon which it was in fact taken. This will be far more effective than a large bundle containing photocopies of accusatory correspondence that the judge will never have time to read.

9–35

3. Identify the Burdens of Persuasion

It never ceases to amaze the writer how infrequently this is done. For example, on an application to set aside judgment, would it not be effective to close by saying:

9–36

"Madam, in order to be able to set aside judgment you must be satisfied that there is evidence before you capable of supporting a defence with a real prospect of success. Madam, in my submission there is no such evidence. Accordingly I would submit that unless there is evidence of some other compelling reason for setting aside judgment, and I would suggest that there is none, this application must fail."

Simple, accurate and to the point. Why is it so rarely done?

4. Be Ready with Evidence on Costs

9–37   With costs so often being the largest issue in a claim you should never miss the opportunity of seeking indemnity costs where appropriate. Bear in mind however that an order for indemnity costs is not a given. It is quite clear from the Court of Appeal decisions in *Reid Minty v Gordon Taylor* [2002] 2 All E.R. 150 and *Kiam v MGN (No.2) Ltd* [2002] 2 All E.R. 242 that, to quote the *White Book* at 44.4.2:

> "The award of costs on an indemnity basis is normally reserved to cases where the court wishes to indicate its disapproval of the conduct in the litigation of the party against whom the costs are awarded."

If you can show that you done all that you can to avoid coming to court in the face of persistent breaches, your chances of an indemnity order will be enhanced. They will be enhanced even further if, having been wholly successful in your application you can produce a letter written "without prejudice save as to costs" in which you offered a consent order in the same or more generous terms. Remember that any admissible offer is relevant on costs see *Petrotrade Inc v Texaco Ltd* [2002] 1 W.L.R. 947 (see further 8–96 and 13–11).

5. Take Careful Notes

9–38   Any note taken by you of:

    (1) The proceedings themselves; and

    (2) Discussions between yourself and your opponent's representative (unless made "without prejudice";

is not subject to any form of privilege. The Court of Appeal decision in *Parry v News Group* [1990] N.L.J. 1719 to that effect is not reported anywhere else and is not as well known as it should be (for a very full discussion of its implications see *Hollander* at 12–18 to 12–30). It may well be that the other side will make various assertions of fact on behalf of their clients that will be relevant to show inconsistency. Your opponent's representative may even, in conceding a point, have made an informal admission (see 7–48) that binds the client. The note itself will be admissible as documentary hearsay (7–48) and, in the unlikely event of your having to give oral evidence, will be a "contemporaneous note" from which you can "refresh your memory" (see 5–29 and 7–46). One cannot help but think that this kind of scavenging hardly accords with the spirit of the CPR, but it is probably wise to take care what you say and keep careful notes in accordance with more traditional practice.

Chapter 10

Disclosure of Documents

In this chapter more than any other, the boundaries between the rules   **10–01**
of evidence and procedure become blurred. However, since documentary evidence, in all its forms, is often the most important source
of evidence in a case, documentary disclosure merits a chapter to
itself. As well as examining the CPR an opportunity will also be taken
to consider other potential sources of documentary evidence, for
example under the Data Protection Act 1998 and the Freedom of
Information Act 2000.

I THE BACKGROUND TO THE CPR

As must now be apparent, "disclosure" is a seriously overworked   **10–02**
word in the CPR, it also marks the point at which, at any rate in commercial cases, the costs start to mount and settlement negotiations
begin in earnest (although under the CPR this now tends to happen
at a much earlier stage).

1. Discovery: The Pre-CPR Position
The duty to give "discovery", which was automatic under RSC   **10–03**
O.24 and CCR O.17 r.11 once pleadings were deemed to be closed,
extended to all documents which:

> "contain information which may enable a party . . . either to
> advance his own case or damage that of his adversary (and extends
> to documents) which may fairly lead him to a line of enquiry which
> may have either of these two consequences".

This was the test laid down in *The "Peruvian Guano"* [1882] 11 Q.B.
55 decision which, over the years, came to be regarded as one of the
main causes of unnecessary delay and expense in litigation.

2. "Peruvian Guano" under Attack

10–04   There were numerous pre-CPR attempts to limit the scope of discovery see, for example, *Baldock v Addison* [1995] 1 W.L.R. 158 (discovery limited to liability only on a "split trial"), *Forrester v BRB* [1996] *The Times,* April 8 (wide ranging discovery application held to be oppressive) and *O Company v M Company* [1996] 2 Lloyds Rep. 347 (application for further discovery limited to those documents that had "substantial evidential materiality"). Nevertheless the expensive and time consuming nature of discovery, especially in large commercial cases, continued to cause concern. As a result the CPR introduced the supposedly narrower concept of "disclosure", a change which was intended to be more than cosmetic. The most important changes introduced were:

(1) The creation of an "industry standard" of "standard disclosure" which did not include "line of enquiry" documents.

(2) The requirement for there to be a "Disclosure Statement" in a list of documents in which the prescribed signatory certified that he understood the duty imposed by disclosure and that to the best of his knowledge and belief the duty had been complied with.

(3) Limiting the scope of inspection by reference to the concept of "proportionality".

(4) Requiring the litigant to assume personal responsibility for signing the Disclosure Statement.

(5) Extending the scope of Pre-Action and Non-Party disclosure to all claims, not simply those involving personal injury and death.

(6) Limiting disclosure to that ordered by the court (or agreed between the parties).

(7) Encouraging the parties to give voluntary disclosure of the most material documents by reference to an individual Protocol or the Protocol Practice Direction.

3. Are the CPR Making a Difference?

10–05   Interestingly (and encouragingly) there has been, Pre-Action and Non-Party disclosure excepted, remarkably little case law on the scope and meaning of any of the new concepts in CPR 31. As a very general summary, the following propositions are advanced. Those seeking a more comprehensive review should consult paras 9–10 to 9–20 of *Hollander.*

(1) So many smaller claims settle early that standard disclosure never becomes an issue.

(2) In fast track PI cases "Annex B disclosure" under the PI Protocol (which is in some ways wider than Standard Disclosure) will have already taken place.

(3) In claims which do reach the disclosure stage, most practitioners are still adopting a "traditional" approach to what goes in the list but are leaving out the "neutral" documents which so clogged up lists in the past.

(4) Case management conferences on larger cases and summary assessments of costs have eliminated the "discovery by attrition" process that was commonplace in the past.

(5) Early meetings of experts may render "full scale" disclosure unnecessary.

(6) In large cases if parties want or need "*Peruvian Guano*" disclosure they can still get it (see especially Part E5 and Appendix 9 of the "*Commercial Court Guide*").

(7) The old process of "disclosure by attrition" will not be tolerated see, in particular, *Morgan v Needhams* [1999] *The Times,* November 5, in which Stuart-Smith L.J. stated:

> "It seems to me that the claimants' whole approach to discovery has been wrong. It has spawned a vast amount of satellite litigation at great expense which is wholly out of proportion to the amount involved in the claim and counterclaim."

Indeed, *Morgan v Needhams* serves as a salutary warning to those who pursue excessive disclosure for tactical reasons. In that case the claimant solicitors pursued their former client, the defendant, for vast amounts of documentation relating to his counterclaim that were either irrelevant or non-existent. They made numerous applications for further discovery backed up by "unless orders" which, in the Court of Appeal's view, should never have been ordered or sought. The court also made it clear that if any form of "unless order" is to be effective it must specify in the clearest possible terms first, what is to be done and, secondly, within what period. Accordingly, the order under appeal, which required the defendant to disclose, "All those documents which are necessary to prove his case" was described as "pathetic" by Stuart-Smith L.J.

II INTER-PARTY DISCLOSURE UNDER CPR 31

The court has power to order disclosure in all types of claim and may do so at any stage of the proceedings (although traditionally discovery orders before full exchange of case statements were exceedingly   **10–06** rare). The objectives of the rules on disclosure are to save time spent and costs incurred in collecting, listing and producing documentation which is often not central to the determination of the issues in the case. Lord Woolf's belief was that these objectives could be best achieved through greater control by the court and by encouraging the parties and their legal advisers to adopt a more reasonable approach. One of the key features is that searches for documents may be subject to a measure of *proportionality*, thus removing the spectre of armies of paralegals sifting through warehouses full of documents in some remote location. In each case the court will have to balance the cost involved in search and retrieval against the potential forensic benefit.

1. The "Industry Standard": Standard Disclosure

10–07   As is pointed out forcefully in ss 9–10 to 9–20 of *Hollander*, identifying the scope of the party's disclosure obligations under the new rule is by no means easy, especially in cases of any substance. The relevant rule, CPR 31.6, requires a party to disclose only:

"(a) The documents on which he relies; and

(b) The documents which could—

(i) Adversely affect his own case;
(ii) Adversely affect another party's case; or
(iii) Support another party's case and

(c) The documents which he is required to disclose by a relevant practice direction."

Standard disclosure will normally be ordered by the court as part of the first set of directions although it is clear from the wording of CPR 31.5(1) that the court may "otherwise direct" more wide ranging or narrower disclosure. Where an order is silent and merely refers to "disclosure", that is to be understood as meaning "standard disclosure" (see CPR 31.5). If, after standard disclosure and inspection have been given, further disclosure is required either because: (1) it is considered that standard disclosure has not been complied with; or (2) additional disclosure is sought of specific documents or classes of documents, an application may be made to the court under CPR 31.12. As *Hollander* rightly points out, it may be that many documents, when viewed in isolation, do not have any apparent forensic significance, but may do so when viewed within a context of which the disclosing party is, as yet, unaware. Faced with this dilemma what is the lawyer to do? The likely response will be "If in doubt put it in". One cannot help but wonder therefore whether the new "industry standard" has made much difference to the average claim.

2. Definitions
The meaning of the term "disclosure" is stated in CPR 31.2 as follows: **10–08**

"a party discloses a document by stating that the document exists or has existed".

As already noted at 5–37 the definition of document CPR 31.4 is very widely drawn, comprising:

"Anything in which information of any description is recorded".

The breadth of this definition is reinforced by para.2A.1 of PD 31 (Electronic Disclosure) which reminds parties that the definition extends not only to those documents that are held in the parties' current systems but also extends to documents stored on servers and back up systems and documents that have been "deleted". It also extends to additional information stared and associated with electronic documents known as "metadata": an obvious example being information as to previous drafts of an "original" document and the dates upon which different drafts were produced.
The term "copy" is equally comprehensive and consists of:

"Anything onto which information recorded in the document has been copied, by whatever means and whether directly or indirectly".

However CPR 31.9(1) states that a party need not disclose more than one copy of any document unless any, "modification, obliteration, or other marking or feature" brings it within the scope of Standard Disclosure (CPR 31.9(2)). Clearly, there may be occasions on which, for example, handwritten notes made on a copy of a document may give it an additional relevance independent of its original contents.

3. Scope of Duty CPR: 31.8
A party used to be under a duty to give discovery of all documents **10–09**
which were in his, "possession, custody or control". Now, under CPR 31.8, a party is only obliged to disclose documents which were or have been in his "control", namely (CPR 31.8(2)) if:

(a) It is or was in his physical possession;

(b) He has or has had a right to possession of it; or

(c) He has or has had a right to inspect or take a copy of it.

As a general rule, it is only the parties to the proceedings that are under a duty to give disclosure, although, on occasions disputes may arise, especially in the case of claims against companies, as to whether the company or an individual member is the person with the right to possession or inspection. These status issues are comprehensively reviewed in *Hollander* at 9–03. One other interesting feature of CPR 31 is the fact that, in possible contrast to the previous position, the obligation to give disclosure is owed by *all* parties to all parties.

10–10   **Example:** C is suing D1, D2 and D3. The court is now considering what orders to make on disclosure.

Prior to the CPR it was generally assumed that, say, D1 could only be ordered to give discovery to, say, D3 if there was an issue between them (the only conflicting decision being that of Rix J. in *Manatee Towing v Oceanbulk Maritime SA* [1999] Lloyds Rep. 876). It is now clear from the wording of CPR 31.6(b) that there is no such limitation.

4. Duration of Duty: CPR 31.11
10–11   The above rule provides that:

"(1) Any duty of disclosure continues until the proceedings are concluded;

(2) If documents to which that duty extends come to a party's notice at any time during the proceedings, he must immediately notify every other party."

The Court of Appeal considered this in *Vernon v Bosley (No.2)* [1999] Q.B. 18, the facts of which have already been given at 8–14). In criticising his failure to disclose the second report to the defendant, the Court of Appeal held that the duty to give discovery was a continuing one. CPR 31.11 places this on a formal footing.

5. The Solicitor's Duty
10–12   The duty to advise the client on the documents that needed to be retained and made available for discovery purposes was always an onerous one as was emphasised by Megarry J. in *Rockwell Machine Tool & Co. v EP Barrus Ltd* [1968] 2 All E.R. 98 in which he stated:

"It seems to me necessary for solicitors to take positive steps to ensure that their clients appreciate at an early stage of the litigation, promptly after the writ has been issued, not only the duty of discovery and its width but also the importance of not destroying documents which might possibly have to be disclosed. This burden extends, in my judgment, to taking steps to ensure that in any corporate organisation knowledge of this burden is passed on to any who may be affected by it".

However, if anything, the burden on the solicitor has intensified, particularly in cases involving large amounts of electronically stored data. Valuable guidance on this can be found by going to USA cases, in particular the series of four decisions handed down by Scheindlin USDJ in: *Zubulake v UBS Warburg* LLC 217 F.R.D. 309 (known as *"Zubulake I, III, IV and V"* respectively). So far as the lawyers' duties were concerned, the judge had this to say (*"Zubulake IV"* at [12]):

"The scope of a party's preservation obligation can be described as follows: once a party reasonably anticipates litigation, it must suspend its routine document retention/destruction policy and put in place a 'litigation hold' to ensure the preservation of relevant documents. As a general rule, that litigation hold does not apply to inaccessible backup tapes (e.g., those typically maintained solely for the purpose of disaster recovery) which may continue to be recycled on the schedule set forth in the company's policy. On the other hand, if backup tapes are accessible (i.e., actively used for information retrieval), then such tapes would likely be subject to the litigation hold. However, it does make sense to create one exception to this general rule. If a company can identify where particular employee documents of 'key players' to the existing or threatened litigation should be preserved if the information contained in those tapes is not otherwise available. This exception applies to all backup tapes."

Bearing in mind that the vast majority of commercial communication is now in electronic format, the burdens on legal advisers are extremely onerous (see further *Hollander* Chapter 1 and 9–05). Section 2A of the revised Practice Direction to CPR 31 now specifically deals specifically with electronic disclosure. Under it (2A.2) parties are expected prior to the first case management conference, to discuss any issues that may arise regarding searches for and preservation of electronic documents, including matters such as storage and retrieval systems and document retention policies. However lawyers need to follow the *Zubulake* guidance so far as advice to their own clients is concerned. One particular trend seen in recent cases in the United States (albeit in front of juries) has been to invite an adverse inference to be drawn from the destruction of potentially relevant electronic data ("despoliation") on the basis of the ancient doctrine of *"omnia praesumuntur contra spoliatorem"* (roughly translated as "if you shred, you are dead"). Although the possibility of such inferences was recognised by the Court of Appeal in *Arrow Nominees v*

Blackledge [2000] EWCA Civ 200, even to the extent of striking a party out if his conduct had prevented a fair trial, there has not, as yet been an English case in which a spoliation inference has been drawn. An attempt to rely on it was made unsuccessfully in *IS Innovative Software v Howes* [2004] EWCA Civ 275. However, Neuberger L.J. (at [90] onwards) recognised the existence of the doctrine and approved the headnote in *Malhotra v Dhawan* [1997] Media L. Rep. 391 which states:

> "If it were found that the destruction of evidence was carried out deliberately so as to hinder the proof of the plaintiff's claim, then such finding of fact would obviously reflect on the credibility of the destroyer. In such circumstances it would enable the court to disregard the evidence of the destroyer in the application of the principle".

It is important that legal advisers make their clients aware of such inferences: there is bound to be a major case that is won or lost on it before too long.

6. Disclosure by List: CPR 31.10

10–13 As already noted, an order for disclosure will usually be made as part of the first set of directions in a claim. Having made a reasonable search for documents falling within the standard disclosure definition, the disclosing party must (although they may agree in writing to dispense with lists and/or disclosure statements, see CPR 31.10(8)) make a list of those documents required to be disclosed and which are or have been in his control (PD 31, para.1.3.). The list of documents, usually in the prescribed Form N265 is then served on all other parties within the time provided by the court's direction. Under CPR 31.13, the court may also direct (or the parties may agree in writing) that disclosure or inspection or both shall take place in stages. This is a particularly useful power where it is clear that there are certain key issues that merit early investigation. An obvious example would be where there was to be a "split trial". It would in that case probably be disproportionate to have full disclosure of *quantum* documents, although the defendant might, even then, be able to argue that he was entitled to sufficient particulars to enable him to make a Pt 36 payment (see the pre-CPR cases of *Baldock v Addison* [1995] 1 W.L.R. 158 and *Kapur v JW Francis & Co (No.1) The Times*, March 4, 1998).

However, as yet parties (and the courts) are not being particularly radical. For example, the court could, in theory, be invited to order that a party list his documents in the categories set out in CPR 31.6, starting with, for example:

"those documents the claimant/defendant intends to rely on at trial".

The writer has never heard of this being done, but it is hard to see why in some cases it would not be entirely appropriate, for example, where:
C serves a list containing 1,000s of documents, many of which are of no obvious relevance, knowing that it will cost D a fortune to inspect them lest the "smoking gun" is to be found somewhere amongst them.

Nor is there any radical departure from the standard sequence of disclosure, followed by exchange of witness statements, culminating in directions on expert evidence. Indeed the Court of Appeal have recently stated (see *Watford Petroleum Ltd v Interoil Trading SA* [2003] EWCA Civ 141, discussed at 11–17) that even in cases where bad faith is alleged, it would need quite exceptional circumstances to justify an order for disclosure to follow exchange of witness statements.

7. The List of Documents: Form N265

CPR 31.10 and PD 31 para.3 set out the detailed instructions for completing the list. A consideration of these requirements is outside the scope of this work and reference should be made to Chapter 30 of *O'Hare and Browne* especially 30–14. Nevertheless it is important to be aware of the three parts into which the list is to be divided. They are:

Part 1 The party giving disclosure states in his list:

"I have control of the documents numbered and listed here. I do not object to you inspecting them/producing copies."

Part 2 Here, the party must state:

"I have control of the documents numbered and listed here, but I object to you inspecting them."

And then state:

"I object to you inspecting these documents because:"

As various commentators have pointed out, this is an odd provision since it appears to require a party not only to disclose the *existence* of privileged documents, but also to *identify* them. If followed it would drive a coach and horses through legal professional privilege. This anomaly is discussed further at 8–16.

10–14

Part 3 Here the party is required to state:

"I have had the documents numbered and listed below, but they are no longer in my control."

The side note to Form N265 requires the disclosing party to then state when each documents in this category was last in his control and where it is now.

8. The Disclosure Statement

10–15   In signing the disclosure statement the party certifies that he has carried out a reasonable and proportionate search for the purpose of disclosing all the documents required by the court's order. The disclosing party may however omit search for certain documents on the grounds the search that would go beyond what is reasonable and proportionate. The disclosure statement is mandatory (CPR 31.10(5)). The factors relevant in deciding the reasonableness of a search are set out in CPR 31.7(2) which states that they include:

"(a) The number of documents involved;

(b) The nature and complexity of the proceedings;

(c) The ease and expense of retrieval of any particular document; and

(d) The significance of any document which is likely to be located during the search".

Paragraph 2A.4 of PD 31 now provides additional guidance as to the factors that might be relevant to CPR 31.7(2)(c) in cases involving electronic disclosure. It is clear that any party who is called upon to justify a limited search will need to be able to adduce *evidence*, for example, of the cost of search and retrieval.

9. Inspection

10–16   In larger cases, inspection may prove to be more expensive than disclosure. This has led on occasions to abuses of the system, for example, the party who disclosed everything knowing that it would cost a fortune for his opponent to carry out a "due diligence" inspection. A fear of missing the "smoking gun" has always given litigators sleepless nights. The new system was set up to police such excesses: here is not the place to comment on whether or not it has succeeded. The procedure for inspection is set out in CPR 31.15 which provides that:

"(1) 'the inspecting party must give the disclosing party written notice of his wish to inspect a document;

(2) the disclosing party must permit inspection not more than sevem days after receipt of the notice;

(3) the inspecting party may request a copy of the document and (provided) he also undertakes to pay reasonable copying costs) is entitled to be supplied with a copy within 15 days."

The right (or duty) to resist inspection on the grounds of privilege or public interest immunity has been preserved by CPR 31.3(1) which states that:

"A party to whom a document has been disclosed has a right to inspect that document except where:

(a) the document is no longer in the control of the party who disclosed it; or

(b) the party disclosing the document has a right or a duty to withhold inspection of it."

However apart from resisting inspection under CPR 31.3(1), CPR 31.3(2) also provides in addition that a party may resist inspection of potentially "adverse" documents disclosed under Standard Disclosure by including notice in his Disclosure Statement that inspection would be "disproportionate" to the issues in the case. Whether inspection would or would not be disproportionate to a particular case is closely allied to the concept of "reasonableness" in disclosure. There is no definition of proportionality in CPR 31 and the only guidance given is provided in CPR 31.7(2) already referred to at 10–15. In cases involving large amounts of electronic disclosure paragraph 2A.3 of PD 31 states that the parties should co-operate at an early stage in as to the format in which electronic copy documents are to be provided on inspection.

10. *"Corporate" Disclosure*
There is no doubt that all common law systems face enormous challenges if they are to maintain a viable system for resolving large-scale corporate disputes. The recent corporate scandals in the United States, the massive paper chase in the *Three Rivers* case and the expansion of electronic communication serve as salutary examples of those challenges. All the following short paragraphs will attempt to do is to summarise the system that is currently in place under the CPR. The practicalities of large-scale disclosure are addressed comprehensively in Chapter 9 of *Hollander*.   **10–17**

(a) *General*
Where the disclosure statement is made on behalf of a corporate litigant, firm, association or other organisation, CPR 31.10(7) requires   **10–18**

that the maker of the statement must also state why he or she is the appropriate person to make the statement. Under PD 31, para.4.3, where CPR 31.10(7) applies, the details given in the disclosure statement about the person making the statement must include:

(1) His/her name and address; and

(2) The office or position she holds in the disclosing party.

(b) *Implications*

10–19 The concept of the disclosure statement represents a significant departure from previous procedure in that, under the former rules, the burden of carrying out the search for documents often fell on the disclosing party's legal advisers. If, at a later stage, it was found that inadequate discovery had been given, then someone within the party's organisation would be required to swear an affidavit deposing that all documents within particular categories had been disclosed. The following points now need to be borne in mind.

(1) Under CPR 31.10(6), and PD 31 para.4.4, it is clear that the person signing the disclosure statement must have an understanding of the duty to search and all that this entails and also that he has knowledge of the documents and issues in the case. The legal adviser is under a duty to ensure that the signatory understands this.

(2) For large corporate parties or organisations such as local authorities, that person will normally be an in-house lawyer with responsibility for the case, but this situation can occasionally present problems. For example, it may be that the person with first hand knowledge of the dispute is a departmental head who does not occupy a senior position in the organisation and it may, therefore, not be fair to expect him or her to take responsibility for a decision that should be taken at a higher corporate level. On the other hand, if the documents are all electronically generated and stored, as will usually be the case, the only person with an understanding of this process may be the client's IT systems manager.

(3) Administrative problems may also arise when documents that have to be disclosed originate from different departments within the organisation. The obligations imposed by the disclosure statement itself will require organisations to have sound and efficient document management systems.

(4) It may well be that a "Disclosure Manager" will have to be appointed within an organisation before specific litigation is even

contemplated to ensure that important data is not inadvertently destroyed before its full significance is appreciated. Opponents will always seek to invite adverse inferences from missing data and in the current climate of cynicism they may be hard to rebut.

(c) *What is a Reasonable Search?*
There is no guidance (save in the case of electronic documents—as to   **10–20**
which see below) in the rules as to the extent to which a search for adverse material would be reasonable, as the requirement will clearly vary according to the circumstances of the particular claim. The extent of the search must be discussed with the client at all stages of litigation planning (see further *Hollander* Chapter 1). It is also incumbent upon clients to provide their legal advisers with realistic information as to the quantity of documents and the time and expense that may be involved in carrying out the search, a task which is not always carried out with a great deal of enthusiasm. So far as electronic disclosure is concerned, para.2A.5 of PD 31 states:

"It may be reasonable to search some or all of the parties' electronic storage systems. In some circumstances, it may be reasonable to search for electronic documents by means of keyword searches (agreed so far as possible between the parties) even where a full review of each and every document would be unreasonable. There may be other forms of electronic search that may be appropriate in particular circumstances".

There is a very useful section on some of the tactical implications of electronic disclosure in *Hollander* at 9–44 to 9–47: what is absolutely essential is that there is a member of the legal team sufficiently computer literate to understand the client's and the opposing parties' IT systems.

11. Specific Disclosure: CPR 31.12
This is the "second stage" of the disclosure process that a party may   **10–21**
need to move on to because he seeks disclosure of "line of enquiry" documents. Note that PD 31, para.5 seems to suggest that if a party fails to give adequate *Standard* Disclosure the application should also be for Specific Disclosure. However, what is clear is that successive applications for further disclosure for whatever reason will incur the court's disapproval unless the applicant can produce evidence first as to the potential *relevance* of the documents sought and, secondly at least some estimate of the likely *cost* of retrieval and inspection. The court cannot be expected to exercise a discretion in a vacuum: of particular relevance is the wide power that the court has to order costs estimates under para.6.3 of PD 43.

(a) *The Power*

10–22   Under CPR 31.12(2) the court may order a party to:

(a) Disclose documents or classes of documents specified in the order; and/or

(b) Carry out a search to the extent stated in the order; and/or

(c) Disclose any documents located as a result of that search.

Relevance will lie at the core of any application along with the ability to put before the court evidence as to the likely cost of search, disclosure and inspection: the court cannot be expected to apply proportionality otherwise. In view of the observations made by the Court of Appeal in *Leigh v Michelin Tyre plc* [2004] 1 W.L.R. 846 as to the value of costs estimates as a tool of case management, it may be prudent to file an estimate as part of your evidence in support in a heavy case (see also Section 6 of the Costs Practice Direction). The applicant is not required to satisfy any specific necessity test, but the court must have regard at all times to the "Overriding Objective" in CPR 1 and the crucial issues of cost and forensic potential. Furthermore, PD 31/5.2 makes it clear that all applications should be supported by *evidence*; in other words advocacy alone will not suffice. Valuable guidance can be found in both the *Chancery Guide* (4.4) and the *Commercial Court Guide* (Section E) as to the correct approach. In particular a party should consider:

(1) Is the further disclosure necessary to do justice?

(2) Is it proportionate to the issue involved?

(3) Could it be dealt with more economically by other means, for example, "sampling" or under CPR 18?

One particularly important feature of CPR 31.12(2)(a) is the reference made to "classes" of documents. By analogy with the case law on applications for non-party disclosure under CPR 31.17 (see, in particular *Three Rivers District Council v Bank of England* (No.4) [2002] 4 All E.R. 881) the court has power to order disclosure of a class of documents even though only some of them might be relevant to the issues in the case: in other words a party may be allowed to "fish" provided he can persuade the court that the lake is not likely to be empty.

(b) *Discussion*

10–23   Paragraph 5.2 makes it quite clear that the application notice must be supported by evidence but does not prescribe what evidence should be tendered. However, at the very least, you will need to set out:

(1) A brief explanation of the nature of the dispute;

(2) The stage that the proceedings have reached; and

(3) The facts which lead you to believe that the documents sought exist, are disclosable (at least within a class), are within the control of the respondent to the application, and do not involve disproportionate expenditure.

Paragraph 5.4 of PD 31 states that in deciding whether or not to make an order for specific disclosure, the court will take into account all the circumstances of the case and, in particular the overriding objective. Paragraph 5.4. goes on to state that:

"Where the court concludes that the party from whom disclosure is sought has failed adequately to comply with the obligations imposed by an order for disclosure (whether by failing to make a sufficient search for documents or otherwise) the court will usually make such order as is necessary to ensure that those obligations are properly complied with."

CPR 31.12 does not specifically state the format for compliance with an order for specific disclosure. Form N265 can be adapted but the court may require a greater degree of formality and could order that the disclosing party file evidence or certify in some form whether or not the documents exist and/or the extent of any search made. Obviously, any order may have sanctions attached under CPR 3.1(3) to (5) in the event of non-compliance.

III MATTERS ARISING DURING DISCLOSURE

The next section deals with a number of additional issues that can cause problems during the case management stage. Many of them touch and concern evidence issues, especially privilege but, for the sake of convenience, they are addressed here.   **10–24**

1. "Documents Referred to" CPR 31.14
As already noted, orders for disclosure (other than under CPR 31.16) are not normally made until the case has been fully pleaded out. However, a party may sometimes acquire the right to *inspect* documents to which this rule applies.   **10–25**

(a) The General Rule: CPR 31.14
Apart from the general right to inspect documents disclosed either by standard disclosure or specific disclosure, under CPR 31.14, a party has a right to inspect a document referred to in: **10–26**

(1) A statement of case;

(2) A witness statement;

(3) An affidavit; or

(4) Subject to CPR 35.10(4), to *apply* to inspect any documents referred to in an expert's report.

These rights arise as soon as the document concerned is referred to, even if this precedes the order for Standard Disclosure. The use of the words, "referred to" indicate that a specific reference must be made before the right to inspect (or apply) arises. Where there is an inference as opposed to a specific reference to the existence of a document, it may be more appropriate to make an application for specific disclosure under CPR 31.12. Where a party makes reference to a document which is *not* in their control, the document may be obtained by seeking an order under CPR 31.17 (Non-Party Disclosure) or CPR 34.2 (Witness Order).

(b) *Experts: CPR 35.10(4)*

10–27   Under CPR 35.10(3), the expert's report must state:

"the substance of all material instructions, whether written or oral, upon which the report is based".

Although, instructions to experts are disclosable, the court will not order disclosure of any specific document referred to in those instructions or permit any questioning in court in relation to them, (other than by the party who instructed the expert) unless (CPR 35.10(4)) it is satisfied namely that:

"there are reasonable grounds to consider that the statement of instructions is inaccurate or incomplete".

It is now clear that no inspection will be ordered unless CPR 35.10(4) is satisfied, and even then, only as a matter of discretion see *Lucas v Barking, Havering and Redbridge NHS Trust [2003] 4 All E.R. 720* discussed further at 12–58.

2. *Authenticity of Documents Disclosed: CPR 31.19*

10–28   As already noted at 5–40, a party is deemed to admit the authenticity of documents disclosed to him under CPR 31 unless he serves notice that he wishes the document to be proved at trial. A notice to prove a document must be served by the latest date for serving witness statements: or within *seven days* (an extraordinarily tight time limit) of disclosure of the document, whichever is later.

3. Failure to Comply with Standard or Specific Disclosure
The court can make "unless" orders under its general case manage-   **10–29**
ment powers (see CPR 3.1). However, care needs to be taken to ensure
that such an order is exercised with sufficient clarity (see *Morgan v
Needhams* discussed at 10–05). A further sanction is imposed by CPR
31.21 which provides that:

> "A party may not rely on any document which he fails to disclose
> or in respect of which he fails to permit inspection unless the court
> gives permission".

There are, as yet, no decided cases on this rule but, since it involves
the application of a sanction, the court's discretion will be governed by the checklist in CPR 3.9 and the extensive case law on late
witness statements (see further 11–20). In the one case in which late
documentary evidence was allowed in by the trial judge, the Court of
Appeal adopted a broad inclusionary approach (see *Hayes v Transco
plc* [2003] EWCA 1261 discussed further at 14–11).

4. Documents Inadvertently Disclosed
Prior to the introduction of the CPR a substantial body of case law   **10–30**
had built up dealing with privileged documents whose contents had
been revealed by mistake (the current law was clarified by the Court
of Appeal in *Goddard v Nationwide Building Society [1987] Q.B.
670*). Although, as a general rule, privilege will be lost by waiver in
such cases (even though unintended), the Court of Appeal in
Guinness Peat Properties Ltd v Fitzroy Robinson [1987] 1 W.L.R. 1027
held that an order could be made for delivery up and an injunction
granted to restrain a party from using any of the information disclosed in the document where:

(1) inspection was obtained by fraud; or

(2) at the time of inspection, the party inspecting the document,
realised that he had been permitted to see it only by reason of
an "obvious mistake".

This principle was further developed in a number of later decisions.
The Court of Appeal in *Pizzey v Ford Motor Company* [1994] P.I.Q.R.
15, a case in which the claimant's solicitors mistakenly sent the defendants' solicitors two "unfavourable" medical reports, held that an
applicant faced a heavy burden in showing that the mistake was
"obvious". If two reports are sent with a covering letter, where is the
"obvious" mistake? In that case relief was refused.
In *IBM v Phoenix* [1995] 1 All E.R. 413 Aldous J. had to consider
whether the test for obviousness was "objective" or "subjective".

In that case, the defendant's "Road Map" (Case Strategy Plan) was inadvertently included in a copious quantity of documents sent to the claimant's solicitors for collation and copying. He held that the test of "obviousness" was *objective*, based on the standard of the reasonably competent solicitor. Blackburne J. took the principle a stage further in *Ablitt v Mills and Reeve, The Times*, October 25, 1995, a case in which counsel's clerk had delivered the claimant's papers to the defendant's solicitors by mistake. Their insurers instructed them to read the papers before returning them. Blackburne J.'s injunction included an order removing the defendant's solicitors from the case.

Initially there was some uncertainty as to whether CPR 31.20 had changed the law in this area. The rule simply provides that:

> "Where a party inadvertently allows a privileged document to be inspected, the party who has inspected the document may use it or its contents only with the permission of the court."

However the Court of Appeal in *Breeze v John Stacey and Sons* [1999] *The Times*, July 8 held that the CPR reforms do not affect the established case law. In that case the defendants had inadvertently exhibited over 100 pages of privileged material to an affidavit in support of a strike-out application. The Court held that:

(1) If a party appeared to rely on privileged material in evidence the recipient was entitled to assume privilege was waived;

(2) The recipient was under no duty of care to check with the sender whether he really intended to waive privilege.

The only difference that CPR 31.20 appears to make is that, at any rate in theory, it is no longer necessary for the disclosing party to apply for a "*Guinness Peat*" order, since the document or the information it contains cannot be used by the other party without the court's permission. The post-CPR position has now been clarified by the Court of Appeal in *Al Fayed v Met Police Commissioner* [2002] EWCA Civ 780. In it the court identified the following principles.

(1) It is for the party giving inspection to decide what privileged documents, if any, he wants his opponent to see.

(2) Although the privilege belongs to the client he clothes his solicitor with ostensible authority to waive it.

(3) The solicitor considering the disclosed document owes no duty of care to ascertain whether or not his opponent is waiving privilege. He is entitled to assume that he is.

(4) If a party permits inspection by mistake it will generally be too late to reclaim privilege.

(5) The court has equitable jurisdiction to intervene where justice requires it, for example where inspection has been procured by fraud.

(6) Absent fraud, the court might intervene where documents have been made available for inspection due to an obvious mistake.

(7) A mistake is likely to be "obvious" where;

    (a) The solicitor actually appreciates the mistake is obvious before making use of the document; or

    (b) It would be obvious to a reasonable solicitor in his position.

(8) Where a solicitor gives detailed consideration to the question and honestly concludes that the material has not been made available by mistake this fact will be a relevant and important pointer.

(9) In many cases within (7)(a) or (b) it may still be unjust or inequitable to grant relief;

(10) Since the jurisdiction is equitable there are no rigid rules.

The decision is noteworthy for two further reasons. First the court held that the same principles apply when Public Interest Immunity is inadvertently waived. Secondly, the defendants had initially objected to inspection of the documents concerned, two opinions from leading counsel supplied to the Crown Prosecution Service, on the grounds of irrelevance. They were, arguably, bound by their objection, having never specifically asserted LPP or PII. The moral of the story is that it is always prudent to "go belt and braces". On the facts, the Court of Appeal held that privilege had been waived, influenced largely by the fact that the documents concerned had appeared, duly indexed and paginated in a lever arch file of copy documents served on the claimant's solicitors as part of Standard Disclosure. There was, therefore, no evidence to suggest that they had been disclosed "by mistake".

5. Undertaking not to use for a Collateral Purpose

(a) Background

The scope and nature of the implied undertaking has its roots in the principle that a party who is compelled to disclose documents, many of them highly confidential, as part of the disclosure process should be protected by a general embargo against their use by an opponent for any purpose other than in the instant proceedings. It is a corollary to   **10–31** that protection that the embargo will generally lift as soon as the document forms part of public proceedings. The rule, surprisingly, is not of great antiquity having first been fully recognised by Jenkins J. in *Alterskye v Scott* [1948] 1 All E.R. 469. Its history and current application is fully covered in Chapter 27 of *Phipson* and Chapter 19 of *Hollander*. It operates both as an exclusionary rule of evidence and provides an aggrieved party with remedies of enforcement, including the right to apply to have any fresh proceedings brought on the basis of such documents struck out as an abuse of process. The undertaking has also been held to apply to documents disclosed during assessment of costs (see *Bourns Inc v Raychem Corp* [1999] 3 All E.R. 154).

Although the undertaking does not prevent a party adding new causes of action to the instant proceedings (see, for example, *Omar v Omar* [1995] 1 W.L.R. 1428), in any other case, a party can only be released from his undertaking in exceptional circumstances if the release would not occasion injustice to the person giving disclosure. This was confirmed by the House of Lords in *Crest Homes v Marks* [1987] A.C. 829 in which leave was granted to use material disclosed under a Search Order in a claim brought in 1985 for the purpose of bringing contempt proceedings in relation to an earlier claim brought in *1984*.

Breaches have traditionally been heavily punished, see for example *Miller v Scorey* [1996] 3 All E.R. 18 in which Robert Walker J. struck out an action brought in breach even though leave would have been given leave if it had been sought. In *Clarke v Ardington* [2001] EWCA Civ 585 a case on non-party disclosure under CPR 31.17 (see 10–37) Tuckey L.J. conceded that a party who made use of information disclosed in an earlier case to assist the conduct of subsequent cases was liable to be struck out for abuse of process. *Clarke v Ardington* involved a series of claims under "Helphire" credit repair and credit hire agreements. Late on in the appeal counsel for the claimants suggested that the defendants, in effect the liability insurers were devising defences of ever-increasing sophistication based on information gleaned from earlier credit-hire cases they had defended. If indeed, the implied undertaking does stretch this far, its consequences could be profound, for example in industrial disease or disrepair cases. As yet no litigant has sought to raise the *Clarke v Ardington* point directly.

(b) *The Position under the CPR*

10–32   This is now governed by CPR 31.22 which provides that:

> "(1) A party to whom a document has been disclosed may use the document only for the purpose of the proceedings in which it is disclosed, except where:

(a) the document has been read to or by the court, or referred to, at a hearing which has been held in public;

(b) the court gives permission; or

(c) the party who disclosed the document and the person to whom the document belongs agree.

(2) The court may make an order restricting or prohibiting the use of a document which has been disclosed, even where the document has been read to or by the court, or referred to, at a hearing which has been held in public.

(3) An application for such an order may be made:

(b) by a party; or

(c) by an person to whom the document belongs".

There have already been a number of important decisions on various aspects of the rule. CPR 31.22(2) (restricting or prohibiting disclosure) was considered by the Court of Appeal in *Lilly Icos v Pfizer Ltd* [2002] 1 W.L.R. 2253. The court, in granting a "confidentiality embargo" on sensitive financial data that had been disclosed by the claimants during the trial of a patent claim, laid down the following principles to be applied on such an application:

(1) There was a strong public interest in securing open justice, hence a gagging order would rarely be granted (even if the documents, as here, had been disclosed "in confidence");

(2) The importance of the documents to the issues was a relevant factor;

(3) It was not enough for the applicant to state that the document was "confidential": specific reasons had to be given as to why the applicant would be damaged if the contents went into the public domain;

(4) Where, as here, the material was highly sensitive and the trial could be followed without reference to it, such an order was appropriate.

It should be remembered that the undertaking will often now cease to apply in relation to documents relied on as evidence on an *interim application* because these will normally be heard in public (see CPR 31.22(1)(a)). It is also important to remember that documents placed before the judge in "open" proceedings are presumed to have been read by him (see *Barings Plc v Cooper Lybrand* [2000] 1 W.L.R. 2353). Note also that the implied undertaking does not arise where the document is inspected under CPR 31.14. It will be recalled that CPR

31.14 entitles a party to inspect any document referred to in a statement of case, witness statement, witness summary, affidavit or (subject to CPR 35.10(4)) expert's report (see 10–25).

So far as *pre-claim* disclosure is concerned, for example under a Protocol, it is probably wise to require an express undertaking in similar terms to that imposed by CPR 31.22, since it is not entirely clear whether the rule applies in this situation. The meaning of "disclosure" in CPR 31.22 once proceedings have *begun* was clarified by the Court of Appeal in *Smithkline Beecham plc v Generics (UK) Ltd* [2003] 4 All E.R. 1302. This appeal, which involved no less than three sets of highly complex patent proceedings, established the following important principles:

(1) Once proceedings have begun, documents which are:

  • Disclosed voluntarily; or
  • Referred to in a case statement, witness statement or expert's report (subject to the inspection provisions of CPR 31.14)

  rather than under an order for disclosure are nevertheless within the definition of "disclosed" in CPR 31.2 and, hence, subject to the implied understanding in CPR 31.22

(2) In deciding whether to permit a party to use disclosed documents for another purpose, the interests of justice were central to the balancing exercise between the interests of the party seeking to use the document(s) and the person seeking the protection of CPR 31.22.

(3) Although each case would depend on its own facts. A material consideration would be whether the document(s) could have been obtained from a third party under CPR 31.17.

(4) The court could always (as here) impose strict conditions as to the use of the documents.

IV PRE-ACTION AND NON-PARTY DISCLOSURE CPR 31.16 AND 17

1. *Pre CPR: The Problem*

10–33   Prior to the CPR coming into force, orders for pre-action discovery against potential parties or discovery against non-parties could only be obtained against a potential party in personal injury and fatal accidents claims under s.34 of the Supreme Court Act 1981, or against an "innocent facilitator" in *Norwich Pharmacal* proceedings (see 10–42). A classic example of the difficulty that this could cause can be seen in

AXA Equity and Law v Nat West Bank Plc [1998] P.N.L.R. 433 in which Rix J. held that the court had no power to give what was in essence non-party discovery under the guise of a *Norwich Pharmacal* action in a case where the prospective tortfeasor's identity was *already known.*

Facts: C made what turned out to be a very unfortunate investment in a hotel company CH plc having placed reliance on a statement made by CH's auditors X as to CH plc's financial health. Knowing that X had been subjected to strong criticism by the trial judge in subsequent criminal proceedings relating to the collapse of CH plc, C now wished to sue X in negligence and breach of the Financial Services Act 1986. They sought disclosure of information relating to CH plc's financial position from various third parties so as to be able to adequately plead their case against X.   **10-34**

Under the law as it then stood they had no means of obtaining pre-claim disclosure from X, and their *Norwich Pharmacal* claim failed due to the limited nature of that form of the relief available (see further 10-42). The position would now be radically different since C could seek pre-claim disclosure from X under CPR 31.16 and follow this up with an application for non-party disclosure under CPR 31.17 once proceedings had commenced. Note also that courts are prepared, exceptionally, to grant *Norwich Pharmacal* relief even where the identity of the wrongdoer is known if that is the most cost effective way of providing the applicant with the information that he needs (see Jacob J. in *Carlton Film Distributors v VDC plc* [2003] F.S.R. 47).

2. *Wider Disclosure under the CPR*

The position has now radically changed. By providing the facilities that had hitherto only been available in personal injury and fatal accident claims to all types of proceedings.   **10-35**

(a) *Pre-Action Disclosure: CPR 31.16*

This is a available against a person who is "likely to be a party to subsequent proceedings" provided: **10-36**

(1) The application is supported by *evidence* (CPR 31.16(2)); and

(2) The documents sought come within the scope of standard disclosure (CPR 31.16(3)(c)); and

(3) Disclosure is "necessary":

    (b) to dispose fairly of the anticipated proceedings (CPR 31.16(3)(d)(i)); or

    (c) save costs (CPR 31.16(d)(iii); or

    (d) it will assist resolution of the dispute without the need to commence proceedings (CPR 31.16(3)(a(ii)).

Pre-action disclosure under CPR 31.16 was first considered by Dyson J. in *Burrells Wharf Freehold v Galliard Homes, unreported, July 1, 1999*, a building claim in which the prospective claimants sought disclosure of Building Regulations correspondence between the developers of a housing project (the prospective defendants) and the relevant local authority. The judge was satisfied that disclosure was "necessary" to reduce the potential cost of a preliminary expert's report by 50 per cent. The Court of Appeal has also considered the new rule in *Bermuda International Securities Ltd v KPMG* [2001] 3 C.P.L.R. 271 and *Black v Sumitomo Corp* [2002] 1 W.L.R. 1562. Following these decisions the following interpretative guidance emerges.

(1) The criteria in CPR 31.16 go to *jurisdiction*: determination of the application involves the exercise of a further discretion under which the applicant has to satisfy the court that the disclosure sought is justified (*Black*).

(2) The applicant does not have a burden of proving on the balance of probabilities, and based on extraneous evidence, that the respondent is "likely to be a party". Following earlier guidance in personal injury claims (see *Dunning v Board of Governors of Unites Liverpool Hospitals* [1973] 2 All E.R. 454) it is enough to show that the applicant "may well" be able to mount a cause of action if the documents sought reveal that he has one (*Black*).

(3) Provided the applicant can establish the jurisdictional criteria prescribed by the rules he does not have to go on and establish "exceptional circumstances" (*Burrells Wharf*) but the bringing forward of standard disclosure should not be seen as a "routine" step (*Black*).

(4) The remedy is designed to cover a vast range of situations and it is not appropriate at this stage for the Court of Appeal to lay down any hard and fast guidelines (*Bermuda*). Relevant factors will include the importance of the material and its non-availability from other sources. The more focused the application, and the more limited the disclosure sought, the more likely it is that the court will exercise its discretion in the applicant's favour (*Black*).

(5) The power is limited to those documents which would, if proceedings were to be commenced, come within standard disclosure. Accordingly, the applicant will normally have to set out the likely issues in the case and explain why the documents sought are material to those issues (*Bermuda/Black*). However, at any rate, in personal injury cases, pre-action disclosure has been ordered in the past purely on the basis of circumstantial

inference analogous to *res ipsa loquitur*, see *Dunning v Board of Governors of United Liverpool Hospitals* [1973] 2 All E.R. 454).

(6) Although the respondent should be entitled to the costs of providing the actual disclosure, the costs of the application may not be his if, for example, he has unreasonably resisted requests for disclosure (see CPR 48.2) (*Burrells Wharf/Bermuda*).

The contents of the order are governed by CPR 31.16(4) which is outside the scope of this summary. Detailed commentary can be found in *O'Hare and Browne* at 30.039 and 2–27 to 2–48 of *Hollander*.

(b) Non Party Disclosure CPR 31.17

The criteria and procedure for such applications are similar to those **10–37** under CPR 31.16 (see further *O'Hare and Browne* 30–034 and *Hollander and Browne* 4–21 to 4–67. Note in particular that the court may only make an order for disclosure where the documents are "likely" to:

(1) Support the case of the applicant; or

(2) Adversely affect the case of one of the other parties.

The power has been considered in a number of recent decisions. The decision of Pumfrey J. in *Re Howglen* [2001] 1 All E.R. 376 in which he held, amongst other things, that:

(1) The jurisdiction must be exercised with some caution;

(2) The non-party should not be left with the task of identifying whether the documents sought come within the class required by CPR 31.17(3);

(3) The court must accordingly be satisfied that the documents sought do in fact exist,

(4) Access should preferably be sought under CPR 31.17 rather than by "advance *subpoena*" under CPR 34.2,

now appears unduly restrictive. A broader approach was adopted by the Court of Appeal in *Clarke v Ardington Electrical Services* [2001] EWCA Civ 585. The case concerned a number of small road traffic claims involving credit hire and repair agreements. Disclosure was ordered by the trial judge against the engineer inspectors and approved repairers of the crash damaged cars to enable him to understand the basis of the underlying transactions. His decision was upheld by the Court of Appeal. A similarly broad approach was adopted in *American Home Products Corp v Novartis Pharmaceuticals UK Ltd (No.2)* [2001] EWCA Civ 165 in which the Court of Appeal held that disclosure of a "class" could be ordered even when some of the documents in that class might not be relevant. This approach was followed by the Court of Appeal in *Three Rivers DC v Bank of England (No.4)* [2002] 4 All E.R. 881 in which the claimants sought disclosure as against the Treasury Solicitor of the 708 files of material held at the Public Records Office in Kew relating to the inquiry of Lord Justice Bingham into the collapse of BCCI (the background to the application is set out in *Hollander* at 4–28). In particular, the court laid down the following principles:

(1) "Likely" means "may well" rather than "More probably those not";

(2) It is immaterial that one or more of the documents in a class might turn out not to be "adverse" or "supportive".

There is much valuable commentary on the rule in *Hollander* at 4–33 to 4–67.

V OTHER FORMS OF PRE-ACTION AND NON-PARTY DISCLOSURE

10–38   Although more a matter of litigation procedure, evidence collection is still of sufficient importance to justify a brief mention. The following additional methods of evidence collection will need to be considered in cases of any substance. Chapter 6 of *Hollander*, especially 6–32 to 6–36, also contains much valuable material. CPR 31.18 specifically provides that:

"Rules 31.16 and 31.17 do not limit any other power which the court may have to order-

(a) disclosure before proceedings have started;
(b) disclosure against a person who is not a party to the proceedings."

Quite apart from that, there are numerous other ways in which members of the public have rights of access to information held by various bodies. Examples include the following.

1. Freezing Injunctions

10–39   This brutal remedy (see CPR 25.1(f) and PD 25 paragraph 6) is only available in the High Court. It has the effect of restraining a party not only from removing assets from the jurisdiction but also from dealing with them save as permitted by the court. It is the subject of detailed commentary in *O'Hare and Browne* at 27.025 to 27.039 and *Hollander* at 3–54 to 3–82. Its relevance to disclosure lies in the fact that courts regularly grant ancillary orders requiring the respondent to file evidence as to his assets, usually in the form of an affidavit. It is now regarded as an essential component of the process (see *Motorola Credit Corp v Uzan (No.2)* [2004] 1 W.L.R. 113). The onerous nature of the order imposed will often have the effect of bringing the litigation to an end.

2. Search Orders

This remedy (see CPR 25.1(h)), like freezing orders, is only available **10–40** in the High Court. It operates in effect, as a form of civil search warrant. Although it confers no right of entry on the part of the party enforcing it, it nevertheless requires the respondent to "permit" the applicant to enter and seize the materials named in the order on pain of punishment for contempt of court. They have somewhat fallen out of fashion since their heyday in the 1980s. This has largely been due to the stringent conditions that have come to be attached to them, especially the appointment of a supervising solicitor. Most of the safeguards developed by the courts have now been incorporated into paragraph 7 of PD 25. The relevant procedure is dealt with in *O'Hare and Browne* at 27–040 to 27–043 and *Hollander* at 3–10 to 3–53.

3. Orders Relating to Property

Pursuing remedies in relation to property can be as vital as securing **10–41** the preservation of documents: an obvious example would be the preservation of an item of machinery or the integrity of a site in a claim for industrial injury. CPR 25.1(c) gives both the High Court and the county court powers to make a wide array of orders in relation to property, for example, as to its preservation or inspection along with the power to authorise entry for any of those purposes (CPR 25.1(d). Equally importantly, CPR 25.5 gives the court power to make such orders prior to the commencement of proceedings and against a non-party as those in CPR 31.16 and 31.17. There is however one material difference; orders can be sought pre-claim against a person who is not a prospective party to the contemplated proceedings (see, s.33(1) Supreme Court Act 1981).

4. "Norwich Pharmacal" Orders

This order, based on the House of Lords decision in *Norwich* **10–42** *Pharmacal Co v Customs and Excise Commissioners* [1974] A.C. 152, requires a person who, albeit innocently, has become mixed up in the wrongdoing of another to assist the person injured by the wrongdoer in ascertaining the wrongdoer's identity. The power has subsequently been extended to include the identity of senders of "threats" letters in *CHC Software Care v Hopkins and Wood* [1993] F.S.R. 241. In *P v*

T [1997] 1 W.L.R. 130 Sir Richard Scott V.C. extended the power even further to cover information which might reveal defamatory statements by a third party even though it could not ascertained whether a defamatory statement had been made without access to the information sought. Finally the House of Lords in *Ashworth Hospital Authority v MGN* [2002] 3 All E.R. 193 has held that the power extends to *any* situation in which an "innocent" party has got mixed up in another's wrongful conduct even where disclosure is not sought in order to bring proceedings against the wrongdoer, but, for example, to dismiss him. Finally, as noted at 10–34, relief may even be granted in a breach of contract case where the other party's identity is *known* (see *Carlton Film Distributors*).

5. *"Bankers Trust" Orders*

10–43   "Bankers Trust" orders are orders in which an innocent person, often a bank as in *Bankers' Trust v Shapira* [1980] 3 All E.R. 353 is required to disclose to a party to proceedings certain confidential information such as copies of correspondence, cheques, debit vouchers, transfer applications and internal memoranda. The purpose of the order is to enable an applicant to trace the existence of and protect the assets he claims when they are in the hands of an innocent non-party see *Arab Monetary Fund v Hashim (No.5)* [1992] 2 All E.R. 911. In the original case, the order was made that discovery be given to the claimant bank against the defendant bank notwithstanding that the defendants had not yet been served. Given the confidential nature of the documents to be disclosed, a party obtaining such an order must give an undertaking not to use the information obtained other than in the course of the proceedings. The jurisdiction to make such orders derives from the court's jurisdiction to order disclosure of documents and is therefore, retained by CPR 31.18.

6. *Requests for Further Information: CPR 18*

10–44   The use of this rule may on occasions offer a cost-effective alternative to an application for specific disclosure under CPR 31.12. CPR 18.1 provides that the Court may, at any time, order a party to:

"(a) clarify any matter which is in dispute in the proceedings; or

(b) give additional information in relation to any such matter, whether or not the matter is contained or referred to in a statement of case."

The rule therefore goes way beyond the previous procedure for requesting Further and Better Particulars which was confined to the contents of case statements, and could, for example, extend to providing details of the unnamed source of an original hearsay statement contained in another person's witness statement. The supporting Practice Direction contains detailed requirements as to the procedure for making such a request. Broadly, it should be made by letter and responded to by letter or more formal reply. In either case, the information must be supported by a signed statement of truth. The remedy for non-compliance is application to the court for a specific order: for further detail, see *O'Hare and Browne* 32–001 to 32–007.

VI OTHER METHODS OF ACCESS TO EVIDENCE

One of the most notable recent developments has been the increase in availability of information from sources other than the parties or prospective parties and through procedures other than the more traditional ones referred to above. Again at the risk of straying from the mainstream of this book, some of the more important examples are listed below. The first two categories are enormously complex and wide-ranging pieces of legislation that, especially in the case of the Freedom of Information Act 2000 ("FOIA"), have not as yet had a chance to fully "bed down". Those seeking detailed commentary are invited to consult *Information Rights* by *Phillip Coppel: (2004) Sweet and Maxwell* and *Freedom of Information Manual (2005) Sweet and Maxwell*. There is also a very helpful list of useful information sources in *Hollander* at 6–32 to 6–36. **10–45**

1. Data Protection Act 1998

The 1998 Act ("DPA") gives individuals a right of access to "personal data" held by a "data controller". The s.7 route has the advantages of speed and cheapness over other court based procedures such as pre-action disclosure, not least because there is no requirement that the data subject and the data controller are in dispute, nor is there any need to satisfy a relevance test of any kind. It does have a number of limitations however, not least the fact that it only permits access to data concerning that individual data subject. It should also be noted that it it operates independently from requests for information under FOIA (see s.40 of the 2000 Act). **10–46**

(a) *Right of Access to Personal Data.*
Section 7 of the 1998 Act provides that: **10–47**

"(1) Subject to the following provisions of this section and to sections 8 and 9, an individual is entitled:

(a) to be informed by any data controller whether personal data of which that individual is the data subject are being processed by or on behalf of that data controller,

(b) if that is the case, to be given by the data controller a description of:

    (i) the personal data of which that individual is the data subject,

    (ii) the purposes for which they are being or are to be processed, and

    (iii) the recipients or classes of recipients to whom they are or may be disclosed,

(c) to have communicated to him in an intelligible form:

    (i) the information constituting any personal data of which that individual is the data subject, and

    (ii) any information available to the data controller as to the source of those data, and

(d) where the processing by automatic means of personal data of which that individual is the data subject for the purpose of evaluating matters relating to him such as, for example, his performance at work, his creditworthiness, his reliability or his conduct, has constituted or is likely to constitute the sole basis for any decision significantly affecting him, to be informed by the data controller of the logic involved in that decision-taking."

Section 8(2) goes on to provide that:

"The obligation imposed by section 7(1)(c)(i) must be complied with by supplying the data subject with a copy of the information in permanent form unless:

(a) the supply of such a copy is not possible or would involve disproportionate effort, or

(b) the data subject agrees otherwise;

and where any of the information referred to in section 7(1)(c)(i) is expressed in terms which are not intelligible without explanation the copy must be accompanied by an explanation of those terms."

(b) *Major Terms Defined*

10–48 Many of the key terms are defined in s.1(1) of the DPA, in particular:

A "Data Controller" is a person (natural or legal) who either alone or with others determines the purposes for which and the manner in which any personal data are, or are to be, processed. Thus, unlike

FOIA, the DPA gives the data subject a right of access to personal data held by the private sector.

"Data" is information which:

(1) Is being processed, or has been recorded with the intention of it being processed, by means of equipment operating automatically in response to instructions given for that purpose (in other words, a computer) ("Category (a) and (b) Data")

(2) Is recorded as part of a relevant filing system or with the intention that it should form part of a relevant filing system ("Category (c) Data") or

(3) Consists of an "accessible record" as defined by s.68, namely health, educational or other accessible public records ("Category (d) Data").

"*Personal Data*" are data which relates to a living individual who can be identified:

"(a) from those data, or

(b) from those data and other information which is in the possession of, or is likely to come into the possession of, the data controller and includes any expression of opinion about the individual and any indication of the intentions of the data controller or any other person in respect of the individual."

It is clear from the above definitions that the DPA in its original form was primarily aimed a creating rights of access to computerised data that was relatively easy and inexpensive to retrieve. This is clear from the way in which "relevant filing system" is defined namely as:

". . . any set of information relating to individuals that is structured, either by reference to individuals or by reference to criteria relating to individuals to the extent that . . . the set is structured, either by reference to individuals or by reference to criteria relating to individuals, in such a way that specific information relating to a particular individual is readily accessible."

The definition is therefore aimed at records such as address directories rather than a randomly collated file in which information concerning an individual happens to appear. This relatively narrow application of the DPA to manually stored data has been confirmed by the Court of Appeal in *Durant v Financial Services Authority [2004] F.S.R. 28* in which Auld L.J. held that what is required is a system in which:

(1) The files forming part of it are structured or referenced in such a way as clearly to indicate at the outset of a search whether

specific information capable of amounting to personal data is held within the system and, if so, in which file or files it is held; and

(2) Has a sufficiently sophisticated and detailed means of readily indicating whether and where in an individual file or files specific criteria or information about the individual can be readily located.

However it should be noted that s.68(1) of the FOIA has effectively made all *manually* stored personal data held by a *public authority* prima facie accessible by adding a new "Category (e)" to the definition of data, namely:

"(e) . . . recorded information held by a public authority [which does not fall into categories] . . . (a) to (d)."

The provision of such data is now regulated by s.9A of the DPA (inserted by s.69 of the FOIA).

10–49 (c) *The Request*
The request must be made in *writing* and accompanied by a *fee* (the current prescribed maximum is £10) (DPA 1998 s.7(2)). An applicant will need to satisfy the data controller of his identity and provide sufficient information to allow the data controller to locate the information sought (DPA 1998 s.7(3)). If the data subject has sufficiently defined his access request in respect of personal data relating to him held by computer or on a relevant filing system, and none of the statutory exemptions apply, then the data controller *must* comply with the request within *40 days* (DPA 1998 s.7(10)) by providing the data subject with a copy of all the information held unless supplying a copy of the information is not possible or would involve the data controller in disproportionate effort (DPA s.8(2)).

10–50 (d) *Exemptions and Refusals*
Part IV of the DPA (ss.29 to 37) contains a number of exemptions to compliance, for example, where the interests of national security arise, commercially sensitive financial information, and confidential references given by the data controller. Section 37 and Schedule 7 specifically preserve legal professional privilege.

Under s.7(5) of the DPA, the data controller may also decline to comply with the request to the extent that compliance would entail disclosing information relating to *another* individual who can be identified from that information unless that individual consents to such disclosure or full compliance with the request is in all the circumstances reasonable without the consent of the other individual.

Conclusion It can be seen that the DPA, in theory, provides a wide **10–51** ranging facility for obtaining information for use in prospective litigation both from a proposed party or a non-party. However, the approach of the Court of Appeal in *Durant* has very much been to condemn as misconceived any attempt to use the DPA as an alternative to disclosure. The court emphasised that the DPA existed as a tool to enable the data subject to protect his privacy rather than an aid to disclosure for the purposes of litigation. Only time will tell whether this narrow approach will stifle attempts to use the DPA as a means of evidence collection.

2. Freedom of Information Act 2000

The FOIA is very much in its infancy therefore it is too early to form **10–52** any clear view as to its efficacy as an additional form of evidence collection. However, as this very brief summary shows, it undoubtedly has its attractions. The Act deals with access to information held by a "public authority". This covers an enormous and ever-increasing range of institutions, the bulk of which are set out in Schedule 1 to the Act (see also ss.3(1) and 5). As well as familiar faces such as central government departments, local authorities, NHS Trusts, the police and armed forces there is a very large number of less well-known organisations such as The Know-How Fund Advisory Board and The Darwin Advisory Committee. Significantly, s.3(2) provides that information is held by a public authority and hence subject to the FOIA if it is:

"(a) . . . held by the authority, otherwise than on behalf of another person; or

(b) it is held by another person on behalf of the authority".

The effect of this is far-reaching since it means that there will be a considerable amount of *private* information received from third parties that will prima facie be liable to disclosure under the FOIA. Conversely, a third party to whom a public authority has contracted out may be in possession of FOIA disclosable information. The *medium* in which the information presents and its method of storage (unlike under the DPA) is immaterial (see s.84).

(a) The FOIA "Right to Know"

Under s.1(1) of FOIA "any person", be they an individual or a cor- **10–53** porate body from anywhere in the world is entitled on written request:

(1) To be informed in writing by the public authority whether it holds information of the description specified in the request; and

(2) If that is the case, to have that information communicated to him, her or it.

It is immaterial *when* the information was created or how long it has been held, and the applicant is under no obligation to state why the information is being sought. Furthermore, there is no restriction on its use once supplied, in contrast to the implied undertaking in CPR 31.22 for documents disclosed in the course of proceedings. Not only that, s.16 imposes a duty on the relevant public authority to *advise* and *assist* applicants who are searching for information.

(b) *The Scheme in Outline*

10–54   The formalities required to trigger the s.1 duties are minimal: simply a request in writing which gives the applicant's name and address and describes the information requested (see, s.8(1)). The basic response period is *20 days* from receipt of the request (s.10(1)), although if the authority needs time to make a public interest decision in respect of "Exempt Information" (see below) they may extend time for a reasonable period (s.10(3)) provided that notify the applicant to this effect within the 20 day period and give a date upon which a final decision will be made (s.17(2)). Applications are *free* provided that the cost of compliance does not exceed £600 (central government) or £450 (other public authorities) costed out at £25 per hour. If the cost will exceed that amount, the authority may refuse the application or negotiate a fee. Compliance is enforced by the Information Commissioner who may issue a Decision Notice, Information Notice or Enforcement Notice, breach of all of which is punishable by contempt proceedings (s.4$(3)). Both sides have rights of appeal to the Information Tribunal from which appeal lies, on a point of law only, to the High Court.

(c) *Exemptions*

10–55   There are three categories of "Exempt Material" in Part II of FOIA (ss.21 to 44). It is not practicable to pretend to provide more than a very brief overview of these complex provisions. Readers are referred to 1–080 to 1–255 of *Turle*, Chapters 14 to 26 of *Coppel*, and the Lord Chancellor's "*Code of Practice*" promulgated under s.45 of FOIA which can be found at *www.dca.gov.uk* and various Codes of Guidance issued by the Information Commissioner, available at *www.informationcommissioner.gov.uk*.

(1) *Absolute Exemptions*

10–56   These include:

- Information accessible by other means (s.21);
- Personal information relating to the applicant (s.40(1)): the concept being that this should be dealt with under the DPA;

- Information received in confidence where disclosure would involve an actionable breach of confidence (s.41).

In such a case the public authority need do no more than write to the applicant within the 20 day period specifying the exemption relied on and advising him of the complaints procedure and right of appeal.

(2) *Conditional Exemption Based on Prejudice*
This category includes information relating to national security   **10–57**
(s.24), defence (s.26), health and safety (s.38) and commercial interests (s.43(2)). The authority must first decide whether disclosure will prejudice the relevant interest. If it *will not*, the information must be disclosed. If it *will*, they must then go on and carry out a balancing exercise similar to that in relation to objections based on PII.

(3) *Conditional Exemptions Based on Classification*
This category differs from the previous one in that there is no need to   **10–58**
show prejudice for the exemption to apply. Nevertheless, the authority still has to go on and carry out a balancing exercise between the factors for and against disclosure. Most notable examples within this category are:

- Personal information relating to third parties (s.40(2)): the concept being that such information will only be released in accordance with DPA principles;

- Information in respect of which a claim to legal professional privilege could be maintained in legal proceedings (s.42).

It is noteworthy that legal professional privilege is not subject to an absolute exemption. This creates the possibility that an applicant could claim to access to legal advice given to a public authority under the Act. It remains to be seen whether the courts take the view that the intention of Parliament is sufficiently clear to override LPP and whether in any event, it is sufficiently "proportionate" to be ECHR compliant. One can see litigation arising in this area.

3. *Access to Health Records*
This Access to Health Records Act 1990 has largely been repealed by   **10–59**
the DPA insofar as it is processed "data". The only operative part of the 1990 Act is s.3, under which the personal representatives of a deceased patient are entitled to be given a copy or extract of the deceased's health records by the relevant record holder. In addition, a person has a right of access to any report on him prepared by a medical practitioner for employment or insurance purposes under the

Access to Medical Reports Act 1988. Compliance may be enforced by application to a county court (s.8(1)).

4. Land Registration Act 2002

10–60   It is now possible, by searching the Property Register, the Proprietorship Register and the Charges Register to obtain information about any person's ownership of land in the United Kingdom. This information is particularly valuable for those seeking to check on the feasibility of enforcement before commencing proceedings.

5. Companies House

10–61   Many documents are available for inspection at Companies House providing information as to, for example, the members and directors, accounts and auditors reports and minutes of general meetings. Section 709(3) specifically provides that a certified copy of any document kept by the registrar and certified to be a true copy is as admissible in evidence as the original and is evidence of any fact stated in it. For reasons already given in Chapters 5 and 7, this is one of a number of similar sections that have been rendered redundant by the Civil Evidence Act 1995.

Conclusions

10–62   We saw in Chapters 5 and 7 just how important a part documents play in civil trials and how, subject to authentication, they can be put in evidence to prove or infer any fact to which they are relevant. This chapter has emphasised:

(1) How important it is to ensure that all documents that have any potential relevance are preserved for possible disclosure as soon as litigation looms;

(2) The term "document" has taken on a new and wider significance now that electronic data has become commonplace;

(3) Relevance and proportionality lie at the heart of both Standard and Specific Disclosure;

(4) The ability of the CPR to curtail time consuming and expensive disclosure exercises has, perhaps, not been as great as was hoped;

(5) The availability of information from other sources means that litigators must at least consider whether they should make wider enquiries when collecting evidence.

Chapter 11

Witness Statements

As with disclosure, many of the rules relating to witness statements are as much matters of procedure as they are of evidence. Nevertheless, they have to be considered part and parcel of the modern law of civil evidence for a number of reasons. Firstly, they affect the rules on examination of witnesses, having largely replaced examination in-chief. Secondly, failure to comply with the relevant case management directions may, in an extreme case, result in oral evidence being excluded altogether. Thirdly, the use of witness statements at trial may give rise to complex evidential issues. Finally, it would be unrealistic not to consider the practical skills required in the drafting of witness statements having regard to the crucial role that they play.

11–01

I ARE WITNESS STATEMENTS WORKING?

Since their general introduction in 1992, witness statements have become the prescribed method for introducing oral evidence before a court of trial. In hearings other than trials they have simply, to a large extent, usurped the role of the affidavit. Their use in trials has had a number of consequences, not all of them beneficial.

11–02

1. "Cards on the table"
Litigants are no longer taken by surprise by oral evidence at trial. The usual requirement for simultaneous rather than sequential exchange prevents (or should prevent) what is sometimes known as "trimming", that is crafting the statement to fit in with the other evidence after it has been disclosed. (Good)

11–03

2. "Defensive" Drafting
Because CPR 32.5 (see 11–63) seriously limits the scope of examination in-chief, statements have tended to grow longer for fear that

11–04

something may have been missed out. This has tended to increase the costs of preparation. (Bad)

3. Tendentious Drafting

11–05 It is naïve to pretend that the average statement, in reality, consists entirely of the witness's own words. To a greater or lesser extent the drafter has, often without realising it, put his own words into the statement. As long as this does not involve "manufacturing" or "doctoring" evidence, this is all well and good but, as we shall see, there have been several notorious cases where witness statements have contained serious "wishful thinking." (Bad)

4. Tactical Misuse

11–06 Again, it has not been unheard of, especially in large scale litigation, for a party to serve a vast bundle of statements in order to intimidate his opponent and facilitate advantageous settlement. On occasions, this practice has even extended to incorporating statements in the trial bundle so that they are pre-read by the trial judge despite the fact that the party tendering them has no intention of putting the statements in as hearsay evidence, let alone calling the maker. As we shall see at 11–68, the use to which an opponent may put such statements is limited. (Bad)

5. "Textual" Cross-Examination

11–07 There is a great temptation to "pick over the bones" of a statement under the pretext that it goes to credit. Although the court has power to control and limit cross-examination under CPR 32.1, valuable court time is frequently wasted, especially in smaller cases. (Bad)

6. Convenience not Justice

11–08 Examination in-chief may have been more time consuming but had the advantage of giving the court (as well as the cross-examiner) the opportunity to evaluate the witness and weigh up his or her credibility. At least one case, referred to at 11–65, has needed a retrial because the real issues never came out in evidence. (Bad)

7. Better Case Management

11–09 Under most case management directions, witness statements will have to be exchanged relatively soon after allocation and standard disclosure. This should enable the procedural judge to "take a grip" of a claim at the Pre-Trial Checklist stage. (Good) However, the reality for most claims is that the thoroughgoing review anticipated by the Woolf reforms simply does not take place. The main reason for this, unfortunately, is because procedural judges are often so hard pressed that there is simply not enough time to study the case papers to the degree of depth required.

Conclusion However one weighs up the good against the bad, on balance, witness statements have resulted in a greater openness between the parties and, hence, facilitated settlement. Gone are the days when a party not only did not know until the trial what his opponent's witnesses were going to say but, in all likelihood, he would only have a general idea of who those witnesses were going to be! As a result, witness statements have become one of the key components, perhaps the key component in trial preparation. The remainder of this chapter will proceed to examine that component in detail.   **11–10**

II CASE MANAGEMENT OF WITNESS STATEMENTS

This section will not only examine the way in which exchange of statements is dealt with under CPR 32, it will also address the extent to which breach may ultimately lead to the exclusion of that witness's oral evidence.   **11–11**

A Oral Evidence at Trial: CPR 32

In practice, oral evidence, given on oath, and tested in cross-examination is regarded as the best way of putting human perception before the court at a trial.   **11–12**

1. CPR 32.2(1): The General Rule

The signed witness statement, supported by a statement of truth has become the means by which a party discloses his oral evidence as part of the case management timetable and also presents his evidence at trial. This duality of purpose is not always fully appreciated. As has already been suggested, many witness statements are drafted primarily with the former purpose in mind rather than the latter. CPR 32.2 (see 5–16) still appears to make oral evidence the norm, but, as already pointed out at 5–04, this is misleading. The only oral evidence of any substance will usually be the witness's cross-examination on his statement.   **11–13**

2. Written Statements: The Common Direction

Directions will invariably be given requiring the service of the written statements of all witnesses as to fact as a prerequisite to calling them   **11–14** to give oral evidence at trial. The process is primarily governed by CPR 32.4 which provides that:

"(1) A witness statement is a written statement signed by a person which contains the evidence which that person would be allowed to give orally.

(2) The court will order a party to serve on the other parties any witness statement of the oral evidence which the party serving the statement intends to rely on in relation to any issues of fact to be decided at the trial.

(3) The court may give directions as to:

(a) the order in which witness statements are to be served; and

(b) whether or not the witness statements are to be filed."

This rule raises a number of practical issues.

(a) *Can the Court Dispense with the Standard Direction?*

11–15   On the face of it the court has no power to dispense with the direction except in very limited circumstances, those being where:

(1) It gives a party permission to serve a summary under CPR 32.9 (see 11–25); or

(2) The claim proceeds directly to a "trial". The only occasion on which this will happen in practice is in landlord and tenant possession actions governed by CPR 55. In this situation, the use of written statements is optional (CPR 55.8(3)) up until the point when the claim is allocated to the Fast Track or Multi-Track. It is, in fact, commonplace for oral evidence to be given at first hearings, often by a local authority housing officer or private landlord, without any witness statement ever having been prepared or served;

(3) In claims allocated to the Small Claims Track. In that case, CPR 32 is one of the rules that are specifically disapplied by CPR 27.2. Although many courts will make orders for witness statements as part of standard directions on allocation there is no requirement to do so, nor is there any automatic sanction if the direction is not complied with (it frequently is not).

In addition, the court retains a general discretion under CPR 32.10 to permit the oral evidence of a witness to be given at trial even though no statement has been served. It would however generally require some special circumstance such as a witness being found at the very last moment; or some unexpected issue arising on which rebutting evidence needs to be given (see further 11–23).

(b) *Simultaneous or Sequential?*
In Multi-Track cases CPR 29 PD 4.10(3) refers to simultaneous   **11–16**
exchange as the "general approach" as does CPR 28 PD 3.12 for Fast Track cases. However it is clearly within the court's power to order sequential exchange. Paragraph 32.4.11 of the *White Book* suggests sequential exchange may become more commonplace in the future and cites *Rayment v Ministry of Defence* [1998] *The Times,* July 6, a clinical negligence case in which the court ordered simultaneous exchange of liability statements, but sequential exchange of *quantum* statements (see further *O'Hare and Browne* 31–005). However orders for sequential exchange are still rare.

(c) *When in the Timetable?*
There is nothing to say that the normal sequence, that is statements   **11–17**
following on after disclosure in the timetable needs to be adhered to slavishly. The court has ample case management powers enabling it, for example to:

(1) Bring exchange forward to an earlier point in the timetable; or

(2) Order witness statements confined to specific issues; or

(3) Direct service of summaries in the first instance.

If nothing else, the court can always invoke CPR 3.1(2)(m) which enables the court to:

"take any other step or make any other order for the purpose of managing the case and furthering the overriding objective",

as well as the powers given to it under CPR 32.1(1) to control the evidence (see 1–52). However the Court of Appeal decision in *Watford Petroleum Ltd v Interoil Ltd [2003] EWCA Civ 1417* suggests disclosure should normally precede service of statements.

Facts: WP Ltd was concerned that if disclosure were to take place   **11–18**
before exchange of witness statements, I Ltd would tailor their witness statements to fit with the documents. They accordingly sought an order for exchange of statements to take place before disclosure. They were so suspicious of I Ltd's intentions that they sought, and were granted the order on a "without notice" application. In allowing the appeal the Court of Appeal, although acknowledging that the court had power to make such an order, considered

that to do so would be highly unusual and require exceptional circumstances. As regards to the claimant's concerns over the tailoring of witness statements post-disclosure, Carnwath L.J. stated at [42]:

"(42) As a matter of principle, I consider the fact that a witness to be called by one party might tailor his or her witness statement in the light and to take account of documents disclosed by the other party should rarely if ever, be a sufficient reason for postponing the disclosure of those documents until service of the statement. The risk of such tailoring is one of the incidents of litigation."

3. Consequences of Breach: CPR 32.10

11–19   In the early days of the CPR, there were numerous hotly contested hearings in which it was argued that the party in default should not be allowed to serve its statements late. These arguments were based on CPR 32.10 which provides that:

"If a witness statement or a witness summary for use at trial is not served in respect of an intended witness within the time specified by the court, then the witness may not be called to give oral evidence unless the court gives permission."

It used to be the thought, following *Beachley Property Limited v Edgar* [1997] P.N.L.R. 197, that late service would often be fatal. However, now that the CPR have bedded down, and following Court of Appeal guidance, it is clear that courts must adopt a more balanced approach. The following cases illustrate the principles to be applied.

(a) *Late Service Involves a "Sanction"*

11–20   Clearly failure to serve in time triggers CPR 3.8 which provides that:

"any sanction for failure to comply imposed by a rule . . . has effect unless the party in default applies for and obtains relief from the sanction".

Theoretically, this means that parties cannot waive a breach once this has taken place, but can only agree an extension prior to the date for service having passed under CPR 2.11. This rule provides that:

"Unless these rules or a practice direction provides otherwise, the time specified by a rule or by the court for a person to do any act may be varied by the written agreement of the parties."

(See also CPR 28.4 (Fast Track) and CPR 29.5 (Multi Track).) However, in reality, parties regularly agree extensions after the timetable date has passed and the court never objects; this accords with common sense.

(b) *Late Evidence will usually be allowed in: CPR 3.9*
In deciding whether to grant relief CPR 3.9 requires the court not **11–21** only to consider "all the circumstances", but also have regard to nine specific factors listed in CPR 3.9 1 (see 1–50). It is the last two:

"(h) the effect which the failure to comply had on each party; and

(i) the effect which the granting of relief would have on each party"

which have made a "hard-line" approach inappropriate. To quote H.H. Judge Geddes at first instance in *Woodward v Finch* [1999] C.P.L.R. 699:

"[As to CPR 3.9(1)(h)] Again, I do not think the failure to serve on time has had very much effect on either party, in so far as their conduct of the action is concerned. [As to CPR 3.9(1)(i)] Clearly if I were to refuse the relief applied for, it would have a devastating effect on the claimant, whose very substantial claim would be lost".

The effect of this approach, which has been applied by the Court of Appeal in case after case, has been to make refusal of relief an order of last resort. The first, and still the leading case, is *Bansal v Cheema* [2001] C.P. Rep. 6, the full chronology of which is set out below:

1997
December, 12 Proceedings Issued in the High Court

1998
January 26   Defence
March 31   *Order (1)* Exchange witness statements by June 2, 1998
October 27   C's solicitors write saying not ready to exchange
October 29   D's solicitors write saying they are ready

1999
March 4   Transfer to C London CC after delay by D's solicitors
June 17   *Order (2)* Exchange WSs by August 4, 1999
August 4   D serves WSs
August 10   C applies for extension to September 10, 1999
                 because C had to leave country urgently
August 27   C's application for an extension of time heard
November 15   Trial listed to start

On *August 27, 1999* the claimant sought an extension until *September 10, 1999* to serve his statements, the reason given being that he had to leave country urgently. A circuit judge refused the application on and proceeded to strike the claim out since it was now doomed to failure. The Court of Appeal allowed the claimant's appeal. Brooke L.J. gave the leading judgment. He stated that:

(1) In every case, the judge must go through each paragraph in CPR 3.9(1) as if it were an application under s.33 of the Limitation Act 1980;

(2) The appropriate order would have been to extend the time for serving witness statements to *September 10*, with a condition that in default the claimant should be debarred from calling oral evidence.

(3) The judge's failure to consider CPR 3.9(1)(h) and (i) had the effect of granting the defendant an unsolicited windfall with a catastrophic effect on the claimant.

There was a suspicion, at least in the early days of the CPR, that some judges were adopting a much harder line on timetable breaches, perhaps having been "fired up" by the words of Lord Woolf M.R. in *Biguzzi v Rank Leisure* [1999] 1 W.L.R. 1926 when he stated (at [1934]):

"Under the CPR the keeping of time limits laid down by the CPR, or by the court itself is in fact more important than it was. Perhaps the clearest reflection of that is to be found in the overriding objectives contained in Part 1 of the CPR. It is also to be found in the power that the court now has to strike out a statement of case under Part 3.4".

An extreme example of this can be found in *Cank v Broadyard Associates*, [2001] C.P. Rep. 47 CA in which the court stated that a judge had been in error to refuse relief to a defendant litigant in person who had served his witness statement only two days out of time and at the claimant's home address rather than on his solicitors. The Court of Appeal, not surprisingly perhaps, described the breach as being "technical in the extreme". However, the next two cases show the Court of Appeal upholding decisions by trial judges who had refused to admit late evidence. The first, *Martin v Steelforce*, unreported, June 13, 2000, is remarkable for the fact that the party in default ultimately "got away with it".

11–22   <u>Facts:</u> C was claiming damages for injuries suffered in an accident at work on April 15, 1997. The claim was listed for trial as a two day fixture commencing on January 28, 2000. At trial D, for the first time, sought to rely on the oral evidence of N, whose statement dated March 6, 1999 had been served on C's solicitors 10 days before the trial. They also sought to call additional evidence from S, whose supplemental statement, dated March 9, 1999, was served on the morning of the trial. No reason was ever given for withholding these statements even though the contents of both of them helped the D's case. The trial judge excluded both statements and refused leave to appeal.

Lord Woolf M.R. gave the leading judgment and, in refusing leave to appeal, went on to say,

"Speaking for myself, I would not be satisfied, that if permission to appeal were granted, I would allow the appeal".

However, the trial judge had taken so long to deal with the issue that was insufficient time left to try the case. Accordingly, it had to be adjourned to the July 13, 2000. The Court of Appeal therefore directed that the additional evidence *could* be admitted, on the basis that although the defendants' conduct had been an "ambush" in January, it would no longer be one July. Although the court did not directly say so, the decision shows how prejudice is usually the central issue. The second case for discussion is *Anderson v Blackpool Wyre and Fylde Community Services NHS Trust* [2002] EWCA Civ 1247, a particularly useful decision for a judge or advocate faced with the problem of the witness who is, quite literally, produced "out of the blue".

Facts: The claim arose out of the attempted murder of the C, a   **11–23**
former merchant seaman, by shooting. As a result he claimed he was suffering from Post-Traumatic Stress Disorder. Unfortunately, he was misdiagnosed as an aggressive psychopath at one of D's hospitals, and consequently did not receive proper treatment for his condition. C claimed that if he had received proper treatment, he would on returning to sea, have eventually become a captain in the merchant navy. Seven days into the trial, C, for the first time, sought to call W, the operations director of a shipping company at which the he had worked. No witness statement had been served before the trial.

The judge, applying CPR 32.10, refused permission on the basis that firstly, the evidence of the new witness was not of great significance: it was simply "confirmatory" of evidence that had gone before. Secondly, the defendants would be prejudiced by not having the opportunity to investigate the evidence. Finally, a different line of cross-examination would have been pursued against earlier witnesses if the defendants had known that W was going to be called. This decision was upheld by the Court of Appeal, Keene L.J. stating (at [24]):

"Justice may sometimes require evidence to be admitted even at a stage as late as occurred in the present case. But that is only likely to be the situation where the evidence is going to be of significance, and where its importance outweighs the prejudice to the other side".

Keene L.J. also implied (at [22] and [23]) that other influencing factors might be:

(1) The existence of a good reason for the lateness, for example the fact that a witness had been hard to track down; and

(2) The fact that a new issue had suddenly arisen.

Although it is hardly surprising to find that the judge's decision was upheld, it important to note that the court did not rule out the admission of evidence even when it was introduced this late in the day. Keene L.J. approved the passage in the *White Book* at para.32.10.2 which (still) states:

"Where a witness statement is served by a party after the time specified for service it will be unjust to exclude the party from adducing the evidence at trial save in very rare circumstances, e.g. where there has been deliberate flouting of court orders, or inexcusable delay such that the only way the court could fairly entertain the evidence would be by adjourning the trial (*Mealy Horgan Plc v Horgan* [1999] STC 711)."

11–24   **Conclusions**   The clear message is that there will be rarely be much mileage in resisting an application for relief from sanction or an extension of the timetable. The Court of Appeal are taking a "broad justice" approach to granting relief. If you are the party in difficulty and confronted by an opponent who refuses point blank to extend the timetable date for exchange any further, you would be well advised to apply for an extension *before* the timetable has expired because, even if it is heard *after* the date for compliance has passed, on the authority of the Court of Appeal decision in *Robert v Momentum Services Ltd* [2003] 2 All E.R. 74:

(1) It will not be a "sanctions case": if the extension is granted it will take effect from the date of the application and, accordingly, the court will not be required to go through the CPR 3.9 checklist,

(2) The only relevant prejudice that the court will required to consider will be that flowing from the period of extension sought; and

(3) The merits of the claim or defence will be irrelevant although it will be open to the opposing party to cross-apply under CPR 3.4 (strike out) or CPR 24 (summary judgment).

However, you should still make every effort to comply so far as you are able. The Court of Appeal commented on the advisability of this course in *R.C Residuals Ltd v Linton Fuel Oils Ltd* [2002] 1 W.L.R. 2782. In that case, the claimants were up against a 4.00 p.m. deadline for service of two experts' reports under an "unless order". They both had to be served by hand because the defendants' solicitors would not accept service by email. Accordingly, although they were both served on that day, they were served slightly out of time. The defendants' solicitors rejected the reports and an Official Referee refused to grant relief, the effect of which was to debar the claimants from adducing evidence in support of a substantial amount of their claim. In allowing the claimants' appeal, the Court of Appeal stated that it would have strengthened their position on costs if they had instructed their two experts to email the reports to the defendants' solicitors as soon as they had become available and followed this up with personal service. Although this would not have amounted to technical compliance it would have placed the defendants in a much weaker position if they had refused to accept late service of the hard copies.

On the other hand, if you are the "innocent" party there is little point resisting an application for extension unless either, you can genuinely argue, having regard to the CPR 3.9 criteria, that the imposition (or upholding) of a sanction is just and proportionate, or that attendance at the hearing is justified in order to achieve some wider case management purpose. There may indeed be costs risks in resisting if your refusal is clearly unreasonable (see *LN Newman Ltd v Adlem* [2004] EWCA Civ 1492). It is equally important to remember that the rules require *mutual* exchange: sanctions bite both ways. Therefore you must take steps to comply yourself. This can be achieved either by:

(1) Simply serving and filing in accordance with the Case Management Direction and then standing back to review the position; or

(2) Filing and serving the statements in sealed envelopes to be marked:

"Not to be opened until after the [Claimant/Defendant] has served/filed his witness statements".

An equally important point to consider is whether you *should* stand back and wait until the party in default applies for relief, or make an early application for an "unless" order. Under the CPR, inaction is not an option. Silence and inaction will be regarded as contrary to CPR 1.3. The recent decision of Lightman J. in *Hertsmere Primary Care Trust v Administrators of Balasubramaniam's Estate* [2005] 3 All E.R. 274, a case on Pt 36 offers, illustrates this approach. In it, Lightman J. stated (at [11]):

> "The [Defendants'] counsel submitted that it was perfectly proper for the [Defendants'] lawyers to act in this way, to withhold information and to take advantage of the non-compliance at a later date. He submitted that there was no duty on the part of the Defendants' lawyers to enable the claimant to perfect the defect and rectify the error. That may have been the law prior to the CPR but it is not the law today."

Furthermore, you are, in effect, *obliged* to apply for an order to secure compliance once the claim has been allocated to the Fast-Track or Multi-Track. Multi-Track PD 29 para.7 states:

> "7.1 Where a party fails to comply with a direction given by the court any other party may apply for an order that he must do so or for a sanction to be imposed or both of these.
> 7.2 The party entitled to apply for such an order must do so *without delay* [author's emphasis] but should first warn the other party of his intention to do so".

Fast-Track PD 28 para. 5 is expressed in identical terms.

4. Witness Summaries: CPR 32.9

11–25 There may be various reasons why it is not possible, or desirable, to obtain a CPR 32 compliant statement from a witness whom a party wishes to call to give oral evidence. Examples are where the witness:

(1) Refuses to sign the statement; or

(2) Lacks the capacity to put his/her signature to a statement; or

(3) A full statement has already been taken in previous proceedings, for example under s.9 of the Criminal Justice Act 1967 and it is a waste of time and money to redraft it; or

(4) It is not possible to interview the potential witness at all and he is being called "on spec"; or

(5) "Proportionality" dictates that the expense of preparing witness statements is not cost effective.

The provisions of CPR 32.9 can be utilised in appropriate circumstances. This rule provides that:

"(1) A party who:

    (a) is required to serve a witness statement for use at trial; but

    (b) is unable to obtain one, may apply, without notice, for permission to serve a witness summary instead.

(2) A witness summary is a summary of:

    (a) the evidence, if known, which would otherwise be included in a witness statement; or

    (b) if the evidence is not known, the matters about which the party serving the witness summary proposes to question the witness.

(3) Unless the court orders otherwise, a witness summary must include the name and address of the intended witness.

(4) Unless the court orders otherwise, a witness summary must be served within the period in which a witness statement would have had to be served.

(5) Where a party serves a witness summary, so far as practicable rules 32.4 (requirement to serve witness statements for use at trial), 32.5(3) (amplifying witness statements), and 32.8 (form of witness statement) shall apply to the summary."

The Practice Direction gives no real guidance as to the circumstances in which summaries might be ordered, but the rule is, in effect, of limitless scope. The most likely, albeit rare, situation in which the use of this rule will need to be considered is where, having interviewed a potential witness, he refuses to sign a witness statement. It may be that you consider his evidence so essential that you decide to serve a witness summary and bring him to court under a witness summons (see 13–15). The extent to which any document, for example:

(1) Containing the notes of an interview with a witness; or

(2) Any other statement, written or oral, that he has made,

may be put in as hearsay evidence to support or contradict the witness is discussed at 14–55.

5. What if the Statement needs Correcting or is Incomplete?
Due to the limited amount of oral examination in-chief allowed at trial (see 14–40) practitioners are often concerned as to how they   **11–26**

should deal with any gaps there may be in the statements. This is by no means uncommon because simultaneous exchange may mean that each side's witness statements have not "engaged" on all of the key issues. Surprisingly, there is no specific rule that covers this eventuality. CPR 32 PD para.22 ("Alterations") appears only to cover alterations that are made prior to service. Strictly speaking, if the time for exchange set out in Directions has passed CPRs 32.10 and 3.8 apply, and an application will have to be made for "relief" in the form of permission to serve a supplemental statement. If the alteration or addition arises from "new" matters arising since service, these can be dealt with under CPR 32.5(3) by way of oral examination in-chief provided there is "good reason" (see 14–40). Appendix 4 to the *Chancery Guide* at para.9 contains helpful guidance:

"Occasionally a party wishes the witness making the statement to give additional evidence, for example to deal with events occurring, or matters discovered, after his or her statement was served, or in response to matters dealt with by another party's witness. In these cases, a supplementary witness statement should be served if practicable and as soon as possible. Permission to adduce the evidence contained in a supplementary witness statement will be needed unless the other party consents. However this need not be sought prior to service; it can be sought at a case management conference if convenient or, if need be, at trial."

Although it is arguable that this is not "playing it by the rules" it represents common sense. Conversely, para.H 1.8 of the *"Commercial Court Guide"* suggests that permission is always required. In practice parties' legal advisers will usually agree exchange of further supplemental statements as circumstances dictate.

6. Is it Always Essential to Prepare Witness Statements?

11–27   Despite the fact that the use of witness statements has brought benefits, it has to be accepted that they have added to the cost of preparing for trial. This has been compounded by the use of word processing software which permits endless revision. Can anything be done to reduce the amount of time spent on this exercise? It should be borne in mind that the court can, under its general case management powers (CPR 3.1(2)(m) order that a document, "shall stand as X's witness statement" for the purpose of the trial. This may be appropriate where, for example:

(1) Lengthy affidavits or witness statements have already been relied on for the purposes of an interim injunction;

(2) The claim is simple and the witness concerned, who is also a party to the proceedings, has already fully set out his evidence in his Case Statement and has signed the Statement of Truth.

The latter direction is particularly useful in Small Claims where it is desirable to keep costs to a minimum.

7. *Implied Undertaking*

CPR 32.12 provides a similar undertaking to that in relation to disclosed documents in CPR 31.22, namely, that a witness statement may not be used for any purpose other than the proceedings in which it is served unless the witness gives his consent, the court gives permission or the statement is put in evidence at a hearing held in public. As with documents used in interim hearings, the use of a witness statement for that purpose will usually release it from the implied undertaking. Note that the rule does not apply to affidavits or witness summaries served under CPR 32.9.   **11–28**

B Use of Witness Statements at Hearings other than Trials

1. *Written Evidence. The Norm CPR 32.2(1)*

As already noted (5–16), CPR 32.2(1)(b) makes written evidence the norm at any hearing other than a trial. This is confirmed by CPR 32.6 which provides: **11–29**

"(1) Subject to paragraph (2), the general rule is that evidence at hearings other than the trial is to be by witness statement unless the court, a practice direction or any other enactment requires otherwise.

(2) At hearings other than the trial, a party may, rely on matters set out in:

    (a) his statement of case; or

    (b) his application notice, if the statement of case or application notice is verified by a statement of truth."

As can be seen therefore there are three different ways in which written evidence can be given, namely by:

(1) Witness statement; and/or

(2) Case Statement; and/or

(3) Part C of the Application Notice,

provided that in each case it is verified by a Statement of Truth. CPR 8.5 contains additional requirements as to the nature of and the time for serving such evidence.

Some commentators take the view that Assessments of Damages come within CPR 32.6 and that accordingly a specific direction is needed for oral evidence (see, for example, *White Book* 32.2.3). There is a specific reference to CPR 32.6 in PD 26 para.12.4(4), which states:

"Rule 32.6 applies to evidence at a disposal hearing unless the court otherwise directs".

However, the term "disposal hearing" only applies to hearings which will not normally last longer than *30 minutes* (PD 26 para.12.1(a)). The writer's own view is that any assessment of damages other than a disposal hearing is a "trial" (especially if it has been allocated to the Multi-Track) and that, accordingly, CPR 32.6 is of limited application. If however a specific direction for oral evidence is required, it can be as simple as:

"CPR 32.6 shall not apply to the final hearing which shall be deemed to be a trial to which CPR 32.2(1)(a) applies".

It should also be noted in conclusion, that the use of statements involves the use of hearsay evidence (see 7–29). This will equally apply to any documents exhibited to a witness statement. Although the use of hearsay in exhibits was permitted in emergency injunction applications prior to the Civil Evidence Act 1995 (see *Deutsche Ruckverischering AG v Walbrook Insurance Co. Ltd* [1994] 4 All E.R. 181), this was not the case for final hearings (see *Re Koscot Interplanetary (UK) Ltd* [1972] 3 All E.R. 829). All these technicalities have now been swept away: there is no need to even serve a hearsay notice (see CPR 33.3(a)).

2. Attendance of Witnesses: CPR 32.7

11–30 The general policy of making oral evidence the exception rather than the rule is underlined by this rule which provides that:

"(1) Where, at a hearing other than the trial, evidence is given in writing, any party may apply to the court for permission to cross-examine the person giving the evidence.

(2) If the court gives permission under paragraph (1) but the person in question does not attend as required by the order, his evidence may not be used unless the court gives permission."

CPR 8.6 makes similar provisions in respect of Part 8 proceedings:

"(2) The court may require or permit a party to give oral evidence at the hearing.

(3) The court may give directions requiring the attendance for cross-examination of a witness who has given written evidence."

Traditionally such orders have rarely been granted. Much of the current case law arises out of applications to cross-examine a party on his affidavit of assets in proceedings for a freezing order (see, in particular, *Great Future International Ltd v Sealand Housing Corp* [2001] C.P.L.R. 293), the principles relating to which are fully rehearsed in *Hollander* at 3–75. Furthermore, CPR 34.3(2)(c) provides that permission is required:

"to have a summons issued for a witness to attend court to give evidence at any hearing except the trial".

The relevant case law, such as it is, has already been summarised at 5–16. The detailed procedure on Pt 8 Applications is to be found in Chapter 8 of *O'Hare and Browne*.

III CONTENTS: PRACTICAL DRAFTING

The skill of drafting witness statements has been the subject of extensive written advice, see, in particular *O'Hare and Browne* 14–007 to 14–017 and *Hollander* 22–01 to 22–25. However the writer would like to add some thoughts of his own on the subject.   **11–31**

A General Points

1. Flexibility
One of the most important consequences of the hearsay rule being abolished is that the rules as to admissibility of the contents of: **11–32**

(1) Witness Statements for use at trial;

(2) Witness Statements for use at hearings other than trial; and

(3) Affidavits for use at either,

are essentially the same. The witness statement prepared for use at one type of hearing can equally be utilised for the other.

2. Abolition of Hearsay: "Information and Belief"

11–33   This is implicitly recognised in paras 4.2 and 18.2 of PD 32, which require that the statement or affidavit must indicate:

> (1) Which of the statements in it are true from the witness's own knowledge and which are matters of information and belief; and
>
> (2) The source of any such matters of information or belief.

Thus, affidavits and witness statements may contain hearsay and, to an extent, opinion evidence. It is *essential* that this rule is observed, particularly in the case of witness statements for use at trial, because this will have the effect of highlighting those parts of the witness statement that contain hearsay. As noted at 7–27, this may be the only notice of hearsay that the other party will get.

3. Attacking Defects

11–34   There is no longer a power similar to that in the old RSC O.41 r.6 to strike out parts of an affidavit which are:

> "Scandalous, irrelevant or otherwise offensive".

Effectively, you can put in what you like, and people often do. However, note the general power to exclude evidence under CPR 32.1(2), which could, in theory, lead to all, or parts, of a statement being struck out. Although Appendix 4, para.4 of the *Chancery Guide* recommends that such an application be made in advance of the trial, it is suggested that, whichever court the claim is proceeding in, this course is only appropriate if the case is being managed by the trial judge (see 14–10).

B   Contents: The Detailed Rules

11–35   The contents of CPR 32 Practice Direction do not make light reading! However, scattered within them are some very helpful practical hints for the proper drafting of witness statements (and affidavits).

1. CPR 32.8: The Starting Point

11–36   This provides that:

> "A witness statement *must* [writer's emphasis] comply with the requirements set out in the relevant practice direction."

Paragraphs 17 to 25 of PD 32 contain a wealth of detailed requirements which are supplemented by additional material in the *Chancery Guide*

(Appendix 4), the *Commercial Court Guide (H1)* and the *Queen's Bench Guide* (7.10). Although many of them are ignored, they do provide some valuable practical guidance as to how statements should be drawn, not least because they tell the drafter what *is* permissible.

2. The Heading: P32/17

This requirement is more or less picked up when you draft your first **11–37** witness statement by copying from a precedent. The paragraph does however lay down detailed requirements, which are not always followed.

"17.1 The witness statement should be headed with the title of the proceedings (see paragraph 4 of the practice direction supplementing Part 7 and paragraph 7 of the practice direction supplementing Part 7 and paragraph 7 of the practice direction supplementing Part 20); where the proceedings are between several parties with the same status it is sufficient to identify the parties as follows:

	Number:
A.B. (and others)	Claimants/Applicants
C.D. (and others)	Defendants/Respondents (as appropriate)

17.2 At the top right hand corner of the first page there should be clearly written:

(1) the party on whose behalf it is made,
(2) the initials and surname of the witness,
(3) the number of the statement in relation to that witness,
(4) the identifying initials and number of each exhibit referred to, and
(5) the date the statement was made."

Often this appears as:

"J.Smith/C/1st/JS 1, 2 and 3/15/8/03"

which is less than helpful to the court. Make sure it is set out more clearly as, for example:

Statement of:	J. Smith
Statement:	1st
For:	Claimant
Dated:	15 Aug 2003
Exhibits:	JS 1, 2 and 3

3. *Layout: PD 32/18*

Many litigators are concerned that they may be accused of "putting words in the witness's mouth" if they edit the witness's language by "cleaning up" vocabulary and syntax. Indeed it is one of the major criticisms levelled on occasions by judges. However, PD 32/18 does afford an element of discretion to the drafter. It provides:

"18.1 The witness statements must, *if practicable* [writer's emphasis], be in the intended witness's own words, the statements should be expressed in the first person and should also state:

(1) the full name of the witness,

(2) his place of residence or, if he is making the statement in his professional, business or other occupational capacity, the address at which he works, the position he holds and the name of his firm or employer,

(3) his occupation or if he has none, his description, and

(4) the fact that he is a party to the proceedings or is the employee of such a party if it be the case.

The words "if practicable" are important. Take, for example, the witness who, when interviewed, expresses himself in a pithy vernacular that you would not wish him to repeat in court. In the writer's view, no criticism can be attached to a lawyer who "sanitises" the witness's language, not least because, if the witness were being examined in-chief, not only would he be more discerning in his choice of language, but, the examining advocate would be able to control the witness's answers to a significant extent (see 14–26). Paragraph 18.2 is also important because it deals with hearsay evidence. It provides that:

"18.2 A witness statement must indicate:

(1) which of the statements in it are made from the witness's own knowledge and which are matters if information or belief, and

(2) the source for any matters of information or belief."

As already pointed out, it is vital that sources are given so that the party against whom the hearsay evidence is tendered can decide how, if at all, he should respond. However, "belief" only embraces belief in the existence of facts, it does not entitle the maker to express opinions, for example, as to why an interim order should be made or who was at fault.

4. *Exhibits*

11–38   The provisions of PD 11.3 to 18.6 are extremely detailed. They tend to be more relevant to interim applications and Pt 8 proceedings than trials. They provide as follows:

(a) *Manner of Exhibiting Documents*
The key passages are to be found in PD 18 which provides as **11–39**
follows:

"18.3 An exhibit used in conjunction with a witness statement
should be verified and identified by the witness and remain separate from the witness statement.
   18.4 Where a witness refers to an exhibit or exhibits, he should
state "I refer to the (description of exhibit) marked . . .".
   18.5 The provisions of paragraphs 11.3 to 15.4 (exhibits) apply
similarly to witness statements as they do to affidavits.
   18.6 Where a witness makes more than one witness statement to
which there are exhibits, in the same proceedings, the numbering of
the exhibits should run consecutively throughout and not start
again with each witness statement."

Thought needs to be given (especially for trial statements) as to
whether documents need to exhibited or referred to at all. It is by no
means unusual to find the same document appearing several
times in the trial bundle, often in places which make it very hard to
follow the witness statement and the relevant document at the same
time. Generally, a reference to the document combined with a
manuscript cross-reference in the margin to the relevant documents
in the document bundle will suffice. Appendix 3, para.8 of the
Chancery Guide contains valuable guidance appropriate to all types
of claim:

"Witness statements often refer to documents. If there could be any
doubt as to what document is being referred to, or if the document
has not previously been made available on disclosure, it may be
helpful for the document to be exhibited to the witness statement.
If, to assist reference to the documents, the documents referred to
are exhibited to the witness statement, they should nevertheless not
be included in trial bundles in that form . . ."

This advice needs to be read in conjunction with Appendix 2,
para.4 which advises:

"If the same document is included in the chronological bundle and
is also an exhibit to an affidavit or witness statement, it should be
included in the chronological bundle and where it would otherwise
appear as an exhibit, a sheet should instead be inserted. The sheet
should state the page and bundle number in the chronological
bundles where the document can be found."

and Appendix 2, paras 24 and 25 which suggest:

"24.   The copies of the witness statements, affidavits and/or expert reports in the bundle should have written on them, next to the reference to any document, the reference to that document in the bundles. This can be done in manuscript.

25.   Documents referred to in, or exhibited to, witness statements, affidavits or expert reports should be put in a separate bundle and not placed behind the statement concerned, so that the reader can see both the text of the statement and the document referred to at the same time."

When considering how to deal with a document in a witness statement, always remember that it would be unusual for a party to need to call a witness to formally prove a document (the reason that this is often the case is explained at 5–58). Therefore, if in doubt, always ask yourself the following question:

"If I was examining this witness in-chief, how would/could I deal with this document?"

This process will be explained more fully at 14–41.

(b) *Letters*

11–40   Vast amounts of correspondence are also frequently exhibited haphazardly to witness statements without any real thought being given as to whether they are needed. The relevant guidance is contained in paras 12 and 13 of PD 32 which provide:

"12.1   Copies of individual letters should be collected together and exhibited in a bundle or bundles. They should be arranged in chronological order with the earliest at the top and firmly secured.
12.2   When a bundle of correspondence is exhibited, the exhibit should have a front page attached stating that the bundle consists of original letters and copies. They should be arranged and secured as above and numbered consecutively."

(c) *Other Documents*

11–41   As already noted, the CPR seem to lay down far more stringent requirements for the presentation of documentary evidence than those demanded by the substantive law (see 5–41).

"13.1   Photocopies instead of original documents may be exhibited provided the *originals* [writer's emphasis] are made available for inspection by the other parties before the hearing and by the judge at the hearing.

13.2 Court documents must not be exhibited (official copies of such documents prove themselves).

13.3 Where an exhibit contains more than one document, a front page should be attached setting out a list of the documents contained in the exhibit; the list should contain the dates of the documents."

The reality is that the court often decides vital issues of fact based on copy documents without the originals ever being produced or anyone raising the point. It is submitted that this is entirely in accordance with the current substantive law.

(d) *Exhibits other than Documents*
Real evidence (see 5–57) may, on occasions need to be introduced as an exhibit, if so, PD 32, para.14 provides

11–42

"14.1 Items other than documents should be clearly marked with an exhibit number or letter in such a manner that the mark cannot become detached from the exhibit.
14.2 Small items may be placed in a container appropriately marked."

(e) *General Provisions*
Paragraph 15 of PD 32 contains particularly helpful guidance on preparation of bundles and exhibits where there is a large amount of evidence to be collated.

11–43

"15.1 Where an exhibit contains more than one document:

(1) the bundle should not be stapled but should be securely fastened in a way that does not hinder the reading of the documents, and
(2) the pages should be numbered consecutively at bottom center.

15.2 Every page of an exhibit should be clearly legible; typed copies of illegible documents should be included, paginated with 'a' numbers.
15.3 Where witness statements and exhibits have become numerous, they should be put into separate bundles and the pages numbered consecutively throughout.
15.4 Where on account of their bulk the service of exhibits or copies of exhibits on the other parties would be difficult or impracticable, the directions of the court should be sought as to arrangements for bringing the exhibits to the attention of the other parties and as to their custody pending trial."

Always check exhibits carefully, especially for any privileged documents included by mistake. Waiver of privilege will almost invariably be assumed (see *Breeze v John Stacey* [1999] The Times, July 8 referred to at 10–30).

5. *Format: PD 32/19 and 20*

11–44   There are a number of detailed but fairly obvious requirements, none of which should cause undue difficulty. There are also some very helpful hints for proper drafting in PD 32, paras 19.2 and 20.1.

"19.1   A witness statement should:

(1) be produced on durable quality A4 paper with a 3.5cm margin,

(2) be fully legible and should normally be typed on one side of the paper only,

(3) where possible, be bound securely in a manner which would not hamper filing, or otherwise each page should be endorsed with the case number and should bear the initials of the witness,

(4) have the pages numbered consecutively as a separate statement (or as one of several statements contained in a file),

(5) be divided into numbered paragraphs,

(6) have all numbers, including dates, expressed in figures, and

(7) give the reference to any document or documents mentioned either in the margin or in bold text in the body of the statement."

This rule may seem at first sight to be unduly prescriptive, but it makes sound forensic sense to follow it for the simple reason that good layout will undoubtedly enhance the perceived quality of the contents. After all, in the days when oral examination in-chief was the norm, the skill of the advocate lay in so structuring the nature and sequence of her questions as to ensure that the witness's testimony emerged in as coherent and persuasive way possible. The same is equally true when it comes to drafting witness statements, as *O'Hare and Browne* state at 14–009:

"The role of a witness statement is to tell a story. The facts should run in chronological order. There must be no confusing flashbacks. The witness must tell his tale, in his own words, frame by frame. However, in telling it he must leave no gaps, no empty frames, no blurred pictures."

The easier a story is to read, the more likely it is that it will make an impact on the court trying the case. The Practice Direction recommends drafting in chronological order, this will usually be the most appropriate method.

"19.2 It is usually convenient for a witness statement to follow the chronological sequence of the events or matters dealt with, each paragraph of a witness statement should as far as possible be confined to a distinct portion of the subject."

The Practice Direction then goes on to state:

"20.1 A witness statement is the *equivalent of the oral evidence* [writer's emphasis] which that witness would, if called, give in evidence; it must include a statement by the intended witness that he believes the facts in it are true."

The full significance of the above paragraph will be explored in greater detail at 14–24, but it is not without its difficulties. The major problem confronting the drafter is that the Practice Direction requires him to prepare the statement by reference to a process which, unless he has trained as an advocate or sat through criminal trials, he will *never have seen* or ever be likely to see in a civil trial. Paragraph 20.2 goes on to require that the witness statement concludes with a statement of truth in the prescribed form, namely:

"20.2 To verify a witness statement the statement of truth is as follows:

"I believe that the facts stated in this witness statement are true."

20.3 Attention is drawn to rule 32.14 which sets out the consequences of verifying a witness statement containing a false statement without an honest belief in it truth."

Although proceedings for contempt of court for false statements are virtually unheard of, CPR 32.14 provides that:

"(1) Proceedings for contempt of court may be brought against a person if he makes, or causes to be made, a false statement in a document verified by a statement of truth without an honest belief in its truth. (Part 22 makes provision for a statement of truth.)

(2) Proceedings under this rule may be brought only:

    (a) by the Attorney General; or
    (b) with the permission of the court."

The circumstances in which such permission should be sought are rare, as was emphasised by Sir Richard Scott V.C. in *Malgar Ltd v R E Leach (Engineering) Ltd* [2000], *The Times*, February 17. The detailed procedure for obtaining permission is set out in PD 32/28. There are also detailed provisions for:

(1) Witnesses who cannot read or sign the statement (PD 32/21);

(2) Alterations (PD 32/22) which must be initialled; and

(3) Filing (PD 32/23) of statements.

The full text with accompanying notes can be found in Volume 1 of the *White Book*.

11–45   *Conclusion*   On the face of it the consequences of failure to comply could prove disastrous because PD 32/25 provides:

"25.1 Where:

(1) an affidavit;
(2) a witness statement, or
(3) an exhibit to either an affidavit or a witness statement,

does not comply with Part 32 or this practice direction in relation to its form, the court may refuse to admit it as evidence and may refuse to allow the costs arising from its preparation.
25.2 Permission to file a defective affidavit or witness statement or to use a defective exhibit may be obtained from a judge in the court where the case is proceeding."

However it is fair to say that most minor defects are ignored by the court and in any event taking technical objections has not found favour with the Court of Appeal. See for example the Court of Appeal decision in *Hannigan v Hannigan*, [2000] 2 F.C.R. 650. However care does need to be taken over detail, especially in those cases where compliance with a timetable may depend upon a formally correct witness statement having been filed and served. See for example, CPR 24.5(1), and CPR 32.10.

B Drafting: Some Practical Thoughts

11–46   In this section we shall examine further some of the ways in which the contents of a statement can be effectively drafted without overstepping the boundaries and substituting your own words for the testimony of the witness. Accordingly let us begin with a warning.

1. Beware of Over Enthusiastic Drafting
There have been a number of cases in which judges have criticised **11–47**
solicitors for "overzealous" drafting of witness statements, see for
example Lightman J. in *ZYX Music Gmbh v King* [1995] 3 All E.R. 1
and the Court of Appeal in *Odyssey Re (London) Limited v OIC Run
Off* [2000] EWCA Civ 71. Some of the most trenchant remarks were
made by Toulson J. in *Aquarius Financial Enterprises Inc v Certain
Underwriters at Lloyds*, unreported, April 30, 2001 in which he stated:

"48. The Law Society's Guide to the Professional Conduct of
Solicitors provides guidance on the taking of witness statements. It
requires a high degree of skill and professional integrity. The object
is to elicit that which the witness is truthfully able to say about relevant matters from his or her own knowledge or recollection, uninfluenced by what the statement taker would like him or her to say.
49. Counsel on both sides expressed anxiety that this is in practice not what generally happens even when are taken by solicitors.
If it is not, the situation is worrying. In the USA pre-trial deposi-
tions of witnesses are a standard feature of civil litigation. The
process is costly and time-consuming. Our system is quicker and
cheaper, but it depends for its proper working on witness statements
being properly taken. Bad practices, like bad money, tend to drive
out good. If bad practices in the taking of witness statements come
to be seen as normal, so that witness statements become lawyers'
artefacts rather than the witnesses' words, their use will have to be
reconsidered. Central to the problem is the ignorance of the court
and the other party about how any witness statement has in fact
been taken. It might therefore be thought salutary that, where a
witness statement is prepared by somebody other than the witness,
there should be a written declaration by the person who prepared
the statement giving information about how, when and where it was
prepared and certifying compliance with any appropriate code of
practice.
50. Moreover where parties are represented in litigation by
solicitors (as is almost invariably the case in the Commercial
Court), I would regard it as part of their duty to ensure, so far as
lies within their power, that any witness statements taken after they
have been instructed are taken either by themselves or, if for some
reason that is not practicable, by somebody who can be relied upon
to exercise the same standard as should apply if the statements
were taken by the solicitors themselves. So far as counsel may be
involved in the preparation of witness statements for use in civil
proceedings, there are rules and guidance in the Code of Conduct
for the Bar and in the Bar Council's supplementary guidance note
dated January 16, 2001."

This case had involved all kinds of extraordinary allegations including the fact that the defendant underwriters' private investigator, when interviewing a key witness, repeatedly tried to get him to change his story, shouted at him when he would not agree, held out the possibility of an *ex gratia* payment by the underwriters to cover his own losses if he co-operated and threatened him with arrest by the Italian police for conspiracy. It is hardly surprising therefore that Toulson J. expressed his concern so strongly.

2. What if English is not the Witness's First Language?

11–48   Paragraphs H1.5 and H1.6 of the *Commercial Court Guide* contain helpful advice which should be followed in all cases.

Fluency of Witness

"H1.5 Where a witness is not sufficiently fluent in English to give his evidence in English, the witness's statement should be in his own language and a translation provided.

H1.6 Where a witness is not fluent in English but can make himself understood in broken English and can understand written English, provided that these matters are indicated in the witness statement the statement need not be in his own words. It must however be written so as to express as accurately as possible the substance of his evidence."

Paragraph H1.6 very much mirrors the approach of Coleman J. in *NRG v Bacon and Woodrow (No.2)* [1995] 2 Lloyds Rep. 404 in which he made similar allowances in respect of a 194 page witness statement in English where the signatory's first language was Dutch. In any case where the court directs the filing of a statement in a foreign language PD32 para.23 must be complied with. This provides that:

"23.2 Where the court has directed that a witness statement in a foreign language is to be filed:

(1) the party wishing to rely on it must:

(a) have it translated, and
(b) file the foreign language witness statement with the court, and

2) the translator must make and file with the court an affidavit verifying the translation and exhibiting both the translation and a copy of the foreign language witness statement."

3. Do I Really Have to Include Everything?
The various High Court Practice Guides contain conflicting messages   **11–49**
on this. Despite criticisms in the Final Report of the Woolf Committee
that witness statements had become "an elaborate, costly branch of
legal drafting", CPR 32.5 gives the drafter little choice but to throw in
everything but the kitchen sink. The *Queen's Bench Guide* says:

"7.10.4 . . . the following matters should be borne in mind:

(1) A witness statement must contain the truth, the whole truth
    and nothing but the truth on the issues it covers,
(2) Those issues should consist only of the issues on which the
    party serving the witness statement wishes that witness to
    give evidence in chief and should not include commentary
    on the trial bundle or other matters which may arise during
    the trial.
(3) A witness statement should be as concise as the circum-
    stances allow, inadmissible or irrelevant material should not
    be included;
(4) The cost of preparation of an over-elaborate witness state-
    ment may not be allowed."

All Paragraph H1.3(d) of the *Commercial Court Guide* has to say is:

"a witness statement should not be longer than necessary and
should not contain lengthy renditions of correspondence."

Appendix 4 of the *Chancery Guide* states:

"2. Witness statements should be as concise as the circumstances
of the case allow . . .
    5. It is incumbent on solicitors and counsel not to allow the cost
of preparation of witness statements to be unnecessarily increased
by over-elaboration of the statements. Any unnecessary elaboration may be the subject of a special order to costs."
    7. A witness statement should simply cover those issues, but only
those issues, on which the party serving the statement wishes that
witness to give evidence in chief. Thus, it is not for example the function of a witness statement to provide a commentary on the documents in the trial. Witness statements should not deal with other
matters merely because they may arise in the course of the trial."

Accordingly the drafter is left with, on the one hand, "Put in everything the witness has to say that might be relevant to the issue"; but,
on the other hand, "Don't make 'everything' too long".

5. "Top Ten Tips" for Sensible Drafting

11–50   The points set out below are very much the writer's personal view, much of it derived from things that he has seen go wrong in practice. It is hoped that they will provide assistance to those working in a hurry and under pressure, the characteristic fate of the litigator.

(1) *Avoid "Lawyer Speak"*

11–51   It is extraordinary how often words and phrases such as "crave leave", "desirous", and "concerns" appear in a lay witness's witness statement. Not only will this provide the advocate with what *Hollander* (22–14) describes as some "fun" on occasions, it has the effect of undermining rather than enhancing the witness's credibility. The problem stems from the fact that, firstly, as lawyers we get so used to using this type of language that it is remarkably easy to insert it unthinkingly in a witness's statement. Secondly, unless you have actually called in the witness to take him through the statement line by line, it is unlikely that he will pick up on the inappropriateness of this type of language, indeed he just as likely to think that since it is for use in court, that type of language is required. Sadly, the problem is becoming worse rather than better, certainly in the case of smaller cases in which the statement has been prepared by a fee earner in a geographically remote firm with whom the witness has had no personal contact.

(b) *Avoid "Traffic Cop" Speak*

11–52   Any person involved in personal injury work, especially road traffic cases will know how commonplace it is to read statements containing language such as "vehicle", "proceed", "observe", and "drove into collision". What is wrong with old-fashioned words like "car", "go", "see" and "crash"? Quite apart from the fact that impersonal language of this kind does not tell any kind of story that grips the imagination just ask yourself how the court would react if during the course of giving oral evidence a witness, having been asked to recount what happened next began thus:

> "I had just travelled in a southerly direction through a traffic light controlled junction that was green in my favour . . ."

It would certainly raise the odd eyebrow, unless perhaps she really was a traffic cop. It is very easy habit to fall into, but represents very poor storytelling. Simple language always tells a better story and is likely to be far more consistent with the witness's own use of language. In an ideal world, witness statements would be drafted with the assistance of a tape recording of the witness's proposed testimony (it is sometimes done in really heavy cases) but the exigencies of cost will often rule out this approach.

(c) *Avoid over use of Value Laden Adverbs and Adjectives*
It may be a personal foible on the writer's part, but words such as   **11–53**
"definitely", "fortunately", "sure" and "certain" always raise a lurking doubt about who has put them there. Quite apart from that, it runs the risk of being challenged in cross-examination if the surrounding facts tend to undermine that certainty. On occasions witnesses genuinely express that degree of conviction, but the reasons for it should be fully gone into before it is included in the statement.

(d) *Avoid Inadmissible Opinion Evidence*
Do not forget that non-expert opinion evidence is generally inadmissible (see further 12–02). Hence, phrases such as "It was the fault of   **11–54**
the driver in the red car" should not appear. Apart from anything else, it creates the suspicion that the statement has simply been created by converting replies to an insurer's questionnaire into a statement without any attempt being made to speak to the witness and take down their account at first hand.

(e) *Avoid Irrelevance*
As already noted (4–44) the writer has always been puzzled by the   **11–55**
statement that invariably appears in road traffic cases along the lines of "I have been driving for ten years and have no motoring convictions". As a general rule, a party's driving record will have no relevance in any type of claim. The circumstances in which peripheral evidence placing the story in context is permitted has already been discussed under the heading of "padding" at 4–22.

(f) *Avoid Unnecessary Comments on Documents*
As already indicated, witness statements are often prepared not so   **11–56**
much with trial in mind but as a means of facilitating settlement or sowing "themes" (see further 14–21) in the judge's mind when she pre-reads the papers. Accordingly sentences such as:

"I would refer this Honourable Court to the letter of October 15, 2002 now produced and shown to the marked "ABC 1" which supports my recollection",

often appear, but should be avoided as far as possible. Once again, the most valuable assistance is to be found in the *Chancery Guide* para.7:

"a witness statement should simply cover those issues, but only those issues, on which the party serving the statement wishes that witness to give evidence in-chief. Thus it is not, for example, the function of a witness statement to provide a commentary on the documents in the trial bundle, nor to set out quotations from such documents, nor to engage in matters of argument."

Always ask yourself how you would wish the witness to deal with the document if he were being examined in-chief on it (see 5–58 for the risks that may flow from failing to do this).

(g) *Do not mix Facts and Advocacy on Interim Application*

11–57   The fact that witness statements are allowed to contain statements of information and belief often means that they read more like skeleton arguments. In the *Moat Housing* case referred to earlier (7–36) Brooke L.J. went so far as to say that one of the claimant's statements read more like an opening speech by counsel for the Crown in a criminal trial. All the rule entitles the signatory state is that he believes certain *facts* to be true based on the sources of information and belief indicated.

(h) *Control the Grammar, Syntax and Order of Topics*

11–58   There is nothing untoward in taking reasonable steps to polish up the witness's language provided it is kept within reasonable bounds. Always start with the premise that the witness's own words are best but do not be afraid to remove or rephrase his language if it is expressed in a way that would not meet with the court's approval. After all, if you were examining him in-chief, you would be able to exercise a considerable degree of control over the witness' answers (see further the section on examination in-chief at 14–24). As already indicated, para.19.2 of PD 32 positively encourages this approach.

(i) *Confine Statements to the Issues*

11–59   In an ideal world witnesses should be interviewed before the decision to embark on litigation is taken, with the results being written up in the form of a draft, traditionally referred to as a "Proof of Evidence". This document should ideally cover everything that could conceivably touch and concern the likely issues in the case including matters that would not be admissible in the proceedings themselves because, for example, they were privileged. It is now downright dangerous to embark on litigation before these steps have been take since, with the current emphasis on early disclosure, allegations and counter allegations in correspondence will need to be expressed with a far higher degree of precision than used to be the case. Once the case has progressed to directions for the exchange of evidence, it will be necessary to examine with care what issues remain in dispute (the technique recommended in *O'Hare and Browne* at 22–005 and 22–006 may be of assistance) and then to prepare statements that are confined to those issues: unfortunately, this does not always happen. However profligacy in the drafting of witness statements may well lead to the costs of preparing them being disallowed.

(j) *Take Drafting Seriously*
If insufficient thought is given to this, the consequences can be disas-   **11–60**
trous (*Odyssey Re (London) Ltd v IOC Run Off Ltd* [2000] EWCA Civ 71 discussed at 5–58 being a classic example). It is also important that you are familiar with Principles 21.10 and 21.11 in the *Guide to the Professional Conduct of Solicitors* (The Law Society (1999)), the most important features of which are:

(1) It is permissible to interview a prospective witness even if they have already been interviewed by another party because there is no property in a witness;

(2) If you are aware that a witness is likely to be called by another party extreme caution is necessary: any interview should normally be carried out in the presence of a representative of the other side;

(3) There is nothing untoward in placing an advertisement inviting witnesses to come forward but care should be taken not to offer too much detail lest there be accusations of prompting;

(4) Although witness other than experts may be offered reasonable expenses and compensation for lost time, they should never be offered payment contingent upon the evidence they give or the result of the case.

IV USE OF WITNESS STATEMENTS AT TRIAL

Throughout this work great emphasis has been placed on the need to   **11–61**
"think trial from day 1". Accordingly, although the trial will be covered in Chapter 14, it is important to be aware of how witness statements are actually received in evidence, because, armed with this knowledge, it will be easier to follow good drafting practice.

A Use of Statements at Trial

1. Compliance with Case Management Directions
CPR 32.10 provides that if a witness statement has not been served   **11–62**
within the time specified:

"the witness may not be asked to give oral evidence unless the court gives permission".

This raises an intriguing point. Does it still permit a party to put in the statement *itself* as hearsay evidence? On the face of it the answer appears to be, technically, "yes" since failure to serve a hearsay notice under CPR 33.2 would not debar the party concerned tendering the statement as hearsay evidence (see 7–26). What weight the court would attach to it is another matter, but it is hard to see how a party could be prevented from using the statement in this way.

2. Examination in-Chief

11–63   Examination in-chief had become unusual as a result of *Case Management Practice Direction* [1995] 1 W.L.R. 262 under which a witness's exchanged statement under RSC O.38 r.2A would normally stand as his evidence in-chief. This process has not been affected by Civil Evidence Act 1995 (see s.6(1) at 7–43), or by CPR 32. However, CPR 32.5 strictly limits the evidence which a witness may give in-chief as follows:

"(1)   If—

    (a) a party has served a witness statement; and
    (b) he wishes to rely at trial on the evidence of the witness who made the statement as direct evidence,

he must call the witness to give oral evidence unless the court orders otherwise or he puts in the statement as hearsay evidence.

(2)   Where a witness is called to give oral evidence under paragraph (1), his witness statement shall stand as his evidence in-chief unless the court orders otherwise.

(3)   A witness giving oral evidence at trial may with the permission of the court—

    (a) amplify his witness statement; and
    (b) give evidence in relation to new matters which have arisen since the witness statement was served on the other parties.

(4)   The court will give permission under paragraph 3 only if it considers there is good reason not to confine the evidence of the witness to the contents of his witness statement.

(5)   If a party who has served a witness statement does not—

    (a) call the witness to give evidence at trial; or
    (b) put in the witness statement as hearsay evidence,

any other party may put in the witness statement as hearsay evidence."

A number of facets of this rule need to be considered in detail.

(a) *Statement as Evidence In-Chief*

In effect this means that all the advocate calling the witness need do is **11–64** introduce the evidence as set out below after the witness has been sworn. However, that would be a somewhat unnerving experience for the witness and so an advocate is generally permitted to ask a few introductory questions to "settle the witness in." Although leading questions are still not permitted it causes no problems in practice because you are always reminding a witness of what he has already given in evidence. This technique is sometimes termed "focusing". For example:

"Focus": "Mr Adams I'd like you to turn to paragraph 8 of your statement, that's on page 21. About half way down you say Mr Johnstone became "very agitated" at this point.

Q. Could you please tell the court in a little more detail exactly how he was behaving?"

You can then move the witness on by use of another technique known as "linking".

"Link": "I'd now like to move on to a telephone conversation you say you had with Mr Johnstone on July 16, 2000."

In this way, it is possible for the examination in-chief to "flow" smoothly from one topic to the next.

(b) *"Amplifying" and "Updating"*

CPR 32.5(3) permits this but only if there is "good reason" (CPR **11–65** 32.5(4)). There is no current case law on how this discretion should be exercised but the approach of the Court of Appeal in *Coles v Kivells* [1997], *The Times*, May 2 is instructive. In it Mummery L.J. stated:

"This case invites comments on the use of witness statements at the trial of this action. Under paragraph 5 of the *Practice Direction* [1995] 1 W.L.R. 262, Vol 2 of the Supreme Court Practice page 270 it is provided that:

'unless otherwise ordered, every witness statement should stand as the evidence-in-chief of the witness concerned.'

That course was adopted, even though there was a conflict of evidence on the crucial issue of Kivells' retainer. In the interests of saving time and costs the opening of the case was short and the documents were not opened before oral evidence was called. The Practice Direction on witness statements should not be inflexibly applied. To the extent that the witness statements reveal that there is no factual dispute, it is sensible that they should stand as evidence-in-chief. That is consistent with the requirements of fairness, expedition and saving costs. It is stated in Volume 1 of the Supreme Court Practice (p.651 38/2A/4) that, even where directions are given for the pre-trial exchange of witness statements, the trial judge retains a discretion to require a witness to give evidence orally. That discretion is unfettered. In this case it would have been appropriate to ask the judge to exercise his discretion, so that the key witnesses, Mr H . . . and Mr R . . . C . . ., could have given their evidence-in-chief orally on the issues where there was a conflict of fact. That course might have clarified the issues of fact and sharpened focus on the conflicts of evidence to be resolved."

The only question mark this passage raises is what constitutes a "good reason" for the exercise of the judge's discretion. It is submitted that the need to determine the claims justly in accordance with CPR I will always supply a "good reason".

(c) The Witness who Fails to Come up to Proof

11–66 If the reason for this is nerves or forgetfulness rather than a refusal to tell the truth, the witness is classified as "unfavourable". However, in practical terms this is unlikely to cause a problem during examination in-chief because of CPR 32.5(1). If the witness is then damaged in cross-examination, the court still retains a discretion to rely on the contents of his witness statement. This approach can be found in *NRG v Bacon and Woodrow* [1995] 2 Lloyds Rep. 404 in which the principal witness, by then retired, signed a 194 page statement. He admitted under cross-examination that he could no longer remember all of the contents. However, Coleman J. was satisfied that at the time he signed the statement he was telling the truth. Accordingly it was admitted as hearsay evidence. The CPR do not specifically deal with the above situation but the statement will be independently admissible under s.1 of the 1995 Act, subject to the court's overriding discretion to exclude it under the CPR 32.1(2). Do bear in mind however that damaging inferences may on occasions be drawn from differences between what is in a witness's statement and what emerges under cross-examination (see, in particular *Odyssey Re (London) Ltd v OIC Run-Off* [2000] EWCA Civ 71 discussed at 5–58).

(d) The Witness who Refuses to Come up to Proof

11–67 If the reason for the witness failing to give evidence expected of him is a refusal to tell the truth at the instance of the party calling him the court may be asked to rule the witness "hostile". The witness may then be cross-examined on the facts of the case and any previous inconsistent statement can be proved (ss.3 to 5 of the Criminal Procedure Act 1865), if he denies making it. Note that, as in criminal proceedings, (see s.119 of the Criminal Justice Act 2003) the statement itself is admissible as evidence of its contents under ss.1 and 6(3) of the Civil Evidence Act 1995, as it was under s.3 1968 Act.

(e) *The Absent Witness*
So far as witness statements served in accordance with CPR 32 are **11–68** concerned, if the witness is not available to give oral evidence there are two alternatives:

(1) The party who served the statement may tender it as evidence (CPR 32.5(1); or

(2) If he chooses not to call the witness or tender his statement, any other party may put it in (CPR 32.5(5)).

If a party adopts the second course, and tenders it as hearsay evidence the use to which it may then be put is restricted as a result of the Court of Appeal decision in *McPhilemy v The Times Newspapers* [2000] C.P.L.R. 335 because, in effect you cannot put it in for the purpose of seeking to demolish it by, for example suggesting that is inconsistent, tendentious or inherently incredible (or all three). In effect, by putting it in, you are making the signatory "your" witness and therefore, by analogy with the restrictions on cross-examining your own witness, there is no general right of impeachment (interestingly, no reference was made to the very wide terms of s.4(2) of the 1995 Act; see 7–35). Brooke L.J. stated:

"I know of no principle of the law of evidence by which a party may put in evidence the written statement of a witness knowing that her evidence conflicts to a substantial degree with the case he is seeking to plead before the jury, on the basis that he will say straight away in the witness's absence that the jury [or court] should disbelieve as untrue a substantial part of that evidence".

This can cause major problems when a party has included in his trial bundle numerous witness statements the contents of which the other party strongly disputes. If they are pre-read by the trial judge and the witnesses are then not called the other party may be at a substantial disadvantage in that:

(1) He will not want to call the witnesses himself because, absent hostility, it will not be possible to cross-examine them; and

(2) He will not be able to put in the statement himself and then attack them.

This issue has been addressed by the Court of Appeal in *Society of Lloyds v Jaffray* [2000] EWCA Civ 1101 in which the Court of Appeal stated that:

(1) A party is entitled not to call a witness whose statement they have served or tender the statement in evidence; but

(2) It is desirable to inform the judge *before* he is asked to read the statements that the witness's evidence will not be tendered:

"It does not seem to us in principle to be desirable that a judge should be asked to read the statement of a witness until a decision to call him has been made, or at any rate unless he is informed of the position."

Furthermore, as already noted at 4–21, in *Wisniewski v Central Manchester HA* [1998] P.I.Q.R. (P) 324 the Court of Appeal held that a court may be entitled to draw adverse inferences from the absence or silence of a witness who might be expected to have material evidence to give on an issue in an action provided certain criteria are satisfied. This case has been followed and applied in *Lloyds v Jaffray*:

"It seems to us that on aspects where the evidence points in a direction against Lloyds in an area which could have been dealt with by Mr R the judge should have drawn an adverse inference from Lloyds' failure to call Mr R to deal with it. This does not mean that any allegation that the names make against Mr R must be accepted because he did not give evidence. It simply means that where the evidence points in a certain direction an adverse inference can be drawn from a failure to call the witness to deal with it."

Another result of putting it in as hearsay evidence is that any other party may then apply for a cross-examination order under CPR 33.4. This situation arose, albeit in somewhat unusual circumstances in *Douglas v Hello* [2003] EWCA Civ 332.

11–69   **Facts:** The famous Hollywood couple Michael Douglas and Catherine Zeta-Jones sought damages against D1 to D5 in respect of unauthorised photographs taken at their wedding. In the course of preparing for trial D4 and D5 obtained a statement from SN who was at the relevant time a picture editor at D1, the publishers of the forbidden photographs. Although her statement was served in their witness statement bundle, D4 and D5 never called her or put her witness statement in as hearsay evidence. However counsel for D1 and D2, after due consideration decided that he would put SN's statement in as hearsay.

The claimants applied for a cross-examination order and the Court of Appeal upheld the judge's order granting their application. It mattered not that they themselves had interviewed SN, taken a statement from her, served it in their witness statement bundle. and had initially declined to call her.

2. Cross-Examination

The opposing party has right to cross-examine a witness. He may be cross-examined on: **11–70**

(1) His entire witness statement whether or not it was referred to in-chief (CPR 32.11);

(2) Any previous inconsistent statement made by a witness may be put to him and, if necessary, proved under ss.4 and 5 of the Criminal Procedure Act, 1865 (see 14–55). Because there is no rule against hearsay in civil proceedings any previous inconsistent statement may be treated by the court as original evidence and can form the basis for findings of fact;

(3) Any admissible and relevant document;

(4) As to credit, subject to the usual restrictions (see 14–51).

The requirement that a cross-examiner must "put his case" is unaffected by the CPR, see *Deepak Fertilisers and Petrochemical Company Ltd v Davy McKee (UK) London Ltd* [2002] EWCA Civ 1006 in which the Court of appeal stated:

"49. The general rule in adversarial proceedings as between the parties is that one party should not be entitled to impugn the evidence of another party's witness if he has not asked appropriate questions enabling the witness to deal with the criticisms that are being made. This general rule is stated in *Phipson on Evidence* (15th Edn) at para.11–26 in the following terms:

"As a rule a party should put to each of his opponent's witnesses in turn so much of his own case as concerns that particular witness, or in which he had a share, e.g. if the witness has deposed a conversation, the opposing counsel should put to the witness any significant differences from his own case. If he asks no questions he will generally be taken to accept the witness's account and will not be permitted to attack it in his final speech. . . . Failure to cross-examine will not, however, always amount to acceptance of the witness's testimony, if for example the witness has had notice to the contrary beforehand, or the story itself is of an incredible or romancing character.""

50. The caveat in the sentence that I have quoted, is important particularly in the context of the Civil Procedure Rules in which, by Part 32 r.1(3) the court is given a power to limit cross-examination. Nonetheless, the general rule remains a valid rule of good practice and fairness. The judge of fact is, however, in a different position from the protagonists. So long as a matter remains clearly in issue, it is the judge's task to determine the facts on which the issue is to be decided. However it seems to me that where, as in the present case, an issue has been identified, but then counsel asks no questions, the judge should be slow to conclude that it remains an issue which has to be determined on the basis of an assessment of reliability or credibility without enquiry of the parties as to their position. The judge should be particularly cautious of doing so if he or she has not given any indication of concern about the evidence so as to alert the witness or counsel acting on the side calling the witness, to the fact that it may be that further explanation should be given in relation to the issue in question.

51. At the end of the day each case will depend upon the way in which the issue arose, and was dealt with in evidence. The present case is a good example of the way unfairness can arise if a judge makes an adverse finding in the absence of a very secure basis for so doing".

3. What if a Witness is Disbelieved?

11–71   All is not lost. It is now clear from the Court of Appeal decision in *Binks v Securicor Omega Express Ltd* 1 W.L.R. 2557. This case establishes that a claimant who has been disbelieved may still seek to amend his claim and seek judgment on any alternative factual basis for finding in his favour that has emerged on *all* of the evidence. This is so even though the alternative case conflicts with the account given in his witness statement and supported by his statement of truth. Maurice Kay J. (with whom Pill and Carnwath L.JJ agreed) stated at [9]:

> "Although I accept that the purpose of Part 22 is to deter or discourage claimants from advancing a case which is entirely untrue or wholly speculative (a purpose which will never be wholly achieved), I do not accept that its purpose extends to the possibility of relieving of liability a defendant whose own evidence may establish a cause of action against him. That would not be consistent with the overriding objective of dealing with a case justly (CPR 1.1(1))."

Accordingly, the court allowed the claimant's appeal against a decision of the trial judge who had refused an application by counsel to amend his Particulars of Claim at the close of the trial on the basis of an alternative case of negligence that had emerged from the *defendants'* evidence.

Conclusions   Although the use of witness statements does have the   **11–72**
beneficial effect of enabling all parties to know well in advance of the
trial the case that they have to meet, they:

(1) Have added to the cost of trial preparation;

(2) Are often drafted more with a view to negotiation than preparation for trial;

(3) Are often filled with irrelevancies and opinion evidence;

(4) In smaller cases are often prepared without the witness ever being seen in person;

they are here to stay. Nevertheless, one should never lose sight of the fact that, certainly in commercial cases, less so in personal injury claims, it is often the contemporary documents that give the better indication of where the truth lies: *Gow v Harker* [2003] EWCA Civ 1160 discussed at 5–09 onwards bears this out.

Chapter 12

Opinion Evidence and Experts

Expert opinion evidence is admissible only because, by statute, it constitutes an exception to the rule against the admission of opinion evidence. It is the last of the mandatory rules of exclusion (see 1–21 onwards) to be considered and has been left until now because it has to be considered in conjunction with CPR 35 (Expert Evidence) and the supporting Practice Direction ("the Expert Practice Direction"). Since June 2005 parties are also required to have regard to the guidance offered in the Civil Justice Council's *Protocol for the Instruction of Experts to give Evidence in Civil Claims* ("The Expert Protocol") which now appears as an Annex to the Expert Practice Direction. Those seeking a fuller commentary on the substantive law should consult Chapter 33 of *Phipson*. There is also much of value in Chapter 23 of *Hollander*. Further commentary on procedural aspects of CPR 35 can be found in Chapter 31 of *O'Hare and Browne*, Chapter 23 of *Hollander* and the relevant section (CPR 35) of the *White Book*.

12–01

I THE GENERAL RULE

As a general rule, opinion evidence is inadmissible because it usurps the function of the court, namely, to interpret the evidence placed before it. It operates, subject to exceptions, as an absolute rule of exclusion. Accordingly a statement of opinion will be equally inadmissible if, for example:

12–02

(1) It appears as a sentence in a witness statement served under CPR 32 (however, statements often *do*, quite wrongly, contain such opinions); or

(2) If it is put in cross-examination to a witness, for example:

Q. "So do you think it was safe to be driving at that speed?"

Such questions are nevertheless frequently (and wrongly) put by inexperienced advocates.

(3) A police officer (unless the court has given permission for him to give expert evidence under CPR 35) expresses an opinion as to the cause of the collision in the Police Accident Report (just because a document is admissible does not mean that its contents are);

(4) An expert authorised under CPR 35 expresses an opinion, either in a written report or while giving oral evidence, which relates to a matter outside of his area of expertise; or

(5) An expert's opinion based on facts which are not proved to the court's satisfaction.

Although there are a number of exceptions to the exclusionary rule (for a full list see *Phipson* 33–02 to 33–09 and 33–69 to 33–75), the only two of any significance are (1) expert opinion evidence and (2) certain categories of lay opinion evidence, both of which are governed in the first instance by the Civil Evidence Act 1972.

1. Experts

12–03 If appropriately qualified, an expert may give opinion evidence on matters within the scope of his or her expertise. Section 3(1) of the Civil Evidence Act 1972 provides:

> "Subject to any rules of court made in pursuance this Act, where a person is called as a witness in any civil proceedings, his opinion on any relevant matter on which he is qualified to give expert evidence shall be admissible in evidence".

Before it can be admitted such evidence must therefore satisfy four requirements:

(1) The witness must qualify as an "expert" within a recognised field;

(2) His or her expertise must be relevant to an issue in the case;

(3) The relevant procedural rules governing the admission of expert opinion evidence set out in CPR 35 must be complied with. Most importantly, no expert opinion evidence is admissible at any hearing unless the court has first given its permission under CPR 35.4; and

(4) The expert's testimony must be based upon admissible facts.

Nearly all the reported cases tend to concern matters relating to (3) above. As a result parties sometimes tend to lose sight of the fact that CPR 35 is rule of *procedure* regulating evidence that is only admissible in the first place as an exception to a *substantive* rule of evidence. It should also be noted that *hearsay* opinion evidence is as admissible as "live" opinion evidence under the Civil Evidence Act 1995: the implications of this are considered further at 12–60.

2. Non-Expert Opinion Under s.3(2) of the Civil Evidence Act 1972
It is by no means uncommon for witness statements to express opinions as to, for example, the speed of a vehicle, the state of the weather or road conditions. Some go even further and openly state, for example, "the bus driver was in no way to blame for the accident" (these words were actually used by a witness in *Rasool v West Midlands Passenger Transport Board* [1974] 3 All E.R. 638 and appear to have been accepted by the court without comment). In practice, as is the case with irrelevant evidence, the court generally tends to simply attach little or no weight to such evidence rather than formally exclude it. However, a witness may, to a limited extent, give value-laden evidence by virtue of s.3(2) which provides that: **12–04**

> "where a person is called as a witness in any civil proceedings a statement of opinion by him on any relevant matter on which he is not qualified to give expert evidence, if made as a way of conveying relevant facts usually perceived by him is admissible as evidence of what he perceived".

Section 3(3) goes on to state that "relevant matter" includes an issue in the proceedings in question. Examples would include:

(1) The speed of a vehicle;

(2) Road or weather conditions;

(3) Identification of an individual; and

(4) Identification of a person's handwriting.

Many of the cases, especially in relation to handwriting, are of considerable antiquity and are fully covered in *Phipson* 33–73. The most important feature of the handwriting cases is that the witness's knowledge of the handwriting must have been acquired from knowledge gained *before* litigation was in prospect.

3. Affidavits and Witness Statements: "The False Exception"
Witness statements and affidavits, whether for use at trial or other hearings may contain statements of information or belief provided the source and grounds are stated. This is expressly provided for in PD   **12–05**

32/4.2 (affidavits) and PD 32/18.2 (witness statements) and has already been discussed at 11–37. However this should not be read as authorising the wholesale introduction of opinion evidence; statements of belief are only admissible insofar as they relate to belief as to facts.

II EXPERT EVIDENCE

12–06   This represents by far the most important exception to the rule against opinion evidence. However, as many commentators have observed (see, for example *Phipson* at 33–10) a great deal of expert evidence is evidence as to observed *facts*, albeit of a highly specialised nature. For example, when an orthopaedic consultant examines a claimant in a personal injury claim, say, as to the degree of flexion and extension in a joint, she is no less a witness of fact than the bystander who observed the accident in which the claimant received his injury. However, this is a distinction that has not, on the whole received a great deal of judicial recognition. Rare examples can be found in *Stevens v Gullis* [2000] 1 All E.R. 227 (discussed further at 12–30) and in some clinical negligence claims (discussed further at 12–62). The distinction is, in theory, important, because the factual parts of the expert's evidence are not subject to the restrictions in CPR 35 and, accordingly, are as admissible as any other factual evidence.

A The Main Rule

12–07   At common law, as stated in *Phipson* at 33–09:

"... the opinions of skilled witnesses [are] admissible wherever the subject is one upon which competency to form an opinion can only be acquired by a course of special study or experience",

this was placed on a statutory footing by s.3(1) of the Civil Evidence Act 1972 (12–03) which, for the first time, made the admission of expert evidence subject to procedural requirements. The headlong advance of scientific and technical progress is such that it would be futile to attempt any catalogue of recognised areas of expertise. In every case where the witness's expertise is novel or unusual, the burden will lie upon the party seeking to rely upon it to establish that it comes within the above definition. This issue was addressed by Evans-Lombe J. in *Barings plc v Coopers & Lybrand (No.2)* [2001] Lloyd's Rep Bank 85. In that case, the judge had given the defendants permission to adduce in evidence the reports of three experts in "banking management". Having obtained the reports and served them on the claimants, the claimants applied for them to be excluded as evidence on the ground that there was no identifiable expertise in "banking management" on which the writers of the reports were competent to express an opinion. After an extensive review of the relevant case law, Evans-Lombe J. refused to grant the order sought. A brief summary of the recognised categories of expertise appears below: for a fuller commentary see *Phipson* at 33–53 to 33–68.

1. Areas of Expertise

Evidence on the following subjects are generally accepted as being within a recognised expertise. This list is no more than a "snapshot": if you can find a person who claims he has an expertise that is relevant to an issue in the case, you are free to seek the court's permission to rely on her evidence. The Academy of Experts maintains a comprehensive list of experts across a wide range of disciplines: their website can be found at *www.academy.org.uk*. **12–08**

(1) The opinions of medical experts as to matters of diagnosis, prognosis, accepted practice and ethics falling within their areas of expertise;

(2) Evidence of accountants as to the interpretation of accounting information including evidence of fraud and the valuation of businesses;

(3) Actuarial evidence as to life expectancy and the cost of annuities;

(4) Engineering evidence in marine and construction claims, and health and safety experts in industrial injury and disease claims;

(5) Evidence as to what is customary practice within a particular trade including, for example, the normal practice on restraint of trade covenants;

(6) Surveyor evidence as to the likely resale or rental value of a building or its state or condition;

(7) Valuation evidence from artists, dealers or restorers as to the value and/genuineness of works of art.

2. Foreign Law

This is the one area in which expert evidence is, in effect, mandatory. The requirement apples equally to Scots and Commonwealth law. The role of the expert is to: **12–09**

(1) Inform the court as to the relevant law;

(2) Refer the court to any relevant authorities explaining their status, for example as binding precedent;

(3) In cases of uncertainty, to assist the court to decide how the foreign tribunal would have ruled if the matter were to have fallen for decision there.

Proof of foreign law has been simplified as a result of changes introduced by s.4 of the Civil Evidence Act 1972.

(a) *Who Qualifies as an Expert?*

12–10   Section 4(1) of the 1972 Act provides that a person is qualified to give his opinion on foreign law:

". . . irrespective of whether he has acted or whether he is entitled to act as legal practitioner there."

Thus there would nothing to prevent an English academic lawyer from giving expert evidence as to a foreign legal system provided her expertise could be established in the usual way. A comprehensive list of those who have either been granted or refused permission to testify appears at 33–57 to 33–58 of *Phipson*.

(b) *Status of a Previous Ruling on Foreign Law*

12–11   At common law, a previous decision was not binding because it was a question of *fact* decided on *evidence* (see 6–24 onwards). However, ss.4(2) to (5) of the 1972 Act now provides that if:

(1) It is a decision of the High Court or above (s.4(4)); and

(2) Reported or recorded in citable form (s.4(2)(b)); and

(3) The prescribed notice is given under CPR 33.7,

the foreign law,

". . . shall be taken to be in accordance with that finding or decision unless the contrary is proved."

It appears that the effect of this presumption is similar to that in s.11 of the Civil Evidence Act 1968 (see *Phoenix v China Ocean* [1999] 1 Lloyd's Rep. 683 at 684–685).

3. *Expert Evidence not Allowed*

12–12   As a general rule, the issue of whether or not a witness is competent to give opinion evidence under s.3(1) of the 1972 Act should be regarded as a question of fact. Clearly, no expert should ever be permitted to express an opinion that is outside his field of expertise. A spectacular example of this can be found in *Liddell v Middleton* [1996] P.I.Q.R. 56 in which an engineer called as an expert in a road traffic claim had been permitted to express a value judgement as to the defendant's standard of driving. The Court of Appeal, not surprisingly, stated that it was not the role of such an expert to make general comments on the evidence. In addition, (see *Phipson* at 33–44 to 33–68) there are a number of situations in which the court has traditionally set its face against the admission of expert opinion evidence, most notable among these are:

(1) The credibility of a witness. The courts have always been astute to reserve this task to the tribunal of fact. Although there seems to be some movement away from a rigid application of the rule in criminal cases, at any rate where the witness is alleged to be mentally ill or suffering from some cognitive disorder (see, for example *R. v Pinfold* [2004] 2 Cr.App.R. 5 and *R. v Blackburn* [2005] EWCA Crim 1349) there is no evidence of a similar movement in civil cases.

(2) The construction of documents. The interpretation and meaning of words and phrases in a document is regarded as a question of fact for the judge, unless there are technical terms within it that can only be interpreted with the aid of expert testimony.

(3) Normal human behaviour. Scientific evidence is not generally admissible as to how a person would be likely to behave when confronted with a particular situation. The only notable exception is in the case of market research evidence where the court, influenced presumably by the more persuasive effect of collective wisdom (or lack of it) has admitted such evidence (see, for example *Reckitt & Colman Products Ltd v Borden Inc (No.2)* [1987] F.S.R. 407).

(4) Probability theories. There have been occasions in criminal cases where statistical evidence as to probability, in particular a form of analysis known as *Bayes' Theorem*, have been placed before juries, in particular for the purpose of evaluating DNA evidence. However the Court of Appeal in *R. v Doheny and Adams* [1997] 1 Cr. App.R. 369 strongly discouraged the use of such evidence.

(5) Lawyers' professional conduct. The courts are particularly unwilling to admit evidence as to, for example, conveyancing practice, being of the general opinion that these are matters of law for the judge to determine. For example, in *Bown v Gould and Swayne* [1996] P.N.L.R. 440 the court held that, in a professional negligence case against a conveyancing solicitor, expert evidence as to conveyancing

practice was inadmissible for the reason stated above. However, it is submitted that this decision is not authority for the proposition that expert evidence on conveyancing practice should *never* be admitted. Each case will depend on its own facts, and if there is some specialised matter upon which expert evidence can assist the court, the evidence should be admitted. An example of this can be found in the decision of H.H. Judge Jack Q.C. in *Macy v Woollcombe Beer & Watts* [1998] 51 E.G. 88.

B The Definition of an "Expert"

12–13   Quite apart from complying with CPR 35 and establishing that the witness is possessed of knowledge that is sufficiently specialised to constitute an "expertise", the party seeking to rely on the expert's opinion must also establish that he or she is an "expert" within that field. In the vast majority of cases, this is taken as a given. Paragraph 13.6 of the Expert Protocol states:

> "The details of experts' qualifications to be given in reports should be commensurate with the nature and complexity of the case. It may be sufficient merely to state academic and professional qualifications. However, where highly specialised expertise is called for, experts should include the detail of particular training and/or experience that qualifies them to provide that highly specialised evidence."

However, it should also be noted that the definition of "expert" in CPR 35.2 is:

> ". . . an expert who has been instructed to give or prepare evidence *for the purpose of court proceedings* [writer's emphasis]".

As is pointed out in *Phipson* at 33–22 and *Hollander* at 23–15, there is a difference between an expert who is merely instructed to *advise* (for which you do not need the court's permission) and one who is instructed for the purpose of giving *opinion evidence* (where you do need the court's permission if you wish to rely on it). The practical implications of this are considered further at 12–28.

1. Purpose of Expert Evidence
12–14   This is now set out in Paragraph 6.1 of the Expert Protocol which provides:

> "Those intending to instruct experts to give or prepare evidence for the purpose of civil proceedings should consider whether expert

evidence is appropriate, taking account of the principles set out in CPR Parts 1 and 35, and in particular whether:

(a) it is relevant to a matter which is in dispute between the parties;
(b) it is reasonably required to resolve the proceedings (CPR 35.1);
(c) the expert has expertise relevant to the issue on which an opinion is sought;
(d) the expert has the experience, expertise and training appropriate to the value, complexity and importance of the case; and whether
(e) these objects can be achieved by the appointment of a single joint expert."

The clear tenor of this passage, in accordance with the philosophy of the CPR, is that it is not sufficient to satisfy yourself that the witness is possessed of the *ability* to express an opinion that is relevant to an issue in the proceedings, you must also be satisfied that his of her instruction is "appropriate" under CPR 1.

2. *Proof of Expertise*

It is commonplace these days for expert reports to contain the writer's **12–15** CV, often listing a most impressive range of qualifications, diplomas and publications. However, formal qualifications are not an essential prerequisite to a witness being accorded the status of an expert. There are numerous instances in criminal proceedings of police officers being accorded expert status by virtue of specialist knowledge gained "in the field" (see the cases cited in *Phipson* at 33–46). However, instances of this in civil proceedings are rarer. A recent example is *Duffy v North Central plc*, unreported, May 5, 2000 in which an unqualified computer technician had been accepted by the trial judge as an expert. The claimant's application for leave to appeal was refused: Mance L.J. stated (at [13]):

"It seems to me, reading his report, reading the account of his evidence in the judgment, he clearly had expertise in order to be an expert. You do not have to have a degree in computing. You can acquire expertise through experience on the ground and [he] certainly had plenty of that."

Conversely, formal qualifications will not, of themselves, lead to the expert's evidence being admitted if it is not relevant to an issue in the case, or is not an issue that is susceptible to expert opinion. For example, in *Larby v Thurgood* [1992] *The Times*, October 27 the defendant wished to rely on the evidence of an employment consultant to show that the claimant had not been making reasonable attempts to mitigate his loss by seeking employment. The evidence was disallowed on the basis that, however expert he might be on matters such as the availability of employment in the area, the issue of the claimant's credibility was for the court to determine.

3. Competence on the Ultimate Issue

12–16   Experts are witnesses: they give evidence, they do not decide cases. This principle was traditionally embodied in the so-called "ultimate issue rule" which in effect precluded an expert witness from stating, for example, that in his opinion, the defendant had undoubtedly been negligent. However, s.3(1) of the Civil Evidence Act 1972 is so widely drawn, it is now generally accepted that the "ultimate issue" rule, has impliedly been abolished. Section 3(1) permits an expert, subject to CPR 35, to give his opinion on any "relevant matter", which s.3(3) of the 1972 Act defines as including:

"An issue in the proceedings in question".

Thus, for example, in a professional negligence case, not only may an expert witness be asked whether or not, in his view, the defendant exercised the requisite standard of care but also, the court may determine liability on the basis of such opinion. This places an additional burdenon the judge where there are conflicting opinions because she will be required to give full reasons as to why she prefers one expert over another (see *Flannery v Halifax Estate Agencies* [2000] 1 W.L.R. 377 and the commentary at 35.0.2 of the *White Book*). Much of the relevant case law (see *Phipson* at 33–12 to 33–15) relates to criminal proceedings where the impact of the jury is manifest. In the non-criminal field, the roles of the expert and the judge have clashed most frequently in children proceedings. However, the Court of Appeal decision in *re M and R (Minors) (Sex Abuse: Evidence)* [1996] 4 All E.R. 239 can be taken to have laid down principles which are of general application. Although the judgment predates the CPR it is equally relevant today both in respect of oral evidence and written reports. Following a full examination of the origins and ultimate demise of the "ultimate issue" rule, Butler-Sloss L.J. concluded (at [252]:

"So the passing of the [1972] Act should not operate to force the court to, in Wigmore's words 'waste its time listening to superfluous and cumbersome testimony', provided that the judge never loses sight of the central truths: namely that the ultimate decision is for him, and that all questions of relevance and weight are for him. If the expert's opinion is clearly irrelevant, he will say so. But, if arguably relevant but in his view ultimately unhelpful, he can generally prevent its reception by indicating that the expert's answer to the question would carry little weight with him. The modern view is to regulate matters by way of weight rather than admissibility. But when the judge is of the opinion that the witness's expertise is still required to assist him to answer the ultimate questions (including, where appropriate, credibility) then the judge can safely and gratefully rely on such evidence, while never losing sight of the fact that the final decision is for him."

These divisions of function are not always easy to reconcile. Do they **12–17** mean, for example, that if an expert puts forward a theory on the facts that is at odds with the testimony of an otherwise credible witness, the court is bound to reject that witness's evidence? The answer to that, following the Court of Appeal decision in *Armstrong v First York* [2005] 1 W.L.R. 2751 is, "Not necessarily". This was a road traffic claim in which the two claimants, a prison officer and a recruitment counsellor, alleged that they had sustained minor whiplash type injuries as a result of a low speed collision with a bus in the centre of York. The defendants admitted negligence but alleged, in effect, that the claim was fraudulent having regard to the low speed of the bus at the point of impact. They relied upon the evidence of a single joint expert forensic engineer, to support this contention. The findings of fact made by the trial judge were, in summary:

(1) Neither of the claimants were lying or had exaggerated their claims;

(2) The expert gave his evidence in a way that was logical and consistent (he had asserted that, on the facts as presented to him, the speed and angle of collision was such that no movement of the claimants' vehicle across the road could have taken place, hence no whiplash injuries could have been suffered either).

The trial judge, faced with either finding that the claimants were lying or that there was some aspect of the single joint expert's evidence that was incorrect, found for the claimants. On appeal it was argued that, as a matter of law the judge had been bound to accept the single joint expert's evidence. The Court of Appeal did not agree. Brooke L.J. stated that:

". . . there is no principle of law that an expert's evidence in an unusual field . . . must be dispositive of liability in such a case and that a judge must be compelled to find that, in his view, two palpably honest witnesses have come to court to deceive him . . ."

The court took the opportunity to discuss an earlier decision, which the defendants had relied heavily upon, *Cooper Payen Ltd v Southampton Container Terminal* [2003] EWCA Civ 1223. In that case, the claimants were claiming in negligence for damage caused to their 600 ton compressor, which had toppled off the defendants' flat trailer while negotiating a corner. The claimants' case was that this was due to excessive speed. They called an expert who stated that the press could not have toppled off unless it was being pulled at at least 9.8 kph (on the facts an excessive speed). However, the trial judge had preferred the evidence of one of the defendants' witnesses who had given otherwise credible testimony to the effect that the trailer had been travelling at "a slow walking pace" that is, not more that 4.8 kph. The Court of Appeal had reversed the decision of the trial judge because, in effect, the expert's opinion, based as it was on scientific calculation was determinative. The difference, according to the court in *Armstrong* was that, in *Cooper Payen*, there was no other rational explanation for the compressor toppling off other that it was being driven too fast. In *Armstrong* on the other hand, the expert evidence was not sufficiently tried and tested to suggest that the two claimants must be lying.

4. The Experts' Duty

12–18   Prior to the introduction of the CPR, there had been a growing concerns at the use of experts in civil cases: many of them, it was feared, were little more than "hired guns" who would express highly tendentious opinions in support of the party instructing them instead of fulfilling their proper role which was to assist the court by providing objective and balanced reports and testimony. The decision of Creswell J. in *National Justice Compania Naviera SA v Prudential Assurance Co Ltd: "The Ikarian Reefer"* [1993] 2 Lloyds Rep. 68 broke new ground by, for the first time, setting out a series of ground rules for the expert giving evidence in proceedings. In it, the judge stated:

(1) Expert evidence presented to the Court should be, and should be seen to be, the independent product of the expert uninfluenced as to form or content by the exigencies of litigation.

(2) An expert witness should provide independent assistance to the Court by way of objective unbiased opinion in relation to matters within his expertise. An expert witness in the High Court should never assume the role of an advocate.

(3) An expert witness should state the facts or assumptions upon which his opinion is based. He should not omit to consider material facts which could detract from his concluded opinion.

(4) An expert witness should make it clear when a particular question or issue falls outside his expertise.

(5) If an expert's opinion is not properly researched because he considers that insufficient data is available, then this must be stated with an indication that the opinion is no more than a provisional one. In cases where an expert witness who has prepared a report could not assert that the report contained the truth, the whole truth and nothing but the truth without some qualification, that qualification should be stated in the report.

(6) If, after exchange of reports, an expert changes his view on a material matter having read the other side's expert's report or for any other reason, such change of view should be communicated (through legal representatives) to the other side without delay and when appropriate to the Court.

(7) When expert evidence refers to photographs, plans, calculations, analyses, measurements, survey reports or other similar documents, these must be provided to the opposite party at the same time as the exchange of reports.

At common law; the *Ikarian Reefer* was held to be of general application following *Vernon v Bosley (No.2)* [1999] Q.B. 18. This was confirmed by the Court of Appeal in *Stevens v Gullis* [2000] 1 All E.R. 527, a case decided after the CPR came into force, in which Lord Woolf M.R. stated that the expert's duties set out in CPR 35 were no more than declaratory of the pre-CPR position as laid down in *Ikarian Reefer*. As we shall see in the next section, the principles laid down by Creswell J. have been reinforced and extended in the CPR, in particular, by making it clear that any expert whose evidence a party wishes to rely upon, in effect, is retained by the *court* and not by the client, and by making oral expert evidence the exception rather than the rule. The relevant procedure is discussed fully at 12–20.

5. "In House" Experts

The definition of "expert" will extend to any employee of a party, for example, an in-house lawyer whose opinion evidence is being tendered in evidence. This was already acknowledged prior to the CPR, see, for example *Shell Pensions Trust Ltd v Pell Frischmann* [1986] 2 All E.R. 911 in which H.H. Judge Newey Q.C. held that, since several of the defendants' witnesses were to be called to give evidence concerning the construction of a building which was the subject matter of the claim, they came within the then definition of "experts" and, as such, their opinion evidence had to be disclosed. Post-CPR, the issue has been considered in a number of decisions, the first of which was *Field v*

12–19

Leeds City Council [2001] 2 C.P.L.R. 129. In it, the claimant sought damages for disrepair against his landlord. The defendants wished to rely upon the expert evidence of an employee in their Housing Services Claims Investigation Section. Although the decision refusing permission was upheld on its facts, Lord Woolf M.R. took the opportunity to issue guidance on the use of employees as experts. He stated (at [19]):

"If the City Council wishes to use a witness such as Mr B . . . , it is important that they show that he has full knowledge of the requirements for an expert to give evidence before the court, and that he is fully familiar with the need for objectivity. In the future I would encourage, if a person such as Mr B . . . is to give evidence, the authority concerned provides some training for such a person to which they can point to show that he has the necessary awareness of the difficult role of an expert, particularly in relation to claims such as these".

It is obvious that there was a strong policy element in this decision because he goes on to state (at [22]):

"these cases have financial implication on local authorities and to the tenants which should not be ignored. The amounts which are in issue can be relatively small. Anything which reduces that expense is to be warmly welcomed".

It is however clear that the decision in *Field* is of general application following *R. (Factortame Ltd) v Transport Secretary (No.8)* [2003] Q.B. 381, a case concerned primarily with litigation funding. Nevertheless, the court, in disapproving of an earlier decision of Evans-Lombe J. in *Liverpool Roman Catholic Archdiocesan Trustees Inc v Goldberg (No.3)* [2001] 1 W.L.R. 2337 took the opportunity to state that although it is always desirable that an expert should have no actual or apparent interest in the outcome of proceedings in which he gives evidence, such disinterest is not automatically a precondition to the admissibility of his evidence. The fact should be made known as soon as possible and can be dealt with as part of case management. Notwithstanding the case law cited above, it will not be easy for an employee to follow the guidance given in para.4 of the Expert Protocol, in particular paras 4.1 and 4.3 (see 12–29).

C The Relevant Procedural Rules

12–20   CPR 35, along with its attendant Expert Practice Direction and the Expert Protocol hold sway over the admission of expert evidence at any hearing, although extracts from reports are regularly prayed in aid at interim hearings without anyone raising the point that, technically speaking, the court's prior permission is required.

1. The Court's Duty: CPR 35.1

This rule could not be more explicit. It provides that: **12–21**

> "Expert evidence shall be restricted to that which is reasonably required to resolve the proceedings."

This power to control the extent of expert evidence should be read in conjunction with CPR 32.1 (general power to control evidence; see 1–52) and CPR 1.1 (overriding objective; see 1–45) in particular the need to control expense and maintain "proportionality". Thus, the court may, for example:

(1) Refuse to admit any expert evidence at all (see *Clarke (Executor of the Will of Francis Bacon) v Marlborough Fine Art (London) Ltd* [2002] EWHC 11 and *Gumpo v Church of Scientology Religious Education College Inc*, [2000] C.P. Rep. 38);

(2) Restrict the number of experts on an issue (for a recent example of this see *Heyward v Plymouth Hospital NHS Trust* [2005] EWCA Civ 939);

(3) Confine the evidence to the contents of written reports;

(4) Refuse late requests for permission to adduce expert evidence (see, for example *Taylor v Brock*, unreported, May 25, 2000);

(5) Disallow the costs of an expert whose evidence has not assisted the court (see *Thomas Johnson Coker v Barkland Cleaning Co* [1999] T.L.R. December 6 CA).

The preamble to the Expert Practice Direction states:

> "Part 35 is intended to limit the use of oral expert evidence to that which is reasonably required. In addition, where possible, matters requiring expert evidence should be dealt with by a single expert. Permission of the court is always required either to call an expert or to put an expert's report in evidence."

2. Court's Permission Essential: CPR 35.4

This rule provides that: **12–22**

> "(1) No party may call an expert or put in evidence an expert's report without the court's permission.

(2) When a party applies for permission under this rule he must identify—

    (a) The field in which he wishes to rely on expert evidence; and

    (b) where practicable the expert in that field on whose evidence he wishes to rely."

The rule does not state that you need permission to *instruct* an expert. Permission is only required if you wish to rely on her evidence (this is confirmed by para.6.2 of the Expert Protocol). The role of the "advising expert" is specifically addressed by s.5 of the Expert Protocol which states:

"5.1 Part 35 only applies where experts are instructed to give opinions which are relied on for the purposes of court proceedings. Advice which the parties do not intend to adduce in litigation is likely to be confidential; the Protocol does not apply in these circumstances.

5.2 The same applies where, after the commencement of proceedings, experts are instructed only to advise (e.g. to comment upon a single joint expert's report) and not to give or prepare evidence for use in the proceedings.

5.3 However this Protocol does apply if experts who were formerly instructed only to advise are later instructed to give or prepare evidence for the purpose of civil proceedings."

The implications of this along with a number of other matters will now be considered.

(a) *Case Management*

12–23 Directions as to expert evidence are part of the standard menu of directions given by the court post-allocation and often appear in an agreed format, or one which the court sends out as part of standard directions, a characteristic formulae being:

<u>Joint Expert</u>

"Expert evidence on the issue of orthopaedic injury shall be limited to the written report of a single expert jointly instructed by the parties. If the parties cannot agree by 4.00pm on February 27, 2006 who the expert is to be or about payment of his/her fees, either/any party may apply to the court for further directions. Unless the parties agree in writing or the court otherwise orders, the fees and expenses of the single expert shall be paid by the parties equally."

Individual Experts

"Each party has permission to use in evidence the written report of an expert in the discipline of forensic accountancy [whose names appear in the Schedule to this order] such reports to be exchanged simultaneously and filed not later than 4.00pm on February 27, 2006. The written reports of the experts shall be agreed if possible and if not agreed, the experts shall hold without prejudice discussions and prepare and serve a statement of issues agreed and issues not agreed with a summary of the reasons for any disagreement by 4.00pm on April 10, 2006."

The practical position in the vast majority of cases, depending upon track allocation is as follows.

(1) *Small Claims* These are largely governed by their own special rules which are set out in CPR 27. CPR 27.2 disapplies many of the mainstream rules, including CPR 35. The only parts that are incorporated into small claims procedure are CPR 35.1 (duty to restrict evidence); CPR 35.3 (experts' overriding duty to the court); and CPR 35.8 (instructions to a single expert). CPR 27.5 specifically provides that, "no expert may give evidence whether oral or written without the permission of the court". Furthermore a successful party cannot generally recover more than £200 towards the cost of instructing an expert (CPR 27.14(3)(c) and PD 27.7.3(2)). The procedure within the various tracks is covered in great depth in *Phipson* at 33–30 to 33–33.   **12–24**

(2) *Fast-Track* CPR 35.5(2) specifically provides that the court should only ever direct oral evidence if it is "necessary in the interests of justice". Quite what this adds to the general restriction on oral evidence in CPR 35.5(1) and the court's duty under CPR 35.1 is unclear. Many fast-track cases will be modest personal injury claims, in which case, the expert selected by the claimant under the Personal Injuries Protocol will be proposed and accepted by the defendant and the court as the "trial expert" and the only further direction that may need to be given will be the ordering of a follow up report.   **12–25**

(3) *Multi-Track* This covers such a vast range of cases that it is impossible to do more than generalise. All the specialist *Guides* have sections dealing with expert evidence, but one is left with the impression that they all follow the same philosophy with minor textual variations. In any case of substance, it is more than likely that both parties will have already instructed their own experts, and at case management the court will merely be asked to place its stamp of approval on that selection by permitting the parties to rely on the written reports. The   **12–26**

only active role that the court will often be asked to perform is to timetable the putting of written questions and the holding of discussions between the experts. Directions may be sought as to the giving of oral evidence, but, this tends not to arise until after the experts have met, and will only be allowed in cases where their presence is necessary to assist the court in resolving contested issues. Generally speaking parties will only be permitted to rely upon one expert in each discipline. However, in those cases where there is a major issue of importance to be determined multiple experts may be allowed. A recent example of this can be found in *ES v Chesterfield and East Derbyshire NHS Trust* [2004] Lloyd's Rep. Med 90 discussed further at 12–62.

(b) *Premature Instruction*

12–27   It is unusual to find that no party has instructed an expert by the time the claim has been allocated to track. Although nearly all the specialist Protocols encourage parties to explore instruction of joint experts, the reality is that parties frequently "jump the gun" and instruct their own experts long before the court is seized with the management of the case. In the early days of the CPR it was feared that such a course might lead to the court refusing permission to rely on such evidence *in toto* and disallowing the costs of the reports. In practice, as noted above, it is rare to find a court forcing the parties to start again from scratch. In any event, even if a party is shown to have breached a protocol, in every case, the key issue will not be, "should reliance on the evidence be refused by way of sanction?" but (see Practice Direction—Protocols para.2.3), has the premature instruction, "led to the commencement of proceedings which might otherwise have not needed to be commenced" or, "led to costs being incurred in the proceedings which might otherwise not have been incurred".

It is therefore arguable that unilateral instruction of an expert prior to commencement of proceedings should not necessarily lead to a refusal of permission to rely on it unless his report does not comply with CPR 35, or there has been serious non-disclosure. Even if a party is refused permission to rely on the report of a prematurely instructed expert, it does not automatically follow that the cost of instructing him or her will be disallowed. In every case the key issue under CPR 44.2 will be whether or not the cost of instruction was reasonable in amount and "reasonably incurred". As the Expert Protocol now acknowledges, experts may need to be instructed at different stages and for different purposes.

(c) *Expert Evidence Outside CPR 35*

12–28   As Section 5 of the Protocol makes clear, the court's permission is not needed to instruct an expert.

"5.1 Part 35 only applies where experts are instructed to give opinions which are relied on for the purposes of court proceedings. Advice which the parties do not intend to adduce in litigation is likely to be confidential; the Protocol does not apply in these circumstances.
5.2 The same applies where, after the commencement of proceedings, experts are instructed only to advise (e.g. to comment upon a single joint expert's report) and not to give or prepare evidence for use in the proceedings.
5.3 However this Protocol does apply if experts who were formerly instructed only to advise are later instructed to give or prepare evidence for the purpose of civil proceedings."

Frequently, a party will consult an expert at the start of the proceedings in order to find out whether he has a case or a defence and to enable him to formulate it with greater precision. Until he decides, firstly to seek the court's permission to rely on that expert as his "reporting expert" and, secondly, to serve his up to date report in compliance with the relevant case management direction, the report remains privileged from inspection by his opponent. However, reports are often voluntarily disclosed at a much earlier stage in order to expedite settlement. Not only that, a claimant in a personal injury claim is required under PD 16, para.4.3 to serve the report of a medical practitioner upon whose evidence he intends to rely at trial at the same time as his particulars of claim. Nevertheless, there may be situations in which an expert is retained in a purely advisory capacity, for example to draft questions to a single joint expert. It may even be the case, that the advisory role taken on at the outset has got him so closely involved with the litigation team running the case, that he no longer possesses the requisite degree of objectivity to fulfil the onerous duties of a reporting expert. "Shadowing" experts of this kind are by no means unusual in larger cases: one interesting implication of the Expert Protocol is that it impliedly authorises their instruction; interesting arguments on detailed assessments of costs lay ahead.

3. Experts' Duties: CPR 35.3

We have already seen how the common law moved in to remind **12–29** experts of the unique role they have in court proceedings. The CPR now take this much further. CPR 35.3 states that:

"(1) It is the duty of an expert to help the court on the matters within his expertise.

(2) this duty overrides any obligation to the person from whom he has received instructions or by whom he is paid."

Thus the expert may no longer appear as the "hired gun" of the party calling her, and indeed, once the report is served in accordance with the relevant direction the expert ceases to become that party's witness. The nature and extent of this duty is expanded upon in Part 1 of the Expert Practice Direction which replicates much of what was said in *Ikarian Reefer* stating:

"1.1 It is the duty of an expert to help the court on matters within his own expertise: rule 35.3(1). This duty is paramount and overrides any obligation to the person from whom the expert has received instructions or by whom he is paid: rule 35.3(2).

1.2 Expert evidence should be the independent product of the expert uninfluenced by the pressures of litigation.

1.3 An expert should assist the court by providing objective, unbiased opinion on matters within his expertise, and should not assume the role of an advocate.

1.4 An expert should consider all material facts, including those which might detract from his opinion.

1.5 An expert should make it clear:

(a) when a question or issue falls outside his expertise; and
(b) when he is not able to reach a definite opinion, for example because he has insufficient information.

1.6 If, after producing a report, an expert changes his view on any material matter, such change of view should be communicated to all the parties without delay, and when appropriate to the court."

If that was not sufficient to ram the message home, Section 4 of the Expert Protocol has this to add.

"4.1 Experts always owe a duty to exercise reasonable skill and care to those instructing them, and to comply with any relevant professional code of ethics. However when they are instructed to give or prepare evidence for the purpose of civil proceedings in England and Wales they have an overriding duty to help the court on matters within their expertise (CPR 35.3). This duty overrides any obligation to the person instructing or paying them. Experts must not serve the exclusive interest of those who retain them.

4.2 Experts should be aware of the overriding objective that courts deal with cases justly. This includes dealing with cases proportionately, expeditiously and fairly (CPR 1.1). Experts are under an obligation to assist the court so as to enable them to deal with cases in accordance with the overriding objective. However the overriding objective does not impose on experts any duty to act as mediators between the parties or require them to trespass on the role of the court in deciding facts.

4.3 Experts should provide opinions which are independent, regardless of the pressures of litigation. In this context, a useful test of 'independence' is that the expert would express the same opinion if given the same instructions by an opposing party. Experts should not take it upon themselves to promote the point of view of the party instructing them or engage in the role of advocates.

4.4 Experts should confine their opinions to matters which are material to the disputes between the parties and provide opinions only in relation to matters which lie within their expertise. Experts should indicate without delay where particular questions or issues fall outside their expertise.

4.5 Experts should take into account all material facts before them at the time that they give their opinion. Their reports should set out those facts and any literature or any other material on which they have relied in forming their opinions. They should indicate if an opinion is provisional, or qualified, or where they consider that further information is required or if, for any other reason, they are not satisfied that an opinion can be expressed finally and without qualification.

4.6 Experts should inform those instructing them without delay of any change in their opinions on any material matter and the reason for it.

4.7 Experts should be aware that any failure by them to comply with the Civil Procedure Rules or court orders or any excessive delay for which they are responsible may result in the parties who instructed them being penalised in costs and even, in extreme cases, being debarred from placing the experts' evidence before the court. In *Phillips v Symes* [2004] EWHC 2330 (Ch.) Peter Smith J. held that courts may also make orders for costs (under section 51 of the Supreme Court Act 1981) directly against expert witnesses who by their evidence cause significant expense to be incurred, and do so in flagrant and reckless disregards of their duties to the Court."

12–30   There is no doubt that the courts have been astute to ensure that experts comply with the new duties imposed upon them. In *Stevens v Gullis and Pile* [2000] 1 All E.R. 527, a case begun before the CPR were operative. The defendant instructed a surveyor to give evidence in a building claim. However, the surveyor had failed to (1) include a Statement of Truth in his report; (2) set out the substance of his instructions; and (3) draw up a joint memorandum of the experts discussions in accordance with an earlier case management direction. The judge managing the case debarred him from giving opinion evidence at the trial although he did give him permission to give evidence as to fact. The Court of Appeal not only upheld the judge's order but took it a stage further by debarring him from even giving evidence as to fact. The Court of Appeal stated that the witness clearly had no conception of the duties required of him as an expert and refused to sanction a consent order that the parties had drawn up under which he was to be permitted to give expert evidence. An even more telling example of what can befall an expert who strays into the arena is the decision of Peter Smith J. in *Philips v Symes* (above) in which a doctor, who had given an opinion as to the defendant's lack of capacity after only an hour's meeting and in the face of overwhelming evidence to the contrary was held to have so disregarded his duties that he was made the subject of a wasted costs order. There have also been a number of instances of an expert who fails in his duty being reported to his professional association, a recent example being *Hussein v William Hill Group* [2004] EWHC (Q.B.) in which two doctors, who were friends of the claimant, were reported to the General Medical Council for providing medical reports which supported his personal injury claim.

4. Restriction on Oral Evidence: CPR 35.5

12–31   The scope of expert evidence at trial is further restricted by this rule which imposes two general limitations on oral expert evidence namely:

(1) Expert evidence is to be given in a written report unless the court directs otherwise.

(2) If a claim is on the fast track, the court will not direct an expert to attend a hearing unless it is necessary to do so in the interests of justice.

This rule represents a major change in that it effectively makes hearsay expert evidence into the change in that it effectively makes hearsay expert evidence into the "industry standard". Pre-CPR, the expert's report had to be served as a prerequisite to his being called to give oral evidence. This often had the effect of keeping even modest claims back for years until both experts were available to give live evidence. Those seeking permission to rely on oral expert evidence at trial will need to convince the court that it is necessary. The court will not generally entertain such an application until the experts have held discussions and there are identifiable issues which require the giving of oral evidence. Although this is sometimes manifest by the first Case Management Conference, it is much more likely that the matter will be raised for the first time at the listing stage. Whenever there is a likelihood that oral evidence will be required, it is incumbent on the parties to ensure that the experts will be available: the court does not look kindly on experts who hold themselves out as expert witnesses and then announce their unavailability for no good reason (see *Matthews v Tarmac Bricks & Tiles Ltd* [1999] C.P.L.R. 463).

5. Contents of Reports: CPR 35.10

Since the courts will now, more often than not, have to base their findings on written expert evidence, it is hardly surprising that the rules lay down detailed requirements as to their content. A new paragraph was added to the Expert Practice Direction in April 2005. Paragraph 6A provides that:

12–32

> "Where an order requires an act to be done by an expert, or otherwise affects an expert, the party instructing that expert must serve a copy of the order on the expert instructed by him. In 6A. In the case of a jointly instructed expert, the claimant must serve the order."

The idea behind this is to assist the expert by directing him or her to the issues on which the court requires assistance. If that objective is to be achieved, orders will have to contain somewhat more detail than at present. CPR 35.10 provides:

"(1) An expert's report must comply with the requirements set out in the relevant practice direction.

(2) At the end of an expert's report there must be a statement that:

    (a) the expert understands his duty to the court; an
    (b) he has complied with that duty.

(3) The expert's report must state the substance of all material instructions, whether written or oral, on the basis of which the report was written.

(4) The instructions referred to in paragraph (3) shall not be privileged against disclosure but the court will not, in relation to those instructions:

    (a) order disclosure of any specific documents; or

(b) permit any questioning in court, other than by the party who instructed the expert,

unless it is satisfied that there are reasonable grounds to consider the statement of instructions given under paragraph (3) to be inaccurate or incomplete."

12–33 The provisions of CPR 35.10(3) are controversial, and some have argued that since it is now clear that legal professional privilege is more than a rule of evidence, the rule is ultra vires. Whatever the position, it is now clear following the cases discussed at 12–53 that the rule does not make as deep an inroad into LPP as was originally thought. Both the Expert Practice Direction and the Expert Protocol contain detailed requirements as to the format and content of reports. Section 2 of the Expert Practice Direction states:

"2.1 An expert's report should be addressed to the court and not to the party from whom the expert has received his instructions.
    2.2 An expert's report must:

(1) give details of the expert's qualifications;
(2) give details of any literature or other material which the expert has relied on in making the report;
(3) contain a statement setting out the substance of all facts and instructions given to the expert which are material to the opinions expressed in the report or upon which those opinions are based;
(4) make clear which of the facts stated in the report are within the expert's own knowledge;
(5) say who carried out any examination, measurement, test or experiment which the expert has used for the report, give the qualifications of that person, and say whether or not the test or experiment has been carried out under the expert's supervision;
(6) where there is a range of opinion on the matters dealt with in the report—

    (a) summarise the range of opinion, and
    (b) give reasons for his own opinion;

(7) contain a summary of the conclusions reached;
(8) if the expert is not able to give his opinion without qualification, state the qualification; and
(9) contain a statement that the expert understands his duty to the court, and has complied and will continue to comply with that duty.

2.3 An expert's report must be verified by a statement of truth as well as containing the statements required in paragraph 2.2(8) and 9) above.

2.4 The form of the statement of truth is as follows:

'I confirm that insofar as the facts stated in my report are within my own knowledge I have made clear which they are and I believe them to be true, and that the opinions I have expressed represent my true and complete professional opinion.'

2.5 Attention is drawn to rule 32.14 which sets out the consequences of verifying a document containing a false statement without an honest belief in its truth."

Part 13 of the Expert Protocol provides further detailed guidance and needs to be read in conjunction with the Expert Practice direction. It is set out below in full. In the writer's view, it should accompany the instructions so that the expert is left in no doubt as to what is required in order to produce a CPR 35-compliant report, in particular as to any "range of opinion" that might exist. A feature of reports that is conspicuous by its absence in the writer's experience.

12–34

"13.1 The content and extent of experts' reports should be governed by the scope of their instructions and general obligations, the contents of CPR 35 and PD35 and their overriding duty to the court. 13.2 In preparing reports, experts should maintain professional objectivity and impartiality at all times. 13.3 PD 35, para.2 provides that experts' reports should be addressed to the court and gives detailed directions about the form and content of such reports. All experts and those who instruct them should ensure that they are familiar with these requirements.

13.4 Model forms of Experts' Reports are available from bodies such as the Academy of Experts or the Expert Witness Institute.

13.5 Experts' reports must contain statements that they understand their duty to the court and have complied and will continue to comply with that duty (PD35 para 2.2(9)). They must also be verified by a statement of truth. The form of the statement of truth is as follows: 'I confirm that insofar as the facts stated in my report are within my own knowledge I have made clear which they are and I believe them to be true, and that the opinions I have expressed represent my true and complete professional opinion.' This wording is mandatory and must not be modified.
Qualifications
13.6 The details of experts' qualifications to be given in reports should be commensurate with the nature and complexity of the case. It may be sufficient merely to state academic and professional

qualifications. However, where highly specialised expertise is called for, experts should include the detail of particular training and/or experience that qualifies them to provide that highly specialised evidence.

Tests

13.7 Where tests of a scientific or technical nature have been carried out, experts should state:

(a) the methodology used; and
(b) by whom the tests were undertaken and under whose supervision, summarising their respective qualifications and experience.

Reliance on the work of others

13.8 Where experts rely in their reports on literature or other material and cite the opinions of others without having verified them, they must give details of those opinions relied on. It is likely to assist the court if the qualifications of the originator(s) are also stated.

Facts

13.9 When addressing questions of fact and opinion, experts should keep the two separate and discrete.

13.10 Experts must state those facts (whether assumed or otherwise) upon which their opinions are based. They must distinguish clearly between those facts which experts know to be true and those facts which they assume.

13.11 Where there are material facts in dispute experts should express separate opinions on each hypothesis put forward. They should not express a view in favour of one or other disputed version of the facts unless, as a result of particular expertise and experience, they consider one set of facts as being more probable or less probable, in which case they may express that view, and should give reasons for holding it.

Range of opinion

13.12 If the mandatory summary of the range of opinion is based on published sources, experts should explain those sources and, where appropriate, state the qualifications of the originator(s) of the opinions from which they differ, particularly if such opinions represent a well-established school of thought.

13.13 Where there is no available source for the range of opinion, experts may need to express opinions on what they believe to be the range which other experts would arrive at if asked. In those circumstances, experts should make it clear that the range that they summarise is based on their own judgement and explain the basis of that judgement.

Conclusions

13.14 A summary of conclusions is mandatory. The summary should be at the end of the report after all the reasoning. There may be cases, however, where the benefit to the court is heightened by placing a short summary at the beginning of the report whilst giving the full conclusions at the end. For example, it can assist with the comprehension of the analysis and with the absorption of the detailed facts if the court is told at the outset of the direction in which the report's logic will flow in cases involving highly complex matters which fall outside the general knowledge of the court.

Basis of report: material instructions

13.15 The mandatory statement of the substance of all material instructions should not be incomplete or otherwise tend to mislead. The imperative is transparency. The term 'instructions' includes all material which solicitors place in front of experts in order to gain advice. The omission from the statement of 'off-the-record' oral instructions is not permitted. Courts may allow cross-examination about the instructions if there are reasonable grounds to consider that the statement may be inaccurate or incomplete."

It remains to be seen how far courts will scrutinise reports to ensure **12–35** compliance with these requirements before they are prepared to give permission for their use at trial. The process of instructing an expert is set out in Sections 7 to 9 of the Expert Protocol: these are not reproduced in full, since they relate to matters of practice rather than evidence. Nevertheless, para.8.1 should now be followed whenever preparing instructions to an expert. It provides:

"Those instructing experts should ensure that they give clear instructions, including the following:

(a) basic information, such as names, addresses, telephone numbers, dates of birth and dates of incidents;
(b) the nature and extent of the expertise which is called for;
(c) the purpose of requesting the advice or report, a description of the matter(s) to be investigated, the principal known issues and the identity of all parties;
(d) the statement(s) of case (if any), those documents which form part of standard disclosure and witness statements which are relevant to the advice or report;
(e) where proceedings have not been started, whether proceedings are being contemplated and, if so, whether the expert is asked only for advice;

> (f) an outline programme, consistent with good case management and the expert's availability, for the completion and delivery of each stage of the expert's work; and
> (g) where proceedings have been started, the dates of any hearings (including any Case Management Conferences and/or Pre-Trial Reviews), the name of the court, the claim number and the track to which the claim has been allocated."

As already noted, the expert must also receive a copy of any order made by virtue of PD 35, para.6A. However it is strange that nowhere does there appear a requirement that the expert receive a copy of PD 35 or any extract from the Protocol as set out above, one imagines because it is assumed that they will have a copy and be familiar with its terms. However, in the writer's view, it is essential that the expert receives both of these extracts, at any rate when he is being instructed for the purpose of providing evidence.

6 Single Joint Expert: CPR 35.7

12–36 One of the major objectives of CPR 35 was to get rid of the perceived "hired gun" mentality that had caused the Woolf Committee such concern.

(a) The Power

12–37 Under CPR 35.7 and 8 there is now power to direct that evidence be given by a single joint expert ("SJE"). CPR 35.7 provides that:

> "(1) Where two or more parties wish to submit expert evidence on a particular issue, the court may direct that the evidence on that issue is to be given by one expert only.
>
> (2) where the parties cannot agree who should be the expert, the court may;
>
> > (a) select the expert from a list prepared or identified by the instructing parties; or
> >
> > (b) direct that the expert be selected in such a manner as the court may direct."

This power, more than any other caused controversy when it was introduced. There were those who predicted that it would lead to "trial by expert", others suggested that it would increase the costs because both sides would instruct their own "shadowing" experts. A list of potential disadvantages appears in *Hollander* at 27–38. In practice, single joint experts ("SJEs") have caused less problems than the pessimists predicted. There is no doubt that the CPR place the court under a duty to consider directing SJEs when giving case management directions of its own initiative. In the Fast Track, the court must "give directions for a single joint expert unless there is good reason not to" (PD 28, para.3.9(4)) and in the Multi Track "give directions for a single joint expert on any appropriate issue unless there is good reason not to do so" (PD 29, para.4.10(4)). This largely reflects what happens in practice. Countless fast track cases, for example relatively low value whiplash claims, now proceed to trial or resolution on the basis of an SJE's report with which both sides are happy. On the other hand, in cases of substance, the position tends to be that, although SJEs are often instructed by agreement on matters of quantum directions for separate liability experts are commonplace. To quote the *Chancery Guide* (at 4–11):

> "There remains, however, a substantial body of cases where liability will turn upon expert opinion evidence or where quantum is a primary issue and where it will be appropriate for the parties to instruct their own experts. For example, in cases where the issue for determination is as to whether a party acted in accordance with proper professional standards, it will often be of value to the court to hear the opinions of more than one expert as to the proper standard in order that the court becomes acquainted with a range of views existing upon the question and in order that the evidence can be tested in cross-examination."

An identical passage appears in the *Queen's Bench Guide* (at 7.9.5). **12–38** Paragraph H2.2 of the *Admiralty and Commercial Court Guides* goes further and states that, "In many cases the use of single joint experts is not appropriate". In *Daniels v Walker* [2000] 1 W.L.R. 1382 Lord Woolf M.R. acknowledged that instruction of an SJE might represent only the "first step" and that it might be necessary to direct the obtaining of further evidence. However, in *Peet v Mid Kent Area Healthcare* [2002] 1 W.L.R. 210, albeit obiter, he suggested that SJEs were the norm and that individual experts should only be permitted in exceptional cases. It is suggested that reality is more accurately reflected in the passages from the *Guides* referred to above. Section 17 of the Expert Protocol also now gives guidance as to the use of SJEs as follows:

> "17.1 CPR 35 and PD35 deal extensively with the instruction and use of joint experts by the parties and the powers of the court to order their use (see CPR 35.7 and 35.8, PD35, para 5).
> 17.2 The Civil Procedure Rules encourage the use of joint experts. Wherever possible a joint report should be obtained. Consideration should therefore be given by all parties to the appointment of single joint experts in all cases where a court might direct such an appointment. Single joint experts are the norm in cases allocated to the small claims track and the fast track.

17.3 Where, in the early stages of a dispute, examinations, investigations, tests, site inspections, experiments, preparation of photographs, plans or other similar preliminary expert tasks are necessary, consideration should be given to the instruction of a single joint expert, especially where such matters are not, at that stage, expected to be contentious as between the parties. The objective of such an appointment should be to agree or to narrow issues.

17.4 Experts who have previously advised a party (whether in the same case or otherwise) should only be proposed as single joint experts if other parties are given all relevant information about the previous involvement.

17.5 The appointment of a single joint expert does not prevent parties from instructing their own experts to advise (but the costs of such expert advisers may not be recoverable in the case)."

The only reference to SJEs in PD 35 appears at para.6 which states:

"Where the court has directed that the evidence on a particular issue is to be given by one expert only (rule 35.7) but there are a number of disciplines relevant to that issue, a leading expert in the dominant discipline should be identified as the single expert. He should prepare the general part of the report and be responsible for annexing or incorporating the contents of any reports from experts in other disciplines."

Quite why it is thought necessary only to apply this to SJEs is unclear. It is by no means uncommon in heavy cases for both sides to have teams of experts out of which a "lead expert" is appointed.

(b) *When is a Single Expert Inappropriate?*

12–39   Instances of parties being "force fed" an SJE against their wishes are rare, but, if this were to happen, and the importance of the claim were to justify considering an appeal, *Oxley v Penwarden* [2001] 1 C.P.L.R. 1 CA provides a useful point of reference. In that case, the claimant sought damages in respect of an alleged failure to adequately treat a vascular ischaemic condition which had led to the amputation of his left leg below the knee. There were major causation issues and, at an earlier case management conference, a district judge had given directions permitting each party to rely on the written evidence of a consultant vascular surgeon and a GP. At a subsequent telephone case management conference a circuit judge had directed that the parties instruct a single joint expert instead and that, in default of agreement, the court would appoint one. The Court of Appeal allowed the claimant's appeal. Mantell L.J. (at [8]) stated that where, as in this case, there were clearly two "schools of thought" on the issues of liability and causation, it was inappropriate to direct a single joint expert. Firstly, the parties would not be able to agree who should be instructed, and secondly, if the judge were left to decide, he would have to choose between the opposing schools of thought. In that event, he would effectively be determining the issue without having heard properly tested evidence.

(c) *What if a Party is Dissatisfied with the SJE?*

This problem arose in *Daniels v Walker* [2000] W.L.R. 1382. The **12–40** claimant had suffered severe injuries as a child in a road traffic accident and would require some form of care for the rest of his life. By agreement, the parties' solicitors instructed an occupational therapist to prepare a report on the most appropriate care regime. The defendants were not happy with that report and sought to have the claimant examined by their own expert. When the claimant's solicitors refused they applied for an order staying the proceedings until the claimant was examined. At first instance, the judge dismissed the application on the basis that, having agreed a joint instruction, the defendants were, in effect, stuck with it. The Court of Appeal allowed the appeal. Lord Woolf M.R. made it clear that it was always open to the court to permit further expert evidence on an issue if this would be in accordance with the overriding objective. He went on to give the following guidance for such cases.

(1) The instruction of a single expert was only the first stage in the process of the court determining what expert evidence was needed to decide the case justly;

(2) Ideally, a joint letter of instruction should be sent to a single expert, but there was nothing to prevent each party sending separate instructions.

(3) If a dissatisfied party could genuinely make a case under CPR 1 for instructing a further expert, the court had power to direct this.

(4) The appropriate sequence was for the dissatisfied party to:

· Write his own letter of instruction; then
· Ask questions under CPR 35.6; if still dissatisfied
· Apply to the court for permission to instruct a further expert and thereafter if the circumstances warranted, to seek permission to call him.

The court directed an early case management conference to consider the issue: having regard to the many hundreds of thousands of pounds that were at stake, one imagines that the defendants were given the permission sought. A somewhat different problem arose in *Cosgrove v Pattinson* [2001] 2 C.P.L.R. 177. This was a relatively small boundary dispute in which the appellants were unhappy with the report of the SJE on the ground that it exhibited bias. By the time they appeared before Neuberger J., they had already obtained the report of their own expert which disagreed in a number of respects with the conclusions of the SJE. The judge set out nine factors that the court should take into account in dealing with such applications, namely:

(1) The nature of the issues;

(2) The number of issues between the parties;

(3) The reason the new expert is wanted;

(4) The amount at stake;

(5) The effect of permitting further expert evidence to be called on the conduct of the trial;

(6) Any delay in making the application;

(7) Any delay that instructing and calling the new expert will cause;

(8) Any special features of the case;

(9) The overall justice to the parties.

Ultimately, the judge allowed the appeal influenced largely by factors (3) (there was a new expert who disagreed with the SJE) and (9), namely that it would leave the appellants with the greater sense of grievance if permission was refused. The most telling passage appears at [19]:

". . . it cannot be enough for a person who wants to call a new expert, simply to say: 'I have a report from another expert and it is inconsistent with the agreed expert's conclusion.' Otherwise anyone who had the money and the inclination to instruct another expert would always have the right to call him. Having said that, it does seem to me that if a new expert can be found who has a contrary view to the joint expert that is a reason for permitting the new expert to be called. It is certainly not a sufficient reason in every case, but if there are grounds for thinking that the joint expert is wrong, because another expert takes a different view, that is certainly a factor which is to be borne in mind."

This is certainly not an invitation to go "expert shopping", but a clear indication that there are two "schools of thought" on a material issue will strengthen your case. A very full summary of other cases in which the issue has arisen can be found in the *White Book* at 35.7.3.

(d) *Instructing an SJE*

Although Lord Woolf M.R. in *Daniels v Walker* made it clear that a **12–41** joint letter of instruction is preferable, he also emphasised that both parties are free to submit their own instructions (naturally, these will not be privileged, so some fear that there is a risk that in so doing they will "give away" their case strategy). The rules themselves make this clear. CPR 35.8 provides:

"(1) Each instructing party may give instructions to the expert.

(2) When an instructing party sends instructions to an expert he must, at the same time, send a copy of the instructions to the other instructing parties.

(3) The court may give directions about:

(a) the payment of his fees and expenses; and
(b) any inspection, examination or experiments which he wishes to carry out.

(4) The court may, before he is instructed:

(a) limit the amount that can be paid by way of fees and expenses to the expert; and
(b) direct that the instructing parties pay that amount into court.

(5) Unless the court otherwise directs, the instructing parties are jointly and severally liable for the payment of the expert's fees and expenses."

Valuable guidance is also now provided in Section 17 of the Expert **12–42** Protocol as follows:

"17.6 The parties should try to agree joint instructions to single joint experts, but, in default of agreement, each party may give instructions. In particular, all parties should try to agree what documents should be included with instructions and what assumptions single joint experts should make.

17.7 Where the parties fail to agree joint instructions, they should try to agree where the areas of disagreement lie and their instructions should make this clear. If separate instructions are given, they should be copied at the same time to the other instructing parties.

17.8 Where experts are instructed by two or more parties, the terms of appointment should, unless the court has directed otherwise, or the parties have agreed otherwise, include:

    (a) a statement that all the instructing parties are jointly and severally liable to pay the experts' fees and, accordingly, that experts' invoices should be sent simultaneously to all instructing parties or their solicitors (as appropriate); and

    (b) a statement as to whether any order has been made limiting the amount of experts' fees and expenses (CPR 35.8(4)(a)).

17.9 Where instructions have not been received by the expert from one or more of the instructing parties the expert should give notice (normally at least seven days) of a deadline to all instructing parties for the receipt by the expert of such instructions. Unless the instructions are received within the deadline the expert may begin work. In the event that instructions are received after the deadline but before the signing off of the report the expert should consider whether it is practicable to comply with those instructions without adversely affecting the timetable set for delivery of the report and in such a manner as to comply with the proportionality principle. An expert who decides to issue a report without taking into account instructions received after the deadline should inform the parties who may apply to the court for directions. In either event the report must show clearly that the expert did not receive instructions within the deadline, or, as the case may be, at all."

Hopefully, if this advice is followed it will avoid difficulties of the type that arose in *Daniels v Walker* and *Cosgrove v Pattinson*. What is abundantly clear is that any party who wishes to obtain a direction for further expert's evidence will have to show that he has followed the guidance given in *Daniels v Walker* and the Expert Protocol if his application is to stand any chance of success.

(e) *Oral Evidence from the SJE*

12–43 Both CPR 35 and the Practice Direction are silent on the subject although there can be no doubt that the court has power to grant an application for such an order under its general powers in CPR 32.1 to manage evidence. As *Phipson* strongly asserts at 33–39, it would surely be unjust to deny a party the opportunity to cross-examine a witness who, even though jointly instructed, was nevertheless expressing an opinion that was adverse to his case. In *Voaden v Champion* [2001] Lloyd's Rep. 739, Creswell J. expressed the view that in any case other than one which involved a report on discrete and non-controversial matters relating to collateral issues:

"the absence of a sole expert may well prejudice the fair resolution of the expert issues in question and make it more difficult for the court to resolve those issues in the light of the other evidence before it."

Additional guidance, based on *dicta* of Lord Woolf C.J. in *Peet v Mid Kent Area Healthcare NHS Trust* [2002] 1 W.L.R. 210 appears in para.17.15 of the Protocol.

"Single joint experts do not normally give oral evidence at trial but if they do, all parties may cross-examine them. In general written questions (CPR 35.6) should be put to single joint experts before requests are made for them to attend court for the purpose of cross-examination."

In practice, the problem tends not to arise because, in the vast majority of cases in which an SJE is ordered, the value of the claim is within Fast Track limits and *quantum* is agreed.

(f) *Privilege and the SJE*

It goes without saying that if an expert is instructed jointly, either **12–44** because the parties agree on this course or because the court orders it, no privilege will attach either to the report or the individual parties' communications with the expert. Most Protocols encourage joint instruction. However the Personal Injuries Protocol is unusual in that it provides for the prospective defendant to approve or disapprove instruction of an expert from a list proffered by the proposed claimant. Does that approval constitute an implied waiver of privilege on the part of the party instructing the expert? This issue was addressed by the Court of Appeal in *Carlson v Townsend* [2001] 3 All E.R. 633. The salient facts of the case were:

Prior to commencement of proceedings, C invited D to select a medical expert from a list and D "approved" Dr X. Dr X's report, it must be assumed, was not sufficiently supportive of C's case. Accordingly, without further reference to D, C instructed Dr Y whose report was more "favourable". Accordingly, on commencing proceedings, C served Dr Y's report with the particulars of claim. D sought an order for inspection of Dr X's report.

A district judge granted the order sought but a circuit judge and the Court of Appeal thought differently. The Court of Appeal held that:

(1) Mere approval of (or failure to object) to an expert does not turn him/her into a "joint expert", hence;

(2) There could be no implied waiver of privilege; accordingly

(3) The claimant could not be ordered to disclose the report of Dr X if he did not wish to do so; but

(4) The court might well refuse permission to the claimant to call the "unapproved" expert (in this case, presumably, Dr Y); and

(5) The trial judge would know (how?) that there was at least one expert who had reported unfavourably.

The decision raises three intriguing issues, all as yet, unresolved. Firstly, will it automatically follow that the court will refuse the claimant permission to rely on the second report? It is submitted that the court will be required to approach it in the same way as any other "unauthorised" instruction, the principles of which have been set out at 12–27 above. It may be that the defendant can argue that the claimant should be ordered to disclose the first report as a pre-condition of being permitted to rely on the second report relying on *Beck v Ministry of Defence* [2003] C.P. Rep. 62 (see 12–53). Secondly, the suggestion that the trial judge will know about the first report must surely be wrong. The claimant is claiming privilege in it, and no adverse inference may be drawn from an assertion of privilege (see 8–84). Accordingly, unless the court applies *Beck*, there is no reason for the trial judge to be informed of the existence of the first report, the fact that an earlier report was obtained is simply irrelevant. Thirdly, it is at least theoretically possible that, subject to the courts' permission being obtained, the defendants could apply on notice to issue a witness summons against the first expert on the grounds that there is no property in a witness (see *Harmony Shipping SA v Davis* [1979] 1 W.L.R. 1380 discussed at 8–45). However, it will be more likely than not that any opinion that the expert will have, certainly in the case of medical experts, will be based on an examination of the client and will therefore be subject to litigation privilege (see *R. v Davis (Keith), The Times*, March 4, 2002 discussed at 08–45).

7. Conditions of Admissibility: CPR 35.13

12–45   The rule states:

> "A party who fails to disclose an expert's report may not use the report at the trial or call the expert to give evidence orally unless the court gives permission."

The usual direction is that parties exchange the reports on which they intend to rely by the specified timetable date as part of the *tranche* of standard directions for disclosure of evidence (see 9–03). As with witness statements (see 11–16) the court has power to order sequential exchange although such orders in practice are unusual. They may be appropriate in cases where the defendant has to answer a large group of litigants (see the pre-CPR decision in *Kirkup v British Railways Engineering Ltd* [1983] 1 All E.R. 147, an industrial deafness claim) or there are complex quantum issues that the defendant's expert is not in a position to respond to until after service of the claimant expert's report. So far as *late service* is concerned, parties frequently run into difficulties over meeting timetable dates as a result of their experts having to meet other pressing commitments. Extensions are often agreed without the need to return to the court. However, the court will take a robust approach if a party is seriously out of time with his expert evidence. In *Baron v Lovell* [1999] C.P.L.R. 630 the Court of Appeal upheld the decision of a circuit judge to debar a defendant from calling an expert whose report had been "sat on" for several months, and had only been disclosed on the day of the pre-trial review. One cannot imagine any party being foolhardy enough to behave in this way again. Conversely, if the breach is minor, the court may well be prepared to overlook it and grant relief (see, for example *R C Residuals v Linton Fuel Oils* [2002] 1 W.L.R. 2782 discussed at 11–24). Late applications for permission to rely on further expert evidence will also be treated robustly (see, for example *Rollinson v Kimberley Clarke Ltd* [2000] C.P. Rep 85 and *Ahmed v Stanley Coleman and Hill* [2002] EWCA Civ 935).

8. Written Questions: CPR 35.6
This rule enables a party to put written questions without leave on one occasion to his opponent's expert witnesses and any SJE. It provides that: **12–46**

"(1) A party may put

(a) to an expert instructed by another party; or
(b) a single joint expert appointed under rule 35.7

written questions about his report.

(2) Written questions under paragraph (1)—

(a) may be put once only;
(b) must be put within 28 days of service of the expert's report; and
(c) must be for the purpose only of clarification of the report; unless in either case,

(i) the court gives permission; or
(ii) the other party agrees.

(3) An expert's answers to question put in accordance with paragraph (1) shall be treated as part of the expert's report."

The questions must be put within 28 days of the original service of the report. In practice, this is rarely done and, accordingly, a direction is often sought at allocation or the first CMC. Although questions are limited in the first instance to extracting "clarification", the court has power to permit wider ranging questions and will be sympathetic to any request properly made especially in view of the fact that the expert is unlikely to be giving oral evidence. *O'Hare and Browne* provides valuable guidance as to the drafting of such questions at 32–028 and 23–029. Any replies are admissible at trial without the need for a further order. This can have the effect of turning the person that you fondly supposed to be "your" expert witness into your opponent's expert (see *Mutch v Allen* [2001] 2 C.P.L.R. 200). In that case, an expert instructed by the claimant provided answers that were favourable to the defendant's defence of contributory negligence. The judge at a case management conference ruled answers inadmissible at trial. The Court of Appeal held that he was in error in so ordering. Although the rule only permits the putting of written questions the court also has power to order a face-to-face meeting with an SJE. In *Peet V Mid Kent Healthcare NHS Trust* [2002] 1 W.L.R. 210, the Court of Appeal stated that it was not possible for a party to have a meeting with a single expert unless all other parties were given an opportunity to be present and had expressly agreed in writing that they did not wish to be present.

9. *Discussions Between Experts: CPR 35.12*

12–47 In practice, the court will almost invariably make an order that experts hold discussion and file and serve a joint memorandum of issues as part of Multi-Track directions. It frequently has the beneficial effect of resolving disputed issues. The rule provides that:

"(1) The court may, at any stage, direct a discussion between the experts for the purpose of requiring the experts to—

   (a) identify the issues in the proceedings; and
   (b) where possible, reach agreement on an issue.

(2) The court may specify the issues which the experts must address.

(3) The court may direct that following a discussion between the experts they must prepare for the court a statement for the court showing—

   (a) those issues on which they agree; and
   (b) those issues on which they disagree and, a summary of their reasons for disagreeing.

(4) The content of the discussion between the experts shall not be referred to at the trial unless the parties agree.

(5) Where experts reach agreement on an issue during their discussions the agreement shall not bind the parties unless the parties expressly agree to be bound by the agreement."

There is much valuable guidance in the notes at 35.12.1 of the *White* **12–48** *Book* as to the appropriate practice. Not surprisingly, the Court of Appeal has held in *Hubbard v Lambeth, Southwark and Lewisham HA* [2001] EWCA 1455 that the procedure does not infringe Art.6 of the ECHR. One notable feature is that the parties' privilege is preserved by CPR 35.12(4). It is not clear what head it comes under (its predecessor RSC O.38 r.38 referred to "without prejudice" meetings) and it would seem to be the most logical head under which to place it. The effect of the rule is as follows:

(1) The discussions themselves are privileged. Since it is a joint privilege, it can only be waived if all parties consent (see 8–98);

(2) No party is bound by any agreement reached in the filed memorandum, but any party who refuses to ratify the heads of agreement is running a major risk on costs (see further, the Expert Protocol at 18.2 below);

(3) The memorandum itself is not subject to privilege and therefore can be deployed in cross-examination if the experts give oral evidence (*Robin Ellis Ltd v Malwright Ltd* [1999] B.L.R. 81).

Further valuable guidance is given in Section 18 of the Expert **12–49** Protocol as follows:

"18.1 The court has powers to direct discussions between experts for the purposes set out in the Rules (CPR 35.12). Parties may also agree that discussions take place between their experts.
  18.2 Where single joint experts have been instructed but parties have, with the permission of the court, instructed their own additional Part 35 experts, there may, if the court so orders or the parties agree, be discussions between the single joint experts and the additional Part 35 experts. Such discussions should be confined to those matters within the remit of the additional Part 35 experts or as ordered by the court.
  18.3 The purpose of discussions between experts should be, wherever possible, to:

(a) identify and discuss the expert issues in the proceedings;

(b) reach agreed opinions on those issues, and, if that is not possible, to narrow the issues in the case;
(c) identify those issues on which they agree and disagree and summarise their reasons for disagreement on any issue; and
(d) identify what action, if any, may be taken to resolve any of the outstanding issues between the parties.

Arrangements for discussions between experts

18.4 Arrangements for discussions between experts should be proportionate to the value of cases. In small claims and fast-track cases there should not normally be meetings between experts. Where discussion is justified in such cases, telephone discussion or an exchange of letters should, in the interests of proportionality, usually suffice. In multi-track cases, discussion may be face to face, but the practicalities or the proportionality principle may require discussions to be by telephone or video conference.

18.5 The parties, their lawyers and experts should co-operate to produce the agenda for any discussion between experts, although primary responsibility for preparation of the agenda should normally lie with the parties' solicitors.

18.6 The agenda should indicate what matters have been agreed and summarise concisely those which are in issue. It is often helpful for it to include questions to be answered by the experts. If agreement cannot be reached promptly or a party is unrepresented, the court may give directions for the drawing up of the agenda. The agenda should be circulated to experts and those instructing them to allow sufficient time for the experts to prepare for the discussion.

18.7 Those instructing experts must not instruct experts to avoid reaching agreement (or to defer doing so) on any matter within the experts' competence. Experts are not permitted to accept such instructions.

18.8 The parties' lawyers may only be present at discussions between experts if all the parties agree or the court so orders. If lawyers do attend, they should not normally intervene except to answer questions put to them by the experts or to advise about the law.

18.9 The content of discussions between experts should not be referred to at trial unless the parties agree (CPR 35.12(4)). It is good practice for any such agreement to be in writing.

18.10 At the conclusion of any discussion between experts, a statement should be prepared setting out:

(a) a list of issues that have been agreed, including, in each instance, the basis of agreement;
(b) a list of issues that have not been agreed, including, in each instance, the basis of disagreement;

(c) a list of any further issues that have arisen that were not included in the original agenda for discussion;

(d) a record of further action, if any, to be taken or recommended, including as appropriate the holding of further discussions between experts.

18.11 The statement should be agreed and signed by all the parties to the discussion as soon as may be practicable.

18.12 Agreements between experts during discussions do not bind the parties unless the parties expressly agree to be bound by the agreement (CPR 35.12(5)). However, in view of the overriding objective, parties should give careful consideration before refusing to be bound by such an agreement and be able to explain their refusal should it become relevant to the issue of costs."

The Court of Appeal in *Stevens v Gullis* referred to at 12–30 held that failure to comply with directions might lead to the expert being debarred from giving evidence. The court has not in the past prescribed the method by which the discussions are to be held. It is not always easy to arrange face to face meeting. It is likely that the same "open ended" orders will be made in the expectation that parties will comply with the guidance given in the Expert Protocol. Any concern that a party's expert might be overawed by the eminence of his opponent's expert can be met by having the discussions recorded and transcribed. It is only in the most exceptional of cases that the parties own legal adviser's should be permitted to be present (see *Hubbard* referred to at 12–48).

12–50

10. Additional Powers
CPR 35 contains two further provisions, neither of which appear to have been greatly used in practice.

12–51

(a) *Provision of Information: CPR 35.9*
This rule provides that:
    Where a party has access to information which is not reasonably available to the other party, the court may direct the party who has access to the information to:

(a) prepare and file a document recording the information; and

(b) serve a copy of that document on the other party.

PD 35, para.3 provides the following additional guidance as to how the rule is to be implemented:

"Under Rule 35.9 the court may direct a party with access to information which is not reasonably available to another party to serve on that other party a document which records the information. The document served must include sufficient details of all the facts, tests, experiments and assumptions which underlie any part of the information to enable the party on whom it is served to make, or to obtain, a proper interpretation of the information and an assessment of its significance".

It is however hard to see what, if anything, it adds to the general powers to order disclosure for example of documents referred to in Chapter 10. However, it may be useful where a party seeks access to information that it would be prohibitively expensive for him to obtain himself. Its clear objective is to ensure that a level playing field is maintained in respect of access to relevant information. Although Section 12 of the Expert Protocol reminds practitioners and experts of the existence of the power it provides no information as to the circumstances or stage at which it might be employed.

(b) *Expert's Right to Ask for Directions: CPR 35.14*

12–52 Under the rule, an expert is entitled to make a written request to the court for directions to "assist him in carrying out his functions as an expert". As with CPR 35.9 this rule does not appear to have been greatly used in practice. Any expert wishing to make use of this facility must notify the part instructing him at least seven days before he makes the request and all other parties at least four days before he files it. Section 11 of the Expert Protocol adds little except for recommending that the expert holds discussions with the party instructing him before taking this step.

D Expert Evidence and Privilege

12–53 The interaction between the CPR and the law on litigation privilege (see generally 6–39) has become ever more complicated as the following cases show.

1. Approved Expert Instructed under the PI Protocol

12–54 The position here, by way of reminder, has been clear since *Carlson v Townsend* [2001] 3 All E.R. 663 CA. If you do not like the report of the "approved" expert, and seek to instruct and rely on a second expert, the defendant is not entitled to call for a copy of the first expert's report. Approval of the first expert's instruction does not constitute a waiver of privilege. However, as the court pointed out, the judge might refuse the claimant permission to rely on the second expert. The new PI Protocol which came into force on April 1, 2005 preserves this situation and at various stages reminds those using it that the approval of an expert under the PI Protocol is not the same as (see for example, para.3.17) a joint instruction.

2. What if the Court has Already Given Permission to Rely on the Evidence of a Named Expert?

CPR 35.4(2)(b) specifically provides that when seeking permission to **12–55** rely on expert evidence a party should "where practicable" name the expert. In practice this is frequently not done, for reasons that will shortly become apparent. If a party is dissatisfied with the report provided by the expert who has been named in the order, he is perfectly entitled to claim privilege (but, if he does he will rather be "giving the game away" because his opponent will be aware of the expert's identity). Although the court's permission is not needed to instruct a new expert, it *will* be needed to rely on the new expert's evidence at trial. In such a case, the Court of Appeal held in *Beck v Ministry of Defence* [2003] C.P. Rep. 62 that, although the court may be prepared to give such permission, it may (and probably will) order disclosure of the first expert's report as a condition. The decision is not entirely easy to follow because, in fact, the direction given namely:

> "each party shall exchange evidence limited to one psychiatrist per party"

did not specifically name the psychiatrist. In those circumstances the defendants could have instructed 20 psychiatrists if they had wanted to and just served the "best" one. The difficulty that they faced was that the new psychiatrist needed to examine the claimant afresh, and it was on this basis that they needed an order from the court granting permission. However the clear tenor of the two main judgments of Simon Browne L.J. and Lord Phillips M.R. is that the position would have been the same if the defendants had simply wished to switch from one "named" expert to another. In particular Lord Phillips M.R. stated [35]:

> "The answer in this case, and in any case where a similar situation arises, is that proposed by Lord Justice Simon Brown, namely that the permission to instruct a new expert should be on terms that the report of the previous expert be disclosed. Such a course should both prevent the practice of expert shopping, and provide a claimant in the position of Mr Beck with the reassurance that the process of the court is not being abused. In this way justice will be seen to be done."

This interpretation has since been confirmed in the later decision of *Vasiliou v Hajigeorgiou* [2005] 3 All E.R. 17 in which Dyson L.J. stated [37]:

"The question of principle that was decided in *Beck* was that the court has the power to give permission to a party to rely on a second (replacement) expert which it should usually exercise only on condition that the report of the first expert is disclosed. This decision is binding on us. We cannot accept that the decision is wrong or that it is conceivable that the court was unaware of the fact that reports prepared for the purposes of litigation are, until they are disclosed, protected by privilege".

3. Would it Make a Difference if the Court Had not Named the Expert?

12–56   The answer to that is "Yes", following *Vassilou v Hajigeorgiou* [2005] 3 All E.R. 17. In that case the direction for experts, as in *Beck*, did not name the expert but simply stated:

"Both the parties do have permission, if so advised, to instruct an expert each in the specialism of restaurant valuation and profitability."

Having instructed Expert A (of whose existence the claimant was aware) the defendant then chose to instruct Expert B. The Court of Appeal held that, in the circumstances, there was no need to seek the court's permission to rely on Expert B's evidence at trial, since all the defendant was required to do under the court's directions was to serve a report of an expert in the relevant specialisation, in accordance with the prescribed timetable. It is likely in future that courts will insist that a party names the expert before granting permission to rely on expert evidence to discourage the practice of "expert shopping": a loosely worded order of the type seen in *Beck* and *Vasiliou* facilitates such shopping. Dyson L.J. also pointed out that the relevant paragraph of the order (which is by no means uncommon) was, in any event, incorrectly drawn because a party does not need permission to *instruct* an expert, only to rely on his or her evidence.

4. Earlier Drafts of the Served Report

12–57   It is by no means uncommon for lengthy discussions to take place with an expert, with draft reports being circulated before the final report is prepared and served on the other party. This situation arose in *Jackson v Marley Davenport Ltd* [2004] EWCA Civ 1225. The claimants had instructed a consultant forensic pathologist to prepare a report for the purposes of a conference with counsel. He subsequently prepared a fuller report which was served in accordance with the case management directions. In it, there appeared the following passage:

"... having gained additional information in relation to the case".

The defendants sought disclosure of the earlier report on the basis that, by implication, there were matters in the earlier report which constituted part of the experts "instructions" for the purposes of CPR 35.10(3). The Court of Appeal made it clear that nothing in the CPR affected the ordinary principles of litigation privilege, provided CPR 35.10(3) was complied with. Longmore L.J. stated:

"13. There can be no doubt that, if an expert makes a report for the purpose of a party's legal advisers being able to give legal advice to their client, or for discussion in a conference of a party's legal advisers, such a report is the subject matter of litigation privilege at the time it is made. It has come into existence for the purposes of litigation. It is common for drafts of expert reports to be circulated among a party's advisers before a final report is prepared for exchange with other side. Such initial reports are privileged.

14. I cannot believe that the Civil Procedure Rules were intended to override that privilege. CPR 35.5 provides that expert evidence is to be given in a report unless the court directs otherwise. CPR 35.10 then changed the previous law by providing in sub-rule (3) that the expert's report must state the substance of all material (whether written or oral instructions) on the basis on which the report was written. By sub-rule (4) it is, moreover, expressly provided that these instructions shall not be privileged. But the reference in Rule 35.10 to 'the expert's report' is, and must be, a reference to the expert's intended evidence, not to earlier and privileged drafts of what may or may not in due course become the expert's evidence.

15. The specific and limited exemption from privilege of the instructions given to the expert as the basis on which the report is to be written, shows, to my mind, that there cannot have been any intention in the minds of the draftsmen of the Civil Procedure Rules to abrogate the privilege attaching in other respects, e.g. to earlier drafts of a final report or to earlier reports whether said, in terms, to be draft reports or not".

5. Documents Referred to in the Report

CPR 31.14 (see 10–25) gives a party the right to call for the inspection of documents referred to in a case statement, witness statement or affidavit on the basis that service of such documents waives privilege in all the documents referred to in them. However documents referred to in experts' reports are treated differently in that a party wishing to inspect documents referred to therein must apply to the

12–58

court for an order. The principles to be applied on such applications have been set out by the Court of Appeal in *Lucas v Barking Havering and Redbridge NHS Trust* [2004] 1 W.L.R. 22. The claimant was making a claim for personal injury allegedly suffered as a result of negligence by the defendant. With his particulars of claim he served two experts' reports relating to his injuries. Those reports both referred to a witness statement of Mr Lucas provided to the experts. One report also referred to a previous report of an expert. The defendants sought disclosure of those documents. In refusing disclosure, the court laid down the following principles:

(1) The mere fact that a document is referred to in a served expert's report is not, of itself waiver of privilege in its contents;

(2) Documents referred to in an expert's report form part of the "instructions";

(3) The applicant must first establish, in accordance with CPR 35.10(4), that the "substance" of the instructions are "inaccurate or incomplete"; and

(4) Inspection will only be allowed as a matter of discretion insofar as it is required in order to remove the inaccuracy or incompleteness.

Waller L.J. stated:

"27 Under CPR 35.10(3) there is a compulsion on experts to set out their material instructions. It is completely up to a party whether in a statement of case, affidavit or witness statement he refers to a document which might otherwise be privileged. CPR 35.10(3) compels disclosure of what would otherwise be privileged material, and indeed compels that material to be referred to in such a way that under the common law there would be held to be waiver of all other privileged material relevant to showing there was no 'cherry picking' at least where that material was deployed at a hearing.

28 The intention behind CPR 35.10(4) seems to me to be to encourage the setting out fully of 'material' instructions and indeed facts. Because a party is compelled so to do, it was thought right that some protection should be given where an expert complies with that requirement."

12–59   *Conclusion*   This group of cases, has, hopefully, clarified the law in an area where, previously there had been much confusion. The position is now, in summary:

(1) Any expert's report obtained for the predominant purpose of reasonably anticipated litigation is subject to litigation privilege until it is waived;

(2) Waiver by advance disclosure is an inevitable consequence of being granted permission to rely on the expert's evidence at trial;

(3) Reference to other documents in the report does not constitute waiver in them if they form part of the expert's "instructions", but a party may apply to inspect such documents if those instructions can be shown to be inaccurate or incomplete.

(4) If permission is granted to instruct a "named" expert a party who seeks permission to rely upon a different expert will probably have to forfeit privilege in the earlier report as a precondition.

E At the Trial: Scope of Expert's Testimony

1. Need to Testify
The expert used to be subject to the hearsay rule (subject to certain modifications). Now his evidence will be admitted subject only to the four statutory safeguards applicable to other types of evidence under the Civil Evidence Act 1995. Accordingly it will now be much easier to adduce evidence from: **12–60**

(1) An expert who is unable to attend court; or

(2) An expert who gives an opinion based on hearsay facts supplied by others.

This has the effect of overturning the practical result of *H v Schering Chemicals Ltd* [1983] 1 W.L.R. 143 in which Bingham J. held that reference in articles and letters as to the side-effects of a drug constituted hearsay evidence which could not be admitted as "records" under the exception in s.4 of the Civil Evidence Act 1968.

2. Scope of Testimony
Insofar as his opinion derives from observed facts and experimentation, under the 1995 Act those facts and experiments no longer need to be proved by non-hearsay evidence. Furthermore, the expert may base his opinion both on matters within his own experience and the "recognised corpus of expert knowledge", for example, by reference to textbooks and published works. See *R. v Abadom* [1983] 1 W.L.R. 126 in which reference by a prosecution expert to Home Office   **12–61**

statistics as to refractive index of different types of manufactured glass was held to be admissible and *R. v Wood* (1983) 76 Cr.App.R. 23 in which the use of a computer to calculate the composition of alloys was held not to infringe the rule, since the calculations were not hearsay; they had been produced by the computer.

3. The Status of the Expert Witness at Trial

12–62   There have been a number of interesting recent cases dealing with both the permissible scope of an expert's evidence at trial and, also, the extent to which a judge is bound to rely upon it. As the Court of Appeal observed in *ES v Chesterfield and East Derbyshire NHS Trust* [2004] Lloyds Rep. Med 90 a professional defendant will often give evidence as to the reasons that he or she took particular steps, in order to allege that he or she was not negligent in the particular circumstances of the case. In so doing he may well refer to literature on the subject or seek to "lock horns" with the court expert witnesses. In that case, the order made at the case management conference was was for one expert in the field of obstetrics on each side. The claimant appealed on the basis that since the two professionals whose conduct was in question would be giving evidence for the defendants, this would create an unfair imbalance. In allowing the appeal and permitting the claimant to rely on two experts, Brooke L.J. stated (at [26]:

"For present purposes it is sufficient to say that in my judgment it is necessary to permit two experts for the claimant in this case for some real purpose . . . and that real purpose is the achievement of justice in accordance with the overriding objective on the particular facts of the particular case."

Of course, such an order may itself create a slightly different potential imbalance: what if the claimant's two experts "going up" against the defendant's single expert during joint discussions? A judge needs to consider all the angles when applying the overriding objective.

A different issue arose in *DN v LB Greenwich* [2004] EWCA Civ 1659 in which the trial judge had ruled that the opinion evidence of an educational psychologist employed by the defendants (in respect of whom no order granting permission to rely on his expert opinion had been made) was wholly inadmissible. The Court of Appeal confirmed that:

(1) Although the evidence of such a person might lack the objectivity of an independent expert witness;

(2) That went to the weight of his evidence, not its admissibility.

The court recognised that, inevitably, such a witness was different from an expert appointed under CPR 35, because there might be a degree of partisanship, especially where, as here, he was defending his own exercise of skill and judgement. It is submitted that this represents a balanced and pragmatic approach to a problem that will inevitably arise in professional negligence cases.

4. *Effect of Disclosure*
CPR 35.11 provides that where: **12–63**

"a party has disclosed an expert's report",

any other party may use that expert's report as evidence at the trial. It is for this reason that when calling an expert the advocate can refer him or her to reports of other experts even though, as yet, they have not been formally admitted in evidence.

This is in direct contrast to lay witness statements (see Chapter 11) which do not become evidence in the case and hence open to comment from earlier witnesses unless or until the individual witnesses are called and finally adopt their statements. However, parties can, and sometimes do, agree that key witness statements be admitted in evidence from the start of the case.

Conclusion
This long chapter shows how: **12–64**

(1) The admission of expert evidence has become progressively weighed down with ever increasing procedural requirements;

(2) The covet is required to act as "gatekeeper" to keep expert evidence to the irreducible minimum;

(3) Even if expert evidence is permitted, oral expert evidence should be the exception rather than the rule;

(4) The use of single joint experts has not created the problems early commentators on the CPR feared;

(5) Once you indicate an intention to rely on an individual expert's evidence by serving the report under case management directions, she ceases to become "your" expert and becomes the *court's* expert.

However, as with so much of the material in Chapters 10 to 12, the vast majority of cases settle on the basis of a single report; a significant improvement on what used to happen.

Chapter 13

From Allocation to Trial

Chapters 10 to 12 have taken us on a journey through all the **13–01** complications that can arise from time to time in heavier cases, and, sometimes, in simpler ones. Perhaps therefore it is time to get our feet back on the ground with a few reminders:

(1) A party can prove facts, more or less, in whatever way he likes provided that the evidence is relevant and not subject to privilege or PII;

(2) All that a party has to do under the CPR to secure the admission of the bulk of his evidence at trial is to serve his evidence in accordance with the timetable set down in the case management directions as to disclosure of:

- Documents (CPR 31: see Chapter 10);
- Witness statements (CPR 32: see Chapter 11);
- Expert evidence (CPR 35: see Chapter 12).

(3) Various other disclosure requirements exist in the CPR which operate automatically without the need for a court order such as the service of:

- Hearsay notices (CPR 33: see Chapter 7);
- Maps and plans (CPR 33.6: see 13–33).

(4) Expert evidence excepted, there are very few occasions on which the court's specific permission is required before evidence can be admitted. One example that we have already seen, is where a party wishes to obtain an order for the cross-examination of the "maker of the original statement" under CPR 33.4 in a case where hearsay evidence is being relied on. A number of other examples will be considered later in this chapter, the most notable being where a party wishes a witness to give evidence by video-link (CPR 32.3, see 13–23).

(5) Although parties are usually prepared to tolerate some degree of "slippage" in the case management timetable, disputes may subsequently arise as to whether late evidence, in whatever form, ought to be admitted. As a general rule, although the leave of the court is required, courts tend to look for ways of achieving justice other than by the outright exclusion of the evidence (see especially, 1–50 and 11–19). Nevertheless in an extreme case the court may exclude late evidence especially if it causes prejudice to the other party that cannot be remedied in a less punitive manner.

(6) The vast majority of cases will settle, sooner of later, after allocation if they have not already done so. Accordingly, we are now moving into a territory which litgators rarely encounter in practice, the case that is likely to go to trial.

As has been stated on a number of occasions through this work, an attempt has been made to avoid getting too sidetracked by matters of pure procedure. Accordingly, those who are looking for a helpful and practical guide to preparing a claim for trial, should consult *O'Hare and Browne* Chapters 36 and 37. Nevertheless, there are a number of matters relating to trial preparation that properly belong in a work on evidence, and these will be considered in turn.

I NARROWING ISSUES

13–02   One of the most notable features of the CPR reforms has been the encouragement it has given to parties to hone issues down to their irreducible minimum. The major danger that parties face if they do not do this is in relation to the costs that have been needlessly incurred as a result. We have already seen one cautionary illustration in *Kastor Navigation v AXA Global Risks (UK) Ltd* [2004] EWCA Civ 277 (see 1–45). Here is another example, *Budgen v Andrew Gardner Partnership (a firm)* [2002] EWCA Civ 1125, a solicitor's professional negligence claim.

13–03   Facts: C was suing his former solicitors AG for negligently allowing his personal injuries claim to be struck out. Liability was admitted early on, so the only dispute was on *quantum*. C beat the AG's Pt 36 payment (£285,000) by a comfortable margin (£329,000). However, the judge awarded C only 75 per cent of his costs. This was because C had failed on the major issue in the trial which related to a claim for an amount exceeding £1 million for a software package which C maintained his injuries had prevented him from completing and marketing. By the time costs arguments were reached it was clear that it was an issue which:

(1) Had taken up a considerable amount of the preparation and trial time (66 per cent according to AG); and

(2) Had been "doomed to failure" on causation from a relatively early stage.

The defendants argued on appeal that the judge should have made an "issues based" order on the basis that two thirds of the total costs were attributable to the issue that the claimant had failed on. The potential difference this could have made can be seen from the hypothetical example set out below:

	C		D
Judge's Order			
(estimated)			
C's own costs	£174,000	D's own costs	£200,000
C gets 75 per cent from D (say)	(£130,000)	D pays to C	£130,000
Total Liability	£44,000	Total Liability	£330,000
Issues Based Order			
(author's hypothesis)			
C's own costs	£174,000	D's own costs	£200,000
C gets on Issue 1 (say)	(£50,000)	D pays C in Issue 1	£50,000
	£124,000		£250,000
C pays D on Issue 2	(£120,000)	D gets on Issue 2	(£120,000)
Total Liability	£244,000	Total Liability	£130,000

However, the Court of Appeal refused to interfere with the trial judge's exercise of discretion.

"[The judge] cannot be forced, however, by *the parties' failure to provide him with more precise information* [author's emphasis]. Accordingly, the central ground of appeal, in my judgment, fails: Wright J. was perfectly entitled to make a percentage costs order in this case."

This was because, in effect, a party wishing to obtain an "issues based" order has the burden of overturning the presumption in CPR 44.3(7). The defendants simply failed to produce any *evidence* on this. It is always easy to look at cases with the benefit of hindsight, but, viewed from the comfort of one's armchair it is perhaps possible to see opportunities for both sides to have protected themselves by tying down the issues in such a way as to put the other side at risk on costs. The diagram on the opposite page illustrates the simplicity of the CPR philosophy. If a party maintains an unduly "high" or "low" position whether it is on the live issues or *quantum*, he is hanging onto the risk of failing on that issue at trial. One should therefore always look at ways in which you can use the evidential strengths of your case to shift the risk to your opponent.

A Notice to Admit Facts CPR 32.18

1. The Rule
13–04 CPR 32.18(1) provides that:

(1) A party may serve on another party a notice requiring him to admit the facts or the part of the case of the serving party specified in the notice.

(2) A notice to admit facts must be served not later than 21 days before the trial.

(3) Where the other party makes any admission in response to the notice the admission may be used against him only:

(a) in the proceedings in which the notice to admit is served, and
(b) by the party who served the notice.

(4) The court may allow a party to amend or withdraw any admission made by him on such terms as it thinks just.

Although it is an enormously effective way of putting costs pressure on an opponent, it appears not to be used as often as it might be. One important change, first introduced in 1980, in the old RSC O.27 r.2 and CCR O.20 r.2, is that a party can serve Notice to Admit part of his case for example simply, "Notice to Admit Liability". Although it was a decision reported under the old rules, the words of Peter Gibson J. in *Baden, Delvaux and Lecuit v Societe General Pour Favouriser le Developpement du Commerce et de L'Industrie en*

France SA [1992] 4 All E.R. 779 ring even truer under the CPR. This was a massive Chancery action for negligence and breach of fiduciary duty, the trial of which had lasted for 108 days. The plaintiffs had failed in their claim but had served a lengthy Notice to Admit Facts. Although putting everything in issue, the defendants did not advance an alternative factual scenario, but simply sought different inferences to drawn. The judge found that some 25 per cent of the trial and 80 per cent of the documentation was devoted to matters covered by the Notice to Admit. As a result, although the defendants, as the successful party, were awarded the costs of the action, the judge also ordered that this should be discounted as to:

(1) 75 per cent of any increase in the defendants' costs attributable to the plaintiffs proving the facts specified in the Notice to Admit; and

(2) 75 per cent of the increase in plaintiffs' costs of proving those facts.

The judge had this to say about Notices to Admit generally (at [276]):

"The policy of the framers of the rules can be discerned to be to encourage the parties to make admissions whenever practicable in respect of their opponent's cases, so that only those matters which are really in dispute between them should fall to be proved and determined at the trial . . . Given the appalling costs of litigation today, this seems to me a wholly salutary policy."

As *O'Hare and Browne* observes at 32–008 to 32–009 the procedure is not used anywhere near often enough in practice. Notices to Admit were first introduced in 1883—some things take a long time to catch on.

2. *Effect of Notice*

One of the anomalies of the CPR is that the consequences of **13–05** refusing to admit are not specifically spelled out. This is strange, because the former RSC O.62 r.3(5) specifically provided that a party who refused or neglected to admit facts contained in a notice would have to pay the costs of proving that fact (unless the court ordered otherwise) irrespective of the overall result of the case. Nevertheless, there can be little doubt that a party who has succeeded overall may well have a significant percentage discount applied in respect of costs incurred as a result of his unreasonable refusal to admit.

3. How do I Know which Facts to Serve Notice on?

13–06 As already noted (5–08), some facts are always more certain of proof than others. Think of it as a spectrum of probability:

"I Know"   "I Disbelieve"
(100 per cent)   (0 per cent)

◄···►

Anything over 50 per cent ("I think") that has not already been admitted should be considered as eligible. Although there are, as yet, no reported decisions under the CPR, the writer's view is that service of a blanket Notice to Admit on every fact that remains in issue after exchange of case statements could be seen as oppressive and might rebound on the server. On the other hand any facts or parts of your case that are well towards the upper end of the probability spectrum should be considered. It is also important to bear in mind that they can be served at any time up to 21 days before the trial date. Three possible uses are listed below by way of example.

13–07 **Example 1:** D serves a defence denying liability, but it is clear that the real issue is *quantum*. He makes a risk discounted Pt 36 payment. C could simply serve Notice to Admit liability in order to put him at risk on the costs of defending the liability issue. Even if C fails to beat the Pt 36 payment, there would be a strong justification for arguing that the normal consequences of failing to beat the Pt 36 payment (see CPR 36.20) should not follow.

13–08 **Example 2:** C is suing D for personal injuries. D is prepared to admit primary liability but C disputes that there is any contributory negligence. D makes a Pt 36 payment based on the prediction that there will be a *20 per cent* reduction for "contrib". At trial C beats the Pt 36 payment because, although D got quantum right and established "contrib", the judge fixed the percentage at *15 per cent*. D could have protected himself to some extent by serving Notice to Admit "contrib". If a large part of the trial had been concerned with establishing the presence of contributory negligence, D would have a strong argument for saying that the "normal" costs consequences of a party beating a Pt 36 payment should not follow.

13–09 **Example 3:** Prior to the commencement of proceedings D's insurers have admitted liability in correspondence. As noted at 6–04, this is not treated as a formal admission. In order to tie D to that pre-claim admission and turn it into a "formal admission" there would be nothing to stop C serving Notice to Admit Liability at the same time as he serves his claim form.

The most remarkable feature of the procedure, provided it is not used oppressively and indiscriminately, is that it is "win/win". If you win overall you can argue that you should get indemnity costs of proving the unadmitted facts, if you lose overall, it may have the effect of mitigating the usual costs consequences of defeat, as in *Baden* (above).

B Part 36 Offers

This is another rule that a party may make use of, albeit somewhat more indirectly, to narrow issues. A full discussion of Part 36 is outside the scope of book on evidence and those seeking a full discussion of the subject should consult Chapter 29 of *O'Hare and Browne* and the very full commentary in the *White Book*. Nevertheless, there are certain aspects of the rule which need to be considered.   **13–10**

1. *"Without Prejudice Save as to Costs"*
CPR 36.1(2) states that: **13–11**

"Nothing . . . prevents a party making an offer to settle in whatever way he chooses."

CPR 36.6(2) (Part 36 Offers) goes on to provide that:

"a Part 36 offer may relate to the whole claim or to part of it or to <u>any issue</u> [author's emphasis) that arises in it."

Thus it is always possible to enhance your chances of obtaining a more favourable costs order by use of "Without Prejudice save as to Costs" offers (see 8–96) which, even when not strictly "Pt 36 offers", will nevertheless have the potential effect of such an offer, even to the extent of giving the court the discretion to award indemnity costs; or even enhanced interest. This was confirmed by the Court of Appeal in *Petrotrade v Texaco* [2002] 1 W.L.R. 947, a case in which a successful claimant had made a discounted offer of settlement on a commercial debt claim in advance of an application for summary judgment at which he recovered the full sum claimed. Lord Woolf M.R. stated that:

(1) CPR 36.21, which creates a presumptive entitlement to enhanced interest and indemnity costs where a claimant beats his own Part 36 offer, only applies where a defendant is 'held liable' at trial.
(2) Accordingly it will not apply where a defendant is 'held liable' on an application for summary judgment.

However, Lord Woolf M.R. went on to remind practitioners that the court has a wide discretion both as to both interest and costs under the general discretions conferred by s.35A of the Supreme Court Act 1981, s.69 of the County Courts Act 1984 (interest) and CPR 44 (costs). As Mance L.J. stated in *Budgen v Andrew Gardner*, "Part 36 is this first line of defence against any party who litigates unreasonably".

2. JSB Guidance on Litigation Conduct

13–12   The Judicial Studies Board Civil Bench Book (accessible at *www.jsb.co.uk*) gives the following guidance to judges on how to deal with "litigation conduct". It serves as an important reminder as to who will be left holding onto the costs risk if they do not co-operate in narrowing issues to their irreducible minimum in advance of the trial.

"The court *must* [author's emphasis] consider the conduct of all the parties; whether a party has succeeded on part of his case, even if he has not been wholly successful, and conduct includes what may have taken place before, as well as during, the proceedings, with particular regard to the extent to which the parties followed any relevant pre-action protocol. Scrutiny of this element includes consideration of whether it was reasonable to raise, pursue or contest a particular issue, and the manner in which a party dealt with the case, whilst an important consideration will be whether the claimant, although successful, exaggerated his claim.

Exaggeration may be intentional, and where apparent it may not be too difficult for the court to decide that it will be appropriate to decline an order for costs, or make a restricted order. Not infrequently however exaggeration of a claim or issues within the claim is unintentional, a claimant being advised, and believing quite sincerely he is entitled to pursue a number of heads of claim, yet after having heard evidence and argument the trial judge is not satisfied as regards one or more. In these circumstances, even if the claimant is awarded more than an amount paid into court by the defendant, the court must be open to argument that because there has been an element of exaggeration, a restricted order for costs may be justified. Defendants are in the same position, for pursuing false points in relation to the defence may fall within the definition of exaggeration, and in any event will fall to be considered in relation to conduct.

However, the position of a defendant as regards costs upon the claimant failing to beat a payment in may not always be as secure might have been anticipated before the CPR came into force, for if the defendant had not enabled the claimant to assess properly whether to accept an offer because of non-disclosure of relevant matters, he might nonetheless be ordered to pay the costs (*Ford v GKR Construction and Others* [2000] 1 AER 802 CA.)

If at conclusion of a case the court is satisfied that although the claimant succeeded in full, he has ignored any relevant pre-action protocol, or to a significant extent failed to conduct the proceedings so as to further the overriding objective, it will be entitled to reflect this in the costs order, reducing or, in a very extreme case, refusing costs."

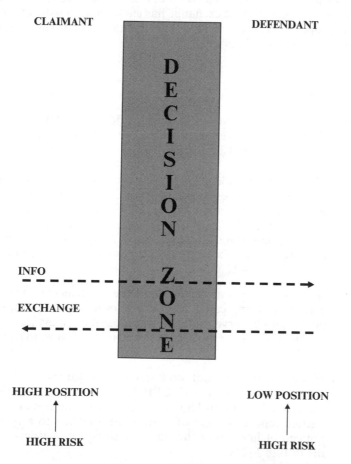

CLAIMANT   DEFENDANT

D
E
C
I
S
I
O
N

INFO ⟶ Z
EXCHANGE ⟵ O
N
E

HIGH POSITION   LOW POSITION
↑   ↑
HIGH RISK   HIGH RISK

These words serve as a salutary warning to those who do not "play the game" according to the letter and spirit of the CPR. They also provided a litigator with a valuable opportunity to exploit any attempt by her opponent to conduct attritional litigation in which nothing is conceded any every issue is made the subject of strict proof.

II WITNESS EVIDENCE

13–13   Provided you have complied with the relevant case management direction and served your statements in time all you now have to concern yourself with is making sure that all those witnesses whose evidence is to be "live" attend court to speak to their statements. As we have seen in Chapter 11, the court tends to be relatively tolerant when dealing with breaches of the timetable (see also 1–50) and parties are usually expected to co-operate in serving supplemental statements where the first exchange has left matters in issue that need to be properly engaged (see 11–26). Remaining matters can therefore be dealt with relatively briefly.

A Hearsay

13–14   What if there is important "eyewitness" evidence that, for one reason or another cannot be given "live"? Here are some basic reminders of the material covered in Chapter 7.

(1) If the hearsay evidence is to be recounted by a person ("W") who will themselves be giving oral evidence at trial, there is no need to serve a hearsay notice. By serving W's witness statement in which the "maker of the original statement" is identified, you have done all that CPR 33.2 requires of you. It will be up to your opponent to decide how, if at all, she is going to respond (see 7–27);

(2) If the hearsay is contained in the witness statement of a witness who is not being called to give oral evidence, then a hearsay notice must be served at the same time as the witness statement. Again, it will be for the person served to decide how to respond (see 7–27).

(3) If the hearsay is not contained in a witness statement served in accordance with CPR 32, for example, a statement made to a Health and Safety Inspector, or the contents of a written report, a copy of it must be attached to a hearsay notice not later than the date for service of witness statements (see 7–27).

As already noted, (2) and (3) tend to be honoured more in the breach than in the observance, but the evidence is admitted without objection with arguments directed as to weight.

B Securing the Attendance of Witnesses

1. The Basic Rules: CPR 34

It is generally regarded as a counsel of prudence to serve all witnesses, **13–15** including experts in order to avoid the embarrassment of their non-attendance. Now that the hearsay rule has gone, it is not as disastrous as it used to be in that their statement can still be put in as hearsay evidence under CPR 32.5(1), but his absence may well have adverse consequences (see 4–20). The means of securing attendance is by serving the witness with a Witness Summons (Practice Form 20). Leave is not required except in the relatively unusual circumstances set out in CPR 34, namely when (CPR 34.3(2)):

(1) It is to be issued less than seven days before the trial date; or

(2) It is for attendance on a date other than the date fixed for trial (see 13–21); or

(3) It is to attend at a hearing other than a trial (see 11–30).

There are, in fact, two varieties of Witness Summons (CPR 34.2(1): (1) to give oral evidence, traditionally known as a *subpoena ad testificandum;* and (2) to produce documents, which used to be termed a *subpoena duces tecum.* They each have their own nuances which will be considered further below.

2. Formalities

The detailed procedure is set out in *O'Hare and Browne* at 36–006 to **13–16** 36–008. The most important features of the procedure are that:

(1) Service is normally by the court (CPR 34.6(1)) by one of the methods permitted by CPR 6 (the court normally serves by first class post);

(2) A sum sufficient to cover the witness's travel costs and reasonable compensation for loss of earnings must be tendered at the same time as service (CPR 34.7): where service is by the court the sum must be lodged in court at the same time as issue; and

(3) A summons is only binding if it is served at least seven clear days before the date that the witness is required to attend unless the court directs otherwise (CPR 34.5).

3. Additional Requirements

A full discussion appears in Phipson at 8–05 to 8–18. These are **13–17** summarised below. Note, in particular that there is no power to direct service of a summons outside of the United Kingdom.

(a) *Summons to give evidence*

13–18 The summons will not be issued unless it is sought in respect of a named individual and is issued bona fide for the purpose of his giving relevant evidence. The court has power to set aside a witness summons if it is considered oppressive. An interesting recent example can be found in two decisions of Neuberger J. In *Brown v Bennett, The Times* November 2, 2000 he set aside a summons against an expert whose fee for attendance the claimant could not afford. In *Harrison and Harrison v Bloom Camillin (a Firm)* (1999) L.T.L. May 14 he set aside a speculative summons against the claimant's father. The judge stated that in each case it was necessary to balance the potential importance of the evidence against the intrusiveness into the witness's affairs.

(b) *Summons to produce documents*

13–19 Applications to set aside such summonses are more commonplace in practice because the most frequent objection that is taken is based on privilege or PII or on the fact that the documents are subject to a duty of confidentiality that outweighs their potential relevance. Obviously, if the objection is based on privilege or PII the application can be dealt with under the standard rules of evidence (see Chapter 8), but what if it is based on other grounds such as confidentiality or oppression? This issue was addressed at length by Gross J. in *South Tyneside Borough Council v Wickes Building Supplies Ltd* [2004] EWHC 2428 (Comm). In it, he gave the following guidance based on earlier authorities:

(1) The documents sought must be specifically identified: the procedure is not to be used as a substitute for non-party disclosure;

(2) The production of the documents must be necessary for the fair disposal of the action and to save costs;

(3) The mere fact that the documents are relevant is not, of itself, decisive. The court is also entitled to examine whether the documents are confidential: it may be that to override confidentiality will be unnecessarily oppressive, intrusive or unfair.

13–20 In that case he set aside a summons issued against B & Q Ltd, a major competitor of the defendants, in an arbitration over a rent review clause. Not surprisingly, the judge held that there were simpler and less oppressive ways of putting comparables before the court than getting them from your major trade rivals. There has been a considerable degree of discussion over the apparent overlap between CPR 34 and non-party disclosure under CPR 31.17; Pumfrey J. went so far as to say that he was unable to understand the respective purposes of the two rules in *Re Howglen* [2001] 1 All E.R. 376. *Hollander* discusses the issue at some length at 4–01 to 4–19. It would appear that the only circumstances in which a party might wish to go down the CPR 34 route would be where:

(1) Production of documents from a non-party is sought in aid of arbitration (CPR 34 is available but it is arguable that CPR 31.17 is not, see *Hollander* at 4–19); or

(2) Under CPR 31.17 the applicant will normally have to pay the non-party's costs (see CPR 48.1), whereas under a witness summons he will only be required to furnish conduct money.

A third possible difference, is that under CPR 31.17 the burden is on the applicant to satisfy the criteria in that rule by evidence, whereas under CPR 34 all he has to do is to identify the documents with a sufficient degree of detail for the court to be prepared to issue the order, leaving it to the witness to apply for the summons to be set aside. One would have thought however that, on the whole CPR 31.17 is the preferable route, not least because it enables the applicant to have access to the documents at a much earlier stage. Not only that, if the request for access is unreasonably refused, the applicant may not end up having to pay the costs of the application. Finally, notwithstanding the suggestion to the contrary in *Phipson* (see 8–10) that the documents sought under an application under CPR 31.17 must be as specifically identified as under a witness summons, it is submitted that this cannot be regarded as correct having regard to the cases on CPR 31.17 discussed at 10–37. Under CPR 31.17 it must be the case that the applicant can cast his net wider.

3. Pre-Trial Orders

A summons to give oral evidence or produce documents may be made **13–21** returnable on a date other than that fixed for trial on application (CPR 34.2(4)). This provision accords recognition to the pre-CPR decision in *Khanna v Lovell White Durrant* [1995] 1 W.L.R. 121. Until that decision a party who wished to summon a witness to give evidence or, more likely, produce documents, took a major risk. Unless the witness was prepared to be interviewed or volunteer pre-trial access to the documents, the party summoning him would have no idea what he was going to say or what the documents might contain until the day of the trial. Accordingly, the "fiction" grew up of giving the trial a notional start date sufficiently in advance of the actual trial date to enable the evidence to be produced in time for the parties to digest it. It should no longer be necessary to make use of the new procedure since, as suggested by Pumfrey J. in *Re Howglen* [2001] 1 All E.R. 376, at any rate so far as documents are concerned, an application under CPR 31.17 will be more appropriate.

4. Evidence by Deposition: CPR 34.8–15

13–22 Where a witness is unable to attend trial a party may apply for him to be examined (and cross-examined) on oath before a judge or (most usually) an examiner of the court appointed by the Lord Chancellor under CPR 34.15. The witness's evidence may be audio and/or video recorded but must in any event be reduced to writing in the form of a deposition (PD 34/4.3). This will then form the evidence of that witness for the purpose of the subsequent trial (CPR 34.11) although the party tendering it must give notice at least 21 days before the trial of his intention to rely on it (CPR 34.11(3)). Suggested uses are where a witness is too ill or infirm to give evidence at trial or will be abroad at the time. The obvious advantage of the process is that, although the judge will not have the benefit of seeing the witness at first hand, his or her evidence will nevertheless have been tested by cross-examination. Although there is no guidance in CPR 34 or its Practice Direction as to the criteria that the court must take into account in deciding whether to grant or refuse a request for an order, the Court of Appeal have made it clear in *Barratt v Shaw & Ashton* [2001] C.P. Rep. 57 that it cannot be used for the purpose of obtaining advance disclosure of a witness's evidence. However, the whole process is extremely time-consuming and expensive and it may well be more practical and cost-effective to consider seeking directions under CPR 32.3 (see 13–23) for evidence to be given by live video link or some other method. It should be noted that, once put in as evidence, unlike in the case of witness statements (see 11–28), the deposition is not subject to any implied undertaking, but until that point it remains subject to litigation privilege (see *Visx v Nidex* [1999] F.S.R. 91).

5. Evidence by Video-Link: CPR 32.3

13–23 The rule provides that:

> "the court may allow a witness to give evidence through a video link or by other means."

Annex 3 to PD 32 should be followed. It is not necessary to recite it in full; the following extracts provide an appropriate flavour:

> "2. VCF may be a convenient was of dealing with any part of proceedings: it can involve considerable savings in time and cost. Its use for the taking of evidence from overseas witnesses will, in particular, be likely to achieve a material saving of costs, and such savings may also be achieved by its use for taking domestic evidence. It is, however, inevitably not as ideal as having the witness physically present in court. Its convenience should not therefore be

allowed to dictate its use. A judgement must be made in every case in which the use of VCF is being considered not only as to whether it will achieve an overall cost saving but as to whether its use will be likely to be beneficial to the efficient, fair and economic disposal of the litigation. In particular, it needs to be recognised that the degree of control a court can exercise over a witness at the remote site is or may be more limited than it can exercise over a witness physically before it.

3. When used for the taking of evidence, the objective should be to make the VCF session as close as possible to the usual practice in a trial court where evidence is taken in open court. To gain the maximum benefit, several differences have to be taken into account. Some matters, which are taken for granted when evidence is taken in the conventional way, take on a different dimension when it is taken by VCF: for example, the administration of the oath, ensuring that the witness understands who is at the local site and what their various roles are, the raising of any objections to the evidence and the use of documents."

The Annex then continues

"6. Those involved with VCF need to be aware that, even with the most advanced systems currently available, there are the briefest of delays between the receipt of the picture and that of the accompanying sound. If due allowance is not made for this, there will be a tendency to 'speak over' the witness, whose voice will continue to be heard for a millisecond or so after he or she appears on the screen to have finished speaking.

7. With current technology, picture quality is good, but not as good as a television picture. The quality of the picture is enhanced if those appearing on VCF monitors keep their movements to a minimum.

8. The court's permission is required for any part of any proceedings to be dealt with by means of VCF. Before seeking a direction, the applicant should notify the listing officer, diary manager or other appropriate court officer of the intention to seek it, and should enquire as to the availability of court VCF equipment for the day or days of the proposed VCF. The applicant for a direction should be made to the Master, Direct Judge or Judge, as may be appropriate. If all parties consent to a direction, permission can be sought by letter, fax or e-mail, although the court may still require an oral hearing. All parties are entitled to be heard on whether or not such a direction should be given and as to its terms. If a witness at a remote site is to give evidence by an interpreter, consideration should be given at this stage as to whether the interpreter should be

at the local site or the remote site. If a VCF direction is given, arrangements for the transmission will then need to be made. The court will ordinarily direct the party seeking permission to use VCF is to be responsible for this. That party is hereafter referred to as 'the VCF arranging party'.

9. Subject to any order to the contrary, all costs of the transmission, including the cost of hiring equipment and technical personnel to operate it, will initially be the responsibility of, and must be met by, the VCF arranging party. All responsible efforts should be made to keep the transmission to a minimum and so keep costs down. All such costs will be considered to be part of the costs of the proceedings and the court will determine at such subsequent time as is convenient or appropriate who, as between the parties, should be responsible for them and (if appropriate) in what proportions."

13–24   The exercise of this power was first considered by Newman J. in *Rowland and Norgen v Bock* [2002] 4 All E.R. 370. In it, Mr Norgen, a Swedish businessman, sought permission to give evidence by live video link, largely on the basis that if he came into the jurisdiction he was at risk of arrest under an outstanding warrant relating to extradition proceedings. His initial application was refused on the basis that the procedure was only to be invoked in cases where the witness was unable to attend trial due to some unforeseen misfortune such as serious illness. His appeal was allowed by Newman J. who held that:

(1) No defined limits could be set to the exercise of discretion under CPR 32.3;

(2) It was certainly not confined solely for cases involving pressing need such as serious illness;

(3) A refusal to attend which could be characterised as abusive or contemptuous might justify refusal;

(4) Where a party was at risk of arrest if he entered the jurisdiction this might, as here, justify an order for evidence by video link;

(5) The court had to be mindful of Art.6 of the ECHR and the need for "equality of arms". An absent party might suffer a real disadvantage over one who was present for cross-examination;

(6) The court could make allowances for any technological consequences of demeanour and delivery being less easy to observe.

The judge went on to try the claim and remarked in his judgment that the giving of evidence by video link had not in any way detracted from his ability to evaluate the evidence or from counsel's ability to test it in cross-examination. However, although approving the above decision, the Court of Appeal in *Polanski v Condé Nast Publications Ltd* [2004] 1 All E.R. 1220 overturned a decision to permit video-link evidence in a case in which the claimant, a famous film director was suing the publishers of a magazine entitled *Vanity Fair*, a publication having its major circulation in the United States, for an article which he alleged was defamatory of him. Having chosen England as his forum, he was unwilling to attend in person to give evidence because he was at risk of arrest and extradition to the United States in respect of an offence for which he had been convicted but not yet sentenced. Although he was given leave at first instance, this decision was overturned by the Court of Appeal on the ground that the case was distinguishable from *Rowland v Bock* because:

(1) The claim was for defamation to be tried in front of a jury so that the *persona* and reputation of the claimant was central to the case;

(2) The claimant was at risk of extradition to the United States for a crime for which he had been convicted; and

(3) He himself had chosen England, a country in which *Vanity Fair* had a very small circulation, as the forum in preference to the United States, whereas, in *Rowland v Bock* the claimant had had no choice but to sue here.

However, on appeal, the House of Lords ([2005] 1 W.L.R. 637) thought differently and overruled the Court of Appeal, holding that:

(1) The fact that a person was unwilling to come to court because he was a "fugitive from justice", was a valid, and could be a sufficient, reason for making a VCO;

(2) A fugitive from justice was entitled to invoke the assistance of the courts in furtherance of his civil rights;

(3) Justice was not brought into disrepute by allowing such a person to take advantage of a technological facility available to all litigants.

There is, as yet, no reported decision on what the words "by other means" in CPR 32.3 are designed to cover, but they appear to suggest that whenever a witness's evidence is to be put before the court other than by calling him as a witness or putting in his written statement as   13–25 hearsay evidence, the court's permission is required. Any number of preferable alternatives exist to having to rely purely on the witness's signed statement. The examples are given below are not in any way intended to be exhaustive.

13–26   **Example 1:** C, a terminally ill claimant in an industrial disease claim is unlikely to survive until the date fixed for trial.

One possible solution would be to attend on him to video record his evidence, possibly even cross-examination if he were able to face it. Supposing the situation was so urgent that there was no time to seek a direction from the court. There appears to be a conflict here between s.1 of the Civil Evidence Act 1995 which, in effect, gives a party an absolute right to adduce hearsay evidence, and CPR 32.3. Assuming that notice of intention to rely on it is given at the earliest possible moment and a copy of the video is served, it is hard to imagine that the court would refuse to admit it, but one must question whether, in any event, they would have power to do so other than under the general power in CPR 32.1(2).

13–27   **Example 2:** A vitally important expert witness is about to embark on an expedition to a remote part of the world in from which it will not be possible to set up a video link. However it will be possible to set up a live link in the nearest city before he disappears into the interior.

A direction could be sought under which his "live link" evidence and cross-examination could be pre-recorded and played at the trial, a course that was approved in the pre-CPR decision of *Garcin v Amerindo investment Advisers Ltd* [1991] 1 W.L.R. 1140.

13–28   **Example 3:** D's solicitors make a video recording of W's evidence when he is originally interviewed because it is anticipated that by the time the claim comes to trial memories will have faded and it will assist D's case if a more contemporaneous record of his recollection is available. D's solicitors nevertheless have every intention of calling him to give oral evidence at trial.

13–29   This commendable practice is becoming more commonplace in larger cases and is indeed one area in which the criminal courts are moving ahead of the civil jurisdiction (see s.137 of the Criminal Justice Act 2003). In the above situation it would appear that, technically speaking, the defendants' solicitors would need to serve a copy of the video along with a hearsay notice if they wished to rely on it as supportive evidence at trial (up until that moment it will, of course, remain subject to litigation privilege). However, since it is a supporting hearsay statement, the court's permission will be required under s.6(2) of the 1995 Act (although it is hard to imagine it refusing, see 7–44).

7. Evidence from Overseas

The availability of video link evidence and the abolition of the rule **13–30**
against hearsay has made it far easier to obtain evidence from overseas witnesses than used to be the case. There is, of course nothing to
stop you flying in witnesses from the other side of the world if they are
willing to attend and your client can afford it, but there is no guarantee that the cost will be recoverable if their evidence could have been
placed before the court in a more cost effective manner. The advances
in video link technology are such that the delay between question and
answer that used to be a feature of earlier systems is no longer present.
However, up until now, we have been assuming that the witness is
willing. What if he does not wish to be interviewed or produce material documents? As already noted, the English courts have no power to
compel the attendance of a witness to give oral evidence or produce
documents unless he or she is within the jurisdiction. The only power
that the court possesses is to request an overseas jurisdiction to use its
powers of compulsion to assist. The manner in which this assistance
is sought is by applying to the English courts to issue "Letters of
Request" to the overseas jurisdiction. The application is made under
CPR 34.13 and the supporting Practice Direction. It is made to the
Senior Master of the High Court, even in case proceedings in a county
court (CPR 34.13(3)). The power to issue letters of request is derived
from various conventions, in particular:

(1) The Hague Convention on the Taking of Evidence Abroad in
Civil or Commercial Matters 1970;

(2) Individual bilateral conventions with various countries;

(3) The Taking of Evidence Regulations on co-operation between
the courts of the member states of the European Union in the
taking of evidence in civil or commercial matters.

A full list of parties to the Hague Convention along with the full text
of the Taking of Evidence Regulation appears in the *White Book* in
the notes to CPR 34. A full review of the appropriate procedure
appears in *Phipson* at 8–27 to 8–31. The most important point to bear
in mind is that the applicant must submit a draft letter of request
which must contain a statement of issues and provide information as
to the subject matter of the questions that are to be put to the overseas witness or details of the documents to which access is sought.
Although the initial application is made without notice, the Master
has power to direct that other parties are notified. Where the witness
is in the United States, it is open to a party to apply direct to a United
States district court under United States Code, Title 28, s.1782. the
applicant must satisfy the United States district court that:

(1) The person from whom disclosure is sought resides or is found in the district of the court;

(2) The disclosure is for the purpose of proceedings in an overseas jurisdiction; and

(3) The application is made by an overseas or international tribunal or another interested person.

Although the English courts are not directly involved in the process, it has power to grant an injunction restraining a s.1782 application if it can be shown that its use is oppressive (see, for example *Omega Group Holdings v Kozeny* [2002] CLC 132).

III DOCUMENTARY EVIDENCE

1. Authenticity and Use of Contents

13–31   As we have already seen in Chapter 5, it is most unlikely that a party will ever be put to strict proof that a document is authentic. If he is, the combined effect of ss.8 and 9 of the Civil Evidence Act 1995, along with the final demise of the Primary Evidence Rule (see 5–54) have made the task much easier. If authenticity is in issue, it will be necessary to consider the best way to prove the document. This may well require calling witnesses who can give oral evidence to prove, for example, its provenance and due execution: each case will be different. However, the greatest task confronting the litigator, at any rate if he is representing the claimant, will be organising the documents into bundles for the trial.

2. Preparation of Bundles

13–32   The detailed requirements for the preparation of documents for the trial judge will either be agreed or contained in the directions given by the court after receiving the Listing Questionnaires or holding a Listing Hearing. They are likely to follow para.3 of the CPR 39 Practice Direction which is frequently referred to the first set of case management directions in Fast-Track and Multi-Track cases almost as a matter of course. It provides:

"(a) Unless the court otherwise orders the claimant must file the trial bundle not more than seven days and note less than three days before the start of the trial.

(b) Unless the court otherwise orders the trial bundle should contain:

(1) the claim form and all statements of case;

(2) a case summary and/or chronology where appropriate;
(3) requests for further information and responses;
(4) all witness statements to be relied on as evidence;
(5) any witness summaries;
(6) hearsay notices served under CPR 33.2;
(7) notices re plans, photographs under CPR 33.6;
(8) any medical reports and responses;
(9) any experts' requests and responses;
(10) any order for directions as to the conduct of the trial;
(11) any other necessary documents."

Putting together a well-organised trial bundle is a craft that is not, in the writer's experience, as widespread as it should be. In particular, it is not uncommon to find that a document has been photocopied several times because it has been exhibited more than once. The helpful suggestion made in the *Chancery Guide* (see 11–39) should always be followed.

IV VISUAL AIDS

Insufficient thought is often given as to the use of these, especially with the opportunities presented by computer graphics. In certain types of case, road traffic claims being the most obvious example, the party who is able to assemble the most plausible visual scenario is the one more likely to succeed at trial.   **13–33**

1. Evidential Status
Plans, photographs, tape-recordings, cine-films and videos are treated as "documents" under s.12 of the Civil Evidence Act 1995. If they are disclosed, as they should be, in a party's list of documents, then, unless Notice of Non-Admission has been served, their authenticity is deemed to have been admitted under CPR 32.19. As already pointed out (see 5–40), you need to be on your guard lest you find that you have inadvertently admitted material whose authenticity you wish to dispute. One potential problem area that the Higher Courts have not yet had to address is the admissibility of photographs taken by digital camera. There may, for example be a dispute as to the order in which a series of photographs was taken which will require production and inspection of the original disc. Issues may even arise as to whether the original photograph has been enhanced.   **13–34**

2. Use of Plans, Photographs and Models as evidence CPR 33.6.
Plans and photographs are usually dealt with at the Listing Questionnaire stage. CPR 33.6 provides a much more detailed code   **13–35**

than that under RSC O.38 r.5. It applies to evidence (such as a plan, photographs or model) which is not:

(1) Contained in a witness statement, affidavit or expert's report; or

(2) To be given orally at trial; or

(3) Evidence in respect of which a hearsay notice must be served under CPR 33.2.

It also applies to "business documents" tendered under s.9 of the Civil Evidence Act 1985 (see 5–42). In all the above cases the party intending to put the document in as evidence must disclose his intention to the other parties not later than the latest date for serving witness statements. The only exceptions are in those cases where either:

(1) There are not to be witness statements (in other words, hardly ever); or

(2) A party intends to put in the evidence solely in order to disprove an allegation made in a witness statement,

in which case notice must be given at least 21 days before the hearing (CPR 33.6(5)). Where a party has disclosed his intention to put in the evidence he must give every other party an opportunity to inspect it and to agree its admission without further proof. Note *Orford v Rasmi Electronics* [2002] EWCA Civ 1672 in which the defendants in a tripping at work claim introduced a factory plan on the day of the trial which the claimant litigant in person had not been given an opportunity to inspect as required by CPR 33.6. In view of the fact that it was a highly material document which went to the credibility of the claimant's version of how the accident had occurred, the Court of Appeal held that the breach was sufficiently serious to justify ordering a retrial.

3. *Are Covert Videos Liable to Disclosure?*

13–36 The Court of Appeal decision in *Birch v Hales* [1996] P.I.Q.R. 307 was the first to confirm that such videos were *not* privileged and hence liable to discovery. It has now been followed (although not referred to) in *Rall v Hume* [2001] 3 All E.R. 248 which also states that:

(1) CPR 32.19 applies to such a video; and

(2) Any party seeking to rely at trial on all or part of it should seek case management directions at the earliest possible opportunity.

It is perhaps not obvious at first sight why such a video is disclosable since one's first reaction might well be that it has been prepared for the purpose of litigation. Unfortunately, no explanation is given in either of the above cases of the basis on which the video is not subject to privilege. The best that the author can come up with is that since privilege only covers "communications" between humans, the recording of light waves on a photo-sensitive film is not a "communication". Whatever the reason, the above decisions must be treated as binding. Their practical importance lies in the fact that if a defendant in a personal injury claim secretly video-records the claimant but, instead of undermining the claimant's case, it *supports* it, it is every bit as much disclosable as the one which damages his claim.

V ADVICE ON EVIDENCE AND BRIEF TO COUNSEL

A Advice on Evidence

It was a standard tradition when the trial date loomed, for a solicitor to bundle up all the case papers and send them down to counsel with little more than a backsheet and a general request to advise on evidence. This often produced an unpleasant shock when counsel indicated that the pleadings required urgent amendment because the evidence placed before him bore no relation to the pleaded case. This is now much less likely to arise because of the fact that both sides are required to disclose much more of their evidence and to disclose it much sooner. However, this does not mean that advice on evidence is no longer necessary. In a large multi-track case, it is likely that trial counsel will have been instructed throughout and will therefore have already played a major role in the assembly of the evidence. In a Fast-Track case or a relatively straightforward assessment of damages, it may have been dispensed with all together (sometimes with unfortunate results, see *McCrae v Chase International* [2003] EWCA Civ 505 discussed at 14–07). Nevertheless, whatever the size of the case, it is important to put together a Case Plan and catalogue the evidence which is to be tendered in respect of each of the Elements that remain in issue. The following template for a few jottings on a simple road traffic claim is given by way of example.

ELEMENT 1: DUTY
Admitted (Defence para.3)

ELEMENT 2: BREACH
Denied plus "contrib" (Defence paras 4 and 5)

Case Theories

We say: "It happened because D took a chance and jumped the lights"

They say: "Lights were green in our favour"

Witness Statements Served in WS Bundle

Claimant (additional exam in-chief to set scene by taking C through pal and photos and deal with allegation of contrib in D's WS)

Mr Smith—driver of car immediately behind D—says D accelerated on the yellow (obtain witness order by 02/02/06; additional exam in-chief to deal with plan and photographs)

Documents Disclosed in List

Vehicle repairer's report to prove point of impact (deemed admitted under CPR 32.19)—crucial shows D hit us on right hand side rear wheel arch therefore we were already in junction.

Scale plan and photographs (admitted under CPR 32.19)

ELEMENT 3: CAUSATION

Fact of collision admitted (Defence para.2). Causation not admitted; prove by same evidence as for Element 2 plus written report of Consultant Orthopod (see below)

ELEMENT 4: DAMAGE

Note: major issue is liability quantum can probably be agreed

(1) Personal Injury

Not Admitted (Defence para. 6)

Witness Statements Served in WS Bundle

Claimant (need to bring court up to date with additional exam in-chief)

Documents Disclosed in List

No Notices of Non-Admission—no need to prove

• Previous salary records
• Statement of current salary
• Travel expenses
• Bills for prescriptions

Expert Evidence

Report of C's orthopod accepted by D

<u>Authorities</u>

JSB Guide (7th Edn) plus specimen awards

<u>(2) Damage to Property</u>

Cost of car repairs and other "specials" agreed subject to liability

This is a very simple example, but even the most complicated case can be reduced to a couple of sheets of paper in this way. The important point to remember is that even if you only spend a few moments on the exercise and do it on a scrap of paper, it will make your preparation more focused than just tying it up in a bundle and sending it to counsel. For further discussion of Advice on Evidence, see *O'Hare and Browne* at 31–026.

B Brief to Counsel

Civil trials are such a rarity that it may sometimes be many years **13–38** before a litigator has to prepare a brief of any substance, or for that matter hear the counsel who has for years produced an immaculate service on documents and interim hearings actually getting to his feet and examining a witness. Drawing a brief is as much of a craft as preparing a trial bundle and there is much of value in *O'Hare and Browne* at 36–021 to 36–025. The only observations that the writer would add to the advice that they give is, firstly, a brief case plan of the type illustrated in the last section will make it much easier for you to give coherent instructions to counsel. Secondly do not hesitate to provide counsel with your own "themes" and "case theory". In a large case, there will probably have already been a great deal of discussion on this, but if the case is relatively small and counsel is only seeing it for the first time, any creative input will be greatly appreciated by her. Finally, it may well be necessary to prepare somewhat fuller statements from the witnesses than those that have been served which deal, for example with comments on the other parties' statements. If there are to be supplemental statements then these will need to be agreed with the other parties.

If the case does not warrant that expense another approach is to **13–39** prepare a separate proof of evidence for each witness which consists of their original witness statement interpolated with comments and additional material in a different font to the main text; alternatively it may sometimes be appropriate to discuss with counsel what format she would prefer.

Chapter 14

Evidence at Trial and Beyond

This chapter deals with that statistical rarity, the civil trial. It is not **14-01** easy to provide a comprehensive review bearing in mind that a "trial" can be anything from a one hour hearing in the small claims court to what has become commonly known as the "McLibel" case which ran from June 28, 1994 to June 19, 1997 when Mr Justice Steel finally concluded delivering his marathon 800 page judgment. Nevertheless, in terms of order of proceedings and the methods of introducing evidence, there is no material difference between them: they both operate to a common set of rules. This chapter will concentrate on the "core" rules of evidence presentation, in particular witness examination. It is not intended to be a chapter on advocacy but, inevitably there will be some general discussion of the basic principles of case presentation. Bearing in mind that throughout this work there has been an exhortation to "Think trial from Day 1" it would hardly be fair not to devote some space to describing what takes place in the average civil trial. The chapter will conclude by dealing briefly with the special rules regarding evidence on appeals.

I CIVIL TRIALS: SOME COMMON FEATURES

A Order of Proceedings

This has already been addressed in some detail at 5-02, but, by way **14-02** of reminder:

(1) (Usually) the claimant's advocate opens. In longer cases this may be followed by a speech in reply from the defendant's advocate, alternatively she may make a short opening address before calling her evidence at (4) below.

(2) The claimant's advocate presents his evidence: (1) oral; (2) documentary; and (3) real during the course of which "live" witnesses will be successively:

- Examined in-chief;
- Cross-examined; and
- Re-examined.

(4) (Extremely rarely) the defendant's advocate will make a submission of no case to answer.

(5) The defendant's advocate will present her evidence in the same sequence as the claimant.

(6) Both sides experts will give oral evidence (assuming the court has given permission).

(7) The defendant's advocate will make her closing speech.

(8) The claimant's advocate will respond.

(9) The judge will pronounce judgment.

However, the court will not always follow that structure: it will very much depend on the track to which the claim has been allocated.

B Small Claims

14–03 The small claims jurisdiction covers such a diverse range of cases and is so devoid of higher authority that it is hard to do more than lay down a few generalisations and refer readers to the few Court of Appeal decisions that provide assistance.

1. Evidence
14–04 A number of specific rules relating to small claims have been mentioned in other chapters, for example as to expert evidence. CPR 27.8(1) specifically provides that the court may adopt any method of proceedings that it considers to be fair. Furthermore, as already noted, the strict rules of evidence do not apply (CPR 27.8(3)). It is not easy to see quite what this adds in view of the fact that the rules of evidence in civil cases are not exactly "strict" as they stand. However it must presumably mean that they are *more* not less permissive than they would be in a trial in the other two tracks. Not, surprisingly perhaps, many cases have reached the Court of Appeal either before or since the CPR came in. However one must assume that the decision in *Chilton v Saga Holidays Plc* [1986] 1 All E.R. 841 would still be regarded as binding. In that case, the Court of Appeal

overturned decisions in the courts below denying the right to the defendants' legal representative to cross-examine the claimant litigant in person. Although CPR 27.8(5) gives the court express power to limit cross-examination, it does not give it the power to dispense with it all together. Another useful Court of Appeal decision is *Bandengani v Norwich Union* [1999] EWCA 1445 which deals with the appropriate method of establishing the value of a motor vehicle. Firstly, the decision establishes that the price paid for a chattel is admissible evidence as to its value at the time the claim arose. Holman J. stated:

> "I quite accept that the price someone has recently paid for a secondhand item may not be very strong evidence of its value and that it may be displaced by other reliable evidence that the true market value is different. (In a case of this kind, namely a small claims arbitration in relation to a car, by referring to 'other reliable evidence' I am not envisaging expert evidence but simply the sort of evidence that can be gleaned from, for example, a reputable publication as to used car prices. Indeed, I, for my part, would strongly wish to discourage the notion that expert evidence, as such, is necessary or desirable in small claims arbitrations of this kind in relation to common items.) But I cannot accept that the price that somebody has recently paid does not amount and cannot amount to <u>any</u> evidence of value. As a matter of common sense, if the issue is as to the market value of an item and the item is widely available, such as a Nissan Cherry car, and it has just been traded at arms' length on the open market, then the price at which it was traded must afford some evidence as to value, even if rebuttable."

Although the case was decided just before the CPR came into force it is clear that the court was mindful of their impending introduction. Henry L.J. had this to say on the use of expert evidence in small claims when the value of a vehicle was in issue:

> "The case was conducted on the assumption that the question of the valuation of the car was a proper matter for the calling in person of expert evidence on both sides. I question that assumption on the grounds of proportionality. I note that now, and as from April 26, the Civil Procedure Rules have been in force in relation to the small claims track. They provide by 27.5:
>
> > 'No expert may give evidence, whether written or oral, at a hearing without the permission of the court.'
>
> I would say nothing to encourage the grant of such a permission in a case such as this for reasons of proportionality. There are published guides available in newsagents and used in the trade that give

some indication as to the market price of second-hand cars which judges may find helpful. I suggest that, in the ordinary case, such guides would give better evidential value for money than the expensive calling of two live experts".

Both passages are arguably statements of the obvious, but they nevertheless provide useful points of reference in a jurisdiction that is largely devoid of authority.

2. Order of Proceedings

14–05 Some small claims hearings will stick to the standard civil format, especially small road traffic claims in which, typically, both parties are represented by junior counsel. In other types of case however, especially where neither side is represented it is not unusual to find:

- The judge conducting nearly all the witness examination;

- The proceedings being conducted more as an inquiry with both sides being asked to summarise their cases and the judge then putting questions to each party in turn as the case progresses;

- A very relaxed attitude to proof with all the evidence, in whatever form, being received, the only issue being weight;

- The judge dispensing with preliminaries and placing very tight time limits on witness examination even where both parties are represented.

There are three final points that need to made. Firstly, claims can still only be determined on *evidence* as in any other type of hearing, rhetoric proves nothing. Secondly, the court is still applying the *law* to defined *issues* (the case of *Sunrule v Avinue* [2004] 1 W.L.R. 634 being a notable example). Thirdly, unlike trials in either of the other tracks, a party may invite the court to determine a claim in his absence based on his case statement and any other evidence he has filed provided that he gives written notice to the court to that effect at least seven days previously (CPR 27.9(1)).

C Fast-Track

14–06 Fast-Track trials are relatively rare, because, frequently, the cost of going to trial is disproportionate to the sum involved. If the case does involve a major issue of principle, such as an allegation of fraud in a low vehicle impact case, it may well be appropriate to put it into the Multi-Track (see *Kearsley v Klarfeld* [2005] EWCA Civ 1510).

1. Evidence

There are few rules that are specific to fast-track trials, the most **14–07**
notable is the additional restriction on oral expert evidence in CPR
35.5 (see 12–31). Accordingly claims have to be analysed, issues identified and evidence prepared in exactly the same careful way as in
larger cases. However, as a general rule, especially in personal injury
claims, it is common to find that:

(1) The only expert evidence will be a report from the claimant's
medical expert along with replies to questions from the defendant;

(2) All the documentary evidence will be in the form of an agreed
trial bundle in which no admissibility points will be taken;

(3) Plans, photographs and diagrams will also have been agreed,
although often they tend to get produced in a rather haphaz-
ard fashion with neither side, or the court, having a common
set;

(4) Much of the time will be taken up in cross-examination, especially because there will often be discrepancies between what
appears in the case statements and the parties' witness statements. This difficulty is compounded by the fact that, not
infrequently, the witnesses, including the parties, will have
never been interviewed face to face by the lawyer preparing the
case;

(5) Costs are often dealt with as an afterthought with very little
information being made available as to the way in which the
litigation has been conducted. Litigators often seem to overlook the fact that arguments as to costs need *evidence* to
support them, albeit that this is usually given in a relatively
informal way.

However, even though time may be tight, the rules of evidence have
to be observed. The same principles apply if liability has been admitted and the only issue is *quantum*. The Court of Appeal made this
very clear in *McCrae v Chase International Ltd* [2003] EWCA Civ 505.
In that case, loss of future earnings had been determined on the most
flimsy of evidence, in particular as to the claimant's pre-accident
work record. The court stated that if this was the usual practice on
damages assessments, the sooner it ceased the better. The remarks of
Kennedy L.J. are apposite to Fast Track trials in general:

"if the methods and presentation adopted in this case reflects a
common circumstance in connection with personal injury cases in

the [county] court it has, in my judgment, departed too far from the basic principle that a claimant must prove his case by evidence capable of supporting the conclusions to which the court is invited to come. It may be that the days of a formal advice on evidence are long gone but the need which such advice fulfils remains. Someone on each side in litigation such as this, with sufficient skill to do so, must, at some timely stage before trial, draw up a list of the issues which remain contentious and then consider whether or not there is evidence available to meet those issues . . . there is no need for an analysis of such evidence; then the judge can make findings of fact by drawing inferences and doing the best he can, but on the evidence which is available."

Advice on evidence has already been considered at 13–37, and often the expense of obtaining such advice from counsel will not be appropriate. Nevertheless, some form of case analysis along the lines suggested at 13–37 is essential.

2. Order of Proceedings

14–08 The whole tenor of CPR 28 is that the fast-track procedure effectively places the court as well as the parties under a duty to "shoe-horn" the hearings into one day (that is, five hours). Indeed the notes to the *White Book* at 28.6.5 set out a "typical" timetable in which the following slots are allocated:

Claimant opens	10 minutes
Defendant opens	10 minutes
Cross-examination of claimant's witnesses	1 hour, 15 minutes
Re-examination	15 minutes
Cross-examination of defendant's witnesses	1 hour, 15 minutes
Re-examination	15 minutes
Defendant closes	20 minutes
Claimant closes	20 minutes
Judge's "thinking time" and judgment	30 minutes
Costs and consequential orders	30 minutes
	5 hours, 0 minutes

In practice there will be significant departure from that format, not least in relation to examination in-chief (see 14–24) but it serves as a strong indicator that brevity is essential: advocates have a particular incentive to keep the trial within its one day slot since they will not get paid for extra days (see CPR 46.2). Although the system works tolerably well in personal injury claims it can place the court under real pressure if there are more detailed issues of fact, for example in disrepair claims or defended possession cases. If a party's legal adviser is genuinely of the opinion that it will not be just to dispose of the claim in five hours, then she should either seek transfer to the multi-track or try to hone down the issues to manageable proportions, serving Notices to Admit in cases where the other side are being uncooperative.

C Multi-Track Claims

A trial in the Multi-Track can consist of anything from a day and a half trial on a relatively straightforward contract claim before a circuit judge to a high value claim before a High Court judge involving many millions of pounds listed to last for several months. However in each case, the basic principles will be the same.   **14–09**

1. Pre-Trial Review

In cases of substance, the court will fix a pre trial review before the trial judge (see CPR 29.7) who may well have been assigned to the case from the outset if it is substantial or appears in a specialised list (see for example, Section D of the *Commercial Court Guide* in the *White Book* at 2A 61). Normally a PTR will be fixed if the trial is likely to last for more than eight days. The judge will expect the trial advocates to attend (see *Baron v Lovell*, *The Times*, September 14, 1999) and will expect the necessary information to be available to: **14–10**

(1) Deal with preliminary issues;

(2) Determine the order in which issues are to be addressed at trial and the order of witnesses;

(3) Deal with expert evidence, for example by identifying the "live" issues, considering whether there is to be oral evidence and determining the stage at which it is to be called.

Three important aspects of the pre-trial review need to be considered. Firstly, it may be that there will be an application for a ruling on the admissibility of a particular item of evidence. As a general rule, notwithstanding the courts' power under CPR 32.1(2) to exclude evidence at any stage in the proceedings, the general approach has always been that this is best left to the trial judge (see most recently Millett L.J. in *Beazer Homes Ltd v Stroude* [2005] EWCA Civ 265 at [10]). However, the position at pre-trial reviews is somewhat different. It might well be appropriate to invite a judge to make evidential rulings in advance of the trial in order to avoid the trial proper being side-tracked by such issues. Secondly, a judge may well be invited to or decide carry out pre-trial reading that goes beyond the material that is to be adduced in evidence. Sometimes this may involve material that is not only inadmissible but highly prejudicial to one of the parties. In *Barings plc v Coopers and Lybrand* [2001] C.P. Rep. 451 the Court of Appeal was asked by the claimants to rule on whether the trial judge, Evans-Lombe J., had exceeded the ambit of his discretion by indicating that he intended to read background material concerning the collapse of the claimants as a result of the notorious activities of Nick Leeson. This background material included two reports and the evidence in the disqualification proceedings brought against some of the claimants' directors that were highly critical of the claimants' conduct. The Court of Appeal held that there was no principle that prevented a judge from reading inadmissible material in order to assimilate the background. Potter L.J. stated that the appellate court would only interfere in the case of obvious error or unfairness. Clearly, the judge must indicate his intentions at the PTR; it will be for any advocate who wishes to restrict his reading to be prepared to make appropriate representations. Finally, there may, unusually, be cases in which a party, having served many witness statements, does not intend to rely on all of them either by calling the maker or putting them in as hearsay evidence. As indicated at 11–68, the trial judge should, as a general rule be informed of this fact before she begins her pre-reading. It may be prudent to enquire or your opponent whether there are any of his witness statements that he does not intend to put in as evidence so that they can be kept out of the trial bundle and, if necessary, away from the judge.

2. Evidence

14–11 It goes without saying that the rules set out in the section on the Fast-Track applies even more in Multi-Track trials. However, the court tends, on the whole to adopt a fairly permissive approach to evidence by letting everything unless there has been a flagrant case of "trial by ambush". We have already seen this approach operating in relation to late tender of witness statements (see 11–21). However, those cases are simply illustrations of the wider principle in operation. The case of *Hayes v Transco* [2003] EWCA Civ 1262 provides an instructive illustration of the "inclusive" approach that trial judges are now expected to adopt. The claimants were three service engineers employed by the defendants. They sought payment of "disturbance allowances" under their contracts of employment. Shortly before the trial, the defendants served lengthy supplemental statements from two of their main witnesses (whose original witness statements had already been validly served). The claimants' solicitors refused to accept service on the grounds that they were way out of time. The defendants accordingly applied for permission to serve the supplemental statements out of time. A district judge refused this application and the defendants did not appeal. At the start of the trial, the claimants were allowed to put in 28 pages of hitherto undisclosed documents which had only come into their possession shortly before the trial via their trade union, who were supporting them in the litigation. Counsel for the defendants then renewed the application to rely on the supplemental statements that had been disallowed by the district judge. The trial judge refused on the basis that the district judge's decision could only be reviewed on appeal. Counsel for the defendants then sought permission to cross-examine the claimants' witnesses on the contents of those statements. The trial judge refused both applications notwithstanding the fact that the supplemental statements touched and concerned many of the matters raised in the supplementary documents that the claimants had been allowed to put in. In ordering a retrial, the Court of Appeal held that the judge had got it wrong on both counts. Clarke L.J. held that the judge should have considered the *totality* of the evidence that needed to be before the court. In failing to do so, he had denied the defendants a fair trial. Having admitted the claimants' late documents, he should have also allowed in the supplemental statements: this was so notwithstanding the fact that the earlier decision of the district judge had, quite properly not been appealed. In other words, once he had allowed the claimants to put in extra evidence, CPR 32.1 placed the judge under a duty to reopen the whole issue of what evidence needed to be before the court to secure a fair trial. In the writer's view this decision gives a very good flavour of the preferred approach to managing evidence in a civil trial.

3. Order of Proceedings
This will very much follow the format set out at 14–02 above. Parties will however be expected to keep within the allotted trial time: any party who is responsible for causing the trial to overrun its allotted allocation can expect to suffer the consequences in costs.   **14–12**

II OPENING THE CASE

Many of the American trial manuals give examples of opening speeches before juries that simply take the breath away as masterpieces of theatre. On the whole, advocates appearing before a judge tend to be somewhat more prosaic, assuming that they are allowed to open at all.   **14–13**

A Preliminaries

Much of the court time that used to be taken up hearing opening speeches is now taken up by the advocates laboriously preparing their   **14–14** paper submissions which the judge will, hopefully, have time to read before the case is called. Although this may work well for heavy specialist commercial cases, the writer is of the view that a good opening speech, perhaps lasting no more than 10 minutes still has much to commend it and actually saves time rather than wastes it.

1. Case Summaries and Skeleton Arguments

14–15 Courts will often give directions as to matters such as skeleton arguments and case summaries as part of standard directions. The specialist *Guides* also contain specific requirements (see, Section G, *Commercial Courts Guide, Chancery Guide* and *Queen's Bench Guide* para.7.11.5)). Arden J. also gave valuable guidance as to the court's expectations in larger cases in *St Albans Court Ltd v Daldorch Estates Ltd*, unreported, May 10, 1999 in which she stated that:

> "(1) It is essential for a case of any size that there should be a Case Summary for the judge to read before the case.
>
> (2) Where there are numerous bundles a Core Bundle should be prepared.
>
> (3) Skeleton arguments should identify any case documents the judge should read before the start of the hearing.
>
> (4) It would be helpful for trial advocates to:
>
> * Draw up a provisional list of issues;
> * Identify the evidence relevant to those issues each witness should give;
> * Identify how long cross-examination of each witness is likely to take."

Further guidance on the preparation of skeleton arguments is given in *O'Hare and Browne* at 36–017 to 36–018. Although not evidence in any sense, a well drafted case summary and skeleton argument is, nevertheless, a potent persuasive device in the right hands because it can "tramline" the judge down the road that advocate ultimately wishes to lead him.

3. Preliminary Points

14–16 If there has not been a PTR, any matters relating to the admissibility of particular items of evidence will be taken at this stage, for example as to whether or not late evidence should be allowed in. On the whole however admissibility points are rarely taken in civil trials: the preferred approach is to let it all in and deal with all the evidence by reference to its weight. If too much time is spent on dealing with evidence points it may result in the trial having to be adjourned over (see *Martin v Steelforce Ltd* at 11–22).

B Opening Speeches

In the past, opening speeches were crucial. Not only did they   14–17
give the advocate an opportunity to impress, they also enabled
her to:

(1) Set the scene in a way that engaged the court's interest;

(2) Summarise the relevant issues of law and fact;

(3) Speak to the strengths of her client's case.

As a general rule, the claimant will open, but there is no hard and
fast rule to this effect. If the principal burden of proof lies with the
defendant, it may be more appropriate for him to open (see *Phipson*
at 11–16). Nowadays, the "old-style" opening speech has tended to
become a thing of the past, other than on the rare occasion that
there is jury trial. However, one should not underestimate the value
of a good concise opening speech. Although this chapter is not
designed to provide a comprehensive advocacy course, some knowledge of the rudiments is necessary. Whatever its length, an opening
speech can effectively be broken down into five distinct stages.
A typical opening in a modest Multi-Track claim of, say two days,
is set out below.

1. Introducing the Advocates
It may be, of course, that the advocates are well known to the judge,   **14–18**
or that they have both handed in their names to the usher so that she
already has a slip with their names on it. However, if you are expected
to formally introduce yourself and your opponent, something along
the following lines should fit the bill:

"(May it please) your Honour, my name is Mr Jones and I appear
for the claimant in this case and Ms Grant appears for the defendant."

2. The "Thumbnail Sketch"
In this you need do no more than provide the court with the kind of   **14–19**
information that would appear, for example, on the claim form. For
example:

"The claimant's case is for damages for personal injuries arising out
of a road traffic accident that took place on the December 7, 2004.
Your Honour, the claimant's case is that these injuries were caused
by the defendant's negligent driving. That negligence is denied by
the defendant who also disputes the amount of those damages."

It is always a worthwhile exercise because it may well be that there are matters that have been resolved since the court received the trial bundle.

3. *Going Through the Documents*

14–20 This is a useful formality because it enables the advocate to find out what the judge already knows about the case. In a case of any substance it involves confirming that the judge has:

(1) The court (trial) bundle (in an ancillary relief case very often just the forms and annexed documents along with any updates);

(2) Any other agreed bundles that there might be.

At this stage it may also be appropriate to put in any agreed chronology and take the judge through the skeleton arguments upon which you propose to rely as well as any agreed plans and photographs. Many courts will have their own "standard" directions for this. As always though, it is a case of "cutting your cloth". It may well be that if you are in a busy list or appearing in a Fast-Track trial the judge is anxious to get on with the case and will more or less expect you to go straight in and start calling your first witness.

4. *"Telling the Story"*

14–21 This is the stage that requires the most creative skill. In it the advocate introduces the main themes which form the basis of her case. The advocate will want to tell the judge:

(1) What the case is about;

(2) What is in issue;

(3) What evidence will be called;

(4) Any preliminary legal issues on which a ruling might be required.

As already pointed out, some courts expect this stage to be reduced to paper and included in the case summary which it will direct should form part of the trial bundle (see para. of PD 39). At present there is still little or no guidance as to the format of a case summary (see para.5.7 of PD 29). However, the following guidelines may be useful.

(1) *Keep it short*. The summary is intended to be a guide to take the court through the major issues. If it is overlong, the law of diminishing returns will apply.

(2) *Make it easy to read*. In particular:

- Make liberal use of headings and short paragraphs;
- Use double spacing;
- Make sensible use of abbreviations e.g. "C" for "Claimant", dates in short form ("1/10/99" etc);
- Adopt a clear and logical structure e.g. split up liability from quantum.

(3) Tie it into the witness statements, documents, plans and photographs.

It is at this stage, that advocacy becomes an art rather than a science. The skilful advocate will, first and foremost, introduce the judge to her "case" theory (remember that a trial is, in essence, a "storytelling competition". Secondly, she will introduce "themes". These are phrases or words that are used to provide recurring points of emphasis and reinforcement at appropriate moments throughout the trial. This technique is a favourite forensic device of American trial lawyers. *Anderson, Schum and Twining* give a classic example (at page 154) from the notorious trial of O J Simpson:

". . . one of the prosecutors challenged OJS to put on the bloody glove that had allegedly been worn by the murderer and found behind his house. It did not fit. Throughout his closing, defence counsel sounded the theme 'if it doesn't fit, you must acquit,' every time he identified items of the prosecution's evidence that could plausibly be interpreted as not supporting OJS's guilt".

Probably not quite the way to go about it in front of an English judge, **14-22** but the technique is regularly employed, albeit with somewhat greater sublety, in English trials. One notable recent example is the marathon opening of Nicholas Stadlen Q.C. for the Bank of England in the *Three Rivers* trial. Having got to his feet with the memorable riposte to Gordon Pollock Q.C.'s soon to be beaten marathon, "After six months the empire strikes back", he kept returning to the "misconceived" and "inherently implausible" nature of the claimants' allegations. He also kept returning to Bank employees' lack of motive for covering up the fraudulent activities of Bank of Credit and Commerce International (see *The Guardian*, July 19, 2004). Finally, it is important to bear in mind that all good stories "paint a picture". Many trials are no different. To a large extent, the many thousands of words that lawyers will throw at a case are only there to serve the higher purpose of creating a visual image of what really happened. Obviously, this is truer in some cases than in others, but many cases are decided on the basis of the more plausible of two competing mental images evidence. This is not confined to personal injury claims. Although the case was ultimately lost on a point of law, the dissenting judgment of Denning L.J. in *Candler v Crane Christmas* [1951] 2 K.B. 164 at 176 is often cited as an example of powerful storytelling which undoubtedly "paints a picture":

> ". . . They were professional accountants who prepared and put before him those accounts, knowing that he was going to be guided by them in making an investment in the company. On the faith of these accounts he did make the investment whereas if the accounts had been carefully prepared he would not have made the investment at all. The result is that he has lost his money."

5. Moving to the Next Stage

14-23 Inexperienced advocates often peter out. Always make sure you end on a positive note. A simple formula is to finish by saying:

> "Your Honour, unless there is any matter upon which I can assist you further at this stage I now propose (with your leave) to call my first witness the claimant, Nigel Davies."

It is at this stage that you have a great opportunity to lay down some major "theme" that you can then run through the whole case. One way of identifying this is to ask yourself whether you can complete the following sentence:

> "My client should win this case/get the order she is seeking because......................................."

If you can complete it you are well on your way to working out how you should finish, if you cannot, then you are missing something in your preparation! Remember that simplicity wins every time.

III EXAMINATION IN-CHIEF

14-24 The claimant's advocate will now call his witnesses, normally starting with the claimant, although there is no hard and fast rule to this effect. In a case of any length, the advocate will however need to give careful thought as to the order in which the evidence is led since he will be endeavouring to ensure that the narrative emerges in a the most compelling and logical way (see *Phipson* at 11–17). Unlike in criminal trials, there is no hard and fast rule that witnesses remain outside court until they are called. The judge has a complete discretion in this regard, but may well decide to adopt this course if there are serious conflicts of fact to be resolved. The dying art of examination in-chief (at least in civil cases) still needs to be examined in some detail because without an awareness of what it entails it will never be possible to draft a witness statement in the way that CPR PD 32 requires (see 11–44).

A Before Exchange of Witness Statements

As will be shown shortly, it is now more or less possible for a witness   **14–25**
to be examined on an exchanged witness statement without any thought being given to many of the difficulties that used to be associated with examination in-chief.

1. The Dying Skill
Traditionally, the principal objectives of examination in-chief were to: **14–26**

(1) Present the witnesses' evidence in a logical sequence. This would usually be chronological or in some case by reference to the pleadings.

(2) Cover all the relevant issues upon which he or she was able to testify.

(3) Structure the examination in-chief so that the witness' evidence emerged in a cogent and credible way.

(4) Anticipate, and if possible neutralise matters that were likely to be raised in cross-examination.

All these tasks would have to be accomplished without the witness being able to see the statement that had been taken from him. As a term of art this was referred to as a "proof of evidence". It differed from the modern "witness statement" in that it remained privileged in the hands of the advocate calling the witness and the opposing party was not given notice of its contents. Although the witness was able to read his proof at any time up to his entering the witness box, once he was in there, he was at the mercy of the advocate calling him. In fact, he was never left quite that "high and dry" because, frequently, all the documents were agreed and, therefore it was always possible to prompt him to some extent by reference to documents in the trial bundle.

2. The "No Leading Questions" Rule
The role of the advocate was restricted by the fact that she could not   **14–27**
ask "leading questions". Thus, for many inexperienced advocates

examination in-chief was more of an ordeal than cross-examination. The traditional style of oral examination in-chief required that no leading questions be asked of the witness. A leading question can be defined as one which suggests its own answer by trying to put words into the witness' mouth. For example, suppose that an advocate was trying to extract from a witness the fact that a car was being driven at speed, it would definitely be a leading question to ask:

Q   "The defendant's car was going very fast <u>wasn't it</u>?"

It would also be leading to ask:

Q   "Was the defendant's car being driven <u>very fast</u>?"

If speed was a major issue, it would arguably be leading to enquire:

Q   "How <u>fast</u> was the defendant's car being driven?"

A safe question would be:

Q   "Could you estimate the speed of the defendant's car?"

It is remarkable how little authority exists for the rule (see *Phipson* 12–20 to 12–21). It is generally accepted that the answers to leading question are not inadmissible, it is simply that in terms of weight they are rendered virtually worthless (see *Moor v Moor* [1954] 2 All E.R. 458, a chilling snapshot of what divorce courts were like in the 1950s). There are three (possibly four) occasions on which such questions are permitted, although it should always be borne in mind that these are not exhaustive (see *Cross and Tapper* at 313): the judge has always had a very broad discretion.

(a) *Matters not in Dispute*

14–28   It has always been permissible to lead a witness up to the disputed point. Accordingly continuing with the above example, if was accepted that the witness had witnessed a road traffic accident on June 18, 2003, it would have been permissible to start the witness off as follows:

Q   "Did you witness <u>an accident on June 18, 2003</u>?"
A   "Yes."

The witness was started. The advocate could now continue, for example by asking:

Q   "Could you <u>describe</u> to the court in your own words what you saw?"

By way of digression, that illustrates another, often overlooked feature of examination in-chief, namely, that commands to a witness such as "explain", "describe" and "tell" are an equally permissible device for extracting information in-chief.

(b) Where a Denial was Sought

This was usually permitted on the basis that it saved time and also cut **14–29** to the core of what the case was really about. So, to continue with the example given above, supposing that the defendant were now called to give evidence, having heard a day's worth of allegations that he had been driving at an excessive speed across the centre line of the road at the time of the accident, he could be asked:

Q   "Mr Smith, were you driving too fast that day?"
Q   "And were you half-way across the white line as has been alleged?"

and so on.

(c) Hostile Witnesses

As noted at 11–67, if a witness did not "come up to proof" you were **14–30** stuck with him. It is still not permissible to seek to contradict your own witness (see at 11–67 how this rule has been extended to witness statements tendered as hearsay evidence) unless the court gives permission to treat the witness as "hostile". The law in this area is, unfortunately, unduly technical, not least because it is not only a mixture of common law and state, but also because the statute governing hostile witnesses is the Criminal Procedure Act 1865. There are, possibly, three issues that the judge may have to consider.

(1) Is the Witness "Hostile"?

This is entirely a question of fact. However, it is not enough that the **14–31** witness gives evidence that is "unfavourable": there must be clear evidence of an unwillingness to tell the truth either because of a point-blank refusal to give any evidence at all (see *R. v Thompson* (1977) 64 Cr.App.R. 96) or because the evidence given is manifestly contrary to previous statements made by the witness either orally or in writing.

(2) What Cross-Examination is Permissible?

This is, confusingly, governed by s.3 of the Criminal Procedure Act **14–32** 1865 (expressly preserved by s.6(3) of the Civil Evidence Act 1995, see 7–45) which provides that:

"A party producing a witness shall not be allowed to impeach his credit by general evidence of bad character, but he may, in case the witness shall in the opinion of the judge prove adverse, contradict him by other evidence, or, by leave of the judge, prove that he has made at other times a statement inconsistent with his present testimony; but before such last mentioned proof can be given, the circumstances of the supposed statement, sufficient to designate the particular occasion must be mentioned to the witness, and he must be asked whether or not he has made such a statement".

Outside of an episode of *Judge John Deed*, it is most unlikely that you will ever encounter this section in practice. However, an example of when it might arise is given below. Almost invariably it will arise in a situation where the witness departs form an earlier statement.

(3) *Does the Earlier Statement Have to be Proved?*

14–33   If the witness admits making the earlier statement, there is no problem, but if he does not, the leave of the judge must be sought to prove it. This will almost invariably be granted. An example of the 1865 Act in operation is given below.

14–34   **Example:** You act for C in a major product liability claim against D plc. X, a former employee of D plc approaches you as a "whistle blower" with evidence that is crucial to your case. You interview him and on the basis of your notes, prepare a witness statement for him to sign. He refuses to do so. However his evidence is so vital, that you obtain leave under CPR 32.9 to serve a witness summary. You issue a witness summons to secure his attendance, but when called he not only refuses to answer questions, but denies ever making the statements contained in the draft you have prepared.

Assuming that the judge has given leave to treat X as hostile, it would now be permissible to call evidence for you to be called to give evidence as to the contents of the interview that you had with him Not only would you be able to "refresh your memory" (see below from the notes you had taken, but the evidence that you give as to X's earlier statement, although obviously hearsay, would be admissible. Thus the judge could be invited to, in effect, treat your evidence as X's evidence. Accordingly, if the judge accepts that what he told you in the earlier interview was probably true, you have succeeded in getting the "whistle blowing" evidence in, albeit by a somewhat tortuous route. Civil trials (perhaps fortunately for one's nerves) are rarely that exciting.

(d) *Cross-Examination on a Hearsay Statement*

14–35   It will be recalled (see 7–32) that the court has power to order the "maker of the original statement" tendered as hearsay evidence to attend for cross-examination. It is not entirely clear whose witness that person is, but, on the questionable assumption that he is the witness of the person summoning him, this is another exception to the "no leading questions" rule.

3. *"Focusing" and "Linking"*

These techniques have already been briefly referred to when dealing **14–36** with witness statements (11–64). They represent an important facet of examination in-chief which, once appreciated, make witness examination seem far less terrifying a prospect. it has always been possible:

(1) To remind a witness of what he has already given in evidence ("focussing"); and

(2) To introduce a witness to a particular topic ("linking").

Thus, to return to the witness to the road traffic accident referred to above, if, having been asked to give an estimate of the speed of the defendant's car he had replied:

A   "It seemed to be going <u>very fast</u>."

The advocate could have proceeded to ask a series of closed questions around that answer, for example, as follows:

Q   "What led you to believe that the car was being driven <u>very fast?</u>"
Q   "Can you remember where the car was in the road when it was being driven <u>at that speed?</u>"
Q   "Can you give the court any idea of <u>how fast it was going?</u>"

and so on. Once the advocate had extracted all the information on that topic in the witness's proof, he could move on to deal with the next topic without being accused of leading, for example by "linking" as follows:

"I'd now like to take you forward to what happened after the collision"

and so on. Once an advocate was aware of these techniques, even an "old style" examination in-chief lost many of its terrors. This technique is still invaluable, not only for taking a witness through his witness statement (see 11–64 and below) but also, for dealing with any answers that he gives on supplemental examination on his statement. Once the techniques have been mastered, it will be possible to prepare an examination in-chief by writing a list of the topics on which you wish to examine and under each of them to write the *answers* that you want from the witness rather than the question needed to extract the required information.

4. "Memory Refreshing"

14–37   Brief mention was made at 5–29 and 7–46 of the fact that, at common law, a witness was, and still is, permitted, subject to leave, to refresh his memory from a contemporaneous note. The note must satisfy two conditions. Firstly, it must have been "made or verified" by him. Secondly, it must have been created more or less contemporaneously with the events to which it relates. As with examination in-chief generally, criminal evidence has moved on where the civil rules have stood still (see, ss.139 to 141 of the Criminal Justice Act 2003). Memory refreshing in civil cases barely gets a mention either in *Phipson* (see 12–09) or *Cross and Tapper* (see page 314). This is hardly surprising in view of the fact that, in the vast majority of cases, the witness's evidence will be in the form of a signed statement that will, where appropriate, refer to any notes made at or about the time of the relevant incident. Not only that, the notes will have been disclosed as part of standard disclosure (see Chapter 10) and, accordingly, their authenticity will, in all probability, have been deemed admitted under CPR 32.19 (see 5–40).

B Exchanged Witness Statements

14–38   The use of witness statements at trial has already been covered at 11–62. Accordingly, it is only necessary to set out a few reminders as to why, in effect, examination in-chief in the traditional sense has disappeared.

1. Use of Witness Statements: CPR 32.4

14–39   As already noted, under CPR 32.4 pre-trial exchange of witness statements is mandatory. The statement will stand as the witness's evidence in-chief unless the court orders otherwise (CPR 32.5(2)) and, having been duly sworn and confirmed his statement, the witness may simply be tendered for cross-examination. This relatively cursory formality could be as short as in the following example:

Q.   "Could you give the court your full name please?"
A.   "John Michael Adams."

Q.   "And your address?"
A.   "15 Barrington Road, Crouch End, London N8 3BT."

Q.   "Could you now turn to page 16 of the bundle in front of you?"
[Witness turns to page 16]

Q. "Do you recognise that document?"
A. "Yes, it's my witness statement."

Q. "Could you turn to page 32? Is that your signature?"
A. "Yes it is."

Q. "Could you wait there please because my learned friend has some questions to ask you?"

As will be explained shortly, it is normal for the witness to be asked a few "supplementaries" before he is exposed to cross-examination, but full examination in-chief in the traditional manner is now most unusual. When would a court ever be likely to order otherwise? Interestingly, it has been done; in *Eagle v Chambers* [2003] EWCA Civ 1107 Moses J. had to try a heavy personal injuries claim arising out of a road traffic accident that had taken place over 13 years previously. He dispensed with statements and took full evidence in-chief. Hale L.J. commented (at [2]):

"the accident took place as long ago as June 22, 1989. The judge was obviously concerned about how he should approach the oral evidence when it had all happened so long ago and the witnesses were more likely to be trying to remember what they had said in their witness statements than what had actually happened. He was therefore anxious first to establish what independent recollection they had rather than relying on their witness statements as evidence in-chief in the usual way".

Another example might be where, as is unfortunately all too common, it becomes clear that the statements have all been churned out from some remote "factory" and sent to the witnesses to sign without any of them ever having been interviewed face to face.

2. *"Amplification"*

The extent to which a witness should be asked further supplementary   **14–40**
questions in-chief will depend very much upon the circumstances of each case. It will be recalled (see 11–65) that CPR 32.5(4) only permits examination by way of amplification or new matters if there is "good reason". As a general rule, most courts will, at the very least adopt the approach suggested by District Judge Frenkel in the *Law Society's Gazette*, June 16, 1999:

"The witnesses will confirm the contents of their statements. A witness of fact may be bowled a soft ball or two to get his or her eye in before cross-examination, but examination in-chief, as we have known it, will be rare."

However if there is conflict on a crucial issue, or credibility is disputed the court retains a discretion to allow examination and should be referred to *Coles v Kivells (a Firm)* [1997], *The Times*, May 2 (see 11–65) and the notes in the *White Book* at 32.5.1. If the court does give permission for a witness to be examined in-chief on his witness statement, many of the problems involved in avoiding leading questions disappear because of the use that can be made of the techniques of "linking" and "focussing" described at 11–64 and 14–36. By way of further example:

"<u>Focus</u>"

> "Mr Smith, in paragraph 4 of your witness statement you describe the weather conditions on December 10, 1998: I would like to ask you some more questions about that.
>
> Q.   In the second sentence you say it was "<u>very gloomy</u>". Could you explain to the court in more detail just <u>how far you could see?</u>"

What the advocate should avoid, is to invite the witness to repeat the contents of his witness statement by asking open questions such as "Can you tell the court what happened?" Not only is this a waste of the court's time, because it is already set out in the statement, but, it is almost certain that the account given will differ, albeit it hopefully in only minor repents, from what he has put in his statement. This will lead to suggestions in cross-examination that the witness statement is does not contain the true version of events. Sometimes the discrepancy is so significant that it may undermine credibility, but more often than not, it is simply an example of a normal human trait: the "story" will always come out slightly differently each time it is told. This type of cross-examination can, on occasions, become exceedingly tiresome.

3. *Introducing Documents*

14–41   In the vast majority of cases, documentary evidence will be in agreed bundles cross-referenced to the witness statements (see 11–39). Accordingly it will not normally be necessary to invite a witness to formally authenticate a document (see 5–38 onwards). Thus it will be possible, for example, in the case of a photograph, to say to a witness:

> "Mr Smith, I would like you to turn to page 3 in the bundle of photographs. As you will see that is a photograph of Park Road looking back to the scene of the accident. I would like you to explain to the court if you can, please, exactly where you say you were standing when you witnessed the accident."

This technique is harder than appears at first sight. However, the experienced advocate will always remember is to adopt a slow pace so that the judge and the witness can keep up.

4. Previous Out-of-Court Statements
These were discussed at 7–43 in the context of s.6(1) of the Civil   **14–42**
Evidence Act 1995. Technically they offend against the so-called "rule
against self-corroboration" and cannot be admitted without the leave
of the court in order to support consistency or fill in any gaps in
recall. However, as stated at 7–44 it is almost inconceivable that a
court would refuse permission and, in practice, since such statements
would no longer be treated as inadmissible hearsay, the s.6(1) point is
unlikely to be taken: everyone will just let it go in.

IV CROSS-EXAMINATION

Cross-examination offers the skilled advocate the opportunity to   **14–43**
strengthen his or her case by putting questions to an opponent's
witnesses in order to elicit facts which support it. It is a skill which
requires constant practice if it is to be perfected and it is a vast
topic for study; the following notes encompass the core principles
of this complex area. The most comprehensive and practically
useful modern treatise is *Cross-Examination: Science and Techniques:*
Pozner and Dodd (1993): The Michie Company. Anderson, Schum and
Twining also contains much valuable food for thought on the subject.
This section will begin by examining the legal rules and then go on to
briefly examine some of the techniques essential to a successful cross-
examination.

A Legal Rules

The most important of these relate to the use of leading questions   **14–44**
and the finality of questions on credit; however there are some
general principles that will need to be discussed as a preliminary. It is
fair to say that in the average civil trial, the technical rules are not
engaged as often as in criminal cases. Nevertheless, they operate by
reference to the same principles and need to be dealt with for the sake
of completeness.

1. General Rules
Quite apart from the express power given to the court under CPR   **14–45**
32.i(3) to limit cross-examination, the *Code of Conduct of the Bar* (see
para.708) and the solicitors' *Advocacy Code* (para.21.09) prohibits
oppressive cross-examination. In particular, suggestions of crime,
fraud or other misconduct may not be put unless they are relevant
and there are grounds to support them. Furthermore, the following
general rules apply:

(1) An advocate is entitled to cross-examine any witness not called by her. In multi-party cases, the order in which advocates cross-examine is entirely within the discretion of the trial judge;

(2) A witness is bound to answer questions put in cross-examination provided that they are relevant. Questions will be regarded as relevant if they either go to an issue in the case or to a witness's credibility. This is however subject to the court's power to control oppressive and unnecessary questions under CPR 32.1(3), and to exempt a party from revealing confidential information if it is insufficiently relevant (see 8–20). A witness may also be entitled to assert privilege or PII under any of the available heads (see Chapter 8);

(3) Under "the rule in *Browne v Dunne*" (see 5–32) a party is obliged to challenge any evidence led in-chief that he intends to dispute (see also 11–70). The duty to "put one's case" is discussed further at 14–61;

(4) CPR 32.11 (see 11–70) specifically provides that a party may be cross-examined on the entirety of his witness statement even though not all of its contents have been referred to in-chief.

The fourth of the above rules is of little practical importance since in normal circumstances, the entirety of the witness's statement will stand as his evidence in-chief under CPR 32.5. In addition he will be liable to be cross-examined on any relevant documents in the trial bundle since they will normally be admissible in evidence from the start of the case.

2. Use of Leading Questions

14–46   What passes for questioning in many modern trials consists of little more than a series of statements delivered by the cross-examiner with little regard to the answers given. An example of this can be seen in the criminal case of *R. v Howell* [2005] 1 Cr.App.R. 1. The defendant was convicted of an offence under s.18 of the Offences Against the Person Act 1861 ("wounding with intent"). At the police station he had declined to answer questions on legal advice. When he gave evidence of his side of the story this, inevitably rendered him liable to cross-examination under s.34 of the Criminal Justice and Public Order Act 1994, for failure to mention when questioned facts which he later relied on in his defence. The following extract is taken from his unsuccessful appeal to the Court of Appeal. Counsel for the Crown concluded his cross-examination thus:

"Q.   Why did you not answer that question, 'Did you try and kill Kevin Johns?' Why did you not answer that question?

A. I would have liked to have answered any of the questions, Sir, but I was advised not to by my solicitor, Mr Andrew Owens.
Q. That was advice. You knew that you were entitled to answer their questions if you wanted to do so, did you not?
A. Well, what was the point of me having a solicitor there, if I wasn't going to actually take his advice?
Q. Because, and this is my final question about that interview, if you were an innocent man you would not have wanted your solicitor to advise you, you would have leapt at the chance to deny the allegations and to give your side of the story, if you were an innocent man. But you did not, did you?
A. I kept to what Mr Owens had told me, a 'no comment' interview. That's why the gentleman was there representing me, sir.
Q. Yes, and of course—
A. But I wouldn't have objected to any of them if I hadn't had a solicitor."

Counsel's cross-examination consists of statements to which a question is tagged on the end. It is almost as if the cross-examiner were giving evidence himself. No evidence is led by the Crown as to what an innocent man would have done when faced with Mr Howell's predicament. This style of cross-examination is commonplace not only in the criminal courts but in the civil courts as well and is often little more than an exercise in creative storytelling. Its significance lies in the fact that it reveals two important features of modern cross-examination.

(1) Cross-examination can often be categorised as an argument directed to the tribunal of fact in the form of questions to a witness; and

(2) Whereas the objective of examination in-chief is to *extract* information from a witness, the primary objective of cross-examination is often to *impose* information on him.

The extract quoted above exhibits both of these features, although its "barnstorming" approach would generally not be appropriate to a civil trial. The use of leading question will be considered further in the next section.

3. Cross-Examination on Credit

Although the credibility of a witness's testimony is regarded as cir- **14–47**
cumstantially relevant (see 4–10) and therefore a proper subject for cross-examination, there are a number of constraints which restrict its scope. In particular:

(a) *Relevance*

14–48   Although a witness's "character" is generally regarded as irrelevant to any of the facts in issue (see 4–38 onwards) it *may* be relevant to his credibility as a witness. Nevertheless the court will, be astute to keep it within proper bounds so as to avoid unnecessary oppression (see 4–38 onwards).

(b) *Proper Foundation*

14–49   As already noted (14–45) a cross-examiner is bound by professional rules of conduct not make allegations of improper behaviour unless there is a proper foundation for doing so.

(c) *Rehabilitation of Offenders Act 1974*

14–50   This forbids the questioning of a "rehabilitated person" in respect of "spent convictions" (see s.5). However s.7(3) permits cross-examination if the court is satisfied that "justice cannot otherwise be done". The only reported case in which this provision has been considered is *Thomas v Metropolitan Police Commissioner* [1997] Q.B. 813. In that case, the Court of Appeal (Sir Richard Scott V.C. dissenting) were not prepared to interfere with trial judge's decision to admit two spent convictions for unlawful wounding and criminal damage in an action for assault, false imprisonment and malicious prosecution. The court held that in each case, the judge had to balance the potential relevance of the convictions top credibility against the possible prejudice that admitting them might occasion. It goes without saying that this is only ever likely to be a live issue in a jury trial which, as we have seen, is now a rarity. In the *Thomas* case, the judge had let the convictions in, not because they went to directly to the claimant's honesty as a witness, but because the jury might otherwise be misled by his appearance as ". . . quiet spoken, apparently sincere, well-educated and generally in every way an upright citizen". Since there was a direct conflict with the police evidence, the majority in the Court of Appeal considered that the judge had exercised his discretion within proper bounds.

(d) *Answers on Credit Final*

14–51   The general rule is that if a party is asked a question in cross-examination that goes only to credit or to a collateral issue then the witness's answer is final. The cross-examiner is not permitted to contradict him by other evidence. The problems caused by this rule arise almost exclusively in criminal trials where there has been much case law on whether a particular line of questioning is "collateral" or goes to and issue in the case (see *Phipson* at 12–46). It is submitted that, in the context of civil trials any issue of this kind should be dealt with under the court's general power to limit cross-examination under CPR 32.1(3) and should no longer be weighed down with the technicalities one finds in criminal cases. There are five exceptions to the rule in any event, which between them largely take care of the circumstance in which an advocate might wish to contradict the witness further, they relate to allegations of:

(1) Bias or partiality;

(2) Previous convictions;

(3) Inconsistent statements;

(4) Evidence of reputation for untruthfulness; and

(5) Medical evidence as to the reliability of a witness's evidence.

They are all considered briefly in the next section.

4. *Answers on Credit not Final*

The vast majority of case law is to be found in cases reported in criminal proceedings which leads one to venture that its significance does not loom large in many civil trials. **14–52**

(a) *Bias or Partiality*

Many of the cases listed in *Phipson* at 12–48 are of considerable antiquity. They read like a roll call from a popular television courtroom drama series and include instances of witnesses who have been accused of taking bribes, bearing a grudge against one of the parties, and "schooling" their daughters to give adverse evidence. The only recent example is *R. v Mendy* (1976) 64 Cr.App.R. 4 in which the trial judge had permitted rebutting evidence to be given in respect of a witness who had denied that he had been talking outside court to a man who had earlier been sitting in court taking notes. **14–53**

(b) *Previous Convictions*

Subject to the previous conviction being sufficiently relevant and not being liable to exclusion under the Rehabilitation of Offenders Act 1974, any witness, including a party who denies a previous conviction put to him may have it proved against him under s.11 of the Civil Evidence Act 1968 (see 4–54 onwards) for the method of proof and the presumption created by it). **14–54**

(c) *Inconsistent Statements*

This topic has already been touched upon when discussing s.6 of the Civil Evidence Act 1995 at 7–45. In theory, it is still governed by ss.3 and 4 of the Criminal Evidence Act 1865, but as pointed out earlier, it is almost inevitable that any previous statement made by a witness will have formed part of standard disclosure and thus will have already been deemed admitted under CPR 32.19. Witnesses are **14–55** regularly cross-examined on documents in the trial bundles, for example letters and emails for the purpose of showing inconsistency without anyone even considering the 1865 Act. With that caveat in mind, s.5 provides that:

> "A witness may be cross-examined as to a previous inconsistent statement made by him in writing or reduced into writing relative to the subject matter of the indictment or proceeding without such writing being shown to him; but if it is intended to contradict such witness by the writing, his attention must, before such contradictory proof can be given, be called to those parts of the writing which are to be used for the purpose of contradicting him; provided always that it shall be competent for the judge, at any time during the trial to require the production of the writing for his inspection, and he may thereupon make such use of it for the purpose of the trial as he may think fit."

There is virtually no commentary on its use in modern civil trials (for example what is meant by "writing" in this day and age). The one practical benefit it nevertheless still seems to confer, is that a witness may still first be cross-examined in general terms on an inconsistent statement before confronting him with its contents. What if the witness denies making the statement? In that case, s.4 provides:

> "If a witness, upon cross-examination as to a former statement made by him relative to the subject matter of the indictment or proceeding, and inconsistent with his present testimony, does not distinctly admit that he has made such statement, proof may be given that he did in fact make it: but before such proof can be given, the circumstances of the supposed statement, sufficient to designate that particular occasion, must be mentioned to the witness and he must be asked whether he has made such a statement".

14–56   Quite how these sections are supposed to interact is not entirely clear. Note that s.4 applies, unlike s.5 to oral as well as written statements. However the evidence is introduced, the most important thing to remember is that, since the abolition of the hearsay rule, the inconsistent statement is as admissible as the witness's testimony (the statement of Buxton L.J. to the contrary at para.[77] of *Denton Hall Legal Services v Fifield* [2006] EWCA Civ 169 is, with respect, plainly wrong). The following (true) example, provides a vivid illustration:

During the course of defended possessions proceedings the tenant D was half way through giving her evidence when the judge rose for lunch. Over the luncheon adjournment D was overheard by an employee of the claimant local authority boasting loudly to a friend that everything that she had said in the witness box was a pack of lies.

On resuming giving her evidence, her statement made over lunch was put to her in cross-examination and she denied it point blank. Counsel for the claimants was then permitted to call the local authority employee to give evidence in rebuttal. The defendant was recalled and she persisted in her denials under cross-examination. In that situation, the court is now permitted to decide which version it prefers without any need to get involve in technicalities over hearsay.

(d) *Reputation for Untruthfulness*
Any television script writer looking for ideas to inject into a courtroom drama might be interested to know that, according to Edmund Davies L.J. in *R. v Richardson and Longman* (1968) 52 Cr.App.R. 317, it is still permissible to call a witness to give evidence as to another witness's credibility and ask him, firstly:

Q.   "What do people think about W's reputation for telling the truth?"

Following up with:

Q.   "Having regard to what people think of his truthfulness, would you believe him?"

Secondly, he could go on to ask him:

Q.   "I'd now like to turn to what you have to say from your own knowledge of his truthfulness. Would you believe him if he gave evidence on oath?"

The second line of questioning could even extend to specific instances, based on the witness's own knowledge, of the earlier witness's untruthfulness. This survival is discussed further in *Phipson* at 12–50.

(e) *Medical Evidence on Reliability*
All of the cases referred to in *Phipson* at 12–51 relate to criminal proceedings, nevertheless the rule also applies, in theory to civil cases. The principle was stated by the House of Lords in *Toohey v Commissioner of Metropolitan Police [1965] A.C. 595* as follows: **14–57**

"Medical evidence is admissible to show that a witness suffers from some disease or defect or abnormality of mind that affects the reliability of his evidence. Such evidence is not confined to general opinion of the unreliability of the witness, but may give all the matters necessary to show not only the foundation of and the reason for the diagnosis but also the extent to which the credibility of the witness is affected".

In a civil case, a party wishing to call such evidence would inevitably face the difficulty of persuading the court that it was just and proportionate to give permission under CPR 35 for such evidence to be adduced.

B Cross-Examination Technique: A Summary

14–58 Although strictly outside the mainstream of a text on the law of evidence, it is unrealistic not to examine some of these techniques in outline. Cross-examination is an essential part of adversarial fact-finding, albeit that its importance has sometimes been overstated. Civil claims are more frequently won on the contents of the documents and application of legal principles.

1. Develop a Theory of the Case

14–59 The starting point for any advocate preparing a cross-examination is to have a fully developed case theory. This must take into account all of the evidence and the client's instructions, and, if accepted, will lead to a successful outcome. This theory will help to focus the advocate's cross-examination by identifying its principal objectives. The Protocols and the CPR on Case Statements require that litigators begin to form provisional case theories at the start of the case. As the case develops, it may well be that some provisional theories will fall by the wayside, not least because, as the other side put their "cards on the table", it will become easier to identify the theories that are likely to be advanced by the opposition. A quotation from a member of the Bar cited in *Anderson, Schum and Twining* at 154 provides a succinct summary of the advocate's task:

> "A primary task of any litigation is to develop a cohesive theory and theme of the case. The theory should be that explanation of the facts which shows logic requires your side to win and the theme should be that explanation of the facts which shows the moral force is on your side. This strategy should provide a framework for assimilating the facts in a manner which is most advantageous to your client. Since there are generally some harmful facts in any litigation, you should choose a strategy which does not rely on those facts and which makes such facts irrelevant . . . Selecting a theory is simply one aspect of careful preparation and is the *sine qua non* of effective litigation . . . While a cohesive theory cannot take the place of thorough preparation and a favourable set of facts, it is the glue which holds together the other elements required for successful litigation."

2. Knowing the other Parties' Cases
The rules as to Exchanged Witness Statements are an important   **14–60**
source of material for the cross-examiner, as are the parties' Case
Statements. As already noted it is possible from this information to
form an early view of the opposition's likely case theories and hence
be in a better position to refine and develop one's own.

C Questioning Techniques

1. Putting the Case
We have already seen how the rule in *Browne v Dunne* (above) requires   **14–61**
that a cross-examiner "puts his case" to the other parties' witnesses,
that is confront the witness with all aspects of the party's case which
conflict with their evidence. In so doing there is no need to preface
each question with the well-worn phrase, "I put it to you" or "I
suggest to you" as in:

> "I put it to you that you are mistaken, it was not the defendant that
> you saw that night."

There are various techniques for "putting the case" but the *R. v
Howell* approach seems to be becoming more commonplace as in:

> "You didn't see the defendant that night did you? You made a
> mistake."

The use of leading question is considered further below.

2. Leading Questions: the Cross-Examiner's Major Weapon
Leading questions are permitted in cross-examination and they can   **14–62**
be very effective in putting across the advocate's theory of the case.
However, an over-use can give the impression that the witness is being
browbeaten, an impression that is not likely to find favour in civil
trials. Nevertheless, they do have a number of advantages, including:

(1) The cross-examiner has complete control over the order of the
    topics;

(2) The cross-examiner has more control over the witness who can
    effectively be restricted to one word answers (unless they are
    super-assertive);

(3) The court hears far more of the cross-examiner than the
    witness. A skilled advocate can cast doubt on a witness's testi-
    mony purely by virtue of the way the questions are put. They

can be put so skilfully that their impact is the same irrespective of the answers.

Voice tone, emphasis and pace can also be adapted to give the questions the desired bias for example, to suggest suspicion, absurdity etc. The same question can be put in many ways depending on the response the advocate wishes to elicit from the witness. Although these techniques can be played with great effect before juries, a civil judge may be somewhat less susceptible to too much amateur dramatics. This section will nevertheless conclude with an extract from one of the more famous cross-examinations in a criminal trial Richard Muir K.C.'s cross-examination of the poisoner Crippen. It shows an experienced cross-examiner taking advantage of all three of the key features of cross-examination listed above. It also shows how the ability to control the subject matter enables the cross-examiner to beak down a particular topic into a number of smaller points to give it greater emphasis. Muir wanted to highlight the fact that Crippen had fled the country under a false name with his girlfriend Ethel Le Neve. Instead of putting this as a general statement he broke it down into a devastating series of leading questions as follows:

"Q. 'You thought you were in danger of arrest?'
A. 'Yes.'

Q. 'And so you fled the country?'
A. 'Yes.'

Q. 'Under a false name?'
A. 'Yes.'

Q. 'Shaved off your moustache?'
A. 'Yes.'

Q. 'Left off wearing glasses in public?'
A. 'For a while, yes.'

Q. 'Took Le Neve with you?'
A. 'Yes.'

Q. 'Under a false name?'
A. 'Yes'

Q. 'Posing as your son?'
A. 'Yes.'

Q. 'Went to another country?'
A. 'Yes.'

Q. 'Stayed in a hotel there?'
A. 'Yes.' "

One imagines that in front of a busy judge in the county court he would have probably been stopped after about the second question with a retort such as "We've got the message Mr Muir, can we move on please". Nevertheless it provides a powerful illustration of the enormous control that a skilful cross-examiner can exert over the presentation of his material.

V RE-EXAMINATION

The need to re-examine has increased due to exchanged witness state-   **14–63**
ments. It is therefore a skill which now needs to be given much greater attention than in the past.

1. Purposes of Re-Examination
There are three principal purposes in re-examining one's own witness: **14–64**

(1) To clear up ambiguities;

(2) To clarify any matters where the witness has become confused;

(3) To give the witness an opportunity to complete an aspect of cross-examination which the cross-examiner did not dare to finish like:

"It was suggested to you by my learned friend that you could not have seen the accident take place from where you were standing. Can you explain to the court how it was you could see what was going on?"

2. The Rules
Although leading questions are not permitted this should never be   **14–65**
a problem because the advocate can always remind the witness what was put to him/her in cross-examination. The "focussing" technique is permissible in the same way as in examination-chief. For example:

"Could you turn back to page 42 in the bundle in front of you please. You may remember that when you were being questioned on that page it was suggested to you that . . ."

The examiner and the witness know exactly where to go. However, this means that the advocate or her instructing solicitor will need to take very careful notes of the cross-examination in order to pick this up and "focus" the witness. Although you are not permitted to go through the whole of the witness testimony again or introduce new matters, subject to relevance, you are free to re-examine on *any* part or on *any* topic that was raised in cross-examination.

VI SUBMISSIONS OF NO CASE

14–66 Submissions of no case to answer, rare in criminal cases are almost unheard of in civil claims. Although it is open to a defendant to argue at the close of the claimant's evidence that he has failed to establish a prima facie case on all the elements of his case such applications were a rarity in view of the fact that a defendant making such a submission in non-jury trials was required to elect that, in so doing he would not be permitted to call any evidence in support of his case. It was though by some commentators that the advent of the CPR with its emphasis on proportionality might bring about a change of approach and, indeed, in the first reported case post-CPR, *Mullan v Birmingham CC* [1999], *The Times*, July 29 David Foskett Q.C. held that a defendant could now make a submission without having to elect not to call evidence if his submission failed. However, in subsequent Court of Appeal cases (see *Boyce v Wyatt Engineering* [2001] EWCA Civ 692, *Lloyd v John Lewis* [2001] EWCA Civ 1529 and *Benham Ltd v Kythira Investments* [2003] EWCA Civ 1794 the status quo was, in effect restored. The most recent decision confirming that a defendant should be put to an election save in the most exceptional circumstances is *Graham v Chorley Borough Council* [2006] EWCA Civ 92. It is important to bear in mind that all the claimant has to do is adduce evidence that is *capable* of proving each element in his case. If the defendant's submission fails, the defendant will not be able to call any evidence. However, relying on *Wisniewski v Central Manchester Health Authority* [1998] P.I.Q.R. 324 (see 4–21 onwards) the claimant will be entitled to invite the judge to draw adverse inferences from the defendant's failure to call any witness whom he might reasonably have been expected to call, thus strengthening the claimant's case and possibly justifying a finding in his favour on all the evidence.

VII FINAL STAGES

14–67 The defendant will now call his evidence which will be rehearsed in the same way as the claimant's evidence followed by closing speeches from each of the parties' advocates with the defendant going first. The skilled trial advocate will have included the drafting of her closing speech in the overall preparation of her case. In fact there are some advocates who recommend that the closing speech is the first task that should be addressed on the basis that it provides an overall target at which to aim. It is based on the premise that producing a rough draft of the closing speech focuses the mind on what one would like to be able to stand up and say in closing if everything were to go according to plan.

1. Objectives
The effective speech should aim to: **14–68**

- Re-assert (and reinforce) your case theory;
- Be simple and as brief as possible;
- Start and end with your strongest points;
- Concentrate on your best points;
- Make a decision in your favour as easy as possible.

2. Structure and Content
Each case is different, but a simple model requires the advocate to   **14–69**
address the following issues.

(a) *Findings of Fact and Law*
Remind the court of the matters of fact and law it has to decide. This   **14–70**
will have usually have already been done in opening, but it is always
useful to have a checklist of matters that remain in issue.

(b) *Case Theory*
Ultimately, the judge will choose to go with the more plausible inter-   **14–71**
pretation of the events. The role of the advocate at this stage is to
emphasis those parts of the evidence which most obviously support
his case theory. It is always important to bear in mind that the simpler
the "theory" or "story" that is being advanced, the more persuasive it
tends to be.

(c) *"Showing the Way Home"*
Adjudication is not easy. On top of that, it is much harder to go with   **14–72**
a theory that will brand one of the parties as a liar than one which
shows them to be mistaken but not wilfully dishonest. To that extent
the speech of Lord Nicholls in *Re H* (see 3–52) reflects reality.
Accordingly, the advocate should always seek out when closing, arguments that make it easier for the judge to let the unsuccessful party

down lightly. However, this is not the time to embark upon a lengthy treatise on how to present a closing speech, nevertheless, it is an important part of the adversarial process. Most importantly, it should not simply repeat the evidence. Not only is this extremely boring but also carries with it the implication that the judge needs to be reminded of what she has just heard given in evidence. The structure of a model judgment was given at 5–07, and it is important to be aware at all times of the difficult task that the judge has to address in giving judgments even in the simplest of cases.

VIII EVIDENCE ON APPEALS

14–73   Appeals based on pure points of evidence are very few and far between. In particular, the appellate court will be very reticent to overturn the decision of a trial judge where the allegation is that he has failed to deal with the evidence correctly . . . the appellate court will have particular regard to the fact that the trial judge had the advantage of seeing the witnesses at first hand (see *Assicurazioni Generali SpA v Arab Insurance Group* [2003] 1 W.L.R. 577). It is particularly important to bear in mind that, firstly, the appellate court will not be able to retry the case, simply review the decision of the trial judge (CPR 52.11) save in exceptional circumstances. Secondly, the appellant will have to show that the judge made a serious error in his interpretation of the evidence or an a legal ruling. Such instances will be, hopefully, rare. Finally, the appellate court will generally determine the appeal on the basis of the evidence that was before the trial judge. There are severe restrictions on the introduction of fresh evidence on appeals and these are set out below. The relevant law and procedure on appeals can be found in Chapters 44 and 45 of *O'Hare and Browne*.

1. First Appeals

14–74   Where, on an appeal brought in the ordinary way, a party wishes to rely on fresh evidence for the purpose of determining the appeal (or remitting it for a retrial) the rules in the well known decision in *Ladd v Marshall* [1954] 1 W.L.R. 1489 will apply. The requirements of the rule are that the evidence:

(1) Could not have been obtained with reasonable diligence for use at the original trial or hearing;

(2) Would probably have had an important (though not necessarily decisive) influence on the result of the case or application; and

(3) It must be credible (though it need not be incontrovertible).

Bearing in mind that permission to appeal is needed in all cases now, this brings home how important it is to make sure that one "gets it right first time round".

2. Second Appeals

Where however a party wishes to rely on fresh evidence in order to **14-75** reopen an appeal that has already been determined, the court must apply the principles laid down by the Court of Appeal in *Taylor v Lawrence* [2003] Q.B. 528 and now set out in CPR 52.17. Although the recent Court of Appeal decision in *Re Uddin (A Child) (Serious Injury: Standard of Proof)* [2005] 3 All E.R. 550 is a childcare case, the principles that it applies and restates are of general application to appeals in which a party wishes to introduce fresh evidence. The court will only entertain re-opening an appeal that has already been determined, in truly exceptional circumstances where:

(1) The integrity of the earlier litigation process, whether at the original hearing or the first appeal, has been critically undermined;

(2) Fraud, judicial bias or a judge who has determined the appeal on the wrong papers(!) are paradigm but not exhaustive examples; and accordingly

(3) The discovery of fresh evidence could, in a truly exceptional case, justify re-opening an appeal, but only if it created a powerful possibility that an erroneous result had in fact been perpetrated.

Clearly any appellant in the second situation (and indeed in the first one) will have a very high mountain to climb.

Conclusion The main theme throughout this work has been that **14-76** proving facts in a civil trial has been made relatively easy as a result of the changes in substantive law and procedure introduced over the last ten years. At first blush, it may therefore seem somewhat profligate to have taken some 200,000 words explaining why. The reality is however that there are still areas of potential complication which litigators will not need to address unless the stakes are high enough or they have no choice. Ultimately however we now have a system of proof in civil cases which:

(1) Encourages early analysis of the relevant issues and the available evidence;

(2) Facilitates the admission of all relevant evidence in whatever format it presents subject only to limited exclusionary rules (of which by far the most important are those relating to privilege);

(3) Expects early voluntary disclosure of material evidence in the pursuit of negotiated settlement;

(4) Requires disclosure of all material evidence as a prerequisite of its admission at trial;

(5) Operates flexibly to ensure that, so far as possible, all material evidence is placed before the court at trial in the interests as fairness; and

(6) Punishes by means of adverse costs orders any litigant who does not abide by these principles.

However, the most important message that this work has set out to deliver is that litigation is no longer a game of bluff in which the mere commencement or defence of proceedings can safely be employed as a tactical device for securing more advantageous terms of settlement. A litigant may still be able to get away with the use of these questionable tactics on occasions, but not only will it turn out to be a very expensive experience if he is found out, but the CPR regime now makes it much easier to detect hoaxers. As the writer stated at the start of Chapter 1 "evidence matters", because if you have no evidence you have no case.

Index

(All references are to paragraph number)